THE ANATOMY OF LONELINESS

The
Anatomy
of
Loneliness

EDITED BY

JOSEPH HARTOG
J. RALPH AUDY

AND

YEHUDI A. COHEN

INTERNATIONAL UNIVERSITIES PRESS
New York

Library of Congress Cataloging in Publication Data

Main entry under title:

The Anatomy of Loneliness.

   Bibliography: p.
   Includes index.
   1. Loneliness — Addresses, essays, lectures.
I. Hartog, Joseph. II. Audy, J. Ralph, III. Cohen, Yehudi A.
BF575.L7A68   158'.2   79-53591
ISBN 0-8236-0146-3

Manufactured in the United States of America

To the memory of

J. RALPH AUDY

human ecologist

Contents

PSYCHOLOGICAL AND PSYCHOANALYTIC VIEWS

ANTHROPOLOGICAL PERSPECTIVES

EFFECTS ON CREATIVITY

PHILOSOPHICAL VIEWS

Acknowledgments

I WISH TO ACKNOWLEDGE the editorial assistance of Suzanne Miller, Carol Fegté, Janice Andersen, and Mary Jane MacDwyer, librarian-editors of the George Williams Hooper Foundation for Medical Research and the Department of Epidemiology and International Health of the University of California, San Francisco. The contributors who waited so patiently through the long gestation deserve my special thanks. I am also indebted to Nicholas Petrakis, Chairman, Department of Epidemiology and International Health, my colleagues at UCSF, my wife Betty, and the friends who made me feel the book was worth the perseverance. My greatest debt is to Ralph Audy who invited me to edit this book and whose untimely death left many of us lonelier without his wisdom and wit to inspire us. He was a visionary scientist who taught that health was more than the absence of illness. He was willing to gamble on the creativity of his faculty and researchers who could join him in stretching medical research beyond the prosaic and the trivial to the human universals.

Contributors

BARBARA G. ANDERSON, PH.D.
Associate Professor of Anthropology, Southern Methodist University, Dallas, Texas

J. RALPH AUDY, M.D., PH.D.
Late Director of the George Williams Hooper Foundation, and Professor of International Health and Human Ecology, University of California, San Francisco, Cal.

PAULINE B. BART, PH.D.
Associate Professor of Sociology, Department of Psychiatry, The Abraham Lincoln School of Medicine, Chicago, Ill.

MARTIN BUBER
Late Jewish Philosopher and Theologian

JOHN B. CALHOUN, PH.D.
Chief, Section on Behavior Systems, Laboratory of Brain Evolution and Behavior, National Institute of Mental Health, Bethesda, Md.

MARGARET M. CLARK, PH.D.
Professor of Anthropology, University of California, San Francisco, Cal.

YEHUDI A. COHEN, PH.D.
Professor of Anthropology, Livingston College, Rutgers University, New Brunswick, N.J.

ERNEST DUNN, PH.D.
Associate Dean, Livingston College, Rutgers University, New Brunswick, N.J.

PATRICIA C. DUNN, PH.D.
Assistant Professor of Social Work, Rutgers University, New Brunswick, N.J.

JON EISENSON, PH.D.
Distinguished Professor of Special Education, San Francisco State University; Emeritus Professor of Hearing and Speech Science, Stanford University Medical Center, Stanford, Cal.

FRIEDA FROMM-REICHMANN
Late Psychoanalyst

JOSEPH HARTOG, M.D.
Associate Clinical Professor of Psychiatry and of Epidemiology and International Health, University of California, San Francisco, Cal.

JULES HENRY
Late Anthropologist

THOMAS B. JOHNSON, JR.
Clinical Psychologist

JOAN B. KELLY, PH.D.
Psychologist, Greenbrae, Cal.

RALPH KEYES
Fellow, Center for Studies of the Person, La Jolla, Cal.

CHRISTIE W. KIEFER, PH.D.
Associate Professor of Anthropology, Department of Psychiatry, University of California, San Francisco, Cal.

MELANIE KLEIN
Late Child Psychoanalyst

JACOB LANDAU
Professor, Pratt Institute, Brooklyn, N. Y.

P. HERBERT LEIDERMAN, M.D.
Professor of Psychiatry, Stanford University Medical Center, Stanford, Cal.

HELENA Z. LOPATA, PH.D.
Professor of Sociology; Director, Center for the Comparative Study of Social Roles, Loyola University of Chicago, Chicago, Ill.

ALBERT J. LUBIN, M.D.
Clinical Professor of Psychiatry, Stanford University Medical Center, Stanford, Cal.

MARGARET MEAD
Late Anthropologist

BEN L. MIJUSKOVIC, PH.D.
Associate Professor of Philosophy, Southern Illinois University, Carbondale, Ill.

DANIEL OFFER, M.D.
Chairman and Professor of Psychiatry, Michael Reese Hospital and Medical Center, Chicago, Ill.

ERIC OSTROV, PH.D.
Research Associate, Psychosomatic and Psychiatric Institute, Michael Reese Hospital and Medical Center, Chicago, Ill.

THOMAS F. PARKINSON, PH.D.
Professor of English, University of California, Berkeley, Cal.

CARIN M. RUBENSTEIN, PH.D.
Social Psychologist; Associate Editor, Psychology Today, New York, N.Y.

WILLIAM A. SADLER, JR., PH.D.
Professor of Sociology; Chairman, Division of Interdisciplinary Studies, Bloomfield College, Bloomfield, N.J.

ROBERT SEIDENBERG, M.D.
Clinical Professor of Psychiatry, Upstate Medical Center, State University of New York, Syracuse, N.Y.

VELLO SERMAT, PH.D.
Professor of Psychology, York University, Ontario, Canada

PHILLIP SHAVER, PH.D.
Associate Professor of Psychology, Research Center for Human Relations, New York University, New York, N.Y.

HENRY DAVID THOREAU
Nineteenth-Century American Philosopher and Naturalist

PAUL TILLICH
Late Protestant Philosopher and Theologian

ILZA VEITH, PH.D.
Professor of Psychiatry, Department of History of Health Sciences, University of California, San Francisco, Cal.

JUDITH S. WALLERSTEIN, PH.D.
  Lecturer, School of Social Welfare, University of California, Berkeley, Cal.

Introduction:
The Anatomization

JOSEPH HARTOG

WE STRUGGLE AGAINST LONELINESS even before we know the adversary. As children, we sense we are alone when we discover that our parents are not omniscient and all powerful. As adolescents, we discover our own mortality and this intensifies our awareness of loneliness. As adults, we come to realize that we are not merely alone within our bodies, but alone in the world. Individuals and cultures expend much effort dispelling and concealing this truth. Religious beliefs, rebirth myths and rituals, ancestor worship, kinship systems, rites of passage, totem beliefs, taboos, and social rules—these are our strategies for denying aloneness.

We avert our gaze. As a result, there is a dearth of scientific writing on the subject. Only recently, under the leadership of Anne Peplau of UCLA and Daniel Perlman of the University of Manitoba, have organized research efforts been stimulated and given academic credibility.[1] For the general public, only Moustakas (1961, 1972), it seems, has confronted the subject in a thoughtful way.

Psychotherapists, whom we would expect to examine the subject, are too close to loneliness to write about it. Perhaps because they reflect at the end of a day of isolated encounters, they are rarely able to share their insights with others. It is revealing that most psycho-

---

[1]Peplau and Perlman recently chaired the UCLA Research Conference on Loneliness, May 10-12, 1979.

therapists who have written about loneliness, especially psychoanalysts, have done so late in their careers. Nonbehavioral scientists,
on the other hand, whose pursuits are often equally lonely, hesitate to
study an experience as emotion-laden and subjective as loneliness.

In an attempt to explore this neglected subject, Yehudi Cohen
organized the symposium "The Anatomy of Loneliness" in 1967 at
the University of California at Davis. He enlisted the help of many
distinguished scholars, some of whom are contributors to this volume.
Since then, an "Anatomy of Loneliness" seminar has been incorporated in the college extension curriculum of the University of
California, and has been presented in communities throughout the
Sacramento Valley and at the University of California at Davis.

In 1977, the late J. Ralph Audy, one of the original participants in
the seminar and one of the world's leading ecologists, suggested the
idea of a book to me after we had both lectured at the invitation of
Ford Lewis. Yehudi Cohen endorsed the project. Although neither of
us began as experts on loneliness, we felt we could not abandon the
subject after having delved into this neglected realm of human
experience. The present volume is the product of our commitment.
Expanding the multidisciplinary approach of the original symposium,
we have sought to create a readable reference work directed at professionals and educated laymen. Our aim was to compile diverse
material, supplemented by a large bibliography, to serve as a text,
baseline, and source book.

By way of introduction I shall attempt to define loneliness with the
knowledge that such a reductionistic explanation does not necessarily
facilitate understanding. I shall then illustrate how the cultural boundaries of the self (sometimes referred to as the ego by others) in different societies define the experience of loneliness in those societies.
Finally, I shall describe the biological, neurological, psychological,
social, and cognitive imperatives that, when violated, lead to different
types of loneliness. In terms of a "cognitive imperative," I shall
discuss verbal and nonverbal aspects as well as the element of meaning. I shall also discuss some ways humans use cognitive mechanisms
to counteract the sense of loneliness.

Two interrelated conditions form the skeletal frame of loneliness:
disconnectedness and longing. Disconnectedness pertains to the
physical and psychological states that tell a person he is alone. Here I

refer to all the voluntary and involuntary victims of such disconnectedness: the hermit and the exile, the runaway and the abandoned child, the divorced and the widowed, the "single rooms only" hotel occupant and the nursing home resident, the assorted bigots and misanthropes and the victims of racial or religious prejudice, the foreign immigrants walled out by the language barrier, and the victims of class discrimination.

Without longing, however, none of these disconnected conditions qualifies as true loneliness. By longing, I mean an anxious, painful, indescribable yearning for someone or something—the yearning of a child for a divorced parent, of a parent for a married daughter or son, of a teacher for a former student, of the griever for a dead friend or relative. Longing also relates to the sufferer who has no conscious object in mind, because the essence of longing is mere separation from something in the past, be it separation from one's relationships, places, or memories. It is the unresolved disconnectedness from past relationships that sustains the failure to cope with the longings of the present. This idea will be developed more fully in my chapter "The Anlage and Ontogeny of Loneliness."

Although longing and disconnectedness convey the essential experiential quality of loneliness, the subject demands further analysis. First, the experiencing of loneliness—its severity and the situations in which it occurs—is determined by the location and boundary of the individual's data-processing self. Because the boundary of the self is culturally determined, the interface at which loneliness occurs varies among cultures.

In urban, Western-type societies, the boundaries of the self are usually coterminous with the boundaries of the body. Such a "self" reflects the cultural value of individualism and the importance of the individual, his personal freedom, choice, responsibility, and bodily integrity. The ideal here is that the individual, with few exceptions, is more important than the group. The individualist cannot have community unless he compromises his individualism. In a society that seeks to cultivate autonomous individuals who have great mobility and tenuous attachments, loneliness will be commonplace. It is suggestive, for example, that a high rate of divorce seems to be a logical outcome of marriage between partners who were both raised as "only" children (Forer, 1969).

In communal societies in which the individual is subordinate to the group, the self's boundaries extend beyond the person to encompass the family, clan, village, or tribe. The individual in such societies experiences loneliness only when separated from the group that defines the boundaries of his self. In this case, the group acts as an individual, taking responsibility, protecting its "self" (its members), carrying grudges, tolerating few independent decisions, and granting little privacy. A person's life is secondary to the life of the group. In such a society, shaming, cursing, ostracism and mortification (from the Latin "to make dead") may lead to "voodoo death," death without apparent physical cause. Outside the group, the life of any one person is meaningless. Outsiders are also without value. In such societies, blood feuds that last several generations are not uncommon. The group usually sees individualist freedom as perverse and destructive to its integrity just as an individual sees institutional and governmental intrusion as a threat to his private life.

In ascetic societies, the self is within but separate from the body. The body is an "outsider" to the soul. The culture of the holy man, the mystic, and the yogi rejects the world of the flesh. Its members do not experience loneliness unless they feel rejected or abandoned by their god or their faith. Other persons are of little importance, and since the body is worthless, its neglect is also of little consequence.

In the subculture of madness, found in all societies, the mind itself, for physical or psychological reasons, is isolated from body and soul. The dysfunction of the self and its withdrawal from the world is so extreme that loneliness threatens annihilation, the self reduced to a mathematical dot in an infinite void. Fortunately, very few of even the most severely mentally ill ever reach this stage.

Different types of loneliness result when an individual violates certain *imperatives*, certain basic drives and supraordinate needs.

The biological drive of gregariousness in primates and many other mammals—dogs and dolphins, for example—must rank as the primary imperative of man. For humans, in most cases, such gregariousness pertains to other humans. But, as exemplified by Robinson Crusoe and his goats, pets can sometimes satisfy this need as well.

We have all read of dogs pining to death over the loss of their masters, and of the high mortality rate of abandoned infants in hospitals. Recent speculations on the psychosomatic theory of cancer point to an association between a history of recent personal loss and the onset of cancer. These are all examples of an outrage to an individual's biological need for company, and, as such, are extreme reactions to loneliness. Undoubtedly, lesser losses produce bodily reactions, though with milder consequences.

Voodoo death, usually described in nonindustrial societies but confirmed in my own clinical experience, may occur unrecognized in modern cultures (where it may be called "dying of a broken heart"). In *The Broken Heart—The Medical Consequences of Loneliness*, Lynch (1977) makes the point unequivocally that the rate for virtually every major cause of death in the United States is significantly higher for the single, the divorced, and the widowed than for married people. The death rate for heart attack (myocardial infarction) may also be higher for the hospitalized patients than for those treated at home because in the hospital the patient is relatively isolated from friends and relatives. Perhaps the cardiac patient feels that the most significant people in his life expect him to die when he goes to the hospital and consequently withdraw from him psychologically when he is hospitalized. Death in some cases may be a self-fulfilling expectation, an instance of *terminal loneliness*.

Phillips' (1977) discovery that there are dips in the death rates of famous people preceding their birthdays, followed by a higher than expected death rate in the months subsequent to these birthdays, is further suggestive of a biological need for company. The explanations are speculative. Perhaps sheer willpower keeps a dying person alive until his birthday. I suggest, however, that a birthday means a reunion with people and a reactivation of memories, and that after a birthday the people and memories abandon the dying person, making way for death.

Humans also have a neurological imperative, the need for an optimal range of sensory stimulation from the physical (Solomon et al., 1957), cultural, and interpersonal environment. Sensory deprivation produces a form of physiological abandonment sometimes resulting in psychosis, while sensory overload creates an experience of entrapment, desperation, and physical pain (Simmel, 1962; Ludwig, 1972). Each in its way leads to loneliness, because both absence and overload of stimulation effectively isolate a person from the environment. The inability to reach out to others fosters a degree of desperation that distinguishes these experiences from mere sensory isolation or solitude. Both sensory deprivation and sensory overload have been used in totalitarian states to torture people. Loneliness makes sense within the context of a crowd because the crowd, like an over-populated cocktail party, effectively prevents meaningful human interaction. On the other hand, the crush of the crowd may be unconsciously sought as a return to the bodily contact that charac-terized infancy. The healing power of the laying on of hands may be, for similar reasons, part of the sensory need.

Population density bears a possible relationship to the degree of loneliness an individual can tolerate. We know that low and high den-sity populations are associated with tolerance to heightened states of loneliness. Perhaps tolerance results from acclimatization to enforced aloneness in sparse populations on the one hand and dense popula-tions on the other. J. Ralph Audy described such tolerance as characteristic of the sparse population of Tarahumara Indians of the Sierra Madre and of the crowded Japanese. A striking exception would be the Australian settlers who postpone adapting to a culture where there are no neighbors nearby by substituting electronic media (radio and telephone) for human contact. Television in American homes and institutions conversely offers an escape for individuals who wish to avoid interacting with others.

John Calhoun, whose work on crowding using laboratory rats first led to the conclusion that an optimal group size is 12, has noted that conceptual space is more likely to explain man's way of coping with population density than pure physical space. In his contribution to this volume, ''Seven Steps from Loneliness,'' Calhoun sublimates physical space into a computer-assisted semantic hypothesis of loneliness as if he were testing the limits of intellectual space.

The psychological imperative directs us to guard against being rejected or left out. The insult of guilt is added to the injury of psychological deprivation when a child is rejected or deserted by a parent. The child feels unloved and guilty, as though he caused himself to be mistreated. The rejected child becomes a lonely child predisposed to become a depressed adult. Clinical evidence tends to confirm that early parental loss increases the probability of later depression (Bowlby, 1960; Winnicott, 1953). At this juncture much of the confusion about the nature of loneliness arises because most descriptions confuse symptoms of depression with those of loneliness. These two entities, though fundamentally different (see Leiderman's contribution to this book), frequently overlap and feed each other.

The social imperative warns us that if we are excluded, we will not be able to get what we need and want in life. This implies that social isolation leads to problems of adaptation, safety, achievement, and the fulfillment of physical—including sexual—reproductive needs. For the social drive to be important, the culture must value it, and to the extent that it does, loneliness, as a felt experience, is a serious matter. Social ostracism can lead to economical and political disenfranchisement, whether the origins are racial, religious, or based on other biases.

The cognitive imperative mandates that we be able to send and receive messages to survive in society. Permanent or prolonged barriers to communication and information, like language differences and primary sensory or speech impairments, may force a person into loneliness. Organic brain disease as a result of stroke (cerebrovascular accident) produces intense frustration in people whose intellectual functioning is intact. Hodgins gives a powerful portrayal of this condition in *Episode: Report on the Accident Inside My Skull* (1964). Certain nonorganic mental disorders may also interrupt communication by virtue of what cyberneticists call "noise in the system." Obsessional thoughts, hallucinations, delusions, intense anxiety or depressive ruminations, severe psychic or physical pain—these would all qualify as noise in the system. The involuntary nature of this painful type of isolation and the human desire to overcome it differentiate such isolation from voluntary withdrawal or noncommunication for whatever reason—be it catatonia or the drive for privacy that prompted Leonardo's mirror writing.

The cognitive imperative to understand and be understood pervades interpersonal relations. We tend to be aware of the problems of the genius and the mentally retarded, but we are oblivious to persons suffering from prevalent but more subtle cultural barriers. We often disregard words and nonverbal signals which we believe do not mean what they seem to mean. These include not only the words of politicians or advertising agencies, but of people from different socioeconomic, ethnic, and geographic backgrounds. Familiar-sounding words like work, bad, naughty, funny, tough, manly, beautiful, honest, criminal, violent, paranoid, love, and poor have such varied meanings that at times they might just as well be foreign words. That is one reason why psychiatrists so often ask, "What do you mean by that?"

The nonverbal mode is more confusing and its effects often subliminal. Those who look down or avert their eyes before an authority figure, for example, are not necessarily admitting guilt or betraying a criminal nature; their culture may prescribe such behavior as a sign of respect. Loneliness does not result directly from verbal and nonverbal barriers, but from missed cues and rebuffs, arising from misinterpretation. Hall (1966) has described the cross-cultural misunderstandings caused by different attitudes about personal distance. For example, the Middle Easterner conversing nose-to-nose with the American as is customary in his culture, feels rejected if the American finds him too forward and takes two steps back.

Whorf introduced the idea that language and its grammar and vocabulary govern the way a person perceives the world (Carroll, 1956). An Eskimo, for example, can identify many kinds of snow; his vocabulary serves this purpose. More recent studies have shown that if a language has no word for a certain color, perception of the color is reduced or absent. This phenomenon filters out even more nuances in the subjective realm of feelings. A Chinese Malaysian medical student on ward rounds in Kuala Lumpur told me that he could not elicit the symptoms of anxiety until he taught his Chinese-speaking patients the word(s) for anxiety.

I have learned that the Japanese have about 50 words for loneliness[2] and related terms (solitude, privacy) based on ideographs (for example, those representing a roof with nothing beneath it, an empty house, an orphan, secrecy-privacy, self-possession, dogs biting each other) and the Katakana (nonideographic) word *pivraibashi* (privacy) from the English. One cannot dismiss the many terms as accidental or merely curious. Any culture that devotes so much vocabulary to the subject of loneliness must be quite aware of and sensitive to its importance. It may be either highly valued, greatly feared, or knowledge of it may have special survival value. For whatever reason, their extensive vocabulary will continue to sensitize and alert the Japanese to loneliness

In their contributions to this volume, Christie Kiefer and Ilze Veith both discuss a unique Japanese psychotherapy called Morita therapy. Kiefer focuses on the sense of dependency and Veith on the renewed relationship with nature that characterize this therapy. The Morita

---

[2]Narae Mochizuki, personal communication to J. Ralph Audy, January, 1967.

process, a form of beneficent, nurturing, isolation therapy, rations the patient's contacts with the outside world, beginning with an enforced isolation and dependence reminiscent of the infantile state, and working toward a full return to normal adult socialization. That such treatment is effective in Japan suggests that in a communal, family-oriented society, language and culture can sensitize people to loneliness (or to solitude, the positive side of being alone), and thereby make the onset of loneliness so painful that a person can be driven to escape into health (as in Morita therapy or as dramatized in Potok's *The Promise*, 1969). Certain social and cultural practices contain built-in defense systems to prevent and counteract loneliness. *Amae*, the Japanese concept of mutual dependency, represents such an intervening mechanism. To be dependent on a significant other means to be well. Not to be in either a nurturing or succoring relationship with another means to be sick (Doi, 1973).

Whether solitude has *meaning* greatly affects the impact of loneliness. Meaningless or self-deprecating loneliness is of a very different order from loneliness that has an understandable cause or that results from an act of the will. One's ability to cope with, and resist, overwhelming stress depends on one's ability to comprehend the meaning of the stress. Adversity implies an opposing force. Fighting back is more conducive to mental health than the passive acquiescence that leads to despair. This is true even when the adversary is nature.

Among the cognitive mechanisms used to counteract the sense of loneliness-without-meaning are intellectual justification and explanation of the condition; the assumption of personal motivation for the activity that led to the lonely condition; reliance on the support provided by the consensus of others; and a belief in the limited duration of the lonely condition. These mechanisms create a sense of *control*. The appeals to spiritual, supernatural, magical, and scientific meanings all serve the same purpose. I recall an incident in a stalled automatic elevator. After a minute of waiting, an impatient passenger began jumping up and down. When the elevator moved again (of its own accord), the passenger felt good because he believed he was in control of the elevator. Highly motivated student volunteers for scientific experiments will tolerate all kinds of abuse, including prolonged sensory deprivation that produces severe psychological reactions. They may justify their predicament either by believing that they are advancing the frontiers of science or by accepting the experimental conditions as a fast way to earn money.

Highly motivated hermits, martyrs, scientists, artists, and explorers usually handle their loneliness better than the abandoned, deserted, widowed, and divorced because their lonely experience has meaning. But the scientist, artist, and explorer, like the executive (and his wife), fail to cope with the loneliness of their lives when they are no longer productive. Their productiveness, therefore, is crucial to their personal sense of meaning and provides an insulation against loneliness. Seidenberg illustrates this point in his chapter on the "Lonely Marriage in Corporate America."

The time-bound grief reaction of a person who has lost someone through death is far different from the almost indelible trauma and psychiatric consequence of loss through abandonment in childhood. In the former case the loss is explainable, in the latter case it is not. I recall a patient who had a history of depression and fear of public places brought on by the death of her husband. We discovered that her resistance to cure stemmed from her inability to deal with her feelings about the way she was abandoned at the age of nine. Her mother had told her to wait for her on a corner in the business district and had never returned. The patient had no way to explain this event.

It is easier to understand and explain the feeling of being cut off and shut out when a language barrier is involved. In such cases, there may be ways to overcome the resulting feelings of loneliness. The sensory aphasia of a stroke victim, however, is of a different order of desperation. Such a patient may read or hear words that look or sound familiar, but the words no longer convey any meaning. The patient usually does not understand the problem and when people act as if he hears nothing, his sense of isolation can easily trigger loneliness.

Researchers have demonstrated how supportive the power of consensus is to members of a group. If nine people in a closed, decision-making group assert a most outlandish idea by prearrangement, a naive subject will find it difficult to resist the pressure to conform. If a group deprecates or appreciates solitude, the ability of group members to withstand it will vary accordingly. Paradoxically, overly high self-estimation in an individual, like low self-esteem, creates an interpersonal wall, blocking the support of others and impeding one's ability to break out of the state of loneliness.

A painful experience that can be justified or explained for an hour or a day, or for which there is consensual support for a week, may not have the same meaning or cause the same degree of pain for an extended period. The worst torment of all is being cut off with no end in sight. The serviceman can tolerate an arctic assignment or submarine tour and the convict can face a fixed sentence more easily than an indeterminate one. Comparably, lonely people would not despair if they could be certain of an end to their pain. In fact, a person confronting a certain circumstance for an indeterminate period of time will become lonely whereas the same person would experience no loneliness in an identical circumstance if its duration was known. Moreover, the sense of time can become distorted by extremes of mood—sadness lengthens the perception of time and feelings of well-being shorten it. The feeling of interminable time aggravates the loneliness of the depressed. The reservoir of hope generated by the earliest mother-child attachment is the source of resilience that a person uses to combat indeterminate loneliness and to return to life among others.

I have tried to analyze the meaning of loneliness. The resulting explanation is not complete, but it is neither spuriously "accurate" nor misleadingly precise. The different outlooks of sociologists, anthropologists, psychologists, psychiatrists, biologists, and theologians would pattern the same data—using some parts, excluding others, and interpolating "missing" pieces—into very different interpretations of loneliness, each valid to a degree, but none complete.

This book is an attempt to let proponents of these various disciplines forge their own meanings of loneliness. Though, as editors, we have not imposed our own definition on the separate contributions, we have chosen to minimize the sociological orientation because there is already an impressive collection of books and articles on anomie and alienation, the societal cousins of loneliness. Sadler and Johnson, however, do contribute a chapter that relates the meaning of anomie to the individual. We were wary of material that dealt with plain unhappiness and depression in the guise of loneliness. Leiderman's chapter on "Pathological Loneliness" helps differentiate loneliness from depression. We sought to steer a course between sentimentality and sociopolitical theory, mainly because the anomie associated with *Gesellschaft* (modern society) says more about the Industrial Revolution than it does about individual pain. Yet this volume still encompasses a broad spectrum of philosophies and professional disciplines, and therefore elaborates many categories of loneliness. The special character of loneliness in various life stages and life crises is presented. Different authors treat variously the loneliness of childhood (Wallerstein and Kelly), adolescence (Ostrov and Offer), widowhood (Lopata), divorce (Eisenson), corporate married life (Seidenberg), being black (Dunn and Dunn), and aging (Bart, Clark, and Anderson). The experience of creativity in relation to loneliness is presented through the eyes of artist (Lubin, Landau) and poet (Parkinson). Calhoun and Sermat present divergent psychological approaches to loneliness, as do the psychiatrists. Rubenstein and Shaver give us the results of a public survey assessing loneliness. I myself employ a developmental model. The psychoanalytic viewpoint is represented by Fromm-Reichmann's article as well as by a relatively unknown posthumous article by Klein. General anthropological overviews are provided by Mead, Cohen, and Henry. A specific look at the Japanese is provided by Kiefer and a slice of America is examined by Keyes. Sadler and Johnson present a fresh and thoughtful formulation of the various levels of loneliness while Audy discusses loneliness from the viewpoint of the biologist. Veith brings a historical dimension to the treatment of loneliness while Buber, Mijuskovic, and Tillich offer thoughtful philosophical reflections. Lastly, Thoreau gives us his joyful ode to solitude and nature. Ultimately, the reader is left alone to synthesize his or her own meaning of loneliness from the elements that are presented, and this, we suggest, can best be done by fusing them with the sensibility of his or her individual experience.

1

The Anlage
and Ontogeny of Loneliness

JOSEPH HARTOG

INTRODUCTION

As THE EMBRYONIC CLUSTER of cells contains the anlage of each anatomical structure, so the childhood cluster of attachment and separation experiences lays the foundation for the individual's eventual
adaptational style. From these anlagen in the child (or infant) develop
the increasingly fixed goals, overall strategies, and coping mechanisms of the growing person.

This model implies a dependent if not causal relationship between
the nature of the child's attachment to his mother (or mother surrogate) and the adult's coping with loneliness and its consequences.
Whether experienced as loneliness or not, the first attachments and
"disattachments" form the prototype of all succeeding reenactments,
and echo through life in the leitmotif of separation. I am not, however,
suggesting an absolute biological determinism or predestination,
whether genetic, congenital, imprinted, or the product of a universal
unconscious. The bits of behavior, particular plans, and life scripts are
learned, not programmed.

Loneliness per se has no objective positive or negative value apart
from subjectively experienced feelings. These subjective feelings
reflect and exacerbate the devaluative effects of solitude or isolation,
sometimes turning a neutral or mildly negative state into a fearful and
painful experience. In an individualistic society, the value accorded
individuality conflicts with the probable primate drive of gregarious-

13

ness, making loneliness a necessary component of life. In such a society, the borders of the ego end with the person or perhaps the immediate family. In the extreme, the ego exists only deep within the body, like the soul or the pineal gland, leaving the flesh without value. Conversely, in traditional peasant societies, "life is with people," individuality is not an assumed right, and loneliness through misfortune is catastrophic. The manifestations of pining merge with those of ostracism, mortification, and voodoo death. In such societies, the ego may extend to the boundary of the family-clan-community. Whereas a hermit cares little about his personal appearance or the society in which he lives, and appears not to need others, the clan member sees himself as part of a larger human system; his ego boundaries and concerns seem remote from his personal desires, and his concerns are thereby subordinate to the larger social good. But the clan member also needs other people. Modern urban man falls in between the hermit and clan member, and feels the conflict of personal needs and societal demands.

Hence the adaptive and maladaptive range of loneliness is defined partly by culture. For instance, we urban Westerners cannot comprehend the Eskimo surviving physically and mentally in the isolation of his kayak in the uncharted ocean under a starless sky. Does he consider himself lonely? Perhaps not. Personality differences notwithstanding, members of different cultures experience identical distances between people or houses differently, as Edward Hall (1968) has noted. Many American suburbanites, formerly city dwellers, have felt terribly isolated and lonely in their roomy dream houses after the closeness of their previous apartments or flats. Chinese apartment house dwellers in Singapore and Hong Kong develop a higher suicide rate after moving from the crowded traditional shop house and village settings. In what follows, my subject concerns how and why the individual survives the inevitable experiences of loneliness.

THE ANLAGE OF LONELINESS

The first and critical loneliness period, probably in all cultures, lies between the ages of six months and three years. This temporal fact virtually assures that this important event will be forgotten years later. But I do not wish to imply that nothing before, or particularly after, the interval is of consequence. Not only can life deal cruel, damaging blows or even compensatory and restitutive experiences before and after this interval, but the infant's health and constitution may prolong or minimize the critical period. In addition to their effect upon the critical period, innate individual differences determine the amount of stimulation each infant needs and how he responds to stimulation. This feedback to parents may, in turn, determine their attitudes toward the child. Family interrelationships and the extrafamilial environment, too, can affect parental attitudes and the psychophysiological timetables. Furthermore, the "mother" may be a mother surrogate, the communal mother that Bettelheim (1969) has discussed, or even haphazardly available relatives within the extended families of some cultures. Such variations also contribute to cultural differences in the impact of separation and loneliness.

The primordial loneliness of early childhood encompasses all of the real, symbolic, and imagined separations from mother, whether they are felt physically, emotionally, physiologically (the empathic organ functions discussed by Greenblatt [1972]) or perhaps extrasensorily (Ehrenwald's [1971] "cradle of ESP"). In an early work, Otto Rank (1929) theorized that the trauma of birth itself, the radical separation from the all-providing amniotic environment, may set the universal tone of primal terror for all succeeding separations, and cause either the return or the continuing concealment of the unconscious wish to return to the womb. Yet, to explain differences in later responses to separation and loneliness, one must seek the corresponding differences in early experiences and not simply look at the universal event that may form the substrate for lifelong anxiety. We must study early mother-child separations beyond parturition.

John Bowlby (1960) and René Spitz (1945) based their pioneering studies of separation on observations of children in pediatric wards of hospitals and other institutions. By studying the effects of separation in these settings they were able to observe the length of separations and the frequency of human contacts. Just as significant are less explicit emotional separations: the subtle withdrawals of love, interest, or attention caused by a shift of the mother's concern to another child; the loss of the child's charm in his mother's eyes that may follow his expression of rivalry, rebellion, or the wish for more autonomy or mobility; or some more indirect event, such as the mother's reaction to some anniversary from her own childhood, as described by Josephine Hilgard (1969).

No real physical or emotional separation need be experienced. The mother's anxiety over a move of the child's toward autonomy, if severe enough, may implant the germ of pathological loneliness that festers for years and may perhaps be acted out as a school phobia. If the child's ability to differentiate his self from that of his mother or other significant family members is impaired, he will be plagued with an unexplainable and refractory loneliness consequent to his feeling of incompleteness. To feel whole, he will need someone else but will inevitably feel disappointed when the other fails to fit the demi-role precisely. In the extreme, if he cannot distinguish his self from the selves of others, he appears schizophrenic, a process discussed in P. Herbert Leiderman's contribution to this volume.

Infants and children probably experience even the most subtly or subliminally neglectful or rejecting attitude as separation, whether or not the culture recognizes the attitude as a rejecting one. Some forms of rejection—abandonment, parental inattention, lack of affection or physical contact, loss of self-esteem, isolation, malnutrition, even direct brutality—may be experienced similarly as separations while others paradoxically are not. Some may even be sought compulsively as antidotes for separation, clear precursors to sado-masochism that simultaneously provide a clue to the meaning of regressive sexual perversions in general. The clue is that any contact is better than none—audience contact (applause, laughter); visual contact for the exhibitionist and voyeur; auditory contact for the anonymous telephone caller; physical contact for the "bad" child (by the whip and rod), the masochist, the rapist, and the pedophiliac. At the same time the symptom allows a distorted return to a wished-for infantile state.

The reactions of the child experiencing separation follow a consistent pattern, according to John Bowlby (1960, 1969). First there is protest: crying, calling, screaming, thrashing about, lasting several hours to several days. This stage is followed by a second stage of despair, withdrawal, and a rejection of attempts by strangers such as nurses to make friends, to entertain, or to play. This stage may produce a period of regression to thumbsucking, encopresis (soiling), enuresis (bedwetting), or other infantile mannerisms that have been outgrown. However, the return of mother during either of these stages will rapidly bring the child back to apparent normality. The third stage is that of detachment and apathy, which roughly begins after more than two weeks of separation. The detached child does not fuss or fight; he will play alone or with adults; he is quiet and well-behaved. Though he will accept gifts and in fact focus on them, he will not recognize his mother or relate emotionally to anyone. He is the early version of the typical long-term institutionalized child, apparently normal but actually isolated in a protective invisible envelope, almost autistic. Extreme forms of this disorder (the "hospitalism" described by René Spitz [1945]) are seen in county hospitals among abandoned infants quietly staring with an inner blindness, easy to care for physically and prone to illness and premature death. In these infants, the feeling for mother is lost (repressed) following prolonged separation or what might be called "attachment starvation," for to the child at this crucial stage, attachment to mother is as important as food. The absence of a proper attachment experience, like food, may result in stunted growth, whereas less complete deprivation may produce overcompensating obesity. "No form of behavior is accompanied by stronger feeling than is attachment behavior," says Bowlby (1969, p. 209). Even infant monkeys demonstrate the detrimental effects of brief separation from their mothers, and for at least two years following such separations, they cling more timidly and react more slowly than nonseparated monkeys (Spencer-Booth and Hinde, 1971).

THE ONTOGENY OF LONELINESS

The need for social interaction beyond the primary attachment to the mother or mother-surrogate becomes increasingly evident as the attachment behavior decreases, though the latter remains important. Early tentative development of sociability appears in the back-and-forth exploratory behavior of infant nonhuman primates. Such behavior may be governed by biological rhythms yet to be delineated. Freud (1926, pp. 169–170) attributed the attractiveness to the child of hide-and-seek games, magic tricks, disappearing acts, rhythmic activities (swinging, bouncing, rocking, yo-yos) and rescue fantasy play to the opportunities such activities provided for reenactment of, and attempts to master the fear of, the cycle of separation and return. I recall an obviously lonely hospitalized child who was endlessly entertained by the appearance and disappearance of the pediatric resident's retractible tape measure. Transitional objects like Linus's blanket, a "pacifier," a special cuddly doll or stuffed animal, or a relationship through prayer with a higher power like God, may smooth the path to autonomy. The child can have attachment and separation at the same time.

In late childhood and preadolescence, companionship with peers, usually of the same sex, is critical. Conformity leading to group acceptance is the means to this end. In the early years pets, dolls, imaginary companions, and the world of fantasy are used at times to fill the companion-free periods (not in lieu of friends). The extent to which these substitutes are used reflects the degree of satisfaction obtained in earlier attachment relationships. The deprived or rejected child will tend to act attached and clinging and may show little independent fantasy play, contradicting the popular notion that fantasy and imaginative play are results of loneliness. The "only" child engages in such imaginary play and, as many writers have observed, is not necessarily lonely in the unhappy sense. And the autism of the psychotic child does not create the well organized and cohesive productions of the healthy imagination.

Resemblance to peers is particularly important during the later stages of childhood; that is when differences in physical appearance due to culture, race, size, or deformity have greatest psychological impact and force some children into loneliness. But even the reactions to such duress vary according to earlier experiences. The attachment-secure child will have a greater repertoire of reactions to threatened ostracism and narcissistic injury while the insecure child will tend to repeat his earlier responses to unfavorable experiences, such as clinging to a rejecting figure, seeking punishment for the sake of attention, regressing, or perhaps withdrawing from all peer social interactions.

It may be during this latency period, the second normal loneliness period, that certain permanent attitudes about "others" develop, such as "people cannot be trusted," "never do anything for anybody," "never depend on others," "no one appreciates what I do," etc. The disappointment of age two is transposed into the distrust of age eight, the beginning of the "loner's" mentality. "Forget you!", like many expressions from black dialect, powerfully gets to the heart of the matter; the phrase projected from "don't forget me" to "forget you" conveys pejorativeness and makes contact with the deepest fears of the child, regardless of his race or economic condition.

Sociability throughout life derives from early attachment behavior, though sociability is less specific in terms of the object(s) of attachment and typically is directed at more than one individual once the "buddy" stage is past. Unlike mother attachment, sociability proves to be merely satisfying in itself, or at least its adaptive value is not as obvious. Early attachment behavior to the mother, on the other hand, is primary, instinctual, and on a par with hunger, sex, and curiosity. Contrary to the assumptions of some psychological theorists, such behavior is not merely the result of pleasant early attachment associations with food, warmth, touch, breast, nor is it utilitarian in the sociological sense of serving the needs of a group.

Adolescence is the loneliest developmental period. Several distinct, unavoidable, crucial events and processes intersect during this period. For one, the physical changes of puberty tend to isolate individuals because the changes are out of phase both within any group (individuals within the group mature at different times) and within an individual (pubescent changes within the individual begin at different times). Such changes pertain to emotions and body, voice and body, growth and secondary sex characteristics. These out-of-phase and uncoordinated changes isolate adolescents from each other and raise questions for the adolescent about who he really is.

The question of identity, which of course does not end with adolescence, causes the third period of normal loneliness. Adolescents care very much about being "true to themselves," not phony or self-deceptive, and about being a "somebody" who is both identifiable and individual. *Individual,* of course, means whole, undivided.

Concern about honesty and deceitfulness, which derives from fragmentation of identity or the awareness of discord within the adolescent subegos (that is, component parts of the ego), has some interesting ramifications. For one, the feeling of not being quite real or genuine can be projected onto the parents or society; hence the accusations of hypocrisy in others, or put more fairly, the heightened awareness of, or sensitivity to, hypocrisy. Erwin Singer (1968) found that children with reading disabilities or other disadvantages more accurately perceived hypocrisy in adults than did children with more advantages. One would predict even more striking findings with adolescents who notice parental double standards regarding the drugs of youth culture (marijuana, psychedelics) and those of the parents' generation (alcohol, amphetamines, barbiturates, tranquilizers, tobacco), or with adolescents who feel the uncomfortable contrast between their own religiosity or idealism and their parents' cynical, acquisitive materialism, or between their own dissatisfaction with society and their parents' apathetic "going along with the system."

Another threat to the delicate identity formation during early adolescence or pre-adolescence is normal, latent homosexuality. It is striking that dissatisfied adult homosexuals are plagued by the same theme of phoniness and dissimulation that adolescents voice. Yet homosexuality, like other sexual variations, still represents an attempt to maintain some form of human attachment (to avoid loneliness) in the face of the threat of, or distaste for, heterosexual closeness.

The feeling of deceit exaggerates loneliness; the adolescent may believe he is the only one in the world who has doubts about his wholeness, purity, and consistency—a logical consequence of identity diffusion and the enormous difference between his own inner life and what he can see of other young people's lives. Imagine (or recall) the adolescent's loneliness and isolation when parents appear imperfect and make contradictory demands (for example, expect him to be successful both socially *and* academically), when friends seem inconsistent, society hypocritical, and education irrelevant to his constantly changing needs and feelings. The adolescent cannot comfortably fit into his family, or into the social institutions of children or adults, but he does not want to dismiss and abandon these worlds either. His position resembles that of the lonely "culture broker"—the marginal person who bridges or stands between two cultures (Press, 1969). To be "somebody" negates the potentially catastrophic loneliness of being "nobody."

A logical consequence then is the hackneyed "adolescent authority revolt" by which, briefly, the adolescent communicates his anxiety and anger about his loneliness and dependency in the no-man's-land of identity formation, while further isolating himself to the extent that he antagonizes the parents or society he still depends upon. In partial compensation he seeks nurturance and support from friends. The guilt resulting from the anger at his parents, the frustration and loss of self-esteem because he cannot be truly independent, and the associated voluntary and involuntary loneliness cause generalized anger and depression. The source of his anger often escapes others, especially participant observers who get caught up in the feelings, and this only aggravates the adolescent further. Yet anger without just cause conceals, if it does not accompany, depression. Bowlby noted that even in infancy separation or threat of loss was likely to arouse anger.

In fact these adolescent crises take on their special importance and intense charge because they reenact problems and solutions of the earlier developmental graduation from around age two. The recapitulation of separation episodes parallels the reawakening at puberty of certain psychosexual conflicts (Oedipal complex) that had been first aroused in early childhood.

The fourth loneliness crisis is that of preparation as it confronts college-age young persons. Planning for the future, obsessing about careers, and undertaking other creative exercises are lonely experiences. One temporary, passive-aggressive solution allows authorities, parents, or peers to lead the way and then gives the young person license to complain about their advice. Certain fluctuations between ascetic withdrawal with fantasy, and hedonistic activity, derive from this dissatisfied compliance with authority or other leaders, and from the attendant identity conflict. College mental health services see the extreme consequences of this crisis in students who appear with the near-psychotic and suicidal symptoms of the "post-adolescent identity crisis."

The importance of the group to the adolescent is so well known that elaboration may not seem necessary. But group activity as a means for coping with loneliness or rather as a means for achieving an attachment to a collective mother-surrogate produces indirect consequences. The immediate positive effects are that the group allows a transitional resolution of the separation from parents by allowing attachment to a higher-order "parent" (or lower-order, depending on one's view). It further allows a displacement of the authority revolt against whomever and whatever the group happens to be opposing; the middle class, communist subversives, capitalists, the Establishment power structure, polluters, foreigners, hippies, radicals, atheists and other "nonbelievers," or special ethnic and religious minorities. The group also relieves the pressure of the identity crisis by submerging individuality and individual differences, while providing a ready-made transitional identity. Even decisions about the future get artificial outside direction via ideologies, or rest in abeyance—in moratorium, to paraphrase Erik Erikson.

As a system for coping with loneliness, however, the group presents potential dangers besides those of mob behavior, reactive totalitarianism, and loss of individual liberty. The adolescent is vulnerable to what I would call pseudoinstitutions. Such pseudoinstitutions may employ group confession (since the adolescent already feels he is not quite honest enough) or various other ritual and often destructive and self-destructive sacrificial activities (as in the Deutsche Jugend, the Red Guard, the Weathermen, the drug culture, group experience panaceas, military and religious fanaticism, and mystical cults). Such groups and institutions can appease the inner opposing authority (superego) by projecting unacceptable impulses on others, seeking punishment, or expiating impurity. The most dangerous effects are anonymity, passive uncritical submission to a leader, and conscience-free behavior.

To prevent being misinterpreted as attacking all so-called youth culture, I should note that the most dangerous groups are those composed of what L. J. West (1969) has called xenophobic cultural conformists, such as superracists. The hippie-type noncomformists, who homophobically direct their hostility towards their own parent culture, do not pose nearly as much of a physical threat in terms of actual mayhem and assault. Most bombings and such in the United States are directed at nonconformists and minority group members, not at the "Establishment."

The two types of groups deal with loneliness from diametrical positions. The conformists handle loneliness by huddling closer to their own kind, attacking outsiders whether they be on the next block or in the next country. The nonconformists try to deny their loneliness and need for conventional acceptance by withdrawing, in behavior or appearance, from their own family's culture. Both groups simultaneously displace and project their authority conflicts—the conformist on strangers, the noncomformists on their own parents' society—while both use the conflict to establish closeness with like-minded individuals in a group. These two groups should not be confused with a third, whose members protest and dissent against society's inequities and injustices in conformity with their parents' moral convictions but in an attempt to correct the hypocrisies and inconsistencies between the ideals taught to them and the reality experienced. They act out of attachment security, not out of the results or fears of personal rejection.

Perhaps nonconforming and lonely "bums" and skid row residents view themselves in a similar positive light. Yet studies of homeless men note their characteristic background of frustrated dependency (attachment) needs. Their alienation syndromes include frozen inner resources, passivity, helplessness, depression, and detachment. But skid row residents also value their independence, freedom, and lack of responsibility, and express their "very low opinion of what motivates others" (Levinson, 1966). The steady decline over the past forty years in the number of skid row residents in the United States does not indicate that homelessness, loneliness, and alienation in general have declined, particularly in view of the new forms of dropping out and of migratory or nomadic life styles, not excluding the unprecedented mobility and rootlessness of the conventional American nuclear family.

The "voluntary" type of individualistic loneliness, more aptly called solitude or aloneness and sometimes termed alienation (à la Camus), deserves special examination. Some marginal individuals sometimes called "culture brokers" typically straddle cultures; they may be misfit deviants, or persons of prestige. They often are the first to welcome outsiders, introduce innovations, and interpret the outside to the traditional group. Examples of such marginal individuals would include the son of a peasant who becomes a school teacher and returns to his own village, the middle-aged hippie, the tomboy, the Mexican who adopts the values and appearance of an Anglo, the English-educated and English-speaking Chinese in Singapore, the ghetto black who receives a college education and attempts to return to help his people, the assimilated nonreligious Jew in an orthodox community (as seen in the powerful Czechoslovak movie "A Shop on Main Street"), or any of countless hybrid professionals, such as the psychiatrist-anthropologist, teacher- or researcher-administrator, politician-sociologist, or philosopher-physicist. Such individuals may facilitate change during times of community stability, and show the way to safety or resolution during times of community crisis. These voluntary aliens aid community adaptability and survival by serving as a pool of human resources awaiting the right time to act and by keeping alive the idea of personal liberty. But the role almost always produces some isolation and occasionally martyrdom, and such marginal people pay a stiff psychological, social, and sometimes political penalty for their deviance.

Another voluntary state of loneliness is that which serves the crea-

tive process. Both loneliness and creativity contain a quality of anticipation and expectation. Perhaps it is a recapitulation of the child's
awaiting the return of mother or the expectation that she will be there
after the early tentative explorations end. The pregnant woman also is
"expecting." It is as though the goal of a creative work was a regression to an earlier state of bliss or a moment of warm security, to be followed by a return to exploration and novelty-seeking. This is a
rhythm seen in children and immature subhuman primates. Some
writers have noted the need to find a comfortable place to write, like
Spain, Italy, or Greece, after highly stimulating and exciting experiences or research, perhaps in New York. The sunny Mediterranean
must have an amniotic quality. Even school children bring their artistic productions back to parents—sometimes for approval but also
because that's what their art is all about. It overcomes the separation
from the family; it maintains the critical attachment symbolically. In
fact the Latin root of the word *relate* means "carry back." For this
reason and for its tangibility, correspondence by letter, even in the age
of telecommunications, will remain emotionally important.

I do not wish to explain all creativity as displaced attachment
behavior any more than the psychoanalyst wishes to consider painting
purely sublimated anal activity. But the childhood past leaves clues to
the meaning of the adult present. Some artists produce when they are
lonely and depressed, but their condition differs from the normal
voluntary solitude that is a necessity for certain kinds of creative work.
The artist may be productive in the presence of depressive loneliness
either to overcome the feeling through the creation of a work of art as
an object of attachment itself, or as "a statement" or message to
make contact with others. Ironically, the very affiliative behavior used
for escaping aloneness and its consequent anxiety defeats the creative
goal. This is why teams or committees, pleasant and productive
though they may be, do not create. Hence, the artist is often forced to
choose between the comfort of uncreative affiliation and the isolation
of creative solitude, or at best to swing from one to the other,
repeatedly reenacting the attachment-separation drama.

Since Stanley Schachter has demonstrated in *The Psychology of Affiliation* (1959) that affiliating with others seems to have an anxiety-
reducing effect, we can begin to guess what the anxiety is all about.
Does isolation, then, increase anxiety? Experiments in sensory deprivation appear to indicate that it does, even to the extent of producing

psychotic-like symptoms. Such were the desired effects of the journey into the wilderness that the American Indian boy undertook in search of a mystical experience that would qualify him for manhood. The experience helped to ritualize and institutionalize the adolescent loneliness, and eventual acceptance into the tribe as an adult offered relief. In other cultures, trance and possession states counteract loneliness. For a time, isolation raises anxiety and, perhaps most important from a creative point of view, increases sensitivity to inner stimulation. These two results combined may light the creative spark, and their extreme manifestations may range from solipsism to reactions resembling psychosis. In this regard, the isolation of creativity appears to have been an important contributor to the near-mad fascination with "the double" shown by Goethe, Maupassant, Dostoevsky, and Poe.

Folk beliefs connecting madness and genius (for example, the belief that "brain-strain" can cause a brilliant student to go mad), while wrong in their assumptions about the causal association between madness and genius, correctly recognize common factors between the two states. Loneliness and hypersensitivity to inner stimuli are two such factors. Is self-imposed isolation during creative activity an inadvertent but essential way of raising the level of psychic output? It may be, but there is a time limit after which the internal stimulation decreases and the result is monotony and boredom, internal as well as external. The central nervous system, like a battery, requires sensory input.

The most common and important adult affiliation is marriage. Generally the potential for its success or failure is written in the childhood of the partners, although economic and cultural stresses and assets also weigh in the balance. My interest here is with the offspring. It is too easy to produce a pseudohereditary pattern of various kinds of psychological and social pathology passed from generation to generation. For instance, "only" children and the children of divorced parents are more likely to be divorced as adults than are children of intact marriages. Abused and battered children tend to become child-battering parents, and "only" children tend to be parents of "only" children. Significantly more children of divorced and deceased parents become college dropouts than those of intact families. Clearly the children of broken partnerships or brutal parents have special problems because of their attachment-deprivation experience. Remedies offered deal with the consequences—delinquency, school failure, drug abuse, and mental disorder—selectively ignoring causes. In a hedonistic society where individual freedom of choice reigns supreme, high divorce and separation rates are predictable. But children have no choice. If the family *and* the society, unaware of the entity "attachment-starvation," fail to protect the interests of children, then we all will eventually pay the cost. The biographies of recent assassins and would-be assassins bear out this assertion. For instance, Prescott and McKay (1972), using R. B. Textor's *Cross-Cultural Summary, 1967,* studied 49 societies that demonstrated a direct correlation between the absence of affection for infants and incidence of killing, torturing, and mutilating enemies. Yet the vastly more numerous but less spectacular private sufferings expressed in depressions and suicides receive less attention. While overall suicide rates in the U.S. have remained fairly stable in the past decade, suicide rates for adolescents (under 20) have almost doubled, making suicide one of the major causes of death in adolescence, in some regions second only to death by accident. Studies of the problems of depression and suicide have confirmed the role of separation and rejection as precipitants. Perhaps the cycle can be interrupted only by new family or communal child-rearing forms, as in the Israeli kibbutz, new family social agencies or child advocacy systems with new legal powers, or, at the very least, a reactionary return to stricter divorce and child-care laws.

As a person passes from the stage of adult creativity to the process of decline in old age, loneliness again takes on new meanings. At this stage, Erik Erikson (1959) teaches that wisdom and psychological integrity can defy despair. Loneliness again provides the medium to prepare for the expected completion (the ultimate separation, closure of life) of the life cycle. The process of disaffiliation allows more time for the creative tying together of personal meanings, for the bequest of integrated knowledge and experience to one's successors, and for some preparation for death. Old age, without these satisfactions and the pleasures of solitude alternating with selected social activities, results in lonely despair. Inability to regress in the service of the ego, as the aging person and artist must, may lead to panic. Harold Voth, Albert Voth, and Robert Canero (1969) have shown that significantly more people who cannot experience their inner psychic selves, who are too rigidly attached to the outer physical world, are likely to commit suicide.

How well a person can tolerate and rebound from loneliness at earlier stages of life will determine later acceptance of death. For those who must deal with the loss of others, ritualized funerals and prescribed mourning are useful at least for confronting the self-deception about death. The loss, separation, and loneliness of death and mourning shorten the life expectancy of the bereaved. Even geographical location of death affects the survivors. The individual whose relative has died away from home is subject to premature death, a vulnerability which may even be related to the relative's distance from home when he died (Rees and Lutkins, 1967).

THE DISGUISES OF LONELINESS

I do not equate loneliness with depression, and yet many people who are involuntarily lonely are also depressed. Conversely, depressed or other emotionally disturbed individuals may choose to be alone. Certain ways of coping with depression and loneliness overlap. From a psychopathological perspective, loneliness, like depression, may be denied, acted out, submerged in a group; it may be painful, despairing, bittersweet, prideful, self-destructive; it may be rationalized ("They do not want me or like me"), philosophized ("It is man's unique fate to be alone in the universe"), sociologized ("It is the impotent anonymity of urban society"), politicized ("It is the hypocritical values of affluent capitalist materialism"), or ecologized ("It is the population explosion, air, water, and noise pollution, and the loss of touch with nature"). It can be *reacted to* (that is, reaction formation) by the choice of isolation as the most delightful way of life or *escaped* through frantic work and social schedules, or in more extreme cases, through fugues, amnesia, multiple personalities (as in Thigpen and Cleckley's *Three Faces of Eve* [1957]), promiscuity, or delinquency. Beneath the surface, however, the escapers attempt to make new contacts and attachments. Loneliness may be *compensated for* through possessed objects, money, acquisitions, accumulations, collections, and pets, in whose absence separation symptoms may return. It may be *combated* from a distance by exhibitionism (for example, please touch me with your shocked reaction, applause, or your eyes) or sexual perversions that allow contact and personal detachment at the same time.

Other psychoneurotic symptoms can be partially understood in terms of the loneliness-attachment relationship. Phobias, for instance, which appear so unrelated to perversions, are really the opposite side of the same coin: the phobic person maintains his detachment physically rather than psychologically out of fear of contact-making behavior that may be associated with sinful impulses—the kind of behavior to which others might resort to overcome or deny their loneliness. What an adolescent (especially a depressed one) might do in the face of loneliness and what a phobic person might be prevented from doing, is to resort to action. Many adolescents convert their feelings of loss and loneliness into delinquent behavior, though not many as transparently as the boy who specialized in stealing women's purses after his mother died. Among a large number of boys in a reform school in Malaysia I noted a high percentage who began their delinquent activities after the birth of a sibling—a relative loss of status and parental attention.

For the person who can experience his psychic life through heightened fantasy or introspection, loneliness, however painful, may be an adaptive defense against stressful events such as personal loss, incarceration, ostracism, and ambiguity. John Nemiah and Peter Sifneos (1970) found that patients with psychosomatic disorders were apparently incapable of producing fantasies. The use of certain drugs may facilitate the experiencing of inner psychic material. This idea underlay the attempted LSD treatment for alcoholics and heroin addicts, who typically have a barren, unimaginative life and who deal with conflict via muscular-motor activity. But, like religious conversion, the treatment for alcoholics provided a transient feeling of well-being and personality change but proved ineffective in the long run. The inability to experience one's internal psychic life must at times create the most unpleasant kind of loneliness, an encircled entrapment, a lack of territory for retreat, reorganization, and restitution. In this sense a schizophrenic psychosis both provides a refuge from an empty, intolerably ambiguous loneliness and at the same time seals the escape back to human involvement. The paranoid, in particular (like the depressive), progressively isolates himself from others by causing his circle of contacts to shrink—through withdrawal, rejection, hostility—until he ends up alone in the small end of a funnel. Yet even then, imagination, fantasy, and hallucinations replace the real self with a delusion and the real objects with imaginary companions (or persecutors), doubles, shadows, and souls, clinging to a hope for eternal attachments, eternal youth, and eternal life.

Drug abusers form another whole class of people attempting to cope with present and past loneliness, using oral compensation and self-defeating drug-induced feeling states rather than psychotic withdrawal. For drug abusers as for psychotics, however, loneliness is still the end product. There are many varieties of drug use, abuse, and misuse undertaken in order to counteract loneliness. In terms of the theme of making human contact one can see that the heroin social system—not just the professional distribution system and the reciprocal police system, but the system of junkie and pusher—entails the continual making of contacts and connections. The need for these human affiliations drives many "cured" addicts back to the use of hard drugs. In one play and film, Michael Gazzo's "Hatful of Rain," the pusher is called "Mother," a metaphor that acknowledges equally the psychodynamics of attachment and the psychosexual equation of drugs with oral gratification. Paradoxically, the opiates seem to force alternating infantile-toned isolation and contact-making, a rhythm caricaturing the earliest attachment-exploration pattern in a pitifully estranged way. It is not just the heavy or hard drugs that almost universally play a part in coping with loneliness. Alcohol, the most obvious, widely used, abused, and destructive drug, at first serves a disinhibiting and socializing function, though it is sometimes employed as a tranquilizer. Tranquilizers and mild sedatives may be used to facilitate interpersonal relations by diminishing anxiety and secondary anger. Teenagers who "drop reds" (secobarbital sodium capsules) readily admit that in addition to the "high" it gives them, the overdose makes it easier for them to get along socially and to tolerate their feelings of estrangement from their families and school culture.

So-called psychedelic drugs of the LSD and mescaline variety may drown out the external world with colorful psychic noise or raise aloneness to the level of saintly asceticism where contact with people is exchanged for anticipated contact with (one's) God, soul, or psyche. This, after all, is what conventional religions offer in less passionate form. Ascetics through the ages have sought spiritual, mystical, or hallucinogenic experiences by various means, including flagellation or several days in the wilderness without food and water. Drugs and sensory or sleep deprivation can produce similar effects, medically categorized as hallucinogenic or psychotomimetic.

Cannabis and its variants, such as marijuana, bhang, ganja, hashish, can be appraised according to their strength and the setting in which they are used. Used when the individual is alone, their action may resemble a mild opiate or tranquilizer or in some cases a psychedelic drug. Used socially, they may resemble alcohol, or again, tranquilizers in their relaxing, socially disinhibiting effects. The psychedelic effect makes loneliness acceptable while the tranquilizing effect makes it easier to overcome loneliness through socialization.

Finally, the energizer-stimulants like the amphetamines and cocaine deal with loneliness by confrontation. They propel toward—not merely facilitating or making possible—social interaction, and at the same time they open up the sensory apparatus to receive communications and sensations from others. In their extreme form, ''speed'' (intravenous amphetamines), they dehumanize interpersonal involvement. People truly become objects, and eventually these objects haunt the reisolated paranoid ''speed freak.''

Drug preferences (assuming free choice and an open market, and the absence of effective religious or cultural sanctions) may reflect the particular character of the early childhood failure of healthy attachment behavior. Since scientific research has not tested this hypothesis, I shall speculate. Opiates may suit those who in infancy had to cope with pain and rejection, accompanied by hyperstimulation from outside; peace and satisfaction could come only from inside via a fantasied oceanic mother. Sedatives and alcohol may suit those who in childhood had some good attachment experiences but became very anxious and angry following sudden separation or parental inconsistency. The sedative effect defends against destructive impulses that, nonetheless, often break out during the disinhibiting phase. Psychedelic users probably missed out on the rich fantasy life of childhood because of the absence of feeling in the attachment to mother, and few should be ''only'' children for that reason. The energizer-stimulants may appeal to those who always had to initiate attachment behavior with mother but always found it unsatisfying. Their stimulant drugs help them overcome their baseline state of boredom, emptiness, depression, and weakness. Of course, since one-to-one direct cause-effect relationships rarely exist in real life, this simplified schema cannot encompass the multiple causal experiences and the mixed reactions and drug preferences that result. Finally, just as the social system provides the opportunity to experiment illegally with drugs, and just as psychological needs and personality govern the selection of the preferred drug, so the chemical effects of drug use may become a physiological end as well as the means to an interpersonal end. This happens through addiction, the self-sustaining biochemical changes which incorporate the drug into the normal physiology by making it an indispensable component of bodily enzymatic systems.

It is noteworthy that the best known treatments for drug and alcohol addictions are community programs that involve strong authoritarian and nurturing elements. Such programs function as obvious substitute families. In exchange for submission to the authority of the organization, i.e., to AA, Synanon, Delancey Street, the Salvation Army, or any of a variety of cults, communes, or conventional religious organizations, they shelter, protect, feed, and rescue the addict. Successful participation often demands that the addict relinquish his own autonomy until he "grows up" into the values and mores of the new family. Blum and his associates (1972) note that children at lowest risk to abuse drugs came from the most authoritarian type families where rules and expectations were clear and consistent. Hence the most effective treatment reflects the most effective prevention of drug abuse. In both cases, it is the shift from individualist or equalitarian to vertical social structures that is central. The message is clearly communicated that "life is with people," and that society is more important than the individual. The danger that such philosophies can be perverted into a kind of fascism must be weighed against the other choices available to the drug abusers. They are already under the fascist heels of their addiction and the drug supply system, or the solitary confinement of their loneliness.

In the extreme, homicide and suicide are displaced attempts to come to grips with loneliness, alienation, and despair. Evidence that those who commit suicide have an inhibited ability to escape pain and personal entrapment through fantasy and thought would most likely be equally applicable to those who commit homicide. The hostile and aggressive intent behind suicide and the message it is intended to carry to relatives and friends substantiates its perverted contact-making significance. Early psychoanalytic findings, and, recently, the research of Herbert Hendin (1969) and Richard Seiden (1972) on suicide among blacks, have noted that, psychodynamically, homicide and suicide are roughly two sides of the same coin. Victim-precipitated homicides and many auto accidents, especially the solo types, if closely examined, turn out to be disguised suicides. For this reason, death penalties do not prevent, and may in fact foster, homicides and airline hijackings, just as Malays will admit that running amok is a form of suicide. Comparably, certain prison inmates cannot tolerate the relative isolation of freedom and quickly manage to return, going out of their way, by all appearances, to be rearrested. One such man, a talented and award-winning artist while in prison with a lucrative postimprisonment job offer, managed to get caught in a burglary within two weeks of release. Like Harlow's monkeys attached to their wire-mesh "mothers," some unfortunate people apparently become attached to wire-meshed institutions.

Even persons who suffer from hysteria or psychosomatic disorders, with their significant component of secondary gain, can be seen as attempting to affect the significant others around them, to achieve a closeness centered about illness or hospitalization. Great personal suffering and incapacitation will be endured for the sake of preventing, avoiding, or counteracting loneliness; in some instances physical disease may be a response or solution to a traumatic separation. Paradoxically, for some, depression replaces people; and for others, even death is not worse than loneliness.

Isolation denies the bio-psycho-social wholeness of the self. For instance, total isolation with acquiescence can lead to death without physical cause. That is the meaning of mortification, sometimes called voodoo death. A statistical study by David Phillips (1977) revealed that people tend to wait to die until after a birthday or other significant anniversary; fewer people died in the month preceding their birthdays, and more in the immediately succeeding months, than in any of the remaining months of the year. The study further demonstrates the unity of mind and body, and suggests that the loneliness of death may be more acceptable after an event such as a birthday that tends to bring together friends and relatives, who are paradoxically the great salve for loneliness though also often the greatest disappointment.

In the future, people will need an even greater ability to cope with loneliness. Loneliness and alienation are not merely by-products of technology and rapid sociocultural value change, but are really unavoidable components of civilization and the human condition. The dearth of scientific writing on loneliness may derive from the immersion of scientists, technologists, and psychotherapists in their lonely pursuits; it may be a subject too close for comfort or objectivity.

In a time of space flights, the relevance of the scientific study of loneliness is increasingly apparent. We can now conjure up thoughts of prolonged periods of isolation, and even periods of prolonged forced closeness that will require at times a tolerance of lengthy isolation while at other times a means of creating psychological isolation in the midst of physical closeness. Judging from the U.S. astronauts, most of whom are firstborn or "only" children, the ability to tolerate loneliness has distinct adaptive value in outer space. Yet the astronauts are Earth dwellers who made the grade by having the most prolonged, the closest, and perhaps the most secure attachment experiences in early childhood.

2

From Loneliness
to Anomia

WILLIAM A. SADLER, JR. and THOMAS B. JOHNSON, JR.

INTRODUCTION

IN THE MIDST of a group therapy session, Mrs. Brown burst out sobbing: "Everything was going all right until all of a sudden I became so lonely. This awful loneliness just came over me and dug into me. I couldn't get rid of it; and I don't know why. There was nothing I could do about it. It was terrible. I couldn't stand it. I wanted to die."

This outburst illustrates many qualities to be found in experiences of loneliness in the modern world. There is an element of surprise. People often do not expect loneliness to be a significant part of their lives. Being unprepared for it, they become confused and worried when it strikes hard. Their loneliness becomes all the more disturbing when it becomes chronic. Most of us can take episodic loneliness in stride, but lingering loneliness gets under our skin and begins to eat away at our vitality. When it digs deep and persists, loneliness has a debilitating effect that can become serious. Furthermore it can contribute to a sense of helplessness that undermines our capacity to respond productively. This situation can become intolerable and contribute to a change in behavior patterns destructive of self and/or society. Loneliness is becoming a pervasive phenomenon in our society. Intense loneliness is a major problem in terms of both personal and social well-being.

Unfortunately professionals as well as lay persons are baffled by expressions of loneliness that threaten human life or happiness. Many of us would be uncomfortably sympathetic with Mrs. Brown. We are unsure of ways to cope with others' loneliness, as we are unsure of how to deal with our own. We are uncertain of the causes of loneliness as well as the consequences of it. This uncertainty and embarrassment may in part explain why there has been so little substantial investigation into loneliness within the social and medical sciences. Another reason for perplexity in the face of the power and pain of loneliness is the failure to recognize the potential complexity of the experience. We do not believe that avoidance of the problems serves any good purpose; nor do we believe that it is necessary to falter in the face of loneliness. One aim of this essay is to delineate structural possibilities of the experience of loneliness, with specific reference to the various social contexts of loneliness in the modern world as viewed from a sociological perspective.

It is possible to increase our understanding of loneliness. If we recognize that loneliness is a universal experience, then we can realize that we need go no further than our own lives to begin to examine it. However, we should not universalize our own experiences precipitously. There are different types and degrees of loneliness. Some forms of loneliness can be a stimulus to growth and creativity; other forms can be debilitating and destructive. To distinguish between different types of loneliness requires careful attention to, and rigorous analysis of, a variety of expressions.

To deal with loneliness adequately, whether scientifically, clinically, or personally, it is necessary to have a workable model that can account for the varieties and complexities of loneliness and can enable us to interpret them in terms of their specific contexts. Much theorizing about loneliness has ignored the situation in which loneliness arises, thereby overlooking many of the dynamic factors that contribute to its meaning. This essay will present a conceptual model that elucidates specific features of loneliness, both as a universal phenomenon and in basic possible variations. The method used here is interdisciplinary, combining psychology and sociology with existential phenomenology. Because there has been so much confusion in the treatment and study of loneliness, we have allotted much space in this essay to the clarification of the theoretical background of basic concepts and of the existential material used in the formulation of the model. By the conclusion of the essay we hope to have demonstrated what loneliness is, how it can develop into four different types and different combinations of these types, some causes for the complexity of loneliness that lie beyond the rather obvious psychological ones, and some consequences of unresolved loneliness in human lives. We shall argue that chronic, unmitigated loneliness, especially when it is suffered on multiple dimensions simultaneously, is a crucial factor contributing to personal breakdowns such as that experienced by Mrs. Brown, and to pervasive problems in our world such as anomia or normlessness. We will offer only a few suggestions regarding how to cope with loneliness effectively. Lest readers be disappointed at the paucity of remarks about coping, we emphasize that no realistic confrontation with loneliness is possible until the experience is identified, carefully diagnosed, and accepted at face value. Hopefully this essay will be useful not only for further research and clinical practice, but to any person who hopes to understand loneliness more accurately and either to mitigate its power or to allow one to live with it in a constructive manner.

FIRST STEPS IN THE DEFINITION OF LONELINESS

To begin an analysis of loneliness we need to set forth some distinctions that should be obvious but are often ignored. In the first place loneliness cannot be equated with a physical condition. Some studies of loneliness have been unsatisfactory because they have reduced the experience to a different phenomenon, such as isolation. The latter is an observable condition which can be measured and to some extent controlled. The meaning of isolation, however, in large part depends upon how a person interprets his situation. We often assume that isolation will be painful; thus we use it as a form of punishment for children and criminals. Sometimes to parental and societal dismay, those isolated learn to enjoy their privacy; instead of feeling deprived, they may find it an opportunity for pleasurable discovery and development. Artists have expressed a craving for isolation in order to create. Most of us want time when we are "left alone." Even the most gregarious social scientists sometime seek isolation "far from the madding crowd." In contrast to isolated existence, which appears to be an objective, external condition, loneliness is an experience which is subjective and internal. Isolation may contribute to loneliness, but the simplistic reduction of the latter to the former ignores the distinctive qualities and the complexities of loneliness. Furthermore, and perhaps more relevant to our own situation, such a reduction neglects the context of some of the most intolerable experiences of loneliness. To many people the most agonizing loneliness is experienced not in isolation but in the midst of a group, in the bosom of a family, and even between friends. Loneliness hit Mrs. Brown not in a desolate region but in the midst of a crowded section of one of the world's largest cities.

Another mistake which we have had to correct in our own approach is the tendency to make loneliness an enormous umbrella concept that covers more phenomena than loneliness implies. There is a tendency, notable in the writings of Moustakas (1961, 1972) and others, to include in the concept of loneliness other factors such as fear, depression, anger, alienation, and guilt. These elements may be associated with it in some cases, but they are not essential to the experience and should be sorted out in the definitional process. What follows is an attempt to identify the essential elements of loneliness and then to delineate some basic structural elements that may constitute the experience.

A PHENOMENOLOGICAL APPROACH TO THE EXPERIENCE OF LONELINESS

To detect isolation one must use one's eyes, but to recognize loneliness one must feel it. Loneliness is felt strongly as a highly subjective, intensely personal, and often unique experience. In everyday comments we frequently hear: "No one else's loneliness is quite like mine; everybody's loneliness is different." There is some truth behind affirmations of the uniqueness of one's loneliness that seem to prevent it from conforming to a universal definition. It is true that my loneliness is mine. No one can experience my loneliness for me. Perhaps no one can fully understand just what I feel when I am lonely. Furthermore, my experiences of loneliness vary from situation to situation and from time to time. Yet for all the uniqueness of any given experience of loneliness, there are certain elements that lonely people have in common. These elements are implied by the term itself and may be noticed by carefully observing the expressions of lonely people. One of the most salient features of loneliness is a special kind of feeling that seems to encompass the entire self. Unlike sensations or localized feelings, the feeling of loneliness is total. Furthermore the feeling of loneliness has a cognitive element. Loneliness is a signal to me about myself; it communicates how I stand in the world. To emphasize both the affective and cognitive elements leads to the realization that *loneliness constitutes a distinctive form of self-perception.* Loneliness is a form of acute self-awareness. It is not necessarily a completely accurate perception of our existential situation; nevertheless, it is one we must reckon with in earnest.

In our ordinary, everyday self-awareness we perceive ourselves as related to a surrounding world. We live out our lives in the context of a complicated and extensive self-world network of relationships. The experience of loneliness conveys a message to us that something is wrong in that network. Often loneliness is a perception that emerges in the form of a need to be included, or wanted, or just to be in touch; but the underlying factor is an awareness of lacking. We experience deprivation, and feel that something is missing, broken, or absent. Or there may be a felt awareness of exclusion or rejection. From the vantage point of existential phenomenology (which is particularly relevant to this study), loneliness represents a threat to or a break in the intentional structure of the experiencing self, especially in the realm of intersubjectivity. Expressed in less technical language, loneliness involves a total feeling that communicates something is missing from the self.

The meaning of this particular form of self-awareness is especially important to the individual when it is related to his deepest personal expectations. Loneliness can cause all sorts of frustrations, but among the worst are those that concern frustrated expectations. These contribute to the distinctive characteristics of loneliness, particularly when it is experienced as a serious problem. In loneliness we feel left out, cut off, lost, bereft, forgotten, unwanted, unneeded, or ignored. These feelings are so bitter because they run contrary to what we expect. Our expectations are for sharing and involvement. Socialization contributes a sense of relatedness and participation, and in shaping a personal perspective we anticipate companionship. Loneliness signifies severed ties and absence whereas our ordinary spatial expectations are oriented toward coherence and connection. Severe loneliness can signal confusion and emptiness, and it can make an individual feel homeless and everywhere out of place. In terms of personal time, loneliness functions to fragment temporal cohesiveness, conveying either a break with the past or a chasm in the future. By fracturing temporality and making the future more uncertain than ever, loneliness may arouse profound anxiety and fear.

Loneliness can so threaten the fabric of relationships that form part of the foundation of personal existence that it can appear as one of the most dreadful experiences imaginable, what Binswanger referred to as a "naked horror" (1942, p. 445). As Frieda Fromm-Reichmann (this volume) has pointed out, loneliness can play a devastating role in the evolution of severe personal disorders. However, even those able to take loneliness in stride admit that it is often a deeply disturbing experience. One factor that contributes to the distress of loneliness is the felt awareness that there is an unnatural or unexpected emptiness at the core of one's personal world. In the context of frustrated expectations we respond to loneliness by longing for a presence to fill an absence, by searching for a bond to connect the broken network of relationships, by looking for a way of sharing that will overcome one's lack of involvement.

Thus far we can offer the following definition: *loneliness is an experience involving a total and often acute feeling that constitutes a distinct form of self-awareness signaling a break in the basic network of the relational reality of self-world.* The disturbance issuing from this experience often motivates the self to search for a remedy for the trouble, especially because it runs counter to basic personal expectations and is thus considered frustratingly undesirable. Though this preliminary definition may seem too complex, it has proven to be effectively workable in both theory and practice.

By delineating loneliness as a specific kind of experience involving a distinctive self-awareness, it is relatively easy to identify it and to differentiate it from other experiences with which it might be confused, such as sadness and depression. Furthermore this definition provides a basis for sorting out elements which are often found within the experience but are not essential parts of it, and it enables us to make an important distinction between the experience itself and attitudes towards it. For example, in our society fear is often associated with loneliness. In some cases fear may precipitate loneliness; in other cases, loneliness produces fear. It should not be assumed that fear is an inherent part of loneliness. On the contrary, we might ask why loneliness is so feared in our culture. There is considerable evidence that it is not universally feared. In cultures where nomadic and hunting life styles require long and frequent periods of aloneness, for ex-

ample, persons have adapted to solitude and presumably have accepted at least a degree of loneliness as an inevitable part of life. Even
in American society young men were once prepared by their families
to face life on their own and to endure loneliness as part of the
challenge to achieve success. Readers will recall that Riesman's (1950)
inner-directed individual was such a person. Why do Americans fear
loneliness so much today? Is it due to a change in social character as
Riesman suggested? Is the nature of loneliness different today from
what it used to be? Are there factors which complicate the experience
of loneliness and so make it more frightening? Certainly these are
important questions which deserve careful investigation. In our
attempt to be faithful to the experience of loneliness the definition
given above provides a basis for making distinctions that can lead to
more fruitful research and greater understanding.

It is possible to be even more specific than the above definition and
to break the experience of loneliness down into different dimensions.
The term *dimension* is of fundamental importance to this model and is
used in a very specific sense. Before developing the model, it will be
helpful to give a brief sketch of the phenomenological background that
has been used in its formulation.

Though the views and claims of individual phenomenologists differ,
the phenomenological movement as it has emerged from its European
tradition is typified by a concern to return to experience in order to
illuminate its basic structures. One important insight that phenomenology has developed is that experience has an intentional structure.
By referring to the intentionality of experience phenomenology emphasizes that experience is not entirely subjective or internal; on the
contrary, experience is inseparable from the lived context of a field of
relationships. This experiential field is complex; it includes meanings
and values as well as nature and society. Furthermore the relational
field of intentionality is a dynamic process, such that experience is
always being directed within a matrix of relationships. The existential
version of phenomenology developing from Heidegger (1967) and
from Merleau-Ponty (1962, 1964), which is particularly relevant here,
has emphasized the dynamic and temporal aspect of the self-world
event of the experiencing self. Further developments of this philosophy have attempted to refine basic notions and to integrate them with
findings of social sciences, as in works by Binswanger (1942, 1957,

1963), Schutz (1962, 1964), and Sadler (1969a,b).

In a previous work, which spelled out the nature of the self-world phenomenon in much greater detail than suggested here, Sadler (1969a) designated the rudimentary phenomenon underlying all experience as the *personal world*. This concept of a personal world develops a Heideggerian reinterpretation of Husserl's intentionality. It is intended to designate the fundamental totality of an experiencing self and is inclusive of what Husserl in later writings referred to as the lived-world. The personal world does not refer merely to a subjective process of reacting to a supposedly preconditioned, external environment nor to a limited area of interest, as suggested by the phrase "the world of sports." Rather it denotes the irreducible self-world phenomenon understood as a dynamic process of interaction that is radically historical; it is the fully human context within which transpire the events, encounters, and becoming that constitute experience. The personal world is an intentionally structured network that establishes the overall frame of reference within which encounters become meaningful. Furthermore, the concept of intentionality as the personal world includes an essentially pluralistic structure. This plurality consists of basic existential possibilities towards which a person may be oriented in his total life history. To put it another way, a personal world has a uniquely human history which appropriately unfolds in several directions towards different possibilities. These possibilities are constituted by types of relationships, and they set the horizon of our world within which we organize experience, make sense of it, and set the course of our personal histories. Basic existential possibilities give shape and substance to our deepest cares. They form the foundation upon which our most personal expectations and our primary values arise.

A major task of Sadler's existential phenomenology has been to elucidate the nature of these possibilities in order to provide a framework within which to understand experiences and, more particularly, modes of human development. When directed towards full humanness a personal world is oriented to the realization of four distinct existential possibilities: 1) the unique destiny of the individual, the actualization of his inherent self, and perhaps some ultimate meaningfulness; 2) the tradition or culture of the individual, which provides many of the assumed values and ideas he employs to interpret his experience and to define his existence;[1] 3) the social environment of the individual which provides the field of organized relationships to other humans and spheres of behavior wherein the terms of his membership, his roles, and his social destiny are established; and 4) the other persons with whom the individual may form I-Thou relationships such that his existence may unfold within the dual reality of a personal We. With this pluralistic structural image of the personal world, it is possible to spell out the essential traits of various life styles in terms of the nature of their orientation towards these possibilities and to compare the essential features of one orientation with those of others. It serves well as a basis for understanding individuals, groups, and cultures; it is also useful for understanding human development and the meaning of significant encounters, accomplishments, conflicts, and disappointments. It has proven to be exceptionally appropriate for illuminating the meaning of love, and more recently it has enabled us to clarify the meaning of loneliness, especially in terms of its range and possible complexity.

THE DIMENSIONS OF LONELINESS

In previous investigations the metaphor of *directions* was employed to stress the distinctive spatial-temporal characteristics of a given life style. In investigating the phenomenon of loneliness the metaphor of *dimensions* has proven to be more appropriate. It is now possible to indicate the specific sense in which the metaphor is used. In ordinary conversation the term dimension is used loosely to suggest levels of dynamics or meanings. In theoretical works it often has a spatial connotation suggesting a distinction between surface and depth levels. In the social sciences it frequently is employed to differentiate between manifest and latent dynamics and meanings. We are not using the term dimension in this ordinary way here. The metaphor of dimension is used instead to refer specifically to the distinct basic possibilities within the pluralistic structure of the personal world. Corresponding to the four directions in which the personal world appropriately unfolds, *the dimensions of loneliness* are fourfold, and they have been

[1]This category is meant to include what some sociologists have referred to as the subjective side of society and what some phenomenologists have suggested as the realm of intersubjectivity.

designated as *cosmic, cultural, social,* and *interpersonal* dimensions. The model of the fourfold dimensions of loneliness has been developed to account for the potential range and complexity of the experience and to illuminate analytically the rich diversity of meanings, which may be found in numerous experiences of loneliness. As we shall point out in greater detail, these meanings can be set forth by portraying basic types of loneliness in terms of the four dimensions. Still more relevant to the agony caused by loneliness in individual lives and the problems attendant to it, this fourfold model enables us to understand how loneliness can cause deep personal distress. We have discovered that loneliness becomes increasingly intolerable when it afflicts an individual in more than one dimension at the same time. Lacking a concept which can account for the varying complexity of loneliness, individuals can neither explain the sources nor account for the severity of their loneliness, as illustrated by Mrs. Brown. This model provides a way of assessing the range and intensity of a given experience of loneliness. Without awareness of these different sources, loneliness may persist without adequate resolution. We shall return to this important point after considering some essential characteristics of the various dimensions.

While it will become clear that loneliness experienced within one dimension will differ from that experienced within others, nevertheless all types of loneliness have in common a feeling that conveys a message about one's self. Each type of loneliness is a form of self-awareness that signals a breach in the basic network of relationships that constitute the personal world. Loneliness communicates significant stress in an important area or areas within one's world. The perception of a threat to the historical unfolding of one's full self produces the distress of loneliness. At least in acute forms, loneliness represents a frustration of deep personal expectations with regard to the realization of a basic possibility that is recognized as an integral part of one's full humanness. In each dimension of loneliness the person is aware that something important is missing or being withheld that he believed he had a right to expect. Each dimension differs from the others, however, so that the content of the message of frustration varies from one dimension to another. The following four sketches are meant to portray some distinctive elements in each of the four dimensions. These sketches draw upon expressions of loneliness in literature, everyday life, research projects, and workshops.

THE COSMIC DIMENSION OF LONELINESS

Of the four dimensions, the cosmic is perhaps the most complex. The cosmic dimension is meant to designate at least three different perceptions of the self: 1) an individual's sense of relatedness to what he conceives to be reality as a whole, often referred to as Nature or the cosmos; 2) a sense of relatedness to a mysterious aspect of life that is of ultimate concern such as God or Being; 3) a sense of relatedness to what an individual believes to be his unique destiny or an ultimate historical goal. Cosmic loneliness is present when only one of these aspects is represented; other expressions of cosmic loneliness may embody two or even three of these aspects.

The sense of loneliness with reference to Nature has been apparent not only in individuals but has typified certain eras and groups. It has recently been expressed with considerable fervency among some groups in industrialized urban societies. Sometimes the feeling of estrangement from Nature which exhibits one type of loneliness connotes a sense of impotence, but the essential element is an awareness of having lost touch with a source of vitality and creativity, even though the awareness may not be patently conscious. Romantic literature provides copious examples of this type of experience. More recently, literature of the counterculture in this country has expressed it. Youths who seek to identify with the perspective of North American Indian cultures that envisaged plant and animal life as part of one vast kinship system are frequently expressing this type of loneliness. It is also evident among some persons greatly concerned about ecology and about restoring the self's relationship with nature. A fervent search for life sources and a close relationship to natural phenomena is often associated with an emergent loneliness of this type. Ironically some people drop out of society, thus creating another type of loneliness in their attempt to resolve this kind of cosmic loneliness.

Cosmic loneliness need not be in terms of a vast vision of nature as a whole; it can be on a smaller scale. For example, some persons are distinctly lonely as they sense their separation from a particular region; they miss their land as other people might long for family and friends from which they had been separated. John Steinbeck provided a penetrating description of this kind of loneliness in *The Grapes of Wrath* (1951) when he portrayed the agony of Okies being driven from their farmlands. The Okies had in common with Romantics and members of the counterculture a particular type of loneliness, an awareness of the self as estranged from a basic part of one's personal world. In this type of loneliness, a fundamental relationship in this world has been strained or severed, but the resulting need cannot be satisfied directly by human companionship.

The individual's sense of a broken relationship with Being or God, which is another variant of this dimension, characterizes certain philosophies and much religious literature. Religious existentialism provides a salient and familiar example of the former in Western literature. In much Eastern philosophical and religious literature the individual is conceived as a lonely soul imprisoned in a realm of earthly unreality or as a pilgrim en route to a true home lying beyond this world. In much mystical theology of both East and West the individual's fundamental problem has been described in terms of a type of loneliness: salvation is said to lie in the "flight of the alone to the Alone." Other examples of this type of loneliness are to be found in modern literature where authors brood over the absence of Being or God. Quite recently distress from this type of loneliness has been expressed in literature referring to the death or eclipse of God, as in the works by Vahanian (1966) and Buber (1952), and even in secular forms as in Maxwell Anderson's song *Lost in the Stars*.

The Judeo-Christian heritage abounds with examples of agonizing expressions of loneliness. The Psalms are filled with complaints of lonely men. "How long, O Lord, wilt Thou quite forget me? How long wilt Thou hide Thy face from me?" "As a hind longs for running streams, so do I long for Thee, O God." The prophetic literature has numerous similar passages. One of the most agonizing cries of cosmic loneliness was uttered during a momentous crucifixion: "My God, my God, why hast Thou forsaken me?" Early Christian liturgies often focused upon this kind of loneliness, in which worshippers corporately anticipated the return of a long expected Jesus. In much contemporary religion, particularly the mystical and evangelical varieties, there are strong strains of loneliness along with claims to resolve it. Some religious groups advertise instant contact with a divine companion who will fill religious lonely hearts to overflowing. There is no doubt that one of the most powerful motivating factors in much highly emotional religion today is loneliness. So far attempts to assess the significance of new cults and religious movements have paid scant attention to it. This model of the cosmic dimension of loneliness provides an indicator that is particularly promising as a means of studying and interpreting some significant aspects of religion both old and new.

The third variant of this type of loneliness may be easily discerned in movements strongly oriented toward some final historical goal or eschaton. It is also to be found in expressions within fiction and humanistic psychology, including works by William James (1902) and Jung (1933, 1951), in which the individual is said to suffer from what he perceives to be a divided self. This type of loneliness is akin to the experience of self-alienation, when an individual is aware that one essential aspect of his personality is missing or that the development of one type of self is canceling another type. Expressions of this aspect of loneliness are sometimes in the form of a longing for a true self that is yet to be realized or which has been lost. Other instances of it may be found in expressions of a belief that "when it comes right down to it, each of us is entirely alone." In contrast to John Donne's famous epigram, some people believe that each man is an island, isolated from all others at the core of his being and even estranged from himself. While that belief may be found most readily in acute forms of autism, we found it expressed by ordinary persons in literature and in workshops dealing with loneliness. Sometimes a fear of loneliness and a tendency to repress recognition of it underlie the belief about isolation as the true state of human existence.

These brief sketches are not all-encompassing. They are pointers referring to countless expressions of loneliness that can be located in history, literature, the arts, and interviews. They are not intended to suggest any metaphysical perspective or religious beliefs. They signify a specific form of felt self-awareness in terms of what some individuals consider to be an interruption within the fundamental dimension of their personal worlds. What is new here is not a discovery of some new form of experience but a presentation of an analytical concept that enables us to recognize a variety of experiences encompassing self-alienation and estrangement from Being, God, or Nature as a specific type of loneliness. Once identified, it becomes possible to analyze the experience of loneliness more carefully, to indicate the source of the distress, and to estimate the significance of the response made or sought after. This concept is also useful in attempting to assess the range and total impact of loneliness in the lives of certain individuals and groups who encounter loneliness on multiple dimensions.

THE CULTURAL DIMENSION OF LONELINESS

In this category of loneliness the term culture is used in the conventional sense within the social sciences to refer to systems of normative meanings and values, usually inherited, that constitute a crucially important element in social intersubjectivity and life styles. A clear example of the cultural dimension of loneliness can be seen in the experiences of immigrants as described by Handlin in *The Uprooted* (1951) and by others. The history of the United States is particularly rich in expressions referring to this type of loneliness. During the waves of immigration in the nineteenth century, for example, many immigrants came to this country in groups that included members of their immediate families, more distant relations, friends, and acquaintances from their native towns and villages. They were often surrounded by loved ones who were most important to them; yet they felt deep loneliness. Frequently they established ethnic communities, which were partly attempts to counter this peculiar type of loneliness. But even within ethnic groups there was a pronounced feeling of estrangement from a cultural heritage that was originally a part of their perspective and style of life. Something which they had come to take for granted had been lost. The term alienation is not always adequate to account for this experience. Alienation refers mainly to their perception of their problematic relatedness to their new country—it does not account for the distress many suffered because of their lonely longing for a constellation of basic ideas, norms, beliefs, attitudes, and values that had been an inherent part of their personal worlds. Cultural alienation may be a part of, or a consequence of, unresolved loneliness on the cultural dimension.

Another example of the cultural dimension of loneliness is found in what some authors have suggested is a distinctive form of experience of man in the modern world. This experience was central in Fromm's now classic study *Escape from Freedom* (1941). In attempting to delineate the dominant social character of modern man, Fromm acknowledged that the key to understanding this type of person was "the specific kind of relatedness of the individual towards the world" (p. 9). For various reasons, which he spelled out in that book, Fromm argued that modern man in an industrialized, highly technical society "feels powerless and extremely insecure. He lives in a world to which he has lost genuine relatedness" (p. 219). Fromm asserted that the new freedom which individuals had won through historical liberation from social, economic, and religious bondage "is bound to create a deep feeling of insecurity, powerlessness, doubt, aloneness, and anxiety" (p. 53). While some of his theorizing is questionable and unsubstantiated, there can be no doubt that his descriptions of an "unbearable feeling of aloneness and powerlessness" have met with widespread recognition and agreement. Many readers have agreed with him that "what man most dreads is: isolation" (p. 15). However, the kind of isolation he referred to was not really the ordinary type which many appear to dread, and Fromm did not indicate how this concept differed from that of ordinary usage. This in part is responsible for the disparate ways his argument has been interpreted. As will be discussed later, Riesman's famous study (Riesman, Denny, and Glazer, 1950), which supposedly was an American adaptation of Fromm's work, actually assumed quite a different type of isolation experience. More important at this point than a critical discussion, however, is the fact that Fromm's presentation called attention to a distinctive type of loneliness which has been recognized as prevalent and powerful in modern societies. This is an experience of the cultural dimension of loneliness that underlies much of the discussion about certain forms of alienation, cultural dislocation, and even anomie.

Cultural loneliness has been barely touched by the social scientists, but it has been brilliantly described in literary works. Herman Hesse's *Steppenwolf* (1929) is an eloquent example. This novel portrays a man who symbolizes the dilemma of many who find themselves caught between two cultures, the old and the new. His loneliness becomes intolerable as he fails to find a home in either one. His loneliness is not something that can be satisfied with love and friendships; it requires a relationship of a different kind. As his personal history developed, his torment increased as his search for a certain kind of involvement proved futile. A powerful poetic expression of loneliness in its cultural dimension was made by T. S. Eliot in *The Waste Land*. Interestingly enough, in his later writings, such as *Four Quartets,* the focus was upon a cosmic dimension of loneliness (see Eliot, 1952).

While tracing examples of this type of loneliness in literature is rewarding, it is more important to detect it in the lives of people. This loneliness is sometimes prominent in situations characterized by anomie, especially if anomie has a subjective impact as suggested by Durkheim in *Suicide* (1897, pp. 254-258) and Merton in *Social Theory and Social Structure* (1957, pp. 160-176). Persons who experience inner turmoil and confusion resulting from a feeling of being divorced from traditional values and normative meanings often express a feeling of loneliness which they cannot quite explain. We have found numerous persons exhibiting the relief of recognition as this type of loneliness was delineated for them; although they could not be characterized as anomic, yet they had experienced cultural dislocation through immigration or through vast, rapid changes in their religion and public morals. The model enabled them to identify a hitherto unknown source of distress.

Cultural loneliness is also apparent in minority groups when individuals perceive that their ties to their own cultural heritage have been broken or that the dominant culture in which they live is hostile to their own. This loneliness is present, waiting to be detected and confronted, in the descriptions of societies undergoing turbulent social change, such as modern Japan (Lifton, 1965) and contemporary America (Toffler, 1970). It is an important element in the lives of youths who cannot find a home in their own culture. This type of loneliness compounds the troubles of persons afflicted by cultural alienation and experiencing an identity crisis. One value of the proposed fourfold model of loneliness is that it enables those who study cultural alienation to concentrate upon particular facets of the situation without losing a sense of the whole constellation and without confusing dynamic processes which should be analytically differentiated.

Cultural differences sometimes intervene and frustrate social and interpersonal communication. In such instances, complex patterns of loneliness often emerge, as in families and institutions where there is a so-called generation gap. Here cultural loneliness contributes to and exacerbates loneliness experienced in the social and interpersonal dimensions. Part of the spin-off of intense social conflict is a complicated loneliness experience, which requires an awareness of the cultural dimension to be understood and dealt with adequately. Loneliness on a cultural dimension is also a frequent inhabitant of the worlds of prophets, scholars, reformers, and cultural critics, especially if they see themselves drifting apart from the cultural mainstream in their attempt to moor themselves to values that have been forgotten or rejected by the public. In such cases this model helps investigators and subjects themselves bear in mind one aspect of personal distress which they should take into account when they set their course against the stream. It is not surprising to find radicals and innovators in history placing great emphasis upon close friendships, thus protecting themselves against interpersonal loneliness as they risk loneliness on the cultural and social dimensions.

THE SOCIAL DIMENSION OF LONELINESS

The term social is meant here in the sense commonly intended within American sociology to refer to enduring patterns of organized relationships that provide the framework within which individuals and groups interact.[2] Furthermore in studying the social dimension of loneliness, the term social pertains primarily to specific groups in society rather than society at large. This kind of loneliness has been widely known, and especially acute forms of it have been designated by terms of social isolation such as exile, ostracism, rejection, and more recently, in some cases, retirement. More subtle forms of social isolation are also intended, including instances where social exclusion deprives persons of membership in groups they deem to be important or desirable. Another example of this type of loneliness may emerge if an individual feels that he is not welcome in his group. In cases of cosmic and cultural loneliness an individual's perception is often that he has lost touch; in the social dimension of loneliness an individual affectively perceives that he has been shoved out, left out, shut out, shipped out, kept out, or lost sight of. In terms of his self-awareness he sees himself as an outcast, an outsider, a loner, an oddball, or a disconnected individual. This kind of loneliness is often inflicted when individuals' roles are rejected, when they are fired, blackballed, cut from the team, not accepted by the college, club, or firm of their

[2]"Social" in the sense of systems of normative meanings which influence an individual's subjectivity and actions is more commonly associated with a European tradition of sociology, represented by figures such as Weber and Durkheim. Insofar as this sense of the term social has bearing upon loneliness, it is included under the category of culture.

choice, or when they are shunned because their behavior, class, or color is deemed socially undesirable.

In addition to these common factors which contribute to the emergence of social loneliness, there are others prevalent in modern societies which help to explain the increase of this type of loneliness in today's world. Some of the most significant of these include the increased fragmentation of society along with growing specialization, the high rate of mobility, the uncertainty of traditional social boundaries, the dissolution of traditional groups and the short life of new ones expected to take their place, and the high level of expectation with regard to social position teamed with discontent or confusion with one's present position. It is a common observation that people today are extremely concerned about where they stand socially. In addition to nervousness over social place and face, there is now considerable doubt about social identity and the meaning of everyday encounters with others. Perhaps more serious with respect to the stability of society is the dissolution of many traditional groups. Homans' warning of more than twenty years ago is as apt as ever: "The civilization that, by its very process of growth, shatters small group life will leave men and women lonely and unhappy" (1950, p. 457). One aspect of vast social change is the emergence of this particular type of loneliness on a large scale. Unfortunately in the attempt to assess the dynamics and consequences of the factors in modern life that contribute to significant social issues, it has not been adequately considered.

There are many obvious examples of social loneliness involving individuals who have been left behind by social change, cast aside, driven out of society or of significant groups, or shunned. Such people are labeled derogatively as criminals, misfits, no-accounts, queers, perverts, parasites, niggers, traitors, or undesirable aliens. However, there is also acute social loneliness experienced by persons who live not outside but on the edge of society. These individuals lack any meaningful social involvement. They include the aged, the poor, eccentric people, deviants, those in occupations publicly considered of dubious worth, and in some cases adolescents and women. There is also a degree of social loneliness in the experience of people who sense political and economic impotence, who feel they are light-years removed from the process of important decision making, who are not so much left out as socially and politically ignored. The complaint of the "forgotten American" often contains an expression of this type of loneliness; so, too, does the statement on a student placard carried during a campus demonstration: "We feel left out." This aspect of loneliness is not restricted to students or radicals; it has also been found to be a disturbing factor among white and blue collar middle-class Americans, as the writings of Coles (1971) and others make clear. Given the rising level of expectation concerning meaningful social involvement in modern democratic societies along with the increasing vastness and complexity that makes such involvement more problematic, we should expect to find this type of loneliness increasingly prevalent. As institutions become larger and roles within them more ambiguous and anonymous, there is all the more opportunity for all kinds of individuals to experience loneliness on the social dimension. This in itself is a problem which should receive attention—much more attention than is possible here.

One purpose of this article is to provide an accurate way of interpreting material pertinent to loneliness in modern societies. This model has a distinct advantage in that it permits us to redeem earlier insights that have been laid aside because of their association with questionable theories. One such insight is that associated with the now famous argument by Riesman and his collaborators (1950) about an emergent social character that has partly been shaped by the fear of loneliness. Apart from the dubious value of his concept of social character, particularly in terms of its correlation with economic and demographic patterns, it is disturbing to discover that nowhere in *The Lonely Crowd* is there a careful definition or description of loneliness. It is a crucial concept, especially in terms of Riesman's assumption that the "terror of loneliness" (p. 186) is assuaged by clinging to a crowd. In numerous instances Riesman acknowledged his indebtedness to Fromm's studies about loneliness and social character. It becomes clear, however, that Riesman and Fromm were not talking about the same type of loneliness. Riesman's "other-directed" individual, who is not socially prepared for loneliness as was his "inner-directed" predecessor, is not frightened by the same dimension of loneliness that supposedly drove Fromm's modern man into mass movements. The new American, as Riesman and others have portrayed him, is primarily concerned about his position in society and his relationship to a group. Consequently he is more concerned about identity and *status* than Fromm's individual who searches desperately for meaning and values. The typical European social character is different in this respect from the typical American one. Hesse's Harry Haller and Arthur Miller's Willy Loman are both agonizingly lonely men, but each character embodies a different dimension of loneliness. The nature of their distress and the kind of solutions appropriate to each should be distinguished.

This distinction is important for purposes of explanation and also for constructive social action and therapy. The kind of loneliness that Riesman pointed to calls for acceptance, inclusion, and affirmation within a group. Symptoms of this kind of loneliness are a nervous concern to be liked and a fear of rejection. To my knowledge Riesman was one of the first to suggest that the American pursuit of success had changed its form: "making it" has come to include, and often to be defined in terms of, making friends, being liked, and winning acceptance. If Riesman is correct, then we should expect to find considerable loneliness on the social dimension as people perceive themselves to have fallen short of success. Creative literature, everyday experience, and workshops on loneliness indicate that this kind of experience is already prevalent. Other factors in our society aggravate this type of loneliness, tending to produce serious problems. Because of the American identification of success with popular acceptance, social loneliness becomes compounded with shame: feelings of loneliness are often indicators of failure to "other-directed" individuals. The consequences of such unresolved loneliness include anxiety, anger, and depression. Careful consideration of this type of loneliness, especially in combination with other forms of distress, will lead to greater understanding of troublesome problems in our society and of more effective ways to cope with them.

The experience of social loneliness is often quite complex. Consider, for example, the problem of identity confusion which may be an integral part of the social dimension of loneliness. Ralph Ellison's novel, *Invisible Man,* (1952) vividly portrays this particular type of loneliness and its consequences. The Invisible Man is a black man plagued by a lack of recognition that contributes to an oppressive loneliness. In his case he finds diverse roles easily enough. Unfortunately, however, he finds that in social confrontations he is met not as an individual but as an embodiment of a stereotype. He is constantly judged in terms of others' expectations pertaining to social roles. The wrong kind of acceptance makes his loneliness more acute.

The proposed model of loneliness helps us to understand the complexity and seriousness of various forms of loneliness, such as the pain of loneliness experienced by victims of prejudice as described so eloquently by Ellison and others. The model also suggests some of the requirements needed to resolve that loneliness. People desire not only involvement in society but an involvement in which personal uniqueness and integrity are recognized and fostered. Consequently, the elimination of loneliness related to social exclusion must involve both genuine social participation and authentic personal recognition.

The above sketches of three dimensions of loneliness, though incomplete, are sufficient to suggest the nature of this phenomenological model and the ways it might be applied to various forms of experience which hitherto have not been assessed in term of the "loneliness content" in them. We can now turn to a brief consideration of loneliness in its more commonly recognized context of interpersonal relationships.

THE INTERPERSONAL DIMENSION OF LONELINESS

Undoubtedly there have been many persons in various societies who have never experienced the cosmic, cultural, or social dimensions of loneliness. Testimony of people through the ages, however, indicates that loneliness as an experience of separation from significant other persons is universal. Sometimes the awareness of loneliness on an interpersonal dimension comes as a shock. In moments of grief or departure it may strike as a thunderbolt, upsetting the equilibrium of a personal world. Often, however, loneliness is a lingering emptiness that corrodes personal well-being. In either event, this type of loneliness is a felt self-awareness that signals to a person that important interpersonal relationships have been severed, weakened, or threatened: it is a communication that something essential is lacking in his personal world.

This type of loneliness is a fact of life. It is not confined to pathological cases or to any particular age, class, race, sex, or interest group. A number of writers have suggested that loneliness is becoming more widespread, more intense, more troublesome in modern societies than at any other time in human history. Since a reliable measurement for loneliness has not yet been worked out, it is difficult to assess the accuracy of such statements.[3] Nevertheless there is an unprecedented outpouring of loneliness in many art forms as well as in clinical experiences, interviews, and ordinary conversations. Modern novelists like D. H. Lawrence and Thomas Wolfe have written about loneliness with a passion that borders on obsession; even less obsessed writers have concentrated upon it to an extent that indicates a conviction that loneliness is becoming a serious threat to personal and social existence. Drama, painting, sculpture, and even music have expressed the pain and anguish people feel in loneliness. Loneliness as a theme has become nearly as prominent in popular music as romance; it flows out not merely from blues and ballads but even from rock. Rod McKuen, reputed to be the wealthiest and most widely listened to American poet of our generation, has capitalized on the loneliness that oppresses the lives of ordinary people. One of the challenges to the social sciences, sociology in particular, is to examine loneliness in the context of modern society and to explain how it has come to loom so large and how it affects different persons and groups. Why in the midst of population explosion, overcrowding, and frequent interaction are so many people so disturbed by loneliness? Before that kind of study can be effectively prosecuted, however, it is imperative to define loneliness carefully so that it can be identified. Hopefully the model presented here will facilitate such study.

While loneliness has largely been ignored by the social sciences, a few works have concentrated on it. One of the best known was Moustakas' *Loneliness* (1961). In that book, his underlying conviction was that modern man was deeply troubled by a loneliness that extended in several directions: "Modern man is starving for communion with his fellow man and with other aspects of life and nature" (p. 25). While alluding to the "other aspects" of loneliness, Moustakas himself examined only the interpersonal dimension. Furthermore he focused upon the subjective aspect of the experience rather than its context and structure, and he confused loneliness with solitude, a positive experience of aloneness. He corrected this error in a later book (Moustakas, 1972). One of the memorable features of Moustakas' earlier study is a distinction between loneliness anxiety, which

[3]Bradley (1970) attempted a measurement of loneliness in her brief dissertation that is a step in the right direction, and especially suggestive of the possible correlation between loneliness and depression.

he claims is pathological, and existential loneliness, which he claims is not. While we share his intention to rescue loneliness from psychopathology, this distinction is unwarranted and promotes further confusion. The former is not loneliness itself but a consequence of a fearful attitude that Moustakas considered unfortunate:

> The fear of loneliness is a sickness which promotes dehumanization and insensitivity. In the extreme, the person stops feeling altogether and tries to live solely by rational means and cognitive directions. This is the terrible tragedy of modern life—the alienation of man from his own feelings, the desensitization of man to his own suffering and grief, the fear of man to experience his own loneliness and pain and the loneliness and misery of others (1961, p. 34).

Although this passage is suggestively rich, it is indicative of Moustakas' tendency to make philosophical pronouncements about a supposedly schizoid social character typical of modern men and thus to make loneliness a huge umbrella concept that is relevant to understanding many different kinds of problems and to reaching authentic solutions to them in a highly individualistic manner.

One point in Moustakas' argument deserves special attention because it helps to illuminate a common fallacy. In numerous programs dealing with loneliness we have heard the conventional wisdom that the answer to loneliness is love. This belief has also found its way into psychological literature, as the following quotation from Hammer (1972) illustrates: "Loneliness is basically a manifestation of egoism and the ego is the big problem-maker and central problem for psychotherapy to deal with. . . . To eliminate the problem of loneliness, the patient's capacity to love is what has to be enhanced" (pp. 25, 27). There is some truth in the belief that a lonely person needs love, but that belief is too simple. Moustakas ably expressed a counter insight: "To love is to be lonely. Every love eventually is broken by illness, separation, or death. The exquisite nature of love, the unique quality of dimension in its highest peak, is threatened by change and termination, and by the fact that the loved one does not always feel or know or understand. . . . All love leads to suffering" (1961, p. 101).

In line with Moustakas' observation it should be emphasized that love can be a bearer of loneliness. It could even be argued that those with the greatest capacity to love and for whom love has been a primary value are those who experience the greatest depths of loneliness on an interpersonal dimension. The most loving people can also be those who are most aware of loneliness in themselves and in others. There are many factors which can frustrate the relationship of love. Intense loneliness may be an honest recognition that the love relation has been badly strained, corrupted, or shattered by death or betrayal. In such experiences there is often an awareness that one's deeply rooted expectation for a common world of love has been frustrated and that the possibility for its realization is impossible or must be postponed. It is of such stuff that the greatest tragedies are made. Our personal worlds are vulnerable to loneliness not only in isolation or in the absence of love but within those interpersonal relationships we cherish the most. In seeking to solve the problem of loneliness, even in its interpersonal dimension, love is not enough.

Careful consideration of this type of loneliness indicates that as a felt need it is ambiguous. The distress may signal a need for companionship and love, but it may also call for honest recognition of a loss within the network of relationships that constitute the personal world. Insight into loneliness certainly does not warrant the conclusion that it is symptomatic either of so-called mental illness or of personal failure. Loneliness can be a healthy indicator of human limitations and much more. It can lead to a self-awareness that is essential for the development of personal integrity, and the testimony of many people indicates that it can be a source of creativity and personal strength as well. But for all the benefits that may be derived from loneliness, there is no reason to conclude, as Moustakas and numerous existentialists have done, that "man is utterly and forever alone." The personal world is constituted by a complex network of relationships that include social intersubjectivity and interpersonal attachments; loneliness is an important signal from that network, but it is neither the most important nor the most authentic one.

Thus far the objectives of this article have been: (1) to define loneliness as a distinctively human experience, (2) to delineate four basic dimensions of the personal world which provide the foundation for the emergence of four types of loneliness, and (3) to indicate the essential nature of these types by reference to a variety of expressions drawn from different kinds of literature and from everyday experiences. By delineating these dimensions, the basic sources of the different types of loneliness have also been indicated. We do not mean to suggest that these are the only major causes; there are important causes awaiting revelation by careful psychological and sociological research. In addition to more detailed studies of causes there is a need for research into the role certain attitudes, emotions, and values have in the development of loneliness. Cross-cultural studies comparing types and occasions of loneliness under various circumstances would also be extremely valuable. As previously mentioned, careful studies should be made of the effects of loneliness in conjunction with other disturbing factors and of consequences resulting from the failure to cope with loneliness effectively. Many other questions come to mind, and no doubt readers have already raised some of their own. What remains to be done in this article is to consider an application of this model to account for the emergence of a serious problem in our society.

FROM LONELINESS TO ANOMIA

Of the utmost importance in our research was the discovery that often the experience of loneliness is not a simple one. There are at least four basic types, and many people experience loneliness on more than one dimension without being conscious of it. When loneliness strikes on only one dimension people usually seem able to live with the distress it produces. However, when loneliness emerges on two or more dimensions simultaneously, the stress is sometimes intensified to the point of serious disturbance, especially when individuals are not aware of the location of the stress within their personal worlds, and therefore cannot cope with it directly. One frequent consequence of being hit by loneliness on multiple dimensions is a feeling of helplessness or impotence that is related to the feeling that vital connections in the matrix of relationships within one's world have been weakened or severed. The proposed phenomenological model enables us to consider personal troubles where loneliness is involved in terms of the possible complexity of the meanings of those troubles and the potential sources of stress. Anomia is a problem that is more complex than we have previously supposed. It is our contention that anomia, at least in many instances, is a consequence of severe unresolved loneliness encountered on two or more dimensions within a person's world.

While working as a clinical researcher in the Tenderloin section of San Francisco, Johnson (1969) attempted to understand how a group of lonely adolescents who were dropouts from conventional society had become anomic. His study was conducted in 1968 on a sample of seventy-five dropouts. Somewhat arbitrarily these were limited to males between the ages of eighteen and twenty-five who had left high school between the ninth and twelfth grades; furthermore they were not enrolled in any other educational program and were without permanent employment. The main thrust of the study at that time was to relate anomia to selected personality and social variables.

During the preliminary phase of his study Johnson had been informed by various helping professionals (social workers and clergymen) that most of the youths coming to the Tenderloin section and similar ones in San Francisco areas like Haight-Ashbury were disaffected and very lonely. Many of them were observed to be developing retreatist life styles, which included frequent drug usage, prostitution, and an unwillingness to pursue educational and occupational opportunities. In interviewing sessions these youths discussed their feelings of alienation, emptiness, and loneliness. Some of them viewed their move to the city in a purposive way: they felt that San Francisco would offer them the chance to deal with their feelings of loneliness positively. McGowan and others have pointed out that their entrance into the Tenderloin section was usually the result of running away from home or migrating from other regions of the country. Publicity and word of mouth acted like a magnet, drawing dissatisfied youths who were looking for freedom and sophisticated culture. Many had read in popular magazines that San Francisco was a fun, open, lively city offering numerous opportunities to meet other young people.

During the course of this study Johnson was puzzled by his observation that while some of the youths had become quite anomic, others, although they expressed loneliness, had not. It was discovered that those who had become anomic had distinctive personality traits. They were generally self-rejecting and rejecting of others, and they tended to operate on the basis of an external locus of control. That is, they felt that what had happened to them was due to outside factors such as the influence of God, the Devil, or fate. They had the attitude that no matter what they did their efforts could have little effect on their general state of being. Those whose state of being included little or no anomia, on the other hand, tended to be more self-accepting, more accepting of others, and operated on the basis of an internal locus of control. That is, they felt that what happened to them was largely of their own doing.

Another finding that added to the puzzlement was that certain respondents were more receptive to therapuetic counseling than others. Some could discuss their feelings of loneliness, and in the context of a warm and caring counseling relationship, found that their loneliness diminished. Others, while discussing their loneliness, actually seemed to become lonelier. The explanation of this according to Carl Rogers' theories (1961) would likely be that the counselor had not worked long enough with the client and thus had not allowed the client to experience the value of therapeutic conditions of empathy, caring, and genuineness.

An alternative explanation to both of the above observations may be found in the proposed model of loneliness. If this model of four dimensional loneliness is valid, we can hypothesize that those youths whose loneliness turned into anomia were experiencing loneliness on more than one dimension simultaneously without resolving it. Similarly, those who responded to client-centered counseling were lonely essentially in the interpersonal and/or social dimensions. The range and complexity of loneliness seem to constitute a differentiating factor in the emergence of anomia.

At this point it will be helpful to clarify the meaning of the concept of anomia as it is used in this study. Some scholars have discussed anomia as if it were essentially the same thing as alienation or loneliness. In contrast to loneliness as a felt perception of oneself as estranged from some vital connection or basic source of meaning, anomia is a more pervasive phenomenon, a general state of being. Especially as developed by Merton (1964) and Lowe and Damankos (1968), anomia is seen as the psychological counterpart to the sociological concept of anomie developed by Durkheim. Durkheim's concept was originally introduced as a strict counterpart of the idea of social solidarity (see Durkheim, 1893). Just as social solidarity is a state of collective ideological integration, so anomie is a state of confusion or normlessness. He suggested that anomie arises when rapid social and economic changes create disruptions in the collective order. These disruptions act to allow man's aspirations to rise beyond their possible fulfillment. The breakdown of traditional norms and the loosening of restraints tend to give people the feeling that they are wandering in empty space with no points of reference. Finding no point of reference, some men tire of wandering; their struggles become futile, life loses its value, and the consequence may be anomic self-destruction (Durkheim, 1897, pp. 246-276, 306-325).

Leo Srole (1956) first proposed *anomia* as the individual's experience of anomie. He conceived of this variable as referring to the individual's generalized pervasive sense of belonging at one extreme compared with self-to-others distance and self-to-others alienation at the other end of the continuum. McClosky and Schaar (1965) later amplified the concept to refer to "a state of mind, a cluster of attitudes, beliefs, and feelings in the minds of individuals. Specifically, it is the feeling that the world and oneself are adrift, wandering, lacking in clear rules and stable moorings. . . . The core of the concept is the feeling of moral emptiness." Drawing on the work of Srole and Mc-Closky and Schaar, and using the techniques of factor analysis, Lowe and Damankos (1965) refined the concept so that it could be measured. According to them, the main factors constituting anomia included meaninglessness, valuelessness, powerlessness, and self-to-others alienation. Lowe's twenty-two item scale included such items as: "As I see it now, the future looks pretty empty for me." "Everything worthwhile is slipping away." "No matter how hard you try, you just end up back where you started." (For those experiencing anomia, all items are scored as true.)

A perusal of the research literature on anomia reveals that most scholars have focused on its sociocultural foundations. For example, they have found that low socioeconomic status, downward mobility, age, and low social participation are important sociological correlates of anomia. Few researchers have looked at psychological correlates of anomia and to our knowledge none has analyzed possible relationships between loneliness and anomia, even though refined definitions point in that direction.

It is logical to assume that those who develop a high degree of anomia have lost touch with more than one source of personal stability. That is, we should expect to find a multidimensional experience of loneliness underlying anomia. Conversely those individuals experiencing loneliness on only one dimension, such as the interpersonal, are not likely to become anomic. Case studies thus far have borne out this thesis.

Consider, for example, the following case. Sandy was a young, male homosexual who had recently migrated from a small Midwestern town to San Francisco. He had had difficulty adjusting to the more conventional and traditional mores of his hometown. He saw in San Francisco an opportunity to meet others who might share his values and with whom he could develop honest relationships. During his adolescence he had lived in fear that his true sexual identity would be discovered by members of his family and community. He was something of a musician and loved the performing arts. Even these interests were difficult for his parents to accept, however, because of their expectations that he should excel in athletics and in other more masculine endeavors. When he finally confronted his parents and told them of his homosexual inclinations, they expressed shock and took him to the family physician, who immediately recommended psychiatric treatment. Rather than enter treatment, he migrated to San Francisco.

Within a matter of months he was able to find a job as a waiter, and he entered an educational program designed to develop his musical talents. He was able to find a homosexually oriented subculture which provided a much higher degree of acceptance than he had previously felt. Several of his friends also helped him to rediscover his Christian faith, which had previously provided him with a strong sense of meaning and purpose.

Sandy came to Johnson's attention as a self-referral after having been jilted by his lover. During the initial stages of counseling he focused primarily on his intense feelings of loss and his loneliness resulting from the breakup of his relationship. Through counseling he gradually worked through his feelings of loneliness and eventually developed another satisfying relationship. At no time did he appear to be anomic. He was supported in his personal world by his homosexual subculture and by his strong religious faith.

On the basis of the four dimensional model of loneliness it is likely that those clients whose loneliness did not diminish during therapeutic counseling were not merely suffering from loneliness on the interpersonal dimension but were experiencing it on several dimensions and as a consequence had reached an advanced stage of anomia.

This point is illustrated in the case of Linda. She had grown up in an upper-middle-class suburb near Detroit. She described her early years of development as typically middle class. She had a number of school friends, participated in various family and community activities, and attended church regularly. Sometime between her senior year in high school and her freshman year of college, however, she became quite disenchanted with her family's values. She felt that her studies in sociology and philosophy had allowed her to see through the hypocrisies of her family's life style and of the practices of her church. In an effort to break with them she decided to drop out and move to the Haight-Ashbury section of San Francisco. She later became involved in the drug scene and had a number of drug-induced hallucinations which moved her even further away from her parents' values.

During counseling sessions she would refer to feelings of loneliness associated with the loss of her family and religious ties. For the most part she tried to repress these feelings. In the search for meaning and community she jumped from one group of friends to another, without ever getting intimately involved. It became apparent after a number of sessions that Linda had become quite anomic. Having broken with her religion, her family, and her community, and then realizing that she could not develop close friendships, she came to feel utterly alone and adrift. Counseling served the purpose of helping her become more aware of her alienation and aloneness, but it did not provide the means for overcoming them. Eventually she decided to commit herself to a mental hospital for more extensive evaluation and treatment.

Another case in which this point is well illustrated is that of Michael. He had grown up in a lower-middle-class, Irish-Catholic family in southern New England. He had been a high achiever in high school and college, and later he went on to get his law degree. His family and friends were very proud of his accomplishments, and he had a feeling of having "made it." However, during his first year of law practice he became involved in a case where he attempted to defend a client using unethical tactics. The immediate result was that he was disbarred and unable to continue any legal practice. He felt intense shame and rejection from both his family and his religion, and he came close to committing suicide. A friend convinced him to move to San Francisco to start a new life. He made several attempts to hold jobs, but he found that he simply lacked the motivation to persist. Eventually he was referred by some of his former employers to the mental health clinic for psychological counseling. During counseling Michael discussed his feelings of purposelessness and loneliness, but he did not seem able to work through these feelings. His sense of hopelessness and powerlessness was so pervasive that the counseling relationship could offer him very little. He was eventually referred to a state mental hospital for further treatment.

We recommend that the counseling and intervention strategies used in cases like these take into account the types of loneliness which contribute to the anomia of suffering individuals. For example, those afflicted by cosmic loneliness might greatly benefit from spiritual or religious counseling. Those grappling with social loneliness might better deal with it through sensitivity training or group psychotherapy. Rogers (1970, pp. 106-116) has in fact reported success working with a special type of loneliness in encounter groups. Truly anomic persons who are afflicted with pervasive multidimensional forms of loneliness will require assistance in recognizing the complexity of their distress and will benefit most from different types of treatment specifically geared to deal with particular dimensions of their problem.

CONCLUSION

Loneliness is a distinctively human, highly significant phenomenon which demands much more careful study by the social and medical sciences than it has hitherto received. Some of the weaknesses and shortcomings of other approaches have been indicated. More importantly, a workable model has been presented that accounts for the potential multidimensionality of loneliness. We have attempted to show the relevance of this model to an understanding of the dynamics of intense, pervasive loneliness in the emergence of personality disorders like anomia.

We have found this model to be a key that unlocks our understanding of many important, disturbing human phenomena associated with loneliness. This understanding has been therapeutically helpful and suggestive for sociological analysis of modern society and for social planning. We invite others to try this key, file its teeth, and mold it to open other doors, thus bringing to science and society keener insight into personal problems that issue from the stresses of loneliness.

3

Loneliness:
An Interdisciplinary Approach

BEN MIJUSKOVIC

PSYCHOLOGICAL MOTIVATIONS, reasons why human nature is what it is, principles by which we may "explain," understand, sympathize, or empathize with other human beings—and ourselves—what a variety of possible principles has been offered by philosophers and psychologists! All men seek happiness, announces Aristotle (*Ethics*). Just as all men delight in imitation (*Poetics*), and human beings universally take pleasure in knowing (*Metaphysics*), in that same sense it may be said that the arche of human conduct or action derives from the self-evident fact that all men desire to be happy. According to Hobbes, each human atom is motivated by self-interest, not to say selfishness, and every individual strives for his own "good" through power over others. Bentham, on the other hand, regards man as under the sovereign twin masters of pleasure and pain, whose dominion extends over the entirety of human conduct. Freud retraces the path of our problematic symptoms to a fund of repressed sexual and libidinal energy, whose fettered strivings result in overt neuroses. Adler employs a Schopenhauerian and Nietzschean "will to power" as a model for understanding a universal feeling of inferiority, whose

Reprinted from *Psychiatry*, 40: 113-132, 1977 by special permission of the William Alanson White Psychiatric Foundation, Inc. Copyright © by the William Alanson White Psychiatric Foundation, Inc.

ultimate origin is grounded in the inadequacy of the infant. And Jung cavalierly splits the human race into the extrovertish and the introvertish, the cosmopolitans and the islanders.

What I have chosen as my concern, in the foregoing, is not a rough survey of conceptions of human nature—whether man is good, bad, or indifferent; a rational creature or essentially a sentient one; whether man's nature has "ever been the same" or whether "man makes himself," creatively. Rather, I am interested in what "motivates" man, I am searching for a universal principle through which we may "understand" why man does what he does, why man is what he is. Obviously, however, the commitment we make in regard to a theory of human motivation will itself necessarily be found to entail a corresponding view of human nature. Confronted with this impressive variety of interpretations, I don't know if I am able to offer a comparable general principle, but I shall try. In a word, that principle is loneliness. Thus, I wish to hold that once man has satisfied his more obviously physiological and biologic drives and comfortably secured the necessities of air, water, and food, he then strives to alleviate his desperate loneliness.[1] It is not so much, then, a fact—correcting Jung, for instance—that we are to be dichotomized into extroverts and introverts, but rather that we all begin by aspiring toward human communion and affection and friendship but that, unfortunately, many of us fail; we who fail are the frustrated extroverts, the retreating introverts; if we cannot enjoy the company of others and command from them the recognition we (abnormally) feel for ourselves, well, then we shall cultivate our own company.

Consequently, in this study, I propose to discuss loneliness, solitude, isolation (I regard these terms as synonymous, hence I shall use them interchangeably) from a variety of perspectives. The idea on which these different aspects converge, as lines toward a center, however, remains essentially a meaning-nucleus, a noematic center (Husserl); or, to vary the paradigm a bit, what A.O. Lovejoy referred to as a unit-idea. But in either case, although the concept of solitude functions in a multiplicity of contexts, and for a variety of purposes, the idea itself remains essentially the same.

I do not intend—and quite likely I am unable—to offer a concep-

---

[1]Cf. J. Howard, 1975, pp. x-xi, 9-10, 17-18, 69, 74 ff., 94 ff., 147 ff., 198 ff. In a striking model, Howard conceives of loneliness as a psychological force analogous to gravity in the physical realm (p. 203).

tual definition of loneliness, partly, I suppose, because it is a feeling as well as a meaning. Like Hobbes, Hume, and Shaftesbury, methodologically, I think that it is something that we can "observe" if we gaze within ourselves. Just as the manifestations of physical gravity are externally observable, so I would contend, loneliness, in the psychological sphere, appears as a gentle force—but also an often violent one—moving us internally. In what follows, consequently, I shall treat loneliness as a psychological drive—one whose internality, or "immanence," is independent of physiological factors. Thus, we obviously have a drive, an overwhelming desire or need, to breathe, to drink, to eat, and to sleep. But my interest in the drive to avoid isolation stems from regarding it as a purely psychological one, not conditioned by environmental or physiological elements. Now this is not to deny that these external factors may be present; or important; or even necessary. I am certain that sensory deprivation experiments, for instance, could result in a mass of data that might parallel or correlate with our assumption and conclusions. Nevertheless, what shall guide our study is loneliness as a mental phenomenon, the self-conscious awareness of isolation; and the model of the self or ego which I shall adopt—as an unargued principle, premise, and paradigm—is basically similar to Descartes' reflexive consciousness. I wish to put aside behaviorist approaches; I would not deny that, upon certain occasions, I have been the last to discover, for example, that I was lonely, just as I'm generally the last one to discover how stupid I've been. As Sartre suggests, I may be the last to discover my anti-Semitism; or my cowardice until I see my "emotion" of fear trickling down my pant leg in a warm yellow stream (*The Wall*). We do not cry because we are sad, says William James, we are sad because we cry. But although this happens, and, if you must, occurs quite often, nevertheless I wish to insist that this sort of "positivistic" perspective is unintelligible unless it is grounded in a prior, more primordial model of self-consciousness, self-awareness of the *meanings* of, for example, bigotry, fear, sorrow, and loneliness. We may not always be able to articulate or communicate our feelings, but we must be able to feel our feelings *as* emotions, we must be (self-)consciously aware of experiencing an emotion. And an electrochemical firing or an explosion in the brain and central nervous system is not "a hatred of Jews"; "a sense of panic"; a "recognition of loss"; or "an awareness of abandonment."

As it will turn out, I shall contend that man is not only psychologically alone but metaphysically isolated as well. Now in saying this I do not mean that we *think* or *feel* we are alone all the time and at every moment; I think we *really* are, but we are not always aware of it. This is important, for it implies that in my account of the affair there is at least a meaningful and possible opposite to loneliness and that is "togetherness" with an interest (when we are "extro-reflecting"); or pursuing a "cause"; or enjoying the proximity of intimate friends. Thus loneliness is *in principle* empirically verifiable because it does have a meaningful contradictory. When I am with my close friend and we are enjoying each other's companionship, I am (apparently) not alone.

In what ensues, therefore, I will maintain that whenever a genuine feeling of friendship is present, then loneliness is not present in consciousness although it, nevertheless, serves as a "structural" (or "transcendental") condition for the possibility of companionship. As Fichte suggests, the lone ego is posited (structurally) prior to the "other."

One last remark before we begin. Since I do not believe man (psychologically) is always or necessarily alone (although he really is metaphysically), it follows that I am not particularly interested in cases of extreme withdrawal, those evidenced in catatonic, autistic, or depressive states. Extreme isolation, I am convinced, will lead to "insanity," and it is quite likely that the sufferer may be nearer to some sort of metaphysical truth in this regard. Nevertheless, I am far more interested in the normal, average, more communicative, and, hence, reflexive cases of solitude as opposed to those individuals who have totally slipped away into a removed psychosis, an insanity whose very structure, I suspect, is yet closer to reality. Therefore, I have no desire to attempt to describe these "lost souls," even if it should promise certain insights. I do not have to inspect a flawless or a perfect diamond in order to learn something about diamonds; ordinary diamonds will do.

THE HISTORICAL ROOTS OF LONELINESS IN WESTERN CONSCIOUSNESS

Is loneliness really ingrained in the conscious structure of Western man? Perhaps it is only a recent aberration, caused by our alienating (or estranging) technological and bureaucratic society. As such, one could argue, it is not an essential or necessary universal structure of man's awareness but merely an unfortunate—but curable—modern distortion. Thus, one might contend that if we were to reflect on the concerns of the early Greeks, we might rather wish to maintain that the presence of loneliness seems to be prominently absent in their literary and philosophic concerns. Hegel conceived of the Hellenic consciousness as the happy consciousness, bathed in sunlight, openness, warmth, and an inclusive unity—as contrasted with the unhappy consciousness, first symbolized by the Old Testament awareness of man and later by the monastic, estranged consciousness of medieval man. Surely in the gregarious spectacle of Athenian communal life, we nowhere discover the dark and gloomy specter of individual isolation. Loneliness may unconsciously haunt the obscure, labyrinthine recesses of Augustine's search for God in the *Confessions,* but where do we read of it in the dialogues of Plato or the treatises of Aristotle? Nevertheless, we might recall, in this context, that Plato's entire literary life was dedicated to perpetuating, from early manhood until old age, the memory of a friend who had died while Plato was still only a young man. *Timaeus* and *Laws* notwithstanding, the bulk of Plato's literary production served as merely the external means for maintaining an internal conscious memory alive. Plato, who may never have committed his deepest beliefs to writing (*The Seventh Letter*), nevertheless clearly believed that at least the flowing conversational structure of his dramas was the best means of keeping and perpetuating the reminiscences of his spiritual master as if he were still alive. (Indeed, the Greeks believed a man was immortal so long as his friends remembered him.) We may remember also that, for Plato, a condition for our progressing toward truth, beauty, and goodness is that we first become friends; otherwise our conversation will be for naught. Friends share things in common; for Plato this usually translates into a common commitment and respect for immaterial truths held mutually by the ''friends of the forms.'' Notice how, in the *Republic,* after Thrasymachus' onslaught against Socrates had dissipated and he assumes the role of a willing listener, if not participant, Adeimantus once more attempts to encourage Thrasymachus to attack Socrates; at that point, Socrates simply says, ''leave us alone, for we have become friends'' (*Rep.,* VI, 498c-d). Similarly, we should remember that Aristotle devotes no less than two entire books, in the *Nicomachean Ethics,* to a discussion of the moral virtue of friendship. One should conclude, I would venture to suggest, that it is not so much, therefore, a fact that the Hellenic Greeks were not motivated by or concerned with solitude but rather that they concentrated on escape from it; and that they did so, primarily, by enjoying the values of friendship. And it is in this sense that they regarded man as a social or political animal.

But is it really the case that we have to ferret out the implications of a stress on loneliness in the Greek mind by indirectly approaching it and inferring its existence through the perspective of their emphasis on friendship? Do we not have available some documentation which might serve as evidence for a direct concern with and fear of aloneness? Indeed, I believe we do. In this regard, I think it would be difficult to find a more gripping and terrifying illustration of man's conception of aloneness than one discovers in *Oedipus Rex*. Granted, it may be challenged that Oedipus' situation was not intended by Sophocles to depict the universal condition of man (Oedipus is special, he is nobler than we are, he is unique). Still, how are we to feel fear and pity unless we are able, at least to some extent, to identify with him? Are we not expected to empathize and sympathize? But obviously we cannot do so unless we somehow imagine his condition as possibly our own, unless we feel his position as at least implicitly a universal one. (Aristotle insisted that poetry dealt with the universal whereas history was restricted to the singular.)

What happens in the tragedy? Briefly, it symbolizes the powerful quest of a man to plumb to the depths of his own identity. Oedipus had solved the riddle of the sphinx by discovering that the solution lay in the universal consciousness of man as finally arising out of and beyond animal awareness (Hegel, 1837, pp. 219-222). Thus Oedipus realized that the essence of man in general is the possession of self-consciousness. But he had not (mercifully) achieved the level of his own individual self-consciousness. Oedipus initiates the search whose own goal is himself; he begins the circle which ends with him. (This is what captured Hegel's imagination in the myth, since, for Hegel, it symbolized the reflexive, circular character of thought; so Plotinus, Descartes, Leibniz, Kant, Fichte, Hegel.) In his desperate, driving search, Oedipus pitilessly subjects Tiresias, Creon, Jocasta, and the old shepherd to remorseless questioning. Oedipus' flaw was a lack of pity; in the end he turned that vice even against himself by condemning himself to utter aloneness, symbolized by blindness, darkness, self-exile, self-abandonment. His self-sentence was harsher than even the god had demanded. Thus, Oedipus refers to himself as "the last man," a phrase which will find a haunting echo in Nietzsche, the loneliest philosopher. The drama ends with the plea of a formerly powerful man not to have his children taken away from him. What more can we say? Is it any wonder then that Thomas Wolfe was convinced that the essence of tragedy lay, not in conflict, but in man's confrontation with loneliness? The symbolism of forced isolation is carried out repeatedly throughout *Oedipus Rex, Oedipus at Colonus,* and *Antigone* by the recurring themes of exile, alienation, homelessness, ostracism, solitary living, entombment in darkness, and explicit references to loneliness. Hegel, of course, believed that *Antigone,* with its conflict of "two rights," Antigone's and Creon's, best stood for tragedy but I think Wolfe is much more insightful in this regard. (If Hegel were right, tragedies would be fairly rare occurrences.)

With the dissolution of the Greek city-states, of course, the Hellenistic and Roman worlds blundered into a disintegration of the "organic bonds" which had essentially, until then, constituted the "good life" of the earlier Hellenic Greeks. For Plato and Aristotle (the early, individualistically oriented dialogues of Plato notwithstanding [cf. esp. *Apology; Rep.* VI, 496b-e]) the "good man" was inconceivable apart from the good polis. The goodness—and happiness —of the individual could only take place within the context of a good society. Later, however, in the Alexandrine period, we suddenly find men fragmented from their fellows. Their subsequent mode of existence, along with a quest for personal salvation, more and more acquires the characteristic of individuals who resemble self-contained and unrelated atoms. Consequently, the struggle for happiness came to consist in an increasingly personal battle for self-sufficiency. It is, as George Sabine has correctly remarked, at time during which men were beginning to "make souls for themselves" (1961, pp. 131ff., 141 ff.)[2] No longer is self-sufficiency to be grounded in the larger unit of the polis; henceforth the way to salvation is to be progressively contemplated as a personal, and, hence, by implication, a lonely path. In their loneliness, the Stoics advocated a theoretical conception of the universal brotherhood of all men as an ideal in which men could share. (Hegel was to condemn this as a merely futile, empty, abstract

[2]Contemporaneously, according to Hegel, the *small* Christian association was grounded in friendship between intimates (1795, sect. 21).

ideal.) The Epicureans, understandably more physically restrictive in this regard, proclaimed a dependence on a few intimate friends (thus mirroring Aristotle's dictum that the essence of friendship is living in communion). And, finally, the Skeptics, with their own distinctive, nihilistic frustration, not only denied truth but also denied any and all possibility of permanence or constancy, including that of their own selves. But by insisting on their imperious will to disbelieve, the Skeptics, in a strange and ironic fashion, ended by affirming, each separately, the nucleus of their own doubting selves. For through an insistence on a limitless power to deny reality, they ironically managed to establish a total concern with their selves, their powers, and their limitations (Hegel, 1807, Sect. "Skepticism"; cf. Loewenberg, 1965, pp. 94-95; and Hyppolite, 1946, pp. 187-188). What skepticism initiated, then, was an involvement with problems regarding the self, with questions that, if not actually centered on the ego, at least were emerging from a nucleus of "personal identity." Later, instead of being resolved, these issues were avoided—for the Middle Ages simply took the metaphysical existence of the soul for granted and as unproblematic—and were internalized within the general structure of Western consciousness. The emphasis on the individual soul, however, quickly engendered a subconscious rift between individual man and absolute being. This, in turn, developed into what Jacob Loewenberg, in his commentary on Hegel's *Phenomenology,* has christened the schizophrenic awareness of monastic medieval man. Indeed, the paradigm itself may be readily extended, chronologically, by portraying it as a symptom which is contemporaneously manifest in all of us who view ourselves—or society—as neurotic, rather than recognize that we are not ill but, worse, alone.

With the advance of Christianity, as it moved forward amid the chaos of the prevailing human condition of extreme social and political alienation, or fragmentation, an increasing need developed to alleviate man's feeling of bondlessness, of abandonment, of desolation. By creating or positing or emphasizing an immutable, eternal, and independent self-conscious being, medieval man managed to discover a vital means of escaping loneliness. For, as early Christian man conceived it, there existed an absolute being with whom one could always communicate, or pray, an external existence whose awareness included every thought of each individual's consciousness. What more secure or ultimate guarantee could there be that one was not alone? But then, of course, the deepest suffering would result in conceiving of oneself as estranged, alienated, separated from God, i.e., in thinking of one's self as absolutely alone or unrecognized, an atom of awareness, an apperceptive monad condemned to a solitary, incommunicable existence (Hegel, 1807, sect. "Unhappy Consciousness"). Far better to be a slave, recognized in some sense—even if it were not a fully human one—by a master, than to be a lord without recognition (Robinson Crusoe, Hegel's example). Accordingly, man's desire, fundamentally and essentially, as Hegel informs us, must be mutually conditioned by other self-conscious selves, with their desires (cf. Loewenberg, 1957, p. 77; and Hegel, 1807, sect. "Lordship and Bondage").

Slowly, after the Middle Ages, a shift began in which man sought to alleviate his sense of isolation not by turning toward an absolute, eternal God but rather by turning toward man himself, or more specifically, toward man as an essence, a universal essence (Hegel; Feuerbach's species-being; Marx's man as class-conscious). But this change in perspective was not to be accomplished until the 16th, 17th, 18th, and 19th centuries, beginning with Montaigne's introspective essays, Descartes' solipsistic meditations, and Hume's concern with personal identity, progressing to Rousseau's and Mill's reflections on individuality, and culminating in the philosophy of Comte, who conceived of *le grand être* not as God but as humanity. (It is in this sense that the father of sociology and positivism advocated a religion of humanity.)

THE PSYCHOLOGY AND SOCIOLOGY OF LONELINESS

Amazingly enough, until recently, psychologists have had relatively little to say about loneliness. There is, for instance, but slight mention of it in Freud. The following passage is one of the few discussions he offers:

> In children the first phobias relating to situations are those of darkness and solitude. The former of these often persists throughout life; both are involved when a child feels the absence of some loved person who looks after it—its mother, that is to say. While I was in the next room, I heard a child who was afraid of the dark call out: "Do speak to me, Auntie! I'm frightened!" "Why, what good would that do? You

can't see me." To this the child replied: "If someome speaks, it gets lighter." Thus a *longing* felt in the dark is transformed into a fear of the dark (1916-1917, p. 407).[3]

Children are not, at least at first, afraid of death, because they cannot comprehend or imagine what a permanent loss of consciousness might mean. But they are frightened by the dark, long before they begin to understand what death might entail. Children initially simply assume they are immortal and eternal. They are, however, terrified of the dark because it symbolizes aloneness. Thus, they are often afraid of going to sleep at night, not because they fear never awakening again, but rather because they are horrified by the prospect of being conscious *and* alone.

We do not fear death, we fear loneliness. We are not frightened by the thought that our senses, our awarenesses, will not operate or exist, for if we were, we would each of us be terrified at the prospect of going to sleep every night. But we are not. Like children, we are not afraid of a loss of consciousness but of being alone, of enduring in an isolated state, often symbolized by a solitude in darkness (Conrad, *Heart of Darkness*). What horrifies us concerning death is the possibility that our consciousness will continue but that it shall be the only one. We imagine ourselves as a solipsistic awareness, existing alone within a dark (or light, it matters not) universe, wandering the solitary, limitless expanses of space (or blackness) and time, in absolute desolation, the only monad of perception, dumbly reflecting, from darkened windows of awareness, a soulless universe—save for one soul, ours alone. "One soul was lost; a tiny soul: his. It flickered once and went out, forgotten, lost. The end black cold void waste" (Joyce, *A Portrait of the Artist as a Young Man,* III). This it is which we (separately) fear; not the mercifulness of an oblivious nothingness, death as Socrates' "dreamless night" (*Apology*); but rather we fear the self's *consciousness* of "nothingness," the awareness of our individual aloneness, an isolation not reflected in the warmth and "reflexive light" of another conscious existence.

Incidentally, the symbol of light in the Freud passage cited above, represents, I believe, the possibility of communication with another

---

[3]A more extended analysis of an essential feeling of isolation, however, is offered by Anna Freud (1954).

consciousness. Light is a spatial medium and a mediating *tertium quid* (Plato, Aristotle) "through" or "by" or "in" which we can see that we are not alone; darkness, by contrast, confines us to an inner solipsistic temporality. The desire to communicate with another awareness and have it reciprocally assure us of our own existence is but the reverse side of the need to escape solitude. This need arises at the very dawn of consciousness within the individual ego. Indeed, when human affection is withheld from the infant, a condition known as marasmus (Coleman, 1964, pp. 130, 665) occurs and it results in both physiological and psychological symptoms carried throughout the sufferer's life. It originates simply as the result of depriving the infant of external human affection and response, of withholding conscious recognition of the infant's existence.

Although Freud's remarks on loneliness are infrequent, nevertheless he does introduce an intriguing model through which we may approach solitude both as a feeling and as a theoretical construct. In what follows it shall be my contention that every individual human consciousness is permeated by an underlying, primordial, pervasive sense (or structure) of the possibility of aloneness and loneliness. And, of course, the question before us is whether there is in fact any psychological evidence for such a theory. Indeed, I believe there is. For instance, we find Freud himself discussing something very much like this in his *Civilization and its Discontents* (1930); he refers to it there as the "oceanic" feeling. It is, as Freud and a colleague describe it, akin to a "sensation of 'eternity'," "limitless, unbounded" (p. 64). For his friend, who is writing to him, this feeling constitutes the source of religion. According to Freud, on the other hand, the oceanic feeling is grounded in the most primitive stage of awareness of the undifferentiating ego (Fichte, Hegel). It is the sensation that the ego originally feels as it experiences itself as a perfect unity with the entire universe, a fusion which excludes any and all distinctions between self and world. In this regard, it is similar to Nietzsche's model of a feeling of primordial unity characterized by Dionysian states of awareness (*The Birth of Tragedy,* sects. 1, 2). Now, for my own purposes, I should like to maintain that this "oceanic feeling" is actually a sensation of nothingness, albeit one which is almost immediately invaded by the plenitude of "material" being, or at least sensory being, as soon as consciousness wakens. The "self" is conscious but not self-conscious yet. At this initial point, awareness mistakes the fullness of the presentation for itself and it identifies itself (incorrectly), not with the nothingness which constitutes the very condition for the given's appearing at all, but rather with the givenness, the otherness. But as consciousness develops toward explicit reflection, it slowly realizes that the fullness is ephemeral and capricious, a vortical mosaic of sound and color; again, it begins to recognize that the plenitude is a contingent otherness and, hence, unessential; but what remains, what stays as an irreducible medium of awareness, which cannot be dismissed or escaped, is its own stark emptiness. Consciousness then increasingly becomes (reflexively) confronted by its own essential nothingness, a black hole of self-conscious existence. When man grasps his true and essential condition—and insofar as he comprehends it—he becomes desperately lonely and he will volitionally create any relation, he will will any meaning which shall afford him an escape from his solitude. And the ultimate evidence of this is in each man's own consciousness. Look within, for there lies an essential element of reality. "Don't go abroad. Truth dwells inside man" (Augustine, *De vera religione*, 39, n. 72).

In a recent study on loneliness, Weiss (1973) undertakes to discuss solitude as if it were a mere disease, like any other. Thus he declares, "Severe loneliness appears to be almost as prevalent as colds during the winter" (p. 1). Since it is an illness, it follows that it is an unnatural condition, albeit fortunately one which may be avoided. Indeed, the little volume adds a litany of remedies and cures of which the orphaned, the divorced, the aged, and the like may avail themselves in order to abate or conquer their affliction. On this model, loneliness is obviously considered almost as a medical problem. Just as malnutrition is defined as a lack of food, so loneliness is regarded as lack of companionship. But this is some sort of gross distortion of the facts permeating individual human existence. Loneliness is not a medical malady, nor even a sociological one. Rather, as we shall see, it is grounded in the intrinsic nature of man, in his very psychological makeup. I admit, I myself have compared loneliness to a biological drive but this is not the same as to regard it as an illness. A desire for nutrition, to take an example, is not itself a disease; instead it is a physiological, structural condition permeating man's states of awareness. My model of loneliness, in direct contrast to that of Weiss, is clearly more comparable to something like Nietzsche's psychological thesis that we are driven by a conscious or unconscious "will to power."

In a brilliant article, entitled, simply enough, "Loneliness," Frieda Fromm-Reichmann points out that there had been, until the time she was writing, practically no discussion in the field of psychological studies regarding the concept of pathological solitude (this volume).[4] The fact that the situation has scarcely improved since the appearance of her paper is a sufficient indication of a glaring deficiency in the disciplines of psychology and sociology. This is not merely a theoretical neglect or oversight but more clearly in the nature of a methodological tragedy. And not because loneliness is a disavowed or an unrecognized illness—like syphilis, a social embarrassment, one which can be cured once it is admitted or diagnosed—for we shall never "cure" it; but because by understanding it, we shall be able better to comprehend man, for the truth of man is that he is essentially—metaphysically and psychologically—alone. Sartre speculated that we are condemned to freedom; but we are more irretrievably and hopelessly sentenced to utter isolation. Thus, despite psychology's and sociology's pretense of dealing with human conditions and realities, it remains manifestly obvious that they have somehow missed this essential structure of human consciousness, of consciousness as constituted throughout by extreme and intrinsic solitude.

Frieda Fromm-Reichmann, however, is certainly not guilty of neglecting what she terms "disintegrative loneliness," but which nevertheless clearly parallels my model of man's isolation. And, as she points out: "The longing for interpersonal intimacy stays with every human being from infancy throughout life; and there is no human being who is not threatened by its loss" (this volume, p. 342; see also Sullivan, 1953, p. 290; and Zilboorg, 1938). As she goes on to suggest, the extremely unnerving experience of "real loneliness has much in common with some other quite serious mental states, such as panic. People cannot endure such states for any length of time without becoming psychotic..." (this volume, p. 345). (One is reminded, in

---

[4]Interestingly enough, the author herself relates her study, at a number of points in her discussion, to Freud's concept of the "oceanic feeling." Compare Freud's psychological description with Hegel's metaphorical interpretation of baptism in Hegel's *Theologische Jugendschriften* (1793-1800, p. 319).

this connection, of some of Kafka's works, such as *The Trial* and *The Metamorphosis*.) Fromm-Reichmann, following Ludwig Binswanger and Harry Stack Sullivan, agrees that the "naked existence," the "naked horror," of loneliness can be an even more compelling drive than the more commonly recognized physiological needs of man: "Anyone who has encountered persons who were under the influence of real loneliness understands why people are more frightened of being lonely than of being hungry, or being deprived of sleep, or having their sexual needs unfulfilled..." (this volume, p. 348).

I wish to claim that wittingly or unwittingly both Freud and Fromm-Reichmann are agreeing with the philosopher Fichte, who had previously theorized that the ego is first conscious—it posits itself—but that it is not aware of itself, as such, it is not reflexively conscious. It next (temporally or logically) posits a non-ego, an-other-than-itself as a condition of its own recognition, its own self-conscious awareness. Later, in Hegel, the "other," which mutually conditions the self, is itself a consciousness (Hegel, 1807, sect. "Lordship and Bondage"). The self then is mutually conditioned by other conscious selves, and one cannot be *self*-conscious unless there are other self-conscious or social selves in existence (contra Descartes, Leibniz, and Kant) (see Loewenberg, 1957, pp. 73 ff.). Consciousness of self is only possible through the existence of other self-consciousnesses. Now this paradigm of the initial state *and* stage of individual human awareness (the ego positing itself as *un*-self-conscious) is taken over by Freud in his discussion of the "oceanic feeling." First there is consciousness as an unconscious, unreflective identification of the ego with the totality of presented being. Slowly, however, with the realization that our desires are not omnipotent, that we are finite and limited, the ego introduces the reality principle, it generates a distinction between itself and the other-than-itself (Hegel's principle of negativity). This is "healthy" and necessary. It leads to the beginning of a "realistic" separation between (a) a reflexive self; (b) inanimate objects; and (c) other selves, most notably the mother. But

> If the omnipotent baby learns the job of being admired and loved but learns nothing about the outside world, he may develop a conviction of his greatness and all-importance which will lead to a narcissistic orientation to life—a conviction that life is nothing but being loved and admired. This narcissistic-megalomanic attitude will not be acceptable

to the environment which will respond with hostility and isolation of the narcissistic person. The deeply seated triad of narcissism, megalomania, and hostility will be established, which is, according to Zilboorg, at the root affliction of loneliness (Fromm-Reichmann, this volume, p. 344).

"Sanity" depends on a tricky balance, on maintaining a distinction between one's self, the external world, and other selves. (As we shall see later, this separateness [Nietzsche's Apollonian principle] itself leads to the paradoxical, but inevitable, need of man both (a) to be distinct, *and* (b) to belong with others. This is another origin of the tragedy of man.) Disrupt this delicate equilibrium by isolating the individual, and the result is an anxiety which, if enforced or prolonged, will culminate in severe disorientation.

> While alone and isolated from others, people feel threatened by the potential loss of their boundaries, of the ability to discriminate between the subjective self and the objective world around them (Fromm-Reichmann, 1959, p. 7; see also May, 1953, p. 32).

Perhaps the best study on loneliness has just appeared, James Howard's *The Flesh-Colored Cage* (1975). The ultimate (metaphysical) presupposition of Howard's thesis concerning man's essential aloneness is grounded in the author's conception of man as a self-conscious being, actually the only one in the animal kingdom. (Animals are conscious but not self-conscious—Leibniz.) According to Howard, then, we are enclosed within the envelope of a radical subjectivity (p. ix).[5] We can never completely overcome isolation but we can reduce it. And we struggle to do so either by "incorporation" or "decapsulation." We either (a) attempt to bring the other within; or (b) we strive "to reach out beyond the limits of our cage and contact some creature in another cage. We do this by communication, touch, expression, transcendence, or some other form of [externally directed] act" (p. xi). "We function at any given time between the

---

[5]There is a conceptual confusion which runs throughout the book. It is uncertain whether Howard wishes to maintain that the physical body is our cage or whether it is our own reflexive awareness, a position akin to solipsism. Obviously, the second alternative is philosophically by far the stronger and the more defensible of the two themes, although it should not be carried out to a subjectivity so extreme that it would deny the conceivability and actuality of communication between two distinct selves.

two strategic poles of complete incorporation of our world, swallowing it all, or complete escape from the boundaries of skin, turning ourselves inside out to join with that which is beyond our direct knowing" (p. xiii).[6] Indeed, I would agree with this model in exactly this way—namely, that consciousness, I am convinced, has just this sort of double-aspect power; it can look outward, "extro-reflect," or it can turn within, "intro-reflect," be reflexively aware of itself. When it performs the latter activity, it is vulnerable to the feeling of loneliness. In one aspect, it struggles to escape; in the other, it is confronted by its tragic essence, its "solipsistic" prison.

As far as insights into radical solitude are concerned, sociology has lagged far behind psychology. In *The Lonely Crowd* (1950) David Riesman and his associates, like Weiss, almost reduce loneliness to an illness, or at least suggest that it is an idiosyncrasy of certain societies. Consequently, they imply in their study that although the inner-directed person and the more predominantly outer-directed person both (often) experience acute feelings of aloneness, this is not the case in the more tradition-oriented societies where the lives of individuals are structured primarily around the multiple-generation family, the tribe, or the community; the latter individual hence exists within a pre-established, meaningful, social life-structure worked out in the context of a basically organically related community or society (1950, pp. v-vi, 68-69, 373). He, by implication, is not lonely or desolate.

More insightful than the foregoing are some remarks of Erich Fromm's (1941). Once more we find some themes we have already repeated: the need for the individual to be related to the world beyond himself is just as compelling as the more readily acknowledged biological drives; and "To feel completely alone and isolated leads to mental disintegration just as physical starvation leads to death" (p. 19). But Fromm adds something new as well. Moral aloneness is defined, by Fromm, as the inability of the individual to relate, not necessarily to other human beings, but to values or ideals in general. In this regard, Fromm points out, the monk in his monastery, who believes in God, or the political prisoner imprisoned in a cell, who feels the solidarity of a common cause, is not alone. Indeed, "Religion and nationalism, as well as any custom and any belief

---

[6]Again, the model offered is a mixed one; the first implies a physiological container; the second, a mental barrier. The basic point, however, is valid.

however absurd and degrading, if it only connects the individual with others, are refuges from what man most dreads: isolation'' (p. 20).

Like Howard, Fromm traces the feeling of extreme solitude to the ''fact of subjective self-consciousness, of the faculty of thinking by which man is aware of himself as an individual entity, different from nature and other people'' (p. 21). Man, once having achieved the level of individual self-consciousness, once having reached a state of distinct personal identity, suddenly is confronted by his extreme and complete aloneness. But just ''as a child can never return to the mother's womb physically, so it can never reverse psychically, the process of individuation'' (p. 30). This is the dilemma of man; he must strive to distinguish his self from the amorphous ''field'' of awareness experienced at the stage of the ''oceanic feeling''; but once that is achieved, he is then confronted by the realization that he no longer ''belongs.'' And then the futile, quixotic road back to ''absolute being'' and unity is undertaken, or at least sporadically attempted. In this sense even the most violent anarchist and political terrorist is desperately involved in a struggle to belong to something more stable than himself.

The only individuals who crave solitude are those who are not condemned to it.

LONELINESS IN LITERATURE, PHILOSOPHY, AND RELIGION

If we really want to show human isolation or loneliness more explicitly and perhaps, to better understand it, to ''intuit'' solitude from within, then undoubtedly we should turn to the province of literature and to some of the Existential writers.

We certainly find a symbolic allusion to forced solitude as early as Dante's *Inferno*. Thus, in the last sphere of hell, the ninth, the sufferers are presented as entombed in ice, almost totally unable to touch, to "communicate"—hence symbolically condemned to eternal solitude. Here, in frozen incommunicable agony, are they who, like Cain, were treacherous against those to whom they were bound by special ties (see also Fromm-Reichmann, this volume, pp. 351–352). The infidelities of these souls were denials of love (represented by God) and of all human warmth. As they denied God's love, so are they furthest removed from the light and warmth of his sun. As they denied all human ties, so are they bound by the unyielding ice (Dante, 1308-1312 p. 266).

In Balzac's *The Inventor's Suffering*, we find the following passage:

> Man has a horror of aloneness. And of all kinds of aloneness, moral aloneness is the most terrible. The first hermits lived with God, they inhabited the world which is most populated, the world of the spirits. The first thought of man, be he a leper or a prisoner, a sinner or an invalid, is: to have a companion of his fate. In order to satisfy this drive which is life itself, he applies all his strength, all his power, the energy of his whole life. Would Satan have found companions without this over-powering craving? (quoted by Fromm, 1941, p. 20.)

A joy unshared is no joy at all; but a sorrow experienced in solitude is inexpressible anguish. Or, as Gabriel Marcel puts it: "Il n'y a qu'une souffrance, c'est d'être seul" (quoted in Sarano, 1970).

Marxist estheticians maintain that the novel as a literary form had its roots in the alienating structure of modern society, with its attendant growth of economic inequalities. In this sense, the novel quickly evolved into a means of explicitly portraying the ills of industrial society in order to condemn them. With this interpretation, Defoe's *Moll Flanders* would be a good example of the novel directed toward social protest, as, obviously, are many of Dickens' works. (Loneliness is symbolized by orphanage in Dickens' works.) But I should like to suggest instead that it would be at least as illuminating to examine the novel from another point of view, and to consider *Robinson Crusoe* as exemplifying the powerful "existentialist" theme of human solitude (see especially the 1972 Oxford edition of Defoe, 1719, pp. 66, 70, 89, 204, 210). In this sense, the novel actually ushers in the literary age of subjective concern, of literary introspection, and a concern with the self and its relation to others, which was impossible in other esthetic forms of expression.

But it is when we turn to more modern and contemporary literature, armed with our model of man's innate loneliness, or sense of isolation, that we read with new insight the novels of: Dostoyevsky (*Notes from the Undergound*); Hardy (*The Return of the Native*); Jack London (*Martin Eden*); Hesse (*Steppenwolf*); Thomas Wolfe (*Look Homeward Angel, Of Time and the River, You Can't Go Home Again*); James Joyce (*A Portrait of the Artist as a Young Man*); O'Neill (*The Iceman*

Cometh, Anna Christie, Long Day's Journey into Night); Camus (*The Stranger, The Plague*); Kafka (*The Trial*); the plays of Tennessee Williams; the novels of Graham Greene (*The Man Within, The Power and the Glory, The Heart of the Matter*); Salinger (*The Catcher in the Rye*, "The Laughing Man"); or Conrad (*Heart of Darkness, Lord Jim, Victory*). Thus, for example, Conrad explicitly posits "the tremendous fact of our isolation, of the loneliness impenetrable and transparent, elusive and everlasting; of the indestructible loneliness that surrounds, envelops, clothes every human soul from the cradle to the grave, and perhaps, beyond" (*An Outcast of the Islands*, IV, 3; quite often, darkness symbolizes loneliness in Conrad's writings just as the atom or a closed door signals it for Wolfe). Zilboorg, in his article on loneliness (1938), catalogs the following artists as representing or suffering from psychopathic solitude: Cervantes, Maupassant, Tolstoy, Dostoyevsky, Nietzsche, Schopenhauer, Wagner, Tchaikovsky, Strindberg, Ibsen, Sinclair Lewis.

It may appear exegetically perverse to lump a good novel, like Hardy's *Return of the Native,* with a poor one, like Salinger's *Catcher in the Rye,* but the only point I wish to make is simply that they are both dedicated to the theme of loneliness, and as such, are classic examples of modern and contemporary literature. Indeed, Egdon Heath and Eustacia Vye symbolize, respectively, natural and human solitude in Hardy's work; in turn, allusions to Hardy's romance and its tragic heroine constitute some of the few explicit literary references found in *Catcher.* Also, it may be remembered that Holden Caulfield's ambition is to be "a catcher" in the rye (= heath field), assigned the task of preventing the (lonely) children from self-destruction, exactly what occurs to the characters in Hardy's book.

Just as a parenthetical note, it might be interesting to compare the notion of friendship in Plato's writings with the strong sense of friendship one finds in Kazantzakis' work *Zorba the Greek.* In comparisons such as these, I am convinced, one would discover an overarching feeling of sympathy and understanding that transcends time, a feeling grounded in the universality of loneliness.

Augustine, even in the *Confessions,* is not alone; he has God just as Fromm's hermit had God. But certainly beginning with the skeptical and introspective essays of Montaigne, at the close of the Renaissance, we begin to see a concentration on the self and, indirectly, unconsciously, on personal identity. Subsequently, with Descartes, not only is the epistemological turn effected but the egocentric commitment is posited which will henceforth haunt Western man and bring him to a more explicit realization of his absolute subjectivity and his metaphysical aloneness (the "egocentric predicament"). In this regard, Descartes merely makes explicit the growing entrapment of Western philosophic thought as it becomes progressively concerned with the problematic relation between an immediately apprehending, self-conscious ego and its (problematic) inferential knowledge of an external world and other minds (cf. Mijuskovic, 1971a). Small wonder, then, given this Cartesian context, that Leibniz, engulfed in this growing concern, proceeds to posit an ontological and epistemological monadology, whose only guarantee for the (apparent) interaction between a plurality of intrinsically distinct consciousnesses becomes completely dependent upon an original intervention, a "pre-established harmony," instituted through the agency of God, the monad of monads. Suddenly, but predictably, a theoretical and moral concern next emerges, with Locke's discussion of possible criteria for the establishment of personal identity, in the *Essay*. No longer are the primordiality and the indubitability of the self taken for granted (Augustine, *Contra Sceptics*). For once Locke assumes command of this voyaging philosophic concern, just as inevitably does the problem, embarked upon "doubt's boundless sea," become shipwrecked on the shoals of Humean skepticism (cf. Mijuskovic, 1971b, 1974, 1975a). And, finally, this, in its turn, culminates in our own contemporary, monomaniacal anxiety, our concern with "identity crises"; neurotic broodings over "popularity" problems; overemphases on extreme orientations toward "other-directedness"; chronic collective "faddism"; violent and distorted attempts at communications through drugs; fanatic involvements in "political causes"; and so forth.

Should we desire to have the feeling of loneliness described more unambiguously, we could do no better than to consult such authors as Pascal and Nietzsche. According to Pascal, man is thrown completely alone into a meaningless existence. And in terror he confronts his own solitude against the background of an infinite and empty universe. The feeling of extreme isolation and abandonment which we discover in certain exaggerated pathological states is perhaps but the finger within the wound of each of us as we singly realize our radical contingency and metaphysical exile.

En regardant tout l'univers muet et l'homme sans lumière abandonné a lui-même, et comme égaré dans ce recoin de l'univers sans savoir qui l'y a mis, ce qui'il y est venu faire, ce qu'il deviendra en mourant . . . j'entre en effroi comme un homme qu'on aurait porté endormi dans une île déserte et effroyable, et qui s'eveillerait sans connâitre et sans moyen den sortir (Pascal, quoted by Sarano, 1970, p. 40; see also Pascal, *Pensées*, sect. 194 and cf. Kierkegaard, 1843, passim; 1844, p. 110; 1849, pp. 102-103).

Similarly, in Nietzsche we find that the death of God simultaneously proclaims the utter aloneness of man. The "last man," in *Thus Spake Zarathustra*, really signifies that we are, each of us, separately, condemned to metaphysical solitude, the "Terrible loneliness of the last philosopher!" (Zarathustra the Hermit and Dostoyevsky's Grand Inquisitor share more than a striking resemblance through their isolation from mankind.)

I call myself the last philosopher because I am the last man. Nobody talks to me but myself and my voice comes to me like that of a dying person! . . . Through you I conceal my loneliness from myself and make my way into the multitude and into love by lies, for my heart . . . cannot bear the terror of the loneliest loneliness and compels me to talk as if I were two (quoted by Jaspers, 1965, p. 56; see also pp. 58 ff., 70, 74, 81, 84-87, 402, 436).[7]

Who of us has not felt—if not uttered so eloquently, profoundly, and desperately—these sentiments of Nietzsche's? And even if we have experienced it but once in our lives, why do we think that it is not in truth our primordial condition, which we continually but futilely strive to escape? Why do so many of us persist in viewing it merely as some sort of momentary, monstrous aberration?

[7]As Jaspers indicates, Nietzsche wrote this in 1876, while he was a young professor and presumably surrounded by friends. *Zarathustra* was not even yet on the literary horizon. But again, this is regarded as a personal fact about Nietzsche himself rather than the representation of the universal condition of mankind. Cf. *The Gay Science*, sect. 50; *The Will to Power*, sects. 985, 988, 993. Actually, Sartre, in "Existentialism is a Humanism" (in Kaufmann, 1958), and Camus, in *The Plague*, are much nearer to conceiving it as the essential nature of man per se. Similarly, Wolfe saw the essence of human tragedy in loneliness, not in conflict. In this sense, the tragedy of Oedipus is the tragedy of each man who is reflexively aware of his aloneness.

Now, we may consider that this sort of extreme psychological and metaphysical melancholy is simply an exaggerated form of monadic hysteria, found in certain unique cases, but surely not in saner, more social natures. Perhaps in the distorted mind of a Pascal or a Dostoyevsky or a Nietzsche we shall uncover such thoughts but never in, say, the healthy personality of a Bertrand Russell. If we believe this, however, it may be illuminating to compare the foregoing with a passage from Russell's own *Autobiography* (1967): "Throughout my childhood I had an increasing sense of loneliness, and of despair of ever meeting anyone with whom I could talk. Nature and books and (later) mathematics saved me from complete despondency. . . ."(p. 30).[8]

To be sure, Russell's reflections on solitude (like Nietzsche's before him) may still be interpreted merely as *individual* outcries or confessions of personal rage and despair, and consequently one would not seem to be entitled to infer that these same emotions are universally prevalent in mankind. But it's a simple enough matter to turn to Russell's own British and Scottish empiricist predecessors in order to discover the general form of the proposition desired. Accordingly, preceding Russell, we find in the English tradition Burke, announcing in no uncertain voice that an "absolute and entire *solitude*, that is, the total and perpetual exclusion from all society, is as great a positive pain as can almost be conceived . . . an entire life of solitude contradicts the purposes of our being, since death itself is scarcely an idea of more terror"*(A Philosophical Enquiry into the Origin of Our Ideas of the Sublime and Beautiful*, I, xi). Similarly, before Burke, Hume had declared that "A perfect solitude is, perhaps, the greatest punishment we can suffer" (*A Treatise of Human Nature*, II, ii, v). Hume's own utterances are but profound echoes of Shaftesbury's statement that "such indeed is man's natural share of [social] affection, that he, of all other creatures is plainly the least able to bear solitude" (1964, p. 315). These 18th-century English-speaking writers are obviously stressing the fear of loneliness as a universal structure of human

---

[8]The rest of the passage, cited by Sarano (1970, p. 41) is as follows: "I searched for love . . . because it delivers us from this terrible solitude, which leads our consciousness to lean itself, shivering, before the unfathomable and icy abyss of nonbeing. . . . The loneliness of human hearts is intolerable. . . . " See also Russell, 1967, pp. 4, 43, 51, 64; 1968, pp. 35-36, 234. R. W. Clark's recent *The Life of Bertrand Russell* (1976) stresses the intense affinity between Russell and Joseph Conrad and suggests their mutual understanding of loneliness as its cause.

consciousness; and given the fact that these same authors were vitally concerned with expounding a "science of human nature," then the foregoing propositions assume the explicit degree of general principle and description. Parenthetically it may be added that Shaftesbury's and Hume's commitment to the "moral sense" doctrine, a feeling or sentiment or sympathy and natural affection for others, is simply the obverse side of the desire to avoid solitude.

Now, of course, it could be argued that Hegel's concept of estrangement (*Entfremdung*) — as opposed to externalization, differentiation, objectification, alienation (*Entäusserung*) and even negation — is essentially a model of loneliness. Thus, we speak of man as estranged from God. On a similar paradigm, Feuerbach views man as estranged, alienated from species-being, the self-conscious universal, his fellow man. Marx likewise believes that under a capitalist economic structure, the atomic individual of competitive, civil society is alienated from himself and his fellow men, through modern technology. Certainly, it would seem that these thinkers were well aware of a philosophical, religious, or social concept of loneliness. And, perforce, in one sense I would never deny this. But the model of loneliness which I have sought to introduce is intrinsically a monadic, individualistic one. (Indeed, it is a conflation of Leibniz's principle of the self-conscious monad and Kant's emphasis on radical subjective temporality.) Still, in this context, I go beyond Leibniz by emphasis and agree with the existentialists: man is essentially *alone* and hence miserable, frightened (Pascal, Kierkegaard, Nietzsche, Sartre). For Hegel and Feuerbach and Comte and Marx the suggestion is clearly that man can overcome alienation through a "dialectic" and/or an increasing humanism. (This is not possible or conceivable in my view of the state of affairs.[9]) Consequently, Hegel believes, for example, that the principle of the family (abstract unity, wholeness, universality through the feeling of love) versus the principle of civil society (concrete atomicity, particu-

[9]In further support of this contention, I might add that when I researched the entry for *alienation* in the *Dictionary of the History of Ideas* and the *Encyclopedia of Philosophy*, I discovered that loneliness is never once mentioned. Again, I take this to imply that I am offering a psychological principle—a phenomenological fact about the individual human psyche—as opposed to a religious or socioeconomic proposition pertaining to man's structural relation to God and/or other men. Nevertheless, I wish to maintain that although this is a phenomenological datum, it yet points to and supports a monadic metaphysics.

larity, fragmentation through egoism) will nevertheless be reconciled or mediated in the ultimate organic unity of the state. Thus, Hegel discusses estrangement, and Bruno Bauer, Feuerbach, and Marx describe the process of alienation. But, again, it is treated as if it were a disease, something which, eventually, can be overcome, either by an immersion of the self within the "absolute" system, or in humanity, or by a restructuring of the socioeconomic system. But this is not to recognize loneliness, it is to avoid it. (It is truly remarkable that Marx, mercifully and indulgently sheltered as he was by his immediate family and devoted friend, never seems to have pondered that alienation may be ingrained in man himself rather than in the "system," which, after all, is merely an "ideological construct" pointing to more fundamental, primordial psychological sources. Simply put, it's not systems that are lonely, but men, individual men. As Freud complained of Marxism, it's not systems that are aggressive but, rather, men.)

SPECULATIVE CONCLUSIONS

The reader, of course, is free to object that I have distorted the facts regarding man's condition. I can only reply that maybe there are a few of us who are seldom (or even ever) *reflexively* aware of their forlornness. Man can obviously concentrate his attention for protracted periods of time on hobbies, tasks, family, promotions, vacations; nevertheless, at these moments, I would contend, he is desperately "extro-reflecting," concentrating in an "interested" manner on external objects or goals. Should he, however, for whatever reason or motive, "intro-reflect," reflexively dwell on his own consciousness, then I submit he shall discover that all his outward-directed focuses are but efforts to escape a confrontation with his "transcendental" and inevitable loneliness, a haunting nothingness that pervades and structures the basic field of each and every purely immanent consciousness (Howard, 1975, p. 15). Then each of us will realize that, in its minor form, loneliness discomforts us as boredom; in its major structure, it results in extreme anguish, when ultimately we are confronted by the possibility of a solipsistic immortality. Indeed, no religious writer, advocating a doctrine of personal immortality, has ever expressed a desire for unique immortality;

rather, it is always an afterlife *with* God and/or other consciousnesses. And when personal immortality is not at stake, and a Plotinian "flight of the alone to the Alone" is contemplated, still, by that very projected immersion of the "self" in the Absolute, the very possibility of loneliness, in principle, is thereby extinguished. In fact, this itself merely seems not unlike Nietzsche's Dionysian impulse toward a mystical oneness, or a Freudian positing of a Parmenidean Ego manifesting itself as the "oceanic feeling."

We are born alone and we live alone. Perhaps Thomas Wolfe expressed it best when, in his first major novel, he described Eugene Gant's dawning consciousness of self:

> And left alone to sleep within a shuttered room, with the thick sunlight printed in bars upon the floor, unfathomable loneliness and sadness crept through him: he saw his life down the solemn vista of a forest aisle, and he knew he would always be the sad one: caged in that little round of skull, imprisoned in that beating and most secret heart, his life must always walk down lonely passages. Lost. He understood that men were forever strangers to one another, that no one ever comes really to know any one, that imprisoned in the dark womb of our mother, we come to life without having seen her face, that we are given to her arms a stranger, and that, caught in that insoluble prison of being, we escape it never, no matter what arms may clasp us, what mouth may kiss us, what heart may warm us. Never, never, never, never, never (*Look Homeward, Angel*, Ch. 4; cf. *Of Time and the River*, Chs. 7, 14, 25, 30).

Again, the central role of loneliness in Wolfe is powerfully illustrated in the Preface to *Look Homeward, Angel*. Indeed, it may be said that the theme of human isolation constitutes the essential unifying concept in all his work, a loneliness which Wolfe conceives as enduring within the temporal consciousness of each individual throughout his entire life.

> *Naked and alone we came into exile. In her dark womb we did not know our mother's face; from the prison of her flesh have we come into the unspeakable and incommunicable prison of this earth.*
>
> *Which of us has known his brother? Which of us has looked into his father's heart? Which of us has not remained forever prison-pent? Which of us is not forever a stranger and alone? (Look Homeward, Angel, Preface).*

But lest we think that Wolfe is merely describing a peculiar state of certain individuals, he goes on to make it quite clear that he regards loneliness as the universal condition of all mankind: "Loneliness, far from being a rare and curious circumstance, is and always has been the central and inevitable experience of every man" (*You Can't Go Home Again*, Book 4, Ch. 31).

And we die alone (Tolstoy, "The Death of Ivan Ilych," a story that considerably impressed Heidegger; Sartre, *The Wall;* Malraux, *Man's Fate*).

Not only are we alone in relation to others, but we are just as inevitably strangers to ourselves. As Hume (at least in certain passages) and Proust argued and showed, respectively, the "continuity" of the self lasts but a brief time. There is reflexive awareness, but anything very much beyond that is either a mere (albeit natural) fiction or a mere remembrance. Thus, if it were possible to split our selves into two persons, or if we could converse with our selves, as we were, when we were children, the enormous abyss that separates us from our own selves would rudely shock us into reveries which could only culminate in bewilderment. Who has not revisited a former friend, or even a favorite haunt, and realized that his "self" has changed through time, that the qualitative structure of each present is intrinsically unique and unrepeatable (Bergson), and hence that the past is gone forever, irretrievable, irreversible? Certainly, we like to imagine that it is our friend, or the place, that has changed. But is it? We are not only strangers to others but even to ourselves.

Contemporary man has been deeply concerned with problems regarding his individuality, his uniqueness; he desperately searches for his "identity" and he fears its loss. This frantic search itself, I believe, originates in the *desire* of the ego (Fichte, Hegel, the ego posits itself as undifferentiated desire)—the ego as an empty structure of a unified self-consciousness—to prevent a dispersion back into the "oceanic feeling." Against this background of an amorphous Nothingness, the ego struggles to maintain its own personal, integrated, unified "nothingness." If it succeeds to any considerable degree, if it establishes a nucleus or center of identity, in opposition to "the mass," "the herd," "the One," "the they," "the others," it suddenly realizes it is confronted with yet a more terrifying prospect—absolute and unredeemable loneliness. And then it (the ego) immediately seeks to achieve some sort of contact through human or even animal affection; through deeds, works, diversions, and amusements. Consequently, what then occurs is a prolonged, and in almost all cases a lifelong, longing for communication, an attempt at unification, a striving for a mutual sharing of feelings and meanings, between apperceptive (self-conscious) monads, who struggle against inevitable frustration, to complete interaction—even apparent interaction will momentarily appease the self—amidst what is in reality a radically disharmonious universe. (But, of course, without Leibniz's God, there is no real interaction.) The paradox, then, is that we struggle to be our selves, a unique unity of consciousness, against the contingency of transient, mutable being, and against the greater nothingness of an unintegrated awareness; but if we succeed, to any great extent, we are then staggered at the absolute loneliness of our position. It is then that we are driven back to the warmth of the crowd, our friends, political, social, and moral causes, the writing of books, the pursuit of fame, each and all of these constituting an attempt at our being assured, by others, that we exist, distinctly, but not alone (cf. Fromm-Reichmann, this volume).

In its less intense or minor form, as I said, we all experience loneliness as boredom (Flaubert, *Madame Bovary*); we continually feel that we must keep ourselves occupied lest we are forced to confront the "nothingness" that is our own consciousness.[10] The dominant element of loneliness that haunts the human psyche, I would contend, allows us to gain a Diltheyan "understanding" or a Bergsonian "intuition" into the striving of: the novelist and his audience; the impulse of radical and reformer alike; the lover and the mathematician; the magazine addict and the athlete; the painter and the stock-manipulator; the performer and the spectator; the student and the professor; the daydreamer and the criminal; the hermit and the tourist; or even the philanthropist and the misanthrope.

Now, the same principle and paradigm of an isolated human existence, which represents the reflexive psyche, testifies also to an accompanying and corresponding model of individual human freedom. As man has being, or exists, alone, so he wills alone, he chooses in utter solitude. Thus, although consciousness is a nothingness, infecting the

---

[10] I have argued for an immaterialist paradigm of consciousness—awareness as an existential nothingness—in a recent article, "The Simplicity Argument *versus* a Materialist Theory of Mind" (1976b). This model is similar to Sartre's outlined in *The Transcendence of the Ego* and *Being and Nothingness,* although unlike Sartre's, mine is based on a reflexive model of consciousness, whereas Sartre's stresses an essential element of intentionality. Cf. also Mijuskovic (1978).

blobby, massive, viscous body of being, it is nevertheless a nothingness which is radically permeated by freedom, a freedom which desperately, futilely manages to endow the mind itself with borrowed or purloined meanings, meanings whose "conditional" reality rests on their continual reaffirmation by the will as it lies embedded in subjective awareness. Like Descartes's God, we conserve a "meaningful" universe at each moment of time by a constant process of free creation. Should we shift our interests, the universe itself would undergo a complete transformation. In this context, and to offer an extreme example, an autistic child may (possibly) become an archaeologist or an astronomer; or his interests may center toward a fascination with extinct reptiles or verge toward a concentration in futuristically oriented science fiction stories.

The Epicurean model of the chance collision of material atoms swerving in empty space may readily be transferred, but only as an illustrative paradigm, to a realm within the mind. Thus transposed, our radically arbitrary choices become a random and discontinuous "passage" through the irreducible temporality of immanent consciousness (Kant, Bergson), a sphere of awareness which is itself characterized by the total absence and negation of spatial metaphors. (The soul is not extended in space although it exists within, nay, it *is* time—Plotinus, Augustine, Kant, Bergson, Husserl.)

Man is free—futilely, tragically condemned to freedom. For Pelagius it was a divine gift, for Sartre, a terrifying curse, but in either case, man is radically free. (Thus, according to Sartre, man is always beyond himself in projects, he pro-jects tasks beyond himself toward the future by positing meanings as goals which transcend him.) The idea of freedom is hardly a new theme in Western thought; the entire great moral tradition of the Christian Middle Ages is predicated upon it. The two interesting questions, however, become: is man free (a) when he thinks as he *should* (Plato, Spinoza; man is free when he self-consciously gives the law to himself—Rousseau, Kant, Fichte, Hegel, Marx); or (b) when he does as he *pleases?* Shall we adopt (a) a rationalist or (b) a voluntarist model of freedom? And, if the latter, how far does man's freedom extend; more specifically, is it actually creative in constituting meanings and thereby reality? Obviously, I shall confine my discussion to the second set of alternatives, since I wish to opt for the model of radical voluntarism. Following Descartes (and Camus' Father Paneloux), I would agree that man's freedom of the will is (potentially) infinite, like God's (which is actually infinite) (see Mijuskovic, 1976a). But in adopting this theory of consciousness, I also wish to exploit interpretationally Kant's concept of the *spontaneous* transcendental faculties of the productive imagination and understanding (*Critique of Pure Reason,* A 99 ff.; *Critique of Judgment,* sects. 22, 49). God's intellectual intuition, according to Kant, immediately *creates* "objects" in conceiving them; man's intuition, by contrast, is, of course, said to be passive—objects must be *given* to it. But, still, the faculties of the imagination and understanding, Kant assures us, both have the power to create from their own internal resources; they are active, originative, generative, productive. What together they produce are the immanent structures of subjective temporality (*Critique of Pure Reason,* A 99 ff.) and the universal principles of order or relations, the categories, underlying empirical meanings. For all consciousness is (a) temporal; and (b) judgmental; and, hence, relationally structured.

Through Fichte's extension of this Kantian theme, we discover that the spontaneity of thought freely posits itself as ego, and an other as a non-ego, as conditions for its eventual return to itself, culminating in the attainment of a true and perfectly self-conscious, reflexive freedom (Hegel, Feuerbach, Marx's social-consciousness, class-consciousness). In Fichte, this results in the productive and practical ego generating an "external world" as a sphere in which it can morally operate; the world then becomes a transcendental, structural condition for the possibility of moral action. For the purposes of our discussion concerning loneliness and a paradigm of voluntaristic freedom, however, we may extend Fichte's model and emphasize and exploit a basically Feuerbachian concept in the following way. Man's consciousness, as we stressed above, is a nothingness, but one which not only *exists,* but exists reflexively, aware of itself and its freedom (at least at certain "privileged" moments). In other words, at certain times, it may become aware of its own emptiness, in violent contrast to the smug, self-contained, self-sufficiency of an opposing matter, sometimes inert, often intermittently heaving and undulating (cf. Roquentin's "experience" of the roots of the chestnut tree in Sartre's *Nausea*). This direct contrast between a void of consciousness and freedom, which desires "it knows not what," and an absolute passiveness (matter) which ignores it, frightens consciousness. It desperately seeks then some kindred being which will always be there (eternally) and whose presence is manifest everywhere (infinitely). But this being must respond, it must care about man's loneliness, it must alleviate his dreadful penalty and burden of individuality by perpetually satisfying him that he is not alone, that he does not exist in vain, i.e., solitary, unrelated, a "useless passion." In short, this being must be itself self-conscious. Man thus freely creates God, a being who hears his every prayer, for he can converse with God; a consciousness who knows, even "sees" his every act and thought, no matter whether it is wicked or laudable, since the really important thing is not whether one is to be punished or forgiven, but rather that man is not to be abandoned, not to be left alone, that one shall not become a solitary atom of consciousness, forsaken to existence among the limitless expanses of space and time. Hell is not suffering, even if it be at the lowest sphere of Dante's inferno, for at least one then suffers with others. Hell is being condemned totally *alone* to eternal consciousness, wandering throughout a darkened universe as a solitary monad, with pathetic windows of awareness reflecting the meaningless blackness. (Solipsism is a "wrong" metaphysical doctrine not because it is false but because it is psychologically terrifying.)

The consciousness of man, a relative and finite nothingness, has freely, spontaneously created an Absolute Nothingness, which will guarantee the mirroring or reflection of its (man's) self-conscious or reflexive thought. Because consciousness exists, and it freely creates or posits meanings (through the constitution, or the positing, of immediate relations), it follows that consciousness thereby originates meanings, "essences" (cf. Mijuskovic, 1975b). In this sense, the ontological argument, although perfectly valid for the individual human consciousness, ironically enough, makes God, at best, a contingent being, while man himself alone is a necessary existence (see Mijuskovic, 1973), but, like the Christian conception of God, infinitely alone.[11]

[11]The Book of Job, as Thomas Wolfe insisted, presents one of the earliest but starkest pictures of man's isolation. Interestingly enough, if it were conceivable to excise all references to God from the Old Testament passages, one would reach something not very different from Sartre's conception of the universal situation of man (see esp., Job 19:13-20, 30:28).

In J. W. Johnson's contemporary spiritual poem, "The Creation," we find the following lines: "And God stepped out on space. And he looked around and said: I'm lonely—I'll make me a world" (1927, p. 17). The verse, of course, ends with the creation of man. Thus, and for the very same motive, I would claim, man has rather created God. Cf. N. Kazantzakis, *Zorba the Greek,* Ch. 13 and D. Turner, *Lonely God, Lonely Man* (1960), pp. 1-13, 41, 48-49. One might say of this little book that it says—or feels—more than it knows.

4

Loneliness and Vulnerability

JULES HENRY

PEOPLE ARE LONELY because they are vulnerable and they are vulnerable because they are alone; they are vulnerable when they are without love and they are vulnerable when they have it. Personal vulnerability and loneliness are inseparable; they are often merely different ways of looking at the same thing.

When a person feels vulnerable—unprotected, easily hurt, and trapped or misled—he shrinks from other people because he is afraid, and he becomes lonely because he shrinks away. In life people pass before him like phantoms toward whom he would reach out, but each time he thinks of doing so he becomes afraid of being hurt, and the motion of reaching stops before it starts. On the other hand, whoever is alone is also vulnerable because there is no one on whom he can rely; he sees the world as made up of things, not people. Things acquire supreme importance because they can be relied on.

When a person is without love, he is extremely vulnerable because there is no one to protect him, and also because, wanting love desperately, he is willing to do anything to obtain it. On the other hand, because he is willing to do anything to get love, he can easily be misused. Recognizing his own vulnerability, and knowing that people

Partially excerpted from "Vulnerability in Education," *Teachers College Record*, 68:135-145, 1966. Reprinted by permission of *Teachers College Record*.

cannot be trusted to deal honestly with a vulnerable person in need of love, he may even shrink from love. In spite of his hunger for what will rid him of his anxiety of vulnerability, that is, he cannot receive love and he remains lonely and afraid. On the other hand, when the feeling of vulnerability and loneliness becomes unbearable, one may rush into love blindly, making the wrong choice. Being aware of all these things, a person may become frozen in loneliness, adopting the motto that "It is better to die for want of love than to be trapped and killed by it."

Love itself can also make a person vulnerable. Having accepted love, he may live in terror that he may lose it, and may be led to give up his self in bizarre and extreme ways to the one who gives love. "Anything for my beloved" then becomes "Nothing for myself *because* of my beloved," and the self is cast away.

Human beings in our society can sense vulnerability in others, and it can either fill them with compassion, wet their appetites, or make them swell with a sense of their own strength. Whoever swells with strength or exploits vulnerability in other ways is bound to be alone, for he can never have a relationship with anyone who needs him. So vulnerability is always reflected in the eyes of other people. It is true that vulnerable people, who are so obsessed by their weakness that they can trust no one, are miserable; but it is no less true that there are those who become lonely because they can do no more than use vulnerable people or react to them with chest-swelling confidence. The good relationship is one in which vulnerability elicits compassion; this destroys loneliness.

Lovemaking is a preferred mode of escape from loneliness and vulnerability in our culture, particularly among divorced women. Lovemaking alleviates, for a short time, the madness of sexual need and simultaneously seems to dissolve loneliness. In the mutual dissolution of the embrace, anxiety seems to disappear.

The mutual attractiveness of vulnerability and exploitation has been immortalized in Mozart's *Don Juan;* there, the rich and satanically irresistible Don Juan takes advantage of women, playing his game with them until he is ultimately destroyed by supernatural powers. In the ideas and idiom of a vanished age, his destruction reveals a traditional attitude of our culture toward anyone who exploits the vulnerability of others for his own purposes. Mozart's creation, of course, occurred before technological "drivenness" made exploitation a kin of nether morality. Nowadays, if one allows his vulnerability and loneliness to push him into being anybody's object, it is simply the way "the cookie crumbles."

Two existentialist formulations show how vulnerability and loneliness become the foundation of philosophies. I refer to those of Søren Kierkegaard and Martin Heidegger. Kierkegaard's model of the perfect man is Abraham, who goes out alone to sacrifice his son in God's name, because he knows that only with God can man have a relationship on which he can rely. It is true that in Kierkegaard's earliest work, *Either/Or,* written while he was still in the deep pain of his broken engagement, he thought that marriage had merit. As it became ever clearer to him that he would never marry, however, and as he spent more and more time alone, he had to conclude that his only relationship—his only escape from loneliness and excruciating feelings of vulnerability—was resignation in God. This is the burden of his *Concluding Unscientific Postscript.*

Borrowing extensively from Hegel and Kierkegaard, Martin Heidegger wrote *Being and Time,* another lonely formulation, with almost suffocating exhalations of Teutonic megalomania. Here again the Self (*Dasein,* a term borrowed from Hegel) stands absolutely alone, concerned only with its self, shunning the "they" *(Mann),* relying on its heritage *(Erbe)* for guidance and on its "freedom toward death" for strength. Kierkegaard and Heidegger were indeed lonely and vulnerable men, the one relying only on God, the other on a curious combination of heritage and a fantasy of absolute courage to keep going. It is interesting that Kierkegaard renounced human love and that Heidegger mentions it merely accidentally in his most important work (1967, note iv to section 190, p. 492). Both men should be carefully studied by students of our age since they objectify man's historic loneliness and fear.

Only certain kinds of lunatics feel invulnerable. The opposite of feeling vulnerable is feeling safe, and only those who are not alone are safe. On the other hand, mere association with others does not make one safe, and that is why one can be lonely in a crowd, a mere collection of people without love. Throughout human history man has struggled not to be alone amid masses of his fellows, and this struggle has found expression in the ordering of society around kinship, a principle according to which every man and woman is bound to a group through ties of blood and marriage.

SEQUELAE OF RANDOMNESS OR REGULATION

It is good, at this point, to consider the difference between stochastic and nonstochastic social arrangements. In a stochastic universe events happen by chance, while in a nonstochastic one events are the result of rules. Marriage in our society, for example, is stochastic, but in most tribal societies marriages is determined by certain rules, such as the one that directs a man to marry his mother's brother's daughter. This practice guarantees the male a wife, and since the female must marry her father's sister's son, it guarantees her a husband. When the designated relative cannot be found, such societies often permit various substitutions. But the important thing is that the individual is, in one way or another, waiting for the spouse even before the spouse is born. Americans may object to this "destruction of individual choice," but the point is that loneliness is nearly impossible in such systems and that millions in Western culture pay for individualism with the loneliness of being unmarried. In all nonstochastic societies, moreover, one is provided with a personal community of supporters from the cradle to the grave. In such societies one's kin are one's social security. If I am old and my children die, moreover, others will step in and assume our responsibilities. In nonstochastic societies one rarely stands alone.

The course of history shows that man, in our culture, has in one way or another always attempted to return to a nonstochastic way of life, even when his rigidly determined social structure has been destroyed. Western man has fought loneliness by real or artificial kinship ties, and when these have been threatened his feeling of vulnerability has compelled him to make efforts to reconstitute the ties to avoid being alone. In the Rome of the early Caesars, the system of kinship began to be destroyed, particularly among the patricians and in the imperial families, when competition for power and absolute power itself undermined the foundations of kinship. When Rome fell, kinship was reconstituted in the outlying dimensions of the former empire and persisted until the breakdown of feudalism began in the thirteenth century. In the Middle Ages fealty became a substitute for, and was as binding as, kinship. It was the fear of the threatened peasantry that underlay the feudal structure of fealty, for the collapse of Roman administration throughout Europe exposed the peasants to pillage by bandits and invaders, and made them willing to give up their freedom to powerful magnates in order to be protected. The lesson here is that when life is threatened and one is alone, freedom becomes an expensive illusion. Throughout history man has been subject to the vicissitudes of changing conditions: on the one hand his *flight from loneliness* has derived from his vulnerability, on the other his *flight into loneliness* has derived from his wish to be free and his fear of those who might protect him. Erich Fromm, in *Escape from Freedom* (1941), deals with some of these issues.

The breakdown of kinship among the Roman aristocracy occurred because of competition for power and for the good will of the emperor. Such competition for resources destroys interpersonal relations and is one of the prime causes of vulnerability and hence loneliness. When one feels unprotected in a world of phantasms, one looks to some absolute power for protection, and metaphysical as well as political systems based on some Absolute thereby come to be expressions of man's loneliness and vulnerability. They express the breakdown of social structures and the resulting need for protection. If I am without friends I can at least feel safe in the Absolute. If I cannot trust my relatives I can feel safe in the shadow of an absolute monarch. Meanwhile, the history of our culture, and of philosophy, shows that there is no safety and no kinship in political or metaphysical absolutes.

I was once invited to participate in a symposium in which the participants were "asked to take a new look at security systems in our society that prevent fluid functioning of the individual ego and creative adaptive response to new experience in both individuals and in the larger society." Translated into vulgar English, this means, "Let us take a look at how people, in defending themselves against their fears, freeze and lose the ability to think freely and handle new situations." Since the security system—or, better, the insecurity system—of all of us is but a reflex of the insecurity—or vulnerability—of the social system as a whole, I take that as my starting point. For if we want to know the roots of our personal feelings of vulnerability, we should look for them in the society in which we live. With this in mind, I shall explore the general nature of vulnerability in contemporary society.

First, people can feel vulnerable either because their societies are contradictory within, or in danger of attack from enemies without. People are also vulnerable from within their own society's protecting walls if they do not behave themselves. Finally, people are vulnerable from within themselves because of unacceptable impulses such as guilt or aggression. I shall examine the feeling of vulnerability in our society along these four lines. I begin with consideration of our economic system.

VULNERABILITY OF THE ECONOMIC SYSTEM

Every epoch presents different sources for feelings of vulnerability. Our present feeling of vulnerability derives in part from the instability of our economic system. The Great Depression, which held us in nightmare for ten years and which my generation has transmitted as a nightmare to its children, destroyed the dream of a self-regulating economy. Even in 1967, during the longest sustained economic boom in American history, it was commonly believed that only the lively efforts of government could prevent recession. Thus belief in economic vulnerability has become economic wisdom and has come to supplant medieval notions of eternal, organic order and stability.

Western economies today are the most vulnerable in history. I mean vulnerability not to natural catastrophe, but to the system's own internal processes—in our case, to the uncertainty of adjustment among the factors of capital, production, distribution, labor, income, international balance of payments, and so forth. In this sense, anthropology has discovered no economic system on earth, outside the West, in which such basic factors repeatedly move so seriously out of adjustment that the economy temporarily collapses and people starve amid plenty. Economic vulnerability is thus a gift of "higher civilization" and wherever the Western system is imposed on simpler economies they too become vulnerable.

It is this vulnerability, as Thomas Cochran has pointed out, that has altered the nature of private enterprise from the daring ideal of nineteenth century economic tradition, to the cautious corporate endeavors of the mid-twentieth, where huge expenditures for research, broad diversification, and steady but moderate profit rates have become an expression of the shift toward security and away from the hope of windfall returns.

Against the reality of economic vulnerability, private enterprise has erected the international corporate network, whose primary object is the attainment of sufficient power to render it invulnerable to economic uncertainty. Driven by this fear to diversify and to develop systems of integration and corporate interlock, it has come about that

135 American corporations own one quarter of the assets of the world, according to Berle. Yet even such power, unmatched in the history of our culture, is still inadequate to convince us that the present economy is here to stay.

As one surveys economic systems throughout the nonindustrialized world and throughout history, one is struck by a surprising phenomenon: in the developed nations there is no separation within the economic system between necessities of life and articles of prestige, and the former can be manipulated in the interest of the latter. Although in some tribal societies manipulation of the economic system is indeed a way to power and prestige, the necessities of existence are rarely the object of manipulation. (R. F. Barton describes a contrary situation.) For example, in Alor, a tiny island in the Dutch East Indies, the natives are driven by the quest for economic honor, but this honor is obtained through the accumulation of purely ceremonial gonglike objects called *mokos,* while it is forbidden to control garden produce or building materials, the mainstays of existence. In this way power and prestige are accessible, but the necessities of life are protected. When necessities can be manipulated for the sake of power, profit, and prestige, the population is highly vulnerable, inasmuch as the necessities are subject to the uncontrolled interplay of strivings that are irrelevant to physical existence.

THE ECONOMICS OF FEAR

I should like to look briefly at the second source of vulnerability mentioned above—danger of attack from enemies without. It is already a commonplace of American economic history that the balance wheel of the American economy and the force that has pushed the economy to unprecedented heights of opulence is war production. Thus, in a curious way, unique in world history, we prosper by our feelings of vulnerability, because fear of a foreign enemy is converted into well-being through the alchemy of the economic system. Hence we literally grow fat with fear; and in a country presumably trembling with fear of destruction, where people should grow gaunt with terror, reducing diets are among the fastest selling items. We have made a Roman holiday of our fear. Yet it is well known that fear is a Mephistopheles that exacts extreme payment for illusory benefits. Thus, the obsession with Communism that binds our economy has made the economy inflexible in response to other needs, and has led to embargoes that cut us off from trade with nearly half the world.

Because of manifold fears inherent in our economy and international relations—because we feel so vulnerable at home and abroad—an American political campaign readily becomes a forest of ambiguities nurtured on the soil of public fear, as each party finds a way to reach us through our feelings of vulnerability. We fly from one candidate to the other not so much because of differences in policy, but because one is less frightening than the other. As far as the voter is concerned, it is no longer possible to make a fruitful distinction between what is chosen because it makes sense and what is chosen because the alternative is more frightful. In our culture they both mean the same thing to the average person.

What is the bearing of this analysis on loneliness? In the first place, since there is practically a direct relation between the intensity of fear and the belief that we need people to protect us, it seems to me that the more we fear, the lonelier we feel. In the second place, each of the sources of vulnerability I have discussed has specific effects on the feeling of being alone.

To the degree that we freeze and lose our ability to think freely and handle new situations, we become inaccessible to other people and they to us. When we become frozen in fear we become encased in loneliness. The more an economic system is threatening or vulnerable, the more people perceive themselves as alone, and the more lonely they feel. Who will take care of us if a depression destroys income? Only the state, and all of us know that the state will do only the minimum or less. So the spectre of a depression serves to remind us of how alone we are. One is afraid of depression not only because of the fall in one's standard of living, but also because one is alone. A curious, even a bizarre, outcome of economic vulnerability is the phenomenon of "corporate loneliness," which is overcome by corporate marriages, called "mergers." Mergers at the corporate level are the analogue of marriage at the personal level, and financial writers often call them marriages. Corporations merge not so much to increase profits as to guard against loss of markets; and there is no end to such mergers, for in business as in personal life there is no end to the feeling of vulnerability.

In our culture, the push to acquire power and prestige exercised in all aspects of life in our culture isolates people—men more than women—through competition and envy. Fear of foreign powers not only intensifies the general feeling of isolation, but it further divides people from one another at home. To the degree that people avoid others with different opinions about the foreign enemy, they become strangers to one another who are more likely to experience loneliness. A person who really cares about Communism, one way or the other, stops seeing others who do not share his opinions; if this person hates and fears the Soviet Union, it is difficult for him to make a lover of one who does not. The same is true of differences regarding domestic politics. Thus, by increasing the general level of fearfulness and by dividing people from those who do not share their political outlook, our political economy creates a probability of loneliness.

It should be clear by now that loneliness has less to do with the physical absence of people than with the complex factors rooted in the personality and in the economic system that affect the availability and acceptability of people to one another. In this connection it will be illuminating to look briefly at loneliness in a tribal society.

The Pilagá Indians of Argentina inhabit an arid region along the Pilcomayo River, which forms the boundary between Argentina and Paraguay. Subsistence is hard for the Pilagá: they live mostly by fishing and gathering forest fruits and they have tiny vegetable plots which are cultivated by men too old to fish. The Pilagá espouse an ethic of independence which affirms that everybody should stand on his own feet, although their life conditions make this absolutely impossible. The Pilagá insist, furthermore, that whatever one obtains through his own labor should be distributed to anyone who asks for it. At the same time they look with contempt on those who ask for aid, because these people are not "standing on their own feet." Meanwhile, hunger often compels people to ask for aid, even though they know that the people of whom they ask will give unwillingly. This unwillingness arises primarily because the requests are substantial, and because there is no recognition for generosity, although death from black magic is believed to follow the failure to give.

The Pilagá do not actually practice black magic, but it is a phantasm in which they believe, and a threat that makes them do what is expected. Almost all the productive people give away more than they receive in return, and they only save themselves from starving by putting aside for themselves a portion of what they produce. In doing so, however, they are afraid of being sorcerized and they fear that people will think them stingy. Thus, in the very act of living up to cultural ideals they suffer fear and imagine themselves hated. Food distributions among the Pilagá are understandably morose affairs, and even housemates call themselves beggars when they sit down at another's pot at *his* invitation. It is easy to understand why a person receiving a gift is frozen-faced: he believes himself a begger who is not standing on his own feet, and he feels that the person who provides for him would rather not.

Under these circumstances it is no wonder that the commonest expressions among the Pilagá are, "I am a poor little thing," and "I am alone," even though these people live in compact villages and their long houses often hold scores of persons. It seems that nothing can blot out the fundamental feeling of being alone. I remember that when the Indians who had been working in the white man's sugar cane plantations returned to the Pilagá village, quite a number of them gave gifts to Sidinki, one of the chiefs of our village; but after telling me what he had received from each, he said, "Nobody gives me anything. I am all alone." The lifelong experience of displeasure and fear in giving and receiving creates a great emotional abyss that cannot be filled. Even when the Pilagá were at the fish trap and tons of fish poured into the villages each night so that the gaunt Pilagá became sleek and the dogs so fat that they looked like pigs, the Indians still complained that they got little or nothing from others.

So, while living amid other people bound to him by economic and kinship ties, the Pilagá *feels* himself alone. He feels this way because his economic system contains many contradictions, is lacking in rewards, and is so conducive to fears. He ultimately expresses the contradictions in the system by adopting contradictory and even negative attitudes toward others. In this way, the lonely, tense, anxious, rather distant and sombre Pilagá is the product of his own economy.

I now return to a general consideration of vulnerability of the self and the relation of vulnerability to loneliness. I will deal first with the ancient problem of how society brings men to heel.

BRINGING MEN TO HEEL

While social scientists consider protection a requisite of society, it is also essential that society make men vulnerable, for if a man is invulnerable society cannot reach him, and if society produces men who cannot be "reached" it cannot endure. Thus society consents to protect us only if we consent to being relatively defenseless. To the end that man can be injured and thereby brought to heel, an array of frightful devices have been created to render men meek and mild, even if such meekness and mildness serve violence, as with the soldier who obeys orders to kill. From all this it follows that for society to survive it must cultivate a vulnerable character structure in its members. The combination of factors that society invokes to make us vulnerable I call the *vulnerability system.*

In what sense is man vulnerable and how is his vulnerability brought about? To begin with we must have a clear idea of the areas of existence in which man is exposed to injury. First there is his reputation, his good name. A person protects his reputation by learning and conforming to the norms of his social class, regardless of whether he endorses or despises these norms. Of course it is always better if one believes in such norms, in the sense that such belief makes it easier to maintain a good reputation. But maintaining a good reputation must also involve a certain degree of concealment, of hiding one's deviations. Since deviation can be in thought as well as in action, invulnerability of reputation involves learning how to conceal deviant (socially unacceptable) thoughts. Of course, it is preferable not to have any deviant thoughts, but this requires either looking away quickly from the socially unpleasant, or better still, never looking at anything closely.

How does society make people excruciatingly sensitive to the possibility of, and the dangers in, losing reputation? How, that is, does society make one sensitive to one's vulnerability? It places reputation—the social person—in the center of consideration and makes reputation destiny; it degrades the inner self to a secondary or merely adventitious place, making the social facade supreme, and ensuring that the self will be sacrificed to the facade at every step of development.

This maneuver is accomplished by exacting acquiescence and by disregarding and even punishing the emerging self. It is not so much that the child is punished for asserting his selfhood, as that the outward expansion of the self is not even seen. What is seen by the parent is largely what is relevant to social requirements, what contributes to a good name, what makes the child socially invulnerable. In this way the child's spirit is insensibly pruned of everything that is not socially acceptable, and his self becomes identical with reputation. This need not be so, for it is possible for a person to lose his good name and yet accomplish good things in the name of his self. Great reformers and creators have often done this.

An important function of the feeling of vulnerability is to make us dependent. As small children we are overwhelmed by our vulnerability and lean on parents, who thereby become exalted in our eyes. Thus another function of vulnerability is to enlarge the image of those who could harm us and those who protect us. While in our culture the child's dependence on parents is necessary and very real, the function of the inflated parental image is to project the child's feeling of vulnerability far beyond realistic boundaries, so that society itself may be protected. Society is built on a foundation of inflated images derived from the individual's vulnerability and upheld by the feeling that what is important are the norms and not the individual self. Behind every inflated authority image lies society's fear that it is vulnerable. Behind every inflated image lies society's determination to eliminate independence.

The child's vulnerability is sustained and intensified by the elementary school where he is at the teacher's mercy. The teacher, clearly through no fault of his own, is the agent who cultivates vulnerability. He transmits the sense of vulnerability to the child through two weapons thrust into his hands, sometimes against his will—discipline and his power to fail the child. Before these absolute weapons the child is even more vulnerable than with his parents, for with his parents the agony of vulnerability is allayed in part by love, and he can, within limits, fight back. In school, however, this usually is not the case. In the contemporary, overcrowded classroom, fighting back negates the necessary order and routine, and the fear of failure is the pulse of school life. Remove the fear of failure and education in America would stop. Yet we cannot blame the feeling of vulnerability solely on fear of failure. After all, without fear of failure nobody would strive for success, and without striving for success there could be no contemporary culture. Thus another characteristic of vulnerability: it has roots in the idea of success.

Fear of failure does not begin in school, for in our culture even the basic biological functions of early childhood are amalgamated with the ideas of success and failure. Moving one's bowels at the right time and in the right place represents great success for a baby, while losing control represents failure, a source of shame and disgrace. Even taking the right amount of milk from the bottle, and eating all one's spinach before getting dessert are successes, while leaving food on one's plate or eating sloppily may be considered failures. Thus in our culture the fear of failure is grafted right onto the biological functions so that the baby is already psychologically vulnerable at the mouth and bowel. In this way the child is prepared for the intensified fear of failure instilled all through school, including college and graduate school.

Related to such fears is the college student's query of, "Will I make it?" For many a student, college is a four-year opium sleep in which he postpones the answer to the question while committing himself to the pleasures of a coeducational school as a courting pavilion and trying to make himself invulnerable to the dangers of the socioeconomic system. And this is the paradox: even as the undergraduate is presumably arming, he gives himself up to pleasure in order to forget the enemy.

Thus fear of failure is the dark aspect of the hope and striving for success. For most of us, our abilities, our good looks, and our social techniques—pleasant, public-relations hellos; the ability to laugh at anybody's jokes; the capacity to hold conventional opinions and never to value or fight too strongly for any position in an argument—never seem quite adequate to ward off all the chances of failure. If a young person succeeds in competition for one grade, one scholarship, one boy or girl or one position today, can he be sure of succeeding next time? In our culture a person's armor of personal capabilities is never predictably adequate, so that like the stock market and the gross national product, today's high capabilities could prove illusory and the person who possesses them could "crash" tomorrow.

From this long training in feeling vulnerable, the graduate student enters the academic world with a greater concern with reputation than with self, and an overpowering fear of failure. Under these conditions he is bound to be a failure to his self and at this point the *coup de grâce* is often administered to it.

The relation of this long process to loneliness is the following: since society can bring men to heel only if they are alone and deprived of the possibility of fighting back, society must, in the first place, devise means of keeping men apart, and, in the second place, develop punitive and threatening instruments that can pierce all available defenses. That is to say, there must be some way in which everyone can be made to fear society. I have already discussed some of the features that keep us apart, like competition and fear of exploitation. But the device through which everyone can be brought to heel is usually some fearful taboo which everybody in his right mind observes, and which leads to the ostracism of the person who breaks it. Examples of such taboo activities include witchcraft and the various forms of heresy in medieval society, and being "red" or loving a person of another race in contemporary society. There is no culture on earth that has not used the "phantasm technique" for bringing men to heel, and the outstanding feature of taboos created by the phantasm is that infraction of them, or putative infraction of them, has the result of separating one from nearly all his fellows. The aim of all cultures, therefore, is to create phantasmic vulnerabilities against which there is no defense other than total acquiescence. The continued attacks on labor unions, especially on moves to organize new ones, is an expression of our society's *need* for people to be alone and vulnerable. Interestingly enough, one of the "ideological" arguments used against organization is that it eliminates independence, destroys individuality, and removes enterprise from society. It is interesting that these same "virtues" create aloneness, loneliness, and vulnerability.

It is perhaps in the classroom that each individual is most alone. For from twelve to sixteen years or more, several hours a day, we receive an excruciating training in living vulnerably and alone. Under the constant goad of our teachers we face failure all alone. Nothing is lonelier, perhaps, than a room full of students taking an examination, unless the students cheat. In cheating, we know, there is often much togetherness. Otherwise the entire experience of success and failure in school is borne alone, and from this a child must surely emerge with the feeling that when he is fighting failure he really is alone. His exquisite educational vulnerability has convinced him of this. Courting on college campuses and in high school, therefore, is not only an expression of maturing sexuality, but also a sigh of relief, a flight from the lonely vulnerability of the classroom.

VULNERABILITY OF THE SELF

The inner self is the part of us that is most vulnerable. The mind is almost as vulnerable, but the course of civilization has shown that although we have mastered techniques for sealing off the mind by educating children to be stupid, people who are safely sealed off from dangerous ideas may still be exceedingly vulnerable to attacks on the self from within.

In a society oriented toward success, where fear of failure is the most common nightmare, people have to find ways of being successful and avoiding failure that go far beyond their means and skills. The most common way of becoming successful is by selling one's self into slavery to the success pirates. In order to get ahead we give in, say yes when we mean no, we praise a book in a review when we think it no good, we are nice to a person we detest, or we merely keep silent. But the self that is sold short in this way gives us no rest. It returns to torment us in our dreams, and we thus become vulnerable from within, held in torment by the self we deemed "expendable." All this we bear alone.

Another important source of inner vulnerability is job choice, for since most of us do the jobs we think we have to do, rather than the jobs we want to do, we give up our job dreams and settle down and do what is expedient. But this is just what the inner self never accepts, for regardless of the external reason for giving up, the inner self never forgives. When we thrust aside our very own job aspirations the inner self sits in judgment on us. A court of law is not primarily interested that one stole because he was hungry or that one killed because he was humiliated. It punishes because one has committed the crime. Similarly, the inner self is the lifelong jury sitting in narrow judgment on us, and if we fail in our aspirations it poisons life with guilt.

By the time we reach adolescence, a congeries of socially unacceptable impulses have made us so afraid of our inner selves that we seal them off. Our motto becomes, "Nobody, including myself, must ever know what I am really like." Against this fear of being discovered we erect the wall that Freud called "resistance." But though resistance prevents discovery it also is a prison, for if people cannot reach us neither can we reach them, and they remain distant from us. In this way, we become facades to one another, living always with the illusion created by the facades. Thus the penalty for invulnerability to discovery is isolation and illusion. This is loneliness.

While Western man in general is thus a vulnerable creature who has generated the very instruments that attack him, some men are more vulnerable than others for inner as well as outer reasons. We all know that the poor are more vulnerable to the system of economic distribution than the rich. It is a platitude that money gives the rich man access where the lack of it excludes the poor. But there is another factor that defends some against vulnerability better than it does others, and that is the factor of hope. Wrapped in a mantle of hope I can confront the future and hope to triumph over the past, but deprived of hope I am assaulted by anxiety. If somebody has made me feel like dirt, and I have no hope, doubts assail me as to whether I can ever become anything. If I am in despair with loneliness and lovelessness I will die if I lose hope. In the past, religion has been a defense against despair, giving man hope, partially defending him against doubts, guilt, and loneliness. But in Western culture man has turned away from religion precisely to the degree that the culture has acquired, along with its heaven-vaulting, productive capability, the capacity to proliferate occasions for a despair that pierces the protective illusions of religion. Outstanding among these occasions have been economic disaster and modern war.

The paradox of man-in-the-West is that the more he has advanced technically the greater his capacity for generating despair, to the point that he has finally made despair itself a factor in production, building armaments, developing advertising techniques, and in general exploiting the feeling of vulnerability itself to keep the system going.

5

Man the Lonely Animal: Biological Roots of Loneliness

J. RALPH AUDY

IT IS SAID that neurotics build castles in the air, psychotics live in them, and psychiatrists charge both of them rent. The psychiatrist Gerard repeated this some two decades ago in writing about the biological roots of psychiatry. He went on to assume that biologists presumably try to build pilings from the castles down to earth. I assumed that I had some such task assigned to me when I was invited to talk on the biological roots of loneliness in 1966; up to that time I had never given any thought to the subject.

I realized at once that I could not confine myself to animals but must pay much attention to man. I decided first to read and think about loneliness in man and especially about my own experiences of loneliness, some of which were vivid. This might allow me to pick out elements of loneliness that lacked biological roots and therefore *must* be purely human, elements, for example, that involved symbolism or a human kind of society. I then considered what happens when man and animals are left alone too long—there is plenty of literature on sensory deprivation (Audy, 1969). Next, I considered whether human cultures handle loneliness in different ways, and whether there are great variations in susceptibility. I also reflected whether there are any

Reproduction of Figure 4 from ''Ecological Factors in Development of Behavioral Anomaly,'' in *Comparative Psychopathology: Animal and Human* (1977), ed. J. Zubin. By permission of Grune & Stratton, Inc., New York and John B. Calhoun.

111

counterparts to such variability among animals. For instance, would individualistic gophers respond very differently from gregarious rabbits? Is the tiger a loner compared with the lion? And how do animals in the field and in the laboratory respond to isolation and ostracism or to the experience of being lowest on the totem pole? How important is the satisfaction of social needs?

I assumed that after thinking about these things I might be able to decide if what seems to be an intensely human experience of loneliness had its counterparts and roots among animals. I believe now that an important part of loneliness has such roots, and I know that biological roots are basic. Nevertheless, man can be lonelier than animals in complex ways.

My first surprise was to find that there is an astonishing lack of information on loneliness in the literature, especially the psychiatric literature. The next surprise was that, although I *thought* I had a clear idea of what loneliness meant, my mind was remarkably vague about this well-known state. I was led to question the differences between voluntary solitude and involuntary isolation, aloneness, loneliness, ostracism, nostalgia, homesickness, pining, grieving for a lost home or a lost one, boredom, withdrawal, anomie, aimlessness, normlessness, wanderlust, and forms of depression having vague relations to loneliness. My first insight came when I looked into myself.

The psychiatrist Harry Stack Sullivan (1953) recognized six phases in the development of the human personality: *infancy,* terminating with the appearance of articulate speech, however meaningless; *childhood,* with a need for adult playmates; *a juvenile era,* with a need for true playmates similar to oneself; *preadolescence,* with a need for intimate relations with a chum or pal of one's own sex; *adolescence,* with a need for an intimate playmate of the opposite sex; and *adulthood,* in which feelings for the selected one of the opposite sex transcend feelings for oneself (it follows that true adulthood or maturity is rarer than one would think). Loneliness, he maintained, accompanies a lack, or a loss, or a fear of losing, elements of human relationships that mature successively with the growth of the individual's personality. These elements include the need for tenderness and contact in the infant, through the fear of ostracism in the juvenile, and to the loss, or fear of loss, of a partner in maturity. In its fully developed and most terrible form, loneliness may express itself from preadolescence onwards. Sullivan did not develop fully the risks of a tendency to pathological adult loneliness that may have its roots in the earlier loneliness of the infant.

Since any form of loneliness is intensely personal and best described personally (as Calhoun has done in his contribution to the present volume), I shall give a few examples of different kinds of so-called loneliness I have experienced. I can recall being miserably lonely on occasions as a child in India when the others were out visiting at night. I had wonderful and considerate parents, but I can remember the agonizing slowness of time and the frightening ghostly emptiness of the bungalow when they were not there. Being able to hear the servants talking or cooking across the compound was sometimes comforting; at others times it intensified the loneliness because of the expanse of the dark no-man's-land between us. One may seek solace from strange things, and I sometimes found it from a friendly star winking through a window. Nevertheless, this experience of intense loneliness, waiting for the sound of my parents' return, was only occasional. Obviously, there were times when I had a need I could not define or overcome.

In contrast, I do not recall feeling lonely at all when, as a child (and incidentally, a truant), I went out exploring by myself in lonely places. I sought solitude.

The word 'loneliness' comes from 'alone,' literally meaning 'all one,' all by oneself. But the state of loneliness is not necessarily related to being alone. It is easy to be alone without being lonely, and easy to be very lonely in a crowd. We now recognize that the healthy development of the mind needs an alternation between periods of intense input of sensations and information, and periods of meditation in solitude for digestion, for so much more thinking goes on in the depth of the mind than in the linear thinking of consciousness that is tied to the outside world.

In adult life, I have sometimes felt aimlessly and vaguely lonely in my own home when my family was far away. All the space in the house, except for my sanctum, the study, is associated with my wife and daughter, so that I feel a sense of incompleteness when they do not share this space. The feeling vanishes when I go to my study or to the University, to sites where solitude is an expectation, as it might be in a chapel. The notion that certain spaces can not only carry certain expectations but can also be incorporated into one's personality is part of the growing understanding of 'the social use of space' or what the anthropologist Edward Hall (1966) calls *proxemics*. This relationship to space and the things in it certainly has deep roots in animal behavior, but I cannot spare time to develop it here.

The only other instances I can recall of anything like loneliness when I was isolated occurred in two kinds of special circumstances. First, I can vividly remember a few times when I encountered some breathtaking scene, or astonishing creature or plant, or even an idea, and suddenly felt the intense need for someone to share my experience, as it is impossible to recapture such things by description afterwards. But the feeling suddenly came as a kind of intense loneliness mingled with awe. Perhaps there is a limit to the amount of awe a man can tolerate alone—too much and it becomes awful, in the earlier sense of the word. The other kind of circumstance was on two occasions when I got lost, once in the desert and once on Mt. Trus Madi in Borneo. On those occasions, I felt anger at myself for foolishly wandering off alone and not checking landmarks, and also a slight element of fear. I seemed to feel lost and very tiny and lonely in a vast expanse of desert or forest. However, I think that these two kinds of experience are not examples of true loneliness as I hope to discuss it: they are rather examples of a *sudden awareness of being alone.*

So much for feelings when alone. I have felt something like loneliness more often when among people than when alone—among people with whom I could not communicate (and I certainly do not mean being unable to speak their language).

Although I have spent much time 'alone' with tribesmen in Africa and Asia I cannot recall ever feeling lonely among them. Nor have I felt true loneliness when in the company of what we call Nature, a point to which I shall return. But I have felt bored, and sometimes painfully lonely and alienated, among people who speak my own native tongue but are 'living in a different world.'

One dreams much of beer and sweet water in deserts. After perhaps an overdose of solitude during two years of Somaliland, I arrived in Nairobi and escaped from my hotel in search of beer. On opening the door to the bar in Torr's I saw a vast sea of faces, groups of close friends laughing together, a babel of voices, both masculine and frighteningly feminine. I was utterly unable to pluck up the courage to go to the bar. I backed out, and had beer in my hotel room. It took over a week to get used to such crowds of one's people and of strangers.

I also recall myself in my early teens, newly arrived in England from

India, often standing aside from a dance as a wallflower, feeling extruded and unwanted. Although I indulged in romantic and even animal fantasies involving the more attractive females, I was too shy to approach them confidently and felt as clumsy as an elephant on the dance floor. There had been no such dancing among young people in India. Later, I came to realize that I was not being excluded but was simply isolating myself and tending to snivel in self-pity about it afterwards.

These last two examples of course represent passing neuroses any person might experience, except that I think I was more neurotic about them than is usual. The common element was social withdrawal interpreted to onself as exclusion or extrusion, accompanied by self-pity. If the situations had continued, they could have developed into mental states requiring treatment, even if I did not have the sense or the courage to seek it. However, as I hope to make clear later, these episodes were what I would now regard as the kind of true loneliness that does have some biological roots. Except perhaps for the occasions when I waited for my parents in the dark as a child, the earlier episodes had no relation to the loneliness that I hope will emerge as a valid concept when we have made comparisons with animals.

Very few works have been devoted entirely to loneliness and only rarely do psychiatric or psychological publications even include a section on this subject. An astonishing number of works to which the student would naturally turn ignore loneliness completely, as well as the several states and processes that can be subsumed under that heading. (Try looking up loneliness and related words in indexes!) The psychiatrist Frieda Fromm-Reichmann (this volume, p. 339) complains that the "writer who wishes to elaborate on the problem of loneliness is faced with a serious terminological handicap. Loneliness seems to be such a painful, frightening experience that people will do practically everything to avoid it. This avoidance seems to include a strange reluctance on the part of psychiatrists to seek scientific clarification of the subject. Thus it comes about that loneliness is one of the least satisfactorily conceptualized psychological phenomena, not even mentioned in most psychiatric textbooks." It is for this reason that I am spending so much time in preamble trying to decide what we should look for in animal behavior to throw further light on loneliness. So far, we can perhaps conclude that loneliness is a vague idea that comprises episodes or states that should be considered separately. Furthermore, we might conclude that loneliness is not basically associated with being alone but more with making oneself alone, regardless of whether one is surrounded by people or by nature. Fear doubtless makes loneliness much harder to bear—fear of ostracism, or fear of meeting a closed and stony heart when one needs tenderness.

SENSORY DEPRIVATION

What happens when ordinary people are alone for a long time, or are subjected to the even more intense experience of sensory deprivation? An extensive literature, much of it autobiographical, describes the subjective experiences, for example, of polar explorers, people alone in boats at sea, and prisoners in solitary confinement or undergoing brainwashing. All these experiences show that when the subjects withdraw into themselves they have hallucinations of astonishing vividness. Bouts of lonely depression may lead to suicide attempts. The hallucinations are sometimes picturesque, like seeing a long file of squirrels carrying packs on their backs and trudging through the snow with their snowshoes. Or they may be saintlike, like the hallucinations experienced by Joshua Slocum (1905) when he sailed alone around the world: on several occasions when he was ill or exhausted during gales, he saw that his boat was boarded by a sort of savior-pilot who would take over the tiller. We can understand how hermits in caves could have similar hallucinations. In fact, isolation for even a few hours may produce notable derangements. This has proved to be a problem to susceptible fighter pilots and isolated navigators in bombers. Flying in a bubble at 40,000 feet, hour after hour, can produce serious disorientation and hallucinations (such as of a monster landing on a wing).

Over the last 25 years many careful studies have been made on volunteers and victims who have been experimentally isolated and subjected to so-called *sensory deprivation* by varying the degrees of their insulation from incoming stimuli. These studies have been largely inspired by wartime brainwashing experiences and by the special problems encountered by astronauts. Although such experiments differ greatly from real life situations in which the duration and outcome are unknown, it is amazing how rapidly experimental subjects may become confused and eventually hallucinate. An intense desire quickly develops for outside stimuli, and the person becomes more suggestible, depressed, confused, and less capable of clear thinking than he would normally be. Similar hallucinations have been observed in polio victims kept in iron lungs, although the patients refer to them afterwards as dreams.

In short, normal functioning of the mind seems to depend on a sufficient level *and variety* of incoming stimuli to keep one in constant contact with the outside world and reality. In the primate laboratories at Yerke and elsewhere, apes brought up in sensorially rich environments have been compared with others reared in sensory isolation. Not only do the latter become deranged, but it soon becomes obvious than an isolated chimpanzee simply is not a whole chimpanzee. Individual minds seem to be at least in part the products of minds in association.

INDIVIDUAL AND CULTURAL DIFFERENCES

Much evidence shows that animals may suffer greatly when isolated. Dogs trained to obey one master, and pet gibbons, for example, may pine away and die when separated from their masters. Zoo keepers are well aware of the social needs of animals and of the fact that such needs can be met by animals of another species, just as man derives company from his dog. A young rhinoceros is unlikely to tolerate, or even live through, a long journey alone to a zoo, but he may become inseparable from a goat or other animal that has been deliberately provided to keep him company. Early in 1967 a leopard was sent to a zoo and was given a live chicken for food en route; instead, the leopard felt greater need of the bird for company in the strange surroundings. A newspaper reported this unusual companionship under the heading "Leopard and chick were pals!"

Man also adapts to the companionship of other species. As a prisoner of war in Germany, Christopher Burney was kept in solitary confinement for 18 months and only on rare occasions was he allowed outside his cell. On one of these he smuggled back a snail. Not only did the snail keep him company for a time, but it also became for him a sort of emissary from the real world (Burney, 1952).

Prolonged isolation can also cause grave derangement, and, in particular, early isolation can do irreparable damage, producing an animal that is greatly withdrawn and socially deranged. Extensive experimental studies confirm this. For the moment I would draw attention particularly to the work of Harry and Margaret Harlow on monkeys (1966) and John B. Calhoun on rodents (1963a; Calhoun and Casby, 1958). Exactly the same sort of reaction noted in animals appears to obtain in the relatively few studies of isolated children (such as the 'wolf-children' or other children who have been neglected by mentally deficient or ill mothers or through chance). The first point to note is that man and animals differ individually in their needs for social feedback or for familiar surroundings and smells. Accompanying these differences in needs are differences in tolerance of the stress of isolation, these varying especially with age, temperament, and training or life experience. The needs also vary according to the species of the animal or the native culture of the man.

The gopher is a very solitary animal. The rabbit and the house mouse are relatively gregarious and sociable. Are there any human groups that show as wide a range of toleration of isolation or of preference for the number of social encounters in a unit of time? I think there are. We must admit, however, that man can be lonely in ways that are emotionally much more complex than an animal, and this leads to much greater individual, transcultural variation. I must also warn you that appearances are often misleading. Sheep that stick together in a flock, for example, are not as dependent on each other as their behavior might lead one to believe. The mother's leadership is imprinted on the memory of the young lamb at an early stage, and that animal, even when full grown, will tend to follow its mother. The leader of a flock of sheep is the head mother, and the others tail along, each grown lamb blindly following its own mother with disinterest in the crowd, contented when jostling others though wholly aloof from the crowd emotionally. Many of our city dwellers are also like this, feeling appallingly isolated or even lonely out in the country, but closer to contentment when being jostled by crowds composed of people from whom they are emotionally remote.

In various human cultures periods of isolation are a recognized part of life, with populations living in hot or polar deserts or populations of seafaring islanders who regularly spend long periods in their canoes when blown off course. These people, I understand, often become accustomed to hallucinating when isolated. Also, many cultures prescribe self-imposed isolation, especially within a priesthood. At the far end of the spectrum are cultures that seem to correspond to the lifestyle of the gopher, making a cult of being alone. My friend Carleton Gajdusek worked with such a group that has recently been in the news, partly because the Mexican Government is trying to make it accessible and partly because the group has an unexpected talent for making violins.

I refer to the Tarahumara Indians in the lonely Sierra Madre of Mexico. A small family may live in a cave 10 miles from its neighbor and keep sheep and a few cattle for manure. The staple food is *pinole*, a parched corn ground into a powder. A little boy of six may take his ration of *pinole* and disappear with the sheep for one or two weeks without seeing a single other person before he returns. In the hinterland these Indians are so accustomed to leading solitary lives that they feel embarrassed and at a loss when called on to converse with others. In fact, they are so shy that they may even start a conversation with their backs toward each other. The only time they seem to communicate freely—verbally, nonverbally, or sexually—is on the occasions of periodic drinking parties or *tesquinadas*.

A man will hoard up portions of his *pinole* until he has enough to brew beer for a *tesquinada*. He then may run (the name Tarahumara comes from the Indian word for *to run*) 10 miles or so to a neighbor to invite him to the coming party. It seems that he is embarrassed by shyness. Let us imagine his arrival while the neighbor is plowing his little corn patch with a primitive plow. Instead of greeting his neighbor face-to-face, the visitor may sit down at the side of the field with his back to the neighbor, who goes on with his work. As the neighbor passes by, plowing a furrow, the visitor calls out a greeting, "Cuida!" Then, as the neighbor later comes back on another furrow, he returns the greeting, "Cuida-ba!" By degrees they strike up enough rapport to face each other, when their shyness often gives way to uncontrollable giggling fits. These fits, combined with digging toes into the sand and much nonverbal communication, may make the whole performance hilariously like a Charlie Chaplin or Laurel and Hardy show. To the Tarahumarans, who have almost a cult of solitude, loneliness obviously does not mean the same thing as it does, for example, to a college student or New Yorker.

Passing attention must be drawn to one remaining sociological feature. This is the *anomie* or feeling of normlessness that arises in a society in which members are urged to strive for certain goals, at the same time that the opportunities for achievement are greatly limited. Man is forced to accept or reject either the cultural goals, the institutionalized means to achieve them, or both. He thus selects, perforce, from among modes that have been described by Merton (1938, 1964) as *con-*

formity (acceptance of both goals and means), *innovation* (acceptance of goals but not of means), *ritualism* (acceptance of means but scaling down of goals), *rebellion* (neither acceptance nor rejection but change of the whole order), or *retreatism* (rejection of both). To the person who must adopt retreatism, the social structure will seem hopelessly anomic or normless, and he may tend to sequester himself from others while blaming his predicament on the society that he may feel is beyond control. The hopelessness of anomie, that is, may encourage a sort of cosmic loneliness in people who are inclined to retreatism.

That is how the sociologist Merton sees anomie. Robert MacIver (1960), on the other hand, recognizes three types of anomie: (1) that which occurs when a life is purposeless in its lack of values; (2) that which occurs when one pursues *means,* such as power, for their own sake; (3) that which occurs when one is isolated from meaningful human relations (and copulation itself is not a meaningful relation in this sense; it may in fact intensify loneliness). Anomie as understood by Merton and in the first two of MacIver's types, seems to be wholly human in origin because it is derived from norms peculiar to elaborate human societies, even though lower primates may presumably pursue power. If anomie is regarded as a type of loneliness, then we may perhaps concede that *this* type has no biological basis, but only a human one. For the other forms of loneliness, such as MacIver's third type, the situation is different and we should seek some roots in animal behavior.

SATISFACTION OF SOCIAL NEEDS

It would seem sensible to start with the extensive experimental work of the Harlows on monkeys, but I prefer to confine myself to the work on rodents by Calhoun (1963a; Calhoun and Casby, 1958) because he is very concerned with group size, trains of social interactions, and the effects of crowding. His work has greatly helped me to further ideas that I have developed without any experimental support, and that I now realize are relevant to loneliness. What follows is the building of a hypothesis.

The temperament or harmonious balance of men and animals requires at least a certain amount of feedback from the outside world, in the shape of familiar objects, smells, and especially, meaningful social contacts or transactions. A general *hunger for input* in men and animals has been thoroughly established by observation and experiment. Confining ourselves for the moment to social intercourse, by far the most important satisfier of stimulus-hunger, I shall use psychiatrist Eric Berne's (1964) term *stroking* for social intercourse. The infant thrives on physical stroking or contact that satisfies much of its social need or stimulus-hunger. In its broadest sense, a stroke may be nothing more than the recognition of another's presence. A wink that indicates recognition or the sharing of an understanding is a stronger stroke than this. It may seem that we have a need for an opposite term such as *ruffle* or *insult* but I think this inessential to the present discussion.

Two rats, A and B, both in a state of social need, encounter and exchange social transaction or stroke(s) that may range from nose-to-nose recognition to an act of mating. Calhoun (1963a) postulated and then showed that the resulting gratification is a refractory state during which the state of social need or the stimulus-hunger is temporarily in abeyance, neutralized. The duration of this refractory state is proportional to the intensity of the gratification.

Now let a third rat C, in a state of social need, approach A while A is refractory. C will not be stroked and will be frustrated. Not receiving an expected response is as frustrating as receiving an equivalent ruffle or insult. Frustration is also a refractory state, the duration of which is roughly proportional to the intensity of the frustration.

Imagine a group of potentially 'equal' juveniles placed together and engaged in a series of such transactions. Chance alone determines which individuals (from whom we select one and call him J) will encounter a series of frustrations while in search of strokes. J's personality and his expectations will be altered accordingly. He may then, in a state of social need, approach yet another individual, K, who is also in a state of social need. But J may not make his approach in the same way: his expectations may have changed, he may have been rebuffed too often, and his approach will at once be recognized by K as in some way incompetent (J might have become somewhat Uriah Heepish in his solicitation). J's personality or behavior patterns may therefore be affected further by the unsatisfactory or inadequate response from K, even though K is also in a state of social need. We may surmise that the summation of such early chance encounters, of genetic and other individual differences that always exist, and of circumstances such as illness or inability to get enough food (due to, say, rebuttals at the feeding-site), are among the factors that determine the development of a pecking order and the relegation of some individuals that may originally have had "normal" potential to the bottom ranks of the hierarchy.

On this basis I propose to discuss first, the balance of gratification and frustration in relation to group size, and second, the consequences of being at the bottom of the totem pole. While doing this, I am painfully aware of the network of supporting evidence I must omit for purposes of brevity.

Gratification, Frustration, and Group Size

Within an enclosure containing ample food and water, we consider groups of increasing size. A solitary rat, as indicated at zero in Figure 1, has no opportunity for social gratification. As the company increases, gratifying encounters increase rapidly as shown in the first part of the 'gratification' curve. But frustrations also increase. The curves in Figure 1 indicate the amount of time spent in one or the other of the two refractory states. A point is reached at which one-quarter of the time is spent in states of gratification and an equal time is spent in states of frustration. The rest of the time is spent in neutral states. If the numbers of rats are increased beyond this point the time spent in gratification starts dropping but that spent in frustration will, due to the crowding, continue to rise. There is therefore an optimum group size that represents a physiological balance at which gratification and frustration balance out (about 12 adults in rats and the other species studied by Calhoun).

A digression is here necessary pertaining to a fact of evolution. Perpetual gratification is unattainable in nature. The expectation is that the evolution of a species will result in an optimal physiological state in which states of gratification are roughly balanced by states of frustration of equal duration. (Frustration therefore constitutes a necessary and healthy part of life—in the right dosages.) Beyond that basic level, N_b, frustration increases at such a rate that at a population of N_b^2 all the individuals would be continually frustrated.

A species can be imagined in which individuals are so adaptable that they could tolerate equally well virtually no social transactions or so many social transactions that time is hardly left for feeding and

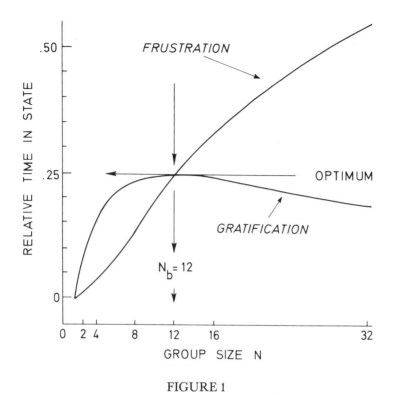

FIGURE 1

Group size, a measure of chances of encounters, is plotted against the relative time spent in the refractory state of either gratification or frustration. Time spent in frustration will continue to increase with group size, but time spent in gratification has its saturation limit, reached when time spent in either state is about equal, i.e., about 0.25 in either state and 0.5 in neutral states. It is assumed that optimal physiological states are achieved with maximal gratification at this stage, when the population size must be regarded as optimal and the set (of group size, of the need for social transactions, and of the physiological systems that regulate the internal processes and stresses involved) has been selected in the interests of evolutionary economy (from Calhoun).

sleeping. In such a case, any group or colony size would be equally viable. This could be achieved only at the expense of extremely elaborate physiological mechanisms and the expenditure of much evolutionary energy. Evolution, however, is strictly economical. We must, therefore, expect the evolution of a limited requirement for the frequency of social transactions and a corresponding optimum group size allowing this requirement to be met with a maximum of gratification—and this can be achieved only by a balance of frustration.

There is evidence that man also has a physiological structure and basic mental requirements suited to a particular group size that corresponds to his need for a certain level of social transactions or strokes. There will be a genetic basis for this, but also great individual phenotypic variation due to cultural factors and especially to the individual's earliest experiences. Calhoun has some evidence that the basic or optimum group size N_b for man is also about 12 adults but phenotypic experiences probably swamp the genetic requirements. Nonetheless, we must never forget that a genetically-based, optimal group-size is accompanied by certain genetically-based physiological mechanisms. Here we may have some basis for further study of the effects of crowding stress and the design of communities.

The above discussion is relevant to the liability of an individual to withdrawal and loneliness in relation to his needs for stroking.

SIGNIFICANCE OF LOW RANKING

Being low on the totem pole is also relevant to the risks of experiencing loneliness through withdrawal. Calhoun uses the term *velocity* as his particular measure of how much an individual is prepared to venture into a place where he has high chances of encounters with others. In the laboratory mouse colonies, each mouse was marked for identification, and observers recorded over a given time span every occasion a mouse was seen in certain places (such as the food and water sites) where chances of encounters were highest. After much observation, each mouse was given a score which was his "velocity." The headman, or alpha mouse or rat, naturally had the highest velocity. The omega mouse had a velocity below which it could not stay alive: it reached a limit of timidity. Low-velocity mice wait for all the others to be asleep before they timorously venture out for food or water, often to scuttle back if a dominant individual twitches.

If individual mice are placed in the order of their velocity scores you have a ranking similar to a pecking order. Calhoun has found that when the velocity score for each individual mouse is plotted against its velocity rank, the plotted points from the alpha mouse at the top left to the omega mouse at the bottom right fall roughly in a straight line. If the group size is increased, the omega mouse cannot score any lower in velocity because he has already reached the limit in subordination. The omega point, on the other hand, will simply move further right because there are more mice to rank. The alpha mouse's velocity drops. The slope of the line flattens. If this process of crowding continues, a stage is reached when the alpha mouse is at about the same low velocity level as the omega. At this stage all mice are equal but at a nadir of activity, and the group is doomed. There is no social interaction and no breeding.

In ordinary colonies, an alpha animal has a rich world of reality, in repeated contact with others and also with the terrain of his colony. It can withstand a great deal of deprivation of these contacts, or "object-losses," without undue suffering. In contrast, the world of reality of a withdrawn animal becomes reduced until its hold on reality is frighteningly slender. Calhoun tells me that he has taken withdrawn rats and simply improved their diets. This seems like a very simple thing, but these withdrawn rats subsequently experienced an object-loss in terms of one of the last important things to which they had become accustomed. As a result of the shock of this new situation, many of these rats withdrew even further and died of starvation in the presence of an improved food supply. I have already mentioned the prisoner Christopher Burney, who smuggled a snail into his cell for company (Burney, 1952). He preserved his sanity during solitary confinement by routinizing his whole waking life with strict discipline. Even though he was starving, he would divide his single ration of food and eat half in the morning and half in the evening. Nevertheless, after a long period of confinement, when his grip on reality had been terribly weakened, he felt seriously threatened by utterly trivial changes. For example, at one point during his confinement, bread was served to him first, followed by soup, thereby breaking a long routine of soup first. He was once moved to a better cell. At such times he felt that his whole equilibrium was threatened and he had to make enormous efforts to retain his hold on reality and his sanity—very much like one of Calhoun's withdrawn rats. If Burney had broken down on one of these occasions, he would perhaps have plumbed depths of loneliness beyond the terrors of his dreams.

CONCLUSIONS: ANIMAL AND HUMAN LONELINESS

We should distinguish *episodes* of simple loneliness from long-standing *states* of loneliness. The former are normal responses unless they are inordinately intense or frequent; the latter are always psychopathological.

At least the higher mammals experience *simple loneliness* when they are cut off from contact with companions. The long howl of loneliness from a dog or wolf may be answered from very far away. When momentarily abandoned, very young animals and many human babies may show almost immediate signs of what seems to be simple loneliness, expressed as obvious distress, and perhaps due as much to a fear of loss as to the actual loss of company. Tiny ducklings stretch out their necks and cheep pitifully when the mother duck races ahead or neglects to quack regularly at the right height above the ground. Is this a form of incipient loneliness?

Periods of solitude are necessary to man and will therefore be sought after. Some can train themselves to retreat into solitude and to meditate in the presence of others, but most must seek sanctuary from time to time. The lack of sanctuaries is a sad feature of urban structure. Solitude must, however, be balanced by human contact. The lack that is felt as loneliness does not merely denote physical separation from people but the lack of intimate relationships with them as well. The presence of people with whom one cannot achieve intimacy and warmth exacerbates loneliness instead of relieving it. The sudden awareness of being alone when encountering something awesome or ineffably inspiring may engender an emotion that imitates loneliness, but only briefly and due to an inability to share the experience.

Pathological loneliness in animals seems to be a voluntary withdrawal and progressive deprivation of the social transactions or strokes that are needed for mental health. The lonely animal's sense of reality becomes enormously reduced and threatened by trivialities. This state seems to be produced by a form of ostracism associated with social hierarchy. The extreme states of loneliness produced in the laboratory, as with Calhoun's rats or Harlow's monkeys, seem, however, to be rare in nature and easily mollified, as when male monkeys extruded from their troupes wander alone until they can rejoin their or another troupe.

Similarly, pathological human loneliness is a voluntary social withdrawal, usually misinterpreted as exclusion or extrusion, often accompanied by self-pity, and leading to progressive starving for meaningful human relationships. The loneliness may be expressed not only by withdrawal but by listlessness, inactivity, depression, and grieving. Its ultimate expression would seem to be a schizophrenic exploration of the desolation of the inner mind in search of something that will become meaningful and loving again.

A man can, however, be lonely in much more complex ways than an animal. The involuntary withdrawal that follows ostracism may produce pathological loneliness, and various forms of ostracism are very common in human communities, so common that some persons gain a degree of consolation by forming groups that are ostracized together as minorities or otherwise. Ostracism has its counterparts in various animal communities also. There seems, however, to be no animal counterpart, or roots, to the defects of complex human societies that evoke the normlessness of anomie. We might find some animal counterpart, probably among primates, to the peculiar and usually simple form of leadership loneliness that occurs when unpleasant decisions must be made, as when Truman had to decide about dropping the first atom bomb.

Species of animals have evolved differently in their responses to separation from others. Tigers are not found in prides, but monkeys are in troupes. Human cultures similarly differ as the result of sociocultural evolution: contrast Eskimos or Somalis with city-dwellers, or Tarahumarans with denizens of a Brazilian favela, or perhaps the Japanese with Tamils. Some human cultures regularly sanction solitude among particular individuals, especially among the priesthood, and such socially sanctioned solitude trains the individual to withstand loneliness as well as attracting those who yearn to be alone.

Great individual differences exist in susceptibility to loneliness in both animals and man, but especially in man as a result of earlier experiences or what René Dubos calls "experience incarnate." There are also differences associated with age. Maturity tends to increase ego strength and also to provide the mind with more diversions and a broader hold on reality. Also, that which is held most dear, and will be most greatly missed, may change with age from mother to pal to a partner of the opposite sex.

Animals require not only satisfactory doses of strokes from other living things, especially their companions, but also, to varying degrees, feedback from objects and places. Contrast the home-bound cat with the more person-bound dog. Objects, and particularly places with their associated sounds and smells, may also be almost as dear to a person as a partner. Their absence may lead to that forlorn form of loneliness that is usually called nostalgia.

Animals may be rescued from loneliness by the company of a partner of another species. So may man. A feeling of unity with nature must have been universal with early man, and although it was generally lost when man began to think of the external world as something he had the power to manipulate, this feeling of unity with nature is still encouraged in some cultures. It is also developed by some individuals in cultures that have practically lost this "ecological awareness." Ecological awareness allows constant communion and company in which a specific pet or even a specific partner is not necessary.

We may conclude that loneliness does have biological roots, but that, in man, it is far more intense and complex than in any of the animals. Why? Because the tremendous development of man's mind initially encouraged him to differentiate himself as something completely separate from the living network around him; then to call it his "environment" and to feel able to manipulate and master it; then to achieve the power to destroy it and alienate himself even more from that network of which he is only a component. Because, parallel with these developments, that part of his mind which is in direct sensory contact with the environment has hypertrophied in his consciousness and has lost much of its ability to communicate with the deep oceans of the rest of his mind; and because with all this he has evolved societies and accompanying structures in which, for lack of insight into himself, his human needs have been largely overlooked. He has only cold and unresponding places whereon to lay his head.

6

Seven Steps
from Loneliness

JOHN B. CALHOUN

INTRODUCTION

FOR REASONS yet unclear to me, I have always elected to explore ideas at the periphery of accepted interpretation or vogue. Until very recently, many aspects of population research, now pursued within the scientific community and appreciated by the broader public, lacked administrative encouragement and financial support. My own interest in the experimental study of animal populations to derive insights for the human scene formerly lay solely within this domain. Anyone dedicated to a direction of inquiry not fully accepted is a frequent companion of loneliness, a loneliness born of the suspicion that the intent and worth of one's efforts are not being recognized. For me, this sense of intellectual alienation was not even fully counteracted by support that provided me with physical facilities for population research between 1955 and 1962 that were unsurpassed anywhere in the world. At considerable personal expense, Eugene B. Casey, a private citizen, remodeled a large dairy barn to meet my research requirements. The Laboratory of Psychology of the National Institute of Mental Health (NIMH) provided me with two assistants and all the animal food and equipment necessary for pursuing large scale studies of animal populations.

One might suspect that this windfall would have erased all feelings of loneliness and rejection. True, I did enter a period of euphoria in which more studies were initiated than could be completed. However, the physical setting of the Casey barn itself had an important bearing on the experience of loneliness. It was located in a then rural area 12 miles from the National Institutes of Health complex. Our staff of three, augmented by Kyle Barbehenn, who joined us as a postdoctoral fellow, was thus physically isolated from the normal work associates. The pressure of work made trips to the NIH reservation rare occasions. Moreover, our small staff had its work spread over an 8,000 square foot laboratory where the different duties often kept each researcher alone except for the lunch period.

Midway during this effort, and just before Dr. Barbehenn arrived, both my assistants decided to seek employment elsewhere. I do not know how much the physical and social isolation influenced their decisions. Suffice it to say, there followed a period of over two months when I was completely alone, and this at a time when the number and size of populations under study, and the number of parallel studies of social behavior, were at their maximum. A quirk in the stipulations for hiring personnel aggravated my sense of loneliness. Prospective employees had to be drawn from employment rolls for the NIH reservation from Bethesda, and yet any person interviewed had the option of turning down the position with me because of the distance of my facilities from Bethesda. Under such circumstances my loneliness became transformed into a mild paranoia, a sense of rejection by the "system." Long hours of work, 10, 12, or 16 hours every day, day after day, began to sap my energies and distort my rationality. Finally late one evening this gradual estrangement and exhaustion flowed over into uncontrolled weeping preceding a brief episode of symbolic violence during which I ruffled up the physical aspects of the laboratory before collapsing and gradually returning to a partial acceptance of reality. This catharsis of transition ushered in an intense period of intellectual synthesis that culminated in my monograph, *The Social Use of Space* (1963b).

These experiences brought me to the conviction that loneliness, withdrawal, frustration, anxiety, and the threat to one's integrity represent essential preconditions for effective creativity. If the present paper, "Seven Steps from Loneliness," does embody some modicum of creativity, the core of its message could have been presented as a cold, "normal science" contribution without these autobiographical comments. However, the way in which a normal scientific, rational activity begins can be as important to its pursuit as the culminating product of the activity. This is particularly true with reference to the concept of loneliness. Without deep involvement in the process of being lonely, and the process of escaping from its bonds, I do not believe that one can become sufficiently sensitive to it as a state of being to contribute to the rational understanding of it.

In 1959 the NIMH secured an appropriation to build a facility where population research could be pursued more closely within the context of related kinds of behavioral research such as neurophysiology and developmental psychology. The initial evaluation of the proposed use of the funds by administrative levels of government came at the time of President Eisenhower's statement of April, 1959 to the effect that the issue of population and family planning lay outside the responsibility of the federal government. As a consequence of Bureau of the Budget decisions, the construction funds could not be utilized for experimental population research since such work had "low priority." Although President Eisenhower retracted this position before his death and subsequently became an ardent supporter of efforts to manage population growth, this retraction did not come soon enough to prevent long delays in securing funds to replace the spacious facilities of the Casey Barn, whose use was discontinued in 1962 by earlier agreement with the owner. Not until 1967, after intense efforts by the NIMH Directors and other administrators, was it finally possible to secure funds for the construction of a large barnlike structure suitable for the study of rodent populations in designed environments. The eight year period 1959-1967 was a time of continuing loneliness for me.

At one point during this period I thought it might be helpful to assemble a panel of experts who could offer advice about the relationship between population and mental health. Such a proposal was prepared and submitted for consideration. I was then advised that before any action would be taken, I would have to prepare a memorandum, not to exceed six pages, in which I simulated the scope of the evaluation that such a panel of experts might make. Although I never completed this memorandum, the intention to write it initiated an effort that continues in this paper on loneliness. It posed quite a problem to develop an unbiased evaluation of what a group of experts might propose about the relationship between population and mental health. As a first step, I focused on the years 1963-1965 and began a search for books and articles which, directly or tangentially, contributed to an understanding of how population and mental health interacted. Each source selected was then abstracted in the author's own words. By the time 350 sources had been abstracted, the redundancy of ideas suggested that the literature search be ended. The final pool of information consisted of approximately 3200 excerpts averaging 20 lines in length.

DEVELOPING THE CONCEPTUAL NETWORK OF RELATED TERMS

When the decision was made to prepare an anthology on population and mental health, no specific attention was given to the concept of loneliness as criterion for selecting material to be abstracted. In fact, it was not until a fairly late stage in the analysis of this anthology that J. Ralph Audy suggested that the pool of information that I had accumulated might shed light upon the topic of loneliness. He had seen a preliminary network of about 100 ideas in which the concept of loneliness was imbedded. This network had emerged from an analysis of the first third of the anthology. Since all the decisions had already been made that would permit the construction of a more comprehensive network, it was apparent that I could make an unbiased investigation of the anthology with specific reference to loneliness. I now wish to trace the development of the strategy through which it was possible to relate systematically the concept of loneliness to other concepts as diverse as "violence" and "responsibility."

After the 3200 abstracted excerpts were assembled, it soon became apparent that I could not recall their contents sufficiently to interrelate concepts contained in the anthology. Adequate information retrieval required indexing. In order to preserve an unbiased perspective, I developed an indexing procedure utilizing the author's own words or phrases assembled into a character-string containing a primary, a secondary, and a tertiary descriptor term or phrase. It soon became apparent that authors were redundant. In the attempts of authors to convey meaning, single excerpts were found to contain at least two, and sometimes as many as five terms that essentially conveyed the same implication. Furthermore, different authors would use different words when dealing with essentially the same idea. If my author's-own-term index was to prove useful, a means had to be developed to pool similar terms to represent generic concepts. Thus, toward a goal that I could not visualize, I adopted the following procedure, which I record for those interested in the process. The reader may care to run through the next few paragraphs rapidly.

Let A and B represent any two words that share meaning. Each represents a subset of a larger generic set. They may be visualized as two overlapping circles, in which the area of overlap depicts the shared meaning. When several words share meaning they form a generic concept. As each excerpt was examined for identification of descriptors to be included in the index character-strings, all such $A \simeq B$ associations were recorded. The final pool contained 2500 such associations. They were put into the computer and permutated into the $B \simeq A$ sequence. The exact excerpt from which most associations arose was also recorded. An alphabetical printout was then made of the descriptors with an alphabetical listing under each of the other descriptors directly linked to it. Cursory perusal of this printout revealed that all generic concepts must be linked together to form a three-dimensional network (Figure 6). This means that it is possible to "travel" from any concept through a series of single step linkages (see, for example, Figure 7).

As soon as Garrett A. Bagley (who has worked continuously with me on the problem) and I realized that the linked concepts formed a three-dimensional network rather than a hierarchial tree structure, we were forced to deal with the structure of the network. As so often happens in such studies, a clue came from a very different area. We found we could adapt a formulation derived from a consideration of habitable planets (Dole, 1970). Most of my investigation of the distribution of animals had considered only two-dimensional space (Calhoun and Casby, 1958; Calhoun, 1963b). The Rand Corporation report of 1964 on habitable planets, however, raised the question of the pattern assumed by particles in three-dimensional space when all the nearest neighbors to any particle are equidistant from it. Figure 1 depicts the solution. The nearest 12 neighbors form corners of an icosahedron, with the particle (planet) to which they related forming a central point bisecting lines drawn from opposite corners. If such a pattern also represents the relationship of any given generic concept to the other, most closely related generic concepts, it means that every generic concept imbedded in the network will be linked to 12 other generic concepts. Similarly, concepts located at the periphery of the network will be linked to six other concepts. Originally we thought that the basic

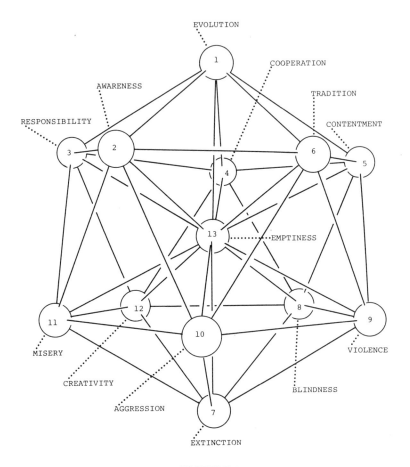

FIGURE 1

The icosahedral central-point pattern of the conceptual network: To the extent that our studies have proceeded, it appears that the six major axes of the conceptual network pass through the central point, the concept of "nothingness or emptiness," as if they were radii representing those connecting opposite corners of the icosahedron. If the adjacent ends of these radii are then connected, their outer surface forms an icosahedron. Both the entire network and included smaller portions of it assume this pattern.

pattern resulted from the packing of 20 tetrahedrons, such that their combined apices formed the central point and their 20 bases formed the surface of the icosahedron. This did not exactly prove to be the case. The external linking bars (assuming that all bars extend to the centers of the balls into which they are inserted) are 1.0526 times the length of the "radial" linkers. As we shall shortly show, this fact leads to an expanding conceptual network (shades of Fred Hoyle!) in which the interconceptual distances between nearest-neighbor concepts increases the farther the pair is from the center of the network.

SEVEN STEPS FROM LONELINESS

At a time when our analysis provided only 100 generic concepts we constructed a crude network of generic concepts that indicated that the observed model approximated the pattern expected theoretically. Given this assurance, we began the parallel effort of refining the model and establishing more generic concepts and the linkages between them. This latter task required that we start with one descriptor and work away from it. Since J. Ralph Audy had invited me to explore the network in relationship to the concept of loneliness, we did just that. This proved a happy choice since loneliness appears to lie very close to the network's actual center represented by the words "nothingness" or "emptiness."[1] Each successive step from loneliness contained more concepts. The more steps intervening between a given concept and loneliness, the more that concept seems unrelated to loneliness. For example, through seven successive steps one can arrive at such divergent concepts as "violence" and "responsibility." As Figure 7 shows, these steps are: *Loneliness* to *Anomie* to *Estrange* to *Fragmentation* to *Distintegrate* to *Chaos* to *Anarchy* to *Violence,* and *Loneliness* to *Abandoned* to *Restrict* to *Compromise* to *Balance* to *Adjust* to *Responsiveness* to *Responsibility.*

As I worked through the tedium of developing the seven steps from loneliness, a growing conviction emerged about the polar concepts forming the extremities of the six axes that pass through the center of the network. They are shown as a two-dimensional diagram in Figure 2, although in fact they form the axes passing through the center of an icosahedron like that shown in Figure 1. Figure 3 arranges these polar

[1]Later (after 1973) more detailed analyses indicated that the center of the conceptual network is actually represented by the word "tradition" in the sense of genetic or learned codes or rules guiding behavior to foster survival. This means that "tradition" and "emptiness" exchange positions as shown in Figure 3. However, since the concept of loneliness will still lie near the center of the network on the negative side, the essentials of the thesis presented here still hold. Prior to more detailed computer analysis about the network's center we had been misled by Osgood's (1971) position about the centrality and primordiality of the concept "emptiness."

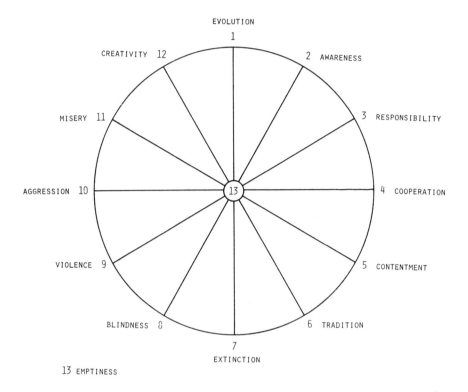

FIGURE 2

The six axes through the conceptual network: In agreement with Charles E. Osgood, the concept "emptiness" or "nothingness" forms the center through which these axes pass. The concept "loneliness" lies very near this center.

concepts to show how they are distributed at the outside corners of the icosahedral net. To get the "feel" of the icosahedral network, "pull" the upper pentagon over the lower one until it forms a pattern shown in Figure 4. Then, after rotating the upper pentagon 36 degrees, connect the polar opposite as shown in Figure 1 by axes passing through the central concept of "emptiness." This then is the bare skeleton of the conceptual network. Seven smaller icosahedral nets are strung along each of the six axes as diagrammed in Figure 5. Our first attempt at theoretical modeling of the inner eight percent of the entire conceptual network is shown in Figure 6.

For our present purpose of exploring loneliness it is easier to deal with this complex network as if it were squashed like a grape to form

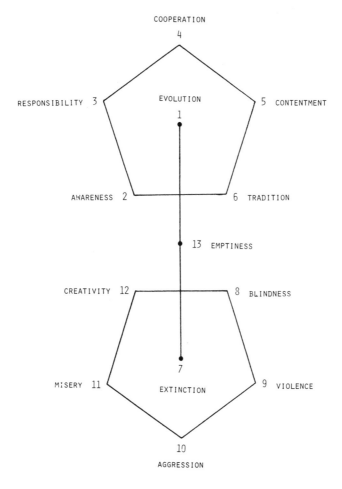

FIGURE 3

Diagrammatic step in the visualization of the icosahedral format of the conceptual network: To get the "feel" of the icosahedral network format, "pull" the upper pentagon over the lower one until it forms a pattern as shown in Figure 4. Then, after rotating the upper pentagon 36 degrees, connect the polar opposites as shown in Figure 1.

two dimensions with the six axes as shown in Figure 1. Having done this, I then identified the sequence of linked concepts that lay closest to these axes and followed each sequence seven steps from loneliness as shown in Figure 7. Two axes (*Responsibility* to *Violence* and *Awareness* to *Blindness*) both terminated at seven steps from loneliness. Two other

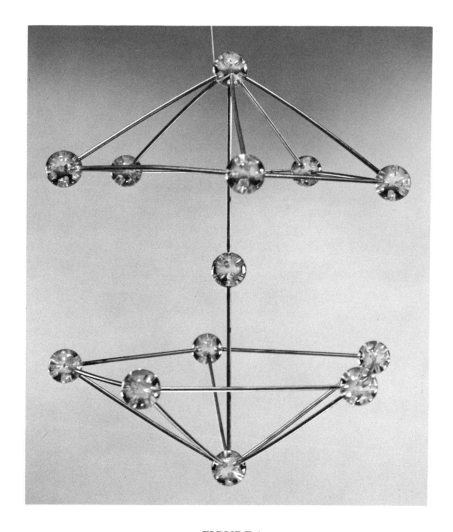

FIGURE 4

Intermediate step in constructing the gross format of the icosahedral conceptual network: This is a 3-dimensional representation of Figure 3.

polar terms (*Aggression* and *Contentment*), lying on different axes, also
lay exactly seven steps from loneliness. Five of the suspected polar
concepts proved to lie less than seven steps from loneliness. In these
steps I still continued to trace the conceptual chain for seven steps.
Only one of the presumed polar concepts, *Creativity*, proved to lie

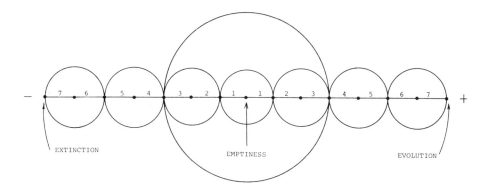

FIGURE 5

Skeletal diagram of one axis through the theoretical model of the conceptual network: Each smaller circle represents an icosahedral center-point network as shown in Figure 2. The larger circle represents the inner 8 percent (i.e., that shown in Figure 6) of the theoretical conceptual network.

more than seven steps from loneliness. This longer distance to the creative pole is actually in error. It should have shown the shorter pathway: *Loneliness* to *Abandoned* to *Emerge* to *Novelty* to *Creativity*. Some of the associational pathways from loneliness to creativity, as shown in Figure 8, exemplify the many routes that may be followed from any one concept to any other concept. At the present stage of developing this conceptual network, it appears that the final structure will include 1625 generic concepts, each of which will reflect a category of named things or images of states as well as a process of change in state or condition. In an effort to put more conceptual "flesh" on the skeletal seven steps from loneliness shown in Figure 7, 184 other concepts were selected. Most of these were directly linked to one of the concepts on the skeleton, and none lay more than two steps away from a concept shown in Figure 7. These 184 additional terms are shown in Figure 9.

A fairly definite line of cleavage separates positively- and negatively-weighted concepts. Shading the negative area resulted in a design resembling that of the Yin-Yang (female-male) concept of Chinese philosophy. This very ancient Chinese design, shown as an insert in Figure 9, is of great symbolic significance. The female principle, yin, also symbolizes darkness, cold, death; the male principle, yang, symbolizes light and warmth. The whole symbolizes life-and-death, oneness, and complementarity. The resemblance of Figure 9 to

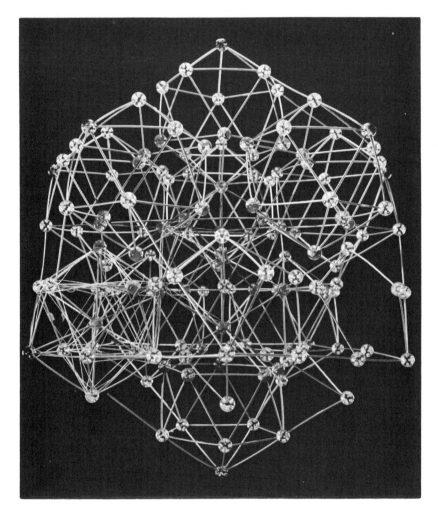

FIGURE 6

Partial representation of the conceptual network: This model depicts the inner 8 percent of the entire theoretical network (see Figure 5, large circle). In 11 of the 13 contained icosahedrons the center point and linking bars to it are omitted.

this symbolic diagram may be pure happenstance, but it raises the possibility that the symbol, and the principles relating to it, represent an intuitive formulation in two-dimensional space of a complex three-dimensional structuring of concepts in the brain.

Opposing segments of Figure 9 frequently contain concepts having

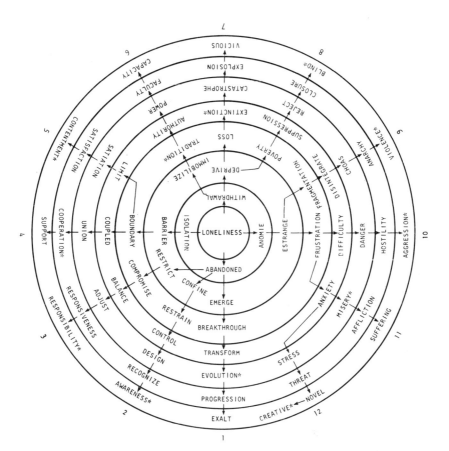

FIGURE 7

Seven steps from loneliness along the 12 major radii: Each arrow represents a conceptual associational step or link.

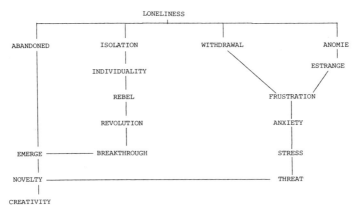

FIGURE 8

Some pathways from loneliness to creativity: Similar multiple routes may be traced between any two noncontiguous concepts.

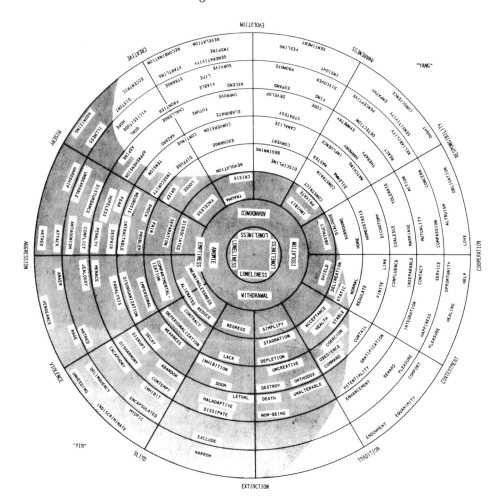

FIGURE 9

A fleshing out of the 2-dimensional representation of the 3-dimensional conceptual
network: Concept descriptors between radii were only one or two conceptual
associational steps from an adjacent concept shown in Figure 7. Shading the
negative concepts produces a configuration resembling the symbolic Chinese yin-
yang diagram.

contradictory meaning. Consider for example the fifth step from
loneliness lying between the axes leading to *Awareness* and *Evolution*.
Here we find the concepts of *Strategy, Code,* and *Develop.* In the opposite
fifth step from loneliness, lying between the axes leading to *Blind* and

Extinction, we find the concepts of *Lethal, Maladaptive,* and *Dissipate.* Although these two sets do not exactly represent antonyms, they do reflect opposing life processes or conditions. Such conceptual structuring characterizes the whole field. One can move from loneliness to any concept in this field through a series of single-step associations. Furthermore, since the concept of loneliness lies so near the true center represented by emptiness or meaninglessness, most trips between a negative concept and its opposing positive concept must pass through, or near to, loneliness. This suggests that loneliness lies at the hub of life; it is a state that cannot be avoided, but one to be sought as a way station between the negative and positive aspects of life.

If this notion of vacillation between negative and positive approximates reality, we should gain insight about loneliness by selecting excerpts from the literature representing successive steps of such trips. To explore this possibility I decided to focus on the concepts along the *Violence-Responsibility* and *Blindness-Awareness* axes of Figure 7, along with those subtended between them as shown in Figure 9. These two axes roughly bisect the yin-yang diagram. Across the transect there are pairs of terms sharing meaning. Pairs of such terms were selected to represent each of the seven steps outward from loneliness in the positive direction toward *awareness* and *responsibility.* Other pairs were selected to represent the seven steps outward in a negative direction from loneliness toward *blindness* and *violence.* Then by employing these pairs of terms, the concept associational index was utilized to identify about seven excerpts from the population and mental health anthology to represent each of these 14 steps across the transect. These 103 excerpts formed a mini-anthology that represented each of these fourteen steps across the transect.

Random perusal of excerpts revealed that most included some amalgam of positive and negative ideas. It is difficult to keep from thinking in terms of opposites. Thus even when one is thinking most positively, images of the negative from which one has escaped come to mind. And when one focuses on the difficulties of life, some glimmer of what life might become percolates up out of the subconscious. For example, consider two passages selected solely because the concept equivalence index noted in them an approximate equivalence between the terms VIOLENCE and ANARCHY. These two excerpts did include such negative terms as *failure, lack of confidence, loss of values, suicide, depression, despair, fear, hopelessness, threatened, disintegra-*

tion, and *unpredictable.* And yet, imbedded in this aura of negativism one finds a modicum of hope reflected in such terms as *creativity, mutuality, improvement,* and *flexibility.*

Each of the 103 excerpts had been indexed for their major concepts prior to the present focus on loneliness. They included 457 entries that could be characterized as having either a positive or a negative overtone. Concepts included in excerpts falling at the loneliness position in the conceptual network were only 10 percent positive in contrast to the 79 percent positive among excerpts representing the last four steps in the positive direction from loneliness. Of the 88 negatively loaded concepts, 16 occurred only in excerpts on the negative side of loneliness. These 24 concepts, as listed below, perhaps provide the essence of the sense of loneliness:

Chaos	Myopic	Unsatisfactory
Void	Impasse	Hopelessness
Absence	Inconsistent	Disillusionment
Encapsulation	Dilemma	Despair
Entrapment	Unwanted	Frustration
Ossification	Denial	Hostility
Restrict	Grief	Aggressiveness
Blindness	Inferiority	Rebellion

This cursory focus on the occurrence of concepts across the transect through loneliness suggested that further insight into the meaning of loneliness might be gained from a more detailed analysis of these 457 concept entries. I particularly wished to understand better the character of the shift between emphasizing positive and negative concepts. To this end the 457 concept entries were condensed to eight negative concepts and their approximate opposite positive representation (Table 1). They are ordered down the page from greatest to least proportion of the total concepts within one step of loneliness that are negative. This ordering revealed four distinct concept sets, A to D.

Set A defines the state of being that one experiences as loneliness.

Set B reflects the further course of withdrawal from reality and loss of identity that may be precipitated by an initial state of loneliness.

Set C represents a state of being, most aptly termed euphoria, that may grow from the state of loneliness. It is a state of realization of opportunities for action.

Set D expresses the changes and course of action that can follow the euphoric C state.

TABLE 1
Kind[a] and Prevalence[b] of Concepts in the Loneliness Anthology

Negative Concepts		Positive Concepts	
Set A: Loneliness		**Set C: Euphoria**	
Blindness	18	Awareness	33
Unaware	(6-7-5)	Consciousness	(11-7-15)
Absurdity		Meaningful	
Weakness	40	Power	42
Threatened	(17-12-11)	Control	(15-4-23)
Anxiety		Potentiality	
Entrapment	15	Freedom	26
Constrict	(4-5-6)	Choice	(3-3-20)
Immobilize		Openness	
Evil	37	Goodness	36
Fear	(19-10-8)	Love	(7-5-24)
Neurosis		Responsibility	
Set B: Retreat from reality		**Set D: Fulfillment**	
Devolution	54	Evolution	31
Lack	(29-13-12)	Transcend	(8-2-21)
Loss		Value change	
Stultify	20	Creativity	24
Inhibit	(14-2-4)	Design	(7-2-15)
Repress		Innovation	
Fragmentation	21	Wholeness	30
Empty	(15-2-4)	Integrity	(6-3-21)
Withdrawal		Fulfillment	
Static	13	Development	17
Compulsion	(8-1-4)	Growth	(2-2-13)
Traditional		Expansion	
TOTAL	218	TOTAL	239
	(112-52-54)		(59-28-152)

[a]The many concepts included within the anthology excerpts were grouped into eight positive and eight negative categories. The key term selected to represent each category is shown in italic. Under each key term, two of the several included concepts are shown in order to give some flavor of the scope of the category.

[b]The total occurrences of concepts within each category is shown after the category name. Just below this total there is listed in parenthesis from left to right the totals in steps − 7 through − 2, − 1 through + 1, and + 2 through + 7.

POSTLOGUE

All the above closely adheres to the 1973 draft of this paper on "Seven Steps from Loneliness" prepared at the request of Professor Audy. By the spring of 1973 I had made the decision to follow my insights that a retreat into a state of loneliness may precipitate a euphoria leading to creative implementation. That is to say, I wished to follow the A-C-D route of Table 1. To this end I spent a large part of the following year isolated in my basement office at home on a sort of sabbatical retreat surrounded by all the records encompassing what I had done and thought during the preceding 30 years. The many unfulfilled goals from prior euphoric episodes surrounded me like the eyes of predators gleaming in the background of a nighttime, fire-lit encampment in the Kenya bush country. If they could not be realized, why look ahead toward more elaborate unrealizable goals? Part of this review tempered despondency with a product—an autobiography (Calhoun, 1977). Its completion served as a goad to try to move out of a state of loneliness toward a euphoric one embellished by nascent objectives.

In a few. more months ideas began to concretize into a plan, a "Scientific Quest for a Path to the Future" (Calhoun, 1976), published under the conviction that a scientist has the obligation to state publicly his intents. By the summer of 1979, as this concluding statement is being written, major portions of these outlandishly encompassing goals have been accomplished with considerable financial and moral support from the administration of the National Institute of Mental Health. However, the course of the past five years has not followed anticipations.

Past experiences had taught me that one must anticipate many crises as one moves from the euphoric state of goal setting, characterized by the implications of Set C concepts, into those of Set D accompanying creative implementation. Both fortunately and unfortunately, the number and intensity of these crises was exacerbated by a decision intended to foster realization of the goals. Four very bright younger men were brought on board to participate in the research program. They had previously not shared much of the broad image of life and evolution that motivated me. Nor did I realize the extent to which they were motivated by a need for job security coupled with a desire to implement their own ideas. And, although their many significant contributions eventually permitted the program to mature effectively, escalating intellectual controversy became sufficiently charged with personal feelings to produce a program-threatening crisis. Each of my four colleagues found, or returned to, a position more in harmony with his desires.

These crises impelled me backward through the loneliness state into a Set B state of devolution and fragmentation of being and behavior as I sought permanent withdrawal from reality. Despite some awareness of the dynamic process of vacillation over the opposing states of being reflected in Table 1, I may well have been unable to extricate myself from the Set B state without the fortunate arrival of two opportunities in the appropriate order. First there came the request to present ideas about the biological basis of the family (Calhoun, 1978) at one of the Georgetown University Symposia on the Family. This provided a warm loneliness emanating from consideration of the evolutionary womb from which we have all emerged. Then came an invitation from the United Nations to discuss the future of humanity as it will be reflected in world population change (Calhoun and Ahuja, 1979). This pushed me from the loneliness state into a euphoric one as I considered the role that we as humans might assume in furthering evolution. Since much of our research program is designed to provide insight about our role in future evolution, this unthreatening task for the United Nations provided the thrust to propel me fully back into the creative implementation phase of Set D concepts.

I can only hope that this conceptual exploration of loneliness, coupled with my personal familiarity with it, may assist in the appreciation of loneliness as a human condition just as essential as security and certainty.

7

The Effects of Parental Divorce: Experiences of the Child in Later Latency

JUDITH S. WALLERSTEIN and JOAN B. KELLY

THE CHILD OF LATENCY AGE has somehow managed to escape the intensive psychological scrutiny with which his younger and older siblings have been regarded. Although no one has disputed the central significance of latency, which Erikson (1959) has characterized as "socially, a most decisive stage," much less is known or conceptualized regarding parent-child relationships during these middle years than of those developmental years which immediately precede or follow them. Moreover, relatively little attention has been devoted to the varying effects of disrupted or fixated development during latency. Although many school-age children come into therapy, the central focus is usually on failure to resolve conflicts that stem from earlier developmental periods. Nor do we tend to learn much about latency from the treatment of adults; there is a relative unavailability of transferences and reconstructions pertaining to these years in most adult analyses. Bornstein (1951) attributed the fact that "One learns relatively little about latency from the analysis of adults" to the distorted and idealized memories of adult patients who recall "the

Reprinted from the *American Journal of Orthopsychiatry*, 46(2):256–269, 1976 by permission of the American Orthopsychiatric Association, Inc. Copyright © by the American Orthopsychiatric Association, Inc.

ideal of latency," namely, the successful warding-off of instinctual impulses during this time.

It is commonly agreed that the confluence of developmental and social forces propels the school-age child outward and away from the family toward peer relationships and new adult figures. Clinicians (Bornstein, 1951; Kaplan, 1957; Harris, 1959; Sarnoff, 1971; Becker, 1974) have stressed the special importance of assuring developmental continuity during these years. Bornstein (1951) specifically cautioned against environmental interruptions, referring to the importance of "free energies needed for character development," and observing that the latency child "fears nothing more than the upsetting of his precarious equilibrium." Erikson (1950, 1959), in addressing the fundamental tasks of this period, called attention to the lasting consequences of partial or total failure to successfully master these at their appropriate times. And Sarnoff (1971), more recently, referring to the fragility of the newly consolidated latency defenses, warned that the drives in latency "may be stirred into activity at any time by seduction or sympathetic stimulation."

It is within this context, stressing the overriding importance of developmental continuity during this life phase, that our understanding of the impact of parental divorce upon the child must be set. For divorce necessarily affects the freedom of the child to keep major attention riveted outside the family circle. Moreover, the decision to divorce frequently ushers in an extended several year period marked by uncertainty and sharp discontinuity which has the potential to move the psychological and social functioning of the latency child into profound disequilibrium and painfully altered parent-child relationships. Alternatively, these changes can bear the potential for promoting development and maturation, as well as the possibility of more gratifying relationships within the postdivorce family structure.

Our data for this paper are drawn from a previously described sample of 57 latency aged children from 47 families (Wallerstein and Kelly, 1974, 1975; Kelly and Wallerstein, 1976), here focused on the experiences of the 31 children from 28 families who were between nine and 10 years old at the time that they were initially seen by us. As elaborated elsewhere, these 31 children from 28 families represent part of a cohort of 131 children from 60 divorcing families referred for anticipatory guidance and planning for their children around the separation, and then seen by us again approximately a year later for the first of two planned follow-up studies.

THE INITIAL RESPONSES

How They Looked When They Came

Many of these children had presence, poise, and courage when they came to their initial interviews. They perceived the realities of their families' disruption and the parental turbulence with a soberness and clarity which we at first found startling, particularly when compared with the younger children who so frequently appeared disorganized and immobilized by their worry and grief. These youngsters were, by contrast, actively struggling to master a host of intense conflicting feelings and fears and trying to give coherence and continuity to the baffling disorder which they now experienced in their lives.

> Robert said, "I have to calm myself down. Everything is happening too fast."
>
> Katherine told us that a long time ago, when she was little, she thought everything was fine, that her parents really loved each other, and that "Nothing would happen to them until they got real, real old." She added with the fine perceptions of a latency age child, "Mom and Dad married 12½ years ago. They met 17½ years ago. I always thought love would last if they stayed together that long."

Some children came prepared with an agenda.

> Anna, after a few general comments from the interviewer, designed to put her at ease, interrupted with a brisk, "Down to business," and went on immediately to describe the diffuse feelings of anxiety with which she suffered these days and which made her feel "sick to her stomach."
>
> Mary volunteered that she was "so glad" her mother brought her to talk about the divorce because, "If I don't talk about it soon I'll fall apart."

For others the opportunity to be with a concerned adult had considerable significance seemingly unrelated to specific content. Some of these children tried in many ways to continue the relationship.

> Janet begged to return the following week. She offered, "I like to talk about my troubles," and drew a heart on the blackboard, writing under it, "I like Miss X. "

Mary tried to extend her interview time, saying that her mother had not yet returned to fetch her, and then confessing that she had just lied.

Still others among these children found these interviews threatening and painful, and barely kept their anxiety controlled by keeping themselves or their extremities in continual motion, the rhythm of which motion correlated with the subject discussed.

Thus, legs moved much faster when Daddy was mentioned to Jim, who was bravely trying to maintain his calm and referred with some disdain to "Mother's divorce problem," adding, "I wonder who she's got now?"

Others maintained their composure by denial and distancing.

Jack stated, "I keep my cool. It's difficult to know what I'm thinking."
David said darkly, "I don't try to think about it."

The Layering of Response

These various efforts to manage—by seeking coherence, by denial, by courage, by bravado, by seeking support from others, by keeping in motion, by conscious avoidance—all emerged as age-available ways of coping with the profound underlying feelings of loss and rejection, of helplessness and loneliness that pervaded these children and that, in most of them, only gradually became visible within the context of the several successive interviews. Actually, testament to the resourcefulness of so many of these children is just this capacity to function simultaneously on these two widely discrepant levels, not always discernible to the outside observer. At times, only information from collateral sources revealed their simultaneous involvement in the mastery efforts of the coping stance and the succumbing to the anguish of their psychic pain. This at times conscious layering of psychological functioning is a specific finding in this age group. It is profoundly useful in muting and encapsulating the suffering, making it tolerable and enabling the child to move developmentally. But it does not overcome the hurt, which is still there and takes its toll.

> After his father left the home, Bob sat for many hours sobbing in his darkened room. The father visited infrequently. When seen by our project, Bob offered smilingly, "I have a grand time on his visits," and added unsolicited and cheerily, "I see him enough." Only later would he shamefacedly admit that he missed his father intensely and longed to see him daily.

A few children were able to express their suffering more directly to their parents, as well as to us. This is the more poignant if one bears in mind Bornstein's (1951) admonition that the latency child is *normally* engaged developmentally in a powerful battle against painful feelings.

> Jane's father left his wife angrily after discovering her infidelity, and ceased visiting the children. He moved in with a woman who had children approximately the age of his own children. Jane cried on the telephone in speaking with her father "I want to see you. I want to see you. I miss you. Alice (referring to the child of the other woman) sees you every day. We only see you once a month. That's not enough."

A very few children succumbed more totally and regressively.

> Paul responded to his father's departure by lying curled up sobbing inside a closet. He alternated this behavior, which lasted intermittently for several weeks, with telephone calls to his father, imploring him to return.

The suffering of these children was governed not only by the immediate pain of the family rupture, but expressed as well their grief over the loss of the family structure they had until then known, as well as their fears for the uncertain future that lay ahead for their newly-diminished family. In a sense, as compared with younger children, their more sophisticated and mature grasp of time and reality and history increased their comprehension of the meanings and consequences of divorce—while enabling some of them better to temper the impact.

> Jim, when told by his parents of the plan to divorce, cried, "Why did you have to wait until we were so old?"

Finally, efforts to master inner distress were conjoined at times with efforts to conceal from the outside observer because of an acute sense of shame. Feelings of shame did not appear in the younger children in our study, but emerged specifically with this age group. These children were ashamed of the divorce and disruption in their family, despite their awareness of the commonness of divorce; they were ashamed of their parents and their behaviors, and they lied loyally to cover these up; and they were ashamed of the implied rejection of themselves in the father's departure, marking them, in their own eyes, as unlovable. Out of such a complex combination of wish to save face and loyalty to parents, some children lied bravely.

> Jesse proudly told us that his physician father had insisted that all of his shots be in his left arm in order to protect his pitching arm. Actually, the father had evinced no interest whatsoever in Jesse's athletic career.

ATTEMPTED MASTERY BY ACTIVITY AND BY PLAY

Unlike the younger latency children, so many of whom were immobilized by the family disruption, the pain which the children in this age group suffered often galvanized them into organized activity. This was usually a multidetermined response geared to overcome their sense of powerlessness in the face of the divorce, to overcome their humiliation at the rejection which they experienced, and to actively—and as energetically as possible—reverse the passively suffered family disruption. In some, this was a direct effort to undo the parental separation.

> Marian, with considerable encouragement at long distance from the paternal grandfather, embarked on a frenzied sequence of activities designed to intimidate her mother and force her to return to the marriage. Marian scolded, yelled, demanded, and berated her mother, often making it impossible for her mother to have dates, and indeed almost succeeding in reversing the divorce decision by mobilizing all her mother's guilt in relation to herself and the other children. In one such episode, the child screamed in anger for several hours and then came quietly and tearfully to her mother, saying softly, "Mom, I'm so unhappy," confessing that she felt "all alone in the world." Following this, the harassment ceased.

Several children in this older latency group energetically developed a variety of new, exciting, and intrinsically pleasurable mastery activities which combined play action with reality adaptation. Many of these activities required not only fantasy production but the enterprise, organization, and skill of the later latency child.

> Ann, whose father was a successful advertising and public relations man, designed and issued a magazine with articles and drawings, announcing the impending divorce of her parents, together with other interesting happenings, which she distributed and sold in her school and community.

In her role identification with her public media father, Ann not only overcame the loss of his ongoing presence. At the very same time, through her newspaper publication, she proclaimed her acceptance of the reality of this loss. But central to this maneuver is the psychic gratification in it—Ann transformed pain into pleasure of achievement, and recaptured the center stage of interest.

> Bill, for his part, spent many after school hours following the divorce in the office of his cold and disinterested father, answering the telephone, playing out the role of executive, and calling his mother regularly to tell her that he was having a grand time.
>
> Elizabeth and her younger siblings found a seagull on the beach on the weekend following the parental separation and announcement of divorce. They spent several hours that day digging a grave, making a cross, marking the grave, and soberly writing the history of their activity on the plaque. One may presume that they were providing not only the seagull but also their predivorce family with a somber and appropriate funeral.

ANGER

The single feeling that most clearly distinguished this group from all the younger children was their conscious, intense anger. It has many sources, but clearly a major determinant was its role in temporarily obliterating or at least obscuring the other even more painful affective responses we have described. Although we have reported elsewhere (Wallerstein and Kelly, 1975) a rise in aggression and irritability in the preschool child following parental separation, the anger experienced by these older latency children was different in being both well organized and clearly object-directed; indeed, their capacity directly to articulate this anger was striking.

> John volunteered that most of the families of the kids on his block were getting a divorce. When asked how the children felt, he said, "They're so angry they're almost going crazy."

Approximately half of the children in this group were angry at their mothers, the other half at their fathers, and a goodly number were angry at both. Many of the children were angry at the parent whom they thought initiated the divorce, and their perception of this was usually accurate.

> Amy said she was angry at Mom for kicking Dad out and ruining their lives. "She's acting just like a college student, at age 31—dancing and dating and having to be with her friends."
>
> Ben accused his mother, saying, "You told me it would be better after the divorce, and it isn't."
>
> One adopted child screamed at his mother, "If you knew you were going to divorce, why did you adopt us?"

Interestingly, despite detailed and often very personal knowledge of the serious causes underlying the divorce decision, including repeated scenes of violence between the parents, most of these children were unable at the time of the initial counseling to see any justification for the parental decision to divorce. (By follow-up, many had come more soberly to terms with this.) Although one father had held his wife on the floor and put bobbie pins in her nose while their two children cried and begged him to stop, both children initially strongly opposed the mother's decision to divorce.

For some, anger against the parents was wedded to a sense of moral indignation and outrage that the parent who had been correcting their conduct was behaving in what they considered to be an immoral and irresponsible fashion.

> Mark said that "three days before my dad left he was telling me all these things about 'be good.' That hurt the most," he said, to think that his father did that and knew he was going to leave all the time.

This kind of moral stance in judgment upon parents is reminiscent of the attitudes we found frequently in the adolescent group (Wallerstein and Kelly, 1974) but not in the younger groups.

The intense anger of these children was variously expressed. Parents reported a rise in temper tantrums, in scolding, in diffuse demandingness, and in dictatorial attitudes. Sometimes the anger was expressed in organized crescendos to provide a calculated nuisance when the mother's dates arrived.

> Shortly after the divorce, Joe's abusive, erratic, and rejecting father disappeared, leaving no address. The mother reported that now she had to ask the boy for permission to go out on dates, was reproached by him if she drank, and had her telephone calls monitored by him; when she bought something for herself, he screamingly demanded that the same amount of money be spent on him. Joe used his sessions with us primarily to express his anger at his mother for not purchasing a gun for him.

Adding to the dictatorial posturings and swaggering expressions that these children enjoyed playing out following the departure of their fathers was the fact that, in many of these households, the father had carried responsibility for a harsh and frightening discipline. His departure thus signaled a new freedom to express impulses that had been carefully held in check during his presence, a freedom to do so with impunity and with pleasure.

> Mary said that she was scared of her father. He had always required that things be spic and span around the house. "In that way I'm glad he's gone," she said.

Many mothers were immobilized by their own conflicts, as well as by their unfamiliarity with the role of disciplinarian. Others indicated in covert ways that they fully expected that one of the children would assume the father's role within the family. For some of these children the taking on of such an aggressive stance clearly reflected an identification with the attributes of the departed father, and thus an undoing of the pain of his departure.

> Anne congratulated her mother warmly on her decision to divorce her tyrannical husband. Shortly thereafter, however, Anne herself began to act out a commanding and screaming role vis-à-vis her mother and the

younger children. This culminated in a dramatic episode of screaming for many hours when an uncle attempted to curb her wild behavior. She became very frightened after this, offering that all men were untrustworthy and that nobody would ever love her again.

Other children showed the obverse of all this—namely, an increased compliance and decreased assertiveness following the divorce.

Janet's behavior shifted in the direction of becoming mother's helper and shadow, and showing unquestioning obedience to her mother's orders. She became known throughout the neighborhood as an excellent and reliable baby-sitter despite her very young age (nine years). She was, however, not able to say anything even mildly critical of her rejecting father, and was one of the few children who openly blamed herself for the divorce. When initially seen by us, she was preoccupied with her feelings of inadequacy and her low self-esteem.

FEARS AND PHOBIAS

Unlike the preschool children and the younger latency group, the children of this sample were not worried about actual starvation, and references to hunger in response to the parental separation were rare. Their fears, however, were nonetheless pervasive. Some, while not entirely realistic, were still tied to reality considerations; others approached phobic proportions. In fact, among this group it was often difficult for us to separate out the reality bases, including their sensitivity to the unspoken wishes of their parents, from the phobic elaboration. Thus, approximately one-quarter of these children were worried about being forgotten or abandoned by both parents.

John, in tears, said that his mother had left him at the doctor's office and didn't return on time. He cried, "She said that she was doing errands, but I know she was with her boyfriend."

Martha said to her mother, "If you don't love Daddy, maybe I'm next."

Some of their responses related to their accurate perception of parental feelings that children represent an unwelcome burden at this time in their lives.

Peggy reported that her mother had said to her, "If you're not good I'm going to leave." Although Peggy knew that her mother had said this in anger, she still worried about it.

Ann opined, "If Daddy marries Mrs. S., she has two daughters of her own, and I'll be Cinderella."

Some expressed the not wholly unrealistic concern that reliance on one rather than two parents was considerably less secure, and therefore the child's position in the world had become more vulnerable.

Katherine told us, "If my mother smokes and gets cancer, where would I live?" She repeatedly begged her mother to stop smoking, and worried intensely whenever her mother was late in arriving home.

Some worried, not unrealistically, about emotionally ill parents.

Ann stated about her mother, "I love her very much, but I have feelings. I'm afraid when Mom takes a long time to come home. She once tried to commit suicide. One day she ate a whole bottle of pills. I think of someone dying . . . how I'll be when I'm alone. Mom tried to commit suicide because of my father. It wasn't until after the divorce that she stopped crying. I think of her jumping over the Golden Gate Bridge. Mom thinks no one worries about her, but I do."

Many of these children experienced the additional concern that their specific needs were likely to be overlooked or forgotten.

Wendy referred several times through her interviews to the fact that her mother insisted on buying Fig Newtons, when she perfectly well knew that Wendy hated them.

RESPONSIBILITY FOR THE DIVORCE

Only a few children expressed concern about having caused the divorce, although we endeavored in a variety of ways, including direct observations, play, and drawings, to elicit such material. We may, perhaps, cautiously infer from the fact that their occasional stealing occurred in situations where the child was assured of being caught, that there may exist some need for punishment relating to guilty fantasies. However, our direct evidence on this issue was limited to a few children in this later latency group, and appeared only in those children who showed a variety of other symptomatic behaviors in addition to the guilty thinking.

> Lorraine, whose petty pilfering and lying and school difficulties were greatly exacerbated with the parental separation, said, "Whenever I think something is going to happen, it goes and happens. Like the time I thought my great-aunt was going to die, and then she died. And like the time I thought there was going to be a divorce." She wished that she could grow up and become a good witch, like Samantha.

SHAKEN SENSE OF IDENTITY

Many of these children experienced a sense of a shaken world in which the usual indicators had changed place or disappeared. For several children, these changed markers were particularly related to their sense of who they were and who they would become in the future. Critical to this new sense of stress is that during latency years the child's normal conception of his own identity is closely tied to the external family structure and developmentally dependent on the physical presence of parental figures—not only for nurture, protection, and control, but also for the consolidation of age-appropriate identifications (Erikson, 1959; Kelly and Wallerstein, 1976). Specifically, the self image and identity which in latency is still organized around "I am the son of John and Mary Smith" is profoundly shaken by the severance of the parental relationship. Some children expressed this confusion and sense of ruptured identity with anxious questions, comparing physical characteristics of their parents and themselves, as if trying in this manner to reassemble the broken pieces into a whole.

> Jack, unsolicited, volunteered a long discussion of his physical features. "My eyes change colors, just like my Mom's. My hair is going to change to light brown, just like my Dad's. Other people say I'm like my Dad. My Dad says I'm like my Mom. I say I'm like a combination."

Another aspect of this threat to the integrity of self which occurs at the time of divorce is posed more specifically to the socialization process and superego formation. The child feels that his conscience controls have been weakened by the family disruption, as the external supports give way and his anger at the parents moves strongly into consciousness. One manifestation of this may be new behaviors of petty stealing and lying which make their appearance in this age group around the time of family disruption. The threat the child perceives to his sense of being socialized is related, as well, to his concern of having to take care of himself; it was conveyed to us by Bob's moving story of his two rabbits.

> Bob volunteered, "I think I want to talk to you today." He told about the two little rabbits he had bought several years ago and cared for in an elaborate high-rise hutch he had carefully constructed. One day, despite his protective watchfulness, vicious neighborhood dogs ripped the cage apart, and the rabbits disappeared or were dragged off. The two rabbits, whom he had named Ragged Ear and Grey Face, may have escaped, he thinks, because recently he came upon two rabbits playing in the woods. They were wild rabbits now, but they resembled the two he had lost.

The two rabbits of this rich fantasy may well have referred to the child and his brother, and his story may reflect his fear of the primitive angers (the vicious dogs) let loose at the time of divorce, his fear that he would be destroyed, and the projected rescue solution—via return to a presocialized wild state in which the child-equals-rabbit takes responsibility for his own care. Clearly, the little wild rabbits who survived had a different identity and a different superego formation than the rabbits who were cared for so lovingly in the elaborately built hutch.

LONELINESS AND LOYALTY CONFLICTS

Children in this older latency group described their loneliness, their sense of having been left outside, and their sad recognition of their powerlessness and peripheral role in major family decisions.

> Betty said, "We were sitting in the dark with candles. Then they (her parents) told us suddenly about the divorce. We didn't have anything to say, and so then we watched TV."

These feelings of loneliness, not observed in this way in the younger age groups, reflect not only the greater maturational achievement of these children but also their more grown-up expectation of mutuality, as well as reciprocal support, in their relationships with parents and other adults. They thus felt more hurt, humiliated, and pushed aside by the events visited upon them, over which they had so little leverage.

It should be noted that these children, in their wrestling with this loneliness, realistically perceived the very real parental withdrawal of interest in children which so often occurs at the time of divorce. In addition to the departure of one parent, both parents understandably at such times become preoccupied with their own needs; their emotional availability, their attention span, and even the time spent with the children are often sharply reduced. Moreover, the families in our study were, by and large, nuclear families, unconnected to wider extended families or support systems of any enduring significance to the children. In this sense the children's feelings of loneliness and of loss reflected their realization that the central connecting structures they had known were dissolving.

Perhaps, however, the central ingredient in the loneliness and sense of isolation these children reported was related to their perception of the divorce as a battle between the parents, in which the child is called upon to take sides (Kelly and Wallerstein, 1976). By this logic, a step in the direction of the one parent was experienced by the child (and, of course, sometimes by the parent) as a betrayal of the other parent, likely to evoke real anger and further rejection, in addition to the intrapsychic conflicts mobilized. Thus, paralyzed by their own conflicting loyalties and the severe psychic or real penalties which attach to choice, many children refrained from choice and felt alone and desolate, with no place to turn for comfort or parenting. In a true sense, their conflict placed them in a solitary position at midpoint in the marital struggle.

SOMATIC SYMPTOMS

Finally, one symptomatic response observed in this group, and not seen in any younger group, was the report of a variety of somatic symptoms of different kinds and degrees of severity, such as headaches and stomachaches, which the children related to the parental conflict and parental visits.

> Martha refused to visit her father, saying that after she visited him she returned with terrible headaches which lasted several hours.
> Bobby had cramps in his legs, which he said were only relieved when his father massaged them.

Two of the children in this group who suffered with chronic asthma experienced intensified attacks, occurring more frequently.

> Jack reported that, during this visits with his father, his asthma increased markedly; he added quickly, "My dad has nothing to do with my asthma."

CHANGES IN SCHOOL PERFORMANCE

Since learning is a central developmental task of latency, it is important to note that, exactly comparable to our figures with the younger latency children, half of the 31 children in this older latency cohort also suffered a noticeable decline in school performance. Unlike the younger latency children, a concomitant deterioration in their peer relationships occurred in this group during and following the parental separation. There was no discernible correlation between prior school performance and the subsequent drop in school achievement, or between the degree of behavioral distress in the home setting and the falling-off in learning. Only one child showed considerable school improvement following the parental separation. This was in a divorce that involved the separation of the mother (and the children) from a seriously ill, manic-depressive husband (Kelly and Wallerstein, 1976).

The behavior of many of the children at school was at considerable variance with that displayed at home. Thus, some children who were feeling pressed and frightened at home began to act out a bossy, controlling, sometimes devious role at school.

> Kay, a gentle girl at home, frightened about the loss of her mother and openly heartbroken by her real rejection by her father, was described by her teachers as a girl who "needs to be queen of the hill," and as "devious, lying, whining, pitting children against each other." Her school work slipped badly as these new social behaviors emerged.

Another school behavior pattern which emerged at the time of separation combined a decreased ability to concentrate in class with increased aggression on the playground.

Some children found the pressure of academic and social expectations at the time of divorce turmoil almost unbearable.

> Jeff, a sober and mild mannered child whose parents were fighting angrily over custody of the children, on receiving an incomplete on his school paper, spurted out of class and ran pell mell across a nearby field, screaming all the way, "I won't do it."

Some children used the school to express what they could not say at home.

> Elsie wrote a composition about a drunken man and his girlfriends, which had clear references to her father's behavior.

We have not been able thus far to distinguish the characteristics of those children who showed change in their school adjustment from those who showed no change at all. All but four of the 15 children whose learning declined at the time of the parental separation had resumed their previous educational and social achievement levels by the time of the one-year follow-up.

CHANGES IN PARENT-CHILD RELATIONSHIPS

We turn now to a necessarily abbreviated discussion of some of the new parent-child configurations that emerged as a response to the marital strife and parental separation. These changed relationships constitute a significant component of the total response of children in this age group. The divorce-triggered changes in the parent-child relationship may propel the child forward into a variety of precocious, adolescent, or, more accurately, pseudoadolescent behaviors. They can, on the other hand, catalyze the development of true empathic responsiveness and increased responsibility in the child. And they can also result, as in the case of alignment with one parent against the other, in a lessening of the age-appropriate distance between parent and child and retreat by the child along the individuation-separation axis of development.

ALIGNMENT

One of the attributes of the parent-child relationship at this particular age is the peculiar interdependence of parent and child, which can become enhanced at the time of the divorce, and which accords the child a significant role in restoring or further diminishing the self-esteem of the parent. Thus the child in late latency, by his attitude, his stance, and his behavior has independent power to hurt, to reject, to confront, to forgive, to comfort, and to affirm. He also has the capacity to be an unswervingly loyal friend, ally, and "team member," exceeding in reliability his sometimes more fickle and capricious adolescent sibling.

Among the 31 children in this cohort, eight (or 25%) formed a relationship with one parent following the separation which was specifically aimed at the exclusion or active rejection of the other. These alignments were usually initiated and always fueled by the embattled parent, most often by the parent who felt aggrieved, deserted, exploited, or betrayed by the divorcing spouse. The angers which the parent and the child shared soon became the basis for complexly organized strategies aimed at hurting and harrassing the former spouse, sometimes with the intent of shaming him or her into returning to the marriage. More often the aim was vengeance. For many of these parents, these anger-driven campaigns served additionally to ward off depressions, and their intensity remained undiminished for a long time following parental separation. It should be noted that none of these children who participated, many of them as ingenious and mischievous allies, had previously rejected the parent who, subsequent to the alignment, became the target of their angers. Therefore, their provocative behavior was extremely painful and their rejection bewildering and humiliating to the excluded parent.

Our data indicate that, although the fight for allegiance may be initiated by the embattled parent, these alignments strike a responsive chord in the children within this specific age group. In fact, it is our suggestion that for children in late latency, the alignment with one parent against the other represents a highly complexly organized, overdetermined, ego-syntonic coping behavior, which serves a diversity of psychological needs and keeps at bay a number of significant intrapyschic conflicts and their attendant anxieties. A central part of the dynamic of this behavior is the splitting of the ambivalent relationship to the parents into that with the good parent and the bad parent. Moreover, in our findings, these alignments have the hurtful potential for consolidation and perpetuation long past the initial postseparation period, especially in those families where the child is aligned with the custodial parent.

> Paul's father was referred to us informally by the court to which the father had gone to complain of his wife's vindictive blocking of his visits with his three children. The father, a successful chemical engineer, expressed sadness and longing for his children, and concern that his children were being systematically turned against him by their mother's unremitting attacks and falsehoods. For example, the children were told by the mother that they had to give up their dog because the father was refusing to purchase food for it, although at that time the family was receiving well over $16,000 a year in support. Paul's mother expressed astonishment and bitterness at his father for the unilateral divorce decision, describing her many years of devoted love and hard work to support the father's graduate education. She coldly insisted that, as a devout Christian woman, she would never harbor anger. Yet she was convinced that, since the father had rejected both her and their three children, Paul would "never forgive his father, nor forget."
>
> Paul's initial response to the parental separation was his regression to sobbing in a dark closet, which we have earlier described, alternating with telephone pleas to his father to return. Later, in recalling this time, the child said to us, "I felt that I was being torn into two pieces." By the time we saw Paul, several months following the separation, he had consolidated an unshakable alignment with his mother. He extolled her as small and powerful, possessed of ESP, and knowledgeable in six languages. Of his father, he stated, "He'll never find another family like us." He volunteered that he never wanted to visit his father—ever. In response to our efforts to elicit fantasy material, he said that he would like best to live on a desert island with his mother and siblings and have a very, very long telephone cord for speaking with his father, and maybe a speedboat for visiting him.
>
> Among Paul's activities during the year following our initial contact was his continuing reporting to his mother, and eventually to her attorney, about his father's "lurid" social life and presumed delinquencies, and his continued rejections of his father's increasingly desperate overtures, including gifts and wishes to maintain visitation. Paul also maintained a coercive control over his younger sisters, who were eager to see their father, and he made sure by his monitoring of them that they

would not respond with affection in his presence. At follow-up he told us, "We are a team now. We used to have an extra guy, and he broke us up into little pieces." His anger and his mother's anger seemed undiminished at this time.

EMPATHY

Heightened empathic response to one or both distressed parents—and siblings—was catalyzed in several children as a specific consequence of the separation and the ensuing divorce.

With unusual insight, Anne described this process in *status nascendi*. She said, "I know that my mother isn't ready for the divorce, because I can put myself in her place. I can think just like I think my mother thinks."

Some youngsters were able to perceive their parents' needs with great sensitivity, and to respond with compassion and caring.

Mary told us, "My mom cried. She was so tired of being so strong for the children, and she asked us to sleep with her." Mary and her brother complied. "It made Mom feel better. Then we got up in the morning and made her breakfast in bed. Sometimes we just tell her, 'We are here, it's going to be all right.' "

We were interested to find that parents were often profoundly appreciative of this sensitivity and consideration.

Jane's mother told us that Jane was a wonderful child who wordlessly responded to the mother's needs and feelings. "Whenever I feel alone in the evening she cuddles me," her mother said.

Some of these children, especially the little girls, worried about their fathers and were concerned about the particulars of where they were sleeping and eating.

Jane told us how much she worries about her father, that he works late, that he only has a couch to sleep on, and that he seems so "extra tired."

Sometimes the children took on responsibility for the younger children, as well as for themselves, and for important routines in the household. Many parents had no adult relationships to lean on, and they relied heavily on these children for emotional support and advice, as well as for practical help.

Sometimes empathic feelings were stimulated by unequal treatment of siblings by the departing parent.

> Jack suddenly began to wheeze as he told us that his father had invited him, but not his sister, to live with him. He added that his father had sent him a Christmas card, signing it, "With all my love," but had only sent his sister a signed card. "I guess it made her feel pretty bad," he added sadly.

A few children were particularly sensitive to the changing moods and needs of their emotionally ill parent, and learned early to dissemble and protect what they understood to be the fragility of the parent's adjustment.

> Jane stated as one of her problems that it was hard for her to be honest with her mother. Her mother kept asking questions about the father's relationship with his new girlfriends. She, Jane, could not tell her mother that her father and his girlfriend didn't fight, because "I'm scared that it will make her sad and cry." At follow-up, Jane solemnly told us, "Mom will probably marry, but she is not ready. She just got the divorce and wants to be settled. I think she has gone through a lot of trouble and sadness and needs more time."

FOLLOW-UP AT ONE YEAR

A first follow-up on these youngsters took place a year after the initial consultation. By and large, as with the younger latency children, the turbulent responses to the divorce itself had mostly become muted with the passage of the intervening year. In about half the children (15 of the 29 available at follow-up) the disequilibrium created by the family disruption—the suffering; the sense of shame; the fears of being forgotten, lost, or actively abandoned; and the many intense worries associated with their new sense of vulnerability and dependence on a more fragile family structure—had almost entirely subsided. But even these children with apparently better outcomes, who seemed relatively content with their new family life and circle of friends, including step-parents, were not without backward glances of bitterness and nostalgia. In fact, the anger and hostility aroused around the divorce events lingered longer and more tenaciously than did any of the other affective responses. Of the total group, 10 (or one-third) of the children maintained an unremitted anger directed at the noncustodial parent; of these, four did so in alignment with the custodial mother, the other six on their own.

> Edward, who was doing splendidly in school and in new friendship relationships with his mother and with an admired male teacher, nonetheless said bitterly of his father, "I'm not going to speak to him any more. My dad is off my list now." (This was a father who, prior to the divorce, had had a very warm relationship with his son.)

Although some of these children who were doing well continued to harbor reconciliation wishes, most had come to accept the divorce with sad finality. Some seemed to be unconsciously extrapolating from these reconciliation wishes to plan future careers as repairmen, as bridge builders, as architects, as lawyers. Others, like Jane, were perhaps extending their protective attitudes toward their disturbed parents.

> Asked what she might like to do when she grows up, Jane responded, "You might laugh. A child psychiatrist. You're one, aren't you?" She talked movingly of working someday "with blind children, or mentally retarded children, or children who cannot speak."

By contrast, the other half (14 of the 29 seen at follow-up) gave evidence of consolidation into troubled and conflicted depressive behavior patterns, with, in half of these, *more* open distress and disturbance than at the initial visit. A significant component in this now chronic maladjustment was a continuing depression and low self-esteem, combined with frequent school and peer difficulties. One such child was described by his teacher at follow-up as, "A little old man who worries all the time and rarely laughs." In this group, symptoms that had emerged had generally persisted and even worsened. For instance, phobic reactions had in one instance worsened and spread; delinquent behavior such as truancy and petty thievery remained relatively unchanged; and some who had become isolated and withdrawn were even more so. One new behavior configuration that emerged during the first postdivorce year in these nine- and 10-year-olds was a precocious thrust into adolescent preoccupation with sexuality and assertiveness, with all the detrimental potential of such phase-inappropriate unfoldings. And amongst all the children, both in the groups with better and with poorer outcomes, relatively few were able to maintain good relationships with both parents.

In a future report we shall present a fuller discussion of the many variables which seem to relate to this bimodal spread of outcomes for the postdivorce course of these children. Here we would like to close with remarks of a 10-year-old sage from our study, whose words capture the salient mood of these children at the first follow-up—their clear-eyed perception of reality, their pragmatism, their courage, and their muted disappointment and sadness. In summarizing the entire scene, she said, "Knowing my parents, no one is going to change his mind. We'll just all have to get used to the situation and to them."

8

Loneliness
and the Adolescent

ERIC OSTROV and DANIEL OFFER

OVERVIEW

LONELINESS CAN BE DESCRIBED as a painful feeling of longing for another person or persons, or, following Ferreira (1962), as an inner craving for intimacy and closeness. Like depression, loneliness is filled with helplessness and pain, but unlike depression, loneliness is characterized by the hope that were the other only present, united with the lonely person, everything would be perfect. Loneliness is part of the normal experience of living since it is engendered by the very process of becoming a person, a separate self. The process of separation and individuation has loneliness as its cutting edge. Mahler and LaPerriere (1965) capture a moment in this process when they describe the very young child who becomes afraid when he realizes that he can not only walk away from his mother, but can walk so far away that he could become lost. Every time we grow more autonomous, create our own thoughts, assert our own identity, we risk moving away from others and therefore risk loneliness.

This kind of loneliness, which we are contending is a normal concomitant of human development, is especially relevant to adolescence. One reason loneliness is especially poignant during adolescence is that during this time the young person develops the ability to reflect intellectually about a whole new range of possibilities regarding values and life choices (Piaget, 1967), while social expectations and physical growth push him toward greatly increased mastery and autonomy.

170

Cognitively, the teenager is capable of questioning old assumptions about life, while new expectations lead him to question who he is, and whether he will be able to find a "career" or place in society where he will receive love and respect (Erikson, 1950). During adolescence, moreover, it becomes clearer that some day he will have to leave his parents and separate from them psychologically. This combination of events mobilizes, to some degree, childhood fears of being helpless and alienated from significant others. The many popular songs dealing with loneliness, sold by the millions, can be seen as expressing a feeling which is psychologically meaningful for the adolescents who buy them.

RELATION TO NORMALITY AND PSYCHOPATHOLOGY

Offer and Offer (1975) studied normal, white, middle-class teenagers over an eight-year period. They used two perspectives on normality to select their population: normality as average and normality as health (Offer and Sabshin, 1974). Using this definition of normality we would hypothesize that in all social classes or cultures, normal teenagers are not lonely often and are not extremely lonely. (We should add, however, that this study is confined mostly to middle-class, white teenagers.) By the time they reach adolescence, these normal young people have a reasonably firm sense of themselves as capable persons, distinct from others. At the same time they have internalized many of their parents' values and accepted their parents' limitations as human beings. Therefore during adolescence their questioning of parental values and assumptions about life is moderate, and their separation from their parents is gradual, with concomitant, increasing identification with them (Offer and Offer, 1975). Normal adolescents are able to relate to other parental figures and friends, who become their allies in maturation, and provide support that prevents trauma during the transitional status of adolescence. Generally, normal adolescents feel they have room and permission to experiment, to play with new possibilities. For normal teenagers, being alone is not necessarily a lonely experience; such teenagers have enough trust in the world, enough sense of continuity of self over time, a sufficiently clear idea of their own values, and enough ability to set restrictions on impulses and fantasy. They are able to "play alone," to use solitude to conduct a dialogue with themselves, to question, to create, to master (Hobson, 1974; Winnicott, 1958). When they are alone they are not driven to engage defensively in omnipotent fantasies or to fantasize union with an idealized other. And they are not driven through the dread of being alone to seek out reassuring but superficial friendships, or to deny continuously feelings of loneliness and helplessness by participating in desperate and grandiose acts.

During adolescence, as at every age, loneliness can be part of a dreadful, pathological adjustment to the world (Fromm-Reichmann, this volume). Our feeling is that the youth who finds adolescence a poignant and lonely time will be vulnerable at every stage of life. The lonely, disturbed adolescent has probably felt disappointed with human relationships for most of his life. Defensively, he may refrain from reaching out to others and nurse his vulnerable self-esteem, simultaneously yearning for someone who will take care of him and make him feel powerful through identification. Conversely, the lonely adolescent may feel a boundless need for attention, approval, and external confirmation of his own worth while experiencing repeated, lonely disappointments in this quest. If he has not experienced enough trust in adults to be by himself and to begin to master reality autonomously, if he has never felt there was a space to play alone safely, he may never have developed the autonomy and mastery needed to feel secure and efficacious as a person in his own right. Solitude, for a disturbed adolescent, may be felt as highly threatening, even annihilating. If, in addition, the adults around him failed to provide adequate models for controlling impulses, being alone could lead to intolerable sexual and aggressive fantasies and feelings. For some disturbed teenagers loneliness can have a desperate quality that they must avoid at all costs.

Adolescents may not be more lonely than people at other points of transition in their lives, but there are common elements in the adolescent process that give loneliness at this stage a specific quality. Characteristically, loneliness during adolescence is intertwined with the mourning of one's own identity as a child and the relinquishing of certain forms of childhood attachments and beliefs. The process of separating and maturing is tinged with loneliness. However, while the loneliness of adolescents shares a common quality, the intensity of the experience ranges from the normal to the highly pathological. Suggestively, there is evidence from other studies that neurotic adults are more lonely than normal adults (Czernik and Steinmeyer, 1974; Siassi, Crocetti, and Spiro, 1974).

AGE DIFFERENCES DURING ADOLESCENCE

For the younger adolescent, typically, the separation process from parents and the readjustment of peer relations temporarily disrupt important interpersonal relationships. For that reason, we would predict that younger adolescents (aged 12 years to 15 years, 11 months) are often more lonely than older ones (aged 16 years to 20 years) who have begun to establish more intimate relationships with peers of the opposite sex (Offer and Offer, 1975). As they grow older, adolescents typically focus less on their own internal changes, and on separating themselves from parents and childhood roles and beliefs. Instead, they concentrate on realizing interpersonal and vocational goals which promise relatedness to significant others and the larger society on a new and more mature basis. While the younger adolescent may be wondering how to define himself outside the context of his family, and whether he is acceptable within a nonfamilial milieu, the older adolescent may be rediscovering similarities between himself and his parents and may, in the light of new certainty about his own identity, be moving toward more open and empathic relationships with others, especially others of the opposite sex.

SEX DIFFERENCES DURING ADOLESCENCE

It is possible that in a male oriented society, females will tend to feel more lonely than males. Opportunities to reach out to others outside the family may be fewer, and mastery of the separation process may therefore be more difficult for females. Teenage girls, for example, may not be able to express and share anger at parents and feelings of increased physical mastery through active sports the way teenage boys can. In addition, teenage girls may feel that becoming independent may conflict with opportunities for intimacy. Generally, passivity may be encouraged among adolescent girls. Rather than find new expressions of autonomy as a way to master separation fears, a woman may look to intimacy with a man as providing both security and a sense of autonomy and status vis-à-vis her parents. The time until that intimacy is possible, however, may be a lonely one.

CULTURAL DIFFERENCES

In a rapidly changing society, the teenager is often confronted with the need to make a more total separation from his parents (who may be committed to adaptations to a different set of social conditions) than that demanded of adolescents in more stable societies. In addition, the range of possibilities for social roles and the lack of clarity about values in a changing society may increase an adolescent's difficulty in deciding who he is and with whom and on what basis he wants to ally himself. All these factors—distance from parents, identity confusion, and lack of clarity about values—can enhance feelings of being separate and unable to communicate with others.

Even apart from considerations relating to the degree of social change, adolescents in our society may tend to feel more lonely than those in less industrialized or competitive societies. In our society, stress on individual achievement and distinction may make alliances with others more difficult. Mobility, or even the anticipation of being mobile, can alienate a young person from the values of friends and family and cause him to feel conflicted about some of his internalized values, leading him to feel both lonely and empty. We would expect, on the basis of these considerations, that adolescents in the United States might typically feel more lonely than youths in other, more traditional, less industrial, and less competitive societies.

METHODS OF INVESTIGATION

The Instrument

The Offer Self-Image Questionnaire (OSIQ) (Offer, 1971) is a self-descriptive personality test that has been shown to measure reliably and validly the adjustment of adolescent boys and girls. This questionnaire has been used in several studies and has been administered to over 5,000 male and female adolescents, including younger adolescents (12 years to 15 years, 11 months) and older adolescents (16 years to 20 years). These studies included normal, disturbed, and delinquent adolescents from various regions in the United States (including minority group adolescents) as well as normal adolescents from Australia and Ireland.

The OSIQ consists of 130 items which are rated by the subject as being more or less true of himself on a scale of 1 through 6. One item is phrased "I am so very lonely." We decided to use this item as a measure of the degree of loneliness of various groups of adolescents because experience with this test had indicated that adolescents are sufficiently sensitive psychologically and sufficiently truthful to report straightforwardly about the extent of this feeling in themselves. We are aware that there are cultural taboos on acknowledging loneliness. In a society like our own, for example, loneliness may be equated with friendlessness or lack of popularity, and therefore with a deficiency in the self. Nonetheless, we felt the anonymity under which most questionnaires were administered and the fact that answers could be qualified (for example, one could answer that loneliness "describes me fairly well" as opposed to "describes me very well") enhanced the probability of obtaining veridical answers.

THE SAMPLES

Boys

1. Younger, 14-year-old, normal American boys from Midwest suburbs, N = 326.
2. Older, 16- to 20-year-old, normal American boys from a Midwest city, N = 141.
3. Younger, 12- to 15-year-old, normal Australian boys from a public school in that country, N = 685.
4. Younger, 12- to 15-year-old, normal, middle-class Irish boys from public schools in that country, N = 167.
5. Disturbed, American boys of various ages (12-20) from five psychiatric hospitals throughout the United States, N = 166.
6. Delinquent American boys of various ages (12-20) from one psychiatric hospital in the Midwest, N = 29.

Girls

1. Younger, 12- to 15-year-old, normal American girls from suburbs in the Midwest, N = 278.
2. Older, 16- to 20-year-old, normal American girls from a Midwest city, N = 154.
3. Younger, 12- to 15-year-old, normal Australian girls from a public school in that country, N = 661.
4. Younger, 12- to 15-year-old, normal, middle-class Irish girls from public schools in that country, N = 163.

5. Disturbed American girls of various ages (12-20) from two psychiatric hospitals, N = 74.
6. Delinquent American girls of various ages (12-20) from one psychiatric hospital and two residential centers for delinquent girls, N = 96.

RESULTS

We compared the extent of self-reported loneliness among the various populations by using Pearson's chi-square. In order to be sure expected frequencies were sufficient in each cell and to avoid making distinctions in degree that might only reflect reluctance to label oneself lonely, we split the six-point scale reflecting degree of loneliness, so that subjects were classified as having said either that they were lonely or that they were not lonely.

1. *Younger Boys versus Older Boys* (Table 1): The proportion of younger American boys reporting that they were lonely was significantly greater than the proportion of older American boys reporting that they were lonely.

2. *American versus Australian versus Irish Boys* (Table 2): Younger American boys more frequently indicated that they were lonely than did their Australian or Irish counterparts.

3. *Normal versus Disturbed versus Delinquent Boys* (Table 3): Disturbed boys in psychiatric treatment in a clinical setting, and delinquent boys, admitted to a good deal more loneliness than normal youths. This was true despite the fact that, unlike the normal groups, the disturbed and delinquent groups contained older as well as younger adolescents and despite the finding that older adolescents are generally less lonely than younger ones. In addition, the data indicate that the disturbed boys felt even more lonely than did those boys who were labeled delinquent.

4. *Younger American Girls versus Younger American Boys* (Table 4): There were no significant differences between these groups in reported frequency of loneliness.

5. *Older American Girls versus Older American Boys* (Table 5): There were no significant differences between these groups in reported frequency of loneliness.

6. *Younger Girls versus Older Girls* (Table 6): The proportion of younger American girls reporting that they were lonely was significantly greater than the proportion of older American girls reporting that they were lonely.

7. *American versus Australian versus Irish Girls* (Table 7): There were no significant differences between these groups in reported frequency of loneliness.

TABLE 1

Comparison of Responses of Younger[a] and Older[b] Normal American Boys to the Offer Self-Image Questionnaire Item, "I Feel So Very Lonely"

Response	Younger Boys ($N = 326$)	Older Boys ($N = 141$)
Feel lonely (%)	22.09	14.18
Do not feel lonely (%)	77.91	85.82

$\chi^2 = 3.8871$; 1 df; $p < .05$

[a]"Younger" subjects were between the ages of 12 years and 15 years 11 months. These data were collected in 1962 by D. Offer from midwestern suburban areas.

[b]"Older" subjects were between the ages of 16 and 20. This sample was studied in 1966 by H. Heath. The data were from a midwestern city.

TABLE 2

Comparison of Responses of Younger,[a] Normal American,[b] Australian,[c] and Irish[d] to the Offer Self-Image Questionnaire Item, "I Feel So Very Lonely"

Response	American Boys ($N = 326$)	Australian Boys ($N = 684$)	Irish Boys ($N = 167$)
Feel lonely (%)	22.09	16.37	12.57
Do not feel lonely (%)	77.21	83.63	87.43

$\chi^2 = 8.179$; 2 df; $p < .025$

[a]"Younger" subjects were between the ages of 12 years and 15 years 11 months.

[b]These data were collected in 1962 by D. Offer from midwestern suburban areas.

[c]These data were collected by A. G. Baikie, A. S. Henderson, and I. L. Lewis from public schools in Australia in 1970.

[d]These data were collected by T. Brennan from Dublin suburbs in 1974.

Eric Ostrov — Daniel Offer

TABLE 3

Comparison of Responses of Normal,[a] Disturbed[b], and Delinquent[c] Younger[d] American Boys to the Offer Self-Image Questionnaire Item, "I Feel So Very Lonely"

Response	Normal Boys (N = 326)	Disturbed Boys (N = 166)	Delinquent Boys (N = 29)
Feel lonely (%)	22.09	36.15	31.03
Do not feel lonely (%)	77.91	63.85	68.97

$\chi^2 = 11.259$; 2 df; $p < .05$

[a]These data were collected in 1962 by D. Offer from midwestern suburban areas.

[b]These data were collected between 1967 and 1974 by A. Anderson from a hospital associated with Cornell University; by P. Beckett from a hospital associated with Wayne University; by E. Mindel, H. Heath, M. Robin, and E. Silverstein from inpatients at the Psychiatric and Psychosomatic Institute, Michael Reese Hospital in Chicago; by E. Coche from first admissions to Friend's Hospital in Philadelphia; and by J. B. McAndrews from a hospital affiliated with the University of Wisconsin.

[c]These data were collected between 1969 and 1973 by D. Offer, R. C. Marohn, and E. Ostrov as part of the Juvenile Delinquency Project at the Illinois State Psychiatric Institute in Chicago.

[d]"Younger" subjects were between the ages of 12 years and 15 years 11 months.

TABLE 4

Comparison of Responses of Younger[a] Normal American Girls[b] and Boys[c] to the Offer Self-Image Questionnaire Item, "I Feel So Very Lonely"

Response	Younger Girls (N = 278)	Younger Boys (N = 326)
Feel lonely (%)	20.14	22.09
Do not feel lonely (%)	79.86	77.91

$\chi^2 = .339$; 1 df; N.S.

[a]"Younger" subjects were between the ages of 12 and 15 years 11 months.

[b]These data were collected by E. Silverstein in 1969 from two midwestern suburbs.

[c]These data were collected in 1962 by D. Offer from midwestern suburban areas.

8. *Normal versus Disturbed versus Delinquent Girls* (Table 8): Disturbed girls in psychiatric treatment in hospitals or clinics reported significantly more loneliness than normal or delinquent girls. Delinquent girls, in turn, reported more loneliness than normal girls. As was the case with boys, this result obtained despite the fact that all the normal girls were younger adolescents while the other groups contained both younger and older teenagers.

TABLE 5

Comparison of Responses of Older,[a] Normal American Girls[b] and Boys[c]
to the Offer Self-Image Questionnaire Item, "I Feel So Very Lonely"

Response	Older Girls ($N = 154$)	Older Boys ($N = 141$)
Do feel lonely (%)	12.34	14.18
Do not feel lonely (%)	87.66	85.82

$\chi^2 = .237$; 1 df; N.S.
[a]"Older" subjects were between the ages of 16 and 20.
[b,c]These samples were studied in 1966 by H. Heath; the data were from a midwestern city.

TABLE 6

Comparison of Responses of Younger[a] and Older[b] Normal American
Girls to Offer Self-Image Questionnaire Item, "I Feel So Very Lonely"

Response	Younger Girls ($N = 278$)	Older Girls ($N = 154$)
Feel lonely (%)	20.14	12.34
Do not feel lonely (%)	79.86	87.66

$\chi^2 = 4.20$; 1 df; $p < .05$
[a]"Younger" subjects were between the ages of 12 years and 15 years 11 months. These data were collected by E. Silverstein in 1969 in two midwestern suburbs.
[b]"Older" subjects were between the ages of 16 and 20. These samples were studied by H. Heath in 1966; the data were from a midwestern city.

TABLE 7

Comparison of Responses of Younger,[a] Normal American,[b] Australian[c], and Irish[d] Girls to the Offer Self-Image Questionnaire Item, "I Feel So Very Lonely"

Response	American Girls (N = 278)	Australian Girls (N = 661)	Irish Girls (N = 163)
Feel lonely (%)	20.14	20.42	20.86
Do not feel lonely (%)	79.86	79.58	79.14

χ^2 = .033; 1 df; N.S.

[a] "Younger" subjects were between the ages of 12 years and 15 years 11 months.

[b] These data were collected by E. Silverstein in 1969 from two midwestern suburbs.

[c] These data were collected by A. G. Baikie, A. S. Henderson, and I. L. Lewis from public schools in Australia in 1970.

[d] These data were collected by T. Brennan from Dublin suburbs in 1974.

TABLE 8

Comparison of Responses of Normal,[a] Disturbed,[b] and Delinquent[c] Younger,[d] American Girls to the Offer Self-Image Questionnaire Item, "I Feel So Very Lonely"

Response	Normal Girls (N = 278)	Disturbed Girls (N = 74)	Delinquent Girls (N = 96)
Feel lonely (%)	20.14	55.41	37.50
Do not feel lonely (%)	79.86	44.59	62.50

χ^2 = 38.384; 1 df; p < .001

[a] These data were collected by E. Silverstein in 1969 from two midwestern suburbs.

[b] These data were collected in 1974 by E. Coche from first admissions to Friend's Hospital in Philadelphia and by J. B. McAndrews from a hospital affiliated with the University of Wisconsin.

[c] These data were collected in 1969 by E. Mindel from a residential treatment home for delinquent girls in a midwestern suburb; in 1973 by P. Agrawal from a correctional facility in California; and in 1969–1973 by D. Offer, R. C. Marohn and E. Ostrov as part of the Juvenile Delinquency Project at the Illinois State Psychiatric Institute in Chicago.

[d] "Younger" subjects were between the ages of 12 years and 15 years 11 months.

DISCUSSION

Earlier in this chapter we suggested that adolescents may not be lonelier than people at other stages in life, but that there are universal issues in adolescence that give loneliness during this period a unique and shared quality. Among adolescents, we found some evidence that the proportion of younger adolescents who report feelings of loneliness is greater than the proportion of older adolescents who report such feelings. We also found that Irish and Australian male adolescents tend to report less loneliness than their American counterparts. Disturbed and delinquent adolescents of both sexes seemed much lonelier than normal youths. Differences between American adolescent boys and girls with respect to frequency of reported loneliness were minimal as were differences between American, Australian, and Irish girls. In what follows, we offer a tentative developmental framework for understanding these findings.

The course of each child's development can be traced to the vicissitudes of his feelings of power and vulnerability. Usually a child's feelings of vulnerability are tempered by (1) the realization that he is surrounded by competent, reliable, and loving adults and (2) the expectation that he can become increasingly like them and ally with them while learning to cope successfully with the environment. Given feelings of relative safety and growing competence, a child can feel free to experiment and accept reversals and failures, in short, to become more autonomous while accepting the reality of the limitations of his power and ability. As he grows more competent and secure, he can also accept and forgive his parent's limitations as humans and use this knowledge of their limitations as a basis for still further identification with them. Through identification, the child acquires the capacity to be apart from his parents and still feel a sense of union with them. Under these circumstances, a child will not suffer chronic or extreme loneliness, since solitude will not be equated with abandonment and aloneness will be countered by feelings of self-sufficiency.

This course of development contrasts with that of the disturbed or delinquent child who is often lonely or engaged in defending against loneliness. We can speculate that the disturbed child's feelings of vulnerability were never adequately allayed. Defensively, such a child fantasizes himself as so powerful or admirable that he need never be afraid. Overtly or covertly, he longs for a powerful, parenting figure who will restore to him what moments of security and comfort he has known. As Sullivan said (1953) "the 'lonely' child . . . inevitably has a very rich fantasy life" (p. 223). Unfortunately, the lonely child may become caught in a vicious circle in which his feelings of vulnerability lead him to retreat from other people and from reality, causing him to feel even more isolated and incompetent and hence, vulnerable. Alternatively, his anger at never having obtained enough from others may result in belligerent actions through which he alienates himself still further from others.

The experience of the normal child and the disturbed or delinquent child entering adolescence will be very different. The normal child may feel lonely at this time because physical and cognitive changes and new, age-graded social expectations make preadolescent modes of adaptation obsolete, with consequent feelings of alienation from parents and lowering of self-esteem. However, the degree of alienation and turmoil will be much greater among disturbed and delinquent adolescents. Thus, the normal younger teenager may find that the sexual adaptations characteristic of latency may not suffice to cope with intensified sexual feelings. Unquestioned acceptance of moral values may become cognitively impossible as his ability to think and engage in formal operations develops (see, for example, Kohlberg, 1964). Relationships may shift away from parents and toward peers, due both to social expectations that the teenager begin to separate from his parents and to the fact that teenagers share something their parents do not: body changes, cognitive changes, and, at least in our Western society, a unique status that confers some adult privileges and status while sanctioning a ''psychosocial moratorium'' (Erikson, 1963) on the need to make long-term career choices. At the same time, the normal, younger teenager may turn inward as he focuses on the changes his body is undergoing and reflects on new insights and his own future within society. Guilt about sexual desires, confusion about ideals, turning away from parents, and focusing inward may all lead the normal, younger adolescent to feel lonely. Nevertheless, he will find his parents are supportive of his need to begin to move away, that they understand his need to question them and his new sexual and other physical needs. He will have the social skills and self-confidence to share his experiences with friends and will begin to form intimate, heterosexual and homosocial relationships. And because his love and respect for his parents are still fundamentally strong, he will not reject them and in fact will begin to reestablish a relationship with them on the basis of a new maturity. The normal teenager, in short, experiences intense loneliness only infrequently, and as he grows older even that loneliness becomes less frequent and intense.

The disturbed child, in contrast to the normal child, will experience adolescence as a threat. The thought of growing up and being on his own may fill him with fear or it may threaten his fantasy of reuniting with an idealized parent (Kohut, 1971). Sexual feelings may be assimilated to grandiose fantasies and longing for an idealized other. Oedipal wishes may be stirred up again with heavy burdens of guilt. The disturbed child may so fear rejection and may be so unskilled at winning friends that he becomes totally isolated when he is expected to form new peer group relationships. At this time such teenagers may become depressed and withdrawn and even suicidal.

To cope with the new demands of adolescence, other adolescents may resort to drugs or join various cults or gangs that promise instant and absolute acceptance. Many become delinquent, acting out either by themselves or with others complex feelings of anger at authorities, grandiosity, and wishes to be apprehended and taken care of.

For both disturbed and delinquent youths, loneliness is a core feeling. Turning to some suggestive empirical evidence for these speculations, we find that Williams (1970) has documented the need for quick intimacy and union with parent surrogates among some "hippies" while Schrut (1968) and Teicher and Jacobs (1966) have shown the role of isolation and disappointment in love among adolescents who attempt suicide.

Before leaving the topic of the relationship between loneliness and psychopathology in adolescence, we would like to discuss a phenomenon that falls within the normal range: the relationship between loneliness and art in adolescence. Adolescence is the time of life when, in terms of career and identity, possibility is more important than actuality, when the critical issue is the choice of what to be. Adolescence is also a time for ideals, when the cognitive ability to conceptualize the ideal is available without many of the experiences of adulthood that temper the ideal. Art, by its very nature, is a realm where everything, including the ideal, is possible, where choice is maximized. Thus art can be an especially attractive medium for adolescents. For many adolescents solitude invites creative expression through poetry, song, or painting. Through art the adolescent reaches out to his imaginary audience, often expressing and hoping to share feelings, especially feelings of loneliness. At the same time, he reaches for the ideal which he fears he is leaving behind in the process of becoming an adult. The essentially adolescent nature of this kind of creativity is demonstrated by its sudden cessation with the end of adolescence.

According to our data, the extent of psychopathology is the most important factor that determines the intensity of loneliness. However, cultural differences play a role as well. According to Bowman (1955), loneliness may be widespread in the United States because (1) mobility tends to separate family members and make relationships with neighbors less close, (2) an emphasis on achievement may make parents less available or make children less respectful of their parents' values, and (3) competitive, bureaucratic, and impersonal social relations increase distance between people. The Irish and Australian populations who participated in our study may represent societies less characterized by mobility, competitiveness, and impersonal social relations than the United States. However, the authors are not familiar with cultural differences in relationships between the sexes that could explain why these differences occurred among males but not females.

We might add that loneliness in modern, industrialized society may have frightening consequences. It is possible, for example, that one source of support for the Nazis was lonely and insecure teenagers seeking an unquestionable identity, as well as a realization of grandiose fantasies and wishes for mystical union with an all-powerful fatherland (Erikson, 1950; see also Hirsch, 1941, who, writing as a Nazi, described how Hitler's soldiers raised youth to a level of supra-individual exaltation and action). Erich Fromm (1941) observed there are many situations in which a person may feel caught between being active and independent and paying the price of feeling alone and unprotected, or belonging and conforming and paying the price of losing his independence. The danger for the adolescent is that he will conform to the demands of others at the expense of not creating, on his own, a synthesis between his values and capabilities and the needs and opportunities in his society.

Across cultures, loneliness may be part of a psychological continuum ranging from introversion to depression. Introversion is similar to the creative solitude Moustakas (1972) describes, a turning inward for self-dialogue and unhampered exploration of possibilities. Loneliness is a feeling of deprivation, of longing that painfully, but hopefully, turns outward for fulfillment. Depression, on the other hand, is laden with feelings of being helplessly and hopelessly alone— where loneliness is hopeful, depression is filled with despair, where loneliness contains longing, depression is filled with helpless anger.

In conclusion, we can state that the individual never becomes so self-sufficient that he can forego altogether the ongoing approval and recognition of others. From the very beginning of life his ability to survive flows from other people. Without the ability to attract the attention and benevolent ministrations of others, he could not survive. As an adult, the individual's need for other people can be understood in cognitive terms. As Asch (1952) showed experimentally, people use other people to help them test what is real and what is not. The less tangible the reality, the more influential the opinions of others are (though for many people the opinions of others are much more important than even their own sensory information). Self-perceptions are an eminently social reality, the convergence of a multiplicity of outside evaluations of behaviors and appearances. While there is a complex interaction between the individual's manipulation and his incorporation of external evaluations of himself, it is apparent that without such outside feedback, the individual may begin to lose his sense of self and even his sense of reality. The threat of not knowing one's own self must blend subtly for most, if not all, people with the threat of annihilation felt by the utterly helpless infant.

The normal person may gain distance from the needs for other people's esteem by increasing competence and internalization of approval-giving functions, but no person can eliminate the need for other people entirely. Therefore, everyone is susceptible to loneliness. The degree, frequency, and quality of a person's loneliness will be a function of the developmental tasks the person is coping with, the degree of emotional health he has achieved, and the society in which he lives. This is as true among adolescents as among individuals at every other stage in life.

9

The Lonely Marriage in Corporate America

ROBERT SEIDENBERG

ALL COMMENTATORS on the corporate wife seem to agree that her principal disease is loneliness. And yet this may not be an endemic but an epidemic illness, contagious in every segment of society.

We learn that corporate men are lonely both in their travels and in their offices. Caught up in what David Riesman has called the "antagonistic" cooperation of big business, they secretly yearn for more trust and genuine friendship, which are absent both from competitors on the outside and inside the organization. Security is always relative: one bad step and everything can be lost. One must maintain a front of confidence and mastery lest someone detect a hidden weakness or deficiency. Despite his success, there is no one such a man can confide in concerning the vital issues that may plague him. He never knows when some conversation or memo may be used against him. Ultimately he must keep his own counsel; he may not talk about certain matters even with his wife, for she might inadvertently betray him. This obviously leads to isolation and loneliness.

This life style contributes to the anger and disappointment cor-

Revised version of "The Anatomy of Loneliness" in Robert Seidenberg, *Corporate Wives—Corporate Casualties?* Copyright © 1973 by AMACOM, a division of American Management Associations. Reprinted by permission of AMACOM.

porate men feel when they come home at night to an unsympathetic wife and family who are seemingly enmeshed in trivial household problems. The corporate husband is continually lamenting, "She just doesn't realize what I go through all day," or "Doesn't a man deserve a few hours peace in his life?" He is responding to the real fears and dangers of his existence and longs for some uncensorious relationship. He is certainly in no condition to receive more of the same when he arrives home.

Yet his experience of loneliness is mitigated by the compensations of challenge and growth that are also an integral part of his work. His personal isolation, certainly painful, is largely relieved by the balm of success, challenge, and achievement. For the corporate wife these compensatory mechanisms are not there. She is much more vulnerable and therefore feels the effects of isolation and estrangement more intensely. There is no comparable balm for injury.

This isolation differs like the whole from its parts, from what I have described previously (Seidenberg, 1973) as the isolation that results from excessive and uprooting mobility, from the difficulties for the wife of transferring her social credentials from community to community, from the great scrutiny (with pitifully small rewards) that she lives under, and from the flagrant sexual double standard and sexism in general to which she is subjected.

Loneliness for the corporate wife is of course also far more than being separated from the "great" man. It means being separated from those resources of culture, community, and people that make up a human existence. Loneliness means being left behind in knowledge, participation, mental growth, and influence. When one hears a wife lament, "He couldn't take me along," or "I have to stay behind with the children," it literally means she has been left out of the opportunity for liberation and growth. And without growth there is stagnation and death. There are many kinds of death; the biological is but one. People worry rightly about their professional, social, and political as well as their biological survival.

To be cut off from communication with other human beings is to feel lonely. But more important, to be out of touch with parts of one's inner self is to feel lonely. This includes the diminution or loss of previously developed talents and interests—the dancing one enjoyed, the music one played, the writing one did. It means the loss of one's skills as an artist, a teacher, or a technician. To be separated from these parts of one's being, these implements of past participation and gratification, contributes to an especially adverse type of loneliness. Erich Kahler writes, ''The estrangement between human beings in daily life, the lack of immediacy in contacts, and the resultant loneliness we frequently witness today have their roots in man's alienation from his own personal human center'' (1957).

It has been my professional experience that loss of self encompasses matters of quality of living, accomplishments or the lack of them, and meeting or falling short of one's ideals as well as success in relationships. Failure at these is as relevant and crucial in fostering hopelessness as the knowledge of one's inevitable demise. I hold with Kierkegaard that we are always well aware of the loss of a limb, a wife, or a five-dollar bill. However, the loss of self in its many subtle manifestations is not well understood. The self sometimes slips away; only the fortunate get a warning signal. Atrophy from disuse, whether of one's limb or of one's liberty, is a particularly painful deprivation since it is a largely self-inflicted condition. It is bad enough that fate, biology, and the ravages of time diminish one, but to allow parts of the self to slip away passively is particularly distressing.

The deprivation often is part of the renunciation that is expected of a wife, even if she had an autonomous life before marriage. In an interview with Arthur Bell, Rhonda Fleming describes what happened to her when she got married: ''I married Hall Bartlett for love and security. He wanted me to quit my career and I was ready to go along with it. I sold my home. I quit acting. I became completely dependent on a man for the first time in my life. Till then I was self-supporting, my career always came first, and I had never been solely dependent on anyone. And till then no one had said the magic words, 'quit working,' in that sweet sweet way'' (Bell, 1973, pp. 81–82).

Gradually she stopped seeing her friends. She began to live his life. ''I was not aware of any resentment, but I began to see what happened to me. I relied on him for every dollar. Sometimes I had to beg for money. We went to Brazil where he was producing *The Sandpit Generals* and I did the dirty work, the typing, the office routine. I put on weight and lost my vivaciousness. I was becoming a dullard, not the woman I was before. I lost my backbone. All my roots were gone and I was frightened.'' Her dependence on her husband was painful and humiliating. In time she got a divorce and resumed her own career.

The loneliness wrought by the separation from one's imaginative and creative processes characterizes corporate life. The exigencies of corporate conformity require the renunciation of those simple pleasures that come from being a little wild, a bit eccentric—from doing one's own thing. The pressure of having to appear mature, cooperative, and conservative necessitates abandonment of play-fulness and far-out behavior. For husband *or* wife to indulge in any of these might jeopardize his status and job. They are given up dutifully—and painfully. Ideally new pleasures might replace the old, new gratifications might be substituted for now inappropriate ones. But there is no guarantee that this does or can happen. As so many older people sadly reflect, nature seems to frown on both regeneration and innovation.

Corporate executives may be paying heavily in little suspected ways for the loneliness that their worklife style imposes on them, like through the stresses generated by uprooting. Less specific but just as dangerous in the long run is their addiction to tobacco and alcohol which is quietly exacting a far higher toll in illness and death than heroin in all the ghettos of America. Also the suicide rate of middle-aged men is greater than that of women, and more management men go mad than are ever reported. The need to live lives of rootlessness without strong community ties, to produce and succeed often at the expense of wives and children, and to work in an atmosphere of chronic distrust and suspiciousness of both competitors and their own team have had brutalizing effects on character and ego.

After years of adherence to *machismo* behavior without truly belonging to a family or supportive community, it is little wonder if later in life the alert and cunning executive develops into a pathetic, paranoid personality. What has happened in essence is that his loneliness, part-ly chosen perhaps but partly forced on him as a condition of his success, has overwhelmed him. Quixotically, if such a man seeks psychiatric help, he frequently presents the complaint that he has been betrayed by—of all people—his wife. And typically, as in the following example, the wife's paramour is named as a good friend and superior at work (Seidenberg, 1967).

In the case of this patient, the circumstances of his life had changed, and the fragile equilibrium by which he lived was seriously disturbed by events a person would ordinarily be expected to deal with. His children were now grown, contemplating marriage. Younger people were coming up in the business, and his position was becoming insecure. He was getting short of breath and had a dizzy spell now and then; his friends were dying of heart disease; his prowess, mental, physical, and sexual, was waning.

His mental health had shown signs of strain at various points in his life, but nothing had led him to seek help. As a child he had suffered night terrors and bedwetting. At puberty he had become panicky at the sight of his newly growing pubic hair. In his late adolescence he had had the feeling that he might have cancer of the throat. During his college years there had been a period of several months of worry that his studying might lead to blindness. Several more brief periods of nervousness during his marriage had occurred. He was usually aloof and restrained in his relations with his wife, but he sentimentalized about his children; he had cried at their birthdays and graduations—his babies were growing up.

He looked back on his childhood as completely happy, and therefore no inquiry was "needed" in this area. His parents had been good to him; he had had only feelings of love for his younger sister. As far as he was concerned, his chief misery had started a year earlier, with his "heartbreak" about his wife and his purported best friend. There never had been and there was not now anything wrong with his mind. Of course he was now nervous and couldn't sleep at night. But who wouldn't be nervous to the point of contemplating suicide if confronted by the agony of such a conspiracy?

Perhaps this man's difficulty was that he had lived long enough for his destiny to catch up with him. If he had died five years earlier, he would have concluded his life a successful individual, with the praise and love of those around him. His name would have been untarnished. Now he had run out of fuel, and he was a pitiable creature, bringing humiliation to himself, his wife, and his children, who were both victims and witnesses of his fall.

Although he was brought down by the rigors of middle age, the roots of his difficulties lay in his formative years. The agonies of childhood, with grave hostilities against and alienation from his parents and his sister, were buried under conventional, acceptable sentiments. He loved happy thoughts and covered his memories with happy, gaily colored wrapping paper. We can only speculate what fantasies of betrayal, infidelity, abandonment, and humiliation he had suffered in that "most happy" home of his childhood. Perhaps it is unfair to do this type of retrospective construction for verification of theory, as psychiatrists do. But it would be naive to believe that this person's troubles were born today. As Santayana said, those who cannot remember the past are condemned to repeat it.

We return to the question of why this man should want to create a world of torment to live in, one in which he was cuckolded and rejected instead of one in which he was loved and respected. Without going into the technicalities, suffice it to say that, in general, he gained relief from lifelong, pent-up, tormenting hostility and rage by creating a *deus ex machina* that cleansed him to pure innocence: the complete perfidy of those who purported to love him. In his role as victim of his wife and best friend, he established that the unholy alliance of woman and man now ruined his life as another union of woman and man had in the past. With such an alignment of tyranny against him, how could he reasonably be expected to function with the dignity and grace of a man of responsibility?

The sense of declining power in his business life added to his isolation. He felt he was losing the respect of others and was being reduced to an inanimate object—deadwood. Few people are lonelier than the man who fails in his work. If he does not succumb to some psychosomatic illness, he may become paranoid, alcoholic, or suicidal. Without success or achievement, the stress of his competitive existence inevitably overwhelms him.

In the real world the patient's importance was lessening. But how did he achieve importance in his created world of perfidy? Strangely enough he had a feeling of personal exaltation that of all the women available, the boss had chosen his wife for his paramour. The president of a large corporation, apparently happily married, a pillar in the community, was risking everything to carry on an affair with his wife! Even if she was a scoundrel, he now had proof that his wife, despite her age and plainness, was a choice woman whom a man of importance would pursue at great risk. Although in fancied defeat, he had the satisfaction of feeling that he had lost a prize to the best of competitors.

Cases like this one are far from rare in clinical practice. More often than not the husband maintains the delusion of his wife's infidelity in spite of massive evidence to the contrary. He hires detectives; their reports are negative. He examines her underclothes for telling spots; there have never been any. If he makes his obsessive suspicions known, her protestations of innocence and the pleas of friends, relatives, and children avail nothing. In just this way did Shakespeare's King Leontes convince himself that his wife had betrayed him with his old friend Polixenes on the single ground that Polixenes had agreed to extend his visit when invited to do so by the queen.

The loneliness that corporate wives universally complain of covers a panoply of feelings, fears, and frustrations that they have neither the rhetoric nor the courage to articulate. "Loneliness" becomes the acceptable word, meaning something entirely different for each woman: "Being away from my familiar surroundings has made me lonely." "My husband's being away so much leaves me lonely." "It's lonely when my children go off to school." "I have no one to talk to, no one to cook for, no one to go to a movie with." "I'm frightened at night."

Left without human companionship a person feels abandoned, a particular form of deprivation that taxes any human being. Yet there is more to this feeling than what results from the departure or absence of the other. In considering adult women who suffer "loneliness," it will not do to label them "children" or "spoiled" or "hysterical."

It is disconcerting to read in *Today's Health* that the Dartnell Corporation has learned, apparently from "experts," that the distress wives suffer is due to their emotional immaturity (Howes, 1970). We are told, therefore, that when a woman feels trapped with her home, children, and husband, and "when sitters become a problem, it is easy for boredom, loneliness and worry to overtake her." In other words the woman's discontent is of her own doing; she had better overcome her childishness for the good of husband and corporation. Instead of being of help to her psychologically, such a message has the effect of increasing her self-doubt and self-hate when the very opposite is desperately needed by this often perplexed and overwhelmed person.

After diagnosing the lonely woman as being emotionally immature, Howes catalogs some "practical" measures in case she is also a worrier: buy a dog for protection, install an extra lock system, and buy electric garage doors. All these plus other devices to allay the fears of apprehensive wives suggest that the dangers lurk from without. It would appear that rather than lessening anxiety, these measures have the effect of increasing it. Such devices can only add credence to irrational fears and fantasies.

The real dangers that women feel are far more complex than can be represented by an intruder. Calling a woman names, psychiatric or other, and locking her in a fortress against purported external dangers may succeed in increasing her self-doubts to the point where she may worry about her sanity. Such "helpfulness" does not address the real problems, as Seidenberg (1960) illustrates in the following cases.

A 26-year-old married woman, a teacher by profession, was referred to me from an adjoining community by her family doctor for an emergency consultation. She came with her husband, who, in his desire to be completely helpful, wished to sit in on the interview and was chagrined when I told him that this was not necessary. The patient was an attractive young woman whose features were distorted by an expression of abject fear. She had a wide-eyed stare that had led physicians to think she might be suffering from a glandular disorder. But thorough examinations proved to be negative.

She stated that in the past six months she had become anxious and depressed and was apprehensive that she was losing her mind and would be committed to the large mental hospital in the vicinity. She reported no current problems other than possibly the possessive demands of her mother. These upset her at times, but they were nothing new. She was very satisfied with her marriage of five years and described her husband as loving, devoted, and now utterly distressed by her unhappiness. He would spare no amount of time and money to get her "over this thing." He had been married once before for a brief period and had suffered a great hurt from the failure of that union. He had extracted the promise from the patient not to refer to that period in his life again, to let it be a completely closed book. This aroused the patient's curiosity, but she abided by her promise.

After this cursory explanation of the current situation, she immediately turned to the facts of her upbringing and early life, which she believed were the causes of her present difficulties. The younger of two children—her brother was three years her senior—she had been indulged because she had been born with a club foot. This had caused a great deal of consternation to the family, but successive operations had corrected the malformation almost completely; there was no noticeable residue. This had entailed financial hardship for the parents, but it had also meant that between the ages of 5 and 11, she had been hospitalized away from home for periods of up to six months. These separations had been very difficult for her, and until recent years when she had come to understand the beneficial results of her hospitalization, she had been bitterly hostile and antagonistic toward her mother for having left her alone in a strange environment. Her bitterness had changed to gratitude when she had realized that a cousin, now an adult, remained crippled with the same affliction because her parents had not been able ''to part with her'' so that she could undergo corrective surgery.

The patient described her father as a successful businessman who had had to retire in his 50s because he suffered episodes of severe depression and hypochondria. She recalled her mother as having been completely unsympathetic to his plight; she on the contrary had had strong positive feelings for her father. But her mother had had fears of her own, particularly of natural phenomena. Whenever there had been a thunderstorm or lightning at night, she had roused her two children from a sound sleep, taken them downstairs, and huddled with them in the basement of their home. Neither the patient nor her brother had had any such fears and at first were puzzled by this behavior. But in her late adolescence she had also become fearful of these things.

During subsequent interviews the patient told me more of her relationship with her mother—how she had written her every day from college, how she had acceded to her mother's wishes about dating, and yet how comfortable she had actually felt on being a considerable distance away from her. After her marriage, however, her husband had felt that they should live in the same community as her mother, which was also near the farm of his own parents. Here they had both entered into the social activities of the village and were quite popular.

His solicitude and attentiveness to her had earned him the reputation of being a model husband. He fully understood her problems with her mother, he told her, and would do everything he could to help her. To get her partly out of her mother's orbit, he had built a home away from the village on a tract on his own parents' farm. To stay close by her so that he could allay her fears of the dark and of thunder and lightning, he had given up successive jobs that might keep him on the road overnight. He had had large floodlights installed around the house to discourage prowlers and had bought a police dog as further protection. On one occasion his company had promoted him to a job in a larger district in another state, but after some deliberation he had decided against it because it would take the patient away from her job which she enjoyed. His company had discharged him, but this had only increased his feelings of nobility. His religious feelings grew in intensity, in contrast with her own. He built an altar in their bedroom so they might pray together, confiding to her that prayer was his mainstay in living.

In this setting, instead of responding with well-being to her husband's solicitude, she became increasingly depressed and fearful. Certain physical symptoms appeared—pain around her heart and feelings of numbness in her arms and legs. Reassurances from her physician that there was nothing organically wrong made her more fearful since she now felt she couldn't even trust her own senses. Her physician treated her principally with sedatives and tranquilizers, which gave her momentary relief but actually lowered her confidence.

The entire relationship with the physician in fact proved to increase her fearfulness. In dealing with her he violated the principles of confidentiality that he would have adhered to in treating "ordinary" physical disease, probably because he too was frightened by her condition. He reported his impressions to her husband and had many private conversations with him about her. The husband was allowed to call him frequently to inquire whether certain activities might be upsetting to her. All this of course made her doubt her own ability to get along.

The final blow, which reduced her to panic, was the regimen of tranquilizers her doctor put her on. Although she got some relief from the medication, the overall effect was to eliminate her last vestige of confidence that she could properly evaluate and deal with things around her. It was when her condition further deteriorated on tranquilizers that she was sent for psychiatric help. The referring physician was very shaken by his experience with this patient and later in an informal communication indicated that he finally realized he was an unwitting accomplice to her husband's machinations.

At this point it was only in the area of her job that she had confidence in her capabilities and judgment. She resisted the suggestions of her husband, friends, and physician that she take a leave of absence. They claimed that perhaps she was working too hard and that the children at school were making her nervous.

In the early months of her marriage, she had enjoyed sexual relations with her husband. After they had moved to his family's homestead, however, sex became fearful and revolting. It made her very ashamed to react this way to a husband who was so kind to her. Her husband had responded to her state by becoming even more solicitous and attentive. Now he would never leave her alone at home; he would forsake any business trip to be with her. When she had expressed her fear of losing her mind, he had suggested that she must confide in him, that married people should keep nothing from each other, reassuring her that no matter what she told him, he would understand. This had puzzled her further since she did not know what she could tell him or what he expected to hear.

These were the data the young woman gave in the initial interviews. We decided to begin psychotherapy. Two years of weekly sessions proved to be successful with her. In the early hours of treatment, there was a barrage of questions from her and, through her, from her husband. Should she continue in her present job? Could she drive alone? Should her husband leave her alone overnight? Should she tell her mother she was seeing a psychiatrist? Should she see a doctor about her palpitations?

I handled each of these questions simply but firmly by taking the traditional neutral position of the therapist. I indicated to her that these were issues to be decided not by her mother, her therapist, or her husband but by herself. When she asked whether she could have a prescription for medication in case she suddenly became nervous or weak, I told her that if this happened, she would deal with it using her own resources, just as she had done during previous stressful times like her separation from home and the death of her father.

As was to be expected, the patient was at first distrustful of this type of treatment and interpreted it as indifference and unconcern. The loudest complaints, however, were from the husband, who declared he would not stand by and watch his wife suffer without medical relief. He would get to the bottom of this and would take her to the finest clinics in the country. But the patient herself resisted this, and the treatment was not interrupted. Appeals for emergency appointments when she felt panicky were refused. Likewise telephone calls for reassurance and for confirmation of appointments were discouraged.

In due course the patient came to grips with a most pertinent truth: that in her daily affairs she alone had the necessary information to make decisions and to act on them. All others—therapist, husband, mother, physician—acted in bad faith if they attempted to take over this function, even if she requested or demanded it of them.

This understanding led the patient to abandon her preoccupation with the past and to examine her present predicament. She saw that she was expected to play the helpless role far beyond actual need. Her feeling of gratitude toward her husband was replaced by a more realistic appraisal of the symbiosis they were involved in. And finally, she allowed herself to understand her husband's emotional difficulties and how they pertained to her. She could then see that he also had a fear of the dark and of being away from home and, most important of all, a need to be near his own parents. He was ashamed of these immaturities and projected them onto her. He hid his own need for parental protection by taking every opportunity to point up her helplessness, real or fancied. She was now angered by the fact that his principal words of endearment had been, "You're my little girl."

Now, without pills in her purse, she actively manages her own affairs. She remains at home alone. She no longer fears going insane or ending up in a mental hospital. A beneficial estrangement has taken place in the marriage, and roles and direction are being reappraised. The husband may enter therapy because of the new stresses placed on him by the realignment.

It is when the self is lost or communication with the self is severed that "the other" becomes so desperately important. Being alone then becomes a particularly fearful experience because there is literally no one at home. The house is empty because the person is. That is the tragic irony of the corporate wife's plight. She is scolded for being fearful and dependent; yet she is literally picked because she is dependent. Selflessness is deemed her most admirable attribute, but when she exhibits the inevitable effects of loss of self, she is labeled troublesome and lacking emotional maturity.

The entire corporate life style encourages her to live solely through and by her husband, while extinguishing personal aspiration or ambition. Any interest in or pleasure with other people is prohibited. And she is not to be fearful or lonely when he is away.

The mad rush to the suburbs has added to her miseries by cutting her off from the civic and cultural centers. The suburbs are like isolation wards, separated from all but the most superficial contact with fellow human beings and from the vitality of the city. Running away from the blacks and the poor, we have created suburban social starvation. We have actually taken pride in the distance we get from community and culture. To avoid being mugged we have accepted an isolation that probably produces more mind damage than could any mugger.

The corporate wife does not suffer this deprivation alone. It is foisted on children, who are located too far from public transportation to get to a library or museum, let alone a movie or playground. Any sense of independence is stifled by this lack of mobility. The enormous chauffeuring burden is placed on the wife, who later wonders why her children are so dependent. Separated from "live" human beings, real art, and civic activities, the mother and children turn to television, and gradually the substitute—the medium—comes to be preferred to real experiences. How audacious of the television announcer to say (as is required by law), "The program originates *live* from New York City."

In his perceptive book *The Pursuit of Loneliness* (1970), psychologist Philip E. Slater writes:

> The emotional and intellectual poverty of the housewife's role is mainly expressed in the almost universal complaint "I get to talking baby talk with no one around all day but the children." . . . The idea of imprisoning each woman alone in a small, self-contained, and architec- turally isolated dwelling is a modern invention dependent on advanced technology. In Moslem societies, for example, the wife may be a prisoner but at least she is not in solitary confinement. In our society the housewife may move freely, but since she has nowhere to go and is not part of anything anyway her prison needs no walls (p. 68).

Of the exodus from the city, Slater observes:

> But the flight to the suburb is in any case self-defeating, its goals subverted by the mass quality of the exodus. The suburban dweller seeks peace, privacy, nature, community and a child-rearing environ- ment which is healthy and culturally optimal. Instead he finds neither the beauty and security of the countryside, the stimulation of the city, nor the stability and sense of community of the small town, and his children are exposed to a cultural deprivation equaling that of any slum child with a television set. Living in a narrow age-graded and class- segregated society, it is little wonder that suburban families have con- tributed so little to the national talent pool in proportion to their members, wealth, and other social advantages (p. 69).

Moreover, as Slater points out, it is the wife who is ultimately left in the suburban trap because the man's work rescues him for most of the week, taking him to the city office, the plant, or on the road meeting real people and challenging problems:

> Consider the suburban living pattern: husbands go to the city and participate in the 20th century, while their wives are assigned the hopeless task of trying to act out a rather pathetic bucolic phantasy oriented toward the 19th. Men in their jobs accept change: even welcome and foster it—however threatening and disruptive it may seem. . . . Such men tend to make of their wives an island of stability in a sea of change. The wife becomes a kind of memento, like the bit of earth that the immigrant brings from the old country and puts under his bed (p. 74).

William V. Shannon calls the suburban housewives "the new servant class," pointing out that with the family's second car, "they spend two to three hours every day as involuntary chauffeurs because there is no other way to get their children to music lessons, dental appointments, or friends' houses" (Shannon, 1972). And this is but one aspect of the service role the suburban housewife is expected to play. The physical care and management of the ever-enlarging, status-proving home becomes her responsibility, and she can no longer find the inexpensive help of yesteryear. Her time is spent on things rather than on people.

In sociologist Alice Rossi's study of young married college graduates, 65 percent of the women reported they conversed with their husbands less than two hours a day (Rossi, 1972). Similarly, research shows that full-time homemakers spend an average of less than two hours a day in direct interaction with children. Women thereby devote to household chores four times as many hours as they do to interaction with husbands or children. Rossi concludes that it is house care that keeps women at home more than child care. A great deception has been perpetrated against suburban women: while they might accept their isolation because they think suburban living enhances communication with mate and children, they find that most of their day and energies are spent on menial, boring, and uncreative tasks—no different from the existence of serving maids of the past.

Even modern technocratic gains have worked against women. It was the expectation for instance that modern appliances would so simplify domestic chores that a woman would be liberated from the household grind that was her grandmother's lot. Studies have shown that the very opposite is the case: the more automatic appliances in a home, the greater—not the fewer—the number of hours of regular household work. For although the amount of physical energy expended per task may be lessened, women have been brainwashed into standards of cleanliness that keep them chronically and inextricably bound. A home economist lamented to me that she met terrible resistance from women to whom she suggested that bed linen didn't have to be changed more often than once a week. One woman put fresh sheets on the bed daily; most changed them twice a week. Some candidly asked just what they were expected to do with the saved time!

It is not wide of the mark to say that such busy work attempts to fill the vacuum made by the absence of meaningful activity and the deprivations wrought by isolation and estrangement from human contact. And loneliness as well as stupefaction inevitably ensues when one is reduced to substituting routinized and contrived activities for the interpersonal and creative endeavors for which the mind was meant. Loneliness can be construed as the dread that results from the loss or diminution of parts of one's self that formerly gave pride and hope. Can these be derived from changing sheets every day?

It is this hierarchy of deprivations that makes the corporate wife appear so pathetically unresourceful. She is lonely, afraid of the night, and lost when her husband is away. To the resourceful and energized person, to be left alone is to be given the blessing of freedom. One becomes free of the onerous aspects of continuous togetherness. Rather than producing loneliness, being alone might leave one free to pursue personal projects, unread books, and cooling friendships. But as existentialist Sartre remarked, probably having the unresourceful in mind, freedom is a curse.

One way of dispelling loneliness is to become a "kitchen sink" drinker. According to the National Council on Alcoholism, there are probably 5 million alcoholics in the United States today, with a ratio of 2 men for every woman. A decade ago the ration was 5 to 1 (*The New York Times*, April 29, 1973).

Drinking in the suburbs is slightly easier than elsewhere, but the suburban housewife has to deal with certain problems, such as how to participate in car pools without causing accidents. One Connecticut woman reported, "I always take the early half of the afternoon car pool because I know I can't handle it later in the day."

Money helps mask the problem. "In a community like ours, it's easier to cover up," said Marie Fitzsimmons, director of the Alcoholism Guidance Center in Westport, Connecticut, a high-income community. "There's money for liquor, for psychiatry, for a housekeeper, all of which may work against coming to grips with the reality of alcoholism."

While the majority of corporate wives in our country continue to follow traditional patterns, increasing numbers are not only hearing but heeding the echoes of Women's Liberation or the promptings of their own independently discovered sense of loss of self. One such woman was featured in a *Life* magazine story (March 17, 1972) of what was termed a drop-out wife. She is a 35-year-old college graduate, mother of three, wife of a "middle-level" business executive. With no great animosity or differences between her and her husband, without frequent separations, and with no money problems, Wanda Adams, finding her life increasingly "frustrating and suffocating," wanted out in her fourteenth year of marriage. There were no villains. It seemed a matter of personal growth. She is seeking this by going back to school and working.

After her separation from her husband, she found herself "happier than I ever was. In spite of the loneliness, the garbage of survival, and the occasional feeling of not wanting to be independent, I like myself better and I like other people better." Still on friendly terms with her husband, she neither asks for nor receives alimony. She lives with her daughter, the oldest child, in a commune arrangement with other women; the two boys are with their father.

Although she says that her life is now full of hassles, Ms. Adams finds solace in their being *her* hassles. She looks back at her married life as neither rewarding nor fulfilling. She was completely absorbed in her family role, with little outside life. "Our friends were always Don's business friends or friends of ours from college."

Her husband has acted as "mother and father" to the boys and has done remarkably well. We read the heading over pictures showing him doing household chores: "Unsuspected joys for a lone father." However, he enjoyed being married and contemplates marrying again. In the separation he has found that caring for his children (for the first time) has given him a sense of closeness he had never felt before. Parenthood after all is alien to most fathers. Many who allow themselves to fulfill the role reap enjoyable rewards.

What are we to make of this story? New sensationalism? The exception that again proves the rule? The story of the Adamses is and will be atypical of how corporate wives in general will behave. Perhaps it is unfortunate that more will not follow in the search.

But this story, along with the movies of recent years, *A Woman Under the Influence, Diary of a Mad Housewife,* and *The Happy Ending,* are signs of the times. They depict dissatisfaction with, and alternatives to, the conventional roles of married life while foregoing tirades against the tyrannies of a husband. This is an era when wives are not railing against villains. On the contrary there is a growing recognition that both marital partners may be trapped by institutionalized expectations that are less than salutary for either, though the wife is more likely to start the rebellion (the greater sufferer understandably feeling more of the pressure). Wanda Adams must be endowed with a remarkable and admirable optimism to have dropped out of a pattern of living (14 years and three children later) to which most wives become reconciled and endure silently.

Brought up and educated to know what one's "normal" role is, performing the duties of wife and mother for years, and obtaining the security and gratifications that accrue from the conventional life make the task of seeking independence no easy matter. That many fall on their face is easy to document.

While some studies find that divorced women are happier than married women, others show that anxiety and depression in divorced women are high. Conditioned from birth to think they should be married, many rush into a frantic search for another man to marry. Because they are actively trained to avoid independence, it is very difficult for them to strive for autonomy, the natural birthright of self-respecting people. When they find Mr. Right, they hope he (unlike the previous, unsatisfactory husband) will truly communicate with them, that alienation will not be the order of the day this time.

Interestingly enough, though a dislike of independence is culturally inadmissible for a man, there are research findings that married men are happier than divorced men, perhaps indicating that marriage, though popularly regarded as the goal of every woman, is really an institution suited to, and beloved by, men.

The loneliness that comes with marriage is particularly severe because there is the expectation of the opposite. Since the Romantic period began, people have hoped that marriage would be a bastion against the disappointments of the world and the fears of self-doubt. Loneliness in marriage is particularly painful because one feels betrayed or abandoned, having had such great hopes. That these hopes were unrealistic and foredoomed to disappointment, that no human being can find in one other person all the passion, intellectual stimulation, warmth, and security that make life exciting as well as safe, makes it no less shattering when they fail.

A colleague, Thomas Szasz, sounds a caveat for those who would live through others: "A person cannot make another happy, but he can make him unhappy. This is the main reason why there is more unhappiness than happiness in the world" (Szasz, 1973, p. 52). Being lonely when one is single is an acceptable idea; being lonely when one is actually eating, sleeping, and dwelling with another is indeed alarming. We can then understand the meaning of Chekhov's seeming contradiction: "If you are afraid of loneliness, don't marry."

10

*Loneliness of
the Long-Distance Mother*

PAULINE BART

I don't want to be alone, and I'm going to be alone, and my children
will go their way and get married—of which I'm wishing for it—and
then I'll still be alone, and I got more and more alone, and more and
more alone.

—Sara

MIDDLE AGE is a time of physiological, psychological, and sociological
changes in women, just as the adolescent period is for teenagers. At one
time the stress thought to characterize both groups was considered
universal since it was associated with the physiological changes taking
place during those stages of the life cycle. In order to test the Sturm und
Drang hypothesis concerning adolescents, Margaret Mead went to
Samoa, where she found what she believed to be an adolescence free
from stress. As there was no reason to assume physiological differences
between Americans and Samoans, she attributed adolescent stress in
Western nations to the effects of culture. Analogously, I went to other
preindustrial cultures (unfortunately only through their anthropological records in the New Haven Human Relations Area Files) to
study middle-aged women, and in addition I studied middle-aged
American women in mental hospitals. I wanted to test the widely held

Reprinted from *Women: A Feminist Perspective*, 2nd edition, by permission of
Mayfield Publishing Company. Copyright © 1979 by Jo Freeman.

assumption that menopausal depression relates to the kinds of roles available to women who are finished child-bearing.

Unfortunately, data on the menopause were scarce; they were available for only five of the 30 societies I studied (when there was a woman investigator). However, there was information on postmaternal roles and some material on the relative status of women in these cultures. The data made it possible to determine whether women's status increased or decreased in middle age.

In every culture, there is a favored stage of life cycle of women. If a woman has a high status when she is young, her power and prestige can be expected to decline as she matures. And the reverse is equally true. Rather than invoking the usual image of society as a pyramid or ladder, one can think of society as a social ferris wheel (Bart, 1969). In view of this model, I attempted to correlate cultural and sociocultural factors in each society with information on the improvement or decline of women's status with age, paying special attention to roles of postmenopausal women.

Most of the cultures I investigated had definite roles that women were expected to fill after they were through with childbearing and rearing. These roles varied from society to society and included, in addition to the wife role, those of: grandmother, economic producer and property holder, mother and mother-in-law, participator in government, performer of magic and ritual, and daughter of aged parents. The roles bringing higher status were those of grandmother, mother and mother-in-law, and participator in government. The available economic role for women in these cultures was restricted to the performance of hard work of little prestige, except in the relatively few matrilineal societies.

Using as indices freedom (especially from taboos), respect, special privileges, and power and influence, I found that in 17 of the 30 cultures women registered *higher* status after menopause than before. In 12 of the 30 they had more respect, in eight they had more power and influence, in seven they had more special privileges, and in four they had greater freedom. In 11 cultures middle-aged women registered neither an increase nor a decrease in social status on any of these indices. In only two cultures, (cultures in a number of ways similar to our own—the Marquesans and the Trobrianders), did women have less power and influence in middle age than when they were younger.

The cross-cultural study therefore indicated that middle age was not usually considered an especially stressful period for women. Consequently, explanations of such stress based wholly on biological change can be rejected. Middle age need not be fraught with difficulty.

I discovered, however, that for women in many cultures facing mid-life problems, the kinship group is a major buffer. The survey showed that a woman's status in middle age is improved if her culture provides a strong tie to family and kin rather than a strong marital tie; an extended family system rather than a nuclear family system; an institutionalized grandmother role rather than a loosely defined one; a mother-in-law role rather than the absence of a role toward a son-in-law or daughter-in-law; and residence patterns keeping children close to the family of orientation (their parents). Thus, as Table 1 summarizes, women's changed status after childbearing can be clearly associated with the structural arrangements and cultural values of a society.

Turning to American society, we can begin to see why there so frequently is stress for women in middle age. In each instance, except for the mother-child bond which in our society is strong but nonreciprocal, American women fall on the right side of the chart, which denotes a decline in the status of women in middle age. For American women whose lives have not been child-centered and whose strong marital ties continue, as for those whose children set up residence near their mothers, the transition to middle age may be buffered. However, even child-centered women claimed that the relationship with their children is nonreciprocal and that they are only entitled to "respect." Once a child reaches maturity in our culture, she/he needs only to honor her/his mother on Mother's Day (unless she is widowed, in which case she/he may do more). Thus for those women who have relied on their maternal role or "glamour" role, middle age may be a difficult and lonely stage in the life cycle. Our emphasis on youth and our stipulation that mothers-in-law not interfere and grandmothers not meddle, make the middle years a time of stress for many American women.[1] This is exemplified by the following two cases selected from my interviews with middle-aged American women in mental institutions.

---

[1] See, however, Neugarten's (1968) work on healthy middle-aged women.

TABLE 1
Cultural Variables Affecting Status of Middle-Aged Women

Raised Status	Lowered Status
Strong tie to family of orientation and kin	Marital tie (tie to family of procreation) stronger than tie to family of orientation
Extended family system	Nuclear family system
Reproduction important	Sex an end in itself
Strong mother-child relationship reciprocal in later life	Weak maternal bond; adult-oriented culture
Institutionalized grandmother role	Noninstitutionalized grandmother role; grandmother role not important
Institutionalized mother-in-law role	Noninstitutionalized mother-in-law role; mother-in-law doesn't train daughter-in-law
Extensive menstrual taboos	Minimal menstrual taboos
Matrilocal, patrilocal, or duo-local residence	Residence that isolates women from kin and grown children, e.g., neo-local, avuncular
Age valued over youth	Youth valued over age

SARA: THE MARTYR MOTHER

In her early sixties, Sara has been admitted to a mental hospital for the second time. At first her condition was diagnosed as "psychophysiological (psychosomatic) gastrointestinal reaction," but with more knowledge, the doctors diagnosed an "involutional (menopausal) depression."

Sara is divorced and in what has been called the "empty nest" stage of life. She represents an almost "ideal" type because she suffers from nearly all of the problems that can beset an aging woman in our society. Sara states she was rejected by her mother, and then successively by her husband, children, and grandchildren. Now she is physically ill, has no access to transportation, and is unable to work or participate in voluntary activities that could give her life meaning. She needs to keep busy, yet her activities are severely restricted. She must live alone, yet she is afraid of being alone.

Sara has had many physical problems including arthritis and kidney trouble. At the time I saw her she had severely swollen feet. Her medical record shows that her frightened, depressed state was induced by fear of living in an apartment in Las Vegas where she felt abandoned and unprotected. This feeling has been present ever since she was asked to move out of her son's home in order to placate the anger of her daughter-in-law who felt she caused trouble by trying to absorb all of her son's time and sympathy. Her psychiatrist characterized Sara as hypochondriacal and self-pitying.

I asked her one question and she immediately launched into a long description of her troubles: her fears of being alone, the failure of medication to alleviate these fears, her physical illnesses, and more:

> I first of all have a lot of fears, and it isn't very easy I guess . . . to do something about it. And . . . these fears just follow me, and just push me in the wrong direction. I'm not really doing what I want to do. I want to go one way, but it just seems to take me the other way and I can't control them. . . the minute nobody's here, and those fears start working with me. Everything seems closed up, and everything looks dark.

Sara was born in New Jersey. Her father was born in Russia and her mother in Austria. She told me that as a child she felt she was "really nothing." Her father died when she was about six, but she always felt close to him. Even now she believes that if he had lived

> He would have always made me feel that I'm not alone, and that someone loves me. I am very strong for love. I feel that this is a very big thing to me, and I wasn't very fortunate because mother didn't give it to me, and I was hungry for it, and when I married I also thought it was going to be a wonderful thing because somebody is going to care, but my marriage never turned out good.

Following Sara's marriage, a son was born, and while he was a baby, Sara's husband started a produce store. She would go to the store four miles from their home at four o'clock in the morning in a horse-drawn wagon, holding the baby in her arms and feeding him: "I worked hard my whole life and I thought that if I worked for him he would—he would be good to me, but he took all that good . . . he didn't feel that I was human, too.''

A daughter was born, but the marriage did not improve. Sara's husband was constantly unfaithful, and apparently contracted venereal disease. Since he had to work during the night, he refused to let her have company during the day or evening when he wanted to rest and sleep. He was rude to her friends. And ''. . . even with sex he was very, very rude about it'':

> He was concerned . . . about himself, nothing about me. . . . He had another woman that he took out, and I found out about it, but I didn't let on. I thought, well if that's a weakness, maybe he'll overcome it. Let me try and, uh, cope with it enough to see if I couldn't get him to reason . . . maybe later I could. But I couldn't. He would always run away when I wanted to reason with him. He would slam the door and go away for a few days, come back and throw the dirty clothes in the bathroom hamper, and everything was coming to him, but nothing was coming to me.

Years later, when her son was in the army but her daughter was still at home, Sara decided she could not ''take'' her marriage anymore. She divorced her husband. After the divorce she became very frightened about having to be on her own. Although she had a job at the time, this did little to reduce her insecurity. In addition, she was ''very hurt'' at having had to get a divorce. This feeling was heightened whenever she sublet her apartment; she said her tenants made her feel it wasn't ''nice'' to divorce. It never occurred to her to consult a psychiatrist, either during her marriage or immediately after her divorce because, ''At those times if you went to a psychiatrist people thought you were insane.''

She became physically ill immediately after the divorce, and had gall bladder surgery followed by anemia. Nine years after the divorce, she underwent a hysterectomy. Ever since this operation she believes she has been ''entirely different.'' When I asked her in what way, she wasn't specific at first. She reiterated what she had been telling me of her desire to be loved, and added, ''It is a death to be alone.'' Then she spontaneously returned to my question of how the hysterectomy had changed her, saying, ''To me it feels like Sara died.''

Sara has four grandchildren. When they were very small she took care of them, but now that they are older she is expected to leave them alone. Their lack of concern and respect hurts her, although she loves them "very dearly." Some years ago, on the advice of her doctor and at the invitation of her daughter-in-law, she left her home in New Jersey and went to Las Vegas to reap the benefits of the Nevada climate and to live with, and help care for, her son's family. But when her grandchildren matured, Sara was no longer needed. She reported that, rather than tell her that they preferred to live alone, her daughter-in-law tried to drive her out with unkind treatment: "She just treated me so that—it just made me go. You know what I mean? You can treat a person enough to make them feel they want to go."

At the time she left her son's home in Las Vegas her daughter in New Jersey was expecting a baby, so she returned to New Jersey to help her. Before she left, her son told her that if she wanted to come back she would have to "go for herself" (i.e., live alone). He pointed out that perhaps she hadn't realized that living with them was a "temporary thing." Sara believes her daughter-in-law pressured him to do this. When she returned to New Jersey she tried to contact friends to see if she could remain in the East after her daughter gave birth, but no one was willing to help her.

She returned to Las Vegas and tried to find work as a saleslady, but this was possible only during the Christmas rush: "It's very difficult in that town to get a job at my age, because it's considered an attraction and they . . . hire the young girls . . . I couldn't get no work and I was pretty disappointed because I felt that there was nothing else in Las Vegas that I could do."

In Las Vegas, she had formerly belonged to the sisterhood of the local synagogue and enjoyed attending services and meetings, and doing volunteer work. Now, living alone, she needed transportation so that she could participate in these activities. Her dependence on her son for transportation became another source of conflict. Furthermore, her daughter-in-law refused to find volunteer activities for her, commenting that social groups needed "young blood."

I asked her at the interview if she had been happier before her children left home, and she said, "Yes and no. Because my husband never let any of us enjoy it." When I asked specifically what changes in her own feelings of self-worth she had noticed since her children left, she replied, "I don't . . . I don't feel like . . . I don't feel at all that I'm wanted. I just feel like nothing." Then I asked what was the worst thing that had ever happened to her. She replied:

When I had to break up and be by myself, and be alone, and I'm just—
I really feel that I'm not—not only not loved but not even liked
sometimes by my own children. . . . They could respect me. If . . . if
they can't say good why should they . . . hurt my feelings and make me
cry, and then call me a crybaby, or tell me that I ought to know better or
something like that. My worst thing is that I'm alone, I'm not wanted,
nobody interests themselves in me. Nobody cares.

Sara couldn't think of the best thing that had ever happened to her,
but the best times in her life, she said, were when she was pregnant
and when her children were babies: "I was glad that God gave
me . . . the privilege of being a mother and—and I loved them. In
fact, I wrapped my love so much around them." She felt grateful to
her husband since, "If it weren't for him there wouldn't be the
children. *They were my whole life, that was it.*"

JEANNE: THE STOIC

A divorced Catholic, Jeanne was diagnosed at the time of the interview as a "psychotic depressive." She is fifty-eight years old and has
had three previous psychiatric hospitalizations for depression, one
twelve years ago following her divorce from her husband. Like Sara,
she has experienced rejection from close family members. In contrast
to Sara, however, she did not express hostility or anger toward them
in the interview.

The breakup of her marriage, according to her psychiatrist, was
precipitated by Jeanne's having undergone a mastectomy for breast
cancer and also by her husband's infidelity. Her psychiatrist was also
of the opinion that her present hospitalization was partly triggered by
her son's graduation from law school because "a large part of herself
was involved in helping him get through and she lost this mission with
his graduation." After graduation, her son moved to another city
about one hundred miles away and he has not come to visit her since
her hospitalization.

Jeanne had also been separated from this son when he was a
teenager and had wanted to go to live with another family which had
two boys. Jeanne let him go because "I thought he'd be much happier
in that environment so I approved of it." When asked if this was a difficult thing for her to do she replied, "No, it wasn't difficult at all. I
didn't think of myself. I thought only of him."

INTERVIEWER: Well, what made you think he'd be happier in that situation?

JEANNE: Well, I don't know, just living alone with your mother, uh, it's kinda trying. You feel you should stay home I think, and uh, I didn't want him to be confined staying with me, and I wanted him to have a normal life.

Although Sara and the other Jewish mothers in the sample were characterized by self-sacrifice for their children, it is hard to imagine that they would have gone so far as to let an only son live with nonrelations except in an emergency situation. Like Sara, Jeanne expressed close feelings toward her children, but unlike Sara and the other Jewish mothers in the sample, Jeanne did not elaborate her answers concerning her relationship with her children during the interview.

Jeanne's older child, a daughter whom she has not seen for eleven years, is married and living in another part of the United States. She felt wonderful about her daughter's marriage and approves of her son-in-law. Her grandchildren have not made much difference in her life and she has apparently not had an opportunity or has not chosen to enter an active grandmother role.

Except for her sister whom she sees about once a week, Jeanne has no close relationships and feels she must be employed to be happy. She states, "I couldn't sit at home day after day. I'd think of myself as being no good at all. I had to get out and do something." Jeanne felt "important" when her children were at home and said that her life was happier when she was "occupied" with them. She also feels that she ought to be independent and take care of herself and expects "nothing" from her children.

When her son went to a law school close to home, he lived in the dorms. When asked how often he came home, she said:

Sometimes twice a week, sometimes once a week, sometimes once every two weeks. Depending if he was studying for an exam or if he had a date. . . . It was understood, you know he wouldn't be around. I wasn't anxious, overanxious to see him, and he wasn't overanxious to—we sort of grew away from that. He'd come home every day, or I'll feel bad and uh. . . .

INTERVIEWER: You said you grew away from it. Was there a time when you had to see him every day?

JEANNE: No. When he first left I had a little anxiety. Now he's in _____, doesn't write. As long as they're happy, I'm happy.

ROLE LOSS AND DEPRESSION

Sara was typical in many ways of the twenty middle-aged women I interviewed who were in mental hospitals in Los Angeles. All but two of these women were depressed. I had predicted that the Jewish mother, especially if she were a housewife, would find the departure of children most stressful, since the departure of children, according to my hypothesis, is most difficult for women whose primary role is that of mother. The devotion of the Jewish woman to her children is legendary, and is eulogized in songs and stories. From the widely selling books of such prominent Jewish sons as Philip Roth (*Portnoy's Complaint*, 1967), Bruce J. Friedman (*A Mother's Kisses*, 1964), and Dan Greenburg (*How to be a Jewish Mother*, 1965), we have come to see that the other side of the coin of extreme devotion to children is overprotection, controlling behavior, and the development of a "martyr complex" by the mother. However, such literature about the Jewish mother should not obscure the fact that such double-edged devotion is not their monopoly. Analysis of the epidemiological data, discussed below, indicates that you don't have to be Jewish to be a Jewish mother, but it helps. Whereas Jewish women were more likely than non-Jewish women to have overinvolved or overprotective relationships with their children, that is, those non-Jewish women who had such relationships were almost as likely as Jewish women to be depressed when their children left. Eighty-six percent of Jewish women with such relationships with their children were depressed, compared with 78 percent of the non-Jewish women.

Though both of the women I have described are depressed and lonely, their self-presentations vary. Jeanne is aptly called "the stoic," for she does not complain. Consistent with her self-effacing life style, she speaks a great deal less than Sara. Her rhetoric about her grandchildren is much less effusive than Sara's. It is almost as if the grandchildren are facts to be taken for granted rather than events potentially to give meaning to her life. She spoke of her need to be independent and assumed her children sought independence as well. These factors generally differentiated the Jewish from the non-Jewish women.

When some crucial items in the interview protocols of the institutionalized American women were analyzed, certain relevant factors that had been suggested by the cross-cultural survey began to emerge. These female psychiatric patients did not have a kinship network to turn to in times of trouble. Though they did not believe that their children "owed" them anything, it was clear from the interviews that the Jewish women in particular had expectations of their children that were not being met. None of the institutionalized women were spending significant time caring for their grandchildren, though several had done so when the grandchildren were younger. These women therefore had had to cope with the loss of both their mother and grandmother roles. When asked what they were most proud of, the women said their children. In general, they were least proud of their failure to have happy homes. Most of the women felt they were expected to keep busy and not to "interfere" once their children were grown. They considered their lives lonelier now than when they were younger, and mentioned that they were less busy. This decline in activity, however, was not viewed as an asset; it merely provided them with an opportunity to ruminate about their problems.

Perhaps the item most relevant to the experience of loneliness was the one in which the women were asked to rank seven possible roles in order of importance. The roles were those of: "(1) being a homemaker; (2) taking part in church, club, and community activities; (3) being a companion to my husband; (4) helping my parents (if one or both are living); (5) being a sexual partner to my husband; (6) doing my paying job (if working outside the home); and (7) helping my children."

Significantly, the maternal role—"helping my children"—was most frequently ranked first or second. The role of homemaker was also ranked high. Roles such as "my paying job" and "taking part in church, club, and community activities" were considered unimportant. It appeared, therefore, as if it were precisely those roles that become constricted as women age that these women viewed as important, while the roles that could be expanded—the occupational and organizational roles—were relatively unimportant to them.

All the Jewish women interviewed, as expected, had had overprotective or overinvolved relationships with their children. It was clear that this factor had led to feelings of depression when the children left. The analysis of the interviews also showed that many of the women had severe physical illnesses before their hospitalization for depression, and that in some cases the physical illnesses were associated with the failure of their marriages, since when ill they were unable to meet the expectations of their husbands. A strikingly high proportion of the women had lost their fathers at an early age. Such a loss may have made them vulnerable to depressions and deprived them of the opportunity to learn role models and relationships in an intact family. It also may have led to compensating overinvolvement in the maternal role with subsequent depression when that role was lost. The departure of their children seemed related to the depression of all the "empty nest" mothers, Jewish and non-Jewish alike. The major difference between Jewish and non-Jewish mothers appeared to be the former group's greater verbalization of this feeling.

The interview material lent support to epidemiological findings I had made earlier in examining the records of 533 hospitalized women between the ages of 40 and 59 who had had no previous hospitalization for mental illness. I used five hospitals varying from one upper-class private institution to two state hospitals. However, it seemed as if maternal role loss was important only for the women who were in the "empty nest" stage. In the women with children still at home, depression seemed associated with factors other than the departure of children.The interview material afforded an opportunity for a qualitative approach to depression, and when the intensity of depression was noted it did appear that those women with multiple role loss were more depressed than those with only one role loss.

Contrary to my original hypothesis that women in high status occupations would be less affected by the loss of the maternal role than other women, the epidemiological data showed that women with professional or managerial occupations had a high rate of depression. From the interview material it had also been apparent that the one woman of the twenty with role loss who had had a job considered professional (she was a nurse) was not greatly involved in her profession. Far from considering it a "calling," she had stopped working outside the home during her first marriage, and had become a nurse only after her first divorce. The norms of our society have been such that a woman is not expected to "fulfill" herself through an occupational role, but rather through the traditional feminine roles of housewife and mother. The fourteen women in the epidemiological sample with high status occupations who had experienced maternal role loss were all either unhappily married or divorced. In view of the cultural expectations of a woman and the considerable discrimination, stresses, and role contradictions a woman with a high status occupation may face, it is not surprising that the occupational role could not be expanded to compensate for a lost maternal or marital role, particularly in those days before consciousness-raising and the women's movement presented alternative bases for identity.

A number of psychiatrists, most notably Helene Deutsch (1945) and Therese Benedek (1950), have advanced the theory that it is the so-called feminine and mothering woman who has the easiest time during the menopause and that it is, in Deutsch's phrase, the "masculine protester" who has the most difficulty. However, our study showed that the women who adopt the traditional feminine role of nonaggressive housewives centering their lives on their children are most prone to respond with depression when their children leave. The depressed women I studied, far from being "masculine protesters," were more feminine by one-half a standard deviation on the Minnesota Multiphasic Personality Inventory than the mean for the criterion group.

The interpretation of these data does not imply that all housewives who are overinvolved or overprotective with their children are hospitalized when their children leave home, or that all married housewives become lonely and depressed in middle age. Under the following conditions such women would continue to find satisfaction in life:

1. Their husbands are financially successful.
2. Their husbands do not become interested in other women, or want a divorce, or die.
3. Their children fulfill their expectations:
   a. The son obtains a good job.
   b. The daughter makes a "good" marriage.
   c. The mother-child relationship can continue through frequent phone calls and visits.

If any one of these expectations is not fulfilled, the vulnerable woman may be in a dangerous situation since all of these conditions depend on activities of other people rather than of the woman herself.

INTEGRATION OF PSYCHIATRIC
AND SOCIOLOGICAL THEORY

Both the psychodynamic and existential theories of depression interpret depression as a result of loss: psychoanalytically oriented (Freudian) psychiatrists consider the loss that of an ambivalently loved object; existentialists, such as Ernest Becker, consider the loss to be one of meaning. In Freudian terms, depressives are understood as individuals who, instead of expressing anger toward the ambivalently loved lost object, turn the anger inward, against themselves. There may be, however, a possible way of combining the Freudian position of anger turned inward with the existential position of loss of meaning. People (and especially women) who are intrapunitive and who do not express their anger, are conforming to our cultural norms. Since they are "good," they expect to be rewarded. Should their husbands or children leave them, their lives may seem meaningless and their worlds may no longer "make sense." Their introjected anger led to "proper" behavior, which in turn led to expectations of reward. If the reward does not materialize, but in fact tragedy strikes, they will suffer from a loss of meaning and will become depressed.

The type of loss that was the independent variable for our study was role loss, especially the loss of the maternal role for middle-aged women who had overinvolved or overprotective relationships with their children. There is no direct evidence that the children "lost" were ambivalently loved, although some of the interviews were suggestive of ambivalence.

It was quite clear in both the interviews and the epidemiological study that these were "norm-following" women. In *The Revolution in Psychiatry* (1964), Ernest Becker says that women who have been too closely integrated into the social structure become depressed when they find their "sacrifices" and their exemplary behavior have been in vain. They discover that it is the exploiters rather than the martyrs who are rewarded, contrary to what they have always believed. They were told that as women they should live for their children. They did so. Their husbands became preoccupied with their occupations, interested in other women, or died. Their children left home. Since their feeling of usefulness stemmed primarily from the traditional feminine roles, they were left alone with no sense of worth.

Durkheim's approach (1897) is also relevant to the stresses a mother may feel when her children leave home, and particularly his concepts of *egoistic* and *anomic* suicide. Durkheim theorized that marriage does not protect women from egoistic suicide as it protects men. Instead, he thought that the birth of children reduced the suicide rate for women, and that immunity to suicide increased with the "density" (number of members residing together) of the family. This density of course diminished when the children matured and left.

Durkheim focused on problems stemming from normlessness, from anomie. His analysis seems relevant to the situation of middle-aged American women, for there are indeed few norms governing the relationship between an American woman and her adult children. When the children leave, the woman's situation is consequently normless. There are no folkways, no patterns, no mores to indicate to Sara just what she should expect from her children or just what their relationship to her should be. There is no Bar Mitzvah for menopause.

All the women I interviewed said their children "owed" them nothing. Yet the women who were Jewish faced an additional element of normative confusion: the norms considered appropriate in parent-child relationships in traditional European Jewish culture—and therefore accepted by the women—may not have been completely internalized by their American children. The children were also exposed to Anglo-Saxon mother-child relationships, which are more restrained and place more emphasis, at least at the verbal level, on the parent's desire for independence, both for her child and for herself.

RECOMMENDATIONS

The cross-cultural study, showing the multiplicity of possible roles for middle-aged women, shows not only that status does not have to drop in mid-life, but that in many cultures it rises. This fact, however, is of little comfort to the American women we have studied who are already isolated and depressed. It is unreasonable to expect them to change their value systems or personality structures or characteristic patterns of interaction at this stage of their lives.

But the broadest implication of the cross-cultural study has to do with the future. It has to do with providing a new sense of worth to girls of all societies, West and East, that will assure them that as women they will not feel useless when their children or their husbands leave them. If one's satisfaction, one's sense of value, comes from other people rather than from one's own accomplishments, it follows that the departure of these significant others will leave one with an empty shell in place of self. If the woman's sense of self comes from her own accomplishments, on the other hand, she is not so vulnerable to breakdown when significant others leave.

The women's liberation movement, by pointing out alternative life styles, by providing the emotional support necessary for deviating from the ascribed sex roles, and by emphasizing the importance of women actualizing their *own selves,* fulfilling their *own* potentials, can aid in the development of personhood for both men and women.

11

Loneliness and the Divorced Post-Middle-Aged Male

JON EISENSON

PROLOGUE

THIS ESSAY was to be a highly personal, autobiographical account of a divorce and the loneliness associated with it. I anticipated that it would be a relatively short, easy-to-write chapter. Soon, however, I realized that the questions I entertained demanded research and a considerable amount of reading. Some of the research proved disappointing because so few of the publications in the fields of sociology and psychology deal with the problems of the elderly who are newly divorced or even those who have been divorced for a considerable time but who have not remarried. There is, however, no dearth of books on the subject of divorce and on the subject of aging. But there is little in the literature that takes up the questions and the problems of divorce *and* aging. Nevertheless, I have tried, and I hope I also succeeded, in bringing together the problems of aging and the problems of the divorced who, by definition, are *older if not aged*. My emphasis and perspective are those of the male, though I recognize that loneliness in the elderly is by no means restricted to the male.

In an important way this essay permitted me to work toward a more objective view of my own divorce. I think it also helped me to see my ex-wife more objectively and possibly even more sympathetically. But this essay is still essentially a subjective view of the dissolution of my marriage.

A marital divorce involves two persons, but each person goes through the process alone. The paths to it, through it, and following it, are lonely ones. The ultimate goal—what is at the end of the path—need not be loneliness but a new capacity for living alone or, in some instances, for living with someone else.

WHO IS OLD?

From physiological and psychological points of view, the state of being *old* is probably more variable in relationship to chronological age than any of the earlier stages of life up to the mid sixties. To summarize the observations of Botwinick and Thompson (1968), if chronological age is the factor for making judgments about who is old, then older adults are more varied in both biological and behavioral functioning than are younger adults. And, as Rosow (1974, p. 22) generalizes: "In the main, people become socially old by drifting into rather than through sharply punctuated events. Hence, a formal *rite de passage* seldom occurs, and except for the funerals of widowhood, there are few public observances of a status change."

HIERARCHY OF NEEDS AND THE AGING (A. MASLOW REVISITED)

Maslow (1962), who had an optimistic view of the potential of human beings to achieve satisfaction in and through living, developed a construct about fundamental needs and the individual's drive to realize them. These needs are prospects for maturing adults. They become retrospects for the senior members of our society. Even though all the needs may have been met adequately if not completely, the post-middle-aged person is likely to have to reevaluate the needs. What may have been accomplished within a family, an extended family, and/or a social group has probably been upset. These upsets result from mobility of family members, the loss of friends through death or geographic relocations, the loss of employment through voluntary or compulsory retirement, and perhaps most disturbing of all for divorced persons, the breaking of ties with family and friends. Persons once loved may be gone. A youth culture that is short on esteem for the elderly creates doubts about self-actualization.

For the post-middle-aged person, then, Maslow's "hierarchy of needs" construct must be faced once again with the basic blocks, *bodily needs, safety,* and *security*. These blocks, however, are more fragile, more demanding, and less supporting than they were in early adult and middle period years. From my conversations with newly single aging persons—our senior citizens who often resent this designation—I am impressed that many do not feel as healthy or as "youthful" as their appearance suggests. To many aged persons, even a favorable physician's report is not reassuring. Interestingly, Pauline Sears (1975) found the same "complaint" among women who were identified as gifted when they were children and who are now in their late fifties and sixties. The subjects were identified and studied by the late, eminent Stanford University psychologist Lewis M. Terman. Sears reported that though the widows in this special population rated their health as good, they nevertheless felt that they had less energy and vitality. This, they thought, was "possibly because of the loss of their spouse and consequent feelings of sadness and depression." I assume that what is cause for sadness and depression among the widowed holds at least as much for divorced men who have not remarried. Perhaps when one is alone, doubts about health begin to occupy the mind.

AGING AND ATTITUDES TOWARD DIVORCE

The banner headline of a story in the November 18, 1975 *New York Times* read "Lonely and Tainted by Divorce, Catholics Unite to Win Respect." Not just adherents to the doctrines of the Roman Catholic Church, but many of those in the Western world still view divorced persons as *tainted*, especially those who disengage from marriage in their middle or later years.

How is *disengagement* from marriage an aspect of a more general social disengagement—the process of mutual withdrawal of the aging members from their social milieu? Is it possible to view divorce, increasing in incidence, as a manifestation of the process of social disengagement that is considered common and possibly even adaptive among senior members of our society? Kalish (1975, pp. 62-64) reviews "disengagement theories" and describes two kinds of disengagement: (1) *social disengagement,* referring to the decrease in number and duration of social contacts (interactions) undertaken, and (2) *psychological disengagement,* referring to the reduction in the extent of emotional involvement and commitment in those relationships which are maintained in the world in general. Despite the recognition that the elderly do disengage, and tend to withdraw into themselves, our culture expects older persons to maintain the semblance of a marital relationship. Elderly persons are supposed to increase rather than decrease their mutual dependence. Some, of course, do. But human beings, including the elderly, are not consistently logical in their behavior.

That needs change among the aging as well as among the younger and pre-middle-aged members of our society seems to be overlooked. Though still an infrequent aspect of their social behavior, especially as compared with members of younger groups, the incidence of divorce among the aging is increasing. Kalish (1975, p. 82) cites the relevant evidence from a Department of Health, Education, and Welfare report of 1971. During the period of 1963-1967, the divorce rate for persons who had been married from 25 to 29 years rose by 36 percent. Kalish speculates that, "Perhaps a combination of less punitive divorce laws and less community disapproval has permitted older people greater freedom to dissolve unhappy marriages. An alternative hypothesis is that marriage, even marriage with a 35- to 50-year history, is simply less satisfying today than in times past. Another possibility is that people are increasingly unable to maintain a commitment to permanent relationships" (Kalish, 1975, p. 82).

The trend toward more divorces among those in the population older than 65 years became clear in the late 1950s, and is revealed in the U.S. Bureau of Census figures for 1960. The figures indicate more than a doubling of divorces among white males 65 years and older in 1960 compared with 1930 (2.3 percent for 1960 and 1.1 percent for 1930 for white males; 2.4 percent for 1960 and 1.1 percent for 1930 for black males). The figures for women 65 years and older are even more dramatic, revealing an increase from .5 percent in 1930 to 2.0 percent in 1960 for white women and .6 percent in 1930 to 2.0 percent in 1960 for black women (Carter and Glick, 1970).[1]

---

[1] These figures represent all divorced persons minus the attrition by remarriage or death (Carter and Glick, 1970, p. 242).

What influence life expectancy has on the increase in divorce among this older segment of the population is worthy of study. When one may look forward to living 10 or more years beyond age 65, how and with whom should these years be spent? If disengagement is a "normal" factor among the aging, perhaps it is both logically and psychologically appropriate for disengagement to be concluded in marital dissolution.

The trend in divorce may be seen by comparing the figures in the 1960 and 1970 U.S. Censuses (Table 1). Although these data do not indicate the number of new divorces, the fact that the percentages increase suggests that the total number as well as the proportion of divorces cannot be attributed to longevity alone. It is of interest to note that the 1970 census shows the same percentage of divorced males and females in the 75 to 79 year range. Time, it would seem, has become the equalizer for differences found in the 65 to 74 year age range.

Any objective interpretation of the statistics on divorce in the United States must lead to the conclusion that attitudes toward marriage and divorce must be changing. Marriage, it becomes increasingly clear, is not forever. Nevertheless there seems to be a lag in attitude toward persons—especially older persons—who are divorced. In a publication as recent as Blau's *Old Age in a Changing Society* (1973) the author generalizes that "Divorce is still an abnormal phenomenon in any age group, although in certain subgroups the divorce rate is so high that people at least once divorced constitute the majority group. Nevertheless, even in such contexts, divorce is experienced and viewed as failure, because it constitutes a premature exit and the violation of the norm of permanency in marriage" (p. 231). This "norm of permanency" is an attitude that is behind the statistics.

Mackey Brown (1974), writing retrospectively and regretfully about her own failure to keep her marriage alive, makes this poignant statement: "Drifting into divorce may be one alternative to living in quiet desperation, but without doubt it is the least affirmative of them all" (p. 101).

As of this writing I can assert that there are no positive attitudes toward newly divorced older persons. The likelihood is that the male will be viewed with suspicion. Regardless of the facts (which are not likely to be determined), sympathy if not understanding will go to the woman. The man is presumed to have been unfaithful, cruel, indif-

TABLE 1

Percentage of Divorced Persons by Age Group
(Range 65-79) and Sex: 1960 and 1970 Census

	Age (%)		
	65-69	70-74	75-79
1960			
Male	2.7	2.4	2.1
Female	2.7	2.1	1.5
1970			
Male	3.5	3.1	2.7
Female	4.1	3.3	2.7

Sources: *Vital Statistics of the United States,* U.S. Department of Health, Education, and Welfare, #(HRA) 75-1103, 1974 and *Marital Status, 1970 Census of Population,* U.S. Bureau of the Census, U.S. Department of Commerce, December, 1972.

ferent, miserly, self-centered. The woman, by and large, is considered to have been long-suffering. If there is any consolation for the man in these attitudes, it is the ironic knowledge that despite this negative view of the elderly divorced male, he is more sought after by women, the widowed, the divorced, and even the never married, than is the ex-wife. Again, there is an evident incompatibility between attitude and practice!

The social attitude may be summed up in Kastenbaum's observation (1973) that "any circumstance that leads an old person to break step with the world around him tends to mitigate against his subsequent integration. He may have to cope not only with the suffering inherent in the grieving process, but also with the increased alienation that often follows in the wake" (p. 705).

ABSENCE OF RITUAL

Elderly persons who dissolve their marriages enter a changed status for which, both by virtue of age and their decisions relative to their marriage, *there are no recognized cultural rites or rituals.* There is a minimum of ritual for the death of a mate—usually a funeral, a period of display of mourning, and a period of actual or accepted grief. But there are no rites for growing old, or for the death of a marriage.[2]

Huyck (1974, pp. 105–106) adapted "processes" that are recognized as important to widowhood for persons involved in the death of a marriage. For the divorced persons, the processes include: grief and mourning,[3] finding new companions who will accept them, learning to solve problems on their own, learning when and from whom to accept advice, and reengagement including, if necessary, establishing a therapeutic relationship. These are not established rites and are far from rituals. But they are processes that may help in preventing loneliness from turning into desperation and depression.

There are, unfortunately, few studies and few guidelines regarding socially accepted behavior in divorced and especially new divorced, older persons. In some ways, the newly divorced older person faces the same adjustment problems as the newly widowed. But death and widowhood are "acceptable" in our society. Divorce among the elderly, on the other hand, catches almost everyone at least a little bit unprepared.

Emotional Divorce

Divorce, as I have suggested, may be a natural outcome of emotional disengagement among aging persons. Divorce rarely happens all at once, even among those few elderly who may have someone "waiting in the wings." In these instances, the waiting "someone" is likely to be a woman appreciably younger than the wife. In most instances, however, divorce among the elderly is accepted, at least at the outset, as an alternative to a marriage that has become destructive.

The Financial Separations: The Division of Wordly Goods and Problems of Support

This aspect of divorce has several facets, depending on the prop-

---

[2] Irving Rosow (1974) discusses the difficulties that come with aging because there are no recognized rites de passage. Rosow observes, "Old Age is the only stage in the life cycle that has systematic social losses rather than gains." The absence of rites of passage is, I think, an important social loss, both for the aging and the younger members of society.

[3] I can recommend in this connection, Krantzler's chapter on "The Healing Process of Mourning" (see Krantzler, 1973).

erty, income, and other worldly goods to be divided. For the elderly, if there is little worldly wealth, the settlement is eased for persons who have continuing or prospective income through social security. Since, by definition, the elderly are persons over age 65, they are assured of income for the remainder of their lives. An appreciable part of medical expenses are also assured.

The present generation of elderly divorced women are less likely to be financially self-supporting than are men. Social security and alimony (or the equivalent) may take care of financial support for the divorced woman who was married to a man of some means. The elderly divorced man may continue in his vocation or profession and so be self-supporting until retirement. If he has a pension, he may continue to do well enough to need no financial assistance other than his social security. There are, of course, other sources of financial support from a variety of legally established community sources. By and large, however, at least until vocational retirement, the older divorced man who is willing and able to work is at an advantage over the divorced woman.

For those with a considerable amount of worldly goods, division of property is likely to be equal, with the ex-wife emerging from the settlement perhaps a bit more equal than her ex-husband. However, the situation varies considerably from state to state. Furthermore, there is no legal requirement that one ex-spouse must insist on obtaining all that the law may provide. The prospective ex-husband may therefore be more generous than required out of a sense of guilt, or to please his children. One prospective ex-husband agreed to a settlement considerably beyond legal requirements to show his true generosity in the hope that his prospective ex-wife would accept this gesture as a basis for reconciliation. He was wrong, because she interpreted his generosity as a sign and proof of guilt. Along these lines, Bohannan (1970) states: "It seems to me that irrational motives such as revenge or self-abnegation are more often in evidence than the facts of relative need, in spite of all that judges and lawyers can do" (p 43).

It would, however, be simple-minded to assume that money and money matters always represent what they seem to. Control of wealth, both during and after the demise of a marriage, represents power and control. Conflicts over the sources and the exercise of power and control may only be what two disengaging persons are able to fight over when they are either unaware of, or afraid to face, the true bases of conflict. These bases may reside in changes of interest, differing physical, social, and emotional needs, and any other differences that accompany the aging process. As Bohannan points out, "When a couple is afraid to fight over the real issue, they fight over something else—and perhaps never discover what the real issue was" (p. 33). Furthermore, Bohannan notes:

> Two of the areas of life that are most ready to accept such displacement are the areas of sex and money. Both sex and money are considered worthwhile fighting over in American culture. If it is impossible to know or admit what a fight is all about, then the embattled couple may cast about for areas of displacement, and they come up with money and sex, because both can be used as weapons (p. 32).

It thus seems that emotional divorce, or the failure to achieve such a divorce, may be expressed in continued conflict over money. An ex-wife may sue an ex-husband for a relatively small sum of money and may thereby incur more expenses in legal fees than the amount she expects to get. The ex-husband, in turn, may refuse to pay inconsequential sums of money "for the principle of the thing" and incur legal expenses beyond the amount he refuses to pay. And so the game may go on until an emotional divorce is achieved.

Conflicts over sex are presumably not concerns of the ex-spouses, at least not with one another after the legal aspect of the divorce has been settled.

DISENGAGEMENTS AND REENGAGEMENTS WITHIN THE FAMILY: CUSTODY RIGHTS AND PRIVILEGES

If there are children, this aspect of divorce is significantly different for newly divorced who are elderly than for those in the middle and younger years. Unless the elderly couple married in their late forties or fifties *and* had children, child custody and visitation rights do not seem to be problems. If they are, they are not likely to remain problems for very long with children who are "grown up." However, determining who visits whom and when may be a problem. Visits on birthdays and holidays may be decided by turn, and there may be quarrels with children if not with the ex-spouse as to whose turn it is. The question of visits with and by grandchildren can also become a sensitive issue that elicits irrational responses.

My impression is that grown children are often caught in the middle by their own ambivalence. If the ex-spouses are living in the same community as the children, it is quite likely that the father will come off second best in regard to visits. For reasons that are not clear, fathers in our culture, even as ex-husbands, are supposed to be emotionally tougher than mothers and ex-wives. The interest and love of the fathers for their children and grandchildren are not denied. However, these needs are not accommodated to the same degree as those of the ex-wife as mother and grandmother.

If there is no problem regarding custody and visitation rights with children and grandchildren, there may still be considerable difficulty for the "custody" of friends. These difficulties may result in the loss of those friends who take the position of "a plague on both your houses." Other friends may take sides, and feel guilty or resentful for having done so. Still others may try to maintain a relationship with each ex-spouse, and may encounter some of the same scheduling problems as the children of the divorced couple. All of these problems are almost completely obviated if one of the ex-spouses moves away and gives way to the other. This is more likely to be the ex-husband than the ex-wife. In that event he faces alone the problems of the community divorce which we will next consider.

DIVORCE, SEPARATIONS, AND NEW AFFILIATIONS WITHIN THE COMMUNITY

Fortunately, and in keeping with their growing numbers, even the newly divorcd "elderly" are likely to find new social communities of others who are divorced. Religious organizations have "new single" groups that often include many more members who are single through death of marriage than through widowhood. However, new contacts and "acquisitions" cannot provide adequate substitutes for old friendships, and often, members of these "singles groups" are lonely together rather than lonely alone. Bohannan, on the other hand, ends his discussion on "Community Divorce" on a positive note. He observes that "the community divorce is an almost universal experience in America. And although there are many individuals who are puzzled and hurt until they find their way into it, it is probably the aspect of divorce that Americans handle best" (1970, p. 52).

Handle best? And yet the rate of suicide among divorced older persons is higher than among the widowed and those still married! Factors such as difficulty in adapting to the divorce role, health, fear of death, and fear of *dying alone* are probably all related to the incidence of suicide among the elderly divorced. In this regard, men and women face different situations. The elderly male, if so inclined, is probably better able to find a "replacement" for his ex-spouse than the elderly female. On the other hand, the elderly divorced woman, like the elderly widow, is likely to be better prepared for living alone than is the elderly divorced male. There are of course exceptions. Some elderly divorced men may have several years of experience living alone and caring for themselves despite sharing a physical residence with their spouses. Along these lines, one of my newly divorced male colleagues assured me, "Whatever else I have and hold against my ex-wife, she did prepare me to live alone. I find it easier to be alone and live alone than for years it was to live alone with her."

Bohannan also reminds us that, "Divorcees are people who have not achieved a good marriage—they are also people who would not settle for a bad one" (p. 54). For the newly divorced elderly, divorce either follows years of trying to maintain a poor marital relationship or points to problems that come with aging and disengagement that can no longer be accepted or solved, possibly because of the psychological distance between the spouses.

RETURN TO LONELINESS, RELATED INDISPOSITIONS, AND SEX DIFFERENCES

A search of the sociological literature for the period 1960-1970 on the relationship of aging, divorce, and psychosocial effects is disappointing. Despite the increasing incidence of divorce among the post-65-year-old population, there are few reported studies on divorce among this age group. Atchley (1972) is one exception. He devotes about two pages to observations about divorce and reports the following:

> While most older couples fit more or less into the happy category, a few are filled with hostility. Some older people feel that their spouses are the cause of all their troubles, and they often wish that they could somehow terminate their marriages. Religious orthodoxy, such as the strong Catholic policy against divorce, has no doubt kept couples together who otherwise would have separated. The same could be said

of social pressure in the community: the stigma of divorce has kept people together for years under a more or less armed truce (pp. 294-295).

In discussing suicide among the aged, Atchley observes, "Suicide rates are . . . higher for widowed older people than for those who are still married. The divorced older people have the highest mortality and suicide rates" (1972, p. 298).

The effects of divorce disturb the general assumptions of sociologists that aging, because it is a gradual process, permits ongoing and gradual adjustments. It belies, for example, Rosow's generalization that, "Aging . . . does not abruptly wrench a person from all his previous groups at one fell swoop. Rather, membership and group supports gradually dwindle away. While isolation and loneliness often do develop, they result from a process that allows the person to adjust continually to his changing circumstance" (1974, p. 125). However, Rosow also observes, "But the crucial factor is that the loss of former groups is not compensated by the acquisition of new ones." My divorced senior citizen associates can vouch for the lack of compensation provided by the acquisition of new friends. They also insist that however prepared they thought they were for divorce—and in some instances the preparation took from five to 10 years—the disruption following their divorce was beyond all expectation.

Some Sex Differences Associated with Divorce

Differences in the effects of divorce between elderly men and women have been considered throughout this essay. In this section I shall highlight some of the differences that are conducive to a state of loneliness.

With important exceptions, elderly women are better able to keep busy with the chores and details of living than are men. Although this may not hold for future generations of the elderly, the homemaker role of the present generation of elderly women is less disturbed and disrupted than the role of men. In his *Proverbs of Hell*, William Blake observed, "The busy bee has no time for sorrow." Most elderly women are better able to keep busy with details than most elderly men. However, if the elderly man does not find the housekeeper role unacceptable, he too can learn to keep occupied with details that he once may have considered trivial.

Biology as well as the social attitude toward the physical changes of aging, however, favor the man. Middle-aged and older men may be viewed as handsome, dignified, or begrudgingly "well preserved." If an older man is seen engaging in physical activity to keep fit, he is likely to be admired. In contrast, a woman of equal age may be considered "not bad for her age." If she is objectively attractive she may still be viewed subjectively as "trying too hard." The unfortunate consequence is that the older male has more opportunities for social contacts, for marriage, or other nonmarital living arrangements than does the older woman.

There is, however, one type of living arrangement more available and acceptable to older women than to men. Women, including older women, may share homes without negative community reaction. Men, whether for fear of negative reaction—an odd couple—or because two poor housekeepers with sloppy habits make sharing quarters more difficult than living alone, are more likely to continue living alone than to enter a two-male household. Also, there are more elderly single women than men.

Now that it is commonly recognized that sexual activity need not end with any given birthday, including birthdays after age 65, we find the satisfaction of these needs viewed somewhat differently in our society. The older male, even though he is identified as "an old swinger" is likely to be accepted and even begrudgingly admired. The older man may "swing" with partners of any age from thirty up; the older woman's choice of a partner is much more restricted. If she chooses obviously younger men, she is likely to be accused of something akin to "cradle snatching." If she chooses obviously older men, she is "surely after something." And if she chooses not to choose, then "That explains it. She's frigid." ("No wonder she is divorced.") Yet, one of the adjustments a post-middle-aged divorced man has to make is how to deal with the assumption that he is a "swinger" merely by virtue of divorce. It is an assumption that seems to require no substantiation in actual conduct. For some it may be a consummation as much feared as desired.

EPILOGUE

"The trouble with insight," remarked a middle-aged divorced colleague, "is that it just makes the behavior that continues all the more painful." My colleague, who like me was divorced at age 64, was talk-

ing about what he once would have called "piddling"—behaviors
such as straightening out a desk to make it not just orderly but neat.
He thought it ironic that he recalled arguing with his wife (even three
years after his divorce, he still could not bring himself to say ex-wife)
that he did not need to be neat for the sake of neatness. That was compulsive. It was enough for him to know where things were on his desk.
The order was in his mind. Following the divorce, he also found
himself putting his slippers in the closet rather than leaving them
under the chair in his bedroom, another compulsive action he had
formerly resisted. And so it was with a host of details and activities
about his apartment. He was doing what he had either refused to do
or done reluctantly or even in anger before his divorce. At first he told
himself that he was engaging in behaviors that he once considered
neurotically compulsive to fill time, to mark the minutes if not the
hours of the day, to do something while he was deciding what he really
should be doing. Then he realized that he was trying to please a wife
who was occupying his house, who now had custody of most of his
possessions, and who was working hard at taking custody of his few
remaining friends.

"Insight is not enough," my colleague insisted. "Insight just
separates your thinking and your actions from your emotions. It
creates a sense of schizophrenic isolation. It leaves you alone with
your loneliness. If you don't suspect or know why in hell you were
doing what you were doing, you might just be angry or even
amused." I once suggested to my colleague that perhaps much of his
present orderly behavior was an indication that he no longer needed
to rebel. He had become his own man. His terse response was, "The
hell I am." So, I let the matter drop, suspecting that, "There, but for
the grace of God, go I." His interpretation was probably as good as
mine. As a colleague in divorce as well as in profession, I understood
his feelings and was just beginning to understand my own. I call this
state "hairshirt loneliness."

Loneliness, I came to realize, must be distinguished from aloneness. It was, of course, nothing new to appreciate that one could be
lonely in a crowd. Perhaps most important in helping me to make the
distinction between being lonely and being alone was the increasing
wish as well as the need to be alone. I have come to relish breakfast
alone, and I enjoy being alone before dinner (though I rarely wish to
be alone at dinner). But the loneliness I felt and still occasionally feel

began years before my divorce. How many years I do not know. At least six and perhaps as many as ten. It was the loneliness of no longer sharing thoughts or feelings or purposes with my wife. It was the loneliness of not wanting to share the recollections of the day's activities. It was the loneliness that grew with the realization that each of us was pretending to hear what the other said, but that neither of us was listening with concern or sympathy.

Loneliness and aloneness have so much in common that I must be cautious not to confuse the two. There is a real danger that finding myself alone, whether or not in the presence of others, I might fall into the mood of loneliness. With considerable frequency I used to settle my mood by asking myself, "Do you really want to communicate with someone else at the moment or do you prefer to be alone?" Alone might mean communicating with myself, or reading, or going for a walk, or just "piddling." If my preference is for any of the latter, I know at that particular time I want to be alone. And that is good. This, I think, is what Alice Roosevelt Longworth had in mind in describing John L. Lewis, who for forty years was the president of the United Mine Workers of America. She said: "He was a lonely man, but very self-sufficient. I think he observes his loneliness with considerable pleasure. He would have enjoyed playing with the idea for a while, turning it over and around" (quoted in Hutchinson, 1975, p. 15).

I think that John L. Lewis was a *loner*, a man who enjoyed being alone. I do not think he viewed loneliness with pleasure, but he relished being alone, just as we can relish being alone.

But loneliness is far from conquered. It would be greedy and unrealistic to view loneliness as a mood and attitude of the past, and not a state of the present and future. Even without the special problems of post-middle-aged divorce, the realities of aging bring with them many causes of loneliness. Old friends die, and though they may be replaced by new acquaintances, it is not always adequate consolation to know that one continues to survive. Grown-up children grow away, sometimes only physically, but often out of the emotional need to be themselves and to have time and opportunity for their own problems and relationships. Aging brings the apprehension and the loneliness that accompany loss of health and the fear of dying. One must die alone! And if illness becomes either chronic or severe, there is the fear of not dying in time, of dying after having drained one's family of emotion, and then of dying both lonely and alone.

There is one aspect of loneliness to which males are more prey than females. It is the loneliness that comes as a result of intellectual as well as physical decline. Women not only outlive men, but are in general more resistant to the effects of aging. Thus, Jarvik, an investigator of the psychobiology of aging, notes that "Not only did men show a greater rate of decline during the 20-year follow-up but they also tended to obtain lower mean scores at the time of initial testing, and the differences between the sexes were maintained over the 20-year-follow-up" (1975, p. 580).

What are the other health prospects for an elderly divorced male? How much company will he have among age if not status peers? Hayflick (1975), a researcher on the physiological and genetic aspects of aging, observes:

> For the first time in man's history significant numbers of people alive today are already aged by usual standards but can still anticipate at least another decade or more of life. Through advancements in medical care and hygiene, industrial societies have produced a large new group of aged individuals, yet the same culture which created them has not yet learned how to incorporate them effectively into the social structure. . . . the 65 and over population constitutes the fastest growing age group in the country. . . . While the entire population of 65 years old and over will rise 43 percent (to 29 million) between 1970 and 2000, persons 75 to 84 will increase by 65 percent, and those 85 and over, 52 percent (pp. 36-43).

In cultures that have expectations about older citizens whose marriage vows included "in sickness and in health," where does that leave divorced males who are facing the prospect of a decade or more of life alone, whether in sickness or in health? Obviously, most divorced males would be better off if they could look forward to years of relative mental, emotional, and physical health rather than illness. Occasional illness, of course, and perhaps more frequent illness than in the middle years, must be expected. Nonetheless, the older male can perhaps begin to share the optimism of Browning's "Rabbi Ben Ezra" who urged:

> Grow old along with me!
> The best is yet to be,
> The last of life, for which the
> first was made.

There is, in fact, some reason beyond faith to be optimistic that ongoing and future gerontological research will not only extend life, but will increase the number of healthy and potentially productive years, so that both those past middle age and their children can look forward to being members of a generation of aging adults who will not spend most of their last years in a state of senility. The establishment in 1974 of the National Institute of Aging as a unit of the National Institutes of Health is evidence that senior citizens are, in their own way, *an important new generation*. Perhaps this new Institute will consider such aspects of aging as the death of a marriage partner, but also the death of a marriage in which two nonpartners survive.

12

Loneliness in Widowhood

HELENA ZNANIECKA LOPATA

LONELINESS is a significant feeling among women who are widowed. Extensive interviews conducted for a role modification study of older widows in Chicago revealed loneliness to be a major problem.[1] However, a careful reading of answers to interview questions indicated that different women who often feel lonely were not referring to the same sentiment and did not feel the same way in the same situations (Lopata, 1969).

If loneliness is defined as the sentiment experienced by a person dissatisfied with the level or quality of social interaction (loneliness of social isolation according to Weiss [1973]) or the lack of an intimate social relation (loneliness of emotional isolation according to Weiss), then I have found at least 11 forms of this feeling pertaining to three major categories of widows (Lopata, 1969). The first category is made up of women who feel lonely for the deceased husband as a person, as a love object and giver of love, as a partner or escort, as a sharer of the work and the parenting role, or as someone around whom time and work was organized.

The second category is composed of those widows who are lonely for the style of life enjoyed when the husband was healthy and alive. Middle- and upper-class women, especially, miss the activities they shared with their late husbands. These activities ranged from atten-

[1] The role modification study included 301 widows 50 years of age and older and was funded by the Administration on Aging, Department of Health, Education, and Welfare (Grant No. AA46703001A1).

dance at conventions to doing things together on weekends (Lopata, 1975a). A woman's income drops considerably in most cases when the husband dies, so she is unable to participate in many of the activities she engaged in as a wife. Her social life may change because of the absence of a male partner.

The third category consists of widows who are lonely because of inadequacy of their relations with other people, in terms of the absence of emotionally meaningful relationships and social interactions. The death of the husband can create tension in relations with others. Children do not help the mother either because they don't know how to assist her through the grief and readjustment or because of their own commitments and problems. Relations with in-laws frequently deteriorate (Lopata, 1973a; Marris, 1958). Friendships with other couples become strained by the husband's death, by the grieving of the widow, by the asymmetry resulting from the absence of the woman's late spouse, and by the difficulty of fitting the widow into the established, "fun" based interaction of polite companionship (Znaniecka, 1965; Lopata, 1975a). In addition, widows experience problems in developing new relations, because of a gamut of self-questioning feelings about self-confidence and their inability to "make friends and influence people" (Carnegie, 1936; Glick, Weiss, and Parkes, 1975). Encounters with men are awkward because of actual or imagined sexual advances or a lack of such advances, and because of the frequent tendency of widows to idealize their late husbands to the point of sanctification, making mortal men unable and unwilling to compete with them (Lopata, 1975b; Hunt, 1966).

In sum, the study of role modifications of older widows in Chicago revealed emotional and social loneliness experienced chronically or situationally, changes in life style, and difficulties in establishing a satisfactory number of social relations of sufficient depth.

These findings, however, leave many unanswered questions. Over three-quarters of the participants mentioned loneliness as one of the major problems of widowhood. Does this mean that loneliness is a passing stage of grief, or that husbandless women continue to be lonely? Do they compare their current level of loneliness to that assumed to be experienced by other people, defining their own in terms of relative deprivation? Which widows are more lonely than they assume others are, and which widows rarely or never feel lonely?

Finally, what are the associations between loneliness and other sentiments, attitudes, and support systems?

WIDOWS OF ALL AGES

In order to answer the preceding questions, I included a very specific question in a new study of metropolitan Chicago widows of all ages who are currently or have recently been recipients of Social Security benefits.[2] In a self-administered segment of the interview, the widows were presented with a set of alternatives to the question, "How would you describe your present feelings about yourself?" (see Table 1). I had been forewarned by reading studies by the Human Development and Family Department at the University of Nebraska, where the loneliness question was developed, that the elderly were the least likely of all studied groups to express loneliness. Nevertheless, I had expected that the frequency of "most lonely" widows would be higher than that for elderly, rural, and urban Nebraskans.[3] The Woodwards (1972) found more women than men to be lonely. Many of the women we studied were younger than those in the Woodward study. Although the Woodwards did not test for loneliness by marital status, they found that people who felt they were loved and cared for were the least lonely. Thus widows could be expected to consider themselves lonely.[4]

[2]The sample was stratified and drawn up by the Social Security Administration's statisticians from lists with different ratios to insure that we had enough cases in some of the less populous strata. The five samples include: (1) current beneficiaries because of dependent children; (2) current beneficiaries over 60 or 62 years of age; (3) former beneficiaries whose children are now adults; (4) former beneficiaries who have remarried; and (5) widows who received only the "lump sum" payment to help defray funeral costs. The 1,169 widows whom we interviewed represent 82,085 women, when weighted by the five ratios. The study was funded with a contract from the Social Security Administration (Contract No. SSA71-3411) with the cooperation of Loyola University of Chicago. Special thanks go to Dr. Henry Brehm of the Social Security Administration, and to the staff of the Center for the Comparative Study of Social Roles, especially Frank Steinhart, Sister Gertrud Kim, Suzanne Meyering, and Sue Dawson.

[3]The Woodwards (1972) used this question with college freshmen, newly widowed and divorced women, the elderly, and housewives, and found the first group to be the most prone to loneliness.

[4]The comparative study of *Old People in Three Industrial Societies* carried out by three teams of scholars in the United States, England, and Denmark under the leadership of

TABLE 1

Distribution of Loneliness Responses by Chicago Area and
Rural and Urban Nebraskan Widows[a]

Response	Chicago area Widows[b]		Nebraskans[c]	
	N	%	N	%
I am the most lonely person I know	2,536	3.2	9	1.7
I am more lonely than most people	5,103	6.4	101	18.7
I am about as lonely as most people	22,866	28.8	110	20.5
I am less lonely than most people	17,983	22.7	191	35.7
I rarely feel lonely	18,725	23.6	124	23.2
I never feel lonely	12,087	15.2	0	0
TOTAL	79,300	100.0	535	100.0

[a]Responses were to the question: "How would you describe your present feelings about yourself?"

[b]From H. Z. Lopata, "Support Systems Involving Widows" study.

[c]From Woodward and Woodward (1972).

In fact we found that a majority of our Chicago respondents reported themselves "less lonely than most people" or "rarely" lonely or "never" lonely. In our sample only 10 percent of the widows feel relatively deprived, compared to the majority of widows who consider themselves not lonely or, at least, no lonelier than other people. Of course, half of these widows have been alone for more than eight years, and three-quarters for more than four years, so they have had time to adjust to the absence of their husbands and to modify other relationships.

Ethel Shanas (1968) found even fewer persons expressing high levels of loneliness. Only four percent of the elderly in Denmark, seven percent in Britain, and nine percent in the United States experience frequent loneliness; 13 percent of the elderly in Denmark, 21 percent in Britain, and 21 percent in the United States experience occasional loneliness; and 83 percent of the elderly in Denmark, 72 percent in Britain, and 70 percent in the United States experience loneliness "rarely or never" (Townsend, 1962, p. 271). Townsend, however, specifies that women are more apt than men to be widowed, to live alone and to be alone during the day, and the widowed are much more likely to say that they are lonely than the married or single women. Also, "In Britain 55 percent of women widowed within the last five years, and in Denmark 35 percent widowed within the last six years, were often or sometimes lonely, compared with 38 percent and 23 percent respectively of women widowed 20 years or more" (p. 272).

Yet, as Weiss (1973) points out, emotional isolation leading to lone-liness is expected whenever there is a loss or lack of intimate ties, par-ticularly, those of marriage. The "never" or "rarely" lonely widows may have had intimate emotional ties with their deceased husbands or they may have been able to substitute others for them. We shall examine these ideas later, after establishing some of the characteristics of women who consider themselves "more lonely than other people" rather than "rarely" or "never" lonely. Several factors affect how a widow defines her level of loneliness in comparison to other people: (1) her background which provides the foundation of her personal resources; (2) her life with her husband and how she remembers it to have been; (3) the number and variety of intimates in her social net-work; and (4) the content of her social and emotional support systems.

BACKGROUND

Previous research on housewives and widows revealed a strong association between the amount of formal schooling a woman has and her social life, that is, her social relationships and roles (Lopata, 1971, 1973a, 1973b). In fact, as Berger and Berger (1975) have pointed out, the life choices of an American are influenced by the social class of the parents, which, in turn, is influenced by their educational achieve-ment. Because urbanization, industrialization, and mass education are recent phenomena, it can be expected that many present widows have been born to parents who were not highly educated, had little or no schooling, and were born in rural areas. Such widows would not likely be highly educated and would be dependent on kinship and ethnic-neighborhood networks for relationships. Because modern cities lack these systems, widows are apt to be isolated (Lopata, 1973b).

We found, however, that although 67 percent of the widows came from families in which the mother had no more than an eighth grade education, there was no significant statistical association between the mother's schooling and the level of loneliness experienced by the daughter. Interestingly enough, the father's educational achievement is more important, but only for daughters of men with no more than a grade school diploma. Ninety-one percent of the most lonely women come from families in which the father has minimal formal education.

The widows' own lack of education is of greater influence. The "most lonely" women or those lonelier than they assume other people to be, are disproportionately liable to have less than 12 grades of schooling. Very few widows with at least a high school education experience a level of loneliness which they considered more than that felt by other people.

Unexpectedly, age at widowhood and length of widowhood are not consistently associated with feelings of loneliness, except that the "most" and "more" lonely groups are apt to have been widowed for either three years or less, or for 11 to 19 years. "Most" lonely widows are also likely to have been young at the time of the husband's death; most of the "never" lonely widows were aged 65 or over (31 percent to the whole group's 24 percent). The husband of a widow in the "most" lonely group likely died in an accident or of cancer; the husband of a "never" lonely widow likely died of a chronic infection, combined illnesses, or other diseases of old age. Husbands of "most" and "comparatively more" lonely widows are liable to have had sudden deaths (48 percent for "most," 36 for "more," to the whole group's 30 percent). There is no association between loneliness and reported family income either the year before the husband's death or at present—a finding that runs counter to all expectations.

SANCTIFICATION OF THE LATE HUSBAND

A widow often idealizes her late husband, sometimes to the point of making him a saint. A sanctification scale was included in the interview in order to determine which widows resisted the temptation to sanctify their late husbands.[5] I hypothesized that the more a woman sanctifies her late husband, the more her current life would appear unsatisfactory, and the more unsatisfactory her current life, the more she would sanctify the late husband. Actually there is only a weak correlation between the characterization of the husband and loneliness except at the extreme levels, and then not in the expected direction (gamma = -0.15). Women declaring themselves "never" lonely tend to sanctify the late husband (64 percent to the whole group's 46 percent). At the other extreme, women who do not have positive

[5]The scale consisted of two segments: (1) a semantic differential set of qualities of the late husband, and (2) a set of statements about their marriage and life together. The most extreme of the statements was "my husband had no irritating habits."

memories of their late husbands are liable to be the "most" lonely. The same tendency appears in the association between loneliness and the idealization of the life the woman shared with her husband before his death.[6] Women remembering their marriages and home lives as being extremely positive are likely to be "never" lonely.

None of the items of the sanctification scale is significantly related to the expressed level of loneliness, although there is a consistent underrepresentation of the very lonely on the side of positive judgments. Although very few women define their late husband as anything but perfectly "good" on a seven-point scale, widows who deviate from the norm declare themselves to be the "most" lonely person they know. The same occurs if the husband is defined as being honest, superior, kind, friendly, or warm, but it does not apply to his being remembered as "useful." The "most" and the "more" lonely widows are likely to agree strongly with several statements in the segment of the sanctification scale which focuses on aspects of the remembered marital situation, such as: "my marriage was above average," "our home was unusually happy," and "my husband had no irritating habits." Although few widows circled the "strongly disagree" answer to these statements, those who did are most apt to be women who declare themselves above average in loneliness. However, they evaluated the late husband as having been a good father. The "never" lonely woman is heavily represented on the positive side of every judgment, in contrast to the "most" lonely widow, in spite of a lack of statistically significant associations due to variations in the distribution of answers of women at the middle levels of loneliness.

SOCIAL NETWORK

The level of loneliness experienced by a widow can be influenced by the number of significant persons available for social and emotional supports. It is therefore surprising that there is no simple, statistically significant difference between the number of people living in the

---

[6]After much debate and testing we settled on the period of time in which the marriage was still "normal" in that it had not been affected by the death process as the "year before your husband's illness (accident) which finally caused his death." We then used that specific year in all questions referring to married life. The respondents did not seem to have any trouble establishing a base year.

widow's household and her feelings of loneliness. Results from widows living alone tend to be distributed along a U-curve; these widows are more apt to be at the extremes of the curve than women at the middle ranges of loneliness. But the differences are not dramatic (51 percent for the "most" lonely to 39 percent for the "less lonely than most"). Women living with four other people are the most likely to declare themselves "never" lonely, whereas women living with seven other people are the most apt to feel "rarely" lonely.

Working in a job outside of the home influences feelings of loneliness, but the pattern is not as clear-cut as expected. Women working before the husband's fatal illness or accident are more frequently "rarely" or "never" lonely (43 percent) than women who have worked at any time during widowhood (32 percent). On the other hand, women working before widowhood are also more likely to feel lonelier than most people, although we expected them to have been less dependent on the marital partner than housewives. However, some of these widows also lost their jobs after their husbands' deaths, so they have two reasons for feeling lonely. Widows currently working declare themselves at the high levels of loneliness less often and at the low levels more often than do full-time homemakers. The trend seems to be that women who have begun working prior to widowhood and have continued working as widows, avoid feeling lonely more successfully than those who have not.

The number of children or siblings a widow has does not affect how lonely she feels. It is difficult to pinpoint why the number of children does not affect the level of loneliness. It is interesting, however, that women with two children often define themselves as the "most lonely person I know" or as "more lonely than other people." No overall association appears regarding the number of siblings. Nevertheless 35 percent of the "most" lonely widows do not have any siblings, compared to only three percent who have four brothers or sisters. Of the women who are "more lonely than people they know," 29 percent have no sibling and only five percent have four siblings. On the other hand, only 14 percent of the very lonely widows lack a sibling now, indicating that the presence of living brothers or sisters does not necessarily prevent strong feelings of loneliness.

A major source of both emotional and social supports can be friendship. We inquired about the number of friends the woman had before her husband's death, if the relationships remained the same, and how many new friends she made during widowhood. Again, there is no significant statistical association between the number of friends and loneliness, except that the loneliest women have no old friends or friends from before the husband's death (42 percent of the "most" lonely and 44 percent of the "more" lonely compared to the group's total of 30 percent). Nevertheless, 27 percent of the "never" lonely women claim no friends before widowhood.

Women with friends before the deaths of their husbands almost inevitably declare the relationships not to have changed, although these friends are not seen as cften as in the past or as often as new friends. Respondents listing only one old friend are apt either to be "more" and "most" lonely or "rarely" and "never" lonely. Widows with two or three friends appear in the medium levels of loneliness; those with four or five friends "rarely" feel lonely. Women without new friends are the most likely to feel very lonely: 62 percent are in the "most" lonely and 69 percent in the "more than others" categories, compared to the whole group's 54 percent. The absence of old and new relations leads to greater loneliness.

A strong association does obtain, however, between loneliness and the desire for more friends (Table 2). Eighty-five percent of the women defining themselves as the "most lonely person I know" agree with the statement "I wish I had more friends." In contrast, only 28 percent of the "never" lonely want more friendships. Even this proportion is high because 25 percent of widows allegedly happy about their emotional and social relations wish to have more intimates. Nevertheless the difference between the two categories is striking.

Recently remarried women are definitely less lonely than those who remarried soon after widowhood, particularly those whose remarriage terminated in divorce. Sixty-six percent of the recently remarried are "rarely" or "never" lonely, compared to 37 percent who did not remarry and only 25 percent who remarried and divorced. This is a dramatic refutation of the assumption that remarried widows do not benefit emotionally from a new marriage.

Of course it is not the number of children or friends a widow has but the quality and frequency of contact with them that can alleviate social isolation and loneliness. A definite inverse relationship obtains between the frequency of contact with the most significant others and feelings of loneliness (Table 3). Average frequency of contact is shown for contact between the widow and at least one child living away from

TABLE 2

Level of Loneliness and Desire for More Friends[a] of Chicago Area Widows

Level of Loneliness		I wish I had more friends				Row Total
		Strongly Agree	Agree	Disagree	Strongly Disagree	
Most lonely person I know	N	1,084	1,072	284	96	2,536
	Row %	43	42	11	4	100
	Column %	9	5	1	1	3
More lonely than most people	N	1,497	1,806	1,628	124	5,056
	Row %	30	36	32	2	100
	Column %	13	8	4	2	6
Same as most people	N	3,836	8,748	9,120	494	22,198
	Row %	17	39	41	3	100
	Column %	33	40	25	6	29

Less than most people					
N	2,253	4,870	9,534	1,244	17,901
Row %	13	27	53	7	100
Column %	19	22	27	15	23
Rarely lonely					
N	1,721	3,444	10,160	3,317	18,642
Row %	9	18	55	18	100
Column %	15	16	29	40	25
Never lonely					
N	1,244	1,959	5,140	2,929	11,273
Row %	11	17	46	26	100
Column %	11	9	14	36	14
TOTAL					
N	11,635	21,900	35,865	8,204	77,605
Row %	15	28	46	11	100
Column %	100	100	100	100	100

Gamma = 0.39.

[a] Desire for more friends determined by extent of agreement with statement: "I wish I had more friends."

home, old friends still being seen, new friends, and with reference to membership in voluntary associations and attendance at church. Twenty-five percent do not have a child or any children living away from home. For those with children living away, frequency of contact is directly related to feelings of loneliness at the high end of the scale, although the association is not linear after that. The "most" lonely women see their offspring on an average of less than once a month but more than several times a year. Women defining themselves as "more lonely than most people" see their children on an average of once a month. Of course, they often see one child more than others, but this still is not frequent enough to alleviate their loneliness. Widows who are "as lonely as other people" or "never" lonely see their children several times a month.

Twenty-seven percent of the widows do not have old friends whom they are now seeing and the average range of contact between the remaining widows and their old friends of once a month to several times a year is not sufficient to influence feelings of loneliness because there is little variation among the groups. Those who are "never" lonely see their friends more often than the others do. Fifty-four percent do not have new friends or did not list frequency of visits; of these, interestingly enough, these widows are "more lonely than other people" yet they have the highest frequency of contact—over once a week. The friends are likely to be co-workers or neighbors, but the contacts, unlike family, do not help to alleviate loneliness. Fifty-one percent do not participate in voluntary associations but those who attend go about once a month. Most belong to only one group; the loneliest have the lowest frequency of attendance. Attendance itself may not alleviate loneliness, but the attitudes which underlie both social involvement and loneliness do. Church attendance is more frequent—only two percent of the total do not list some involvement, but the average ranges from once a month to several times a year. Interestingly enough, the "most lonely" women attend more frequently.

SUPPORT SYSTEMS FOR WIDOWS

In the interviews, we included four support systems with 65 different supports; the systems are economic, service, emotional, and social, with an in- and out-flow between the first two. Data on the emotional supports were obtained for the year before the husband's

TABLE 3

Mean Frequency of Contact Between Chicago Area Widows and Significant Others[a]

Level of Loneliness	Contact with			Attendance	
	Children	Old Friends	New Friends	Groups	Church
Most lonely person I know	4.7678	4.9108	6.8863	4.4014	5.2910
More lonely than most people	5.2848	4.6485	7.4725	5.7226	4.5454
Same as most people	6.2274	4.8125	6.9761	5.1927	4.2909
Less than most people	5.8790	4.7918	6.3015	4.9753	4.8297
Rarely lonely	5.7751	5.0605	6.9149	4.7393	4.4472
Never lonely	5.9092	4.9300	6.8035	4.7331	4.8841
TOTAL	5.9092	4.9300	6.8035	4.9607	4.5874
N	59,742	57,513	36,768	38,607	77,694

Code: Daily = 9; Several times a week = 8; About once a week = 7; Several times a month = 6; About once a month = 5; Several times a year = 4; About once a year = 3; Less than once a year = 2; Never = 1.

[a] Significant others include children living away from home, friends, and acquaintances seen at church or the meetings of voluntary associations.

death and the present. Each respondent was given the opportunity to list three different persons in each support for a total of 195. In general, the widows were independent in that they were not involved in many economic supports, nor were they givers or receivers of money in the form of gifts, or financial help with the payment of rent, food, clothing, or other bills. They also are not involved with many exchanges of services and, when they are so involved, there is no effect on their feelings of loneliness. Examination of the emotional and the social support systems thus complemented nicely Weiss's (1973) two reasons for loneliness—the lack of intimate relations and the lack of social ties.

Our scale for the emotional system has two components: in the first one we asked the widow to whom she felt the closest, with whom she most enjoyed being, who comforted her when she was depressed, who made her angry most often, to whom she turned in a crisis, and who made her feel especially important. In the second part of the scale we investigated six "feeling states." We asked what persons or groups made the widow feel respected, useful, independent, accepted, self-sufficient, and secure (Tables 4 and 5).

We had two hypotheses about the association between the emotional supports and loneliness. In the first we expected that lonely women would more frequently answer "myself" or "no one" because they have no one to turn to or they would not be so lonely. Secondly, it is possible that the very lonely are not emotionally self-sufficient and therefore cannot depend on themselves in a crisis. The feeling-states segment of the scale in particular provided opportunities for the self to appear at least once because other people really cannot provide the feeling of self-sufficiency or independence.

The self occurs more frequently in the feeling-states segment, but it appears in confusing ways. The women who are "less lonely than others," "rarely" or "never" lonely, depend on themselves for at least one of the six feelings more often than the lonelier widows. The second hypothesis anticipated this. Widows "more lonely than most people" omit themselves in the feeling states, but the "most" lonely mention themselves frequently—as much as three times. This distribution confused the hypotheses that the lonely have no one but themselves to draw on, but that they nevertheless cannot draw even on themselves for important feelings of self. This suggests that there is more than one type of widow lonelier than other people. Some of the

TABLE 4
Percent Distributions of First-Listed Contributors to the Present Emotional Support Systems of "Most Lonely" and "More Lonely" Chicago Area Widows

Emotional Supports	Self		Pres. Husb.		Boyfriend		Child		Sib.		Parent		Relative		Friend		Other		No one		Total
Sentiments																					
Closest	0[a]	5[b]	0	1	0	0	64	49	1	10	4	3	1	16	2	10	12	0	16	5	100
Enjoy	2	0	6	4	4	0	51	41	0	8	0	2	11	13	14	18	11	0	6	12	100
Tell Problems	0	6	6	1	1	1	39	29	0	11	3	1	2	8	7	7	13	12	34	18	100
Comforted	2	1	6	0	1	1	33	30	0	10	5	0	11	6	17	15	2	7	39	23	100
Important	0	1	6	2	2	1	44	49	0	6	4	1	12	12	13	2	0	7	24	14	100
Angry	0	0	1	4	4	0	44	20	0	1	0	0	1	6	2	5	13	4	36	61	100
Turn to in crisis	2	7	6	3	3	0	41	35	1	12	4	1	2	12	1	3	13	16	32	12	100
Self-feelings																					
Respected	0	6	6	1	1	0	46	50	0	6	2	3	11	8	13	3	18	13	8	6	100
Useful	6	12	6	0	2	0	49	36	0	7	4	4	2	14	0	1	7	3	30	17	100
Independent	64	56	0	0	2	0	6	7	0	6	2	2	0	0	0	0	3	7	22	23	100
Accepted	15	11	6	0	2	6	36	38	0	7	2	4	7	6	5	10	16	15	8	8	100
Self-sufficient	57	55	6	0	0	0	6	7	0	6	2	2	1	1	0	3	4	7	29	14	100
Secure	38	34	6	0	3	1	7	12	0	6	4	4	1	1	1	1	14	2	31	34	100

[a] I am the most lonely person I know. $N = 2{,}536$ on "Closest" and similar on other supports.
[b] I am more lonely that most people. $N = 5{,}092$ on "Closest" and similar on other supports.

TABLE 5

Percent Distributions of First-Listed Contributors to the Present Emotional Support Systems of "Rarely Lonely" and "Never Lonely" Chicago Area Widows

Each cell shows two percentages: the first for "rarely lonely"[a], the second for "never lonely"[b].

Emotional Supports		Self	Pres. Husb.	Boyfriend	Child	Sib.	Parent	Relative	Friend	Other	No one	Total
Sentiments												
Closest		1[a] 0[b]	5 6	1 1	58 60	14 10	2 1	4 7	10 3	3 4	0 7	100 100
Enjoy		1 2	8 7	6 2	49 41	6 7	1 0	5 10	17 20	0 0	0 11	100 100
Tell Problems		8 10	7 6	2 1	34 32	8 4	1 0	3 5	12 12	6 9	18 21	100 100
Comforted		3 10	8 7	4 2	37 29	6 3	2 1	1 7	9 3	4 10	27 29	100 100
Important		5 12	9 9	6 2	45 43	2 0	1 0	4 12	9 10	5 0	14 12	100 100
Angry		1 0	2 1	2 0	16 10	2 0	0 0	3 5	2 0	11 12	60 69	100 100
Turn to in crisis		3 10	9 8	1 1	48 50	10 2	2 1	5 16	7 5	4 8	11 6	100 100
Self-feelings												
Respected		6 11	8 6	2 2	45 50	1 3	0 1	4 5	10 6	21 9	2 6	100 100
Useful		10 20	7 7	2 1	41 38	2 3	1 0	4 3	9 5	16 8	7 15	100 100
Independent		62 72	4 3	0 0	14 5	2 3	0 0	2 2	0 0	6 4	8 11	100 100
Accepted		9 14	7 6	2 2	37 28	1 0	0 0	6 4	16 23	18 18	4 5	100 100
Self-sufficient		66 67	4 3	1 1	10 8	1 3	0 0	2 0	23 36	6 3	8 10	100 100
Secure		37 50	8 7	3 1	26 24	2 3	0 0	2 0	3 1	12 12	5 3	100 100

[a] I rarely feel lonely. N = 18,710 on "Closest" and similar on other supports.

[b] I never feel lonely. N = 12,087 on "Closest" and similar on other supports.

lonely women can draw on themselves, others cannot. We know that women without much loneliness feel self-sufficient.

Women who list a new husband in any of the supports are "rarely" or "never" lonely, whereas those who are "more" or "most" lonely overwhelmingly lack such a reference (gamma = 0.33). Boyfriends do not affect the sentiment segment but they are important sources of feelings of self (gamma = 0.26). The frequency with which children are mentioned in either segment does not affect the mother's level of loneliness.

Few of the Chicago area widows have living siblings available as supports or they are not included in their emotional lives; 75 percent fail to mention them in the sentiment segment and 88 percent in the self-feeling segment of the scale. Most widows do not have living parents to whom they can turn, and surprisingly few mention relatives outside of parents, siblings, spouse, and children.

The frequency with which other relatives are mentioned by widows at the extremes contrasts sharply: 77 percent of the "most" lonely, but only 59 percent of the "never" lonely do not list a friend in the sentiment segment and 79 percent and 65 percent respectively do not mention someone in the self-feeling segment. Again, friendship appears to be an important source of emotional supports; its absence intensifies loneliness. Other persons or groups, such as co-members of church or voluntary associations, co-workers, or those "helping professionals" who are not friends, do not influence the degree of loneliness experienced.

In the social support system there is the same lack of association between the frequency with which a significant other person is mentioned and the degree of loneliness. Although only five percent are presently married, they are definitely less lonely than the women without a husband (gamma = 0.42). The frequency with which significant others appear in the social support system is not as important as whether they are mentioned at all or left unmentioned. The most lonely women are not apt to engage in social activities or to list associates even if they engage in some activity such as going to church. Thirty-four percent (compared to 20 percent) of the whole group never mention children as companions; 94 percent (compared to 74 percent) never mention siblings; 68 percent (compared to 51 percent) never mention other relatives; and 90 percent (compared to 74 percent) never mention other persons or groups. The difference is not as strong between the extreme category and the whole group when it comes to friends; the women most likely to lack such companions are "more lonely than others" (47 percent compared to 37 percent for the "most" lonely and 33 percent for the whole group).

The differences in the emotional support between the "more" lonely women and the "rarely" or "never" lonely can be examined in the distributions of contributors to each component of the emotional support system of these widows (see Tables 4 and 5). There are some interesting differences between the widows located at the four extreme levels of loneliness and an overall trend. The women who are the "most lonely person" and "more lonely than most people" have fewer contributors to each of their sentimental and self-feeling supports than do "rarely" or "never" lonely women. Table 4 details the first listed contributors to each support at the two highest levels of loneliness; Table 5 presents the same data for widows at the two lowest levels.

There is a significant difference between the "most" lonely (64 percent) and the "rarely" (40 percent) or "never" lonely widows who list someone in answer to the question "Who makes you angry most often?" The "most" lonely widows are thus the ones who are the most angry of this sample of women, or the most willing to admit that there are people who anger them. In fact the very lonely women remember being angry with other people frequently before the husband's death. Only 14 percent claim not to have been angry with anyone, compared with 45 percent of the comparatively lonely and 54 percent of the "never lonely." The anger of very lonely women was directed at the late husband 54 percent, at the children 15 percent, and at siblings 10 percent of the time.

Not only are the very and the comparatively lonely widows angry, but they also do not feel secure; 31 and 34 percent, respectively, list "no one" when asked who makes them feel secure, compared with five and three percent, respectively, of the "rarely" and "never" lonely. Children provide the "never" or "rarely" lonely with security much more often than the children of the "most" lonely, and 50 percent of the "never" lonely obtain this feeling from themselves, compared with 38 percent for the "most" lonely. The extensive use of the self as a source of feelings of self-sufficiency and security by the "never" lonely, when compared with the very lonely, supports our hypothesis that emotional desolation (Townsend, 1962; Weiss, 1973) signifies alienation from the self, leading to problems not only with self-feelings but also with relations with others.

In spite of the complexity of the social network from which "never" lonely women draw supports, there are some "never" lonely widows who lack close associates to whom they can tell problems (21 percent), who comfort them when they are depressed (29 percent), who make them feel important (12 percent) or useful (15 percent). Nevertheless, they are able to differentiate loneliness from the absence of intimacy in relations with others.

SUMMARY

We posited that Chicago-area widows who are or have been recipients of Social Security are frequently lonely, or at least assume other people to be experiencing much less loneliness than they suffer. This expectation proved wrong. Most widows assumed that their loneliness was similar to, or even less pervasive than, that of most people. In fact, almost 40 percent of the widows claim "rarely" or "never" to feel lonely. We expected to find a strong association between levels of loneliness reported by widows and background variables such as the educational achievement of parents and self, ethnicity, race, and income when the husband was alive and at the present. These variables proved statistically insignificant in distinguishing levels of loneliness, although the "most" lonely tend also to be the most disadvantaged. Age at widowhood and at the present had an influence opposite to that expected. Lonelier women were and are younger and length of widowhood affects the level of loneliness only for the recently widowed. Our expectation that the "most" lonely would tend to sanctify the late husband more than "never" lonely widows also proved wrong.

The following findings are significant: (1) the lonely lack resources in terms of people to whom they can turn for emotional and social supports and their support systems are thereby restricted; (2) lonely women are and have been angry people. They cannot draw strength and other emotional supports from themselves or from others; their attitudes undoubtedly antagonize potential intimates, although they definitely want more friends. Table 6 contains a summary of their own loneliness and supports systems derived from comparing the level of loneliness experienced and agreement with the statement "I am very satisfied with the way my life is going now" (see Table 6). The

TABLE 6

Association Between Level of Loneliness and Satisfaction with Life[a] of Chicago Area Widows

Level of Loneliness		Satisfied with Present Life				
		Strongly Agree	Agree	Disagree	Strongly Disagree	Row Total
Most lonely person I know	N	129	414	774	1,219	2,536
	Row %	5	16	31	48	100
	Column %	1	1	6	25	3
More lonely than most people	N	621	1,516	2,192	727	5,056
	Row %	12	30	44	14	100
	Column %	2	5	18	15	7
Same as most people	N	4,325	10,712	5,428	1,686	22,150
	Row %	20	49	24	8	100
	Column %	14	35	45	35	28

Less than most people	N	7,770	7,093	2,046	512	17,421
	Row %	44	41	12	3	100
	Column %	25	23	17	10	22
Rarely lonely	N	9,340	7,620	1,370	384	18,714
	Row %	50	41	7	2	100
	Column %	30	25	12	8	24
Never lonely	N	8,487	3,086	168	345	12,087
	Row %	70	26	1	3	100
	Column %	28	10	2	7	16
TOTAL	N	30,671	30,440	11,978	4,874	77,963
	Row %	39	39	16	6	100
	Column %	100	100	100	100	100

Gamma = -0.53.

[a] Responses indicated extent of agreement with the statement: "I am very satisfied with the way my life is going on."

distribution of responses documents the fact that loneliness is not a sentiment enjoyed by those who experience it and that it is not possible to be satisfied with life when feeling lonely. Lonely and dissatisfied women have no one to tell their problems to, no one to comfort them, no one to make them feel important or secure, and they are as angry now as when their husbands were alive. In fact, they are more often angry at resource persons not providing the needed emotional supports than are other widows. They are also more socially isolated, but emotional isolation is even more important as a source of loneliness than social isolation. The presence of, and frequent contact with, children, siblings, and friends does help to alleviate loneliness when such contacts provide emotional supports and positive self feelings. Many widows depend on their adult children because they do not have other intimates, but some women do not even receive emotional supports from their children. The lonely are definitely not satisfied with their present life.

13

Loneliness and Old Age

MARGARET CLARK and BARBARA GALLATIN ANDERSON

GROWING OLD ON SKID ROW

GREGORY MAKRINOS* lives at the Paramount Hotel south of Market Street. It is a hotel for men only—dark, airless, and very run-down. His second-floor room is small, occupied largely by an old iron bed, a bureau, a washstand, and two straight chairs. On the wall has been thumbtacked a full-page newspaper photograph of John F. Kennedy. Under it, Mr. Makrinos had crisscrossed a tiny American flag and a plastic rose. Above the bedstead are four calendars, one with a picture of a nude and the others showing nature scenes. Under one of these, in bold black type, is MARTIN'S MEATS with the yellowed legend, 1943—OUR TENTH YEAR IN YOUR SERVICE. Beneath this, the curling pages of the obsolete calendar remain apparently intact. On the single bureau is a mound of old newspapers, a glass with a spoon in it, and a small collection of medicine bottles. Tucked into the mirror-frame are several holy cards, new pennies taped on two of them. There is also a photograph of a young man with slicked black hair and a tight black suit. "That's me," Mr. Makrinos says, "when I come to this country 51 years ago."

Reprinted from "Self and Society in Old Age," in *Culture and Aging: An Anthropological Study of Older Americans* by permission of Charles C. Thomas, Springfield, Ill., Copyright © 1967 by Margaret Clark and Barbara Gallatin Anderson.

*Names of all individuals and of many specific places—hotels, clubs, business establishments—have been camouflaged in this report in order to protect the identity of members of the sample.

Mr. Makrinos was born in Greece, but has been in the United States since he was 14. Though he completed high school in Greece, he was, upon his arrival in this country, put to work almost immediately as a dishwasher by his older brother, an earlier immigrant. Mr. Makrinos spent his first few years in the United States living and working in Greek colonies, first in New York, and later in North Dakota, where he was a water boy for the Great Northern Railroad. He has never learned to speak English well. In 1918, when his brother joined the Army and went to France, Mr. Makrinos came to San Francisco. "America's a great country," he says. "The best in the world. But North Dakota—that was too cold. San Francisco, I like it because I like to stay in one place. I like the climate—all the time. I'm 43 years here; I can find the places here."

Mr. Makrinos is a slight man, greatly underweight. His clothes are very old and patched and far from clean. Somehow, however, his frailty and poise lift him above the makeshift quality of his clothing and surroundings. His face is very lined for his 64 years, and his complexion yellowish, though his eyes are very fine and bright.

He has lived in the Paramount Hotel for almost 15 years. "When I went to the hospital with a busted spleen, I guess they [the hotel management] thought I'm gonna die. Well, they give this guy my room. They was sure surprised when they see me walking back in. I got my room back. I'm a good tenant. Always ready with the money." That was seven years ago. "From that time on, I've never been real well. Always sick." Nevertheless, Mr. Makrinos continued to work with some regularity as a dishwasher until two years ago, when he was again hospitalized briefly and released. Asked if he misses work, he replies, "What to do? I'm not strong to work. But I was 27 years in the union as a dishwasher. Pension's okay—I don't drink or spend money foolish."

His already limited world has now shrunk to an area that encompasses the Kentucky Bar and Grill, his usual eating place, the Greek Orthodox Church a few blocks away, and a neighboring hotel where Biff, his closest friend, lives. He makes maximum utilization of meager financial and social resources, retaining a strong sense of pride in his continuing autonomy. "I pay a fella [Biff] one dollar a day to take me up and down to the restaurant. Can't make it alone no more. The restaurant is the only place I go. No, that's not right. I'm still Greek Orthodox. I go to church—with Biff—pretty close to every Sunday."

Mr. Makrinos has friends within the hotel and "guys I know in the restaurant or on the block. They come up to see me and ask me if I want money. I say no." There is a local self-help culture in this part of town. "You see a lot of boozers. Well, I'm telling you, there's lots of guys like me. I no spend one penny on booze. I have lots of appetite to eat. Everything is high. It costs me at least $2.50 a day to eat. This other guy, he lives just this side of the restaurant. He has a little kitchen. Well, if he sees something cheap at the grocery—'Come on and eat,' he says. Sometimes stew. He cooks pretty good. Well, I always give him something. He tells me what it costs."

How else does he spend his time? "Well, I sleep in the lobby. I talk and look at TV." The hotel man later said that Mr. Makrinos does not usually sleep in his bed. He curls up in a corner of the lobby on an overstuffed chair at night. "But sometimes I can't sleep," he explains. "I only slept two hours last night. I ask myself, 'What you gonna do up there alone anyhow? And who's gonna know if you get sick or something...?'"

He has few complaints. "I feel stronger, better. I like to be with friends and with everybody. I say to that doctor, 'Listen, Doctor, if I stay in this hospital, I die. Already I feel dead inside.' If I'd'a stayed two more weeks, it would have been the end...I'm not afraid. I wasn't afraid when I came here. I'm never afraid. What was in my mind when I came to San Francisco was to work a couple of years, save money, and go back to Greece. But then I decided no. America's a great country and San Francisco is a pretty good place to live. I'm glad I stayed. I don't bother nobody. I laugh. A good life, lots of friends. Not so bad off for an old guy."

Like the majority of the old people with whom we spoke, Mr. Makrinos begins and ends his days a man alone.

Although aging is an inevitable biological event, it is nevertheless influenced by the cultural setting in which it occurs. There is probably no life process built into the human organism that is not shaped in some way—intimately or remotely—by society and its cultural norms. All the subjects of this study, in spite of their differences, have two things in common: all are growing old, and all are faced with the task of adapting to that process within the cultural framework of American urban society. We have postulated, therefore, that most subjects will share certain views of later life, its character, and its problems in our society.

The men and women whose lives we studied are San Franciscans. While few were born in the city, the majority have lived a third or more of their lives within this urban environment. They occupy a wide range of subcultures within a city famous for its heterogeneity— a cosmopolitan area of Latins and Orientals, Polynesians and Slavs, Negroes and Caucasians. The aged are everywhere in San Francisco. They constitute 18 percent of the city's population—a proportion found in few other places in the country, despite the growing numbers of old people in the nation generally.[1]

A minority of the men and women we studied are still a part of the business world of San Francisco. In a Market Street building, not too far from the Tenderloin district, an ancient janitor goes home at noon to prepare lunch for his bedridden wife. Chic and vital at seventy, an indomitable Austrian refugee aids her son in his gift shop. In a Montgomery Street employment office, Miss Potter lies with moderate success about her 70 years and finds temporary stenographic employment in an insurance office. A few individuals—for the most part, men and women in their early sixties—continue their work as shopkeepers, teachers, nurses, clerks, and technicians. Among our subjects is a bank guard, a tailor, and even a longshoreman who puts in a good day's work—when he can get it. Some have part-time jobs now, often different from and more modest than their major life occupations. They are servants, handy-men, baby-sitters, messengers, and dishwashers. The majority live on retirement income, savings, Social Security, charity, or a combination of these. Some live with or are supported by their children—a situation regarded as categorically undesirable by the vast majority of our subjects.

For the most part, they deplore dependency and value self-reliance and autonomy. To achieve these precious goals, they create for themselves manageable worlds within which they can perpetuate for a

---

[1]The sparsest statistics dramatize the phenomenal increase in longevity that is taking place in this country. The "senior citizens," as they are often referred to by our legislators and social workers, constitute the second fastest growing age group in our nation, exceeded only by children aged five to fourteen. Today, people 65 and over number more than 17 million. Each day their numbers experience a net increase of 1,000. By 1970, they will total 20 million. Today the "very old" age group—those eight-five and over—exceeds 900,000, an increase of 920 percent since 1920 (United States Senate, 1963, p. ix).

little while longer their meaningful patterns of life. But their degree of participation in social life often comes to depend upon proximity to stores, churches, or friends. One's own San Francisco then shrinks to the boundaries of an immediate world—one's room or apartment, one's two-or-three-block neighborhood.

It seems clear that American culture defines mental health as *social involvement;* at times of personal distress, social interaction and the support of others are vital to the aging individual's well-being. Yet, urban American society does not automatically provide a matrix within which that interaction may occur, at least between the elderly and the younger members of society. The distance between the generations is too great, and there is no ongoing cultural tradition to cement bonds between young and old.

THE SOCIAL ALIENATION OF AMERICA'S ELDERLY

Cumming and Henry (1961) have quite rightly pointed out that some writings in the field of aging have ''. . . sometimes suggested that every man ages alone, in the sense of being cut off, by the fact of his age, from others. . . . It seems to be assumed that the 'one' who is the reference point is the only one doing any aging. . . . There is little indication of people aging in ranks, echelons, or generations, but rather some feeling that growing old is a solitary experience, unique to each individual'' (p. 17). From the evidence of our study the elderly do indeed interact with each other, and depend upon collateral relationships (with spouse, siblings, or friends) more than they depend upon their offspring or other younger people.

Yet, there are some older people in our sample who do not have the necessary mobility and strength to seek out others of their own generation—others who, too, may be partially housebound. Someone must *come to them,* if they are to have social contacts beyond their own quarters, their own city block, or, at the most, their own small neighborhood. These visitors would have to be people more active and vigorous than they themselves—people almost by definition, somewhat younger than they.

Then, too, we have encountered older people who hate the idea of growing old—are, in fact, horrified and depressed by the passage of years. And many of these do not want to be reminded that they are growing older; they do not want older associates, particularly if those associates have serious health problems—it is too painful a reminder of their own vulnerability. As Mrs. Trocopian says, "Some older people lose their hearing and their memory. It's hard to get along with them. It's unfortunate if you lose your memory. *I* don't feel old at all! If I don't feel right, I blame it on the food; I never say it is because I am old. Most of my friends are younger."

Some of our subjects, too, have outlived all the age-mates with whom they had formerly been close. A little later in this chapter we will describe such a man, Mr. Hart, who, at 93, has long survived his peers.

For these reasons, many of the elderly turn increasingly to members of the succeeding generation for social contacts, but, in this undertaking, they are often deterred by the conviction that the young despise the old, and that the old have no place in American society.

Responses regarding youth-age relationships fall into two groups: those who emphasize the lack of communication between the generations—a condition often recognized as unavoidable and accepted with understanding and resignation—and those who disparage the young and their assumed negative attitudes toward older people. These latter subjects report these perceptions with some bitterness and consider them a threat to their self-esteem. Mr. Czernich exemplifies the first sort of perception: "You cannot get along with young people. They talk about different things together. Usually our conversation does not mix." Mrs. Kramer has somewhat similar ideas: "I don't get through to younger people as good. I can't get on common ground with them." Mr. Jespersen emphasizes how technology has created a gulf between the generations: "Younger people have more modern ideas which, in many ways, are better than the old ones. The increased use of machines and the more education the younger ones have, the more advanced they are from the older generation." Mrs. Miller perceives younger people as moving in a separate sphere of activity: "Younger people have different things to do—different ways in life from what is mine." Those who disparage the young generally do so mildly as Mrs. Langtry does: "Reactions of young people are entirely different; some say that I'm 'just an old woman,' but some will listen," or as Mr. Ebenhauser does: "Younger people want to travel among their own age. Quite a lot have no respect for older people." Others are harsher, such as Mr. Mersky: "Young people don't want to have somebody old around. Most of the time they feel that older people are old-fashioned," or as Mr. Albert Jay says: "Some

call me 'Pop.' I dislike that. Some say 'old timer'—that's all right. I
don't say nothing, but it gripes me!'' Miss Potter accuses younger
people of very unpleasant behavior toward the old: "In the offices—some places—they [younger co-workers] sort of ridicule you."
In general community women report the least number of negative
experiences vis-à-vis the younger generation.

When we ask the elderly to *generalize* about what younger people
probably think of old people, they tend to draw a considerably darker
picture in the abstract than they do when they describe their own personal interactions with the young. They seem to suspect young people
of harboring thoughts that the old are more or less an inferior and
useless class of people, essentially superfluous and—at times—a
nuisance. Only two nonhospitalized individuals, Mr. Bauer and Miss
Wimsatt, think younger people perceive older people at all benignly.
"Lots of younger people have a lot of respect for older people," says
Mr. Bauer. "If they think they can do elderly people a favor, they will
do it. Some won't, but nice people will." Miss Wimsatt feels that
relationships would be good, if the elderly were not overly critical of
the young: "I think if a younger person meets an older person in a
proper way, they can have as much fun [as if they were the same age];
but if older people are critical, they won't get along." The majority
mention negative attitudes only. About one-third mingle favorable
and unfavorable attitudes, as is evident in such replies as: "Some take
cognizance of the elderly, others think they are fogies," or: "Some
will listen to your problems, others won't." In general, negative
evaluations center on themes of indifference, avoidance, and on
stereotypes of the aged as backward and mentally inferior. For instance, young people were thought to: "put up with" older people,
"not pay any attention," "not care," or be "oblivious" to them.
They were thought to consider older people as "old-fashioned" or
"dumb." Mrs. Bruzinsky thinks the young regard the old as "in the
way and not very up-to-date on things. That's why many of them
have no use for old people." Mr. Fox thinks that younger people
"want to keep away" from their elders. "They don't want anything
to do with them," he continues. "I hear them talk, and they say, 'Oh,
an old crowd goes there; let's not go.' " Mr. Jespersen has the opinion that the young feel "the old fogies are fools and in the way." Mrs.
Tully's criticism is not as stringent as these: "Oh, they don't consider
older people at *all* any more. They are polite, but they don't pay any

attention to you—that's all." While some community subjects can be bitter and some hospital subjects moderate in their opinions about the attitudes of the young, it is the mentally ill who make the most devastating statements. As Mr. Hopland puts it: "They are ashamed of older people, especially when you've got white hair." Mrs. Harris points to the theme of avoidance: "Most of them don't like older people and avoid them. They just want to get away from you."

Older people do not always place the blame for unsatisfactory relationships between the generations on the young alone. Almost half the female subjects—both community and discharged—imply that the behavior and outlook of the aged themselves have much to do with poor intergenerational relationships. If the elderly would take the effort to come to terms with younger people, if they would be less critical of them, and try to understand the ways of youth, the age barrier, they suggest, could be overcome and the elderly could "keep abreast of the times." Mrs. Willoughby states very clearly that the attitude assumed by younger people depends upon the behavior of the old: "If you're going to throw your weight around and say, 'When *I* was your age...,' why, I'm afraid that won't go over very good. Naturally, they would resent it. I used to hear that sort of stuff myself and *I* didn't like it." Older women seem more sensitive to this problem than men do; it is a rare man in our sample who expresses any conviction that the elderly themselves should exert restraint and relinquish authority when relating to the young. Their solution to the problem of intergenerational conflict is more often phrased in terms of social withdrawal and age-segregation.

Although morale levels are dependent on social interaction, only the mentally healthy perceive themselves on the whole as active participants in the social system. They enjoy being useful to others and having the ability to keep old friends and make new ones. Community subjects shy away from troublesome over-involvement with others, although they seek out and enjoy pleasant social encounters. The mentally ill are more likely to perceive interaction as difficult and unrewarding, even with age-mates—but infinitely more so with younger people. Both groups, with a few notable exceptions in the community group, are aware of some social alienation of the old from succeeding generations. Nearly all feel that the aged are somewhat devalued, but only half perceive this as a significant problem. Hospitalized subjects are particularly bitter about what they perceive to be derogatory attitudes of younger people towards the elderly. Men, especially, feel that their authority and instrumentality are threatened by younger men, and tend to see age-segregation as the preferred solution to intergenerational conflicts. Elderly women are just as likely to feel devalued (particularly if they are emotionally disturbed), but about half express the belief that social skills and graceful acquiescence to the ways and desires of the young can ease many of the strains between younger and older people. Several of the women prefer younger friends out of a seeming desire to disassociate themselves from reminders of their own advancing years.

It seems clear, then, that personal function is adversely affected not only by role loss (among the mentally ill) and constriction of interpersonal contacts, but also by disturbances in the *quality* of human relationships; those between the generations are particularly troublesome for men and women who perceive themselves as members of a devalued class. Elderly people who have an unstable emotional life—particularly the hospitalized men—often prefer the demoralizing loneliness of social seclusion to the denigration they perceive in exposure to the sneering arrogance of their juniors.

In our study we have encountered some curiously provocative findings that seem almost contradictory: (1) As we have already shown, mentally healthy older people are more socially involved than are the mentally ill; yet community people are more likely to report that they enjoy being alone at times. (2) Women, on the average, have more social roles and a larger number of friends than men do; yet, women are considerably more likely than men to complain of loneliness and a paucity of social contacts. (3) Although the mentally ill subjects in our study have lower levels of social interaction on the whole than community subjects, some of the most highly involved people are in the hospital—but still these subjects often complain of loneliness.

Returning to the first finding, our data indicate that, in general, solitude has a different meaning for mentally healthy and mentally ill elderly people. Despite their concern with active participation in social life, the interest of the mentally healthy group in others is not inordinate. They are content to be by themselves some of the time. As Mr. Knight says, "Partial solitude doesn't bother me. I have plenty of entertainment—television, magazines—I can even go to the theater alone if I have to." Mr. Wheeler states, "I like to be with people, but sometimes I like to be alone, to read and work in the garden—I love nature. We all change with age, and that change is so slow from year to year that we cannot follow it. We get more from quietness as the years go by.''

The mentally healthy aged seem to feel that they can afford to structure and limit the extent of their interaction with others, if they so desire. Mr. Knight explains this: ''As an individual, I keep my own counsel. I am not sympathetic to opening my life to just anybody. Not many people tell me their problems. I'm not much of a chaplain.'' Such reservations are not to be confused with isolation. These subjects have friends and enjoy social activity when they choose to; however, they limit the degree of involvement. As Mr. Schwann says, ''I don't spend a lot of time talking to people I don't know.'' ''I never get *too* involved,'' says Mr. VanDamm. Socializing is something to be enjoyed, but not tedious, demanding, and unrewarding relationships. Earlier in life this might have been necessary—to pacify the neighbors, curry the boss's favor, please one's mate, or gain a client. Now, however, such considerations are less compelling—life is just too short.

Most mentally ill subjects do not *seek* solitude; rather, they *avoid* others. They rarely refer to being alone as an opportunity for simply doing the solitary things one enjoys. They more often perceive it as an escape from their difficulties in dealing with others. Mr. Jackson describes his feelings in this way: ''I'm getting very ornery lately—cranky. I'm very much afraid of meeting people, but I don't know why.'' For some of these people, retirement is a loss greater than widowhood—being out of work may mean the loss of nearly all contact with the world around them. For Mr. Jackson, for instance, having a job provided a kind of enforced socialization. It kept him in contact with people in a relationship that was defined and understood. The role-play was spelled out for him. His difficulties in dealing with people may have been due to a long-standing inarticulateness or personality conflicts, but work and family formerly provided a rampart between this subject and the world around him. With the loss of these structured supports, he became frightened and defensive. Alone now, he is afraid of becoming an object of ridicule. He says, ''If I feel someone is poking fun at me, I take umbrage—very much umbrage.''

We were interested in discovering if these varying attitudes toward solitude were reflected in attitudes toward living alone. Since living alone was one of the control variables in selecting our community subjects, and since—willy-nilly—we had gathered quite a few social isolates into our hospital sample, we turned with special interest to those living alone. We asked them if they wanted to live otherwise. A few freely voiced dissatisfaction with their aloneness, but many more expressed the opinion that living with others had not worked out for them. Some had tried it in earlier years of their lives, driven by either loneliness or economy, but had abandoned it. A number have deliberately turned down invitations from friends to come and live with them. One male subject describes the circumstances of his refusing such an invitation: "I hesitate because I don't want to be a burden. Two guys—buddies of mine—got a house with about five or six rooms in it. They asked me to come and live with them. They said it would cost me nothing. Well, I refused, not because I didn't like them, but I like to be free, by myself." Yet, this man often complained in the interviews of increasing loneliness. His statement points to the overriding influence of a need to avoid dependency (interestingly, he thinks of this avoidance as maintaining his "freedom").

Returning to the subject of solitude, approximately a quarter of those interviewed report that they *do* mind being alone from time to time, that their tolerance for solitude has decreased with their old age. Of these, all but one had at some time been married and about half were currently living with their spouses. This finding suggests what Lowenthal (1964), in a study of social isolation, uncovered relative to a group of lifelong social isolates. She found that these extreme social isolates—"lone wolves" for all their lives—"liked being alone, and. . . rarely mentioned loneliness as a problem of their past or current lives" (p. 64). Commenting further on this group, she writes: "While such an alienated life style might in itself be culturally defined as a form of mental illness, lack of interpersonal relationships, which is one of its main characteristics, may help [in old age] to prevent the development of overt psychogenic disorder [or to prevent its detection if it does develop]" (p. 69). On the other hand, she found that "lifelong marginal social adjustment may be conducive to the development of [mental] disorder [in old age]" (p. 70). Essentially, elderly people with a marginal social adjustment—called "the defeated" and "the blamers" in the study—are those who, early in life, tried to satisfy their dependency needs with others and, because of some failure in the transaction, partially withdrew from social intercourse:

These are the subjects who, according to her findings, were "more likely than the [lifelong] alienated to mention loneliness as a problem" (p. 65). In short, feelings of loneliness in old age appear to arise more often within those who have *tried* to effect satisfactory personal relationships with others during their lives, but, for one reason or another, have failed to secure the satisfaction they required. Consequently, they have retreated to marginal positions in the social system in order to defend themselves better. On the other hand, there are those who have never—in adult life, at least—really made the effort to set up a workable *entente cordiale* with others. Very early, they struck out on their own and have ever since maintained a rigid, solitary course through life. Ironically, these—the "loners," confirmed bachelors or spinsters, and itinerants—are often better equipped, when old age arrives at last, to confront the solitude and alienation forced upon so many of the old in American society today. They are well-rehearsed in this life pattern. But, as we shall see, if incapacitating illness forces them to rely on others, if the hard shell of complete self-reliance is shattered—the fragile self-system which it houses may be seriously damaged as well.

Generally, however, it is among those who have made a tenuous and inadequate adjustment to society—the hurt who still hope— where loneliness brings the greatest threat to equilibrium and self-esteem. For such as these, solitude is dangerous. One touching example of this can be seen in the case of Mr. Makrinos with which we introduced this chapter. He is typical of those with a marginal social adjustment. This man, living now in a squalid hotel on Skid Row, has been severely ill for a number of years. At 64 and ancient for his age, the only source of security he has is the familiar hotel in which he has lived for 15 years. He rarely goes out of doors, rarely speaks with anyone except the desk clerk, and seems incapable of extending himself to anyone who might become his friend. "I tell you, I'm very afraid," he says. He desperately needs the presence of others—though they be strangers—to feel secure.

More often, however, it is the individual who is or has been psychologically disturbed who expresses the terrors of loneliness most eloquently. Such is the case of Mr. Jackson, who voluntarily committed himself to a state hospital for alcoholism and its severe physical consequences. "No one could have helped me, unless they locked me away from liquor," he explains. He spent 18 months in this institution. When he was due for discharge, his anticipated loneliness was so intense that he begged his caretakers not to release him until after the Christmas season was over. Today, faced with inoperable cancer, poignantly aware of his imminent death, and alone in a cheap downtown hotel, he is a desperately unhappy man. He is tortured by self-recriminations for having wasted the one life given him. He finds it intolerable to remain in his room alone with his dreary thoughts. He must be around where he can hear people talk, although he is disinterested in what they are saying and takes no part in the discussions. "What else can I do?" he asks. "It's lonely here—you don't get to know people. It's a very unhappy life."

We now turn to a second finding of our study which gives us some insight into why many women, although they generally have more social contacts, complain of isolation more often than the men do. Women are more apt to admit openly their loneliness than are the males. Many of them are even desperate for companionship. "I would like to get work," says Mrs. Willoughby. "That would mean being with people and I just can't take this being alone." The women who complain of loneliness are generally widows and are further distinguished in that, earlier in their lives, interpersonal relationships were fraught with difficulties—they are either not very accepting of others or, as the data suggest, are too self-centered. Women whose relationships have always been good continue to maintain friends into their later years. Among those complaining, we catch a note of this contrariness. Mrs. Kramer, for instance, remarks: "No one drops in. Maybe I'll see someone in the street, but I don't ask them in either." She, too, admits: "I get very lonely" and is trying to avoid this by seeking work, but, at the same time, she expresses the opinion: "I do not try to get too intimate. It seems to breed contempt." Similarly, Mrs. Viet, who is not on good terms with her own daughter, states: "I don't have nothing to do with neighbors. I never went in people's houses to confess or gab or whatever you call it. I always stay by myself or go to the park." This woman lists two former co-workers whom she has known for many years as her friends, but her contact with them is limited to telephone conversations: "I worked with them. They know me. Nobody could say nothing bad about me to them." Mrs. Viet feels that people "don't have the interest in me they do in other people. I imagine this is so because of the way I am. They don't want to be bothered with me. When you need help, they won't be bothered with you." Apparently unable to form a close relationship, this woman goes to the park every afternoon, where on Sundays she distributes programs for the band concerts. "A lady at the concert said I was the sweetest person there is," she muses.

A note of jealousy creeps into Mrs. Miller's description of the one friend she likes to be with: "She's a dressmaker, not furs, like me. As far as making dresses is concerned, I could do as well, but I don't anymore. My line is coats." In much the same way, Mrs. Trocopian wants people but alienates herself from them, in this case because of a grandiose self-image. "Right now, I have only one friend that I am very close to," she explains. "Unfortunately—she is a good person—but her mind is not trained enough. If she were more intelligent, I would be happier with her. I have always been choosy about my friends." Mrs. Trocopian glamorizes her loneliness as the foredoomed isolation of the elite: "Others try to hurt you when you are more talented, creative, or something. They get jealous instead of appreciating it."

All of these women seem to present a state of mind summed up in an epigram by one subject who says: "I don't enjoy being with anybody or being alone either." This is a very different attitude from that held by Miss Wimsatt who describes changes in friendship as follows: "You always go through different stages with friends. Start as an acquaintance, then you begin to know they love you and you love them and can trust them."

Feelings of loneliness following the attrition of friendships among elderly males are not expressed as freely as is the case among the females. We have already touched upon the sensitivity of many men in this area and their tendencies to describe the atrophy of friendships as a deliberate choice. This reticence is particularly evident in the reports of male subjects from the lower economic statuses. It may be that the harsh social atmosphere prevailing in the Tenderloin and Skid Row districts of the city, where many of these men live, has fostered much of the mistrust and embittered withdrawal they express. The main centers of social activity for men of these districts are bars and cheap restaurants where social contacts are superficial and without any real warmth. A sense of resignation permeates their descriptions of the lives they lead. Mr. Alioto in former years used to "go to poolrooms and sit down and play cards—used to love to go around with the boys—all that stuff," but now he has almost no interaction with friends at all: "I'm just a distant person. Don't talk too much. I worked with four hundred people. I'd say hello to them, but that's as far as my talking went. When you get to be 80, you're no good." Before Mr. Pillsbury's stroke, he found relaxation and sociability at the horse races, but now he sits sullenly in his cheap hotel and exhibits marked contempt of other down-and-outers who share his fate: "I don't mix much. I just get disgusted with them, that's all." He lists the manager of the hotel as his only friend, but adds, "I didn't think much of him until he came to see me at the hospital." Mr. Ebenhauser has been a loner all of his life and, until his sixties, rarely spent more than two or three years in any one location. He has worked at countless numbers of odd jobs: baker, team driver, barber, harvester, painter, orchard manager, and finally, dishwasher. He has never been sociable, preferring to make only the casual contacts of an itinerant. He claims to be quite satisfied with only one friend—and at that, a person living at some distance. "I like this fellow in Reno," he says. "I can depend on what he tells me. He isn't double-faced. We think similar thoughts—congenial." Mr. Ebenhauser does not miss social interaction. He is more interested in developing himself. Strongly narcissistic, he is satisfied to contemplate his own individuality, improving himself and nurturing his yet hidden potentialities. His enthusiasm for steam baths, vegetariansism, and spiritualism keep him so preocupied that he has little time for people. He has never questioned his abilities and retains supreme confidence in himself.

Mr. Czernich, also a working-class man, perpetuates instrumental roles to compensate for a friendless old age. This bachelor, now in his seventies, strives consciously to maintain his gift for "positive thinking," while denying the need for social interaction. The core of his self-esteem rests upon his remarkable physical prowess. He exercises daily and feels he can still challenge anybody to a fight. His days are filled working on many "inventions" which he hopes to put on the market—if he can find some trustworthy individual to help him. He prides himself on his creativity and ingenuity. Chatting and visiting with friends, he says, are a waste of time which can be more usefully spent working on his inventions. At the same time Mr. Czernich is apparently insecure in social relationships these days, assiduously avoiding all of his former friends. He limits himself to casual exchanges of talk he might strike up with passersby on the street: "If strangers talk to me, I talk to them. I talked to a fellow the other morning. I am willing to talk to strangers, but strangers have nothing to say—maybe afraid. You can notice in streetcars—nobody talks unless they're together. Most people won't talk to strangers.''

That there are subjects in the study who are socially involved to the point of exhaustion—but who still claim to be lonely—we have already shown. Mrs. Powers, despite her frenetic social schedule, complains of thoughts of loneliness, describing them as times of gloomy ruminations. "I hate being alone," she says, "even for an hour." On the rare occasions that her husband leaves the house, she phones a friend to come and keep her company. At the age of 77, suffering from considerable physical debility, this woman will exert every ounce of energy to take part in each and every social activity that comes along. Almost pathetically, she clings to old and new friends alike, and is desirous of making still others. Her very security in life appears to be based on distracting activity. Asked when thoughts of death are likely to arise in her mind, she says bluntly: "Don't you think it is something in your mind at *all* times?"

Questions about solitude, social isolation, and loneliness among the aged naturally usher in a consideration of what has been called disengagement. But, before embarking upon a discussion of this process, we must examine an allied issue of great significance for older people: dependency *versus* autonomy. The successful resolution of the grave problem inherent in this issue will often mean the difference between mental health or mental illness. Since the older one gets, the more likely one will need help of some kind, old people are often obliged to admit this need and seek this help. Unfortunately for some—and especially for men in our culture—these very real and very serious circumstances often run counter to an individual's additional need for anchoring his self-esteem upon autonomy—the ability to keep on managing for oneself, to go it alone, to reaffirm that one is still a self-governing adult. It is within the crux of this primarily cultural dilemma that social disengagement must be analyzed and understood.

What in one case might seem to be a dangerous withdrawal from all social intercourse into a hermitage might, in fact, be a valid attempt to preserve self-esteem in the face of acknowledged decrements in physical and mental functioning. If such decrements are not yet so severe as to merit professional or institutional care, we are obliged to acknowledge such withdrawal as reasonably functional to the individual's culturally sanctioned need for autonomy and self-reliance.

However, in other cases—those where withdrawal from others represents a pathological denial of physical and/or mental illness—the greatest circumspection is required in assessing the disengagement as functional or malfunctional.

Among our hospitalized subjects, we have observed the most tragic consequences of this conflict between dependence and autonomy. These older people have great difficulty in reconciling within themselves what they *ought* to do (the value culture) and what, clearly, they *must* do (the reality culture). They fail in their struggle to bridge these polarities. For some—and this is especially true of subjects whose needs for dependency have been strong throughout life— being and living alone is a threatening circumstance, for the risk is great that one's emotional and physical needs will simply not be met. For those with long-ingrained impulses toward autonomy — a primary value for American males and especially those males in the generations we are now studying—disruption of one's life-space even in the interests of health may be perceived as an aggressive, hostile development—a threat to one's integrity as an adult, an event to be resisted at all costs. Thus, the feelings one entertains about one's solitude can be a good index of one's dependency needs. Contrariwise, denials of need—especially in circumstances of physical illness, poverty, and few social supports—can be a good index of the strength of urges for independence and self-reliance.

Because of the unique, often tenuous, balance each aging individual is required to make between his own unavoidable claims upon others and his personal demands upon himself, the question of the wholesale desirability of disengagement is a burning one in gerontological research.

From our various discussions of personal and social function in later life, certain features with great relevance to the so-called disengagement theory of aging should now be apparent. We have found that decreases in social function, apparently related to age, are in fact related to other factors—physical disability, emotional disturbances, and poverty are the main ones. High levels of social interaction promote high levels of morale in all subgroups within our sample, and we have demonstrated that mental illness leading to hospitalization accompanies a lack of social supports and involvements to a much greater extent than personal disturbances alone.

Our findings, then, seem to be in contrast with some of those described by Cumming and Henry (1961) in their study of an elderly sample in Kansas City, Missouri. Those authors have maintained, as their first major proposition, that social involvement *inevitably* decreases with age. The findings from our San Francisco sample bear this out only conditionally. The lessening of interactions through poverty, illness, or decrease of energy secondary to psychological depression we do find related to increased age—but only indirectly, through the mechanisms indicated. In very old age (past 80), those in relatively good physical and mental health, with reasonably adequate incomes, are just as outgoing and involved as the younger members of our sample (those 60 to 65).

The loss of friends and others through death is an unfortunate but natural consequence of aging. However, in our sample, the majority of mentally and physically healthy old men and women are capable of replacing lost relationships through a variety of substitutions. Widows or widowers sometimes remarry, or at least establish a close liaison with a friend of the opposite sex; those who lose old friends make new ones, or intensify their relationships with those remaining; voluntary associations and other activities are pursued as strength and inclination permit. There may indeed be losses, but remaining or new resources can be mobilized.

Our findings are also in contrast with the disengagement theory at the point of another of its propositions: that accepting decrease in social involvement in old age and even enhancing it with willful disengagements from the social system is adaptive and beneficial to one's morale. Our findings show, instead, that in old age, social engagement rather than disengagement is more closely related to psychological well-being. Furthermore, we found, in our analysis of the sources of high and low morale, that—at least for our intensively studied mentally healthy subsample—social contacts are specifically named as sources of satisfaction. Without social contacts, subjects became demoralized, and anxiety and pessimism characterize their attitudes toward later life. Among some of the emotionally disturbed subjects, however, we found that social withdrawal served a positive function in insulating the self-image against critical attack.

We have no reason to deny that disengagement from the social system may be the line of least resistance for white, middle-class, Midwestern Americans between the ages of 50 and 90—*who do not need help*. The presence in our San Francisco sample of those who have succumbed to physical and mental illness and a careful examination of the self-evaluation and morale of the ill and the healthy demonstrate that retreat from social involvement is associated with maladaptation, here defining maladaptation as that kind of functioning in mood, thought, and behavior which eventuates in a mental hospitalization.

At the present point in our research, we cannot determine whether this decline in social activity is cause or result of the mental and physical difficulties manifested by our hospital subjects. It may be one or the other or both, according to the individual case. Regardless, in a comparison of our community and hospital subjects, the healthier subjects showed a deeper and wider commitment to the social milieu —they had more personal associations with others and showed greater flexibility in making new friends in compensation for those lost—than did those in our hospital sample. This finding is further corroborated by case review in the intensive sample, showing that emotionally disturbed males, in contrast with men in the community, could not point to *a single close relationship with anyone.* Whenever a friend was named, it was the most cursory type of acquaintanceship. On the other hand, community sample subjects, both male and female, reported a greater number of friends and, especially in the case of those women who had but few friends, complaints of loneliness were easily and frequently articulated. Among the males, only those in the community appeared to demonstrate any capacity for making new friends. We are left with the conclusion that relatively healthy old people—sometimes to an advanced age—cherish their liaisons with social reality and will do everything they possibly can to preserve that level of social functioning which is customary and comfortable for each individual; that mentally *healthy* older people, pressured to disengage by personal illness or the deaths of others, will show remarkable talents for compensating and replacing these losses with renewed creative extensions of themselves into social reality; but that mentally *ill* older people distinguish themselves by retreats and retrenchments, often to a point of hermetic isolation, where they look out upon the world with mock indifference, contempt, rigidly paranoid superiority, or mute, hopeless resignation.

However, none of this implies that our findings support the opposite of the disengagement theory—the activity theory which has developed primarily out of the philosophy of recreational and social workers who have, in the last 20 to 30 years, concerned themselves with ameliorating the lot of older people in our society. (For more scholarly statements of the theory, see Havighurst et al., 1949; Albrecht, 1962; and Havighurst and Albrecht, 1953.) We have seen in some of our case analyses that an obsessive, hyperactive involvement with others in old age can itself be indicative of maladaptation. Rather than this, the key to successful adaptation appears to be a judicious assessment of strengths and resources and a continued application of these to the flux and reflux, the rhythmic exertion and relaxation which characterize social relationships at any age level.

From the earliest moments of living organisms, we can observe this systolic-diastolic movement from solitary, self-absorbing activities to those where the individual is actively engaged in meeting and absorbing the environment—from periods of rest, sleep, digestion, and homeostatic contentment to restless searching for food, animated self-assertion, and hungering for stimulus and pleasure. Our most successfully adapted subjects witness to a continuation of systolic-diastolic rhythm of engagement and withdrawal from others, sometimes under the most incredibly delimiting of circumstances.

Mr. Ed Hart is an excellent example of how one man of an advanced age has been able to maintain a viable sociability in spite of disabilities. Mr. Hart has outlived three successful marriages as well as the lifetimes of his own sons. At the time of our last interview with him, Mr. Hart was 93 years old, maintaining himself quite satisfactorily in his own apartment, doing his own cooking, and getting about with a cane. Mr. Hart's physical impairment had—he admitted—curtailed much of his social activity, but he was certainly continuing to interact with others at his optimum under the circumstances. Following the death of his third wife, when Mr. Hart was 90, he invited a younger man of 60 to live with him and share expenses. This man—his "roomie" as Mr. Hart called him—was his companion and admirer. When, for instance, Mr. Hart was asked to describe his own temperament, he replied: "Very even. Well, Gino has learned about my temperament. Sometimes, though, I get angry and fly off the handle quick." To this self-criticism, Gino, Mr. Hart's roommate, responded with an emphatic: "No!"

Mr. Hart has a deep love and respect for people, and, for this reason, has earned many loyal friends. When recalling friendships out of his past he says: "I cannot recall any individual I considered a close friend who ever proved disloyal." But many of the old friends are gone now and making new ones is a bit hard for him because of his limited mobility, yet "if I had a friend without having to do anything *physical* for them, it's not difficult at all." This man readily admits that, right now, he has the fewest number of close friends he has ever had in his life ("They're all passed away"), but this is not to say he is friendless ("I have lots of friends; I can't keep up with them"). He draws a fine distinction between "close" friends and merely "dear" friends: "My neighbors are very dear friends but I can't be *close* to them." When Mr. Hart was 91, he stopped sending Christmas cards to his many friends: "I quit. I told them I wouldn't be sending any more. For two reasons, one I couldn't send to all so I send to none, then no one is hurt; two, it was too much for my strength— about 150 cards—addressing them, writing notes." This man's social charm has enchanted every interviewer and has seemed to draw people to him as a magnet. Even his neighbors and landlady are within the radius of his loving care and concern: "Even my landlady is my friend. She had me for Christmas dinner. She never comes but she grabs me and kisses me. The lady across the street who owns those four flats – if my blinds aren't up by 7:30 A.M., I get a telephone call from her. Then next door – the two ladies are spinsters. One just retired. They come in and see if I need anything. They are my immediate neighbors. Yes, I'm blessed with lots of neighbors and friends. I . . . I will say this. Lots of people love me or they're darned good actors. Hmmm, they must like my ways or something." When asked to cite the person who had the most influence on him at present, he replied: "If it were necessary, I think I would listen to my three neighbors. They treat me like a father and they're old enough to have good judgment. One's past 70."

In comparison with other men in our sample, Mr. Hart is somewhat exceptional in that he is a letter-writer. In this regard, he mentions a long letter he must soon answer from a young woman whom he has helped with advice for many years and who has told him: "You're the only father I know." He readily awakens trust in the young who confide their problems to him: "I've had a lot of friends in my time who placed me on the spot, wanting to know what to do." At this point, he showed the interviewer some postcards he had received from a young friend. "I've corresponded with several young people. I can't do much of that now though." (His eyesight is beginning to fail.) He then proceeded to describe a young man with whom he has long corresponded, "of parentage that was not very elevating at all—haphazard, rough drinking." Mr. Hart was mentor to this young man as he progressed through army and college years: "In each letter, I'd give him a line of philosophy, but I didn't preach to him. I have a number of correspondents very similar to that one." Finally, in completing his roster of friends, there is "Hank, who is on the staff of the Senior Citizens. He's taken me under his wing."

Mr. Hart is also exceptional among elderly men, for he keeps in touch with his many friends over the telephone, sometimes two to four times a day. Generally, these are lady friends who had also been friends of his deceased wife. It might be added here that Mr. Hart's role as parent and grandparent is still intact. He will make regular monthly trips to stay with his daughter and her family who live out of the state. Often he will spend a week or two with his granddaughter.

This subject's capacities for social intercourse are most remarkable in the light of one of the major cultural problems of American aging: how to replace collateral relationships, which are bound to atrophy through illness and death, with lineal ones. In other words, as the ranks of one's peers are decimated, how are substitutions to be recruited from younger generations? In societies more traditional than our own, it is less of a problem, for the cultural system of such groups (and the folkways of Old Japan and Old China are good examples here) does not generally force the generations to march lock-step through life with little exchange of wisdom and experience between them.

Traditional cultures will often reserve for the elderly crucial roles as patriarch, village elder, counselor, storyteller, sage, and friend. In this way, the old still participate in the power structure of the society and maintain lineal relationships. The only possibility for American aged to maintain such relationships lies in whatever individual strength and talent an older person might have to forge these links across the generations. Mr. Hart clearly has this talent.

There is an additional liability resulting from this age-segregation. The aged who sink into what we have called "pockets of anonymity" essentially lose contact with available lines of communication to the younger members of society who are in gatekeeper or aid-dispenser positions—or to those individuals who receive and transmit messages about needs for help or problems requiring external aid to appropriate social agencies. Quite a number of the subjects we talked to in these secluded situations treated the interviewers as though they were the long-sought saviors at last arrived to help them get medical aid or increase their welfare payments. For people such as these, any contact with the younger generation becomes a possible pipeline to those who are instrumentally involved in welfare functions.[2]

To return for a moment to the disengagement theory, we suspect that the psychological benefits that Cumming and Henry found accruing to the elderly by social withdrawal were due to three factors: (1) The group of older people in their sample did not need help—either physical, psychiatric, or financial—and were thus in a better position to pursue the cultural goal of individual autonomy. (2) In American society, age-grading has been extended to age-segregation; the young have little to hear from or say to the old. A predictable reaction to this situation on the part of the elderly might be summed up in the words of one of our subjects: "If they don't want me, I sure don't want them. Why should I stick my neck out?" (3) These first two factors (a drive for independence and age-segregation), compounded by the attrition of social relationships through death or illness of peers, might well lead to a decrease in social involvement—and this might be dubbed disengagement.

In addition, it may be that, by their term "disengagement," Cumming and Henry were, in part, thinking of what we call "relaxation" or substitution of terminal for instrumental values. In the case of "relaxation," the constraints of social sanction are loosened a bit for the elderly and they take advantage of their exemptions. They are permitted to be more themselves, to conform a bit less, to cultivate

---

[2] A collection of papers edited by Shanas and Streib (1965) contains several discussions of interest to the problem of dependency of the aged on children or welfare agencies. Margaret Blenkner, the author of one of these papers, "Social Work and Family Relationships in Later Life with Some Thoughts on Filial Maturity," comments on: "...the unease, ambivalence, and plain ineptitude with which the average professional worker, in agencies not devoted specifically to serving the aging, meets the problem of alienation, or worse still, may compound or exacerbate it under the mistaken notion that his sole responsibility is to free the child from the parental tie, in line with his theory of personality development and nuclear family orientation. . . . The number of case records in which one reads of the worker 'relieving his client's (the child's) guilt' or 'alleviating separation-anxiety' is depressing as is the number of times the worker is supported in this by the agency's psychiatric consultant. . . . Most older persons under 75 are quite capable of taking care of themselves and their affairs. They neither want nor need to be 'dependent,' but they do want and need someone they can *depend on* should illness or other crises arise. There is a vast difference in these two conceptions which is sometimes overlooked" (Blenkner, 1963, pp. 50, 55).

their individuality—even to the point of eccentricity; but, at least in our sample, such people are not withdrawn from social life. Those in our sample who do hide themselves away from the young, those who pay ritual service to modern society's decree that the elderly should be neither seen nor heard, those who gather themselves up into a fragile shell of righteous self-reliance—these are not the happy and fulfilled elderly men and women we have met in San Francisco. They are those who, when sickness, poverty, and need at last threaten their defended little worlds, often succumb to madness.

CONCLUSION

The single most critical problem of the aged we have studied in San Francisco is not the issue of disengagement *versus* engagement. We have already seen how, for some, social isolation has been a functional lifelong pattern unrelated to aging per se—and how, for others, it is a late-life defensive maneuver serving to hide one's needs or aberrations from public appraisal. Nor is the issue of continued instrumentality in later life the central problem, although we have found *preoccupation* with instrumental values to be maladaptive for many older people.

For our sample as a whole, there are two basic goals—survival and self-esteem. The elderly—like people of all ages—must try to survive as long as life holds more rewards than pain. And the elderly—like people of all ages—must somehow preserve self-respect in order to avoid the emotional torment that can end only in death or derangement. For most of this generation of older Americans, self-esteem is indelibly linked with the personal and cultural value of independence—autonomy and self-reliance. Yet, old age in reality is often a time when one must have help and support in order to survive. This is the fundamental dilemma. In our sample, the tragic contradiction that American culture generates for the elderly between these two basic goals is the major problem in adaptation to aging.

These elderly people, products of the "Protestant ethic" (or immigrants into it), *must* be independent in order to maintain their self-esteem. To many, even death is preferable to "becoming a burden." They do not mind receiving financial aid—and are often glad to have it—as long as they can maintain some semblance of autonomy: a room of their own, freedom of movement and choice, and avoidance of the stigma of "being paupers on charity." However, in times of real need—illness, impoverishment, emotional distress, failing sight or strength—survival may rest on the assistance and support of others. But our society finds it inefficient to make special provisions for special cases; this is expensive, time-consuming, and wasteful of trained personnel. We centralize these functions, efficiently, in large institutions—state hospitals and homes for the aged or, more recently, "homes for the care of the ambulatory aged." And there even the illusion of self-determination melts away.

Some of the aged in our sample feel that, if help can be obtained only at the expense of institutionalization, if the small sphere of respectable autonomy that constitutes the aged person's shrunken life-space can be punctured like a child's balloon—then it may be best to gamble on one's own with survival. Such people will draw their curtains to avoid critical appraisals of their helplessness; they will not get enough to eat; they will stay away from the doctors and forego even vital drugs; they will shiver with the cold; they will live in filth and squalor—but pride they will relinquish only as a last resort when failing health forces them to be hospitalized.

But there are other elderly people who seem better able to adapt to the inevitable, however distasteful that may be. If they must have help in order to survive, they opt for survival. They may have to surrender self-determination in the end, but they find compensations in staying alive. When we last saw Miss Wimsatt, she was hospitalized for a broken hip which was not mending properly. Yet, she said, "Even if I have to stay here, I'd like to be a part of life long enough to see how some of it turns out."

14

Loneliness and the Black Experience

ERNEST F. DUNN and PATRICIA CRAWFORD DUNN

> Why should it be my loneliness?
> Why should it be my song?
> Why should it be my dream deferred overlong?
> (Hughes, 1958, p. 96)

THE LONELINESS of the human soul is a condition that is "widely distributed and severely distressing" (Weiss, 1973). Loneliness is an inevitable fact of human existence—it is innately woven into the fabric of the human circumstance.

In spite of the universality of loneliness and the toll it takes on mankind, social scientists have generally ignored the subject. Artists, poets, songwriters, and novelists, more than social scientists, are the ones who have most often commented upon the agony, the anguish, the aching void, the fear, and the many symptoms of loneliness. "Only a handful of psychiatrists, psychologists and sociologists have studied the ordinary loneliness of ordinary people" (Weiss, 1973, p. 9).

In reading the studies on loneliness, we have discovered that one area which has received almost no attention is loneliness within the black experience. This paper, therefore, will focus on ordinary loneliness and some of those potential loneliness-producing situations and circumstances within the black experience which result in part from the overlay of racism.

DEFINITIONS OF LONELINESS

Modern man's loneliness in society is the central theme of several books. Erich Fromm, in *Escape From Freedom* (1941), describes man's plight as a moment in which he discovers that he is alone and lacks the ability to establish new and emotionally satisfying social relationships. Man has a horror of aloneness: "To feel completely alone and isolated leads to mental disintegration just as starvation leads to death" (p. 34). The relatedness one seeks is not physical contact, asserts Fromm. One may be physically alone, yet feel a sense of belonging through an association with ideas, values, and social patterns. Through such association man is able to transcend his feelings of insignificance and minuteness in the large universe; feelings that constantly threaten to reduce his life to meaninglessness—a particle of dust to be blown in the wind. Through this transcendence, doubt gives way to assurance and man is allotted the capacity to act, to decide—to live.

In the *Lonely Crowd* (1950), David Riesman describes one of the ways in which man seeks to escape from loneliness essentially as an "escape from freedom." He writes of "a mode of conformity" which inhibits spontaneity and personal creativity. A kind of "group loneliness" results in which man sacrifices his autonomy and social freedom for acceptance into a pattern of conventional conformity.

In *Solitude and Privacy* (1969), Paul Halmos explains man's loneliness on the premise that it is man's biological nature to be other-directed, to be dependent on primary group attitudes. According to Halmos, man has a gregarious instinct, a "drive towards an identification with the species, toward a phylic union or rather—re-union" (p. 4). He asserts that "The experience of a 'birth trauma' seems a plausible hypothesis; for birth means the termination of an even, secure dependence on the mother . . . and the end of an antenatal life of absolute sharing, of full participation" (p. 5). Throughout his existence, man is continually plagued with a loneliness engendered by the limitation of his biosocial participation. Halmos uses the term "dissocialization" to designate the reduction of modes and opportunities of social participation and significant sharing (p. 31).

Man's susceptibility to loneliness as part of his biological inheritance is echoed by the psychoanalyst Eric Mosse (1957). He views loneliness as a "constitutional susceptibility" which is reinforced by a multitude of social and cultural factors. Loneliness is a disease of the emotions to which everyone can fall victim. It is not the disease of being alone, for being alone is a human condition. Rather, it is a disease of feeling alone, isolated, shut out of or shut off from human support and warmth. The struggle to come to grips with the universal fact of the human condition—each human separated from another—is a battle some wage all their lives. Only when the person transcends his physical limitations by forming close ties with others is the battle won.

Moustakas defines loneliness as a "time of crucial significance, an entering into an unknown search, a mystery, a unique and special moment of beauty, love or joy, or a particular moment of pain, despair, disillusionment, doubt, rejection" (1972, p. 19). Loneliness, then, is an "entering into" which could either have redeeming features or result in pain. The key is the entering into process, the position one takes in relation to loneliness.

For Moustakas, there are two categories of loneliness, existential loneliness and loneliness anxiety. Existential loneliness is innate in the human condition; it proceeds from the necessity of coming to grips with the extremes of existence, namely, birth, maturity, and death. It is a recognition of the fact that no one escapes experiences of tragic and cataclysmic change. Existential loneliness has many variations, but expresses itself in two basic forms:

> The *loneliness of solitude*, which is a peaceful state of being alone with the ultimate mystery of life—people, nature, the universe—the harmony and wholeness of existence; and the *loneliness of a broken life*, a life suddenly shattered by betrayal, deceit, rejection, gross misunderstanding, pain, separation, illness, death, tragedy and crisis that severely alter not only one's sense of self, but the world in which one lives, one's relationships and work projects (1972, p. 20).

Moustakas describes the anxiety of loneliness, by contrast, not as a true loneliness, but merely a defense that attempts to eliminate loneliness by constantly seeking activity with others, or continually keeping oneself busy to avoid facing the crucial questions of life and death.

Loneliness anxiety is a widespread phenomenon. It is an acute problem, asserts Moustakas, because man has lost his rightful place in his world. He is a stranger, an alien, cut off from vital experience of neighborliness and community life. Man experiences a feeling of estrangement. Not only has he lost *camaraderie* with his fellow humans, but, further, the advanced technological society in which he endures has snatched away his intimate sense of relatedness to the food that nourishes him, the clothing he wears, and the shelter that protects him.

This separation from the companionship, support, and protection of his neighbors, and the separation from the creative processes of nature, combine to produce the unhappiness, misery, fakery, pretense, the surface meetings, the glib assurances which all contribute to the continuation of nongenuine human contact. Such contact further results in a fear of loneliness, "a smoldering but helpless rage and a desire for revenge for being left out of life." Feelings of inferiority and aggressiveness are engendered as well as manifestations of one's inability to resolve the crises of loneliness anxiety (Moustakas, 1961, p. 28).

Moustakas has taken the concepts of aloneness and loneliness and redefined them, respectively, as existential loneliness and loneliness anxiety. The former is considered positive, perhaps desirable, the latter is generally considered negative and is to be avoided. Within his system, however, it would seem advisable to recognize different variations or levels of loneliness anxiety. One can readily distinguish, for example, between the anxiety that results from a refusal to deal realistically with the situation of one's loneliness and the anxiety that results from a serious yet futile attempt to resolve the loneliness-producing situation. In the latter case, the agony, the turmoil, the desperation may be more deeply felt.

In his essay on the topic, Hobson (1974) defines loneliness as the pain of a felt inability to satisfy that urgent need for relations with other persons which is a basic characteristic of a human being. In a manner reminiscent of Moustakas, he also distinguishes two kinds of loneliness, "non-being" and "cut-offness." Both varieties contrast with "aloneness" (p. 75). "Non-being" is a psychotic loneliness, a naked horror that inspires terror in all of us. It is a serious confrontation with the possibility that I am no one, that "there are no images that call 'me,' 'mine' or 'my own' " (p. 76). By implication there is no one or nothing out there to affirm that "I am me." If, indeed, anything is there, it only anticipates as a "kaleidoscope of disconnected fragments," floating aimlessly across an abyss of nothingness (p. 76).

The ability to create one's own fantasies and ideas allows for Hobson's other kind of loneliness, "cut-offness." Within this realm of loneliness there is self-recognition and recognition of others. Still, life is intolerable in that there is a lack of communication and an inability to enter into significant relationships with others.

By contrast, aloneness portends a sense of what it means to say "I am myself." This is formulated in the context of an "ideal wholeness embracing togetherness with another, with all others—and perhaps with nature" (Hobson, 1974, p. 77). (This notion is similar to Moustakas' concept of the loneliness of solitude.) Loneliness in both of its manifestations is avoided through the ability to "maintain the stability of important bonds and yet remain alone with my own middle" (p. 77).

ORDINARY LONELINESS

We have examined definitions of loneliness as isolation from values, ideas, or social patterns (Fromm); as an escape from autonomy and social freedom for the sake of group conformity (Riesman); as engendered by limitation of man's biosocial participation with other persons (Halmos and Mosse); and as existential loneliness and loneliness anxiety (Moustakas). These definitions refer in some manner to the innate need for human intimacy. It is not surprising, then, that Harry Stack Sullivan described loneliness as "the exceedingly unpleasant and driving experience connected with inadequate discharge of the need for human intimacy" (1953, p. 290). According to Weiss (1973), this common yet perplexing condition may be characterized as ordinary loneliness.

Ordinary loneliness is uniformly distressing but can be distinguished from other forms of distress such as depression and grief. Loneliness is characterized by an urgency to find new relationships in order to alleviate the distress. "The lonely are driven to find others, and if they find the right others, they change and are no longer lonely" (Weiss, 1973, p. 15).

Depression, unlike loneliness, is not alleviated by forming new relationships. The depressed are "often unwilling to impose their unhappiness on others, their feelings cannot be reached by new relationships" (Weiss, 1973, p. 15).

Grief is distinguished from loneliness and depression, but it contains aspects of both. Grief is the response to a traumatic loss, though not necessarily a death. The grief process has identifiable, successive stages: (1) disbelief; (2) denial; (3) symptoms of somatic distress;

preoccupation with images of the deceased; guilt; anger toward the deceased and others, including doctors, friends, and relatives; loss of usual patterns of behavior and the emergence of depression, withdrawal, and dependence; (4) emancipation from the bondage to the deceased; (5) readjustment to an environment without the lost attachment; and (6) the establishment of new relationships and behavior patterns (Lindemann, 1944).

If grief runs its normal course these symptoms will subside (Lindemann, 1944). However, if the process does not culminate in finding a new, significant other to replace the lost one, loneliness can persist long after denial, anger, and somatic distress have subsided.

Ordinary loneliness cannot be remedied by ending aloneness. Rather, the remedy consists in forming relationships that possess significant meaning. Weiss (1973) contends that loneliness appears to be a response to the absence of some particular type of relationship, or, more accurately stated, a response to the absence of some particular relationship provision. The response could be to the absence of an intimate attachment to a mate, child, lover, or friend. The response could also be to the absence of linkages to social communities composed of work colleagues, club members, and church members. Weiss labels these two forms of loneliness the "loneliness of emotional isolation" (need for a significant other) and the "loneliness of social isolation" (need for a cohesive social network).

Loneliness within this context is neither ennobling nor enhancing. It is a feared, chronic distress which contains none of the enriching creative features of Moustakas' "loneliness of solitude" or Hobson's "aloneness." In ordinary loneliness there is an urgent, intense drive to find others in order to relieve pervasive feelings of fear, apprehension, and dread.

The remedy for such a state is access to others. It is important to recognize in Weiss's findings that the two different loneliness syndromes have symptoms and remedies peculiar to each as well as common to both. All loneliness syndromes result from a relationship deficit and create a need to satisfy the deficit by forming intimate relationships. The drive toward satisfaction produces distress that is manifested in impatience, irritability, and dissatisfaction with relationships that do not satiate the need for intimacy.

The syndrome of loneliness, which Weiss has labeled the loneliness of emotional isolation, is characterized by symptoms of abandonment and apprehensiveness which are reminiscent of early childhood fears. Weiss states:

> Associated with apprehensiveness is sometimes vigilance to threat, a readiness to hear sounds in the night, which keeps one tense, unable to relax enough to sleep. Often though, vigilance seems less to be directed to threat than to possible remedy; the individual is forever appraising others for their potential as providers of the needed relationship, and forever appraising situations in terms of their potential for making the needed relationships available. The lonely individual's perceptual and motivational energies are likely to become organized in the service of finding remedies for his or her loneliness (1973, p. 21).

This form of loneliness may be remedied only by access to another who is significant and "right." The remedy cannot be effected by entering into the kind of relationships provided by clubs, churches, or organizations that merely prevent one from being alone. Nonetheless, loneliness can benefit from such relationships, inasmuch as it reflects the yearning for a life style that is sustained by a meaningful social network.

The primary symptoms of social isolation are boredom, a sense of alienation, anomie, cut-offness, not belonging, and marginality. The symptoms differ from those feelings of abandonment and emptiness that are characteristic of the loneliness of emotional isolation. Hence the remedy would be to form meaningful linkages in a social community; an emotional attachment to a significant other would not be sufficient.

RACISM AND THE BLACK EXPERIENCE

The black experience is not uniform. It varies according to time, place, and individual endowment; it is complex and diverse. The black experience, nevertheless, possesses certain elements that, directly or indirectly, pertain to the lives of all black people. Pettigrew argues that "the ubiquity of racial prejudice and discrimination in the United States guarantees that virtually every Negro American faces at some level the impersonal effects of discrimination, the frightening feeling of being a black man in what appears to be a white man's world" (1964, p. 3). Similarly, Grier and Cobbs contend that every "black man in America has suffered injury as to be realistically sad about the hurt done him. . . . He develops a sadness and intimacy with misery which has become characteristic of black Americans'' (1968, p. 149).

History immediately reveals that the misery to which Grier and Cobbs allude has a long legacy. Black people were snatched from their families in the villages and cities of Africa, brought to this country, and forced into that "peculiar institution" which was designed to crush their spirits through calculated, uncontrolled, physical and emotional abuse. From the outset, black Americans were "marginal men," cut off from family, clan, friends, their cultural heritage, their land, and, in most instances, even their languages. The slavery system was designed to divest the Africans of all feelings of "belonging" save that of belonging to the slave owner.

Blacks were not afforded the privilege granted to other Indo-European ethnic groups who came to these shores of maintaining their cultural heritage. For these groups, the cultural heritage preserved continuity and a vital link with the homeland, the "melting pot" effect notwithstanding. Blacks, on the other hand, experienced a rupture of continuity, the annihilation of a meaningful past. While steps were being taken to destroy all vestiges of their African experience, devastating steps were simultaneously taken to prevent blacks from assimilating into American society.

With the dissolution of the legal sanction for slavery, the marginal position of the black American in society remained virtually unaltered. The black American encountered new, illegal bondage, i.e., "Jim Crowism," while other racist movements contrived to maintain the status quo of the slave-master relationship. Such movements, functioning as veritable extensions of slavery, were able to implant in the national character the notion that blacks are inferior and, therefore, not worthy of the rights and privileges accorded whites. "This belief permeates every facet of this country, and it is the etiological agent from which has developed the national sickness" (Grier and Cobbs, 1968, p. 25).

As a result of decisions made years ago, black Americans continue to be perhaps the most mistreated and neglected group in American society. Even after the passage of considerable civil rights legislation, a disproportionate number of blacks live below the poverty level, and a disproportionate number of blacks receive inferior education in the public schools. For a disproportionate number of blacks, the "scales of justice" are inequitably tipped, and a disproportionate number have restricted access to the privileges guaranteed nonblacks. Such discrimination stirred St. Clair Drake to write:

> Negroes in America have been subject to victimization in a sense that a system of social relations operates in such a way as to deprive them of a chance to share in the more desirable material and nonmaterial products of a society which is dependent, in part, upon their labor and loyalty. They are "victimized," also, because they do not have the same degree of access which others have to the attributes needed for rising in the general class system—money, education, "contacts" and "knowhow" (in Knowles and Prewitt, 1969, p. 1).

Poverty, hardship, misery, and ruggedness of life are conditions that persist in the communities of black Americans. However, in the words of Ralph Ellison, "There is 'something else,' something subjective, willful and complexly and compellingly human. It is that 'something else' that challenges the sociologists who ignore it, and the society which would deny its existence. It is that 'something else' which makes for our strength, which makes for our endurance and our promise" (1967, p. 162).

It is a mistake to overgeneralize the handicapping impact of oppression, but no less a mistake to underestimate its harmful consequences. "It is one thing to recognize the social handicaps that impede the fulfillment of an individual's potential. It is quite another to conclude the handicap has 'crippled him' " (Thomas and Sillen, 1972, p. 47).

There is a tendency to minimize or deny the impact of prejudice and discrimination on blacks, a refusal to understand them as irreparably scarred as a consequence of prejudice. These two views seem contradictory. According to Thomas and Sillen (1972), however, they are committed to a common postulate—that black Americans are to be understood in terms of intrapsychic pathology. They are deviant because they are victimized or they are deviant because their behavior, adopted as a realistic response to oppression, is viewed apart from the social context in which it occurs.

Black Americans must be viewed as unique individuals, but that uniqueness does not spring from any special psychological or genetic determinants. The American black has been influenced by certain experiences, or by certain elements within an experience which, to some degree, touch directly or indirectly the lives of all blacks. "There is a timeless quality to the unconscious which transforms yesterday into today. The obsessions of slave and master continue'' (Grier and Cobbs, 1968, p. 27). All blacks are exposed to a culture spawned by the experience of bondage. Yet in spite of the victimization and the wounds inflicted by racism, the uniqueness of the black American is also reflected in his genius and his tenacity to survive. That ''something else,'' to which Ellison alludes, has helped to develop a vigorous style of life that has touched all facets of American society. In order to survive, blacks have had to be constantly suspicious of the motives of the dominant society while at the same time careful not to allow their suspicions to distort the reality of the situation.

ORDINARY LONELINESS WITHIN THE BLACK EXPERIENCE

> I could tell you
> If I wanted to,
> What makes me
> What I am.
>
> But I don't
> Really want to —
> And you don't
> Give a damn.
> *(Hughes, 1967, p. 85)*

When racism is a prime factor in human interaction, barriers are constructed that foster alienation and loneliness. Racism inhibits ready access to social networks and emotional attachments. Belief in the innate superiority/inferiority of the races stands steadfast as a granite-like obstacle to shared activities and mutual understanding. The "we/they" mentality results in exclusion, leaving the "out group" members feeling snubbed, ignored, rejected, scorned, used and laughed at — the "outcasts."

Living within the restrictive confines induced by racist attitudes, loneliness and loneliness-producing conditions are not easily alleviated. Individual efforts to ward off or to remedy loneliness become Herculean in scope and often may result in the resigned futility echoed in the familiar phrase, ''I have been down so long, getting up ain't even crossed my mind.'' With this in mind, let us examine some of the loneliness-producing conditions which racism has engendered that are so pervasive in the black experience.

Poverty and discrimination, arch enemies of justice and upward mobility, power, and self-esteem, are two great contributors to loneliness and alienation. In America, poverty and discrimination catabolically feed upon each other. To be poor often is the result of having been subjected to discrimination. To be subject to discrimination usually results in powerlessness and helplessness. In a culture in which the Protestant ethic is entrenched, to be poor is to be a ''sinner'' unworthy of the merits of a benevolent God and deserving of the penalty—mistreatment. Poverty so permeates the life of many black Americans that poverty and blackness are often viewed as synonymous.

Poverty, like a virus, can affect every aspect of life—housing, education, family patterns, recreation, employment, religion, and individual self-esteem. The norm for the treatment of the poor in America has been ostracism. The norm for the poor who are also black has been ostracism and discrimination. ''Jim Crow,'' considered to have been slain by civil rights legislation, reappears in the guise of zoning restrictions, unjustly dispensed prison terms, informal quota systems, ''gentleman's agreements,'' required union-sponsored apprenticeships, ''private'' schools, and special work experience and educational requirements (subtly denied many blacks) for employment.

Ordinary loneliness within the black experience, in part, results when societal racism is experienced in personal terms. A prevailing cause of loneliness articulated by black women living in inner city apartments is the isolation in a ''sea of people.'' Often these women are constrained by neighborhood conditions that discourage the establishment of social ties, including occupancy of the top floors of high rise apartments with elevators chronically out of service, inhibiting visits to other apartments and making all outside movement an inconvenience. Similarly, children may suffer loneliness as a result of inadequate play space as well as limited accessibility to peer group interaction. Children, especially young children, may become virtual prisoners, confined to their apartments, cut off from ground level activity.

Loneliness may also be produced in black children when they are too often forced to observe their parents and other black adults being ignored, humiliated, and reduced to seeming insignificance. This kind of loneliness stems from the aching fear that there is no one to provide for their individual security—their defenders are defenseless. There is also the loneliness of the moment described by Martin Luther King in "A Letter from a Birmingham Jail." King wrote:

"You suddenly find your tongue twisted as you seek to explain to your six-year-old daughter why she can't go to the public amusement park. . .and you see the ominous clouds of inferiority beginning to form in her little mental sky" (1963, p. 771).

In the attempt to rise from or avoid poverty, far too many blacks find a type of employment that may also contribute to loneliness. Recently, in a seminar dealing with the subject of loneliness, a number of participants reported that their jobs were so draining of their emotional and physical energies that they lacked the time and enthusiasm to engage in recreational activities with family, friends, and neighbors.

The middle-class black faces other problems. In order to facilitate his chances for employment success, the corporate nomad may choose to live in a suburban neighborhood with his colleagues. Such an arrangement makes extra-job related contacts more probable; it may also severely curtail interaction with members of a black community and possibly retard the development of intimate relationships. The situation is intensified in proportion to the degree and extent of ethnocentrism and/or racism in the suburban community in question.

Black token representatives on a work force may also be exposed to situations that are potentially loneliness-producing. With the advent of affirmative action demands, many black workers, hired to work in the virgin territory of white corporations and institutions, have gained marginal positions in the social networks of the dominant group. "Being on the outside looking in" may also result in feelings of powerlessness, anomie, alienation, and loneliness.

Some blacks have suffered from the psychological effects of racism but for many others counterinfluences or buffers in the black experience have helped to establish and maintain healthy self-esteem. After all, loneliness is not an inevitable consequence—a malady from which all within the black experience will suffer. In spite of many common experiences, each individual has his own unique personality which is also shaped by special endowments and personal reactions to experiences. Therefore, when social networks are not available, discriminatorily denied, or when emotional attachments are deficient, loneliness as a response is not a universal consequence. Loneliness emanates from the inability of the individual person to find the inner resources and the external ties to combat these circumstances.

In order to cope with loneliness and other psychological maladies, blacks historically have created a number of channels for resolution, or buffers for living. We suggest that several of these buffers are helpful aids in the resolution of ordinary loneliness. We also think that the buffers we discuss are by no means the only—or most common—means used by blacks to resolve loneliness. Our brief examination of the buffers provided by the spiritual and blues, the church, bonds of kinship, and participation in the struggle for freedom and equality is meant to serve as a suggestive approach for a more in-depth study of loneliness and the black experience.

SPIRITUALS AND BLUES—KEEPING HOPE ALIVE

To ease the burden of anxiety and loneliness, and to retain social consciousness, blacks in bondage sang mournful songs and uttered "field hollers." This transmission of misery and trouble into song led to the development of the spiritual. Feelings of loneliness are evident in such spirituals as "Sometimes I Feel Like a Motherless Child," "Way Down Yonder By Myself," and "I Couldn't Hear Nobody Pray." The spiritual eventually became "the key to the slave's description and criticism of his environment" (Lovell, 1953, p. 456). The spirituals were, according to Frederick Douglass, "tones loud, long and deep, breathing the prayer and complaint of souls boiling over with the bitterest anguish" (1855, p. 99).

Writing on the social implications of the spiritual, Sterling Brown (1937) provides this insight:

> Against the tradition of the plantation as a state of blessed happiness the spiritual speaks out with power and tragic beauty. Too many rash critics have stated that the spirituals showed the slave turning his back on this world for the joys of the next. The truth is that he took a good look at this world and told what he saw (p. 18).

While the spiritual expressed feelings of loneliness and despair, it was also an affirmation, a folk group's answer to the problem of coping with their enforced life style. Contrary to the cherished notion (mentioned by Brown) that the spiritual was exclusively or primarily a mode of escape from their troublesome plight into a fantasy world of freedom, the spiritual in reality encouraged hope for betterment in *this* life, "on this side of the Jordan." The singing of spirituals eased the isolation and loneliness as it helped to create a network of social relationships and life-sustaining ideas. The spiritual was a perpetual testimony against the ills of slavery; it constantly expressed the desire for justice and proper retribution and finally offered a strategy by which to gain a meaningful future—a future in which the slave's work and presence would be significant and personally pleasing.

When the opportunity would come, and it was coming, the slave was going to "shout all over God's heav'n," making every person and every community feel his power. The spiritual constantly reinforced the determination to make that coming day of justice a reality: "Though all may not sing those songs openly, they sing them in their souls. They are a part of the very breath they breathe and of the life they live" (Work, 1969, p. 120).

The spirituals, along with the sorrow songs and hollers from which they sprang, were the antecedents of the blues. Eileen Southern suggests that "the dividing line between the blues and some kinds of spirituals cannot always be sharply drawn" (1971, p. 336). The spiritual tends to be more figurative than direct in its language when compared to the blues (no doubt because the spiritual was often used covertly to convey messages of the times and routes for escape). More importantly, however, the distinction between these two expressive forms tends to be that spirituals express group feelings and longings whereas the blues express individual ones. Generally, but not always, the blues reflect the personal response of its inventor to a specific occurrence or situation. By singing about his misery, the blues singer effects a catharsis and life becomes tolerable again. The blues become a community affair when those listening are able to identify in one way or another with the experience described.

Sometimes blues songs are sorrowful. Often they express the heartache and loneliness resulting from a fickle or departed lover or the uncertainty of tomorrow when a job is lost. But not all blues are sorrowful. Eileen Southern sheds light on this aspect of the blues:

Almost always there is a note of humor and sometimes the blues singer audaciously challenges fate to mete out further blows. Sure, he has lost his job, and his woman has left him and he has the blues, but he will go out the next morning to look for another job, and perhaps another woman will come along. Such a blues may have all of the jubilance of a shouting, foot-stomping spiritual (1971, p. 194).

In a somewhat similar vein, Alain Locke (1936) writes that beneath all the grief, hard luck, self-ridicule, and bitter disillusionment, the blues express revenge. Building upon this perceptive comment, Ames asserts that:

The fantasies of poetry are seldom purely passive or escapist, but are psychological preparation for action. A human problem, no longer a puzzle or a mystery when it is defined in poetry, is solved in poetry symbolically or fantastically, and this gives the singer the hope and assurance to go forward in real life to the actual completion of the task. The blues outline and sharpen consciousness of suffering and injustice (1953, p. 494).

The blues often express defiance, endurance, a plan for action, and they sometimes provide a hero to emulate. Like the spirituals, the blues reveal a desire for freedom and personal respectability. Unlike the spiritual, however, the blues sometimes reflect the ambivalence of being in a minority—the fear that one's dreams are hopeless, inviting despair along with a highly believable assumption that one is, in spite of obstacles thrown in one's path, capable of establishing for oneself a richer and fuller life.

THE CHURCH

Another crucially important buffer against the perils of loneliness and isolation in the black experience has been, and continues to be, the church. Franklin Frazier in his treatise *The Negro Church in America* (1966), asserts that "for the Negro masses, in their social and moral isolation in American society, the Negro Church community has been a nation within a nation" (p. 44). The church was a shelter, a refuge in a hostile world. The church provided a structured social life, a system of social networks in which blacks were able to give expression to their deepest yearnings, feelings, and frustrations. "Moreover, it turned their minds from the sufferings and privations of this world to a world after death where the weary could find rest, and the victims of injustices would be compensated" (p. 415).

Frazier goes on to propose that the black man paid a heavy price for the refuge offered by the church. The Negro Church from the outset could offer such refuge only so long as it posed no overt threat to the dominant white society in the economic and social realms. As long as the church did not overstep its bounds and made no menacing gestures, it was not invaded but rather looked upon with amused condescension. To the church the black man often gave his deep loyalty; in return he found refuge from a hostile environment. In the process, concludes Frazier, he accommodated himself to an inferior status.

There is some justification in the argument that the black church should be condemned for its otherworldly outlook. The church has been guilty of dismissing or glossing over the privations and injustices of the present existence as ephemeral and transient, fitting them into a glorious design that will eventually vindicate the black man's suffering. Nevertheless, the argument does not negate the fact that the church was the community which afforded blacks an opportunity for self-expression and status—a place to be somebody. Furthermore, it can be argued that for the sake of mental stability, an occasional escape from the painful experience encountered in the daily routine was essential.

While it is true, as some critics state, that the church was often used as an agency for social control from within and without, from a positive standpoint the church has been and continues to be a meaningful and significant factor in the lives of many blacks. Frazier provides this appraisal: "They may develop a more secular outlook on life and complain that the church and the minister are not sufficiently concerned with the problems of the Negro race yet they find in their religious heritage an opportunity to satisfy their deepest emotional yearnings" (1966, p. 73).

Although the church may have been an opiate for the slaves that diverted their attention from the oppressive system and eradicated any desire to rebel against the harsh conditions of slavery, blacks transformed the church into a positive institution to serve their particular needs. Initially, African traditions of religious ritual and ceremony were introduced into the church and the African cultural heritage has been maintained. "The traditions of the past are reinforced and perpetuated, faith is renewed, values are conveyed and deeply imbedded in the consciousness of the participants'' (Staples, 1976, p. 160).

The black church also provided the means for developing leadership abilities. Blacks were afforded an opportunity to display their talent and initiative. A janitor, unknown and almost invisible at his place of employment, could hold the esteemed position of Sunday School Superintendent. A domestic servant, known only for her ability to polish silver, could be the lead soloist, moving the congregation to tears with her rendition of a spiritual. An alternative, humanizing experience was thereby provided. Recently, the eminent psychiatrist, James Comer, suggested that the recent decline of the black church has contributed to a marked increase in the suicide rate among blacks (1971, p. 160).

> The black church has provided one of the primary vehicles for the relief of emotional tensions accumulated through the experiences faced in a racist society. Its structure and content are designed to reduce emotional states of tension. The singing of spirituals, styles of preaching, and group interaction all help to promote a group solidarity and give the participants a sense of identity (Staples, 1976, p. 167).

In addition to worship, the black church is a center for recreational activities: suppers, socials, plays. For many the church is a place where gossiping, courting, and friendly conversation take place. In its strengths and weaknesses, the black church has functioned in the community as the place where individuals could be accepted, achieve a sense of importance and prestige, and participate in a revitalizing activity.

BONDS OF KINSHIP

A fourth counterinfluence to loneliness-producing situations is the kinship bond. The family has been and continues to be one of the most important mechanisms for the psychological well-being of black Americans. Billingsley states that:

> In every Negro neighborhood of any size in the country, a wide variety of family structures will be represented. This range and variety does not suggest, as some commentaries hold, that the Negro family is failing but

rather that these families are fully capable of surviving by adapting to the historical and contemporary social and economic conditions facing the Negro people. How does a people survive in the face of oppression and sharply restricted economics and social support? There are of course numerous ways. But surely one of them is to adapt to the conflicting demands placed on it. In this context, then, the Negro family has proved to be an amazingly resilient institution (1968, p. 21).

The adaptability of the black family cannot be overstressed as a means of combating ordinary loneliness. Kinship ties extend beyond the bonds of blood to include those who are bound by special friendships. In our own family there are at least four reunions each summer. Our clan and its various branches number in the hundreds. At these gatherings there are numerous "uncles, aunts, and cousins" who do not appear on the family tree as they are not related to us by blood or marriage, but are bound to us by special friendships which approximate the claims and obligations of blood relationships. Staples (1976) noted that black "kinsmen" help one another with financial aid, child care, advice, health care, and other functions. They also perform the most important function of enhancing emotional relationships beyond the kinship group.

The kinship group creates channels for interaction with significant others. When problems occur and this accessibility is denied, the potential for ordinary loneliness increases. All too often black families have been blamed for the problems of accessibility breakdown. The problems faced by blacks are not related to family stability, but to the socioeconomic conditions that disrupt families—poverty and racism.

STRUGGLE FOR LIBERATION

The final counterinfluence to loneliness we shall discuss is the by-product of the black struggle to cast off the bonds of poverty and racism. In this struggle blacks have become involved in numerous experiences which are cathartic and socially binding. Devotion to a common cause, even when the means were not convergent, has fostered the creation of social networks. Staples (1976) indicates that as blacks struggle for liberation, they become more secure and satisfied with themselves. They express compassion for all oppressed people and become more active in the community.

A shared goal, coupled with group identification stemming from the sharing of a history of oppression, allow for a unity typified by the manner in which blacks approach one another—the knowing glance when a kindred soul is spotted across a "sea of white faces"; the warmth of the familiar salute or handshake of black men who previously were strangers; and the sharing of common experiences in the church or school or place of employment as an entree for social interaction. The experiences serve as an important source of group identification. On the individual level group identification is translated into feelings of self-worth and self-value. These feelings are constructive weapons in the war against ordinary loneliness.

Individuals who like themselves behave in ways that facilitate ties with others. Common involvement in social organizations, educational institutions, political activities, and religious organizations in the struggle to eliminate poverty and racism, provides social networks which make possible not only group attachments, but attachments with individuals who could become primary and significant.

Only a few studies have attempted to examine the subject of loneliness. In these studies little if any attention has been directed to the problems of loneliness within the black experience. In the process of researching and writing this chapter, we engaged a number of professional colleagues, black and white, in conversations about loneliness. All with whom we spoke conceded that from time to time they experienced ordinary loneliness. Yet from the conversations we discerned that few had considered loneliness as a topic or concern that might direct their research endeavors.

Several colleagues have become interested in the subject as a result of our attempts to elicit their ideas on loneliness and plan to engage in future research. We hope that our chapter will stimulate interest in the study of loneliness and will serve as a catalyst for further research on loneliness within the black experience.

15

Poem on Loneliness

ANONYMOUS

THE POEM BELOW appeared in *Guy's Hospital Gazette*, the newsletter of Greenwich District Hospital, London, on February 2, 1974. It was written by a lady in a geriatric ward and found in her locker after she died by staff who thought her incapable of writing.

What do you see, nurses, what do you see?
Are you thinking when you are looking at me—
A crabbit old woman, not very wise,
Uncertain of habit with far away eyes.
Who dribbles her food and makes no reply,
When you say in a loud voice, "I do wish you'd try."
I'll tell you who I am as I sit here so still
As I rise at your bidding, as I eat at your will.
I'm a small child of ten with a father and mother
Brothers and sister who love one another;
A bride soon at twenty my heart gives a leap
Remembering the vows that I promised to keep;
At twenty-five now I have young of my own
Who need me to build a secure happy home;
At fifty once more babies play round my knee,
Again we know children; my loved one and me;
Dark days are upon me, my husband is dead
I look to the future I shudder with dread.
My young are all busy rearing young of their own.
And I think of the years and the love that I've known.
I'm an old woman now and Nature is cruel

'Tis her jest to make old age look like a fool.
The body it crumbles, grace and vigour depart.
There is now a stone where I once had a heart.
But inside this old carcase a young girl still dwells
And now and again my battered heart swells,
I remember the joys, I remember the pain,
And I'm loving and living all over again.
And I think of the years all too few—gone too fast
And accept the stark fact that nothing will last.
So open your eyes, nurses, open and see,
Not a crabbit old woman, look closer—see me!

16

Some Situational and Personality Correlates of Loneliness

VELLO SERMAT

FOR A NUMBER OF YEARS the author, with the assistance of a group of graduate and undergraduate students at York University in Toronto, Canada has been collecting data on people's loneliness experiences in the form of autobiographical statements, structured interviews, questionnaires, and personality tests. In addition, the author previously collected several hundred essays on loneliness experiences from three other universities: the University of Oregon, San Francisco State University, and the University of Toronto. Practical considerations, such as the unavailability of research funds for this type of investigation during its early stages, limited the earlier work to university populations, although more recently we have been able to start investigating populations outside the academic setting.

In our experience to date, no more than one or two percent of the people studied report never having experienced loneliness, while between ten and thirty percent of the individuals in various samples state that they have experienced a pervasive feeling of loneliness, with up-and-down fluctuations, during much of their lives. The distribution of the types of reported loneliness experiences seems to be fairly consistent between the academic and nonacademic populations, although a higher percentage of those who have volunteered to participate in our study in response to an appeal published in newspapers and magazine articles seems to have experienced severe and traumatic loneliness episodes, as indicated by self-reported suicide attempts and psychiatric treatment.

We started our investigation by asking a large number of persons to describe in considerable detail their own loneliness experiences, or those of someone they knew well and about whom they could provide detailed information. Next, we carried out a content analysis of these written documents. It appeared that the wide variety of personal experiences could be grouped together under certain common themes and categories. For example, three out of four writers spontaneously attributed their loneliness experiences to difficulties or breakdowns in personal, intimate communication with other people. They seemed to feel the lack of any opportunity to share those thoughts, feelings, and concerns that were most important to them with someone who would understand, accept, and care about what they wanted to say. The death of a close person, a failure in some important personal undertaking, or a more general feeling of having failed to measure up to one's own expectations and norms were among the other experiences that were frequently seen by these persons as having caused, or contributed to, loneliness feelings. We also found a group of responses in which loneliness was not related to any particular precipitating event or crisis, but rather seemed to be of an existential nature. Such existential responses related loneliness to the realization of one's basic separateness from other people, the impossibility of sharing feelings and experiences fully with anyone, the need to make important decisions alone and in the face of uncertainty, and the state of being mortal.

Eventually, we developed a series of questions designed to obtain the same information in a more systematic and structured way. We compiled these questions into a "situational loneliness" questionnaire. Although the rank order of the importance of the items varied slightly from population to population, certain situations and experiences were consistently associated with higher levels of self-reported loneliness than were others.

The following items tended to receive average ratings between 6.5 and 8.0 on a 10-point "intensity of loneliness feeling" scale in predominantly young and university-educated samples:

> "Feeling lonely when someone close to you died (parent, child, spouse, or friend)."

"When your relationship with girlfriend, boyfriend, or marital partner broke up (opposite sex only)."

"Feeling lonely in the company of a person with whom you were supposed to have a close, intimate relationship (for example, your spouse, lover, boyfriend, or girlfriend)."

"Feeling that you did not belong where you were; that people around you were strangers who had no interest in you as a person."

"When a close friend (someone you were not romantically involved with) left for a distant place."

"Feeling that it was impossible or useless to talk to anyone about your most important and deepest feelings, concerns, thoughts, etc., because you expected that others would not understand or would not be interested and sympathetic, or might even react negatively."

"When people who were important to you seemed to have a low opinion of you, or expressed unfavorable or unpleasant opinions or judgments about you."

"At a time when you wanted to talk to a good friend and realized that they were all living far away, outside an easily reachable distance."

Each person responded only to those items that related to his or her personal experience. All of the items listed above were relevant to the experience of a substantial majority of people in all samples. In addition, there were some items that seemed to be more characteristic of particular sub-groups of people. Men, for example, appeared to have higher loneliness ratings associated with "feeling that they had not lived up to their expectations; that they had let themselves down." Young people who identified themselves with small ethnic groups and who were either born abroad, or whose parents had immigrated to North America just prior to their birth, reported fairly strong loneliness experiences when they felt that "no one could possibly understand the experiences they had had."

Although a high proportion of the respondents reported having experienced physical isolation from all other people at one time or another, the average ratings of loneliness feelings associated with such isolation tended to be moderate. There is evidence that prolonged and complete isolation from all human contact can have a severely disturbing and incapacitating effect on the person (such as solitary confinement in a prison cell or being marooned in an unpopulated area as a result of a shipwreck or airplane crash). However, only a very small percentage of the people we have studied reported experiences that involved physical isolation from other people even for a few days, and less than one percent had been isolated for more than a week. Approximately three out of four people reported feeling lonely while they were not physically isolated from other people in any way, and of the remainder, approximately one-half indicated they could have easily gone out to meet people or to see their old friends while lonely, but that they made no effort.

Inspection of the content of 401 essays about loneliness experiences revealed no significant relationship between the degree of physical isolation from other people, and the intensity of loneliness experiences. In fact, the inspection suggested that, if anything, more severe loneliness experiences tended to occur in situations where the individual was not lacking human company. It is apparently more difficult to cope with loneliness that persists in spite of the fact that one is in the company of friends or family.

We used the self-report measures to assess the presence and intensity of loneliness because loneliness is a subjective experience, rather than an external state that can be objectively observed and rated by independent judges. The kind and extent of human company a person needs in order to overcome his loneliness also seem to vary from person to person. Our present view is that the intensity of loneliness is proportional to the discrepancy that an individual perceives between the kinds of interpersonal relationships he sees himself as having at the time, and the kinds of relationships he sees as desirable or that he would ideally like to have. By this, we are not suggesting that every person is necessarily able to describe the relationships that he would like to have, however dissatisfied he may feel with his present situation. This may be particularly true of individuals who have been more or less chronically lonely all through their lives and may therefore find it very difficult to imagine what the ideal state might be.

A person may also mislabel the nature of his distress and not perceive it as loneliness at all. For example, he may express contempt for, angrily plan legal action against, some people whom he thinks have done him injustice, instead of recognizing that he is really hurt by their failure to extend to him their approval and friendship. All self-report measures are further vulnerable to errors and distortions, attempts at portraying oneself in a more socially desirable light, and the possibility that one might deny or be unaware of aspects of personality or ways of life that suggest weakness and vulnerability. Thus, I have met people who categorically deny that they have ever experienced loneliness, and who claim to be independent and self-sufficient. These same people behave in a way that strongly suggests they are very preoccupied with seeking out relationships with others, even though they do it in a way that usually leads to failure and disappointment. Since we therefore cannot assume that the manner in which people answer questions about their loneliness feelings always yields a true and complete picture of the person's inner state, we have begun to develop other and more indirect measures of loneliness that can be compared against the self-reported data. Nonetheless, the notion of loneliness as a subjectively experienced discrepancy between perceived reality and the desired ideal state still seems to come closest to describing the nature of the problem.

Although the approach we have taken focuses on the individual—on his life history, his perceptions of the present, and his ways of coping with loneliness—we do not intend to ignore or minimize the importance of social conditions and cultural norms that may contribute to the loneliness experiences of many people in our society. Furthermore, the factors contributing to widespread loneliness may also have important social consequences. Recently collected evidence, for example, suggests that the suicide rate among teenagers and young people in their early twenties has doubled within the past 10 years, and that one of the major contributing factors seems to be an intense and almost uncommunicable sense of loneliness. The staff at the Toronto Distress Center, which maintains a 24-hour telephone service for people who wish to talk to someone during a crisis, has reported that approximately 80 percent of all the incoming calls deal with the topic of loneliness. In the present discussion, however, we will not consider the social ramifications of loneliness, but will limit ourselves to discussing some aspects of the individual's subjective experience of loneliness and his ways of coping with it.

One potentially interesting approach is to compare those people who seem to have maintained generally satisfactory interpersonal relationships during much of their lifetimes, but suffer loneliness due to some crisis such as death or separation, with people who have been continuously lonely for years, without any clearly identifiable external cause. Although we do not have any long-term follow-up data, the biographical data we have collected suggest that a person with a history of good interpersonal relationships is likely to have sufficient interpersonal skills and social resources eventually to reestablish satisfactory new relationships. Temporary support and comfort at the height of the crisis may be sufficient to carry him through. There are, of course, people whose interpersonal skills have proven adequate up to a drastic change in their life situation, such as the immigrant who moves into a different cultural environment, or a person who had a very satisfactory marriage and suddenly finds himself or herself placed in a very different social situation by the death of the spouse. Under these circumstances, previously adequate interpersonal skills may no longer be functional in the changed social environment. In contrast, there is the person with a long, almost continuous history of loneliness who appears to have inadequate or inappropriate ways of relating to others. Indeed, sometimes he appears to act in ways that bring about, or perpetuate, the conditions which make him lonely.

Two personality variables which seem to correlate with self-reported loneliness are hostility and passivity or submissiveness. A doctoral dissertation by Joseph Moore (1972) at York University found that first-year female college students who obtained high scores on the Sisenwein Loneliness Questionnaire (1964) also obtained significantly higher scores on both the hostility and submissiveness dimensions of the Leary Interpersonal Check List (ICL) (1957) than did female students with low loneliness scores. Subsequently, the author of this paper asked the students in a psychology class to rate themselves anonymously on both overall loneliness feelings and on their tendency to become angry with other people. The resulting correlation of + .39 was significant at almost the .01 level of confidence.

In another study, two independent observers rated the interpersonal behavior of the members of three small groups which met for 10 weekly three-hour sessions (Sermat, Cohen, and Pollack, 1970). The ratings were concerned with behavioral characteristics such as expressing feelings, attempting to control and to manipulate the behavior of others, offering help to other members of the group, and addressing one's remarks to what was going on in the group at the time rather than being concerned with personal preoccupations. The ratings for each individual were combined over all variables and over several sessions, and were scored in the direction which was assumed, by the authors, to be facilitating interpersonal relationships. After the tenth group meeting, each member was asked to name (anonymously) the three persons in the group with whom he would feel comfortable while discussing very personal matters, and also to select three people with whom he would prefer not to be placed in another group of this nature. The combined behavior ratings of judges correlated + .52 with the choice of a person with whom to discuss intimate topics, and – .46 with the exclusion of a member from further group membership. In spite of the very small number of people involved in these observations (16), both correlations were significant. It thus appears that observers can reliably identify certain interpersonal behaviors in a group setting that can predict the reaction of other group members toward the individual.

In a study of 125 York University undergraduates who applied to a group program designed to improve the participants' interpersonal skills, Moore and Sermat (1974) found that individuals who reported having been lonely "frequently" or "all the time" during the past year differed significantly on the Shostrom Personal Orientation Inventory (POI) (1966) from those who reported that they had been "not at all" or "a little" lonely during the same period. The lonelier individuals seemed to be more concerned with regrets and guilt feelings about their past, and with rigid or overly idealistic goals for the future. They appeared to be guided less by internal motivation than by external pressures and influences. Other significant differences suggested that lonelier individuals had greater difficulty in the area of recognizing and acting upon their own feelings, less ability to express themselves spontaneously, less tolerance for anger and aggression in themselves, and greater difficulties in developing personal, intimate relationships with others. They also scored lower on the POI subscales of Self-Actualizing and Self-Regard.

The evidence is correlational that people who report themselves more lonely also tend to have higher personality test scores on hostility and submissiveness, but lower capacity to handle their own angry feelings, lower self-regard, less spontaneity, and less ability to form interpersonal relationships. Observation of individual behavior in groups and more intensive study of selected persons has suggested that one of the contributing factors to loneliness is the individual's unwillingness to enter into interpersonal situations that involve the risk of being rejected, embarrassed, or disappointed. Hostility and passivity may be the result of past, unsatisfactory interactions, and the lack of a sense of security and warmth in parent-child relationships may well predispose a person to perpetuate social isolation and loneliness in his subsequent life style (Farber, 1968). If we find that fear of social risk-taking makes it more difficult for an individual to cope with loneliness, and indeed brings about in certain ways the conditions that result in feeling lonely, we may arrive at an increased understanding of loneliness, as well as a workable point of departure for both preventive and remedial intervention.

With this goal in mind, we have attempted to develop a measure of social risk-taking. The original scale consisted of 52 items which described a variety of interpersonal situations, ranging from relatively impersonal to fairly intimate ones. Among the items included in the scale were: Would a person who has just taken a new job find it easy or difficult to ask others whether his performance is satisfactory, if he has doubts about it? When he expected to be alone on a weekend, and wanted company, how would he feel about approaching someone and suggesting that they do something together? If he had the impression that a friend was angry or annoyed at him, but did not know the reason and was not sure that this was the case, how would he feel about asking him whether anything was wrong? We administered this scale to 169 women and 32 men who volunteered to participate in our research in response to an appeal published in a Canadian magazine, and we found that most of the items, regardless of their content or level of intimacy, were highly interconnected. A set of the best 15 items correlated .85 with the total score of the scale; a set of 30 items produced a correlation of .91. It appeared as if we were dealing largely with a unidimensional scale: those who found it difficult to cope with one "risky" situation also tended to find the others difficult.

When we looked at the relationship of this risk-taking measure to self-reported loneliness, however, we found a striking difference between males and females. In spite of the relatively small number of males, their total risk-taking score correlated relatively highly and significantly ($r = .53$, $p < .001$) with loneliness, while for women there was practically no correlation between these two measures ($r = .09$, $p = .131$). Subsequently I administered the same 52-item scale to a whole psychology class at York University consisting of 23 males and 44 females. On another occasion, several weeks apart, this same class was also given a self-report measure of loneliness in a questionnaire that contained a number of other items. Both measures were obtained under anonymous conditions in which the participants were identified by code numbers known only to themselves. Only 16 men and 34 women completed both measures; the missing cases resulted from absenteeism on one of the two occasions. In spite of these very small numbers, the correlation between loneliness and social risk-taking was again significant for men ($r = .52$, $p = .019$) but not for women ($r = .08$, $p = .326$). This lack of a significant relationship between the two measures for women, along with the consistent positive relationship for men, was confirmed in several other tests with students from other universities using a shorter form of 15 risk-taking items. There was one exception: in a study of 20 male and 20 female students, in which both direct and indirect (projective) measures of loneliness were employed, risk-taking and loneliness appeared to be significantly correlated for both men and women. Until this study is replicated with a larger number of participants, however, we are reluctant to draw any conclusions from it. The finding of sex differences with regard to the risk-taking measure has also held when the 15-item short scale has been correlated with various other personality measures: the short scale scores seem to relate to somewhat different personality configurations in men and women.

In comparing the individual correlations of the 52 items with the total score of the whole risk-taking scale, we also found that they varied considerably between the first administration of the scale to a nonuniversity population, and the second administration to university undergraduates. Yet the total scale correlations with loneliness were almost identical. Here are eight of the 52 items, chosen because they showed substantial correlations with the total risk-taking score and/or with the self-reported loneliness score for both men and women in both samples. They are rank-ordered according to their correlations with the 52-item total score in the first sample of 201 men and women, which ranged between .68 and .54 for the first six items which were also included in the shorter 15-item version. Table 1 shows the correlations of each item with the scale total and with self-reported loneliness for both men and women in the second sample, consisting of undergraduates.

1. "If I were at a party where there were many unfamiliar faces, would I take the initiative and try to meet some of these new people?"

2. "If I wanted company and was invited to a party where I knew no one, would I go?"

3. "When I am introduced to someone and I don't hear their name, would I ask them to repeat it?"

4. "If I saw someone I greatly admired at a party, and there appeared an opportunity to approach him or her, would I go up and introduce myself?"

5. "If I lived in a private home in an area where I knew nobody, and I wanted to meet people, would I go over and introduce myself to my neighbours?"

6. "If someone I knew only moderately well had something—such as a tool—that I badly needed, would I go and ask whether I could borrow it?"

7. "If I was attracted to a person of opposite sex and I had a friend who knew him (or her), would I ask my friend to introduce us?"

8. "If I was in a store and unable to locate an item, would I ask a clerk for help?"

Each subject rated each item on a 6-point scale in terms of "how easy or how difficult (uncomfortable, or requiring courage) he or she would find this specific situation or task." In a preliminary study, we also asked each person to rate the items in terms of whether or not he or she would be "likely to do what the item says," but found that the subjective rating of the difficulty of the situation produced higher correlations with self-reported loneliness than the rating of "whether or not they would do it."

An inspection of the above items shows that the first seven all have to do with taking the initiative in social situations. Only the last item (which incidentally shows the highest correlation with loneliness for women among all the 52 items), and possibly also the sixth item, pertain to a kind of dependent relationship in which the person's actions are not exposed to any significant amount of risk of rejection or embarrassment. On looking over those items which had the highest correlations with loneliness for women, we felt that loneliness tended to be related to difficulties in dealing with dependency needs and with relatively personal and intimate communication. These difficulties are usually irrelevant to the initial stages of forming an acquaintanceship, but rather characterize a more advanced stage of an intimate relation-

TABLE 1

Selected Items from the Social Risk-Taking Scale.
Correlations with the Total Scale (52 items) and with Self-Reported Loneliness in Men and Women.

| Item Description | Correlation with Total | | Correlation with Loneliness | |
	Men (n = 23)	Women (n = 44)	Men (n = 16)	Women (n = 34)
1. Approaching unfamiliar people at a party	.502	– .013	.494	.245
2. Going to a party where the person knew no one	.234	– .145	.394	.172
3. Asking the other to repeat his/her name	.037	.206	.324	.346
4. Introducing oneself to an admired person	.316	.019	.327	.392
5. Introducing oneself to neighbours	.492	.450	.323	.169
6. Asking to borrow a tool from an acquaintance	.451	.122	.607	.292
7. Asking to be introduced to person of opposite sex	.473	.242	.620	.197
8. Asking store clerk for help	.475	– .045	.470	.415

ship. The items which showed the highest correlations with loneliness for men, on the other hand, appeared to emphasize the ability to take initiative in social relationships, a trait typically associated with the male role in our culture. Thus, the item having the highest correlation with loneliness for the 169 females in the first (cross-Canada) sample, involved calling up a friend when feeling depressed, upset, or lonely (r = .273), while the highest item for the 32 men involved asking a stranger at a party for a dance (r = .673). In the second (York University) sample, the top item for males retained its position (r = .699 with loneliness), while the top item for women dropped to twelfth place out of 52 (r = .213). Conceivably, female students find it easier to discuss, or have more opportunities to talk to their peers about, their emotional problems than do women outside the university.

The risk-taking scale is still being developed and has not been used with sufficiently large and representative samples from different populations. We are now trying to develop items related to the more intimate, social risk-taking situations that might be relevant to loneliness experiences in women. In the meantime, our hunches about sex differences in relation to social risk-taking and loneliness must remain speculative, although there is little doubt that such differences do exist.

A major problem which has been hardly touched upon in loneliness research is that of determining the validity and reliability of the measures of loneliness. We have attempted to obtain test-retest reliability data on our ''situational loneliness'' questionnaire with two samples of university students. The retest returns were disappointingly low, however, and the number of males and females who filled out both forms was so small that we are reluctant to draw any conclusions, except to note that the test-retest reliability varied greatly from item to item and from sample to sample. One particular item, for example, ranged from .155 in one group of female undergraduates to .904 in another group of female undergraduates. The reliability coefficients appeared to be considerably higher when the second testing took place within four to six weeks rather than three months after the first one; they were also higher for students attending a course taught by the author than for students obtained from other classes through an appeal for volunteers, and they appeared to be higher for women than for men. When a group of 20 undergraduates in a fourth-year seminar taught by the author was administered the loneliness scale at weekly intervals, their self-ratings appeared to remain quite stable over two months, except for a few occasions where the change in the scores was found to be related to important changes in the individual's interpersonal relationships.

It seems likely that people will be less guarded in revealing their feelings of loneliness if they are interviewed by someone who first attempts to build up personal rapport and makes them feel comfortable about the purpose of the investigation. Differences in the degree of openness in discussing this topic probably also exist between different populations. When approaching individuals in senior citizen homes and housing developments, for example, we have found that a high percentage of them refuse to be interviewed at all, and that even those willing to talk often deny that they are at all lonely at the present time, although they may readily admit that they felt lonely in various specific situations—when someone died, or when their children failed to keep in touch with them as often as they would have liked. Perhaps the denial of loneliness is a way these people protect themselves against diminished self-esteem, rejection by the larger society and their kin, and the realization that they have very limited resources for making their own lives meaningful and rewarding.

The stability or lack of stability of self-ratings of loneliness is probably also related to the age and current developmental stage of the subject. In late teens and early twenties, when the individual is undergoing rapid changes in his home environment, study and work setting, and interpersonal relations, his day-to-day feelings of loneliness can be expected to show less stability than during a period of life when he has "settled down" in an occupation and established his own home and family. Recently, however, several researchers (for example, Gould, 1972 and Levinson et al., 1974) have suggested that there are recurrent and predictable points of crisis throughout much of the adult life cycle. Therefore measures of loneliness are also likely to change over time, and there is little reason to view loneliness as a stable personality trait in most people. The exception may be the person who is chronically lonely because he has not succeeded in establishing satisfactory interpersonal and social ties at any point in his life.

An approach to the investigation of loneliness that would minimize many of these methodological difficulties would be a longitudinal study. It would provide continuous contact between the individual and the researcher, so that the precipitating factors of loneliness, the nature of the experience, and the individual's ways of coping with it would be observed at the time when the events were taking place, instead of depending upon the individual's ability and willingness to recall the past. A long-term relationship would also help to build up the necessary rapport and trust, so that the person would be less defensive about revealing his feelings and experiences. However, even with the more limited methodology described above, certain regularities in the types of situations and personality characteristics that are related to loneliness have already become apparent. It is a field of study that has only recently begun to attract the attention of researchers, but it is a field of study that appears to have considerable importance for society, the individual, and those who function in various kinds of helping relationships.

17

Loneliness
in Two Northeastern Cities

CARIN M. RUBENSTEIN and PHILLIP SHAVER

LONELINESS is a topic of growing concern in the United States. Newspapers and popular magazines are publishing an increasing number of articles about it; organizations use it to sell everything from perfume to religion; it is a recurrent theme in recent fiction and the focus of a raft of self-help books. But despite the intense national interest in loneliness, social scientists are just beginning to explore its nature and causes. This is not to say they have had trouble theorizing or speculating about loneliness. Some believe it is due to geographic mobility, others connect it with the high divorce rate, while still others see it as a natural consequence of American society's overemphasis on self in the "Me Decade" (Wolfe, 1976). Among journalists, a negative stereotype of lonely old people, especially widows, seems to be current: these people, having outlived their industrial value and their spouses, supposedly pine away in isolation until they die. The grandest and grayest portraits have been painted by historical sociologists, who believe that widespread loneliness is the result of a long assault by industrial society on religion, meaningful work, the extended family, and now even the nuclear family. According to this line of reasoning, the "Me Decade" is the logical, final stage in the atomization of Western society.

Research reported in this chapter was funded in part by a grant from New York University. A more complete account of the project will appear in *What It Means to Be Lonely* (Delacorte Press, forthcoming), by the same authors.

319

Are these theories valid? Searching for preliminary answers, we designed a survey questionnaire about loneliness that could be printed in Sunday supplements of American newspapers. Part of the questionnaire, as it appeared in the New York *Daily News* and the Worcester (Mass.) *Telegram,* is printed at the end of this chapter. Here we will discuss the results from these two large Northeastern cities. Since the results for the two cities proved to be very similar, we believe they can be cautiously generalized to other urban areas.

HYPOTHESES

To the best of our knowledge, no large-scale empirical studies of loneliness have ever been published. It was therefore necessary to construct our questionnaire around our own hunches (based partly on survey results obtained by Shaver and Freedman, 1976) and the theoretical speculations of prominent scientists and journalists who have written about loneliness and conceptually related topics.

One such writer is psychiatrist John Bowlby (1973), author of the two-volume classic *Attachment and Loss.* According to Bowlby (1973), humans have evolved "proximity-promoting mechanisms," since it has generally proved safer for them to live and travel together. Thus, being alone is (for human beings and many other animals) a "natural clue" to danger. During infancy, this natural "separation anxiety" becomes associated with parental (especially maternal) absence. If this absence is frequent or prolonged, it can contribute to lasting insecurity and neurosis. Summarizing his volume on *Separation*, Bowlby (1973) offers three theoretical propositions: (1) If a person is confident that an attachment figure will be available whenever necessary, he or she will be less prone to separation anxiety than a person without this confidence. (2) The feeling of confidence is built up gradually during childhood and adolescence, when expectations develop that will remain with the individual throughout life. (3) Parental behavior is the crucial determinant of a child's sense of attachment or separation anxiety.

If Bowlby is correct, it seems likely that chronic adult loneliness can be traced back to childhood experiences of separation, loss, or neglect. Several of our survey questions (#25–31 at the end of this chapter) were designed to test this possibility. They ask about loss of parents through death and divorce, closeness to mother and father, reliability of mother and father, and the extent to which "you considered your parents to be *trusted* and *secure* bases of support. How much could you really count on them?''

Another factor that might be expected to cause separation anxiety or distress is geographic mobility. Vance Packard argues in *A Nation of Strangers* (1972), that the average American moves 14 times during his or her lifetime, and each year at least 40 million Americans change their addresses. Packard describes what he believes is the resulting ''rootlessness'' of Americans, citing as evidence the great interest in encounter groups, the popularity of radio ''talk-jockeys'' and call-in programs, the advent of bars, clubs, and apartment complexes for singles, and the trend toward generational segregation.

In order to test Packard's claims, we designed questions concerning the number of times people moved during their childhood (#23) and adulthood (#24), the length of time they had resided in their present community (#5), and the number of people they could rely on in an emergency (#53). We also asked, if the respondent was lonely, whether ''moving too often'' was one of the reasons (#66).

Another possible correlate of loneliness is age, but the direction of this correlation was difficult for us to anticipate. On the one hand, journalists have made us increasingly aware of the growing number of ''senior citizens'' who live alone, often portraying them as socially isolated and miserably lonely. On the other hand, pilot studies at New York University, and Erikson's writings (1950) on the developmental crisis of ''intimacy vs. isolation'' that typically occurs during young adulthood, alerted us to the fact that many young people suffer from intense loneliness even though they are less likely than old people to live alone.

A fourth area of inquiry has to do with self-esteem and regard for others. Our pilot studies, and research by Rosenberg (1965), suggested that lonely people tend to dislike themselves. There are at least two different kinds of explanations for this: (1) A person who desires but cannot find friendship or companionship is likely to blame himself for this failure. (2) People who doubt their own value are less likely than their self-confident peers to take the risks that are sometimes necessary to establish social ties. Moreover, previous research (for example, Scheerer, 1949 and Berger, 1952, 1955) has shown that people who dislike themselves are prone to dislike others as well, perhaps because this protects them from rejection. Whatever the reason, the disliking of others probably contributes to the persistence of social isolation, loneliness, and low self-esteem.

In order to investigate the relationship between loneliness and self-esteem, and the potentially vicious cycle involving self-dislike and dislike for others, we asked questions about personal attractiveness (#77), likeability (#78), and self-esteem, friendliness, shyness, and the liking of others (all in #81).

Do lonely adults actually have fewer friends than their nonlonely counterparts? Do they belong to fewer groups and socialize less often? Do they spend less time on the phone? Are they more likely to live alone? Or are they merely dissatisfied with what other people might consider a satisfactory number of social relationships? In other words, is loneliness due to objectively defined social isolation or is it a subjective feeling that can befall some people even in the midst of friends and family? Several items on our questionnaire were aimed at these issues.

We believe that at least one important loneliness theorist, James Lynch, has assumed too quickly that loneliness and aloneness are synonymous. Moreover, Lynch has argued, in his provocative book *The Broken Heart: The Medical Consequences of Loneliness* (1977), that people who live alone are unusually susceptible to serious illnesses and prone to premature death. We suspected that Lynch's hypothesis might be valid for loneliness but invalid for aloneness. We therefore included a list of questions about mental and physical health (#32) which could be tested for relationships with (1) living alone (Lynch's focus) and (2) feelings of loneliness (our focus).

EXPLORATORY QUESTIONS

In addition to hypotheses outlined in the previous section, three general questions interested us: (1) How do people feel when they are "lonely"? Is there a small, specifiable set of factors that define loneliness for most people? (2) To what do people attribute loneliness? Do they blame themselves or the situations in which they find themselves? What personal and situational factors are commonly called upon to explain loneliness? (3) What do people do when they feel lonely? Can reactions to loneliness be organized into a few meaningful categories?

In order to answer these questions, we completed a pilot survey and conducted intensive interviews. These yielded the lists of answer alternatives for items 65, 66, and 84 of our newspaper questionnaire.

THE SURVEYS

Most of the 84 items on our questionnaire can be divided into five categories: demographic, family background, social involvement, personal satisfaction, and loneliness. The demographic questions are concerned with age, sex, marital status, income, education, and occupation. Family background questions assess the quality of the relationships between the respondent and each of his or her parents. Questions in the social involvement category map the respondent's social world, inquiring about the number of organizations he or she belongs to, the number of personal and business conversations engaged in each day, and the frequency of participation in various social activities. The personal satisfaction questions ask how pleased or dissatisfied respondents are with everything from their houses or apartments to the way their lives seem to be going. Finally, the loneliness questions cover all aspects of being lonely: *how* lonely the respondent is (based on eight separate questions), his or her *reasons* for being lonely, how he or she *feels* when lonely, and what he or she *does* when feeling that way.

RESULTS

WHO RESPONDED IN NEW YORK?[1]

People of all ages, from 18 to 88, answered the questionnaire. The mean age was 35.4 (31 percent of the respondents were between 25 and 35). All education and income levels were represented, as was almost every conceivable occupation. Over one-third of the respondents were single, 30 percent were married for the first time, and 23 percent were either separated, divorced, or widowed. Fifty percent of the respondents had children.

Members of all major religious groups responded, as did members of 25 racial or ethnic categories. Fifty-one percent of the sample was Catholic, 19 percent Protestant, and 15 percent Jewish; 14 percent were Black, 22 percent were Italian, 13 percent were Irish, and 7 percent were Hispanic.

---

[1]Figures reported in this section are for the New York sample only, but except for the racial distribution the results were almost identical to figures obtained from the Worcester sample.

The only way in which the sample seemed obviously unrepresentative of the New York area was that 74 percent of the respondents were women. We do not know whether this high response rate among women reflects differential reading of the *News* magazine, different levels of interest in loneliness, or greater willingness on the part of women to fill out a questionnaire concerned with personal feelings. We do know that among those who responded, women were no lonelier than men.

Most important, however, was the variety of lonely and nonlonely people who responded. Although some people wrote on their answer sheet, "Only a lonely person would bother to fill this out," about half of the respondents indicated that they are infrequently lonely ("occasionally," "rarely," or "never"). Only 16 percent are lonely most or all of the time.[2]

THE BOWLBY HYPOTHESIS

In both the New York and Worcester samples, significant relationships were found between parental helpfulness and closeness, on the one hand, and degree of reported loneliness on the other. Respondents who had warm, helpful mothers and fathers were less likely to be lonely than those who had disagreeable, unhelpful parents. Similarly, we found a significant relationship between being able to trust parents and degree of loneliness: the least lonely people were the most likely to say that they considered their parents to be "trusted and secure bases of support." As long as parents were considered somewhat helpful and close, adult loneliness was not a problem. However, a conflicted relationship with parents who could not be relied upon for help was associated with a moderate degree of adult loneliness, and the absence of a parent produced the highest degree of adult loneliness.

In terms of adult loneliness, the loss of either parent by divorce proved more detrimental than loss by death. Respondents whose parents were divorced before age 18 were significantly more lonely in adulthood than respondents whose parents were divorced later or not

---

[2]Loneliness was determined by computing standard scores for each of eight loneliness items and then summing them. The internal consistency reliability of this eight-item loneliness scale is .88 (which is quite high for a brief measure).

at all. In addition, there was a negative relationship between age at parents' divorce and adult loneliness (the younger the respondent at the time of the parents' divorce, the lonelier he or she is as an adult). We found no significant difference in loneliness between respondents whose parents *died* before the respondent reached the age of 18 and those whose parents either died after the respondent was 18 or are still living.

These preliminary results lend substantial support to Bowlby's (1973) theory. Our findings suggest that chronic "separation anxiety" leaves a person more vulnerable to situational pressures that can cause loneliness. The least vulnerable adults are those who grew up with supportive parents; the most vulnerable are those who lost a parent through divorce or separation (but not through death). Perhaps a potentially available, divorced parent is perceived by the child as *choosing* not to be present—that is, as rejecting the child—whereas a deceased parent is usually understood not to have chosen separation.

The implications of these findings for future generations of Americans are disturbing, considering that census bureau demographers (Glick and Norton, 1977) predict that 45 percent of all children born in 1977 will probably live for *at least* several months with only one parent.

THE PACKARD HYPOTHESIS

Adult loneliness was *not* related to the number of years the respondent had lived in his or her present community (unless this was less than one year), the number of moves during childhood, or the number of moves during adulthood. (This pattern of results was obtained for both the New York and Worcester samples.)

Packard's notion that geographic mobility is a primary cause of loneliness appears to be incorrect, at least for the majority of frequent movers. Perhaps people who move often are more willing to take social risks or are more skilled, because more practiced, at initiating new friendships. People who move more often have no fewer friends than people who remain rooted in one area, nor are frequent movers less satisfied with their friendships.

AGE AND LONELINESS

Perhaps our most striking finding, in both New York and Worcester, was that elderly respondents were significantly *less* lonely than young respondents. Moreover, elderly respondents say they have more close friends (although they spend less time with them) and are more satisfied than the young with their friendships. The elderly participate in more groups, watch TV less often, and get "drunk or stoned" less often. They also seem to have different attitudes about themselves. People over 60 have *higher* self-esteem than respondents under 25 and also feel more "independent." For them, "having a romantic or sexual partner" is less important than it is for the young. Surprisingly, the elderly respondents even complain less than the young about most physical and psychological symptoms (such as headaches, poor appetite, crying spells, feeling irritable or angry, and having poor concentration).

Of course, we should keep in mind that truly isolated or lonely elderly people may not buy newspapers or be able to fill out questionnaires. But statistics do not support the popular stereotype, fostered by the mass media, of elderly Americans as ill, hospitalized, or institutionalized. Actually, people over 65 have a lower incidence of acute illnesses, and according to the 1970 Census Report, only four percent of people over 65 live in nursing homes or institutions for the aged. Moreover, our findings are sufficiently strong and consistent (and have been corroborated often enough by others) to suggest that loneliness is mainly a problem of the young. Similar results, for example, have been reported by Rosow (1962), Shanas et al. (1968), and Lowenthal, Thurnher, and Chiriboga (1975). In a study of social integration in retirement housing, Rosow found that only a "minority of old people are lonely." Shanas et al. (1968) used area-probability sampling in three countries (the United States, Great Britain, and Denmark) to study the role of the aged in industrial societies. They reported that 80 percent of the elderly (those over 65) "rarely" or "never" feel lonely. Only nine percent feel lonely "often." Fifteen years ago, Shanas and her colleagues stated: "Relatively few old people feel lonely often. [These results show] how wide of the mark has been much of the pessimistic and misleading speculation about the loneliness of the elderly in industrialized countries." They concluded that loneliness is not necessarily a reaction of those who are physically isolated, but is "an individual response to an external situation" (see Shanas et al., 1968, p. 270).

More recently, Lowenthal, Thurnher, and Chiriboga's (1975) investigation of four stages of adult life, beginning with graduation from high school, revealed that the youngest subjects (the high school graduates) were the loneliest. Reported loneliness decreased in frequency from high school graduation, to first marriage, to middle age, and finally to preretirement where it was the least common. (They also found that depression, boredom, and restlessness decrease steadily with age.)

These age trends are compatible with Erikson's (1950) theory of psychosocial development. The characteristic crisis of young adults, "intimacy vs. isolation," deals with establishing an intimate relationship, so people in this age group are especially concerned about being "unattached." Often, their notion of ideal intimacy is quite discrepant with their actual relationships, and the pain and disappointment of this discovery leaves them feeling lonely and alienated.

Older people are less lonely even though they are more likely than the young to live alone. Thus, loneliness and living alone are quite distinct, contrary to Lynch's (1977) suggestions (see below). Some of the loneliest respondents live with their parents, some are married, and a few live in institutions. A woman from New York wrote: "It is possible to be alone and never be lonely. It is also possible to be lonely and never be alone. Since the death of my first husband there has been an inner core of loneliness within me, a void that is never filled. This is true despite the fact that I remarried within less than a year after his death."

REGARD FOR SELF AND OTHERS

Lonely people have low self-esteem; this was one of our strongest findings ($r = .59, .57$)[3]. Moreover, lonely people tend to like others *less* than nonlonely people ($r = .22, .27$).

All self-descriptive items in the questionnaire are related to loneliness. The more positively a person sees himself, the less lonely

[3]The correlation coefficients in parentheses indicate the strength of the relationship between the two variables—in this case, loneliness and self-esteem. Where two figures are listed, the first is for the New York sample and the second is for the Worcester sample. The reason for listing both is to show how remarkably similar they are.

he feels. This positive self-image includes perception of oneself as "likeable," "attractive," "friendly," "not shy," and in control of one's life (see #80; all of these correlations are in the .20 to .50 range). In addition, people who believe that their lives have "meaning and direction" are less likely to be lonely ($r = .46, .49$). (This measure is *not* synonymous with religious belief; there was no correlation between religiosity and loneliness.) Finally, people who are lonely also tend to be "bored" ($r = .51, .51$) and "unhappy" ($r = .57, .64$).

The fact that lonely people dislike others probably has something to do with self-defense. If a person feels vulnerable to rejection, one way to protect himself is to claim that other people are undesirable anyway. In fact, low self-esteem correlates with denying that "I like most people I meet" ($r = .21, .35$). Also, people with low self-esteem have fewer friends, participate less in social and civic groups, are less "busy" during the week and on weekends, and are more often bored.

One possible route to chronic loneliness is suggested by these and earlier results. Some lonely people may have experienced real or imagined rejection during childhood which led them to question their own value and feel angry or suspicious toward others. This in turn could lead to reduced social risk-taking, greater social isolation, and less satisfying friendships—and finally to increased loneliness. In other words, loneliness and low self-esteem augment each other.

Social Life

Since lonely people *do* have fewer social ties, their need for others may be realistic in a sense, but their *dissatisfaction* with the ties they have is an even more important determinant of their loneliness. They belong to fewer groups, have fewer friends, attend social events and church and civic groups less often, and receive fewer telephone calls than nonlonely people. They spend fewer hours socializing each week, are able to rely on fewer people to help them in an emergency, and tend not to know their neighbors very well. However, these relationships (all in the .10 to .30 range) are not nearly as strong as the relationships between loneliness and the items measuring satisfaction.

Lonely people are dissatisfied people. They are dissatisfied with their living situation ($r = .42, .54$), with the number of friends they have ($r = .47, .46$) and with the quality of their friendships ($r = .41, .35$), with their marriages or love relationships ($r = .43, .52$), with the number of casual (r = .20, .22) and personal (r = .30,.33) conversations they have each day, and with their sex lives (r = .38, .41). Unfortunately, we cannot tell from our results how much of this widespread dissatisfaction is due to objectively substandard relationships and how much to unrealistically strong needs or high standards.

THE LYNCH HYPOTHESIS

Degree of loneliness is *not* related to the number of years a person has lived alone (r = .06, .02). People who live alone are *not necessarily lonely*; neither are they necessarily in poor health (contrary to Lynch, 1977). We found no differences in self-reported mental and physical health between people who live alone and people who live with others. Lonely people are, however, more troubled by *all* of the symptoms, particularly by feelings of despair and guilt, irrational fears, irritability, and anxiety. We developed a composite index of health and stress (via factor analysis; see Nie et al., 1975) based on a weighted sum of all the items included in question #32 (the psychosomatic symptom list). There was *no* difference in scores on this index between people who live alone and those who do not. However, a very strong relationship was found between the health/stress index and self-reported loneliness (r = .60, .63).

Similar findings have been reported by Shanas et al. (1968) and Townsend (1957). In both studies, loneliness was associated with reports of relatively poor health, and this was true regardless of living arrangements (alone or with others). Townsend's study, conducted in London, focused on the difference between social isolation and loneliness among the elderly. He found that those living in relative isolation were often *not* as lonely as those "living at the center of a large family." He concluded that the loss of a loved one is more important than social isolation in explaining loneliness.

HOW DOES LONELINESS FEEL?

When people label themselves "lonely," the feelings they mention having most often are: depression, sadness, boredom, self-pity, and longing to be with one special person. We performed a factor analysis on the 27 feelings associated with loneliness (question #65) in order to discover whether there are clear-cut sets of feelings that define loneliness. Four such factors emerged in both the New York and Worcester samples (see Table 1).

The first and statistically most important factor we have named "Desperation." It indicates that a large part of loneliness is anxiety about one's inability to satisfy a powerful need. The third factor, "Impatient Boredom," represents a milder form of loneliness, the kind that many people feel when they are uncharacteristically left alone on a Saturday night or find themselves alone during an uneventful business trip. Factors 2 and 4, "Self-deprecation" and "Depression," are probably reactions to prolonged feelings of loneliness. Self-deprecation could be viewed as hostility toward the self (feeling "unattractive," "stupid," "down on self"); depression, as defined here, is a more passive state characterized by self-pity. These feeling-clusters call to mind two of the major theories of depression due to loss: psychoanalytic theory (Freud, 1917), according to which depression is due to inwardly directed aggression, and Seligman's theory (1975), based on the concept of "learned helplessness."

To What Do People Attribute Loneliness?

People are most likely to attribute their loneliness to (1) "being alone," (2) being bored, and (3) being without a spouse or lover.

TABLE 1
Factor Analyses: Feelings When Lonely

Factor 1 Desperation	Factor 2 Self-Deprecation	Factor 3 Impatient Boredom	Factor 4 Depression
Desperate	Feeling unattractive	Impatient	Sad
Panic	Down on self	Bored	Depressed
Helpless	Stupid	Desire to be	Empty
Afraid	Ashamed	elsewhere	Isolated
Without hope	Insecure	Uneasy	Sorry for self
Abandoned		Angry	Melancholy
Vulnerable		Unable to	Alienated
		concentrate	Longing to be with one special person

Thus, in both New York and Worcester the blame is placed primarily on the *situation* in which the lonely person finds himself. A factor analysis performed on the list of 20 reasons for being lonely (question #66) yielded five distinct categories in both New York and Worcester (see Table 2).

The categories are nearly self-explanatory. The first factor reveals a desire for one special person, a spouse or lover. The second factor reflects a need for a comfortable and understanding friend or group of friends. The third and the fifth factors pertain to forced social isolation. The fourth factor, "Being Alone," describes simple situations in which the general absence of other people is noticed. "Forced Isolation" applies mainly to the infirm aged and the handicapped, while "Alienation" applies predominantly to young adults. "Being Unattached" is especially important to young singles and to the recently separated and divorced of all ages.

What Do People Do When They Feel Lonely?

We offered a list of 24 possible responses to loneliness (question #84). The most frequently chosen alternatives were watching TV, listening to music, calling a friend, and reading. Four distinct factors emerged from a factor analysis of the 24 items (see Table 3). "Sad Passivity" (Factor 1) is a characteristic reaction to loneliness among those who are chronically or severely lonely. They have reached a state of lethargic self-pity which is not likely to attract other people and which probably contributes to the vicious cycle of low self-esteem and loneliness discussed earlier. The passive and oral reactions to loneliness will not ameliorate the feeling, but only prolong it. It is interesting to note that television viewing falls in the same category as taking tranquilizers.

The three remaining factors represent different solutions to loneliness chosen by people who are only infrequently lonely. "Active Solitude" reflects a creative and rewarding use of time spent alone; it is an alternative to loneliness. The profligates, who react by "Spending Money," seek compensation for their negative feelings, or at least attempt actively to distract themselves. "Social Contact" deals with the problem of loneliness head on, by "calling a friend" or "visiting someone." For people who use this strategy, loneliness is likely to be a transient state.

TABLE 2
Factor Analysis: Reasons for Being Lonely

Factor 1 Being Unattached	Factor 2 Alienation	Factor 3 Forced Isolation	Factor 4 Being Alone	Factor 5 Dislocation
Having no spouse	Feeling different	Being housebound	Coming home to an empty house	Being far from home
Having no sexual partner	Being misunderstood	Being hospitalized	Being alone	Moving too often
Breaking up with a spouse or lover	Not being needed	Having no transportation		Being in a new job or new school
	Having no close friends			Traveling often

TABLE 3
Factor Analysis: What People Do When They Feel Lonely

Factor 1 Sad Passivity	Factor 2 Active Solitude	Factor 3 Spending Money	Factor 4 Social Contact
Cry	Study or work	Spend money	Call a friend
Sleep	Write	Go shopping	Visit someone
Sit and think	Listen to music		
Do nothing	Exercise		
Overeat	Walk		
Take tranquilizers	Work on a hobby		
Watch TV	Go to a movie		
Drink or get 'stoned'	Read		
	Play music		

CONCLUDING COMMENTS

Loneliness is a complex phenomenon, meaning different things to different people. To one person it represents a desperate need for a lost love or an intimate friend; to another, it represents a temporary feeling of boredom due to an absence of social stimulation; to a third, loneliness might be a part of general alienation, a feeling of not fitting in. Like all complex emotions, loneliness is caused by an interaction of personal dispositions and situational forces.

Our studies suggest that the loss of a parent through divorce, or lack of confidence in parental support during childhood, can leave a person vulnerable to adult loneliness. This vulnerability lasts for a long time, perhaps throughout life, causing some people to react more strongly than others to separation and social isolation.

Separation and social isolation may be misleading terms. Many of the lonely people we surveyed were not isolated from others in any simple, objective sense. Indeed, many were married or living with friends or family. Most were working or studying in a social setting of some kind. Although lonely people do have somewhat fewer friends and engage in fewer social interactions on the average, a much more powerful determinant of loneliness is *dissatisfaction* with available friends and relationships.

Lonely people are inclined to dislike other people in general, a defensive reaction which easily precludes the formation of new social ties. Even more evident is their dislike of themselves, suggesting that their defenses ultimately fail. If loneliness continues for too long, the lonely person can no longer blame his or her dissatisfaction on circumstances or on the faults of others (even if the latter interpretations are valid). The eventual results of self-blame include apathy, depression, disease, and even premature death.

Since concern over loneliness in America is unlikely to subside, given our high divorce rate and the unavoidable difficulties of adolescence in modern society, effective treatment approaches are needed. Results from our studies offer suggestions for treatment (see also Perlman, Gerson, and Spinner, 1978 and Peplau, Russell, and Heim, 1979) but more detailed studies are required. Since the causes of loneliness are diverse, no single remedy will be suitable for all lonely people. We have yet to discover the appropriate match between types of loneliness and different treatment methods. Of course, to the extent that widespread loneliness reflects societal dynamics rather than individual deficiencies, no array of personal remedies is likely to be sufficient.

APPENDIX

Selected Items from the N.Y.U. Loneliness Questionnaire

Below are all of the items from our questionnaire that are referred to in the preceding pages. Original item numbers have been retained so that item references in this chapter will be consistent with those in our other publications.

5. How long have you been living in your present community? _____ years

23. During the first eighteen years of your life, how many times did you move? _____ times

24. Since the age of 18, how many times have you moved? _____ times

25. On the answer sheet, please make a list of the persons close to you who have died. Use words like mother, brother, grandparent, friend, and *not* their names. Give *your* age when each of these people died.

26. If your parents were divorced or permanently separated, how old were you when it happened? If they didn't divorce or separate, skip to the next question. _____ years old

27. Which of the following describe your mother and her relationship with you while you were growing up?
   1. She and I had a warm, loving relationship; we were very close.

2. She and I had a good relationship; we were fairly close.
3. She and I had almost no relationship; we were not very close.
4. She and I had a very conflicted relationship; we argued often.
5. I didn't live with my mother during most of those years.

28. How much could you rely on your mother for help when you had any kind of problem?
   1. Very much
   2. A fair amount
   3. Some
   4. Not very much
   5. Not at all
   6. Not applicable

29. Which of the following describe your father and his relationship with you while you were growing up?
   1. He and I had a warm, loving relationship; we were very close.
   2. He and I had a good relationship; we were fairly close.
   3. He and I had almost no relationship; we were not very close.
   4. He and I had a very conflicted relationship; we argued often.
   5. I didn't live with my father during most of those years.

30. How much could you rely on your father for help when you had any kind of problem?
   1. Very much
   2. A lot
   3. A fair amount
   4. Not very much
   5. Not at all
   6. Not applicable

31. While you were growing up, how much did you consider your parents to be *trusted* and *secure* bases of support? How much could you really count on them?
   1. Very much
   2. A lot
   3. Some
   4. Not very much
   5. Not at all

32. How much have each of the following problems bothered you during the past year? Use the scale described here.

   0 = Not at all
   1 = A little bit
   2 = Quite a lot
   3 = A lot

0 1 2 3	**32.1**	Headaches
0 1 2 3	**32.2**	Loss of interest in sex
0 1 2 3	**32.3**	Digestive problems
0 1 2 3	**32.4**	Pains in heart or chest; heart disease
0 1 2 3	**32.5**	Feeling tired or low in energy
0 1 2 3	**32.6**	Poor appetite
0 1 2 3	**32.7**	Crying spells
0 1 2 3	**32.8**	Feeling irritable or angry
0 1 2 3	**32.9**	Constant worry and anxiety
0 1 2 3	**32.10**	Irrational fears
0 1 2 3	**32.11**	Trouble falling asleep or staying asleep
0 1 2 3	**32.12**	Trouble getting your breath
0 1 2 3	**32.13**	Being overweight, feeling fat
0 1 2 3	**32.14**	Feelings of worthlessness
0 1 2 3	**32.15**	Feelings of guilt
0 1 2 3	**32.16**	Trouble concentrating
0 1 2 3	**32.17**	Feeling that you just can't go on
0 1 2 3	**32.18**	Had a disabling accident
0 1 2 3	**32.19**	Suffered from a serious disease (Specify: _____)

53. Besides members of your family, how many people in your neighborhood or community could you rely on to help you in an emergency? For example, to take you to the hospital, help you when you are sick, etc.
   _____people

65. How do you usually *feel* when you are lonely? Circle all that apply.
   1. Down on myself

2. Sad
3. Unable to concentrate
4. Uneasy
5. Impatient
6. Sorry for myself
7. Insecure
8. Afraid
9. Melancholy
10. Bored
11. Ashamed of being lonely
12. Without hope
13. Stupid, incompetent
14. Depressed
15. Longing to be with one special person
16. Vulnerable
17. Empty
18. Alienated, "out of place"
19. Unattractive
20. Isolated, alone
21. Desperate
22. Abandoned
23. Desire to be somewhere else
24. Panic
25. Resigned
26. Helpless
27. Angry, resentful
28. Other (Specify: _____)

66. Listed below are some reasons that various people have given for feeling lonely. If you have been lonely during the past year or so, circle all the *major* reasons.
    1. Having nothing to do, feeling bored
    2. Being alone
    3. Having no close friends; no one to talk to
    4. Being far away from friends or family
    5. Death of a loved one
    6. Breakup with spouse or lover
    7. Having *no* spouse or lover
    8. Being in a new job or new school
    9. No convenient means of transportation
    10. No telephone
    11. Not being needed
    12. Coming home to an empty house
    13. Being hospitalized

14. Being housebound, due to age, illness or handicap
15. Traveling often
16. Having a loved one who travels often
17. Having no sexual partner
18. Being misunderstood
19. Moving too often
20. Feeling different from everyone else, alienated
21. Other (Specify: _____)

77. How attractive are you compared with others of your age?
    1. Much more attractive
    2. Somewhat more attractive
    3. About the same
    4. Somewhat less attractive
    5. Much less attractive

78. How likable are you compared with others of your age?
    1. Much more likable
    2. Somewhat more likable
    3. About the same
    4. Somewhat less likable
    5. Much less likable

80. In your opinion, how much control do you have over the things that happen in your life?
    1. Almost total control
    2. Quite a bit of control
    3. A moderate degree of control
    4. A little bit of control
    5. Almost no control

81. Using a 4-point agree-disagree scale, indicate how much you agree with each of the following.

    1 = Strongly agree
    2 = Agree
    3 = Disagree
    4 = Strongly disagree

1 2 3 4 **81.1** I feel my life has meaning and direction.

1 2 3 4 **81.2** I like most people I meet.

1 2 3 4 **81.3** I generally take a positive attitude toward myself.

1 2 3 4 **81.4** On the whole, I am satisfied with myself.

1 2 3 4   **81.5**   At times, I think I am no good at all.

1 2 3 4   **81.6**   I am introspective, I I often examine my thoughts and feelings.

1 2 3 4   **81.7**   I am a shy person.

1 2 3 4   **81.8**   I am an independent person.

1 2 3 4   **81.9**   I am a friendly person.

1 2 3 4   **81.10**   I *am* a lonely person.

1 2 3 4   **81.11**   I always *was* a lonely person.

1 2 3 4   **81.12**   I always *will be* a lonely person.

1 2 3 4   **81.13**   Other people think of me as a lonely person.

84. When you feel lonely, what do you usually do about it? Circle your *most common* reactions.

   1. Go for a drive
   2. Nothing
   3. Take a walk
   4. Exercise
   5. Sleep
   6. Do housework
   7. Call a friend
   8. Read
   9. Go shopping
10. Visit someone
11. Read the Bible or pray
12. Drink or get "stoned"
13. Go to a movie, a play, etc.
14. Sit and think
15. Listen to music
16. Watch TV
17. Work on a hobby
18. Overeat
19. Study or work
20. Cry
21. Write
22. Spend money on myself
23. Play a musical instrument
24. Take tranquilizers
25. Other (Specify: _____)

18

Loneliness

FRIEDA FROMM-REICHMANN

I AM NOT SURE what inner forces have made me, during the last years, ponder about and struggle with the psychiatric problems of loneliness. I have found a strange fascination in thinking about it—and subsequently in attempting to break through the aloneness of thinking about loneliness by trying to communicate what I believe I have learned.

Perhaps my interest began with the young catatonic woman who broke through a period of completely blocked communication and obvious anxiety by responding when I asked her a question about her feeling miserable: She raised her hand with her thumb lifted, the other four fingers bent toward the palm, so that I could see only the thumb, isolated from the four hidden fingers. I interpreted the signal with "That lonely?" in a sympathetic tone of voice. At this, her facial expression loosened up as though in great relief and gratitude, and her fingers opened. Then she began to tell me about herself by means of her fingers, and she asked me by gestures to respond in kind. We continued with this finger conversation for one or two weeks, and as we did so, her anxious tension began to decrease and she began to break through her noncommunicative isolation; and subsequently she emerged altogether from her loneliness.

I have had somewhat similar experiences with other patients; and

Reprinted from *Psychiatry*, 22:1-15, 1959 by special permission of the William Alanson White Psychiatric Foundation, Inc. Copyright © by the William Alanson White Psychiatric Foundation, Inc.

so I have finally been prompted to write down what I have learned about loneliness from my work with these patients and from other experiences of my own.

The writer who wishes to elaborate on the problems of loneliness is faced with a serious terminological handicap. Loneliness seems to be such a painful, frightening experience that people will do practically everything to avoid it. This avoidance seems to include a strange reluctance on the part of psychiatrists to seek scientific clarification of the subject. Thus it comes about that loneliness is one of the least satisfactorily conceptualized psychological phenomena, not even mentioned in most psychiatric textbooks. Very little is known among scientists about its genetics and psychodynamics, and various different experiences which are descriptively and dynamically as different from one another as culturally determined loneliness, self-imposed aloneness, compulsory solitude, isolation, and real loneliness are all thrown into the one terminological basket of "loneliness."

Before entering into a discussion of the psychiatric aspects of what I call real loneliness, I will briefly mention the types of loneliness which are *not* the subject of this chapter. The writings of modern sociologists and social psychologists are widely concerned with culturally determined loneliness, the "cut-offness and solitariness of civilized men"—the "shut-upness," in Kierkegaard's phrase (Kierkegaard, 1844, p. 110; see also Fromm, 1941), which they describe as characteristic of this culture. While this is a very distressing and painful experience, it is by definition the common fate of many people of this culture. Unverbalized as it may remain, it is nevertheless potentially a communicable experience, one which can be shared. Hence it does not carry the deep threat of the uncommunicable, private emotional experience of severe loneliness, with which this chapter will be concerned.

I am not here concerned with the sense of solitude which some people have, when, all by themselves, they experience the infinity of nature as presented by the mountains, the desert, or the ocean—the experience which has been described with the expression, "oceanic feelings" (Freud, 1930; see, for instance, p. 64). These oceanic feelings may well be an expression of a creative loneliness, if one defines creativity, with Paul Tillich (1952), in the wider sense of the term, as "living spontaneously, in action and reaction, with the contents of one's cultural life" (p. 46).

I am also not concerned in this chapter with the seclusion which yields creative artistic or scientific products. In contrast to the disintegrative loneliness of the mental patient, these are states of constructive loneliness, and they are often temporary and self-induced, and may be voluntarily and alternately sought out and rejected. Nearly all works of creative originality are conceived in such states of constructive aloneness; and, in fact, only the creative person who is not afraid of this constructive aloneness will have free command over his creativity. Some of these people, schizoid, artistic personalities in Karl Menninger's nomenclature (1930), submit to the world, as a product of their detachment from normal life, "fragments of their own world—bits of dreams and visions and songs that we—out here—don't hear except as they translate them" (p. 79). It should be added that an original, creative person may not only be lonely for the time of his involvement in creative processes, but subsequently *because* of them, since the appearance of new creations of genuine originality often antedates the ability of the creator's contemporaries to understand or to accept them.

I am not talking here about the temporary aloneness of, for instance, a person who has to stay in bed with a cold on a pleasant Sunday afternoon while the rest of the family are enjoying the outdoors. He may complain about loneliness and feel sorry for himself, for to the "other-directed" types of the culture, "loneliness is such an omnipotent and painful threat . . . that they have little conception of the positive values of solitude, and even at times are very frightened at the prospect of being alone" (May, 1953, p. 26; see also Riesman et al., 1950). But however much this man with a cold may complain about loneliness, he is, needless to say, not lonely in the sense I am talking about; he is just temporarily alone.

Here I should also like to mention the sense of isolation or temporary loneliness which a person may feel who is in a situation of pseudo-companionship with others, with whom an experience cannot be shared, or who actively interfere with his enjoyment of an experience. To convey more clearly what I have in mind, I quote Rupert Brooke's poem, "The Voice":

> Safe in the magic of my woods
> I lay, and watched the dying light.
> Faint in the pale high solitudes,
> And washed with rain and veiled by night,

Silver and blue and green were showing.
And the dark woods grew darker still;
And birds were hushed; and peace was growing
And quietness crept up the hill;
And no wind was blowing.

And I knew
That this was the hour of knowing
And the night and the woods and you
Were one together, and I should find
Soon in the silence the hidden key
Of all that had hurt and puzzled me—
Why you were you, and the night was kind,
And the woods were part of the heart of me.

And there I waited breathlessly,
Alone; and slowly the holy three,
The three that I loved, together grew
One, in the hour of knowing,
Night, and the woods, and you—
And suddenly
There was an uproar in my woods,

The noise of a fool in mock distress,
Crashing and laughing and blindly going,
Of ignorant feet and a swishing dress,
And a Voice profaning the solitudes.

The spell was broken, the key denied me
And at length your flat clear voice beside me
Mouthed cheerful clear flat platitudes.

You came and quacked beside me in the wood.
You said, "The view from here is very good!"
You said, "It's nice to be alone a bit!"
And, "How the days are drawing out!" you said.
You said, "The sunset's pretty, isn't it?"

*   *   *   *   *   *   *   *

By God! I wish—I wish that you were dead.[1]

[1]Reprinted by permission of Dodd, Mead & Co. from *The Collected Poems of Rupert Brooke*, copyright 1915 by Dodd, Mead & Co., Inc. Copyright 1943 by Edward Marsh.

While the loneliness of the person who suffers the sense of loss and of being alone following the death of someone close to him is on another level, it too does not concern me here. Freud (1917, 1923) and Abraham (1911) have described the dynamics by which the mourner counteracts this aloneness by incorporation and identification; this can often be descriptively verified by the way in which the mourner comes to develop a likeness in looks, personality, and activities to the lost beloved one. By such incorporation and identification the human mind has the power of fighting the aloneness after the loss of a beloved person. Somewhat similar is the sense of lonesomeness which lovers may suffer after a broken-off love affair. Daydreams, fantasies, and the love songs of others—or sometimes original compositions—help the unhappy lover to overcome his temporary solitude: "Out of my great worry I emerge with my little songs," as the German poet Adelbert von Chamisso put it.

The kind of loneliness I am discussing is nonconstructive if not disintegrative, and it shows in, or leads ultimately to, the development of psychotic states. It renders people who suffer it emotionally paralyzed and helpless. In Sullivan's (1953) words, it is "the exceedingly unpleasant and driving experience connected with an inadequate discharge of the need for human intimacy, for interpersonal intimacy" (p. 290). The longing for interpersonal intimacy stays with every human being from infancy throughout life; and there is no human being who is not threatened by its loss.

I have implied, in what I have just said, that the human being is born with the need for contact and tenderness. I should now like to review briefly how this need is fulfilled in the various phases of childhood development—if things go right—in order to provide a basis for asking and answering the question, What has gone wrong in the history of the lonely ones? That is, what has gone wrong in the history of those people who suffer from their failure to obtain satisfaction of the universal human need for intimacy?

The infant thrives in a relationship of intimate and tender closeness with the person who tends, and mothers him. In childhood, the healthy youngster's longing for intimacy is, according to Sullivan, fulfilled by his participation in activities with adults, in the juvenile era by finding compeers and acceptance, and in preadolescence by finding a "chum." In adolescence and in the years of growth and development which should follow it, man feels the need for friendship and intimacy jointly with or independently of his sexual drive (see Sullivan, 1953, especially pp. 261-262).

A number of writers have investigated what may happen, at various stages of development, if the need for intimacy goes unsatisfied. For example, René Spitz (1946) demonstrated the fatal influence of lack of love and of loneliness on infants, in what he called their "anaclitic depression." An interesting sidelight on this is provided by experiments in isolation with very young animals, in which the effect of isolation can be an almost completely irreversible lack of development of whole systems, such as those necessary for the use of vision in accomplishing tasks put to the animal (Lilly, 1956). Sullivan (1953) and Suttie (1952) have noted the unfortunate effects on future development if a person's early need for tenderness remains unsatisfied, and Anna Freud, in her lecture at the 1953 International Psychoanalytic meetings in London, described sensations of essential loneliness in children under the heading of "Losing and Being Lost" (A. Freud, 1954).[2]

Both Sullivan and Suttie have particularly called attention to the fact that the lonely child may resort to substitute satisfactions in fantasy, which he cannot share with others. Thus his primary sense of isolation may subsequently be reinforced if, despite the pressures of socialization and acculturation, he does not sufficiently learn to discriminate between realistic phenomena and the products of his own lively fantasy. In order to escape being laughed at or being punished for replacing reports of real events by fictitious narratives, he may further withdraw, and may continue, in his social isolation, to hold on to the uncorrected substitutive preoccupation. An impressive example of the results of such a faulty development has been presented by Robert Lindner (1955), in his treatment history of Kirk Allen, the hero of the "true psychoanalytic tale," "The Jet-Propelled Couch."

Incidently, I think that the substitutive enjoyment which the neglected child may find for himself in his fantasy life makes him especially lonely in the present age of overemphasis on the conceptual differentiation between subjective and objective reality. One of the outcomes of this scientific attitude is that all too frequently even

[2]An interesting description by a layman of the impact of loneliness in childhood is given by Lucy Sprague Mitchell in her *Two Lives: The Story of Wesley Clair Mitchell and Myself* (1953). In this book she vividly contrasts her own childhood loneliness with the affection, approval, and security her husband had as a child.

healthy children are trained to give up prematurely the subjective inner reality of their normal fantasy life and, instead, to accept the objective reality of the outward world.

The process by which the child withdraws into social isolation and into his substitutive fantasies may occur if the mothering one weans him from her caressing tenderness before he is ready to try for the satisfactions of the modified needs for intimacy characteristic of his ensuing developmental phase. As Suttie (1952) has put it, separation from the direct tenderness and nurtural love relationship with the mother may outrun the child's ability for making substitutions (pp. 87-88). This is a rather serious threat to an infant and child in a world where a taboo exists on tenderness among adults. When such a premature weaning from mothering tenderness occurs, the roots for permanent aloneness and isolation, for "love-shyness," as Suttie has called it, for fear of intimacy and tenderness, are planted in the child's mind; and the defensive counterreactions against this eventuality may lead to psychopathological developments.

Zilboorg (1938), on the other hand, has warned against psychological dangers which may arise from other types of failure in handling children—failures in adequate guidance in reality testing. If the omnipotent baby learns the joy of being admired and loved but learns nothing about the outside world, he may develop a conviction of his greatness and all-importance which will lead to a narcissistic orientation to life—a conviction that life is nothing but being loved and admired. This narcissistic-megalomanic attitude will not be acceptable to the environment, which will respond with hostility and isolation of the narcissistic person. The deeply seated triad of narcissism, megalomania, and hostility will be established, which is, according to Zilboorg, at the root of the affliction of loneliness.

The concepts of Sullivan (1953), Suttie (1952), and Zilboorg (1938) are all based on the insight that the person who is isolated and lonely in his present environment has anachronistically held on to early narcissistic need fulfillments or fantasied substitutive satisfactions. According to Sullivan and Suttie, it may be the fulfillment of his early needs which has been critical; or, according to Zilboorg, the failure may have been in meeting his needs later on for adequate guidance in reality testing.

Karl Menninger (1930) has described the milder states of loneliness which result from these failures in handling infants and children in his "isolation types of personality" (p. 79)—that is, lonely and schizoid personalities. The more severe developments of loneliness appear in the unconstructive, desolate phases of isolation and real loneliness which are beyond the state of feeling sorry for oneself—the states of mind in which the fact that there were people in one's past life is more or less forgotten, and the possibility that there may be interpersonal relationships in one's future life is out of the realm of expectation or imagination. This loneliness, in its quintessential form, is of such a nature that it is incommunicable by one who suffers it. Unlike other noncommunicable emotional experiences, it cannot even be shared empathetically, perhaps because the other person's empathetic abilities are obstructed by the anxiety-arousing quality of the mere emanations of this profound loneliness.[3]

I wonder whether this explains the fact that this real loneliness defies description, even by the pen of a master of conceptualization such as Sullivan. As a matter of fact, the extremely uncanny experience of real loneliness has much in common with some other quite serious mental states, such as panic. People cannot endure such states for any length of time without becoming psychotic—although the sequence of events is often reversed, and the loneliness or panic is concomitant with or the outcome of a psychotic disturbance. Subject to further dynamic investigation, I offer the suggestion that the experiences in adults usually described as a loss of reality or as a sense of world catastrophe can also be understood as expressions of profound loneliness.

On the other hand, while some psychiatrists seem to think of severe psychotic loneliness as part of, or as identical with, other emotional phenomena, such as psychotic withdrawal, depression, and anxiety, I do not agree with this viewpoint, in general. I shall elaborate on the interrelationship between loneliness and anxiety later. So far as psychotic withdrawal is concerned, it constitutes only seemingly a factual isolation from others; the relationship of the withdrawn person to his interpersonal environment, and even his interest in it, is by no means extinguished in the way that is true of the lonely person. So far as depressed patients are concerned, every psychiatrist knows that

---

[3] Some attention has been given to this interference of anxiety with the freedom of utilizing intuitive abilities by a seminar in which I participated, dealing specifically with intuitive processes in the psychiatrist who works with schizophrenics. See Szalita-Pemow (1955).

they complain about loneliness; but let me suggest that the preoccupation with their relationships with others, and the pleas for fulfillment of their interpersonal dependency-needs—which even withdrawn depressives show—are proof that their loneliness is not of the same order as the state of real detachment I am trying to depict.

The characteristic feature of loneliness, on which I shall elaborate later, is this: It can arouse anxiety and fear of contamination which may induce people—among them the psychiatrists who deal with it in their patients—to refer to it euphemistically as "depression." One can understand the emotional motivation for this definition, but that does not make it conceptually correct.

People who are in the grip of severe degrees of loneliness cannot talk about it; and people who have at some time in the past had such an experience can seldom do so either, for it is so frightening and uncanny in character that they try to dissociate the memory of what it was like, and even the fear of it. This frightened secretiveness and lack of communication about loneliness seem to increase its threat for the lonely ones, even in retrospect; it produces the sad convictions that nobody else has experienced or ever will sense what they are experiencing or have experienced.

Even mild borderline states of loneliness do not seem to be easy to talk about. Most people who are alone try to keep the mere fact of their aloneness a secret from others, and even try to keep its conscious realization hidden from themselves. I think that this may be in part determined by the fact that loneliness is a most unpopular phenomenon in this group-conscious culture. Perhaps only children have the independence and courage to identify their own loneliness as such—or perhaps they do it simply out of a lack of imagination or an inability to conceal it. One youngster asked another, in the comic strip "Peanuts," "Do you know what you're going to be when you grow up?" "Lonesome," was the unequivocal reply of the other.

Incidently, one element in the isolation of some lonely psychotics may be the fact that, perhaps because of their interpersonal detachment, some of them are more keen, sensitive, and fearless observers of the people in their environment than the average nonlonely, mentally healthy person is. They may observe and feel free to express themselves about many painful truths which go unobserved or are suppressed by their healthy and gregarious fellowmen. But unlike the court jester, who was granted a fool's paradise where he could voice his unwelcome truths with impunity, the lonely person may be displeasing if not frightening to his hearers, who may erect a psychological wall of ostracism and isolation about him as a means of protecting themselves. Cervantes, in his story, "Man of Glass," has depicted a psychotic man who observes his fellowmen keenly and offers them uncensored truths about themselves. As long as they look upon him as sufficiently isolated by his "craziness," they are able to laugh off the narcissistic hurts to which he exposes them (Cervantes, 1613).

I would now like to digress for a moment from the subject of real, psychotogenic loneliness to consider for a moment the fact that while all adults seem to be afraid of real loneliness, they vary a great deal in their tolerance of aloneness. I have, for example, seen some people who felt deeply frightened at facing the infinity of the desert, with its connotations of loneliness, and others who felt singularly peaceful, serene, and pregnant with creative ideas. Why are some people able to meet aloneness with fearless enjoyment, while others are made anxious even by temporary aloneness—or even by silence, which may or may not connote potential aloneness? The fear of these latter people is such that they make every possible effort to avoid it—by playing bridge, by looking for hours at television, by listening to the radio, by going compulsively to dances, parties, the movies. As Kierkegaard has put it, " . . . one does everything possible by way of diversions and the Janizary music of loud-voiced enterprises to keep lonely thoughts away . . . " (Kierkegaard, 1844, p. 107).

Perhaps the explanation for the fear of aloneness lies in the fact that, in this culture, people can come to a valid self-orientation, or even awareness of themselves, only in terms of their actual overt relationships with others. "Every human being gets much of his sense of his own reality out of what others say to him and think about him," as Rollo May puts it (1953, p. 32). While alone and isolated from others people feel threatened by the potential loss of their boundaries, of the ability to discriminate between the subjective self and the objective world around them. But valid as this general explanation for the fear of loneliness may be, it leaves unanswered the question of why this fear is not ubiquitous.

Generally speaking, I believe that the answer lies in the *degree* of a person's dependence on others for his self-orientation, and that this depends in turn on the particular vicissitudes of the developmental history. Here, you may recall, I am talking about aloneness, and not what I term real loneliness; and whether the same holds true for loneliness, I do not know. Only an intensive scrutiny of the developmental history of the really lonely ones might give the answer; and the nature of real loneliness is such that one cannot communicate with people who are in the grip of it. Once they emerge from it, they do not wish—or they are unable—to talk about their loneliness or about any topic which is psychologically connected with it, as I suggested earlier.

Descriptively speaking, however, one can understand why people are terrified of the "naked horror"—in Binswanger's term—of real loneliness. Anyone who has encountered persons who were under the influence of real loneliness understands why people are more frightened of being lonely than of being hungry, or being deprived of sleep, or of having their sexual needs unfulfulled—the three other basic needs which Sullivan assigns to the same group as the avoidance of loneliness. As Sullivan points out, people will even resort to anxiety-arousing experiences in an effort to escape from loneliness, even though anxiety itself is an emotional experience against which people fight, as a rule, with every defense at their disposal (1953, p. 262). Needless to say, however, the person who is able to do this is not fully in the grip of true, severe loneliness, with its specific character of paralyzing hopelessness and unutterable futility. This "naked horror" is beyond anxiety and tension; defense and remedy seem out of reach. Only as its all-engulfing intensity decreases can the person utilize anxiety-provoking defenses against it. One of my patients, after she emerged from the depths of loneliness, tried unconsciously to prevent its recurrence, by pushing herself, as it were, into a pseudo-manic state of talkativeness, which was colored by all signs of anxiety.

Another drastic defensive maneuver which should be mentioned is compulsive eating. As Hilde Bruch's (1957) research on obesity has shown, the attempt to counteract loneliness by overeating serves at the same time as a means of getting even with the significant people in the environment, whom the threatened person holds responsible for his loneliness. The patient I have just mentioned, who resorted to psuedo-manic talkativeness as a defense against loneliness, told me that her happiest childhood memory was of sitting in the darkened living room of her home, secretly eating stolen sweets. In her first therapeutic interview, she said to me, "You will take away my gut pains [from overeating], my trance states [her delusional states of retreat], and my food; and where will I be then?'' That is, if she gave up her defenses against her loneliness, where would she be then?

Sullivan, it should be added, thought that loneliness—beyond his description of it in terms of the driving force to satisfy the universal human need for intimacy—is such an intense and incommunicable experience that psychiatrists must resign themselves to describing it in terms of people's defenses against it. Freud's thinking about it seems to point in the same direction, in his references to loneliness and defenses against it in *Civilization and its Discontents* (1930).

SOME DESCRIPTIONS OF LONELINESS BY POETS AND PHILOSOPHERS

I think that many poets and philosophers have come closer to putting into words what loneliness is than we psychiatrists have. Loneliness is a theme on which many poets have written—for instance, Friedrich Hölderlin, Nikolaus Lenau, and Joseph von Eichendorf among the German romanticists, T.S. Eliot in England and Walt Whitman and Thomas Wolfe in this country. Let me remind you, for instance, of Walt Whitman's poem ''I Saw in Louisiana a Live-Oak Growing'' (1855, pp. 273-274) which, although it is not a song of real loneliness, depicts beautifully the experience of the alone person:

> I saw in Louisiana a live-oak growing,
> All alone stood it, and the moss hung down from the branches;
> Without any companion it grew there; uttering joyous leaves
>   of dark green,
> And its look, rude, unbending, lusty, made me think of myself;
> But I wonder'd how it could utter joyous leaves, standing alone
>   there, without its friend, its lover near—for I knew I
>   could not. . . .

More recently, Thomas Wolfe[4] has written of the development from Judaism to Christianity as the development from loneliness to love. To him, the books of the Old Testament—particularly the Book

---

[4]Originally reprinted from ''Death the Proud Brother,'' by Thomas Wolfe (copyright 1933, Charles Scribner's Sons) with the permission of the publishers. See Wolfe (1957, pp. 179-180).

of Job and the sermon of Ecclesiastes—provide the most final and profound literature of human loneliness that the world has known. Wolfe, in contrast to all the dramatists and most of the poets, sees the essence of human tragedy in loneliness, not in conflict. But he senses a solution of the tragedy of loneliness in the fact that the lonely man is invariably the man who loves life dearly. His hymn to loneliness must be understood in this spirit:

> Now, Loneliness forever and the earth again! Dark brother and stern friend, immortal face of darkness and of night, with whom the half part of my life was spent, and with whom I shall abide now till my death forever, what is there for me to fear as long as you are with me? Heroic friend, blood-brother of Proud Death, dark face, have we not gone together down a million streets, have we not coursed together the great and furious avenues of night, have we not crossed the stormy seas alone, and known strange lands, and come again to walk the continent of night and listen to the silence of the earth? Have we not been brave and glorious when we were together, friend, have we not known triumph, joy and glory on this earth—and will it not be again with me as it was then, if you come back to me? Come to me, brother, in the watches of the night, come to me in the secret and most silent heart of darkness, come to me as you always came, bringing to me once more the old invincible strength, the deathless hope, the triumphant joy and confidence that will storm the ramparts of the earth again.

Incidentally, Wolfe's polar concept of loneliness as such and yet also as an expression of great potentiality for love is reflected in the psychiatric hypothesis about the childhood experience of the lonely schizophrenic. Many psychiatrists now believe that the lack of real attention and acceptance by the significant adults of his infancy and early childhood hits him especially hard because of his innate, specific potentialities for sensitive responsiveness to love and intimacy. This situation forms the cradle of his later loneliness and simultaneous yearning for, yet fear of, interpersonal closeness. The lonely schizophrenic's capacity for love is the reason why he is able sometimes to develop intense experiences of transference in his relationship with the psychotherapist—something with which psychiatrists are now familiar, although they used to be misled by his simultaneous fear of closeness into doubting the possibility of establishing workable therapeutic relationships. I think that Thomas

Wolfe's concept of loneliness is useful to the psychiatrist in attempting to understand this bipolarity of schizophrenic dynamics.

Among philosophers, I think Binswanger (1942) has come nearest to a philosophical and psychiatric definition of loneliness when he speaks of it as "naked existence," "mere existence," and "naked horror," and when he characterizes lonely people as being "devoid of any interest in any goal" (pp. 130, 177-178). Tillich (1952) describes, by implication, the people whom I would call lonely as those in whom the essentially united experiences of the courage to be as oneself and the courage to be as a part are split, so that both "disintegrate in their isolation" (p. 90). Kierkegaard (1843, 1849), Nietzsche, Buber, and others are also able to say more about loneliness than we psychiatrists have said so far. Buber, in particular, has presented psychiatrists with the understanding of an important link between loneliness, schizophrenic states, and psychotherapy (Buber, 1947, pp. 135, 397). He states that isolated and lonely people can communicate and be communicated with only in the most concrete terms; one cannot break through their isolation with abstractions. Buber's remarks add an emotional basis for understanding the concreteness of schizophrenic communication and thinking, which psychiatrists and psychologists have so far primarily studied from the viewpoint of the theory of thought processes.

PATIENTS' DESCRIPTIONS OF LONELINESS

One of our patients at Chestnut Lodge, as she emerged from a severe state of schizophrenic depression, asked to see me because she wished to tell me about the deep state of hopeless loneliness and subjective isolation which she had undergone during her psychotic episodes. But even though she was now in fine command of the language, and even though she came with the intention of talking, she was just as little able to tell me about her loneliness in so many words as are most people who are engulfed in or have gone through a period of real psychotic loneliness. After several futile attempts, she finally burst out, "I don't know why people think of hell as a place where there is heat and where fires are burning. That is not hell. Hell is if you are frozen in isolation into a block of ice. That is where I have been."

I don't know whether this patient was familiar with Dante's

description of the ninth and last, or frozen circle of the Inferno. It is in essence quite similar to the patient's conception of hell—the "lowest part of the Universe, and farthest remote from the Source of all light and heat," reserved for the gravest sinners, namely those "who have done violence to their own kindred (like Cain who slew Abel), and those who committed treachery against their native land." Among others, Dante met there "two sinners that are frozen close together in the same hole" (1308-1321, p. 169).

Despite the difficulty of communicating about loneliness, every now and then a creative patient succeeds in conveying his experience of essential loneliness artistically after having emerged from it. Mary Jane Ward succeeded in doing so in her novel, *The Snake Pit* (1946).

The most impressive poetic document of loneliness from a mental patient of which I know has been written by Eithne Tabor (1950, p. 36), a schizophrenic patient at St. Elizabeth's Hospital:

Panic

And is there anyone at all?
And is
There anyone at all?
I am knocking at the oaken door . . .
And will it open
Never now no more?
I am calling, calling to you—
Don't you hear?
And is there anyone
Near?
And does this empty silence have to be?
And is there no-one there at all
To answer me?

I do not know the road—
I fear to fall.
And is there anyone
At all?[5]

Another patient, after her recovery, wrote the following poem, "The Disenchanted," which she dedicated to me:

[5]Reprinted by permission of the author.

The demented hold love
In the palm of the hand,
And let it fall
And grind it in the sand.
They return by darkest night
To bury it again,
And hide it forever
From the sight of men.[6]

In another poem, "Empty Lot," also written after her recovery, she depicted symbolically what loneliness feels like:

No one comes near here
Morning or night
The desolate grasses
Grow out of sight.
Only a wild hare
Strays, then is gone.
The landlord is silence.
The tenant is dawn.[7]

All these poems have—only seemingly coincidentally—a common feature: They are not entitled "Loneliness," but "Panic," "The Disenchanted," and "Empty Lot." Is this because of the general inclination of the word-conscious and word-suspicious schizophrenic to replace direct communications and definitions by allusions, symbols, circumlocutions, and so on? Or is it an unconscious expression of the fear of loneliness—a fear so great that even naming it is frightening? If one remembers that fear of loneliness is the common fate of the people of this Western culture, be they mentally healthy or disturbed, it seems that the choice of the titles of these poems is determined by this fear.

ENFORCED AND EXPERIMENTAL ISOLATION

There are two sources of verification for the assumption that severe loneliness cannot ordinarily be endured more than temporarily without leading to psychotic developments—if it does not, in fact, oc-

---

[6]By permission of the author.

[7]By permission of the author.

cur as an inherent part of mental illness. One source of verification is found in the psychoses which develop in people undergoing an experience of enforced isolation, the other in the psychosis-like states ensuing from experimentally induced states of loneliness.

Three types of nonexperimental isolation may be differentiated. The first is the voluntary isolation which comes about in the course of polar expeditions, or in the lives of rangers at solitary outposts. Such isolation may be tolerated without serious emotional disturbances. Courtauld's (1932) "Living Alone Under Polar Conditions" may be mentioned as representative to some degree. Courtauld, who was isolated on the Greenland icecap in a weather station, writes that there is no objection, in his judgment, to a solitary voluntary mission if one is certain of adequate measures for one's safety and of ultimate relief. He recommends, however, that only persons with active, imaginative minds, who do not suffer from a nervous disposition and are not given to brooding, and who can occupy themselves by such means as reading, should go on polar expeditions.

The second type of isolation is represented by solitary seafarers, who seem to be in a considerably more complex situation than the polar isolates or solitary rangers. Most of the solitary sailors seem to suffer from symptoms of mental illness. Slocum (1905), for instance, developed hallucinations of a savior who appeared in times of particular stress—a reflection, probably, of his inner conviction that he would survive.

The third group consists of those who are subjected to solitary confinement in prisons and concentration camps. They are, of course, seriously threatened by psychotic developments, and they do frequently become victims of mental illness.

Christopher Burney (1952) has written a report about his survival, without mental illness, of eighteen months of solitary confinement by the Germans during World War II. His isolation was made worse by cold, physical and emotional humiliation, and a near-starvation diet. On the few occasions when he had an opportunity for communication, " . . . I found that the muscles of my mouth had become stiff and unwilling and that the thoughts and questions I had wanted to express became ridiculous when I turned them into words" (p. 86). "Solitude," he says, "had so far weaned me from the habit of intercourse, even the thin intercourse of speculation, that I could no longer see any relationship with another person unless it was introduced gradually by a long overture of common trivialities" (p. 105).

Burney describes the systematic devices he developed to counteract the danger of becoming mad; he forced himself to divide his lonely days into fixed periods, with a daily routine made up of such items as manicuring his fingernails with a splinter of wood he had managed to peel from his stool, doing physical exercises, pacing up and down his cell, counting the rounds he made, and whistling a musical program made up of every tune he could remember. He forced himself to divide the eating of his one meager meal per day between noon and evening, despite the craving of his hungry stomach. On one of the rare occasions when he was allowed to go outside for exercise, he brought back with him to his cell a snail: "It was company of a sort, and as it were an emissary from the world of real life. . ." (p. 109). He disciplined his mind to work on intellectual and spiritual problems, whose starting point had frequently to come from the torn and ancient sheets of newspaper, or sometimes pages of books, given him for toilet paper.

Secretly routinizing his life proved to be an important safeguard for his mental equilibrium. The importance of this device can be measured by the degree to which Burney felt threatened by even small changes, such as a change in the sequence of receiving first soup and then bread, to receiving first bread and then soup. He also felt being moved from one cell to another was a threat to his equilibrium, even though the new cell, as such, was obviously preferable to the old one.

While Burney survived his ordeal without mental illness, he was aware, toward the end of the eighteen months of solitary confinement, that isolation was threatening his mental health. "As long as my brain worked," he says, "solitude served a purpose, but I could see that it was slowly exhausting the fuel with which it had started, and if it stopped from inanition I would have nothing left but cold and hunger, which would make short work of me. Metaphysics were not enough: they are an exercise, weakening rather than nourishing; and the brain requires food of real substance" (p. 150). The intensity of the effort it had taken to stay adjusted to his solitary life may be measured by the fact that, at the first opportunity to communicate, he did not dare to talk, "because I thought it quite probable that if I opened my mouth I should show myself to be mad" (p. 151). "I tried to talk . . . and succeeded a little, but constantly had to check my tongue for fear of uttering some impossibility" (p. 152).

The reports of Ellam and Mudie (1953), and Bernicot (1953) include statements similar to these last remarks of Burney's (1952). As Lilly says, in discussing these accounts, "The inner life becomes so vivid and intense that it takes time to readjust to the life among other persons and to reestablish one's inner criteria of sanity" (1956, p. 4).

One more remark about Burney's experience: I believe that his unquestioning, matter-of-fact belief in the spiritual validity of the political convictions which were the cause of his imprisonment may have been an additional factor which helped him to survive his ordeal without becoming mentally ill. In this sense, his confinement was more of a piece with the voluntary isolation of the polar explorers than, for example, with the imprisonment of a delinquent. The delinquent prisoner is not likely to have the determination and devotion to a cause which helped Burney to stay mentally sound, even though he was deprived of the opportunity to work or to receive stimulation through reading—which for many others seem to have been the two most effective antidotes or remedies for the humiliation of confinement and the rise of disintegrating loneliness.

My suggestion that Burney's conviction and determination were factors in his remaining mentally healthy raises a question about the inner emotional factors which determine whether a person can tolerate isolation or will be particularly vulnerable to its dangers. So far, I have not succeeded in finding specific psychodynamic or descriptive data which could be helpful in differentiating between people who react to solitude with or without succumbing to psychotic loneliness. However, it should be possible to learn more by interrogating persons who have exposed themselves voluntarily to a life of solitude and isolation.

The last important source of insight into the psychodynamics of loneliness is the significant experimental work of Donald Hebb and his group (Heron, Bexton, and Hebb, 1953; Bexton, Heron, and Scott, 1954; Heron, 1957) at McGill University and of John C. Lilly (1956) at the National Institute of Mental Health, who have exposed their subjects to experimentally created states of physical and emotional isolation. Both investigators have brought about marked temporary impairments of people's emotional reactions, mental activities, and mental health by cutting down the scope of their physical contact with the outside world through experimental limitations of their sensory perception and decreased variation in their sensory environment. In the Canadian experiments the aim has been to reduce the *patterning* of stimuli to the lowest level; while the National Institute of Mental Health experiments have endeavored to reduce the *absolute intensity* of all physical stimuli to the lowest possible level.

The subjects of the McGill experiments spent twenty-four hours a day, with time out for eating and elimination, on a comfortable bed with a foam rubber pillow. Although communication was kept to a minimum, an amplifier connected with earphones was provided, through which an observer could test the subject verbally. Other noises were masked by fans and the humming of air-conditioners. The subjects wore translucent goggles which transmitted diffused light but prevented patterned vision, and gloves and cardboard cuffs reaching from below the elbow to beyond the fingertips. The most striking result of these experiments was the occurrence of primarily visual, but also auditory, kinesthetic, and somesthetic hallucinatory experiences. The subjects, even though they had insight into the objective unreality of these experiences, found them extremely vivid.

In Lilly's experiments at the National Institute of Mental Health, the subject was immersed, except for his head, in a tank of water at such temperature that he neither felt hot nor cold. In fact, he tactually could feel the supports which held him, and a blacked-out mask over his whole head, but not much else. The sound level was also low, and the total environment was an even and monotonous one. Lilly has reported the various stages of experience through which subjects go, with, eventually, the projection of visual imagery.

LONELINESS AND ANXIETY

My impression is that loneliness and the fear of loneliness, on the one hand, and anxiety, on the other, are sometimes used interchangeably in our psychiatric thinking and in our clinical terminology. For instance, it is probably true that what psychiatrists describe as separation-anxiety can also be described as fear of loneliness. Furthermore, most authors agree, explicitly or implicitly, with the definition of anxiety as a response to the anticipated loss of love and approval by significant people in one's environment. Tillich (1952) expresses a similar idea when he postulates the ability to accept acceptance in spite of the anxiety of guilt as the basis for the courage of confidence (p. 164). Does that not imply that man with his imperfections is threatened by loneliness if his anxiety prevents him from accepting acceptance? And does this in turn not mean that anxiety is closely related to the fear of isolation or loneliness? Or, when Tillich says that "the anxiety of meaninglessness is anxiety about the loss of an ultimate concern" (p. 47), is that not synonymous with Binswanger's (1942) depiction of loneliness as a state of need in which people are bare of any interest in any goal?

Yet I suspect that if we psychiatrists can learn to separate the two dynamisms more sharply from one another, we will come to see that loneliness in its own right plays a much more significant role in the dynamics of mental disturbance than we have so far been ready to acknowledge. I find good reason for this hypothesis in my own experience with my patients and on the basis of the many reports about other patients which I have heard from my colleagues.

This, in turn, makes me wonder about the origin of this conceptual merger between anxiety and loneliness. I have already suggested that this may have been brought about originally by the fear of loneliness, which the psychiatrist, of course, shares with his nonprofessional fellowmen. But perhaps this is an oversimplification. Perhaps a contributing factor is the ever-increasing insight of psychiatrists into the enormous psychodynamic significance of anxiety for the understanding of human psychology and psychopathology, which has brought about such a degree of preoccupation with this universal emotional experience that it has limited our ability to study other ubiquitous emotional experiences adequately. For instance, the neglect accorded loneliness has also existed, to a lesser degree, for grief, which has, by and large, been mentioned only as a part of mourning, depression, and melancholia; as far as I know, nowhere, except in Sullivan's writings (1956, pp. 105-112), has its significance as an independent emotional experience in its own right been recognized. Hope, as an outcome of memories of previous satisfaction, as a stimulus for efforts focused upon positive goals, and as a means of relieving tension, has only recently been introduced as an important concept by Thomas French (1952). The psychodynamics of realistic worry in its own right have been recently investigated for the first time by Judd Marmor (1958). Very little is known about the psychodynamics of pain. Envy is a universal human experience whose significance as an independent emotional experience has again been noted only by Sullivan (1956; pp.

128-138), as far as I know. And above all, real loneliness has only quite rarely been mentioned, in so many words, in the psychiatric literature. Thus I believe that the suggestion is justified that the interrelation of loneliness and anxiety be thoroughly scrutinized, with the goal of accomplishing a new and more precise differentiation between the two dynamisms.

PHYSICAL LONELINESS

I would like to add to this discussion of emotional loneliness a word about physical loneliness. The need, or at least the wish, to have, at times, physical contact with another is a universal human phenomenon, innate and constant, from the time when the human infant leaves the womb and is physically separated from his mother. Physical and emotional disturbances in infants due to consistent lack of physical contact have been repeatedly described, and such a wise and experienced psychotherapist as Georg Groddeck has repeatedly elaborated on the topic of loneliness for nonsexual physical contact in adults.

In the middle and upper social strata of Western cuture, physical loneliness has become a specific problem, since this culture is characterized by so many obsessional taboos with regard to people's touching each other, or having their physical privacy threatened in other ways. I agree with Gorer's suggestion that American drinking habits can be understood as a means of counteracting the threats of physical loneliness (1948, p. 130).

People who give massages or osteopathic treatment are quite aware of the fact that their treatment, irrespective of the specific physical ailment for which it is primarily applied, often helps their patients emotionally by relieving their physical loneliness. Pointing in the same direction is the pacifying influence which an alcohol back rub often has on mental patients, and the eagerness with which many of them ask for it.

PSYCHOTHERAPY WITH THE LONELY

Now I would like to make some observations drawn from my experience in psychotherapy with lonely patients. I have said that most patients keep their loneliness hidden as a secret from others, often even from themselves. In Otto A. Will's recorded interview in psychotherapy, the doctor and Miss A, the patient, talk about an internist whose patients go to see him allegedly for physical treatment, but actually because they are lonely. And while Miss A herself "may talk of many things . . . one of her most essential problems is that of loneliness" (Will and Cohen, 1953, p. 278).

I think that this great difficulty of patients in accepting the awareness of being lonely, and their even greater difficulty in admitting it to the therapist in so many words, explains the relief with which some lonely mental patients respond if the psychiatrist takes the initiative and opens the discussion about it—for example, by offering a sober statement to the effect that he knows about the patient's loneliness. Of course, I do not mean to say that such a statement can be offered to patients before they have overcome at least some fraction of their isolation. This can be accomplished by the doctor's mere presence, without therapeutic pressure; that is, the doctor should offer his presence to the lonely patient first in the spirit of expecting nothing but to be tolerated, then to be accepted simply as a person who is there. The possibility that psychotherapy may be able to do something about the patient's loneliness should, of course, not be verbalized at this point. To offer any such suggestion in the beginning of one's contact with an essentially lonely patient could lend itself only to one of two interpretations in the patient's mind: Either the psychotherapist does not know anything about the inexplicable, uncanny quality of the patient's loneliness, or the psychotherapist himself is afraid of it. The mere statements, however, that "I know," and "I am here," put in at the right time, by implication or in so many words, may be accepted and may replace the patient's desolate experience of "nobody knows except me." I have tried this device with several patients and have been gratified by its results. It has helped patients to make an initial dent in their inner loneliness and isolation, and has thus become a beneficial turning point in the course of their treatment.

The psychiatrist's specific personal problem in treating lonely patients seems to be that he has to be alert for and recognize traces of his own loneliness or fear of loneliness, lest it interfere with his fearless acceptance of manifestations of the patient's loneliness. This holds true, for example, when the psychiatrist, hard as he may try, cannot understand the meaning of a psychotic communication. He may then feel excluded from a "we-experience" with his patient; and this exclusion may evoke a sense of loneliness or fear of loneliness in the doctor, which makes him anxious.

I have made an attempt in this paper to invite the interest of psychiatrists to the investigation of the psychodynamics of loneliness, as a significant, universal emotional experience with far-reaching psychopathological ramifications. Such investigation may identify certain trends in the developmental history as specific for persons suffering from real loneliness.

I have postulated a significant interrelatedness between loneliness and anxiety, and suggested the need for further conceptual and clinical examination of loneliness in its own right and in its relation to anxiety. I expect that, as result of such scrutiny, it will be found that real loneliness plays an essential role in the genesis of mental disorder. Thus I suggest that an understanding of loneliness is important for the understanding of mental disorder.

19

On the Sense of Loneliness

MELANIE KLEIN

IN THE PRESENT PAPER an attempt will be made to investigate the source of the sense of loneliness. By the sense of loneliness I am referring not to the objective situation of being deprived of external companionship. I am referring to the inner sense of loneliness—the sense of being alone regardless of external circumstances, of feeling lonely even when among friends or receiving love. This state of internal loneliness, I will suggest, is the result of a ubiquitous yearning for an unattainable perfect internal state. Such loneliness, which is experienced to some extent by everyone, springs from paranoid and depressive anxieties which are derivatives of the infant's psychotic anxieties. These anxieties exist in some measure in every individual but are excessively strong in illness; therefore loneliness is also part of illness, both of a schizophrenic and depressive nature.

In order to understand how the sense of loneliness arises we have—as with other attitudes and emotions—to go back to early infancy and trace its influence on later stages of life. As I have frequently described, the ego exists and operates from birth onwards. At first it is largely lacking in cohesion and dominated by splitting mechanisms. The danger of being destroyed by the death instinct directed against the self contributes to the splitting of impulses into good and bad; owing to the projection of these impulses on to the primal object, it too is split into good and bad. In consequence, in the earliest stages, the good part of the ego and the good object are in some measure protected, since aggression is directed away from them. These are the particular splitting processes which I have described as the basis of relative security in the very young infant, in so far as security can be achieved at this stage; whereas other splitting processes, such as those leading to fragmentation, are detrimental to the ego and its strength.

Together with the urge to split there is from the beginning of life a drive towards integration which increases with the growth of the ego. This process of integration is based on the introjection of the good object, primarily a part object—the mother's breast, although other aspects of the mother also enter into even the earliest relation. If the good internal object is established with relative security, it becomes the core of the developing ego.

A satisfactory early relation to the mother (not necessarily based on breast feeding since the bottle can also symbolically stand for the breast) implies a close contact between the unconscious of the mother and of the child. This is the foundation for the most complete experience of being understood and is essentially linked with the preverbal stage. However gratifying it is in later life to express thoughts and feelings to a congenial person, there remains an unsatisfied longing for an understanding without words—ultimately for the earliest relation with the mother. This longing contributes to the sense of loneliness and derives from the depressive feeling of an irretrievable loss.

Even at best, however, the happy relation with the mother and her breast is never undisturbed, since persecutory anxiety is bound to arise. Persecutory anxiety is at its height during the first three months of life—the period of the paranoid-schizoid position; it emerges from the beginning of life as the result of the conflict between the life and death instincts and the experience of birth contributes to it. Whenever destructive impulses arise strongly, the mother and her breast, owing to projection, are felt to be persecutory, and therefore the infant inevitably experiences some insecurity. This paranoid insecurity is one of the roots of loneliness.

When the depressive position arises—ordinarily in the middle of the first half of the first year of life—the ego is already more integrated. This is expressed in a stronger sense of wholeness so that the infant is better able to relate itself to the mother, and later to other people, as a whole person. Then paranoid anxiety, as a factor in loneliness, increasingly gives way to depressive anxiety. But the actual process of integration brings in its train new problems, and I shall discuss some of these and their relation to loneliness.

One of the factors which stimulates integration is that the splitting processes by which the early ego attempts to counteract insecurity are never more than temporarily effective and the ego is driven to attempt to come to terms with the destructive impulses. This drive contributes towards the need for integration. For integration, if it could be achieved, would have the effect of mitigating hate by love and in this way rendering destructive impulses less powerful. The ego would then feel safer not only about its own survival but also about the preservation of its good object. This is one of the reasons why lack of integration is extremely painful.

However, integration is difficult to accept. The coming together of destructive and loving impulses, and of the good and bad aspects of the object, arouses the anxiety that destructive feelings may overwhelm the loving feelings and endanger the good object. Thus, there is conflict between seeking integration as a safeguard against destructive impulses and fearing integration lest the destructive impulses endanger the good object and the good parts of the self. I have heard patients express the painfulness of integration in terms of feeling lonely and deserted, through being completely alone with what to them was a bad part of the self. And the process becomes all the more painful when a harsh superego has engendered a very strong repression of destructive impulses and tries to maintain it.

It is only step by step that integration can take place and the security achieved by it is liable to be disturbed under internal and external pressure; and this remains true throughout life. Full and permanent integration is never possible for some polarity between the life and death instincts always persists and remains the deepest source of conflict. Since full integration is never achieved, complete understanding and acceptance of one's own emotions, phantasies, and anxieties is not possible and this continues as an important factor in loneliness. The longing to understand oneself is also bound up with the need to be understood by the internalized good object. One expression of this longing is the universal phantasy of having a twin—a phantasy to which Bion drew attention in an unpublished paper. This twin figure as he suggested, represents those un-

understood and split off parts which the individual is longing to regain, in the hope of achieving wholeness and complete understanding; they are sometimes felt to be the ideal parts. At other times the twin also represents an entirely reliable, in fact, idealized internal object.

There is one further connection between loneliness and the problem of integration that needs consideration at this point. It is generally supposed that loneliness can derive from the conviction that there is no person or group to which one belongs. This not belonging can be seen to have a much deeper meaning. However much integration proceeds, it cannot do away with the feeling that certain components of the self are not available because they are split off and cannot be regained. Some of these split off parts, as I shall discuss in more detail later, are projected into other people, contributing to the feeling that one is not in full possession of one's self, that one does not fully belong to oneself or, therefore, to anybody else. The lost parts too, are felt to be lonely.

I have already suggested that paranoid and depressive anxieties are never entirely overcome even in people who are not ill and are the foundation for some measure of loneliness. There are considerable individual differences in the way in which loneliness is experienced. When paranoid anxiety is relatively strong, though still within the range of normality, the relation to the internal good object is liable to be disturbed and trust in the good part of the self is impaired. As a consequence, there is an increased projection of paranoid feelings and suspicions on others, with a resulting sense of loneliness.

In actual schizophrenic illness these factors are necessarily present but much exacerbated; the lack of integration which I have so far been discussing within the normal range is now seen in its pathological form—indeed, all the features of the paranoid-schizoid position are present to an excessive degree.

Before going on to discuss loneliness in the schizophrenic it is important to consider in more detail some of the processes of the paranoid-schizoid position, particularly splitting and projective identification. Projective identification is based on the splitting of the ego and the projection of parts of the self into other people; first of all the mother or her breast. This projection derives from the oral-anal-urethral impulses, the parts of the self being omnipotently expelled in the bodily substances into the mother in order to control

and take possession of her. She is not then felt to be a separate individual but an aspect of the self. If these excrements are expelled in
hatred the mother is felt to be dangerous and hostile. But it is not only bad parts of the self that are split off and projected, but also good
parts. Ordinarily, as I have discussed, as the ego develops, splitting
and projection lessen and the ego becomes more integrated. If,
however, the ego is very weak, which I consider to be an innate
feature, and if there have been difficulties at birth and the beginning
of life, the capacity to integrate—to bring together the split off parts
of the ego—is also weak, and there is in addition a greater tendency
to split in order to avoid anxiety aroused by the destructive impulses
directed against the self and external world. This incapacity to bear
anxiety is thus of far-reaching importance. It not only increases the
need to split the ego and object excessively, which can lead to a state
of fragmentation, but also makes it impossible to work through the
early anxieties.

In the schizophrenic we see the result of these unresolved processes. The schizophrenic feels that he is hopelessly in bits and that he
will never be in possession of his self. The very fact that he is so
fragmented results in his being unable to internalize his primal object (the mother) sufficiently as a good object and therefore in his
lacking the foundation of stability; he cannot rely on an external and
internal good object, nor can he rely on his own self. This factor is
bound up with loneliness, for it increases the feeling of the
schizophrenic that he is left alone, as it were, with his misery. The
sense of being surrounded by a hostile world, which is characteristic
of the paranoid aspect of schizophrenic illness, not only increases all
his anxieties but vitally influences his feelings of loneliness.

Another factor which contributes to the loneliness of the
schizophrenic is confusion. This is the result of a number of factors,
particularly the fragmentation of the ego, and the excessive use of
projective identification, so that he constantly feels himself not only
to be in bits, but to be mixed up with other people. He is then unable
to distinguish between the good and bad parts of the self, between
the good and bad object, and between external and internal reality.
The schizophrenic thus cannot understand himself or trust himself.
These factors, allied with his paranoid distrust of others, result in a
state of withdrawal which destroys his ability to make object relations and to gain from them the reassurance and pleasure which can

counteract loneliness by strengthening the ego. He longs to be able to make relationships with people, but cannot.

It is important not to underrate the schizophrenic's pain and suffering. They are not so easily detected because of his constant defensive use of withdrawal and the distraction of his emotions. Nevertheless, I and some of my colleagues, of whom I shall only mention Dr. Davidson, Dr. Rosenfeld, and Dr. Hanna Segal, who have treated or are treating schizophrenics, retain some optimism about the outcome. This optimism is based on the fact that there is an urge towards integration, even in such ill people, and that there is a relation, however undeveloped, to the good object and the good self.

I now wish to deal with the loneliness characteristic of a prevalence of depressive anxiety, first of all within the range of normality. I have often referred to the fact that early emotional life is characterized by the recurrent experiences of losing and regaining. Whenever the mother is not present, she may be felt by the infant to be lost, either because she is injured or because she has turned into a persecutor. The feeling that she is lost is equivalent to the fear of her death. Owing to introjection, the death of the external mother means the loss of the internal good object as well, and this reinforces the infant's fear of his own death. These anxieties and emotions are heightened at the stage of the depressive position, but throughout life, the fear of death plays a part in loneliness.

I have already suggested that the pain which accompanies processes of integration also contributes to loneliness. For it means facing one's destructive impulses and hated parts of the self, which at times appear uncontrollable and which therefore endanger the good object. With integration and a growing sense of reality, omnipotence is bound to be lessened, and this again contributes to the pain of integration, for it means a diminished capacity for hope. While there are other sources of hopefulness which derive from the strength of the ego and from trust in oneself and others, an element of omnipotence is always part of it.

Integration also means losing some of the idealization—both of the object and of a part of the self—which has from the beginning coloured the relation to the good object. The realization that the good object can never approximate to the perfection expected from the ideal one brings about de-idealization: and even more painful is the realization that no really ideal part of the self exists. In my experience, the need for idealization is never fully given up, even though in normal development the facing of internal and external reality tends to diminish it. As a patient put it to me, while admitting the relief obtained from some steps in integration, "the glamour has gone." The analysis showed that the glamour which had gone was the idealization of the self and of the object, and the loss of it led to feelings of loneliness.

Some of these factors enter in a greater degree into the mental processes characteristic of manic-depressive illness. The manic-depressive patient has already made some steps towards the depressive position, that is to say, he experiences the object more as a whole, and his feelings of guilt, though still bound up with paranoid mechanisms, are stronger and less evanescent. More, therefore, than the schizophrenic, he feels the longing to have the good object safely inside to preserve it and protect it. But this he feels unable to do since, at the same time, he has not sufficiently worked through the depressive position, so that his capacity for making reparation, for synthesizing the good object, and achieving integration of the ego have not sufficiently progressed. In so far as, in his relation to his good object, there is still a great deal of hatred and, therefore, fear, he is unable sufficiently to make reparation to it, therefore his relation to it brings no relief but only a feeling of being unloved, and hated, and again and again he feels that it is endangered by his destructive impulses. The longing to be able to overcome all these difficulties in relation to the good object is part of the feeling of loneliness. In extreme cases this expresses itself in the tendency towards suicide.

In external relations similar processes are at work. The manic-depressive can only at times, and very temporarily, get relief from a relation with a well-meaning person, since, as he quickly projects his own hate, resentment, envy, and fear, he is constantly full of distrust. In other words, his paranoid anxieties are still very strong. The feeling of loneliness of the manic-depressive centers, therefore, more on his incapacity to keep an inner and external companionship with a good object and less on his being in bits.

I shall discuss some further difficulties in integration and shall deal particularly with the conflict between male and female elements in both sexes. We know that there is a biological factor in bisexuality, but I am concerned here with the psychological aspect. In women there is universally the wish to be a man, expressed perhaps most clearly in terms of penis envy; similarly, one finds in men the feminine position, the longing to possess breasts and to give birth to children. Such wishes are bound up with an identification with both parents and are accompanied by feelings of competitiveness and envy, as well as admiration of the coveted possessions. These identifications vary in strength and also in quality, depending on whether admiration or envy is the more prevalent. Part of the desire for integration in the young child is the urge to integrate these different aspects of the personality. In addition, the superego makes the conflicting demand for identification with both parents, prompted by the need to make reparation for early desires to rob each of them and expressing the wish to keep them alive internally. If the element of guilt is predominant it will hamper the integration of these identifications. If, however, these identifications are satisfactorily achieved they become a source of enrichment and a basis for the development of a variety of gifts and capacities.

In order to illustrate the difficulties of this particular aspect of integration and its relation to loneliness, I shall quote the dream of a male patient. A little girl was playing with a lioness and holding out a hoop for her to jump through, but on the other side of the hoop was a precipice. The lioness obeyed and was killed in the process. At the same time, a little boy was killing a snake. The patient himself recognized, since similar material had come up previously, that the little girl stood for his feminine part and the little boy for his masculine part. The lioness had strong links with myself in the transference, of which I shall only give one instance. The little girl had a cat with her and this led to associations to my cat, which often stood for me. It was extremely painful to the patient to become aware that, being in competition with my femininity, he wanted to destroy me, and in the past, his mother. This recognition that one part of himself wanted to kill the loved lioness—analyst—which would thus deprive him of his good object, led to a feeling not only of misery and guilt but also of loneliness in the transference. It was also very distressing for him to recognize that the competition with his father led him to destroy the father's potency and penis, represented by the snake.

This material led to further and very painful work about integration. The dream of the lioness which I have mentioned was preceded by a dream in which a woman committed suicide by throwing herself from a very high building, and the patient, contrary to his usual attitude, experienced no horror. The analysis which was, at that time, very much occupied with his difficulty over the feminine position, which was then at its height, showed that the woman represented his feminine part and that he really wished it to be destroyed. He felt that not only would it injure his relation to women, but would also damage his masculinity and all its constructive tendencies, including reparation to the mother, which became clear in relation to myself. This attitude of putting all his envy and competitiveness into his feminine part turned out to be one way of splitting, and at the same time seemed to overshadow his very great admiration and regard for femininity. Moreover, it became clear that while he felt masculine aggression to be comparatively open and, therefore, more honest, he attributed to the feminine side envy and deception, and since he very much loathed all insincerity and dishonesty, this contributed to his difficulties in integration.

The analysis of these attitudes, going back to his earliest feelings of envy towards the mother, led to a much better integration of both the feminine and masculine parts of his personality and to the diminution of envy in both the masculine and feminine role. This increased his competence in his relationships and thus helped to combat a sense of loneliness.

I shall now give another instance, from the analysis of a patient, a man who was not unhappy or ill, and who was successful in his work and in his relationships. He was aware that he had always felt lonely as a child and that this feeling of loneliness had never entirely gone. Love of nature had been a significant feature in this patient's sublimations. Even from earliest childhood he found comfort and satisfaction in being out of doors. In one session he described his enjoyment of a journey which led him through hilly country and then the revulsion he felt when he entered the town. I interpreted as I had done previously, that to him nature represented not only beauty but also goodness, actually the good object that he had taken into himself. He replied after a pause that he felt that was true, but that nature was not only good because there is always much aggression in it. In the same way, he added, his own relation to the countryside was also not wholly good, instancing how as a boy, he used to rob nests, while at the same time he had always wanted to grow things. He said that in loving nature he had actually, as he put it, "taken in an integrated object."

In order to understand how the patient had overcome his loneliness in relation to the countryside, while still experiencing it in connection with the town, we have to follow up some of his associations referring both to his childhood and to nature. He had told me that he was supposed to have been a happy baby, well fed by his mother; and much material—particularly in the transference situation—supported this assumption. He had soon become aware of his worries about his mother's health, and also his resentment about her rather disciplinarian attitude. In spite of this, his relation to her was in many ways happy, and he remained fond of her; but he felt himself hemmed in at home and was aware of an urgent longing to be out of doors. He seemed to have developed a very early admiration for the beauties of nature; and as soon as he could get more freedom to be out of doors, this became his greatest pleasure. He described how he, together with other boys, used to spend his free time wandering in the woods and fields. He confessed to some aggression in connection with nature, such as robbing nests and damaging hedges. At the same time he was convinced that such damage would not be lasting because nature always repaired itself. Nature he regarded as rich and invulnerable, in striking contrast to his attitude towards his mother. The relation to nature seemed to be relatively free of guilt, whereas in his relation to his mother for whose frailty he felt responsible for unconscious reasons, there was a great deal of guilt.

From his material I was able to conclude that he had to some extent introjected the mother as a good object and had been able to achieve a measure of synthesis between his loving and hostile feelings towards her. He also reached a fair level of integration but this was disturbed by persecutory and depressive anxiety in relation to his parents. The relation to the father had been very important for his development, but it does not enter into this particular piece of material.

I have referred to this patient's obsessional need to be out of doors, and this was linked with his claustrophobia. Claustrophobia, as I have elsewhere suggested, derives from two main sources: projective identification into the mother leading to an anxiety of imprisonment inside her; and reintrojection resulting in a feeling that inside oneself one is hemmed in by resentful internal objects. With regard to this patient, I would conclude that his flight into nature was a defense against both these anxiety situations. In a sense his love for nature was split off from his relation to his mother; his de-idealization of the latter having led to his transferring his idealization on to nature. In connection with home and mother he felt very lonely, and it was this sense of loneliness which was at the root of his revulsion against town. The freedom and enjoyment which nature gave him were not only a source of pleasure, derived from a strong sense of beauty and linked with appreciation of art, but also a means of counteracting the fundamental loneliness which had never entirely gone.

In another session the patient reported with a feeling of guilt that on a trip into the country he had caught a field mouse and put it in a box in the boot of his car, as a present for his young child who, he thought, would enjoy having this creature as a pet. The patient forgot about the mouse, remembering it only a day later. He made unsuccessful efforts to find it because it had eaten its way out of the box and hidden itself in the farthest corner of the boot where it was out of reach. Eventually, after renewed efforts to get hold of it, he found that it had died. The patient's guilt about having forgotten the field mouse and thus caused its death led in the course of subsequent sessions to associations about dead people for whose death he felt to some extent responsible though not for rational reasons.

In the subsequent sessions there was a wealth of associations to the field mouse which appeared to play a number of roles; it stood for a split-off part of himself, lonely and deprived. By identification with his child he moreover felt deprived of a potential companion. A number of associations showed that throughout childhood the patient had longed for a playmate of his own age—a longing that went beyond the actual need for external companions and was the result of feeling that split-off parts of his self could not be regained. The field mouse also stood for his good object, which he had enclosed in his inside—represented by the car—and about which he felt guilty and also feared that it might turn retaliatory. One of his other associations, referring to neglect, was that the field mouse also stood for a neglected woman. This association came after a holiday and implied that not only had he been left alone by the analyst but that the analyst had been neglected and lonely. The link with similar feelings towards his mother became clear in the material, as did the conclusion that he contained a dead or lonely object, which increased his loneliness.

This patient's material supports my contention that there is a link between loneliness and the incapacity sufficiently to integrate the good object as well as parts of the self which are felt to be inaccessible.

I shall now go on to examine more closely the factors which normally mitigate loneliness. The relatively secure internalization of the good breast is characteristic of some innate strength of the ego. A strong ego is less liable to fragmentation and therefore more capable of achieving a measure of integration and a good early relation to the primal object. Further, a successful internalization of the good object is the root of an identification with it which strengthens the feeling of goodness and trust both in the object and in the self. This identification with the good object mitigates the destructive impulses and in this way also diminishes the harshness of the superego. A milder superego makes less stringent demands on the ego; this leads to tolerance and to the ability to bear deficiencies in loved objects without impairing the relation to them.

A decrease in omnipotence, which comes about with progress in integration and leads to some loss of hopefulness, yet makes possible a distinction between the destructive impulses and their effects; therefore aggressiveness and hate are felt to be less dangerous. This greater adaptation to reality leads to an acceptance of one's own shortcomings and in consequence lessens the sense of resentment about past frustrations. It also opens up sources of enjoyment emanating from the external world and is thus another factor which diminishes loneliness.

A happy relation to the first object and a successful internalization of it means that love can be given and received. As a result the infant can experience enjoyment not only at times of feeding but also in response to the mother's presence and affection. Memories of such happy experiences are a stand-by for the young child when he feels frustrated, because they are bound up with the hope of further happy times. Moreover, there is a close link between enjoyment and the feeling of understanding and being understood. At the moment of enjoyment anxiety is assuaged and the closeness to the mother and trust in her are uppermost. Introjective and projective identification, when not excessive, play an important part in this feeling of closeness, for they underlie the capacity to understand and contribute to the experience of being understood.

Enjoyment is always bound up with gratitude; if this gratitude is deeply felt it includes the wish to return goodness received and is thus the basis of generosity. There is always a close connection between being able to accept and to give, and both are part of the relation to the good object and therefore counteract loneliness. Furthermore, the feeling of generosity underlies creativeness, and this applies to the infant's most primitive constructive activities as well as to the creativeness of the adult.

The capacity for enjoyment is also the precondition for a measure of resignation which allows for pleasure in what is available without too much greed for inaccessible gratifications and without excessive resentment about frustration. Such adaptation can already be observed in some young infants. Resignation is bound up with tolerance and with the feeling that destructive impulses will not overwhelm love, and that therefore goodness and life may be preserved.

A child who, in spite of some envy and jealousy, can identify himself with the pleasures of gratifications of members of his family circle will be able to do so in relation to other people in later life. In old age he will then be able to reverse the early situation and identify himself with the satisfactions of youth. This is only possible if there is gratitude for past pleasures without too much resentment because they are no longer available.

All the factors in development which I have touched upon, though they mitigate the sense of loneliness, never entirely eliminate it; therefore they are liable to be used as defenses. When these defenses are very powerful and dovetail successfully, loneliness may often not be consciously experienced. Some infants use extreme dependence on the mother as a defense against loneliness, and the need for dependence remains as a pattern throughout life. On the other hand, the flight to the internal object, which can be expressed in early infancy in hallucinatory gratification, is often used defensively in an attempt to counteract dependence on the external object. In some adults this attitude leads to a rejection of any companionship which in extreme cases is a symptom of illness.

The urge towards independence, which is part of maturation, can be used defensively for the purpose of overcoming loneliness. A lessening of dependence on the object makes the individual less vulnerable and also counteracts the need for excessive internal and external closeness to loved people.

Another defense, particularly in old age, is the preoccupation with the past in order to avoid the frustrations of the present. Some idealization of the past is bound to enter into these memories and is put into the service of defense. In young people, idealization of the future serves a similar purpose. Some measure of idealization of people and causes is a normal defense and is part of the search for idealized inner objects which is projected on to the external world.

Appreciation by others and success—originally the infantile need to be appreciated by the mother—can be used defensively against loneliness. But this method becomes very insecure if it is used excessively since trust in oneself is then not sufficiently established. Another defense, bound up with omnipotence and part of manic defense, is a particular use of the capacity to wait for what is desired; this may lead to over-optimism and a lack of drive and may be linked with a defective sense of reality.

The denial of loneliness, which is frequently used as a defense, is likely to interfere with good object relations, in contrast to an attitude in which loneliness is actually experienced and becomes a stimulus towards object relations.

Finally, I want to indicate why it is so difficult to evaluate the balance between internal and external influences in the causation of loneliness. I have so far in this paper dealt mainly with internal aspects—but these do not exist in vacuo. There is a constant interaction between internal and external factors in mental life, based on the processes of projection and introjection which initiate object relations.

The first powerful impact of the external world on the young infant is the discomfort of various kinds which accompanies birth and which is attributed by him to hostile persecutory forces. These paranoid anxieties become part of his internal situation. Internal factors also operate from the beginning; the conflict between life and death instincts engenders the deflection of the death instinct outwards and this, according to Freud, initiates the projection of destructive impulses. I hold, however, that at the same time the urge of the life instinct to find a good object in the external world leads to the projection of loving impulses as well. In this way the picture of the external world—represented first by the mother, and particularly by her breast, and based on actual good and bad experiences in relation to her—is coloured by internal factors. By introjection this picture of the external world affects the internal one. However, it is not only that the infant's feelings about the external world are coloured by his projection, but the mother's actual relation to her child is in indirect and subtle ways influenced by the infant's response to her. A contented baby who sucks with enjoyment allays his mother's anxiety; and her happiness expresses itself in her way of handling and feeding him, thus diminishing his persecutory anxiety and affecting his ability to internalize the good breast. In contrast, a child who has difficulties over feeding may arouse the mother's anxiety and guilt and thus unfavourably influence her relation to him. In these varying ways there is constant interaction between the internal and external world persisting throughout life.

The interplay of external and internal factors has an important bearing on increasing or diminishing loneliness. The internalization of a good breast, which can only result from a favourable interplay between internal and external elements, is a foundation for integration which I have mentioned as one of the most important factors in diminishing the sense of loneliness. In addition, it is well recognized that in normal development, when feelings of loneliness are strongly experienced, there is a great need to turn to external objects, since loneliness is partially allayed by external relations. External influences, particularly the attitude of people important to the individual, can in other ways diminish loneliness. For example, a fundamentally good relation to the parents makes the loss of idealization and the lessening of the feeling of omnipotence more bearable. The parents, by accepting the existence of the child's destructive impulses and showing that they can protect themselves against his aggressiveness, can diminish his anxiety about the effects of his hostile wishes. As a result, the internal object is felt to be less vulnerable and the self less destructive.

I can here only touch on the importance of the superego in connection with all these processes. A harsh superego can never be felt to forgive destructive impulses; in fact, it demands that they should not exist. Although the superego is built up largely from a split-off part of the ego on to which impulses are projected, it is also inevitably influenced by the introjection of the personalities of the actual parents and of their relation to the child. The harsher the superego, the greater will be the loneliness, because its severe demands increase depressive and paranoid anxieties.

In conclusion I wish to restate my hypothesis that although loneliness can be diminished or increased by external influences, it can never be completely eliminated, because the urge towards integration, as well as the pain experienced in the process of integration, spring from internal sources which remain powerful throughout life.

20

Pathological Loneliness:
A Psychodynamic Interpretation

P. HERBERT LEIDERMAN

LONELINESS, a theme common to the pleadings of a biblical Job and to the contemporary writings of the social philosophers (Josephson and Josephson, 1962; Riesman, Denny, and Glaser, 1950), has become of increasing concern in the Western urban society. Considering the fact that psychiatrists, as a group, are not reluctant to deal with and write about contemporary issues, one might reasonably expect loneliness to be mentioned frequently in the psychiatric literature. However, examination of this literature reveals few papers on this subject. Although the basis for this dearth may be attributed to psychodynamic reasons, perhaps hinted at by Menninger (1959) when he describes loneliness as the psychiatrist's own clinical problem, it is my contention that the lack of papers is attributable more likely to the absence of an adequate theoretical model to aid in understanding the psychodynamics of loneliness. The purpose of this chapter is to develop a psychodynamic model for states of pathological loneliness and thereby to differentiate loneliness from depression, with which, I believe, it has frequently been confused. In so doing, I

Reprinted from *International Psychiatry Clinics* 6(2):155–174, 1969 by permission of Little, Brown & Co., Inc., Boston, Mass. Copyright © 1969 by Little, Brown & Company, Inc.

hope to point the way for more adequate therapy for this frequently occurring symptom of contemporary American life.

The framework for the development of this model will develop from the psychoanalytical viewpoint, since this theory has proved to be most useful so far in understanding the phenomenology of psycho-pathological states. I shall deal only with the psychodynamics of loneliness, ignoring sociological and philosophical approaches, not because they are considered less important, but rather because they have been more widely discussed, while the psychodynamics of loneliness have been neglected by comparison.

DEFINITION OF LONELINESS

Some definitions are in order. The term loneliness, in this chapter, refers to an affective state in which the individual is aware of the feeling of being apart from others, along with the experiences of a vague need for other individuals. Loneliness has an unpleasant connotation in contrast to mere solitude or aloneness, in which the individual may be alone physically but does not experience the negative or unpleasant aspects of loneliness. Loneliness does not imply physical isolation. It can occur in the presence of other individuals. In my opinion, it cannot be considered a clinical syndrome, but should be considered present when reported as the predominant mood accompanying a patient's symptoms. As such, it can be part of several recognizable syndromes such as depression, schizophrenia, psychoneurosis, and phobic reactions. Undoubtedly, it is associated most frequently with clinical depression and is most likely to be confused with depressive affect reported by depressed individuals.

DEPRESSION AND LONELINESS

Since loneliness frequently accompanies depression and is readily confused with depressive affect, I shall first review briefly the psychodynamics of depression, before presenting the three clinical cases and developing a theory of the psychodynamics of loneliness.

One of the first formulations of a theory of depression was that of Abraham (1924), who in 1911 used Freud's concept of ambivalence in formulating the psychodynamics of the manic-depressive psychosis. He concluded that manic-depressive psychosis resulted from an attitude of hatred that paralyzed the patient's capacity for love. Abraham's major theoretical contribution to the understanding of depression was his introduction of the concept of repressed hostility as a central feature of manic-depressive psychosis.

The next major step in the development of the psychoanalytic theory of depression was the introduction by Freud of the concept of "loss." In his paper "Mourning and Melancholia" Freud (1917) contrasted the process of normal mourning with the profound grief and self-reproaches of the melancholic patient. Though mourning and melancholia resemble one another in that both occur after a loss of some individual or object, mourning usually involves a loss in the real world, while the loss in melancholia involves the intrapsychic representation of that world.

The normal person in mourning gradually withdraws his libidinal cathexis or attachment from the loved object. At a later stage in the course of the mourning process he transfers his attachment to a new object, thereby restoring the psychic balance of cathectic forces. The melancholic patient, on the other hand, upon the loss of an object, withdraws his cathexis not only from the real world but also from an intrapsychic representation of that object. Any loss in the real world is experienced as a loss of part of his own ego. According to Freud, this intrapsychic representation is suffused with positive and negative feelings, and any withdrawal of cathexis from this intrapsychic representation or introject leads to feelings of hostility directed toward the negative portions of the object, as well as to feelings of guilt about destruction of the positive portion of the object. In delineating mourning from melancholia, Freud not only clarified the psychic process involved but also introduced a concept of the ambivalent introject.

The next major development of the psychoanalytical theory of depression was that of Bibring (1953), who formulated the mechanism of depression and its accompanying depressive affect in terms of psychology of the ego. He suggested that the common core of these conditions is the affect involved with a loss of self-esteem, the ego's painful awareness of its helplessness to achieve its aspirations. Bibring's major contribution to the conceptualization of depression was his emphasis on conflicts within the ego in the genesis of depressive affects.

Edith Jacobson (1957) further clarified the theoretical model of depression. She distinguished between the ego, as part of a psychic system, and the self, as an object within the system ego. These self-objects are differentiated from other-person objects. Like Bibring (1953), she believed self-esteem to be the central problem in melancholia, with depressive affect reflecting the degree of discrepancy or harmony between the self-representations and wished-for concept of the self. Jacobson suggested that for the melancholic, the worthless object-images merge with the self-representations, and she further postulated that an inadequate separation of the self and object-images from one another facilitates this process. It is this concept, inadequate separation of self and object representations, which, I believe, is critical for the development of pathological loneliness.

DISCUSSION OF LONELINESS IN THE PSYCHIATRIC LITERATURE

Although the psychiatric literature on loneliness is scant compared to the amount of work on depression, several authors have explored the topic and presented relevant concepts.

Gregory Zilboorg (1938), writing in the *Atlantic Monthly*, was one of the first psychodynamically oriented psychiatrists to deal specifically with the topic of loneliness. Although he attributed pathological loneliness to damage to or loss of the narcissistic image of self, Zilboorg questioned the presumed relationship of pathological loneliness to normal loneliness. He described normal lonesomeness and nostalgia as transient states of the normal process of mourning. He contrasted this type of transient lonesomeness with chronic loneliness, which involved a narcissistic wound. He postulated three fundamental urges, (1) narcissism, (2) megalomania, and (3) hostility, which, in their various combinations, manifest or hidden, are to be found in chronically lonely individuals. He postulated two types of loneliness, one of which he likened to a transient state akin to the normal mourning process; the other type follows the classic Freud-Abraham model of melancholia. For Zilboorg, the psychodynamics of loneliness were similar to, if not identical with, the psychodynamics of depression.

Frieda Fromm-Reichmann (this volume) contributed one of the first papers on loneliness in a professional journal. She approached the problem of loneliness from the vantage point of her work with hospitalized schizophrenic patients. In a paper left incomplete at her death, she summarized her investigations of the psychodynamics of loneliness. She pointed out that loneliness "can arouse anxiety and fear of contamination which may induce people—among these the psychiatrists who deal with it in their patients—to refer to it euphemistically as 'depression.'"

She suggested that the fear of loneliness may be due, in part, to our culture's insistence that valid self-orientations depend upon overt relationships with others. Individuals feel loneliness when the boundary between the subjective self and others is threatened. She raised the question as to why this fear develops in some and not in others, and answered it by suggesting that fear of loneliness and separation anxiety of the infant are closely linked developmentally. For her, separation early in the course of development was the clue to the detached loneliness of the schizophrenic.

In contrasting loneliness in schizophrenics with loneliness in depressed patients, she noted that even in the withdrawal phase of depression, the individual frequently may maintain a strong interest in his interpersonal environment, whereas in the schizophrenic there is detachment from the real world. Considering the preoccupation of depressed patients with relationships and their pleas for fulfillment of interpersonal dependency, she felt that the loneliness of psychotic depression was not of the same order as the loneliness of the schizophrenic.

Fromm-Reichmann brought some additional conceptual issues and problems into the open. She emphasized the importance of object relationships in the development of loneliness and suggested that the genesis of these pathological relationships occurs early in the course of psychological development. She believed loneliness to be one of the more predominant affects in the schizophrenic patient and suggested that preoccupation with anxiety had led to relative neglect of loneliness by psychiatrists. While she did not have the opportunity to develop her ideas further, nevertheless, she did use psychological material from depressed and normal individuals to stress the universality of the human experience of loneliness and to draw the attention of the psychiatric world to its fundamental importance.

A paper on loneliness by von Witzleben (1958), published in honor of Fromm-Reichmann shortly after her death, further elucidated the psychodynamics of loneliness. Von Witzleben distinguished between two types of loneliness, one accompanied by loss of an object in the real world, and the other the "loneliness of one's self," the feeling of being alone and helpless in this world. This latter type of loneliness, inborn in everyone, he terms *primary loneliness*; for him it was independent of the loss of an object. The loneliness of the schizophrenic patient described by Fromm-Reichmann exemplifies this primary loneliness, while the loneliness of the depressed patient, involving loss, illustrates secondary loneliness. Although von Witzleben differentiated the type of loneliness seen in the schizophrenic patient from that of the depressed patient, he did not develop his ideas on possible mechanisms for the development of these differences, nor did he discuss the relationship of secondary loneliness to loss of self-esteem and the hostile mechanisms so often attributed to depressive patients.

Although the psychodynamic concepts reviewed above set the stage for formulation of the psychodynamics of loneliness, it is the examination of case histories that will reveal the importance of distinguishing loneliness from depression. Three cases will be presented. In the first, the predominant complaint is pathological loneliness; in the second, loneliness and anxiety, along with depression; and in the third, depression with little or no loneliness. Each of these patients was in intensive therapy for at least eighteen months and, therefore, provided a good amount of information on early development, predominance of various affects, current object relationships, and also some assessment of intrapsychic self and object representations. By contrasting these three cases, each with a varying mixture of depressive and loneliness affects, the psychodynamics of loneliness as differentiated from the classic theory of depression will be formulated.

CASE NO. 1

A 32-year-old engineer sought psychotherapy because of intense feelings of loneliness, indecision about his future work, tension, and concern about his bachelor state. His symptoms, which extended back several years, appeared to have exacerbated about a year prior to starting therapy. He attributed the exacerbation to moving away from the South where he had been near his family, but also attributed some of his uneasiness to the fact that he was "one-half of an identical twin."

The twins had been inseparable through grade school, high school, and college, separating for the first time in their lives when they decided to attend different graduate schools. The patient found this separation intolerable and, after one year, rejoined his brother at his graduate school. This contact lasted two years before they separated again, in the year prior to beginning therapy. The patient was aware that he missed his brother, as well as his father and mother. He experienced loneliness in relationship to a large number of friends left behind.

Despite making new friends, the patient continued to have these feelings and reported that they had become more intense.

The patient's father was a professional person, in a field different from the patient's. He is described by the patient as a very rigid and opinionated man who, although kind to his wife and children, had very little time for them. The patient was disturbed in particular because the father never differentiated him from his brother, as indicated by the fact that he addressed both of them by a singular noun, "Brother."

The patient's mother was described by him as warm, friendly, and loving, quite ignorant of the ways of the world. Her life revolved about her family and, although she continued to be a source of warmth and refuge, devoting herself to her family, she played a less important role in his life currently.

The twin brother, who resembled the patient so closely that even the parents, on occasion, confused them, worked in a field related to that of the patient. He was described by the patient as more relaxed and carefree than the patient, although the patient himself was warm, open, and friendly. The twin brother, like the patient, was unmarried.

The patient had numerous male and female friends as a youngster and adolescent. As an adult, there were fewer friends although he was engaged briefly four years ago, but broke the engagement because he "wasn't ready for marriage." Currently, he dates a number of women rather infrequently. He is emotionally involved now with one young woman but doesn't know whether he loves her or not. He is desperately searching for someone he can marry, who would be acceptable to parents and brother.

The patient brought up several examples of situations in which his feelings of loneliness became overwhelming. While working in graduate school, he had increasing difficulty going to the laboratory, especially at night when technicians and other graduate students were absent. Despite the fact that he loved the scientific aspects of his work, he could not bring himself to work in laboratories alone. He decided after a year that he would have to satisfy his need to be with people by changing the emphasis of his work so that he would not have to spend time alone in the laboratory.

The problem of working alone in the laboratory persists for this patient currently. He arranged his schedule so that he could work with others, and, although he dislikes collaborative projects, he usually arranges to do his work in conjunction with one or more colleagues, a pattern reminiscent of the relationship with his twin brother.

A further indication of his poor tolerance of being alone was suggested by his associations to a dream in which he saw himself as sick. "I get depressed when I think of getting sick. It's nice to be taken care of. I suppose this goes back to my mother." In another session, he talked about lumbar disc symptoms which necessitated his being placed on bed rest. "The isolation; I really was alone; I felt very sorry for myself." He could not tolerate being on bed rest, and, after one week, signed out of the hospital. When he developed symptoms again this past year, he refused hospitalization because of his previous experience. Later on in this same hour, when asked to tell how he felt when he described himself as lonely in the hospital, he went on to say, "I felt in need of something that I didn't have and couldn't get. I felt isolated and alone, not depressed." Other associations were to his brother, in which he wondered aloud how his brother might feel in these circumstances. It should be noted that loneliness is not an invariable accompaniment to being alone. For example, in another hour, he mentioned wanting to go into the woods for solitude. He enjoys these periods alone, just being with himself, but realizes in a short while that he would like someone to be with him.

The patient was quite aware of various affective states within himself and could clearly differentiate and describe their occurrence. Aside from his feelings of loneliness, he was aware on occasion of being depressed and, much more rarely, of being angry with himself or with others. When asked to describe his feelings about loneliness and depression, he said that loneliness could sometimes occur with feelings of depression, but they were not the same. He gets depressed when he spends a week in the laboratory and the experiment does not work out, but he usually does not feel lonely then. "Loneliness is something that if found in myself, I don't share it with the outside world. When I'm depressed, I withdraw; when I'm lonely, I try to reach out—or I would like to." The feeling accompanying loneliness is one of incompleteness.

DISCUSSION

There are several points concerning depression and loneliness brought out by this case that deserve emphasis. First, loneliness is clearly differentiated from depression. Minor depression, when reported by the patient, followed a loss of self-esteem in relation to his work. This relative lack of depressive affect was consistent with his very adequate maternal relationship during his earliest years. The absence of overt hostility and anxiety also attested to the adequacy of this relationship in these early years.

Loneliness, on the other hand, was the predominant symptom for this patient, and he had only to arrive home to an empty house after work, or be wrapped in the quiet of an evening drive to the city, to be reminded of it. While it would be easy to ascribe this loneliness to a longing for the absent twin, it is undoubtedly more complex than this. The clue for understanding loneliness in this patient is presented by his statement of "incompleteness," that he believes himself to be "one-half a twin." It would appear that self and object representations are poorly differentiated, if not incomplete, in this patient. This psychological maldevelopment is particularly facilitated in the case of an identical twin, where the peer intrapsychic object-representation is a carbon copy of the self. Thus, this case suggests that loneliness might be accounted for by a maldevelopment of the ego which is the basis for the patient's chronic feeling of loneliness. Loneliness is not experienced as a sense of loss, but rather as a sense of incompleteness. The psychological task for the patient was to overcome or compensate for this developmental arrest and to direct whatever cathectic capacity he had available toward further self-object differentiation.

CASE NO. 2

Case 2 was that of a 24-year-old student, in whom depressive affect and anxiety were accompanied by feelings of loneliness. This patient initially sought therapy because of feelings that he was "losing control of his temper," usually in relation to his parents, though also toward his wife of recent marriage and toward an occasional classmate. He felt tense a great deal of the time, would "panic during exams," and thought that he was doing poorly in his academic work. Although many of these symptoms had been apparent to him since mid-high school, he believed them to be worsening, especially since entering graduate school.

The patient was born in a large city, the second son of a professional family. His father, a college graduate, was very involved in his work and set high standards for his sons, particularly for the patient, who was directed toward his father's profession. The patient's mother was professionally trained, having given up her career for charitable work after being married. She spent very little time with the patient, leaving child care to full-time help.

The patient's brother, three years his senior, was married and successful in a professional career. The patient described him as more intelligent and more artistic than himself. The older brother graduated with honors from the "right" schools; the patient did neither. Despite the rivalry between the two boys over the years, the patient looked to his brother as a model for success.

The patient was reared by nurses and governesses until age six. During much of this period, he reports having little contact with his mother, who was involved with social and charitable activities. The relationships with two nurse-governesses are recalled by the patient with both fondness and resentment. However, it was during a period of his rage at one nurse that his parents dismissed her, much to the regret of the patient. He recalls being both sad and happy following this, sad that he lost her, happy in the thought that his mother might pay more attention to him.

High school and college years were spent in considerable superficial heterosexual social activity, usually accompanied by feelings of intense competition with his brother. He tried to avoid friends and families with whom his brother was particularly successful. However, his interpersonal relationships seemed to be varied and satisfying.

Unlike the patient in Case No. 1, feelings of loneliness were not initially a prominent feature of this case. As therapy proceeded, the patient reported several incidents that illustrated the importance of this affect in his symptomatology. One of the earliest concerned his wife's leaving the room when he was studying at home. He immediately felt a wave of anxiety coming over him. He felt all alone with no one there to reassure him. He reacted to this situation by getting angry at his wife for not studying with him, clearly projecting his own anxiety about classwork onto her, displaced from his panic of loneliness.

On another occasion he was in the laboratory when he suddenly felt he couldn't tolerate the silence and absence of people. He deliberately sought out classmates at the other tables, asking them their opinions about the forthcoming examination, realizing all the time that he was doing it to relieve his terror-like feelings of facing his work alone.

On a third occasion, he was traveling alone in Europe and found himself in a dingy hotel in Paris. He began to think of how lonely he felt and how he longed for his girl friend and parents. He was aware of angry feelings toward them, and he gradually became more and more withdrawn and depressed. During this period of depression he remained in the hotel room for several days, going out only to eat, essentially out of contact with the world. This episode terminated fairly abruptly when he received a letter from home.

Discussion

In this patient, loneliness is compounded with feelings of depression which the patient is able usually, though not always, to distinguish. A prominent feature in this case is the presence of hostile feelings frequently directed outward toward objects in the real world, though more often directed toward ambivalent introjects, typical of a classic depressive reaction. As a further illustration of his ambivalence toward his father, he said, "I looked to him for things, like sending me food in college, but when he did, it wouldn't be what I wanted." His father did not have the patient's respect, despite the fact that he is successful in his profession. "Father must have something, though I can't understand what it is," summarized his ambivalent feelings.

Loneliness, on the other hand, for this patient frequently involved peer relationships, usually those related to his older brother. In discussing feelings of being alone, he talked about getting praise from his brother as an indication that he was liked by him. "I try to get his praise. It helps me feel I am not alone." Unlike the previous case, self-object relationships were reasonably well delineated, especially in reference to his brother, though less so in relationship to his parents, with whom there was strong identification. On the basis of the formulation of the previous case, it would be anticipated that loneliness would be a less prominent symptom, and this appeared to be so. Anxiety and depression, which were prominent symptoms, can be attributed to the separation and multiple mothering relationships experienced by this patient in his earliest years. Early separation anxiety, according to Bowlby (1963), may lead to states of chronic mourning. These would appear to be the conditions which obtain in this case.

The major point to be made about this case concerns loneliness affect accompanying depressive and hostile affects. Though these affects are present together, they are differentiated by the patient. I have attempted to show that these affects are probably derived from different stages in development, depression from the earliest stages and loneliness from a later stage. The prominence of hostility in this case, contrasted with its virtual absence in Case 1, further emphasizes the close relationship of hostility to depressive affect, as pointed out by Freud and Abraham.

In contrast to the first case, in which loneliness played a prominent part in the symptomatology, and in contrast also to the second case, in which depression and loneliness were found together, the third case stands out because of the absence of feelings of loneliness in a patient with marked depressive affect.

CASE NO. 3

A 37-year-old woman, mother of a 15-year-old girl, sought therapy because of her "inability to get any happiness out of life," "dissatisfaction with marriage," and "feeling that it is not worthwhile to carry on with life." The patient's presenting problems were said to have dated from the time of her second marriage. Although she had known her second husband for about a year, she realized after marriage that he was not the romantic, considerate individual whom she thought she had married. Each made demands on the other which were not fulfilled. The patient experienced intense guilt, accentuated because of the failure of her first marriage. She became depressed frequently, and these feelings became so intense that she made an abortive suicide attempt. She began therapy after this episode.

Her childhood was marked by a disrupted home life, with frequent moves. Her parents separated when she was two and were divorced when the patient was four. Her mother remarried four years later. During the period of separation and divorce, her mother was forced to work, and, hence, the patient was frequently alone or cared for by others. The patient complained about lack of affection from the mother, in contrast to an overindulgent stepfather. Her adolescence was marked by impulsive heterosexual activity, characterized by many superficial friendships. While in college, she fell in love with a classmate and was married before graduation.

Her marriage was unsuccessful from the start, and, despite the birth of a daughter, the patient separated from her husband after two and a half years of marriage. She lived alone with her daughter and supported herself by working. She described this period of her life as being very satisfying because she was independent and could do things on her own. After several years, she felt the need for male companionship, met a widower, and decided that she was prepared to be a wife and mother again, rather than to pursue a career. She remarried after a six-month courtship.

DISCUSSION

Noteworthy in this patient's history is a strong ambivalent relationship with her mother, intense feelings of hostility expressed toward self, high self-esteem, preference for independence, and absence of feelings of loneliness. In comparison to the other cases, she preferred solitude, actually seeking it out for opportunities to do creative work. She was self-sufficient, perhaps suggesting that her self-object representations had an autonomy which could tolerate physical and psychological isolation, not evident in Case No. 1 and Case No. 2.

SELF-OBJECT DIFFERENTIATION: DISCUSSION

In presenting fragments of these three cases, I have attempted to isolate some of the differences between depressive and loneliness affects, and to set the stage for a formulation of some of the dynamics of loneliness.

In the first two cases, both patients were aware of this feeling of loneliness, a feeling so incapacitating at times as to interfere with their work. In Case No. 1, this affect was predominant, while in Case No. 2 this affect was associated with other affects of anxiety, depression, and hostility. In Case No. 3, depression was the predominant affect, with virtual absence of loneliness. The contrasts among these cases suggest that one can differentiate the symptoms of loneliness from those of depression on the basis of phenomenology. A further clue to this differentiation can be found in the absence of hostility in the patient with loneliness as the predominant affect. Thus, on a phenomenological basis, loneliness does occur without depression and depression, when present, is accompanied by hostile affect. This might imply that the affect of loneliness is related more to libidinal drive components, whereas depression is related more to aggressive drive components.

If loneliness is not related specifically to clinical depression, it is necessary to postulate separate mechanisms for the development of loneliness. The dynamics which appear crucial are the development of object relationships and self-object differentiation. Case No. 1 experienced good, though superficial, object relationships, and was highly cathected to one major relationship, that with his twin brother.

His description of himself as "half a twin" was the initial clue to the incompleteness of his self-object differentiation. The loss of this object left him with a feeling of incompleteness, suggesting that the task of "self" differentiation had either been arrested or was not yet completed. He yearned for someone or something to make him whole. When his brother was not around, he became aware of the loss, and of the incomplete image within him. At this point, he would become lonely. Because of adequate maternal contact during his early years, however, he generally did not experience anxiety with separation and, therefore, lacked the basis for development of pathological depressive affect.

These observations suggest that an important element in the development of pathological loneliness may be poorly differentiated self-object representations within the ego. Although this differentiation is not clear in Case No. 2, and hence loneliness is less well delineated, the presence of depressive affect can likely be attributed to the multiple mothering situation in the patient's earliest years.

In Case No. 3, in which loneliness affect was essentially absent even in the presence of marked depressive affect, the patient had developed good object relationships, and probably good self-object differentiation. She was an only child, had the exclusive attention of her mother (when available) until age four. However, mother was frequently absent from the home because of work. The patient did not experience loneliness, but readily developed feelings of hostility and depression when she felt rejected by her mother and husband. She was particularly sensitive to losses and criticism, consistent with the predominant affect of depression.

PSYCHODYNAMICS OF PATHOLOGICAL LONELINESS

From the previous observations on self-object differentiation, I should like to suggest the following formulation of the psychodynamics of pathological loneliness.

Loneliness is an affect within the awareness of the individual. It appears as a sense of incompleteness, a longing for or yearning for another individual. In its normal manifestation, it is probably clearly related to feelings of nostalgia. In its more pathological manifestations, it can be associated with feelings of anxiety, guilt, or hostility. It typically is associated with libidinal rather than aggressive drive components. Its presence does not depend on the loss of real objects or introjected ambivalent object representations. Pathological loneliness reflects not loss but uncompleted or undifferentiated self-object representations, or both, within the system ego. Its frequent association with depressive affect can be explained best by the fact that inadequate mothering, along with separation, frequently accompanies situations where self-object differentiation is also pathological, a pattern that leads to confusion of depression with loneliness.

The question now arises as to what might produce this lack of self-object differentiation. The classic psychoanalytical model is useful here. Freud (1926) described the development of the relationship between an infant and its mother through the infant's pain and anxiety that accompany intermittent separation from, and restoration of, its mother. Repeated situations of satisfaction for the infant gradually create an intrapsychic object representation out of mother. The major objects incorporated during this period are, of course, mother and father. I would suggest that other objects in the environment of the infant and young child, such as siblings, would also be part of this internalizing process. The pathological process in self-object differentiation occurs when the appropriate individuals in the infant's environment are not available, or are idiosyncratic, as in the case of identical twins.

Since this self-object differentiation takes place over a relatively long period of time, throughout childhood at the very minimum, we should expect considerable variations in the clinical manifestations of loneliness. When the self-object differentiation is least developed, as in the typical schizophrenic reaction, loneliness occurs in its most pathological form, frequently accompanied by panic and terror. This is the type of loneliness described by Fromm-Reichmann. Where self-object differentiations are more developed, as in the manic-depressive or melancholic patient with ambivalent introjects, loneliness is accompanied by depressive affect along with hostility projected or reintrojected toward the offending objects. This circumstance is typical of Case No. 2 and Case No. 3. Where self-object differentiation occurs in the presence of an exactly equivalent individual, as in the case of identical twins (Case No. 1), loneliness can arise without including such accompanying affects as hostility or anxiety.

The important point, if this formulation has merit, is that symptoms of loneliness can vary from a most pathological form, as seen in the panic-stricken schizophrenic patient, to a most benign form, as seen in normal individuals as part of the vicissitudes of everyday life. Furthermore, since self-object differentiation is a dynamic process, symptoms of loneliness vary in the course of development as well as under conditions where self-object relationships become obscured, that is, under conditions where drugs such as alcohol and LSD disrupt normal perceptual and cognitive processes.

IMPLICATIONS FOR THERAPY

Perhaps the most important aspect of this model for loneliness lies in the implications that it has for therapy. First, it should be apparent that we must be prepared to recognize the symptoms of loneliness as different from those of depression. All too frequently, these loneliness symptoms are overlooked. Fromm-Reichmann (1959) recognized this when she stated, "The psychiatrist's specific personal problem in treating lonely patients seems to be that he has to be alert for and recognize traces of his own loneliness or fear of loneliness, lest it interfere with his fearless acceptance of manifestations of the patient's loneliness" (p. 14).

The importance of differentiating loneliness symptoms from those of depression, from the therapeutic viewpoint, is laid to the fact that psychotherapeutic and pharmacological techniques dealing with depressive illness are reasonably well delineated, even if not always successful, whereas those for loneliness are less well understood. Therapy for pathological loneliness requires a therapeutic tactic different from that for depression. I should suggest that, in addition to the fundamental strategy of establishment of basic trust between doctor and patient, a crucial tactic for the therapy of loneliness would be the encouragement of self-object differentiation. This differentiation probably can be accomplished best through increased contact with appropriate object sources in the environment. Group therapy would seem to offer the best opportunity for achieving this type of contact. It is through the kinds of intensive peer relationships experienced in group therapy that further self-object differentiation can occur. While the use of social relationships for the therapy of lonely individuals is certainly not original, what is novel here is the suggestion that the mechanisms for success in group therapy should be looked for in the area of self-object differentiation. Whitehorn (1961) makes a similar point in discussing pathological loneliness in relationship to the self-image of patients.

CONCLUSION

In presenting portions of three cases, I have emphasized the dynamics related to depression and loneliness. There are many other facets of the psychodynamics of these patients, particularly those involving defensive and coping behaviors, which would be important in understanding the total clinical picture. In developing a psychodynamic formulation of loneliness, I have ignored the social components of isolation and anomie, which are undoubtedly critical for a more comprehensive understanding of the problems of loneliness and depression. They are beyond the scope of this chapter. I agree with Rubins (1964), who commented that pathological loneliness affects have to be considered from the viewpoint of the psychodynamics of the individual. Whatever influence social factors might have, they act to "light up preexisting [or] predisposing factors within the personality" (p. 165).

My chief purpose has been to spell out the psychodynamics viewed in a psychoanalytical framework. I have intended to develop the model in order to permit explicit statements of hypotheses that will require much systematic empirical verification. My hope is that, through the explication of this model, I have further stimulated the process of scrutiny leading to understanding, an objective which Fromm-Reichmann (1959) so aptly expressed: "to invite the interest of psychiatrists to the investigation of the psychodynamics of loneliness, as a significant universal emotional experience with far-reaching psychopathological ramifications. . . . as a result of such scrutiny, it will be found that real loneliness plays an essential role in the genesis of mental disorder" (p. 15). It is by understanding this genesis that psychotherapists may be in a better position to treat this all-too-human universal condition.

21

Loneliness, Autonomy, and Interdependence in Cultural Context

MARGARET MEAD

ONE ACCUSATION frequently aimed at Americans, with the assumption that it is a national trait, is that they are lonely people. This statement is supported by a variety of sociological and quasi-sociological statements, many of them bolstered by references to the concept of anomie, a sociological disease believed to afflict men in modern cities. This assertion of the frequency of American loneliness is a cultural statement, because behind it lies the assumption that other people, the English, the French, the Germans, the Russians, are somehow less lonely than Americans, or the assumption that at some other period Americans were less lonely than they are now. The evidence either way is often poor.

In this brief paper I propose to examine the American conception of loneliness as a state, and to place it within the context of other American valuations of related conditions, such as to have no friends; to be alone, separated from others in space, without the expected support of relatives, acquaintances, colleagues, and friends; and to be nostalgic or homesick or lovelorn, separated from a past or a place or a person

---

This text is a revision, dated November 18, 1967, of a taped version of Dr. Mead's talk for the "The Anatomy of Loneliness" symposium at the University of California at Davis, February 8, 1967.

that has been endowed with a special aura of desirability. Loneliness in this sense may be said to be a completely negative condition, one which any normal person will shun and prevent if he can, as he will these other related states of intense unsatisfied longing. But loneliness is distinguished from these other more intense states by its lack of particularity.

THE INTRUSION OF
HOMESICKNESS AND BEREAVEMENT

Homesickness is an intense, almost unbearable longing for home, based in the enormous delight that one felt as a child, or in terms of childhood satisfactions: delicious food and delightful dream-wrapped sleep in a place called home from which one is now separated and of which one is reminded. Characteristically the feeling overwhelms a child as he is put to bed in a strange place by a strange person—unless in fact his early childhood has included among its delights strange beds and new places. If this has been the case, the first moment of settling down in a strange hotel room, placing the traveling clock or the shaving set on the dresser, may recall the pleasures of traveling at other times in other places. But the sense of being engulfed by a wave of remembrance of things past, as Proust expressed it, or the *Heimweh* of German literature, the intense longing for a particular place and time and set of people, is not often recognized in American life. Instead homesickness tends to be interpreted as not liking the place where one is in contrast to other places. Homesickness is often transformed from a positive attitude toward particular persons, toward the smell of freshly baked bread or the scent of freshly cut hay, or early morning chatter of sparrows, to a sense of unfamiliarity, or repugnance toward the present environment. Food that one does not like because one is not accustomed to eating it, a hard bed or a too soft bed, poor ventilation or lack of air conditioning or central heating, a table set without a glass of water, no drugstore and no hot dog stand, meals at wrong hours, people speaking foreign languages, no eggs for breakfast—these make Americans say they are homesick. This is an inversion of the typical homesickness that reinvokes the appeal of a particular past; it lacks the particularity and the poignancy of true homesickness. The American who is claiming that he is homesick is not necessarily carried away with longing for his childhood home or even for his wife and children; he is simply repelled by the general unfamiliarity of the present circumstances. However much a mother may treasure her son's letters saying he is homesick, they usually mean not that he wants to see her, but that he wants to stop being in an unfamiliar place.

This generalized objection to the strange and unfamiliar, in contrast to a particular longing for the acutely remembered, is congruent with the extent to which Americans change homes, cars, schools, work, wives, roommates, playmates. Home, in the United States, is where you live, and real estate dealers advertise still unoccupied houses as "beautiful homes." This attitude shocks the English commentator, who finds it hard to call a new house that he's never lived in "home." The transient child learns to sleep in approximately the same beds, eat approximately the same food, and drink approximately the same orange juice, and to deal with the curiosity and transient hostility of new sets of schoolmates. Such adaptation to a variety of somewhat like conditions, made familiar by the same tone in mother's voice or the same early morning growl or whoop in father's, may demand—although we are not sure—somewhat more difficult adjustments from a young child than the adjustments demanded from an infant who is always rocked to sleep in the same rocking chair, with the same scents blowing in the window from the fields outside. There is suggestive evidence, however, that people cling harder to learning that has been difficult—in the cases of prisoners who cannot sleep on a soft bed after the hard prison bed, or sharecroppers who cling to the fatback hated and imposed in childhood. American early childhood situations—being carried about on trains and buses, set down in a basket on a plane seat, strapped in the front seat of the car, left strapped in a car in a strange street while mother shops, put to sleep on strange beds in other people's apartments, left with a long string of strange baby-sitters— may require a kind of adjustment that although superficially good and easy may be rigid at a deeper level. A child who learns to tolerate a whole range of small differences as "home" may, at some level of unfamiliarity where suddenly nothing looks like home, reject everything. As an adult he will give anything to talk to any other American if he is outside the United States, and to any other Georgian or Tarheel or Hoosier or Californian if he is inside the country. This sense of rejection of the generally too different, often loudly expressed and cast in terms of "homesickness," can easily be misinterpreted as loneliness, especially by Europeans or those steeped in European literature and concepts. And indeed most Americans will describe themselves as more lonely in places where they are also homesick. But the feeling is nevertheless an impersonal, negative response to situation and environment rather than an acute desire for particular people and places.

In contrast to their generalized dislike for a too unfamiliar place or set of people, Americans on the whole disapprove of those who mope or are inconsolable over the memory of a particular place or person. It is no longer fashionable to die of love, to "carry the torch" for a faithless lover, to pine over a deserting husband, or to grieve very long for the dead. The best compliment that the living can pay a deceased spouse is to marry again, thus showing that the departed spouse was really a good husband or good wife, has commended the general state of matrimony to the survivor. People comment at the funeral of a member of a happily married pair, "I do hope he (or she) will marry again." The bereaved are expected to be brave, go places and see people, make friends again, and seek to replace the dead spouse, child, or companion. Bereavement, like homesickness, is treated as a general loss rather than a particular one. People may comment, "She'll find it hard to find someone like Sam," but in a sense this comment is an insistence that she try. The young man whose wife of three years has just left him, dazed because he had thought he was being a satisfactory husband, comments wearily, "Now I'll have to start hunting all over again." He does not devote even a few weeks to setting his loss in perspective. The stiff upper lip, the well-known Anglo-Saxon fortitude, requires in the case of Americans replacement of the missing.

INFANCY AND EARLY CHILDHOOD: BEING ALONE

It is also necessary to explore the American attitude toward being alone, because the state is often equated with loneliness. We do indeed require infants to spend a great deal of time alone: in their cribs, in a room without a night light, with the door shut. A baby should get used to sleeping through the night with no friendly hand and voice within easy reach, from the moment it comes home from the hospital. Ideally, a good baby falls asleep at once, learning that it is no use crying, no one will come.

A few years ago, I participated in making one of the Canadian Film Board's comparison films, comparing a day in the life of a Japanese, an Indian, a French, and a North American family (Mead, 1959). The

three other babies were each sung to sleep by a mother who stayed close
by the cradle until they were fast asleep; the North American baby was
put firmly down in a room of its own, no lullaby, lights out, door shut.
American audiences sigh with envy over the beauty of the foreign lullabies but this does not mean that as parents they would approve of putting children to sleep as the others do. After all, a child has to learn independence and autonomy; to go to sleep by itself is the first lesson.
(Incidentally, foreign observers often confuse American sighs of expressed envy with either acute nostalgia or a genuine desire for some
other state. So American women's expressed desire for strong, fierce,
dominating, "masculine" men is sometimes taken to mean that they
are deeply dissatisfied with their own American mates when actually
they would be most unwilling to exchange their companionable, good-
humored, helpful husbands for the lovers in the movies, who should in
fact stay in their place as a fortunately unrealizable daydream.)

American babies are expected to spend a good deal of time alone, lying on their backs, with nothing to look at but the ceiling or the canopy
of the baby carriage. Sometimes today the baby is provided with a
cradle gym, a string of bright objects hung across the crib or baby carriage, within reach of its exploring hand movements. A "good baby"
is willing to stay alone, to lie cooing and talking to itself, or at most
shaking the cradle gym, later to sit quietly in the car. A good baby
doesn't insist on getting up at night to see what is going on; a good baby
doesn't demand to be picked up or carried all the time. In contrast to
the demands of many other cultures, these are rigorous demands on a
young child, especially on the infant recently separated from the comforting balance of its mother's womb. By clothing both baby and
mother, we deprive the baby, even the breast-fed baby, of skin contact
with its mother's body, and we prefer to locate it out of reach of her
hand and away from her arms.

While it is impossible to say that one way of child care will produce a
specific and unvaried kind of character in an adult, we can say that the
whole constellation of adults' attitudes and evoked child behavior are
positively related to the child's later expectations of life. What the
American baby, not less loved because less fondled and less sung to,
learns would seem to be that being alone is something you have to put
up with in order to be rewarded by human company the rest of the
time. The peevish, crying baby, the child who summons his mother for
five drinks of water and three trips to the bathroom, is not being

"good." He is not rewarded with smiles of welcome and approval when he climbs out of his crib at 1:00 A.M. and appears in the living room. So he learns to tolerate loneliness in order to enjoy approval the rest of the time. Not for him the search for some place away from the continuous pressure of others' presence, the relief of a closed door, the sanctuary of his own room. Sending a child to his room is a typical American punishment, and in many modern American homes there are no locks on bathroom doors. Later the American child learns that he can go with them if he will not outrage the feelings of parents or older siblings with more activity and noise than is permitted. Going along, going too, not being left alone when the others go, not being sent to bed early—these are the expected and cultivated aims of the American child and counterpoint the insistence that children do go to bed and stay there, that they consent to stay at home with the nice baby-sitter, that they in fact endure being left out in order to be let in later.

This insistence of adults on what may well be premature toleration of being alone is followed, as children grow older, by adults' distrust if a child seeks to be alone while he is awake. Sleep is essentially a guarantee that a child is not doing anything it shouldn't do. But leaving a waking baby alone in its crib conjures up forbidden infantile orgies of destruction and disapproved play. Babies who are left alone take off their socks, tear the bedclothes, get undressed—or worse. The good mother insists that her child sleep alone, rewards it by attention when it wakes, and keeps an eye on it during its waking hours. And the good mother is wary of the moment when a child is out of her sight, and quiet. "Go see what Johnny is doing and tell him to stop," sums up the general belief that children who are avoiding adult attention are getting into mischief. As children get older, this avoidance of adult attention is associated with "reading too much," an undefined state which contends with the parallel danger—in the minds of literate parents—of "not being interested in reading." But, characteristically, parents worry about the child who always has his nose in a book, masking their genuine fear of long periods of unsociability as a fear that he will ruin his eyes, not learn to get on with other children, not get enough fresh air.

Even more is the daydreaming child disapproved. Carpenter, one of the first astronauts, to whom the American people extended a captious and ungracious public response, was pictured as a "loner," a child seated alone in a great cleft of rock. The implied moral: no wonder he made a slip. Among the pictures used in the Thematic Apperception Test to evoke stories from children is one of a lone child confronting his violin. The Manus, of New Guinea, saw in the picture happy, purposeful ambition: "He is thinking of what he will be." But in the United States, he is a disappointed, wistful child, oppressed by failure and longing. He is not dreaming about what he will be, but fantasying about what he can never become, engaged in what is at best a waste of time. These American taboos on being alone and daydreaming are historically explicable. The severe taboos on too close a relationship to one's own body call for screens interposed between the body and the self, such as the garment in which the convent-bred once bathed. Being completely alone may be interpreted as being tempted to unmentionable acts; the identification of a state of temptation automatically raises the tempter's appeal, and the American mother's "Find out what he's doing and tell him to stop" echoes down the corridors of adult life. The taboo on daydreaming was serviceable in the early days of pioneer hardships; too much long, backward looking disqualified the pioneer settler from making the best of his coarse food, crude cabin, and untamed or harsh and unfamiliar landscape. The American child born of immigrant parents, or later of parents who had left the lilacs and magnolias of the eastern seaboard garden for the stark, windblown plains of Kansas and Nebraska, learned from his determined parents to look forward, realistically, rather than to daydream about unobtainable delights. Characteristically the European fairy tale of Jack and the beanstalk ends with Jack sitting with his mother after the giant is dead in a blissful oedipal twilight; whereas in the American version, a much older boy, a nuisance around the house, is sent off to get on with life and grows like the beanstalk. So as an infant and little child, the American child learns to endure being alone and to greet company as a reward for this endurance. As a school child, he is continually urged toward social activity. He himself learns to distrust solitary occupations as wasteful and inefficient, if not actually sinful. Then comes adolescence.

ADOLESCENCE AND THE SEXUAL PARTNER

Among those civilizations from which our own stems, adolescent boys were expected to form firm, lifelong friendships with other boys. Part of the expected weaning from the home was finding a friend, equally anxious to become someone in his own right, and in the delight of mutual confidence and introspection to grow toward individuality. Family relationships were inevitably asymmetrical, with differences in age, sex, authority, and temperament. But the best friend was chosen in the belief that here was virtually a symmetrical mirror image of the self: a person of the same age and sex, with the same problem parents from whom to escape and schoolmasters to outwit or emulate, and the same preoccupying and rewarding need to explore the mysterious and tempting mystery of sex, choose a career, and embrace a philosophy of life. Such adolescent friendships often became the prototype of true intimacy. They provided an escape from adolescent loneliness and were enormously productive in developing young men as persons in their own right. Marriage, in contrast, catered to quite different needs than any desire for intellectual, artistic, or philosophical companionship. In every other highly creative civilization on record, one-sex friendships between students were an integral part of the educational process.

But in the United States, the tradition of student friendships has been steadily eroded by the lowering of the age for heterosexual relationships, including dating, going steady, premarital sex relations, and marriage. The institution of the junior high school isolates adolescents of enormously discrepant states of physical, emotional, and intellectual development. It has added a grim note to the whole practice of dating, accentuating the difference in development between boys and girls in their early teens. The presence of so many more mature girls exacerbates for the boy, not yet full-grown, tentative and needing time, the desirability of the girl who will neither challenge nor threaten him. From all sides boys, as well as girls, are pressured into premature dating by mothers who have come to associate an interest in chess or mathematics with a liability to be homosexual, if not traitorous. At the very moment when increased and unrealized possibilities of introspection are aroused in the adolescent boy, possibilities that could be fruitfully explored with friends of his own age and sex, he is forced into an inappropriate and exacting association with girls, more mature, more purposefully bent on conquest, less intellectually awakened than he. The capacity for tenderness, idealization, and warmth is prematurely directed toward girls, and relationships to other boys are restricted to sports, overlaid with the appropriate roughhouse and competitiveness. So American boys, and as a by-product of the early dating style, American girls, lose the opportunity to learn those things about themselves that make for intellectual intimacy and toleration for being alone. In one-sex friendships, with their assumption of symmetry and like-mindedness, there is enormous room for self-exploration, experimental daydreaming, tentativeness, and dreams. Each friend gives the other permission to pursue aloud his private thoughts. And private thoughts, in turn, require periods alone to perfect the figures of speech and grandiloquent sentences in which they are then couched for the admiring ear of a friend. As the child learns from his mother that being alone is something that is to be endured as an infant and avoided as an older child, so the American adolescent learns, from his parents, his teachers, and his girl friend, that private intellectual exploration and play are useless, to be foregone in the interest of active social life and purposeful career direction. Unrealistic career aspirations are snuffed out by the questions of his 16-year-old girl friend, her ruthless crushing of high aspirations with "How many years will it take?" The kind of thought and introspection that could have been shared with an equally immature and questing member of his own sex is discouraged and stunted.

LIFE STYLES, LOVE, AND LONELINESS

It is possible to contrast this sequence with those cultures in which infants are swamped with affection, or insulated in cradle boards or swaddling bands, kept from the evil eye of others for many months, or carried about on a mother's arm, held rigid for their own greater autonomy, by the time they are five days old. Every life style has its own internal consequences. It may be argued that the American style produces people who move easily within wide limits of social and spatial mobility, who make friends easily and quickly, recover from barely broken hearts with great speed, are able to form many new associations in a lifetime, can fall in love and marry, and can work and cooperate with many more kinds of people than has been customary in precursor societies with narrower and deeper channeling of emotion. We may ask in fact if the American is ever lonely as the thoughtful European is lonely, especially in America where Europeans complain they cannot find any friends, nor any time to be by themselves and think.

But what then do Americans mean by that undoubted pejorative, *loneliness?* It is not acute nostalgia for particular persons or places; it is not failure to find friends with whom intellectual intimacy is possible; it is not, surely, the continual presence of those who do not matter very much which the European tends to find accentuates rather than relieves his sense of loneliness. And if not these, what? American loneliness may, I think, be defined as being alone when one has not elected to be alone, when the state of being alone will be recognized by others as inappropriate. It is typified by the teenager without a date on date night. As Geoffrey Gorer noted, an American date is not a person, but a state. If one should have a date but does not, and if other people, particularly one's peers and one's overobservant family, know one does not, life is unbearable for a girl and increasingly unsatisfactory for a boy. For he who has asked and been refused, the situation carries the stigma of rejection. There is no one whom he wants to ask out who will go out with him. For a girl it carries the additional misery of passivity; she hasn't been asked and there is nothing she can do about it. The misery is the sharper for its impersonality. These are no Romeos and Juliets sighing for each other, but young people in search of a respectable public image, whose public image is destroyed by enforced, nonelective loneliness. The situation is similar throughout life. To be unmarried when one should be married, to be alone on a vacation, to be unaccompanied to a party, to attend a theater alone, to be condemned to an evening alone, and above all to eat Thanksgiving dinner alone—these are recurrent unhappinesses that Americans identify as loneliness. Geoffrey Gorer (1948), in writing anthropologically about the American people, has described the American search for company as a search for reaffirmation that one is loved. To begin with, Gorer argues, mothers show love for their children not in return for love, but as a reward for showing up well in comparison with peers. Thus children are taught to feel that love is not a two-way, reciprocal affair. Rather, it is earned outside a relationship, by accomplishment or other demonstration of worthiness. Following from this notion of love is a need for feedback—assurance of worthiness and adequate accomplishment. Most vulnerable to doubts about their worthiness when no one is there to assure them otherwise, Americans tend to devise constant opportunities for contact and conversation—even just a radio playing—at home, at work, and at play. Most cannot stand to be alone for long, and the sanity of those who choose to be alone is suspect. Gorer continues:

The presence, the attention, the admiration of other people thus becomes for Americans a necessary component to their self-esteem, demanded with a feeling of far greater psychological urgency than is usual in other countries. This gives a special tone to the social relationships of Americans with their fellows (with the exception, on occasion, of marital and parental relationships): they are, in the first instance, devices by which a person's self-esteem is maintained and enhanced. They can be considered exploitative, but this exploitation is nearly always mutual: "I will assure you that you are a success if you will assure me that I am" might be the unspoken contract under which two people begin a mutual relationship. The most satisfying form of this assurance is not given by direct flattery or commendation (this by itself is suspect as a device to exploit the other) but by love, or at least the concentrated, exclusive attention which shows that one is worthy of interest and esteem.

The misery imposed by nonelective and known aloneness has a reciprocal American state: guilt at being alone. Cultivated by parental disapproval in childhood, this guilt is accentuated by the knowledge that each person who chooses to spend an evening alone is, or at least may be, condemning another person to nonelective loneliness. No sooner has one settled down comfortably to a meal alone, a good book, or an early bedtime, or tentatively put on one's coat to go to a movie alone, than the miserable faces of those with whom one might have spent the evening crop up: the faces of lonely parents, widowed and divorced women, strangers, foreign students, or just the over-eager man or the woman with whom one has become a little bored, crowd in upon one. An evening alone becomes selfish; because it is elective it can be delightful, but because it is delightful, then, reinstating the childhood taboos, it becomes sinful, selfish, even cruel. Edna St. Vincent Millay (1956, pp. 173-174) expressed this in "The Betrothal":

I might as well be easing you
As lie alone in bed
And waste the night in wanting
A cruel dark head.

You might as well be calling yours
What never will be his,
And one of us be happy.
There's few enough as is.

Early childhood training in autonomy and independence undoubtedly accentuates the tendency to see the alleviation of another's loneliness as essentially nonreciprocal, a gift of companionship from one person to another, rather than an act of mutually rewarding interchange. The emphasis on independence as an aspect of autonomy makes the ideal person the one who is sought—in ordinary parlance the one who is popular—and who then in turn out of his or her good fortune seeks those who are less fortunate, who are lonely, are left out. It is perhaps this element of nonreciprocity, nonsymmetry, that is most distinctively American, that makes American loneliness so easy to alleviate, so that everyone has a date and no one lives in a new suburb, friendless because without acquaintances. Recent studies have shown that a new young mother, living in a new suburb without acquaintances, far from her female relatives and female friends, is especially prone to postpartum psychosis. But the recommended and effective cure is joining a group of people who are also themselves far away from their sisters and mothers, finding comfort and solace in mitigating each other's loneliness.

Lack of cross-cultural knowledge may contribute to baseless assertions that lack of intimacy based on seeing people every day, in unstructured contacts, is a terrible deprivation, and that intimacy can be established only in situations of ubiquitous unplanned contact. At the same time, we may well see our present style of autonomy, independence, and flight from our own and other people's loneliness as well as responsibility for the loneliness of others as aspects of a period of rapid change and great mobility. These follow on and are associated with immigration and internal migration and the rapid growth of cities, against which we may want to guard in the future. We may do well to plan for greater stability in the social and physical environment of the young child and for greater willingness of parents for children to be alone. We might even go to the extent of institutionalizing aloneness —say on Wednesdays—as churches have institutionalized silence in retreats. If being alone could be disassociated from being either the one who is rejected or the one who is rejecting, and could be seen instead as a human and desirable state, we would reduce the miseries that accompany culturally imposed loneliness.

22

We, The Lonely People

RALPH KEYES

KIDS have taken over the shopping centers.

Especially on weekends you see them, arrogant occupiers, an army marching up and down the mall, mugging at each other and stabbing their cigarettes at passersby.

While working for *Newsday*, I went to Long Island's Walt Whitman Shopping Center to expose this latest chapter in modern materialism.

The first day in, I hung around and asked kids why they spent so much time there. They seemed genuinely puzzled and usually could only mumble things like, "Well, you know, it's warm . . . and I have friends here."

An Englishman I know who grew up in a small village in Yorkshire says the most striking quality of the town, and the thing he misses most, was the feeling of being *known* there. He said it wasn't even a spoken thing. Nobody would say anything out loud about your beating your wife. But they knew, you knew they knew, they knew you knew they knew—and in that there was comfort.

Today we talk about our "loss of community" in city and suburb. Often we discuss it intellectually while sipping Scotch. Sometimes mystically, passing a joint. Or nostalgically over beer.

When we try to be more specific about just what "community" means, we usually think first of a place, the place where we live. I

Abridged and adapted from Ralph Keyes, *We, The Lonely People*, by permission of Harper & Row, Publishers, Inc., New York, N.Y. Copyright © 1973 by Ralph Keyes.

think this is what Carnation Milk has in mind when they implore me on their carton to "help keep our community litter free."

But when we consider where we find a "sense of community," it's rarely where we live. We use the word interchangeably, but it really means two different things.

A *sense* of community is what we find among the people who know us, with whom we feel safe. That rarely includes the neighbors.

It wasn't always so. For most of history man found his sense of community where he lived, with the people among whom he was born and with whom he died. For some that remains true today. But most of us in city and suburb live one place and find "community" in another. Or nowhere.

So many of us want back the more intimate sense of community, the one where the grocer knew our name and the butcher could comment on meat and life.

Business knows, and they're trying to sell that feeling back to us, some sense of community.

None of it works, and it won't work. The qualities that make a good mass marketer can't also produce a feeling of community. I find it a toss-up as to who loves me more, my local Shakey's Pizza Parlor or Howard Johnson's.

But business is hardly pernicious for trying. Their job is to be sensitive to markets, and there's obviously a market for intimacy. The market, however, is a package deal, part of a consumer's double message: give us all the advantages of a supermarket with all the familiarity of the corner store.

Sixty-nine percent of 200 Bostonians surveyed in 1970 agreed that "stores are so big these days that the customer gets lost in the shuffle." But 81 percent believed that "supermarkets are a great advance over the corner store."

We want both, and business tries to comply. It's an impossible task. If they're confused, it's because we're confused.

It's not that we don't want more community. We do. We crave community. We lust after it. "Community" is a national obsession. But we want other things more. I wanted to write this book more. Not getting involved with the neighbors is worth more to us than "community."

It's this confusion, this ambivalence, that confounds our quest for community. We yearn for a simpler, more communal life; we sincerely want more sense of community. But not at the sacrifice of any advantages that mass society has brought us, even ones we presumably scorn.

We didn't lose community. We bought it off. And rediscovering community isn't a matter of finding "the solution." We know how to do it. It's a question of how much we're willing to trade in.

I could find a Mom & Pop store if I really wanted one. But I don't. I prefer a supermarket's prices and selection. Also the anonymity, the fact that I'm *not* burdened by knowing the help.

Even as we hate being unknown to each other, we crave anonymity. And rather than take paths that might lead us back together, we pursue the very things that keep us cut off from each other. There are three things we cherish in particular—mobility, privacy, and convenience—which are the very sources of our lack of community.

"It is astonishing," wrote Scottish journalist Alexander McKay in 1849, "how readily . . . an American makes up his mind to try his fortunes elsewhere." One historian says that "the M-factor"—movement, migration, and mobility—is the shaping influence of our national character.

In nearly two decades of studying top corporation executives, industrial psychologist Eugene Jennings has found an increasingly close relationship between mobility and success, leading to what Jennings calls "mobicentricity." "To the mobility-centered person," he explains, "a new American phenomenon, movement is not so much a way to get someplace or a means to an end as it is an end in itself. The mobicentric man values motion and action not because they lead to change but because they are change, and change is his ultimate value."

Those studying communes have found a curious paradox. Experiments in communal living are top-heavy with the root-seeking children of nomadic corporation men. Yet these same utopian ventures are witness to a perpetual flow from one to the next, communards changing communes just as their fathers transferred between corporations. "Repeating the quintessentially American trait," writes an analyst of this movement, "when conditions of communal life become intolerable, the residents simply move elsewhere."

The worst part of mobicentricity may not be the moves themselves so much as the certainty that one will move again, and again and again. Why get involved with people, when you know you'll soon be leaving them? Why get close to anyone, when you know in advance that making friends, close friends, only means more pain at parting?

It all leads to a kind of "stewardess syndrome"—smiling warmly at strangers as you part after a few hours, or minutes, as if you had shared the intimacy of a lifetime.

I get this stewardess approach a lot in the counterculture. When I meet someone bearded and barefoot like myself, or a girl in work shirt and Levis, we're supposed to lock thumbs, whisper "brother" or "sister," and exchange the warmth of friendship for a few moments in passing. If there isn't time to get close, we may at least smoke some grass together, which is almost the same thing, or at least seems like it.

While we are on the move, appearances become all. Without time to come to know each other we must depend on outer signals. Eventually it becomes hard to remember that there's an inner person not so easily exhibited, a person more important than any badge or secret handshake. The worst part of mobicentricity is being doomed to travel about seeking one's identity in the eyes of near strangers.

Mobility is a major enemy of the community of intimate friendship. But I'm not clear where it is cause and where effect: whether we're afraid to get close because we're always moving on, or whether we're always moving on because we're afraid to get close.

Mobility has also made a major contribution to the decline of neighborhood life, of our community of place. But in that it's had help, in particular from our love of privacy.

Privacy as an ideal, even as a concept, is relatively modern. Marshall McLuhan says it took the invention of print to tear man from his tribes and plant the dream of isolation in his brain. Historian Jacob Burckhardt says that before the Renaissance, Western man was barely aware of himself as an individual. Mostly he drew identity from membership in groups—family, tribe, church, guild.

But since the Renaissance, Western man has sought increasing amounts of isolation, of distance from his neighbors. In America, with more land in which to seek elbow room, and with more money to buy it, the ideal of the unfettered individual, rugged, free, and secluded, has reached its zenith. Howard Hughes is only the logical conclusion, an inspiration to us all.

Increasing numbers of us suffer from an "autonomy-withdrawal syndrome," according to the architect-planner C.A. Alexander. Most people, explains Alexander, use their home as an insulation against the outside world, a means of self-protection. Eventually this withdrawal becomes habitual and people lose the ability to let others inside their secluded world. What begins as a normal concern for privacy soon resembles the pathological.

"The neighbors are perfect," reports University of Southern California football coach John McKay. "I don't know any of them."

A study of 75 white, middle-class, male Michigan suburbanites showed that most of their relationships with other men on the block took place standing up. This group of men defined a good neighbor as one who "is available for emergency aid; can be called on to trade mutual aid; lends and can be loaned to; respects privacy; friendly, but not friends." Only four of the men said they had neighbors they also considered friends.

I'm constantly horrified/fascinated by the regular accounts of crime and carnage perpetrated by "respectable" but highly private men who turn out not to have been known at all by shocked friends and neighbors.

Recently an insurance executive apparently killed his wife, three children and mother-in-law, then left the bodies in their $90,000 New Jersey home. No neighbor noticed anything amiss until the newspapers started piling up on the porch and the lights burned out over a month's time. A news account explained that "the disappearance of the family caused little notice in the suburb, where executives move in and out frequently without making close friends."

We not only use our homes to avoid each other, but we also can do the same thing within the home, with just a little help from modern technology.

I once gave a speech on "The Generation Gap" to a women's club. In the discussion afterward, one fiftyish mother stood up and said: "I'm gonna tell you what brought on the whole thing—dishwashers. That's right, dishwashers. I got to know my kids better, they told me more, when we washed dishes together. One would wash, another rinse, and a third dry. We'd fight, but we'd also talk. Now that we have a dishwasher, there's no regular time when we get to know each other."

She had fingered clearly something I was sensing only vaguely; that our household conveniences—our whole drive for a *convenient* life— have cut us off from each other. The cooperation and communication that used to accompany life's chores are being built out of our social systems.

Eating, according to contemporary nutritionists, has become less and less a family affair and more and more a matter of "slot-machine snacking." According to one estimate, 28 percent of our food intake is now in the form of snacks outside mealtime.

Consider, for example, the effect of individual pudding servings in a can. These not only make it unnecessary to work together in the kitchen preparing dessert, but also reduce the need to consider one's family as a unit, to compromise between chocolate and banana cream when it comes to fixing pudding. All members get their own flavor, right out of the can, whenever they want.

"The basic theme underlying food practices in contemporary American society is *individualism*," writes nutritionist Norge W. Jerome. "The structure, timing, and ordering of meals (and snacks) as traditionally defined are yielding to individual patterns of food use."

This evolution of our eating patterns has been hard to document. "It may be easier to get people to talk with complete frankness about their sex life than about the eating patterns of the family," says motivational psychologist Paul A. Fine, who has conducted several surveys of meal habits for food manufacturers.

Fine says that today's average family eating pattern includes little or no breakfast, snacks during the morning, maybe lunch (but not for Mom unless little kids are home), big eating after school, a smaller and smaller supper, and TV snacking that may be supplemented by after-bed refrigerator raids. The sit-down family dinner, he says, seldom takes place more than three nights a week in any family.

That seems a shame. Our family meals were warm, together times, times when the talk rivaled the food for attention. My best memories of home take place around the dining room table.

With our comings and goings inhibiting friendship, a love of seclusion eroding our neighborhoods, and our passion for convenience atomizing the family, it's hardly any wonder we feel a "loss of community."

But the distinctions are artificial. Mobility, privacy, and convenience are like a trio, first one playing, then the other, and all three finally coming together to play their song—at our request.

More than any single thing on the American scene, cars unite the triumvirate of values that are wrecking our sense of community. Automobiles are at once our main agent of mobility, the most private place to which we can retire, and a primary source of convenience.

When one asks what it is that we must trade in on community, the answer could very well be: our cars.

I once heard a woman describe in a most appealing way her two-and-a-half years on a commune. More than most, this commune seemed to have kept a stable core of people together over its brief/long life. She talked of their deep feeling of commitment to each other.

But she also pointed out that although most property was held in common, each communard kept a car—just in case he or she wanted to split. And if I lived on that commune, I'd probably want to keep a car too—just in case I wanted to split. I prize my mobility, my right to get up and go, as much as anyone—and I love the car that permits it. It's freedom, and in San Diego as on Long Island, the car is an absolutely indispensable tool for survival. Without it you're crippled, a virtual prisoner.

The great, overlooked seduction of this earth module, the car, is privacy. Cars and bathrooms are the only places where most urban-suburbanites can be completely and blissfully—alone. And a car is better than the bathroom. No one can knock and tell you to hurry up.

I initially grew interested in the car as private space when friends of mine began screaming inside their automobiles.

The first person to tell me about this, a father of five in his late thirties, explained that within his van, driving to and from work, was the only time he felt free to rage—spit and holler—let it all out. He called it his Private Therapy Van. Just roll up the windows and howl, go crazy if you like. No one will ever know.

This intrigued me, and I began to talk with other friends, asking what they did alone in a car, mentioning that one guy I knew screamed. With striking frequency faces would light up and heads nod vigorously as they heard this: "Hey, me too," they'd say. "I scream in my car too sometimes, but I didn't know anyone else did."

Traffic patrolmen with whom I talked said singing is common within cars, especially among women, and many drivers seem just to be talking to themselves. They say you can tell the difference by whether the driver's head is keeping time with the movement of his lips.

The only problem with criticizing the way cars make us anonymous, unknown, and nasty to each other is the assumption that we'd prefer it any other way. We do, of course, and yet. . . .

It's that ambivalence. We say we'd like to be less cut off from and uncivilized with each other, but another voice within speaks differently. The private car is a place safe to be our other self.

The car itself has had a lot to do with cutting us off from each other by sealing us in cocoons on wheels and making it easy to drive away from each other. But its greater impact may be in the environments we erect to suit the car, environments built for mobility, privacy, and convenience.

The process is self-feeding. The more we drive, the less pleasant it becomes to walk down streets that have become noisy, dangerous, and smelly from cars. The less pleasant it becomes to walk, the more we drive. Eventually, custom becomes law.

In 1971 the city council of Dallas passed an antiloitering ordinance that made a crime of: "the walking about aimlessly without apparent purpose; lingering; hanging around; lagging behind; the idle spending of time; delaying; sauntering and moving slowly about, where such conduct is not due to physical defects or conditions."

Beverly Hills is the logical conclusion. There the police are notorious for questioning anyone caught walking at night. Long Island, also built to suit cars, is not much better. I spent a lot of my two years on Long Island feeling sorry for its residents—like myself. In all that time I can't remember ever meeting anyone by accident. Or having a place to hang out, a store within walking distance or anything within walking distance. Life in such environments can be ghastly.

The suburbs are simply not designed for congregation. One suburbanite says that in the subdivision where she lived the better part of a decade, seeing more than three people gathered on the street made her wonder whether a disaster had just occurred and perhaps she ought to inquire.

When we lived on Long Island, a small "7/11" was the only store close by—our neighborhood grocery. It was also a hangout for local kids in this purely residential area. When you went in to buy something, you'd have to plow through compacted youth, like police breaking up a demonstration.

Shortly after arriving in San Diego, my wife and I checked out the stores close by. The nearest one was 7/11. On their parking lot, kids were hanging around outside, with identical banana-seat bikes. Inside the store was just as I remembered it: refrigerated goods in the rear, magazines up front, Slurpee machine by the cash register. All of this made me feel good, secure. There was a familiar place in this strange setting.

It seemed like a fresh insight—that I felt right at home at my local 7/11, almost as if we'd never left. Then I started reading up on franchisers and found that's exactly what they want me to feel.

Mobility has a built-in paradox. We move on in search of change. But the more we move, the more identical things become in every region. And the process feeds itself. The more we move, the more alike things become. The more alike things become, the easier it is to move.

We fret about this growing sameness for a variety of cultural and aesthetic reasons but without considering the comfort uniformity provides for a people constantly on the move. As Lewis Mumford points out, the common grid pattern of our towns and cities has historically made strangers as much at home as veterans.

Since franchises grew up after World War II right along with the auto and freeway explosion, they have housed themselves in very visible buildings that have the advantage of being easily seen from a speeding car. When everything else is a blur through the windshield, Holiday Inn's green, red, and yellow logo is a comforting point of stability. Their 1,500 buildings may seem distinct, but that's an optical delusion. There's really only one Holiday Inn, just as there's only one 7/11, one McDonald's, and a single Colonel Harlan Sanders.

In Oakland the Institute of Human Abilities is franchising communes and human growth. They buy up dilapidated houses in the Bay Area, redub them "More Houses," then charge the young and lonely $200 a month to live there and fix up the places. For their money and effort, residents get more than just a place to live. They also get a hero, Victor Baranco, the "heavy" founder/philosopher-king of the Institute; a medallion with the More symbol; a variety of courses in human growth; *Aquarius* magazine; and 16 More Houses to be welcome at.

The More Houses people know what they're up to. "We are like Colonel Sanders," admits the institute's president and *Aquarius* editor, Ken Brown, 51. "We can reproduce our thing anywhere. The product is words. And the attraction is love."

The counterculture generally has built up a rather impressive network of familiarity within the national hometown—ranging from informal places to sleep, through friendly homes listed in guidebooks, communes, and spiritual centers. The new nomads needn't feel much stress on the road.

Laundromats have become an excellent place to meet other citizens of the national hometown, straight and hip alike. Usually unguarded, often open all night, laundromats have become major American hangouts. There's something about laundromats that makes them a much safer, less threatening space than other public mixing points. It's just hard to seem dangerous with a box of Tide in your hands.

As a place to gather and share, laundromats differ only in form from the streams running by old hometowns where washers used to congregate. But laundromats have many more purposes to serve in the national hometown. After the Holiday Inn, they may be our leading community center.

Trust is what all these comfort points are about—the laundromats, the ashrams, the communes, the franchises. No matter how they clothe it or what they call it, the uniform gathering places—franchises in particular—are basically marketing trust. When we lived on a smaller scale, we would learn which merchants were trustworthy. Living now as we do throughout the country, we can only grope at symbols, and consistency is the best substitute for intimate knowledge.

Ironically, the last encounter group I attended spent its final day in the Holiday Inn room of one participant. In that room, on Sunday morning, one of the men in the group gave me an "Esalen massage." The experience made my body tremble and my mouth moan—as loudly as I would let it in the Holiday Inn. It felt great, great to let go, at least partway, and trust that group of people to see me shaking and exposed.

Afterward I exchanged hugs with all the participants and addresses with a few. We promised to visit, though it was months ago and we haven't yet. I still think we may.

A unique breed of "grouper" has grown up in southern California, and perhaps across the nation. With so many encounter groups going on, such people go from group to group getting stroked, enjoying their intimacy *seriatim*. To this group you reveal what a cad your wife is, to that group you cry about your vicious mother, and to the other about your brother. Then maybe trot out your wife again. If you handle the situation right, and it's not hard, each group of people will love and console you. A weekend's intimacy can sustain you till the next group.

I once asked a leader of a student-adult encounter group in a Long Island school district if they had a gossip problem, since participants lived near each other and could tell tales. "Oh, no," he replied. "We make sure that people in the group are strangers to each other." Then he leaned forward affirmatively. "It's not the sort of thing you'd want to do with friends and neighbors."

Swinging is only the most obvious example of the growing acceptability of intimacy with strangers. Swingers have taken the trend a step further, removing even the need to feel good about the person with whom you're sharing intercourse or to seek actual closeness in the sex act. "It's fun," explains one New York swinger, "but I don't like most of the people involved in it."

It's as if we're trying to make our opportunities for intimate community, the times when we'll peek from behind the mask, as handy and convenient as a TV dinner. A time to cry, to reveal, to take off one's shoes and relax is a human necessity. To do so with friends, even with family (especially with family), is scary and risky. It might lead to rejection, even worse—to commitment.

The safest, most convenient alternative is to seek a few days' intimacy with strangers, love and let loose.

Psychologist Richard Farson says, "The people who will live successfully in tomorrow's world are those who can accept and enjoy temporary systems."

So what we're doing is developing temporary love systems, hit-and-run intimacy, self-destructing communities that are making closeness just as convenient and just as disposable as a two-week guided tour.

I'm fascinated, driving down the highway, by the number of campers that are complete with name-and-address plates just as if they were home. "The Newman's," a plate will say, "Bayside, Texas." Sometimes a little message will be added, like "Y'all come see us."

And the new campers find the community they seek. Their changing cast of neighbors will be gone in a few days, so there's little risk in getting close.

This is a lot of the appeal of hitchhiking. "It's a special feeling," wrote one guy hitching across the country. "Meeting other people and throwing in for a while together. There's a trust."

I once discussed this with Julie, my sister-in-law. She's a Berkeleyite who enjoys hitching around that town. Julie likes meeting people and talking with them. I commented that I really used to resent it when people would pick me up just for company, especially when I didn't feel like talking.

"Well, how far were you hitching?" she asked.

"Usually hundreds of miles," I replied.

Her face brightened. "Oh, I see the difference. I'm usually just hitching around town. Anything over ten blocks is a heavy commitment."

Airlines understand our hunger for intimacy-in-passing better than any sociologist alive. Disposable community has become their bread and butter.

United wants me to fly their "Friendly Skies," in "Friend Ships."

Southwest Airlines calls itself, "The Somebody Else Up There Who Loves You." Passengers boarding one of their flights are greeted by a stewardess saying, "Hi, I'm Suzanne, and we're so glad to have you on our flight. You-all buckle up your safety belts and don't dare get up. We don't want anything happening to you now, because we love you."

Airplanes are forced to *become* community and serve up intimacy because their customers' hunger is so great. The airlines knew that they had become the community they once served long before most of us had a notion. But we're beginning to catch up. That transformation—from *serving* community to *being* community—is revolutionizing our social institutions.

Now courts and juries have entered another incarnation and are floating free of any community except the one they have become themselves. Today's jury *is* the community, a family even.

And so the circle is completed. When we lived on a smaller scale, juries consisted of community members *known* to another member on trial. As we grew larger, we sought refuge in the objectivity of anonymity, of jurors *unknown* to the person being tried.

Now we're in the third stage. The courtroom is a community, the judge a father, each jury a family, and the defendants prodigal sons. Trials provide the opportunity to come to *know* each other once again, to become community. Justice has been communalized.

The evolution is from bureaucracy to brotherhood. Do you dislike waiting anonymously in line? Get to know the other people and make the queue family. Is the multiversity giving you "just-another-number" blahs? Shut it down and become a community.

Families Anonymous is just one of the self-help groups that are springing up in this country like dandelions after a rain. Many are anonymous, patterned after Alcoholics Anonymous. These range from Survivors Anonymous (for those left behind by suicides) to

Pussy Anonymous (for men who are compulsive philanderers). Other groups, without being "anonymous," are bringing together Vietnam veterans to talk about their fears, POW wives to share frustrations, or unemployed aerospace engineers to share despair.

Tocqueville anticipated this development a century and a half ago. He saw our drive to associate, even in the early 1830s, growing inevitably out of our rootlessness and the lack of relatedness he considered inherent in a democratic society. The only thing new in our drive to belong is the degree of disconnectedness Americans feel, and the added weight we put on our associations to be not only community but also family.

A biker says of his gang, "Our chapter is like a brotherhood. Strong. Strong. We're real tight. One of us cries, we all cry. One laughs, we all laugh. That's the thing about the Aliens. We're a family."

The Aliens. A family.

After completing the Dale Carnegie course, an insurance executive boasted, "Now there's a lot more cooperation in our department. . . . We enjoy working together so much we're really more like a family."

A family.

When Oregon's Governor Tom McCall decided against running for the Senate in 1972, he explained, "My prime commitment is to Oregon and the Oregon family. I feel I can do the most effective job for Oregon by finishing what the Oregon family reelected me to finish two years ago."

The Oregon family.

I don't know much about lexicography, but when a word becomes that popular and that diverse in the ways it's used, some of the original meaning has obviously been lost.

Dave Walden once belonged to the sports car community. He worked on cars and officiated at rallies. Dave had friends within the community, friends who really cared. When he had to go to the hospital, they visited.

But then Dave lost interest in sports cars and soon lost all contact with that community, as they with him. Their commitment was only to the sports car buff, not the person. The community was only in part.

We do seek community. There's no question about it. But also we're scared of it. So we seek a safe community, one in which we needn't be fully known. We want to preserve as much as we can of our privacy, our conveniences, as well as the freedom to pick up and move on.

The logical conclusion, the direction we're headed, is what Henry Burger calls "agapurgy," the industrialization of affection. An anthropologist at the University of Missouri, Burger says that although America has done badly at providing enough "tender loving care" to go around, we do have a demonstrated genius for mass production and sophisticated technology. Therefore, why not apply the strength to the weakness: build love machines; Friend-O-Mats; or as he calls it, "the mass production of affect."

We're already in the primitive stages of agapurgy.

But it won't work. Agapurgy won't work any more than TV and magazine communities work—or dialed counseling, franchised friendship, bumper-sticker conversation, thumb-lock trust, encounter-group love, tribal clubs, or self-help groups. None of them work as community because none is a place where we're known whole.

We want to be known, whole, and yet . . .

If any or all of our approaches worked, we wouldn't be suffering such an epidemic of loneliness.

A year before his death. W. H. Auden left New York and returned to England. The poet said he regretted leaving his adopted home of more than three decades but explained: "It's just that I'm getting rather old to live alone in the winter, and I'd rather live in community. Supposing I had a coronary. It might be days before I was found."

Auden fingered what, for me, is the minimum criterion of being in community, for being known: that my absence, as well as my presence, be noted.

The minimum question about whether a group of people is really a community for me is: "Would anyone notice if I didn't show up?"

It's a frightening question, perhaps the most scary one I could put to a group of people. I'd dread what the answer might be.

Better not to ask it at all—anywhere.

This fear, I think, fuels a lot of our frantic rushing around—the feeling that if we just keep moving we'll have an excuse never to raise such a question with any group of people.

Today we're free to choose and reject, be chosen or rejected. This right to choose is a liberation, and also a tyranny. It's much easier to be thrust into community from your mother's womb, with the alternative only to leave. The opposite choice—to ask to be included in community—is terrifying and excruciating, a choice rarely made.

Millions of us have gladly rejected the suffocation of total community, and even the partial oppression of churches or clubs, where we were once known and scrutinized. We feel well rid of that kind of oppression. At least I do. But we forget to provide anywhere for the fellowship that went hand in hand with suffocation. The sermons may have been a drag, but the potlucks weren't so bad.

Rather than moon about the old potlucks, though, we'd do better to build a new community now, at home. We keep remembering the small towns and stores because we want back some of their qualities—manageable size, familiar faces, a sense of being known. Few of us will ever again know the kind of total community that intermingled place and kin, work and friends—and fewer of us want to. Far more helpful is to find out where it is that we do feel community *today*, and to set about enhancing that feeling without getting hung up on obsolete notions of what a community should be.

Some see the building of community as a job for the government, the best path a political one. There is much that the government can do to create a climate more conducive to community. The government, for example, could evaluate all social and political programs according to a "community index," one that would judge programs purely in terms of their effect on human intercourse, whether they brought people together or drove them apart. A community index should not be the only one, but should weigh more heavily than it does now.

Urban renewal, for example, might get a zero for putting high rises and freeways above neighborhoods, people, and community. Local laws that prevent unrelated groups of people from living together would rank at the bottom of a community index.

Some trends in America are encouraging, such as the growing "community-based" orientation in mental health, corrections, and education. Most of what's going on in the ecology movement is an encouragement to community and ranks high on the community index. Anything that helps develop alternatives to cars has to be good.

Still, neither political reform nor revolution can bring about the kind of community I'm concerned about, the kind where people really know each other. The job of government is to mediate among millions of people. This gives it a set of priorities in which community building ranks low, and should. Feeding the hungry must come first, then redistributing income and keeping us from killing each other.

Take the issue of busing. From a political standpoint the crosstown busing of schoolchildren may be a necessary tool for integration and social justice. From the standpoint of community, busing is a disaster, another wrecker of our neighborhoods. In this case, as in so many, political priorities are at variance with those of community.

Building a sense of community will always be the work of those who want it. The government at times may be able to lend a hand, but only a hand.

An ideal community would be like a good family: the group from which one can't be expelled. Or like Robert Frost's definition of home—the place where, when you have to go there, they have to take you in. But that's ideal, and few of us will ever build such a community.

I've defined my attainable community as "the place where it's safe to be known." This has meaning for me, because trusting people to see me is so hard, and it feels so good when I do. It feels like community. And that kind of community can be built in a range of settings from a commune to a bar or a church.

The elements that strike me as especially important for building a community include manageable size, a willingness to be exclusive, acceptance of oppression, and at least some modicum of commitment.

Size is of the essence. Manageable numbers are basic to any group of people hoping to get close. Trust can be built only among familiar faces.

There's a simple experiment that can be done with a group to discover one's "comfort peak." Break down in pairs and chat with one other person. After a few minutes, join with another couple to become a foursome and chat some more. Then become eight people and talk again, then 16, and 32 if you have enough time and people. The point at which you become uncomfortable, even stop talking, is probably your "comfort peak." For me, it's anything over 12.

I have a hunch that one reason juries get so intimate is their legal limit of 12 members.

The need to exclude is one of the harshest realities with which would-be community builders must cope. It grates against every humanistic instinct to openness, hospitality, and tolerance.

But there's no alternative path to a truly intimate community.

If you have done the 2-4-8-16 experiment mentioned earlier, check yourself out. Did you resent the intrusion of newcomers once you had some rapport built with one or more members?

I usually do.

I'm not saying that it's necessary or even good to exclude *all* outsiders. A community with completely stable membership would get dull very quickly. But the crucial point for an intimate community is that it controls its own access, chooses new members, and is not just like a hotel.

Recently I've been reading about an outfit called Leadership Dynamics Institute, which has developed a weird cross between encounter and the Inquisition. Participants in LDI's four-day groups are beaten, deprived of food and sleep, and subjected to hours-long harangues from other members until they break down, confess their shortcomings, and plead for the group's forgiveness. The late businessman William Penn Patrick, father of this method, says all but a few of the 2,000 participants in his $1,000 weekends have loved it—"a claim," says one news report, "that hotelmen who have sponsored the seminars somewhat incredulously support."

But it's not incredible at all. Individualism is a terrible burden, and when it is ripped away from us in exchange for submersion in a group, we're ecstatic, reborn, free at last from the tyranny of ourselves.

There is an inescapable relationship between brotherhood and oppression. Any group setting out to build community must anticipate this relationship and deal with it. Being in community doesn't make you more free; it takes away some of your freedom in exchange for the warmth of membership. Ignoring or denying that trade-off just makes it harder to confront.

To deny the relation between community and conformity, to call them two different things, is to make community that much more difficult to achieve. To be in community requires the sacrifice of at least part of your individuality. To belong to a group you must accept the group's will at least sometimes, like it or not. That's as true at Esalen as it is in Levittown. For me and for anyone seeking community, it then becomes a question of how much autonomy to trade in. Is the community I want Synanon or a radio talk show?

A community simply cannot be built from people crouched and ready to take off, like foot racers awaiting the crack of a gun. Commitment is basic. There is just no way that a community can be forged from people trying to make up their minds about whether to belong—community-seekers who keep their bags packed and ready.

Fear of commitment may be the biggest barrier to the rediscovery of community, including marriage.

When I say "commitment," I don't mean a signature in blood, or even a long-term contract. What I do mean is a willingness to stay through friction, to work on problems when they occur, to be a little stuck with each other. That may not be "commitment" according to Webster, but it's more than many of today's "communities," even today's marriages, enjoy.

Without confusing temporary and committed community, some opt for the former. That's the approach of Richard Sennet, a young sociologist, who says that his kind of community is best found in the disorder of a city. "In the adult society I envision," writes Sennet, "there would be no expectation of human love, no community of affection, warm and comforting, laid down for the society as a whole. Human bonds would be fragmented and limited to specific, individual encounters."

That's an honest vision of a society in which I wouldn't want to live, one in which disposability would infect every relationship. But it's an alternative not masquerading as anything other than a community of transients. Confusion of that alternative, of disposable communities, with ones based on commitment is what creates problems.

As I wrap up three years of work on a book about community, I'm sitting here wondering—What is it that I have to say, in a nutshell? What's the essence, the kernel of what I've learned from studying community and seeking it?

I began with a fairly conventional perspective on how we became such a lonely people—that mass society dehumanized and cut us off from each other—but believed that with imagination and new approaches we might defeat these influences and restore our sense of community.

The more I studied the issue and tried to build a community for myself, the less I found that to be the case. The villain whose trail I kept stalking turned out really to be ourselves—myself; our—my—ambivalence about community; our wish—my wish—not to get too close, thwarting a real hunger to join together.

Something I've realized only slowly is that seeking "community" in the abstract dooms the search. Community is people. I find community only when I find other people. I'm open to a group only when I'm open to its members. When I start looking for some mystical "community" I usually miss the people.

The problem of community, which sociologist Robert Nisbet calls "the single most impressive fact in the twentieth century in Western society," is relatively modern. For most of man's history, group life was a given, and grew naturally out of the ways we were forced to be with each other—to live, work, wash clothes, and die.

This is no longer true. We have less and less necessity to be together and fewer ways of knowing each other, while our need for community remains constant. So we're forced back on the only immutable reason for joining hands; the human need for company. Without place, cause, common work, or religion, most of us must make that humiliating admission: I can't live alone.

Once someone—once I—can take the risk, break the ice and say how I really feel, it's amazing how many others turn out just to have been waiting their turn. Then the community begins.

23

Loneliness
and Japanese Social Structure

CHRISTIE W. KIEFER

IT IS PRECARIOUS to begin a scientific paper on loneliness by depicting man as somehow hopelessly alienated from his world, his kind, and himself by virtue of his self-conscious brain. Such a picture is metaphysical and slippery; it is not derived directly from objective knowledge, but rather from the accumulated personal experience of many lifetimes of introspection. I don't know how many great minds have discovered within themselves some Fall from Eden going back to the acquisition of symbolic thought in human evolution. My reading has uncovered the idea in the works of Goethe, D. T. Suzuki, Nietzsche, William James, Ernst Cassirer, Joseph Campbell, Loren Eiseley, and Gerald Berreman. Eiseley sharpens his point with a quote, moreover, from Ralph Waldo Emerson: "It is very unhappy, but too late to be helped, the discovery we have made that we exist. That discovery is called the Fall of Man. Ever afterwards we suspect our instruments. We have learned that we do not see directly" (from Eiseley, 1969, p. 47).

We can neither *see* directly nor *be* directly, and our need for intimate contact and support from our environment inevitably leads to a more or less conscious examination of our "instruments" themselves. We are apt to get lost in what the poet E. E. Cummings called "the enormous room," and Eiseley called "the ghost continent" of our individual selves.

What these writings—and my own experience—suggest is that a certain increment of loneliness comes with our inherited equipment, and this increment comes pretty much the same to all of us. I have to say this first, because my present task sets me a little beyond (or beneath) pure introspective philosophy, and requires that I examine how the cultural patterning of experience might affect the quality and distribution of loneliness in Man.

The word "lonely" is probably used by most people to cover a vague range of emotions having in common a sense of the absence of satisfying companionship. If I examine the emotions which I have identified in myself as "loneliness" at one time or another, I find that they have overtones ranging from aesthetic rapture to fairly intense anxiety and disgust. Sometimes I have trouble deciding whether I am experiencing loneliness or some other emotion; at other times I am quite sure.

One solution to the problem of defining loneliness is to identify those situations that evoke it. One finds that such situations are extremely diverse, that they differ from person to person, and that they have no necessary connection with the presence or absence of either specific companions, or companions in general. I think, rather, that feelings of loneliness occur only when a person *experiences deprivation of an emotional gratification, and the deprivation is perceived to result from the inability of the lonely one to communicate his or her need to another being or other beings.*

Thus loneliness can be the result of joyous feelings which we cannot share, of nurturant feelings which we cannot discharge, or a sense of our deprivation relative to real or imagined others who could provide us with supportive social contacts. Please note that physical absence of the object to which one needs to communicate is not necessary for loneliness. The feeling can arise as a result of social taboos or other barriers to communication between physically close beings. Such obstructions appear *necessary* but not *sufficient* for loneliness. They may lead instead to feelings of aggression (toward some obstacle preventing the gratification) or self-disgust (for needing the gratification in the first place).

If I may be allowed to use the above as a partial definition of loneliness, then, it seems to me that the following sorts of cultural norms contribute to the creation of the necessé   conditions for loneliness:[1]

a. Norms that limit the range of emotions deemed appropriate in a given situation.
b. Norms that limit the classes of beings with whom an individual might legitimately interact.
c. Norms that limit the contexts within which one individual might legitimately interact with another.
d. Norms that limit the kinds of information that might legitimately be exchanged between one individual and another in a given context.

Such norms, of course, are never clear-cut or dictatorial. They may be contradicted or supported by individual experience. In addition, conflicting norms may be espoused by parties to an interaction, just as different parties might variously interpret situations so as to invoke different norms. Still, if we are to seek regularity of any kind in the study of loneliness, it might be useful to propose the following normative aspects of the experience of loneliness:

a. One tends to interpret one's *own* feelings in terms of cultural expectations (for experimental support, see Schachter, 1959). Norms regarding the appropriateness of the feeling, and of the communicative act in a given situation influence whether or not one is conscious of a desire to communicate a feeling to another being.
b. If one experiences or anticipates a conscious desire to communicate with another being, norms influence one's level of expectation regarding whether, how, where, when, and with whom one might have gratifying communication, and what the repercussions will be.

Professor Mead's example of being lonely on shipboard without a male companion (M. Mead, this volume) is a good illustration of the influence of norms. One *ought* to have a male companion; *others* have

---

[1] Students of the *interactionist* genre in social psychology will recognize here the influence of W. I. Thomas, C. H. Cooley, and G. H. Mead.

male companions; therefore one is *likely* to be lonely without one. Dr. Audy's observation of the *lack* of loneliness among strange people in the desert (J. Audy, this volume) might also be taken as an illustration of this very human (to me "human" and "symbolic" practically coincide) expectation-setting activity. In a crowded place, where one finds evidence of civilization, there *ought* to be people with whom one can share feelings. Not so in the wilderness among tribesmen. Moreover, in both situations, one cannot just communicate with *anyone*, or even with any sympathetic and receptive person. Cultural "reasons" for the communication must be added to individual motives. For example, a lonely person may go to his mother for comfort in our culture only under certain limited circumstances without being considered immature and wishy-washy. In Japan, the appropriate circumstances for going to one's mother are much more inclusive, but the chances of having a lover for a confidante in Japan are probably much more limited than in our culture, except for the well-to-do.

Before we consider the application of these observations to Japanese culture, we must mention one other sense in which cultural norms can be said to affect loneliness. As I said earlier, perceptions of the norms circumscribing loneliness are rarely clear-cut or incontestable. Since no cultural system is flawless, there are often conflicting norms which might apply to a given situation. This appears to be especially true in complex, rapidly changing societies like the United States and Japan. Our third hypothetical cultural influence on loneliness, then, is:

c. By placing role demands on individuals that simultaneously create and frustrate needs for communication, some norms might be said to add to the incidence and severity of loneliness.

American culture, with its emphases on independence *and* spontaneity *and* "happiness" offers plenty of illustrations of this principle. Hence the selection of such titles as *The Lonely Crowd* (Riesman, Denny, and Glazer, 1950) and *The Pursuit of Loneliness* (Slater, 1970) for essays on American character. Later I will give some Japanese examples.

In the following essay, I will try to take each of these hypothetical cultural influences in turn, discussing their expression in Japanese culture.

CONSCIOUSNESS OF LONELY FEELINGS

It is impossible to say whether the Japanese are more often or less often conscious of lonely feelings than Americans. However, there are a number of tendencies of Japanese culture which are likely to influence the consciousness of loneliness by attaching cultural meaning to such feelings.

FEELING-ORIENTEDNESS

Many Western writers have remarked on the formality of Japanese social relations. The Japanese are seen by outsiders often as excessively polite, "inscrutable," and guarded. The facade of formality is so hard to penetrate that Seidensticker, a highly respected American expert on Japan, observed that "The foreigner who complains, 'But I just can't get in with them,' should not worry too much about the failure. They have trouble getting in with themselves" (1961, p. 16). Whereas the culture certainly places a high value on the self-control of gross, verbal displays of emotion under most circumstances, it would be a great mistake to assume that this indicates an emphasis on the repression of feelings themselves. Rather, the opposite is often the case. I will have more to say in the next section on legitimate channels of communication. Here I want to discuss a class of social attitudes toward the emotional life of the individual which I call "feeling-orientedness."

The traits which I have lumped together under "feeling-orientedness" include a general recognition of the emotional (as opposed to the rational) nature of man: a taste for nuances of subtle emotional expression well documented in Japanese arts and well expressed in the language; a high value placed on anticipating and gratifying the feelings of others with a minimum of direct communication; and the elaborate cultivation of emotionally titillating experiences.

Perhaps the best way to characterize the differences between American and Japanese culture in evaluating the emotional component of relationships is to compare highly instrumental encounters in the two cultures. When business is conducted in America, the parties rely heavily on the telephone, discuss directly and precisely the instrumental reason for each encounter, and make face-to-face contact only when convenient, or when the complexity, delicacy, or importance of the matter demands it. In Japan, the telephone is used almost exclusively in business to find out *when* and *where* the business can be conducted in person. The meeting which ensues rarely begins with any mention of the business at hand, but rather with the drinking of tea, sake, or whiskey and some pleasant conversation, setting the mood for a congenial discussion. During this period, the participants are alert to facial and postural expressions, gestures, verbal nuances, and other cues regarding how the other is feeling at each turn of the discussion. (Morsbach [1972] has written an excellent paper on nonverbal communication in Japan.) If rapport does not emerge after some time, the meeting may be adjourned without any discussion of the business each person knew was the reason for the meeting. People tend to know when things are going "well" or "badly," and can act on this knowledge without detailed discussion about the expectations of others.

Complementary to the recognition of another's feelings is an attention to interior states that makes the Japanese more inclined to think of their selfhood in terms of these states than in terms of social attributes. For instance, when I asked 28 Japanese high school seniors to describe themselves in 20 statements, they were much more inclined to express private feelings than to list social roles (Kiefer, 1968, pp. 171–172). This contrasts sharply with American norms (Kuhn and McPartland, 1954) and is substantiated by other studies in Japan (Hoshino and Atsumi, 1960).

Another important aspect of "feeling-orientedness" is the taste for aesthetic and bodily pleasures that characterizes Japanese culture. Not only Japanese graphic art, but drama, film, architecture, landscaping, and industrial design show an unusual sensitivity to the aesthetic qualities of texture, form, and color (although this by no means implies that the Japanese have "innate good taste" any more than Americans do). Likewise in matters of food and drink, the average Japanese is much more likely to have a gourmet's knowledge about his favorites than the American, and to go to extreme lengths to satisfy his palate at least once in a while. In Japan a great deal of physical satisfaction seems to be gained through various forms of muscle and skin stimulation and relaxation such as bathing, exercise, and massage. Some say that the Japanese submit to pain and physical discomfort philosophically, and that this shows a lack of physical sensitivity, but I do not agree. Now that such things as heated rooms and air conditioning are becoming economically obtainable on a large scale in Japan, there is a great demand for them. I recently read a news item about a Japanese businessman who equipped an aerial cableway with bathtub-carrying cars, so that customers could enjoy sumptuous visual and tactile experiences at the same time. What other culture would encourage such a use of modern technology!

The Japanese have even elevated the titillation of the ego to a high art form. Whereas, for instance, the sexual mastery of a woman enhances most men's sense of power and competence, it takes the art of the geisha[2] to make the bore feel witty and the dull plodder feel charming and intelligent. This art requires extensive training, and is procured at heavy expense. The legions of bar girls that inhabit the entertainment centers of Japan use sex itself as their main form of compliment, but even here sexual consummation is by no means the only criterion of quality service. In general, the ability to flatter one's superiors and customers extravagantly without appearing unduly obsequious is a mark of a cultured person—male or female.

In general, I believe these emphases on the nonrational and the sentimental in Japan encourage free expression of appropriate feelings and self-awareness of emotions, *when emotions do not conflict with specific role demands*. However, rigid self-suppression becomes necessary when the expression of certain emotions would threaten proper role behavior. One expression of this fact is the common use of the term *makoto*, usually translated "sincerity," but also carrying the connotation of social aptness. Related to the concept of *makoto* is that of self-examination (*hansei*). When things go badly between people, the cause is often thought to be a lack of harmony between role demands and inner feelings, and the actors are often encouraged to search out and rid themselves of feelings that stand in the way of proper behavior—in other words, to become "sincere" in the performance of their respective roles.

Now, obviously feelings which give rise to loneliness may or may not conflict with role performance, depending on the intensity of the feelings and the social context in question. Are there any traditions in Japan that might serve to *remove* lonely feelings from the list of socially dangerous emotions? I think there are, and I will give three examples from the realms of epistemology, aesthetics, and ethics.

[2]I have used the system of romanizing Japanese words used in most modern Japanese-English dictionaries such as Kenkyūsha and Ōbunsha. Long vowels are indicated by a stroke (ā), and "shi," "ji," and "tsu" are used instead of the less common "si," "zi," and "tu."

NON-DUALITY

It is characteristically Western to view loneliness as a specific and often undesirable entity that is understandable but can be attended to—much like pneumonia. This sort of thinking arises from our tendency to divide the world into dualities: good and evil, life and death, growth and decay, truth and falsity. For the Japanese, the world is not so constituted. Reality is seen as multifaceted and ultimately enigmatic (when approached logically), and value results from a pragmatic appraisal of reality, rather than being an intrinsic feature of it. For example, I have had many conversations like the following:

> Kobayashi-san, why do the Japanese wear those knit wool belly-bands in the summertime?
> Nobody wears those anymore.
> But I have seen dozens of people wearing them right around here. Today I saw three or four.
> [Laughing] That old custom died out ages ago!

In this example, my friend was conveying a feeling about the relative importance of belly-bands and their wearers—a feeling more important in his world view than the mere "fact" that many people wear them. Another Japanese friend of mine lecturing at the Institute of Buddhist Studies in Berkeley, found himself condemning the tendency of institutions to suppress human creativity. Suddenly he stopped in full stride and exclaimed, "But . . . how interesting! This is an institution, isn't it?" Conflicting observations are often seen by the Japanese as equally valid nuances of a complex truth. The term *rikutsuppoi* ("reason-freak") is an epithet reserved for those who want the facts more orderly than nature meant them to be.

This friendship with paradox is especially evident in Japanese social relations. Truth and morality are socially constituted. They are specific to the interaction at hand. At a Buddhist funeral, Buddhism is right. At a Shinto wedding on the same day, Shinto is right. The same husband who is roundly scolded in the bath for some shortcoming deserves absolute respect and obedience in the presence of his children (if his wife is a traditionalist).

According to this world view, loneliness is neither "good" nor "bad" *in itself*; many people suffer from it but some do not, so it is neither inevitable nor eradicable. Being a common fact of life, it is best regarded as ''natural.''

LONELINESS AND AESTHETICS

Ah, kankodori,[3]
Deepen this wanderer's loneliness.
—Basho

The fact that Japan is a crowded country, where social life is often formal and burdensome, has resulted in a cultural premium being placed on solitude, communion with nature, and silent contemplation as aesthetic experiences. The traditional Japanese home and garden are carefully designed to create the illusion of empty space. The ritual of tea dramatizes the union of man and nature, and creates by artifice a welcome moment of aloneness in the thick of human life. Solitude is a very frequent theme in Japanese painting, where much aesthetic use is also made of blank space. In his popular novel, *The Buddha Tree*, Niwa Fumio contrasts the tormented life of a popular priest, besieged by lonely women and solicitous parishioners, with the serenity of a poor and solitary old man. Much of Japanese poetry dwells on the pleasures of the solitary moment, when the clatter of society has fallen still and one hears the elusive voice of the timeless and the nameless:

Awakened by the wind in the mountain village rice leaves,
in the deep night I hear the cries of deer.
—Morotada, Eighth Century

Loneliness and solitude are clearly not the same thing. However, they frequently occur together in such a way that the aesthetic feelings which occur in solitude are tinged by loneliness. As a result of this association, the word *sabishii*, ''lonely,'' is often meant to convey the aesthetic experience too—the bittersweet sensuality of a poem, a desolate place, or something very old and fine.

BUSHIDO, DEATH, AND ZEN

From the beginning of the year to the end, day and night, morning and

---

[3]R. H. Blyth (1949, p. 172) describes the *kankodori* as a bird which lives deep in the mountains, far from the haunts of men. Its wood-pigeon-like cry is said to announce the approach of rain.

evening, in action and repose, in speech and in silence, the warrior must
keep death constantly before him.

— *Yoshida Shōin*

Nietzsche cynically remarked that what is most valued by a cultural
group is what the group finds most difficult to practice. True or not,
the Japanese seem to have a way of turning hard necessity into virtue.
The necessity of being ready to lay down his life at any time for his
liege lord was a fact of life for the feudal warrior, or *bushi*, and the
ability to keep the thought of death constantly in mind came to be
viewed as a prerequisite of moral excellence.

This fact isolated the warrior from society in at least three important ways. For one thing, he could not share his preoccupation with
death with nonwarriors, except in an intellectual way. For another
thing, he was forced to regard all personal ties as tenuous and subject
to abrupt termination. But most important, while receiving instruc-
tion on how to face death from others in the same dilemma, the warrior ultimately had to accept the problem as a wholly personal one.
No one else was capable of viewing *his* death the way he himself
viewed it, and no one could provide him with a personal solution to
the problem of making sense of it.

Zen Buddhism (the religion of the warrior) offers a solution to the
problem of death and the problem of loneliness at the same time. Zen
teaches that the fear of death and the experience of loneliness are both
products of the illusion that there is such a thing as "self"—a skin-
encapsulated ego distinct from the rest of the world. The self, according to Zen, is a collection of attitudes, beliefs, tastes, and desires.
These preferences can be abandoned, however, and when they are,
experience reveals itself as value-neutral, with dualities like life and
death and solitude and company having no preconceived, extrinsic
value. Although any experience may be painful or joyous *at the time,*
Zen instructs one neither to avoid nor embrace it.

The figure of the hero as a self-sufficient, solitary man, although by
no means exclusive to Japan, is well developed in the folklore, art,
and moral philosophy of that country. Not only the magnificently
lonely samurai—epitomized by the hero of Kurosawa Akira's well-
known films, *Yojimbo* and *Sanjuro*—but also the Buddhist hermit, or
yamabushi, personify courage and wisdom. Mastering (*not* banishing)
the need for companionship, and other human comforts, is widely

considered a difficult but desirable possibility, and almost a necessary quality of the truly heroic character.

To summarize: For Americans who value rationality, not only are the stigmatized lonely, but loneliness itself is a kind of stigma. It is a dualistic opposite of "happiness." In Japan, in contrast, irrationality is human and to be lonely is to suffer the natural complexities of human life—especially the complexities of a virtuous life—and is not necessarily a wholly unpleasant experience. For such reasons as these, the Japanese might be more inclined than Americans to identify their feelings with loneliness. We now turn to the question of the circumstances under which a Japanese might feel lonely, and of what he thinks should be done about it.

LONELINESS AND EXPECTATIONS

THE HUMAN NEXUS

> Everybody lived and worked for some household; every household for some clan; outside of the household, and the related aggregate of households, there was no life to be lived—except that of criminals, beggars, and pariahs.
>
> —*Lafcadio Hearn*

Japanese social organization is often described by Western observers as "collectivistic" and "particularistic." This refers to the fact that Japanese, when compared with Americans, tend to prefer social relations that are binding, stable, and all-encompassing to those that are fleetingly contracted and dissolved on the basis of utility. Although kinship (and fictive kinship) is no longer the basis of nearly all important social relations as it was in ancient times, roles and attitudes characteristic of the family continue to provide models for much of social life.

Durability and generality of function are complementary characteristics of social relations. In order to endure, groups require a high degree of commitment from their participants. One cannot be highly committed to many relationships without experiencing severe role conflict; therefore, the more functions served by each enduring relationship, the better. Conversely, the willingness of partners to a relationship to attend to a wide range of reciprocal needs helps to assure mutual loyalty and the stability of the relationship.

Outside the sphere of the family itself (which remains in many ways the most important unit of social life), we find enduring and profound relationships in Japan between office workers, classmates, employer and employee, teacher and student, and a host of other role sets. Male office workers look after each other's emotional needs, spending a great deal of leisure time together. Bosses arrange their employers' marriages, see to their housing, and feel little hesitancy about judging their moral conduct off the job. Teachers function as confessors and employment agents for their students, and demand many personal services in return. Old classmates rely on one another to procure tickets to the kabuki theatre, get discounts on their employee's products, and settle questionable insurance claims. So close is the identification of the individual with particularistic groups that he often feels his identity to be coextensive with that of one group or another. The Japanese personality can be called "sociocentric" as opposed to "egocentric." DeVos (1964) refers to the "blurring of ego boundaries" to characterize such group identification.

All this helps to minimize the loneliness of anonymity. When I compared 57 middle-class Japanese responses and 86 middle-class American responses to Thematic Apperception Test cards showing a person in a dejected pose,[4] I found that the Americans were twice as likely to tell stories involving interpersonal loss or separation (50 percent vs. 25 percent). My experience with the Thematic Apperception Test,[5] both personally and through the literature, leads me to accept

[4]The American responses were to the feminine version and the Japanese to the masculine version of Murray Card no. 3. However, the latent stimulus demand of these two cards is very similar for both sexes. Half of each sample was high school seniors. In the other half, ages ranged from nine to 67 in the Japanese sample, and from 39 to 61 in the American sample. Sex was roughly equal in both samples. Both samples were lower middle- to upper middle-class urbanites. There are two internal indications of the validity of the test. First, the high school seniors in both samples gave considerably more separation/isolation themes. This follows, since they are at a time of life when they face major role changes including the attenuation or loss of childhood ties. Second, economic deprivation was a theme in 8 percent of the Japanese stories, but was missing in the American stories. One would expect the difference to be in this direction, given the relative economic security of the two populations in the late 1960s, when the subjects were tested.

[5]A projective technique which consists of pictures that depict a number of social situations and interpersonal relations, presented to the subject who is asked to tell a story about what is going on in each picture. Ten to twelve pictures are used typically.

this as empirical support for the hypothesis that a *generalized* fear of isolation is a greater source of anxiety in American than in Japanese middle-class culture.

Any system of social organization of course has its drawbacks. If human relations are more reliable in Japan, they are more oppressive in their demands on the individual, and therefore harder to establish or change. Involvement with others on more than a polite, superficial level carries the risk of incurring heavy obligations, and one does not lightly ask or accept favors. Spontaneous relationships are easily crushed by the weight of enduring prior commitments, and for that reason casual friendships are rare and highly tentative when they occur. American bachelors in Japan, for instance, are often horrified to learn that three or four dates with the same girl constitutes something like a marriage proposal; pressures become great at that point either for the suitor's permanent disappearance, or for his eternal commitment, depending on what the girl's family thinks of him. Even straightforward business transactions are maddeningly cautious outside the networks of lasting personal associations that run like fibrin through Japanese society.

Under the circumstances, the Japanese would have a high expectation of loneliness should they be expelled from their particularistically constituted groups. That this is true is borne out by the common use of ridicule and ostracism—(and threats thereof)—as means of social control. Punishing children by confinement in an isolated (and often dark) place such as a closet, storeroom, or outbuilding was reported by 23 percent of Japanese parents surveyed as late as 1952, and the practice was apparently more common in earlier times (Lanham, 1956).

A group of more severe isolation practices which also prevailed in premodern Japan is still sporadically used. Here I am referring to the banishing or ostracizing of deviants and political rivals. In the case of important men with large followings, banishment traditionally took the form of exile to a desolate place, usually an island, as indicated by the term for exile, *shima-nagashi* (literally, "island-floating"). Ordinary deviants, however, did not have to be removed physically from a traditional society in which kinship and community provided the bases for nearly all human exchange. Simply to be identified as a deviant by one's community usually produced enough suffering to bring about a return to noxious conformity, and when this failed, other measures were at hand. Formal withdrawal of community support from a deviant household (called *mura-hachibu*) was one such measure employed in Japan, disinheritance from family (*kando*) another, and banishment of the individual from family and community (*oi-dashi*) still another.[6]

In order to test this hypothesis further, I took the same Thematic Apperception Test stories mentioned above, and tabulated the *contexts* in which separation or quarrel were seen as the cause of depression. I found that 92 percent of the Japanese stories dealing with quarrel or separation clearly saw the context as a family one, whereas only 44 percent of the American stories of the same type specifically mentioned kin. Apparently, anxiety regarding conflict and isolation is more closely bound to the family context in Japan than in America.

My impression of Japanese fiction and films also supports this finding. Loneliness is a major theme of Niwa's novel *The Buddha Tree*, as we have already mentioned. The chief sources of loneliness are the orphanhood of the protagonist and his consequent moral decay, the separation of the protagonist's son from his mother, and the separation of the heroine from her parents. Natsume Soseki's *Kokoro* ("Heart"), another novel of loneliness, dwells on the psychological isolation of a man from his wife due to a guilty conscience. Several of director Ozu Yasujiro's postwar films deal with the erosion of the family in the modern metropolis, and the loneliness which results.

There are of course functional associations between the life-style of a cultural group and the group's normative expectations regarding loneliness. Middle-class Americans have adopted, as William H. Whyte (1956) demonstrated, an attitude of diffuse sociability as an adaptation to a highly mobile life-style and an "atomistic" social structure. Whyte's Park Foresters, for instance, were veritable gluttons for short-term, voluntary sociability between neighbors. It is in-

---

[6]*Mura-hachibu* was formally outlawed after 1868, but continues to be practiced in modern times (Smith, 1956, p. 17; Plath and Sugihara, 1968). The term means "village eight-parts." Plath and Sugihara note: "According to tradition, neighborly village social interaction consists of ten parts, including the right to such near-necessities as disaster relief and the use of common land. When a family is ostracized, it will be deprived (at least in theory) of eight of these ten parts. To have them restored, the head of the household must repent, persuade a village influential to stand as his guarantor, and then make appropriate restitution" (1968, p. 31). Formal disinheritance is still occasionally practiced, although I have never witnessed an incident. I have no data on the modern practice of banishment.

structive to compare this attitude to concepts of neighborliness in a physically similar Japanese apartment complex, which I studied in 1965–66.

The *danchi*, or apartment complex that I studied, was only about five years old at the time. It was largely inhabited by young, college-educated, white collar families. Having been created out of whole cloth, with no traditions of its own, and being mostly populated by nuclear families, the community was a symptom of the vast changes in social life accompanying urbanization. Inhabitants knew very little about their neighbors, and were typically anxious to avoid appearing "different" in any way. One 37-year-old housewife, for instance, described her great embarrassment when, shortly after arriving in this Osaka suburb, she found herself using Tokyo dialect in the heat of a neighborhood discussion. There is no stigma attached to being a Tokyoite, she explained, it simply makes you *different*. She felt others were silently laughing at her.

Her case illustrates the relative normlessness of the neighborhood, and the anxiety of many residents toward the possibility of doing the wrong thing. To the American way of thinking, this looks like an intolerably lonely situation: a society in which one is taught to dread the criticism and ridicule of one's neighbors, but where one has no reliable guide to what one's neighbors are thinking. What is the typical response of the Japanese individual to this situation? Table 1 summarizes responses drawn from three *danchi* regarding the isolation factor in this type of community. It shows the percentage of residents who agreed with various characterizations of living in a *danchi*.

More than 70 percent of both sexes found living in a *danchi* desirable because it provided circumstances where it is possible to withdraw from neighbors (items one and three); an almost equal percentage preferred the anonymity of the *danchi* to more traditional communities for that reason (item one). My own observations in a *danchi* confirm this trend. Many people simply avoid their neighbors, and only a handful of potential community organizers (derisively called "self-government vendors") find this disturbing.

The aloofness of these middle-class *danchi* residents can be explained in part by reference to their expectations about loneliness and its cures. Husbands typically seek companionship among their coworkers, with whom they may spend upward of 60 hours a week, including a good part of their leisure time. This is the stable, func-

TABLE 1

Isolation and Privacy in Japanese *Danchi*

Item	Men %	Women %
Living in a *danchi* is desirable because you can get away from people if you want to.	70	60
Living in a *danchi* is lonely, because people withdraw from each other.	8	15
Living in a *danchi* is annoying, because you can't get away from people.	6	10
Living in a *danchi* is desirable because people can't withdraw from each other.	14	11

Adapted from Takenaka, 1964, p. 20.

tionally diffuse group which serves many of the functions of the family for them. Wives have a harder time finding companionship outside of the neighborhood (notice that, compared with men, a higher percentage of women view living in the *danchi* as lonely and a lower percentage as desirably aloof). Even when their family roles are not satisfactory, social expectations do not point to gregarious neighboring as the solution to women's loneliness.

The Unity of Self and Role

I mentioned earlier the necessity of suppressing emotions which conflict with role demands. This is true of any culture, but the norms governing self-expression appear more clear-cut in Japan than in middle-class America. Whereas we Americans recognize the frequent necessity of suppressing our feelings, we think of this as unfair. We believe in self-expression. We feel ''out of character'' when we consciously deny feelings, and we resent it:

Love has no limits; it swallows us. It stuffs us, it crowds the air with false pretenses. Love assigns us a supernatural value in which we struggle frantically, like a king still alive in his gorgeous sarcophagus.

—*John Updike*

The Japanese are no less aware of the distinction between the inner, spontaneous man and the outer, social man—indeed, they are if anything more aware of it than Americans are. The difference is that Japanese culture takes account of the highly whimsical character of the "inner man," and demands his submission to a stable, predictable, social character. Whereas the American emphasis is on selecting roles that satisfy the inner man, the Japanese emphasis is on suppressing those feelings that are out of step with roles. Even the highly individualistic tradition of Zen teaches that there is no "self" at all, and therefore no contradiction between self and role. One of the aims of Morita Therapy, a Japanese form of psychotherapy akin to Zen that I will discuss below, is to get the patient to feel this at the gut level. Likewise, a metaphor familiar to students of Japanese Buddhism illustrates this principle in moral thought. The mind is likened to a mirror, which is prone to accumulate the "dust" of attachment to worldly phenomena (ambitions, memories, desired objects). Right thinking occurs when this dust is wiped away, so that the mind reflects instantly and perfectly that which impinges on it. This is the highly desirable state, *mushin*, or "no-mind," where reality is not bent to fit any personal order.

The significance of this for Japanese expectations about loneliness, it seems to me, lies in the relative absence of anxiety stemming from ambiguity about inner-outer conflicts. The Japanese can probably judge with greater confidence what can be expressed and when, how, and to whom it can be expressed. At the least, the Japanese can judge what the risks are of generating conflict versus getting gratification. If one does not demand autonomy for the expression of one's own feelings, one can assume role-appropriate responses from others as well. The opposite of this equation, which often holds in America, helps to account for our mistrust of stable relationships, and our reliance instead on ad hoc solutions to loneliness.

Role Loss, Dependent Status

What are some of the circumstances under which a Japanese can confidently expect to communicate personal feelings successfully? Up to now we have been discussing the heavy reliance on kinship and kinlike stable relationships to provide such circumstances. Under these conditions, feeling-oriented people are closely attuned to each other's needs, and very subtle signs are usually sufficient for the communication of everyday emotional needs. What appears to the outsider to be a thorough-going stoicism may in fact be an understated but nonetheless passionate, emotional dialogue.

Whereas subtlety helps to assure that such dialogue does not disrupt normal day-to-day behavior patterns, it is apparently costly in terms of the suppression of certain kinds of spontaneous feeling. One cultural solution to this dilemma is the use of cathartic rituals (see V. W. Turner, 1969). Because such rituals take place in an extraordinary context, and are marked off from day-to-day behavior by limits of time and place, they can provide safe settings for the release of normally disruptive sentiments. Normal role behavior is temporarily set aside in the class of rituals that I will refer to as "rituals of role loss." The American Christmas Office Party offers an illustration of a ritual of role loss in our own culture.

There are many occasions in Japan, some formal and public, and some private, when the principle of spontaneous affective display is made normative in a circumscribed context. On these occasions, the special status of the participants is explicitly recognized, and their behavior is deemed irrelevant to, or supportive of, the fulfillment of their normal roles. Cherry-blossom season, for instance (at least in the Osaka area, where I lived), lasts only a couple of weeks, and it circumscribes a period during which individuals and whole families may respectably appear drunk and giddy in public at high noon, neglect certain duties, and spend a little money traveling, feasting, and generally enjoying themselves. Office workers, business associates, and members of the myriad cooperative associations that suffuse Japanese life, periodically engage in drinking and feasting bouts during which sentimental weeping, lewd humor, and general clowning are encouraged in everybody, from the highest official on down.

I suspect that in most cultures, negative consequences follow the communication of dependent feelings in a very wide variety of contexts, and for this reason loneliness and the need for nurturance are often linked. Certainly in America, the ethic of self-reliance dictates that most emotional exchange (for an adult) should not be one-sided, but should take place in egalitarian, mutual relationships. Except when one talks about God, "interdependency" is a nice word; "dependency" is a bad one.

Such conflicts are by no means absent in Japan (as the example of *bushido* illustrates). Again, however, once one enters a formally dependent relationship with another, I suspect there is less ambiguity attached to the expression of dependent needs. A valued quality of those who wield power over others is *ninjo*, meaning "human feeling." Through *ninjo* a superior is supposed to be sensitive to his subordinate's needs for nurturance, and to take these into account in his dealings with him. Together with *giri* (duty), *ninjo* is often mentioned as one of the pillars of good character (cf. Benedict, 1946). The reciprocal of *ninjo*, under some circumstances, is *amae*. Doi (1962) has translated it, "to avail oneself of the nurturant feelings of another." Although too much *amae* is undesirable, it is considered natural for a subordinate to invoke it from time to time, and the inability to give or receive nurturance in the sense of *amae* is considered pathological in Japanese culture (Doi, 1973). If such expressions of dependency are thwarted, a feeling of loneliness is likely to result. In addition to kinship and patron-client relationships, there are certain special statuses that enable a Japanese to adopt a position of temporary dependency with much the same effect. There is some evidence, for instance, that physical or emotional illness is used as a special status for the communication of normally forbidden dependency cravings (Caudill, 1962).

Drunkenness is another special status which, if not employed too frequently, exempts the Japanese from normal demeanor and responsibility. In sharp contrast to the United States, solitary drunks (often in a very fine humor) may express their feelings openly in public and expect a sympathetic if slightly amused audience. Until recently, some legal offenses committed when drunk carried lighter penalties than if the guilty party had been sober.

To summarize what I see as the contrast between Japan and America in these respects: In America, communicative acts involving personal feelings appear to be regulated more by universal principles such as "reason" and "freedom" than by specific considerations of status, role, and setting. Americans mistrust obvious rituals that are contrary to normal reasoning. American individuality suggests that people are internally consistent, integrated personalities, and that the expression of an emotional need reveals something basic about the person, rather than the role he or she happens to be playing. It is "irrational" to be "inconsistent" about such things as one's own emotional self-sufficiency. As a result of these traits, Americans can depend less on explicit ritual and role definitions in the communication of personal impulses, and must instead negotiate their communications on a case-by-case basis. What is often deplored as the conformism of Americans (Riesman, Denny, and Glazer, 1950; Hsu, 1961) often results from the loneliness which this situation entails.

SOCIAL CHANGE AND NORM CONFLICTS

Had the world come to praise the profligate as loyal servant and pious son, he would have declined, even at the cost of selling his property, to hear the voice of praise. Indignation at the hypocritical vanity of proper wives and at the fraud of the just and open society was the force that sent him speeding in the other direction, toward what was from the start taken for dark and unrighteous.

—*Nagai Kafu*

Nagai is of course writing about himself. But as an artist of stature he is also voicing the inarticulate sentiments of his time and place. The loss of life's meaning amid the rapid change of the industrial age has been so widely attended to in literature that Paul Tillich has called it the core experience of our time (1952, p. 139). So widespread is this feeling in Japan in our era that the very names of many of Japan's best-known modern writers—Natsume Soseki, Dazai Osamu, Mishima Yukio, Nagai Kafu, Akutagawa Ryunosuke, Tanizaki Junichiro, and even Nobel laureate Kawabata Yasunari—immediately evoke a mood of brooding nihilism reminiscent of Kafka or Camus. Dazai, Akutagawa, Mishima, and Kawabata all committed suicide. One can point as well to the widespread disaffection of Japanese college students which led them to serious riots in 1960 and in 1968–69, to the popularity of "absurd" theatre and films, and to the ubiquity of phrases such as *seiji no hinkon*—"the poverty of politics," and *ekonomikku animaru*—"economic animal."

UNWANTED DEPENDENCY

> Some time ago the labor unions called a meeting in Hiroshima having as its theme: 'We should do our best to help the Atomic Bomb survivors.' When I saw this motto. . . I felt resentful. . . because I thought they were using the A-Bomb for their own purposes. But maybe the fact that I had this reaction means that I am an Atomic Bomb Survivor.
>
> *—A-Bomb Survivor*

Not only disaster, but also social dislocation resulting from urbanization and industrialization can cut the individual off from supporting social networks. This is a particularly alienating experience in Japan, where the acceptance of nurturance from others is demeaning and carries a heavy moral debt *unless* it is dictated by explicit role requirements like those that accompany a kinship or patron-client relationship.

When studying the lives of several atomic bomb survivors in Japan, Robert Lifton (1967) noticed that many of those who had lost all social supports in the disaster felt considerable conflict about receiving help and sympathy; they felt that others often had ulterior motives for offering help, or were merely being polite out of pity. Thus loneliness compounded the social isolation. This conflict, which Lifton calls "suspicion of counterfeit nurturance," is familiar to people everywhere whose self-concept has been damaged by some stigmatizing status or experience. I think the conflict is particularly widespread and severe in Japan. In my research with elderly Japanese both in Osaka and in San Francisco, I was repeatedly told by these grandparents that they prefer to live apart from their children, even though the children are dutiful about material support, and even though cultural norms support their presence in the home. Their feeling seems to be that the children are simply fulfilling their duty, and do not *really* have the well-being and happiness of the elderly at heart, or do not recognize the moral debt they owe their parents.

In the case of the A-bomb survivors, the lack of reciprocity in the nurturant relationship is obvious. In the case of the elderly, a similar lack of reciprocity arises due to the economic, spiritual, and intellectual liberation of the nuclear family in an urban-industrial milieu. Since in both cases the recipient has not previously paid for the proffered nurture, and cannot expect to repay it in the future, the debt of gratitude weighs heavily upon him. He is likely to feel hostility toward the giver, which he can only explain to himself by assuming that the giver is not sincere. This explanation is reinforced by the feeling-orientedness of the culture, which places a premium on harmony in interpersonal relations, and suppresses the direct expression of aggression.

Another related component of the feeling of counterfeit nurturance is the implication of prestige attached to giving. Giving is a characteristic of high status. Material means, for instance, can be converted to social status by the distribution of favors. In fact, this is a commonly accepted avenue to power and prestige in modern Japan (cf. Pelzel, 1954). To be the recipient of nurturance from others without the possibility of immediate repayment is demeaning—doubly so if one considers the donor to be one's social equal or inferior. In the case of the elderly, I have often found an unwillingness to surrender the reins of family authority or to accept a loss in community social status lurking behind the refusal to accept filial nurturance.

WHITE-COLLAR WIVES

The erosion of cooperative functions of neighborhoods and families as a result of geographical and status mobility in industrialized Japan is a huge subject, and one I cannot do justice to here. Perhaps, however, the effects of these forces on the experience of loneliness can be partly understood by looking at one group severely affected by social change: the wives of young, white-collar employees of large industries.

According to traditional norms, women should go through a period of loneliness when they get married, since they have to leave their natal family (and usually their natal village or neighborhood) and join their husband's household. However, they should eventually acquire friends in their new surroundings through the gradual establishment of stable relationships with neighbors and conjugal kin. Whereas deep mutual affection is not a traditional Japanese criterion for the selection of a mate, it was still supposed that such affection would develop gradually between spouses. The weakening of family authority has led to a greater emphasis on love as an important criterion of successful marriage in recent decades. The devotion of the white-collar husband to his job away from home deprives the wife of an expected source of companionship.

In traditional Japan, the young wife's social status in the community was more or less fixed by the status of her husband's family. Such status, in turn, was based mainly on stable factors like land ownership and occupation. Since there was little geographic mobility, people's status in the community was a matter of common knowledge. Poor people were probably less lonely on the average than their wealthy neighbors, since they had nothing to hide or suppress for the sake of their status. The opposite is the case for young, white-collar wives, because they are by education (or at least by husband's education) members of an elite, but often by income worse off than less educated neighbors. This ambiguity is compounded by the fact that they are intellectual, educated women—a contradiction in traditional terms.

Many white-collar wives, then, go through a period of relative social isolation and loneliness while their children are small and their husbands are on the bottom rungs of the pay scale. The factors which contribute to this situation, and their effects, are listed below:

Factor	*Effect*
Upward status mobility	Necessity of defending status (maintaining economic self-sufficiency, observing decorum, avoiding scandal, competing with neighbors).
Husband's commitment to career; physical separation of home and husband's job	Husband's long hours away from home; husband's socializing with office peers, taking business trips, etc.
Geographic mobility (due to transfers-of-post on husband's part)	Separation from childhood community, family, friends; repeated "newcomer" status.
High status/low income discrepancy	Shame regarding poverty plus inability to travel or to join certain mutual interest groups lowers rate of contact with neighbors, friends, family.
High educational achievement/ low recognition discrepancy	Many roles (e.g., community organizations, heterosexual friendships) limited or closed.

| Nuclear household structure | Heavy responsibility for children's achievement; excessive time spent in child-rearing at the expense of peer relations; absence of kin as advisors, helpmates, companions. |

Although it is difficult to document the actual incidence of loneliness in a population, there are some things that suggest an epidemic of it in this group. Feelings of depression and anxiety are so frequent among new residents in middle-class *danchi* that a folk disease—*danchi noiroze* (or "apartment-town neurosis")—has been invented to describe the syndrome. In a recent study (Nihon Jutaku Kodan, 1972), 24 percent of a large sample of *danchi* wives said that they had suffered *danchi noiroze* at one time or another. Although the physical environment was frequently mentioned as a cause of the difficulty, by far the most frequently listed cause (59 percent) was "human relations."

Other indirect indicators come from the popular image of the young, white-collar wife. She is often referred to as *kyoiku mama* ("education mama"), and said to suffer from another folk syndrome, *ikuji noiroze* ("child-rearing neurosis"), because of her intense, isolated, and anxious involvement in her child's education. Her husband is often called *geshukunin papa* ("lodger papa"), referring to his long hours away from home.

In my research of a white-collar, Japanese community in 1966, I identified two main types of response to the problem. By far the most popular response was resignation for the time being, along with the hope for a better future. Most women complained mildly about their husbands' absence and the distance of their relatives, but made little or no effort to find intimate relationships outside their families. The other response was to draw on traditional roles to justify involvement in new social pursuits. Part-time employment, for instance, was justified on the grounds that the family needed the income, and it was the wife's responsibility to provide it if she had spare time. Involvement in local politics or the PTA was justified on the grounds that schools and other institutions were not providing adequate services for one's children, and it was one's responsibility as a mother to correct this. The value of community consciousness (*kyōdo ishiki*) was occasionally invoked as justification for formal cooperative activities as well. At the same time it was clear that these activities, which were decidedly untraditional for middle-class wives, provided many opportunities for companionship. In the case of political groups, they often appeared to provide very little else.

A study done by Morioka Kiyomi in 1961 in another *danchi* in Tokyo (Morioka, 1968) reveals some interesting demographic patterns associated with styles of informal socializing. For one thing, he found that informal sociability was particularly difficult for women with small children. Over half of the women interviewed who had children under three years of age reported having *no* intimate friends or neighborhood relations whatsoever. There are probably several reasons for this. Obviously, women with small children have less free time and less freedom of movement than those with no children or older children. Also, middle-class Japanese norms regarding ideal motherly and wifely behavior tend to proscribe recreation and the pursuit of personal enjoyment for young mothers. I suspect that yet another factor is the relation between having young children and having a tight family budget. The mothers of babies are married more often to younger men with lower salaries than the mothers of older children, and they have many more necessary expenses than nonmothers.

Further analysis of Morioka's findings reveals an important pattern in *type* of informal social interaction: the higher the education and income of the woman, the more likely she is to associate with (a) people in voluntary "circle activities" centering on educational and handicraft pursuits, (b) friends living outside her neighborhood within the *danchi*, and (c) friends living outside the *danchi*. Conversely, the lower a woman's education and family income, the more likely she is to have her intimate relationships restricted to her neighborhood. It would appear that the possession of these two commodities broadens the range of possibilities in informal relations for Japanese women. In either group new friendships must be hindered by the cultural expectation that friendship carries serious obligations and responsibilities such as the privilege of practicing *amae*. Nonetheless, I think the cultivation of purely voluntary relationships based on mutual interest represents a new pattern for young, middle-class wives, and one that could lead eventually to major changes in Japanese society and personality (see Kiefer, 1976).

CONCLUSION

If, as I suggested at the beginning, we consider loneliness as something always coiled in the convolutions of our overdeveloped cortexes, ready to catch us in an introspective mood, we can then see the very idea of culture partly as a weapon on the side of relatedness. Culture insists on the reality of symbols; it gives men histories, names, and essences; it certifies our instruments. In the process, culture severely limits spontaneity. Seen from the vantage point of Western individualism, Japanese culture is a fairly repressive system. On the other hand, its orderly traditions seem to offer as adequate a solution as one can expect to the problem of loneliness in a complex, crowded society. We have seen how the breakdown of repressive traditions sometimes threatens patterns of companionship and solidarity. Moreover, if we believe that *real* intimacy and *real* relatedness must lie at the end of an uninhibited individual development, we must be ready for the sleeping dragon beyond the protective walls of socially constituted reality. We must recognize that while those walls often separate us from each other, they also shelter us from the "ghost continent" of introspection. As Victor Turner says, "There is a mystery of mutual distance, what the poet Rilke called, 'the circumspection of human gesture,' which is just as humanly important as the mystery of intimacy" (1969, p. 139).

24

"*You're O.K., How Am I?*"
Loneliness and Its Institutional Frames

YEHUDI A. COHEN

EVERYONE'S LIFE—male as well as female—is governed by cycles. In addition to diurnal and lunar rhythms that control many physical functions, there is also periodic regulation of psychological processes. Whether or not these mental features of our lives are under the jurisdiction of biochemical or hormonal processes is beside the point here. Whatever their origins, certain emotional and psychological needs seem to have a pulse of their own, a requirement that they be periodically satisfied.

It is a characteristic sanction of all cultures that prohibits the promiscuous gratification of the individual's psychological and physical needs; in all societies, physical and emotional needs may be satisfied only with specially designated people. The individual's need to be reassured that he makes a difference to others, to know there is a fellowship that embraces him—this need also has periodic oscillations. This need also may be satisfied only by people with particular ties to the individual. It is not a satisfaction that may be derived from just anyone if it is to have meaning.

People who have been geographically very mobile are acutely aware of this fact. I am one of them. I have lived in seven different cities and two countries during a ten-year period. Under such circumstances, it is difficult to strike roots that are lasting and meaningful. My long-distance telephone bills reflect this difficulty. I have noticed for a number of years that my phone calls all over the United

States to relatives and close friends tend to cluster together at different times of the billing periods. I not only need to be reassured that there are people who care about me and view my experiences as part of their lives (just as my own life would be diminished without their experiences); it is also to hear them tell me how important they feel my work is and what a splendid fellow I am. There are a few such people where I now live, but they do not make up a community. In fact, some of those on whom I rely for such reinforcement are barely aware of the existence of others who provide the same kind of support.

Many people whose work and life opportunities require mobility have experienced a vacuum in the institutions in which they participate. They try to fill the void in different ways that they hope will be satisfying. But let us not overrate the elements of choice and volition in filling the voids of our institutional lives.

It is necessary to keep in mind as a starting point that the place one lives, the kind of work one does, and the people with whom one associates and who touch one's life in different ways are not always matters of personal choice and decision. Increasingly, one's residence and affiliations are governed by impersonal agencies, by opportunities too good to miss, and by unanticipated events, the outcomes of which we cannot control.

The depths at which impersonal and often capricious institutions strike were illustrated during the U.S. Senate's Watergate hearings. I was neither surprised nor upset by the criminal activities disclosed; if anything, I found the deviousness of the president and his underlings expectable and entertaining in their Keystone-Kop ingenuity.

I was shocked by one disclosure, however. This disclosure was not part of the agenda, and I am not aware of any analysts or journalists who saw it as a theme deserving comment. But it was the kind of serendipity every anthropologist hopes for during field work because it is just the kind of information that often sheds the most light on a culture and on the lives of its members. I was intrigued as I sat and heard this disclosure; I could just as well have been sitting with a notebook doing field work among these exotic natives.

On several occasions witnesses were asked whether they knew others whose guilt was also being gauged. With some variations, the exchanges between questioner and witness went as follows:

"Do you know so-and-so?"

"Yes."

"Would you describe him as a friend?"

"Yes."

"A close friend?"

"Yes, a close friend."

"How often do you and he see each other?"

"I've had lunch with him two or three times."

I was incredulous at each exchange of this type. Imagine what such an exchange signifies, I thought to myself. Forget the desecration of the term "friend," one of the few words I consider sacred. But imagine how lonely, how inwardly empty these men must feel. They are the quintessential products of the institutions they work so hard to maintain. I wondered: What is it like to live that way after having died so long before?

I was very impressed a few years ago by the skillfulness of two brothers whom I knew. One is a surgeon with an established and lucrative practice, the other a high-ranking engineer employed by a large corporate firm. They are emotionally very close and were unhappy over the great distance that separated them; they missed each other badly. The engineer maneuvered his employers into transferring him to another city about fifty miles from where the surgeon lived. By the most incredible luck, the engineer was able to buy a house next door to his brother. He did so and commuted daily to his job. Later, however, he was transferred back to the city from which he had initially moved. No stratagem could alter this decision; he was finally told that his choice was either to return to the distant city or leave the firm entirely. He valued the position he had reached after many years of hard work and he finally acquiesced in the return.

Such recurrent uprootings leave us standing alone. Whether we live or die, are healthy or ill, triumphant or depressed, successful or unsuccessful, married or divorced, remain in our present location or move away—these things make little difference in our neighbors' lives, assuming they even know what has happened to us. Aside from a few relatives and close friends, these things matter most to employers who must replace us, to real estate agents who have another house to sell, to tax collectors, and to anonymous people who keep demographic records.

But these facts are not cause for voicing gloom and doom. Rather, these are facts of life in a modern industrial society to which we have to adapt, just as we must make accommodations to hunger, fatigue, climatic changes, traffic regulations, and so forth. We may not like the features of the social landscape into which we have been "dropped," even though there is much to be said in favor of the variety of experience that comes with mobility and the resulting weakening of bonds. The point is that we must come to terms with the distinctive aspects of the social environment; this is part of the sociology of everyday life.

Left to stand by itself, this may sound banal; everyone knows that each of us must come to terms with the social as well as physical environment. But I want to pursue the thought further.

When I first undertook to write this paper, I considered another title: "Hooray for Anomie." That, however, meant the adoption of a different central theme. But it is an important theme that needs some exploration.

I begin with an observation that is periodically unpopular among American academic social scientists. The United States is an extraordinary and remarkable society; its accomplishments—social and humane as well as material—far outstrip those of any other society, present or past. No society in history has gone *as* far as the United States in getting people of different ethnic, religious, language, racial, and class backgrounds to live together and work at the same jobs. No other society has gone as far in eliminating barriers to marriage between the members of different ethnic, religious, and other groups. These processes are often referred to in social science treatises as the "breakdown" of kin, ethnic, religious, and language groups. This is an important part of the point I want to make.

Some of the greatest achievements of American society have been in the realm of ideas in the broadest sense of the term—in literature, music, philosophy, natural science, social science, art, political thought, planning; and the list goes on. I do not want to imply that all —or even one-tenth—the ideas produced in America are good, though some are certainly quite good, if not brilliant. That is not the central issue.

What is to the point is that in its mere 200 years about 25 times as many original and innovative ideas—at least—have come out of American society than out of Europe, Africa, and Asia during the past five thousand. I do not know how one measures or counts ideas; I am speaking impressionistically. But relative to the total span of time during which ideas have been recorded, the intellectual ferment of American society has been staggering.

But think beyond the quantity of ideas produced in America. Though approximately 90 percent of all the scientists who have ever lived are alive today and most of them live in the United States, only a small proportion of the ideas coming out of America have been put forth by scientists. For better or worse, some of the most popular and highly regarded thinkers in American history have been pamphleteers, businessmen, historians, inventors, lawyers, longshoremen, clergymen, dissidents who fit no categories, and the like.

Talent, skills, ability, native intelligence, and articulateness are obviously necessary for the production of new and innovative ideas. But the United States may not be said to have had a monopoly on people with these attributes.

Nothing—be it a plant, a person, an idea—grows unless it has a fertile milieu. One of the environmental elements necessary for innovation in the sphere of ideas is a political climate in which people may express new ideas without fear of politically inspired punishment. That much is obvious. But there is another element that ideas need if they are to be conceived and brought to fruition: a strong measure of alienation, anomie, a sense of isolation, of loneliness.

Academic social scientists periodically go through phases in which they rhapsodize about the sense of community and belonging that people derive from the strong bonds of kinship and religious fraternity in tribal and peasant groups. Implicit in these songs of praise is a nostalgia; sometimes the modern psalmists explicitly suggest that we adopt the *Gemeinschaft* of these societies by grafting it onto our own.

Fortunately, that is impossible. Kinship, religion, strong ethnic consciousness, and all the other ingredients of tight communal forms are deadweights; they mire the mind in the sands of conservatism. It is probably true that there is little loneliness where kinship, religion, linguistic traditionalism, and the like, predominate in the sociology of everday life. But it is also true that people in such groups keep each other under constant surveillance to make certain that no one breaks step. And when people do break step, they pay terrible economic and legal prices. The pressures to conformity are exceedingly tight, not only in the realm of daily social behavior but also in thought. The old debate about whether religion and science are incompatible misses the point slightly: religion is antithetical to the innovativeness that is one of the *sine qua non* of science.

To be innovative in the realm of ideas one must be prepared to be heretical and say to himself daily, repeatedly, almost catechetically, "I don't care a whit for anyone else's opinions." But such a commitment also entails a troth to an existence of loneliness. The United States has been a fertile seedbed for ideas because the way the society was founded guaranteed a climate of alienation. Though the first communities in the Northeast (Puritan New England) were tightly knit and were exquisitely sophisticated in their control of individual behavior and thought, dissidents had virtually no limit on where they could reestablish themselves when they found the Puritan social environment too oppressive or restrictive.

True, the settlers of frontiers in North America did not have much time for the life of ideas; they were too busy keeping their bodies and souls together and separating Indians' bodies from *their* souls. But an important tradition had been established, the shared idea that everyone could make his own way regardless of his parentage and his intellectual commitments.

To accomplish this—though it was not the stated or conscious goal —the founders of American society established a social system free of the constraints of kinship; in their periodic encouragement of frontier settlement, they prodded individuals, not whole families or kin groups, to go westward. In the separation of church and state, they deprived government of one of the oldest weapons against innovative thought. The reality as well as the ideology of the "Melting Pot"— and make no mistake about it, the United States is still a melting pot, though the cauldron is merely simmering instead of boiling as it used to—freed men and women from the strangleholds of ethnic subcultural separateness to think and create autonomously. The linguistic homogenization brought about by compulsory free education provided people with the tools with which to communicate with the entire society instead of only with the ghettoized minds of their ethnic groups. (The current fad of bilingual education in public schools is an aberration that will pass; history is always marked by two steps forward and one step backward.)

One pays a price for these discarded shackles. But that has been the case with all evolution, be it physical, cultural, or intellectual evolution: prices are always paid. No kind of evolution (to anthropomorphize for a moment) cares for the individual; it cares only for the survival of new forms exhibiting fitness. Intellectual history is no different; it cares not for the anguish of loneliness that innovative ideas require. As new ideas multiply at accelerating rates, it gloats and chortles, "Hooray for anomie, long life to loneliness."

But just as intellectual history cares not a whit for the individual, the individual thinks of evolution only in the abstract (unless he makes a living of studying it), as something that happened only long ago to Neanderthal and tribal societies. What, however, is the personal and subjective experience of loneliness within the context of society's institutions?

When people are self-consciously concerned about an experience like loneliness, they are not only saying something about themselves, but are also commenting on the inadequacy of established social institutions. I am not talking about the sense of loneliness that follows the death of a loved one, a divorce, or a move to a new town or city where everyone is a stranger. I am talking instead about the inner void that lonely people carry inside them all the time, or at least very often. I am speaking of the pervasive, characteristic, and gnawing feeling of these people that something is missing from their lives, and of the cheerless solitude, depersonalization, and dejection or depression that comes from their sense of being alone. This is the core of loneliness.

Everyone has the experience of periodically asking in one way or other, "You're O.K., how am I?" Assuming that the question elicits the response that one seeks, one experiences a sense of good fellowship and of being welcome in the world; one feels at home with oneself and others. But there are times when the plea for reassurance goes unanswered. Then there follows a void, a feeling of personal meaninglessness, a lack of self-definition. This experience of loneliness is painful, if not anguishing, because it drains one of personal identity. It results from a lack of feedback.

Loneliness in this sense connotes longing; we always long for others when the lack of reassuring feedback threatens the integrity of the personal self. This is not the loneliness we experience when we long for a particular person who is absent or when we are homesick while on a trip. It is rather the loneliness that signifies a longing for people in the abstract whose feedback is personally meaningful and who can validate our sense of worth and being.

This experience is painful because no one is able to subsist emotionally on inner feedback alone. When people experience loneliness —when there is a persistent and constantly unsatisfied longing for people—due to a lack of feedback from others, there is a breakdown in communication that needs repair. But what are the impediments to communication in such cases? Has there been a breakdown in the individual's own circuitry or is there something wrong with the wiring in people's links with each other?

There are, of course, certain people who are unable to metabolize the inputs made by others. These are people who are unable to convert stimuli from others—approval, reward, criticism, physical contact or avoidance, a gaze, or even a passing or casual remark—into sustaining and energizing forces. The causes of this are varied. They may be dietary or nutritional. Abnormally high or low glucose levels may interfere with the emotional metabolism of the inputs of others. Painful or consistently confusing past experiences with others may make it difficult to know how to respond to people. Moving from one culture to another or from one social class to another may make people uncertain about the cues and signals that others send out. Richard Hoggart described his own experiences in this connection in *The Uses of Literacy* (1957), where he recounted the social and psychological trek from an English working-class background to the university-based upper-middle class. Many women currently experience such uncertainty as they make the hegira from their home-bound statuses and roles into professional or business careers. Comparably, many men who used to feel very comfortable with women now experience a sense of anguishing isolation when they are with them because the women have been developing new ways of relating to people and the men do not know how to interpret the signals or metabolize the inputs.

This brings me to my central theme. There are many people— perhaps a majority—who have receiving equipment that is perfectly intact, who are ready and able to transform social and emotional messages into the personal energy that is necessary to get from one day to another, from week to week, and from year to year. But, in these people the communications are not forthcoming. They make sounds and gestures, but they are either on the wrong wavelength or they transmit so much interference that their messages are unintelligible. There are, in other words, communicational barriers that may underlie the dejected and depressing solitude that is referred to as loneliness. Such barriers are not of the individual's own making, but they nevertheless account for his sense of anguishing solitude.

We tend to see ourselves as others see us. This means that there must be others whose opinions are important to us when we try to gauge whether we are "measuring up." Not only must there be people whose opinions count, but there must be ways—organized, systematic, predictable ways—by which the assurances of these people are conveyed. Such lines of communication may be found in family gatherings where pats on the back are given overtly and subtly, in a local pub or club where we are stamped with social approval by quiet attention when we speak or by being included in a round of drinks, or in town meetings when the glints in the eyes of others convey happiness at seeing us there. When others hold us in such esteem, we feel that our lives have meaning, that there is an embracing good fellowship, and that we are welcome in other people's consciousness.

But the social climate becomes greatly chilled and we feel in the cold when these organized validations of our identities are no longer available. We lack social mirrors when family members are so scattered that Christmas cards and birthday greetings must be substituted for gatherings of the clan, when developers and planners omit pubs and clubs from their designs, or when we stop frequenting existing facilities because we are trying to rise socially in the world. We experience a similar loss when town meetings are rubber stamps for larger political agencies or when the community itself is reduced to a way station for executives on their way elsewhere. When changes like these occur in the society's institutions, our cards of identity are not suddenly invalidated or withdrawn. Instead, and almost without realizing it while it is happening, others give us the impression that the identifying marks on our cards are becoming too dim to recognize —just as we do not understand the identifying marks on their cards. After a while, we no longer bother even to show cards of identity. Instead, we take others out occasionally and socialize superficially while nursing a scotch-and-soda or through a haze of sweet-smelling smoke.

Identity has many wellsprings. It is unlikely that a person can survive very long or effectively if his or her self-image rests on only one support. The exigencies of life in all groups are such that a person must be prepared to cope with setbacks, failures, rejections, and losses. When a sense of personal worth or success is built on only one criterion or achievement, a person becomes brittle. We are all familiar with the type of person whose sense of "I am" rests exclusively on the amassment of great wealth and who is driven to suicide—the ultimate expression of a total loss of identity or sense of self—when his financial principality crumbles. The same is true of the person whose subjective existence rests exclusively on the care (or control) of children who then assert their independence or the person for whom the aim of life is literary, scientific, or artistic creativity and who runs dry at some point during his or her career. This also applies to the person whose sense of continuity as an individual rests on sexual conquests and performance but whose abilities in this regard suddenly slacken or the person whose identity is bound up exclusively with social status —high or low—but whose sense of being is lost when society's existing hierarchical organization is suddenly turned topsy-turvy. Such people—those who have only one self-defined place in the scheme of things—are among the most fragile members of the species.

Everything we do to obtain a sense of personal meaning serves to place us in the midst of others who give us the psychological validation we need. In the words of William James, "a man's social self is the recognition which he gets from his mates" (1925, p. 127). The person who takes from only one source to maintain a sense of personal meaning is landlocked. If the one thing on which any of these people builds an identity—work, amassing a fortune, parenthood, beauty, sexual conquests—gives way, that person is cut off entirely from social recognition, approval, and the wherewithal of sustenance. When this happens, there is nothing else to keep the person going. He is thoroughly isolated, socially and psychologically alone in the fullest sense of the term. One of the reasons farm women traditionally were able to feel they led full lives (even though they were prevented from engaging in worldly affairs) was through the sewing-bees and circles they devised; they did not restrict themselves to being housewives and parents. These associations not only provided them with people to talk to, they were social and emotional shock absorbers as well.

Every person has a variety of needs and interests which require orchestration with different people. "Properly speaking," James wrote, *"a man has as many social selves as there are individuals who recognize him* and carry an image of him in their mind . . . But as the individuals who carry the image fall naturally into classes, we may practically say that he has as many different social selves as there are distinct *groups* of persons about whose opinions he cares. He generally shows a different side of himself to each of these different groups" (James, 1925, p. 128).

The "different sides of himself" that a person shows in the various institutional contexts in which he participates correspond to the fact that the organization of a human community does not reduce to a single set of roles and groups; it is rather a series of several sets of roles and groups which appear and disappear according to people's assignments. In slowly changing societies, people's roles and memberships are more or less fixed. In contemporary industrial societies, on the other hand, organizations of social relations undergo rapid and drastic change.

As suggested earlier, the disestablishment of groups (like kin groups) that help maintain conservative traditionalism provides the individual with an incalculable measure of freedom to maneuver autonomously on the social landscape. But the attenuation of kin, religious, ethnic, and other such primordial ties under the impact of economic modernization and political centralization produces serious problems in self-definitions because the social referents that had supported these definitions no longer exist. We often observe this among men who had been productively employed for thirty or forty years and who suddenly retire from work. Their gainful labor had often been an important source of identity for them, and though they may have looked forward to their retirement, they suffer severe "identity crises" when this buttress is removed. The crisis is one of anguishing loneliness. Some women face similar problems when their children mature and leave the parental home or when they lose their symbolic expression of productivity at menopause.

But it is not only the loss of activity that is experienced as a threat to identity. That is only a small part of the picture. The major part of the assault is the sudden termination of specific social relations that had been significant to these people. In traditional societies in which every stage of a person's history from birth through death has a corresponding, predefined social category embracing many people who are inextricably bound to each other, there is little likelihood that a person ever doubts who (or what) he or she is. The problem becomes notably acute, however, in societies like the United States where there are few formal categories that are recognized and used to support the sense of identity.

Though every society provides people with several sources of identity, one stands out everywhere as the most important. This is the kind of work that people do. Seifer, for example, has noted that:

> Psychiatric studies have shown a much higher rate of depression among housewives than among women with jobs outside the home, suggesting greater insecurity about both their value to society and their fate, should they lose either their husbands or their children. . . . A negative self-image characterizes depressives, and in our society, where worth is equated with money, social psychiatric studies demonstrate that it is better to be young and rich than old and poor. Housewifery is menial work and we do not regard our menials highly (1973, p. 39).

As they work and gain a livelihood, so people live and experience their unique sense of being. "To imagine life without work for many urban men is like trying to imagine life without a self" (Wright, 1971, p. 321). This probably applies to all people, not only those who live in cities.

Why is work so important in people's lives? The kind of work people do sets the basic theme in their experiences because, in every society, people spend more time and effort at work than at any other activity. Additionally, whenever people meet for the first time, they immediately try to "place" one another prior to engaging in significant social relations; this seems to be true in all societies. In placing themselves, people identify themselves — they present their selves — to one another and, in this respect, the question frequently asked is, "What do you do?" The question obviously refers to work. The underlying premise is that a person's fundamental social attributes — his or her identity — may be deduced from the kind of work performed and the kinds of people he or she associates with.

Work is almost never done in isolation; even if one is physically alone while working, one's efforts are always oriented to an audience or market. Work almost always provides the groundwork for making friends. It is the basis of the social recognition that one gets from one's mates (in James's terms) and from one's family. It is the medium for the validation that one needs to maintain an awareness of self. It is the wavelength along which approval and praise are transmitted and which lead one to feel worthwhile.

Sennett and Cobb have observed that industrial laborers whose lives are filled with endless rounds of meaningless work on assembly lines and elsewhere often find a sense of personal meaning in personal sacrifice, self-denial, and abnegation. These attributes provide them with a sense of dignity and self-worth. Furthermore, their sacrifice is a means of raising their children's status and of helping them across the divide that separates them from those who have political power and who exercise control over their life opportunities. In these people's lives, "only sacrifice is supposed to make a person 'worth' something to those he loves" (Sennett and Cobb, 1972, p. 138).

A predominant element in the anguish of pervasive loneliness is the feeling—real or imagined—that one makes no difference in other people's lives. Sacrifice and denial for others help create the illusion that one does make a difference. Sacrifice and self-denial are idioms through which people may communicate; they make up an emotional language through which the person who has eschewed his or her own wishes may elicit feedback, approval, gratitude, a reassurance that the meaningless grind of labor that fills more hours and takes more energy than anything else has purpose.

These observations must be seen in a broader context. Much has been said in recent years about the meaninglessness of work, the sense of alienation experienced by people in modern industrial societies, and the demise of the Protestant Ethic. What is often lost sight of in this connection is that work devoted to keeping body and soul together has probably always been meaningless. I often expect that the pop sociologists' medieval cobbler will turn over in his grave the next time a pseudoMarxist talks about the satisfactions that came from creating a shoe from beginning to end. Imagine the disgust that man must have felt after making the same shoe day in and day out for forty years. Whatever pride, dignity, and self-esteem the idealized cobbler had was not from his monotonous shoe-making. It came instead from his immediate, local, primary groups who thought him a wonderful fellow—and repeatedly told him so—for remaining on his treadmill and providing the best he could for his household.

Prior to the eighteenth century in Western Europe, as Ariès has observed,

> material success, social conventions and collective amusements were not separate activities as they are today, any more than professional life, private life and social life were separate functions. The main thing was to maintain social relations with the whole of the group into which one had

been born, and to better one's position by skillful use of this network of relations. To make a success of life was not to make a fortune, or at least that was of secondary importance; it was above all to win a more honorable standing in a society whose members all saw one another, heard one another and met one another nearly every day (1962, p. 376).

What happened in the eighteenth century to create the sense of alienation that has come to characterize people in modern industrial societies? The sense of estrangement had its origins in the barriers to validations of self from significant others that followed the Industrial Revolution. One of the foremost consequences of the Industrial Revolution is that groups and attachments that traditionally provided validation of self have disappeared from the social map or are in the process of being seriously weakened. This pertains to kinship groups, ethnic enclaves, religious groups, communities, and so forth.

The modern inefficacy, if not the triviality, of these bonds has extended even into the most intimate of family relationships. As Sennett has observed,

> The anxieties [working-class men and women in their forties and fifties] feel about being men and women concern not so much getting into bed as feeling that the tasks of nurturing children and working that society has set out for them create barriers to love between themselves and their children; the children often think of their parents simply as functions, with low status outside the family, rather than as human beings (1972, p. 23).

People in agrarian localities are able to maintain a strong sense of personal dignity and self-worth because of the repeated validations of self provided by kinsmen and those who are regarded as kin in tight local groups. In a modern industrial society's urban locales, on the other hand, people rarely see—or are seen by—those whose recognition and validation of self mean the most. Commercial advertisements in the United States periodically remind us to telephone relations on ritual occasions or to send them flowers (in death as well as in life) or other gifts because we see them so infrequently. These advertisements tap a vital chord of life in a society in which most social relationships are with strangers. Those with whom we are in contact during our workdays this week may be gone the next, often unaccountably, because of decisions made by impersonal agencies which may be unknown. Kinsmen and friends may eventually know of one's accomplishments and setbacks, but such knowledge is usually obtained some time after the event. What has been removed from industrial society's urban institutions are the means for regularly and repeatedly communicating the recognitions, the approvals, and the reassurances that we need from those who are most important to us and who are indispensable to our sense of personal identity.

The thrust of life in a modern industrial society like the United States is that, to survive, the individual must develop a self-portraiture that is based on an important measure of passivity before the forces that directly affect him or her. One may be jailed for refusing to work, to pay taxes, to serve in the army when called, to send one's children to school, and for countless other acts. Though one may occasionally obtain emotional support for unpopular actions, most of the social relations that derive from such actions are temporary and with strangers. There is a dimension of self-experience in a modern industrial society that may only be described as hearing echoes in a room without walls. The social enclosures that are necessary to orient oneself and to keep one's bearing—the significant people that one needs for validation—have fallen away under the pressures of modern life.

What are these pressures? They are the requirements of a particular kind of economy, a social order in which people are recruited to jobs in ways that disregard kinship, friendship, ethnic and religious affiliation, and so forth. When people moved from farms to cities—whether because of burdensome taxes or the promise of a better life—extended families, kinship networks, church groups, and communities weakened and died. When an urban person looks for a first job or later tries to find ways for advancement, he or she goes where the job is. One of the ways in which I often make this point to my classes is to ask how many were born and brought up in the vicinity of the university. Rarely do more than 10 percent raise their hands. I then ask how many plan to return to their home communities or neighborhoods after completing their university studies. In the more than twenty years that I have been asking this, no more than about five or six have raised their hands—not in any one class, but in more than two decades. Almost every one of these people is going to make several major moves to different cities and different regions—and in some cases to different countries—in the course of a lifetime. Each will be spending an entire life among strangers, a situation that is exacerbated by increasingly frequent divorces and remarriages.

The mobility that increasingly characterizes people's lives, the inadequacy of institutions that formerly provided a sense of purpose and meaning, and the voids in the sociology of everyday life require new institutional adaptations. I think this is why people have become so interested in "consciousness-raising groups," communes of one sort or another, or what are often referred to as "alternative life styles." These are searches for new institutions and associations in which people may develop the meaningful relationships from which they can receive the self-validations they need to feel that they make a difference to others, and that they have self-worth, self-respect, and dignity. These are substitutes for older institutions and organizations of social relations that are no longer able to provide these necessities of life. New ones are being fashioned out of shared experiences and common needs.

25

Loneliness of the Poet

THOMAS PARKINSON

LONELINESS begins with the recognition of one's singularity—the fact that a deep communication of one's self and recognition by others of its legitimacy is not fully possible. Individualization is painful, and individuality is therefore a mixed boon. The sense of being a voice in a void—speaking in a vacuum—is unsettling and disturbing. With this sense comes the desire for comrades; of homesickness for one's own kind. This desire for companions grows from a sense of exile, of being part of the social world that does not resonate in harmony with the buried genuine self that we take to be our most certain reality. Realizing our separateness, we are moved toward understanding—a noncensorious passion, a fellow feeling that asserts that the world really is a community of spirits who all know one another. Mature men and women of sensitivity are often delighted on meeting another who is inhabiting the same world and can thus mitigate the sense of being banned from one's proper milieu. The imagination, the capacity for seeing others as other and yet as part of our being, and ourselves as part of theirs, leads to work, study, and affections that extend, subtilize, and confirm the initial sense of separateness.

The classics of modern literature by Joyce, Pound, Proust, and

Eliot are largely populated by characters who live in isolation. They are encapsulated and walled in so that meaningful relations are canceled for them. They do not find the comradeship that relieves the burden of individuality. They have no place. Their condition is further aggravated by the sense of helplessness that has permeated literature and life in the last half of the twentieth century. W. H. Auden could speak of the 1940s as the Age of Anxiety. Perhaps we are in the Age of Panic in which the human condition in the world is without the supports of the firm, unchangeable natural order; without a set of ordered rituals and sacraments. For as the general human ability to control the environment increases, the specific individual capacity to control the forces of the world diminishes to the vanishing point. The individual vanishes into a condition of laconic impotence.

The poet suffers less from this condition than most men. This may be one of the major reasons for the sudden growth of interest not only in reading poetry or attending poetry readings, but in the actual writing of poetry. Twenty years ago the student who wanted to write had idle dreams of becoming another Ernest Hemingway, living a romantic life, and drinking gin with the international set on the Riviera. Now the more attractive model is the more private figure of the poet working modestly without publicity and social status. The freedom for contemplation and exploration is more attractive to such students than the glare of public attention. Nor is this privacy viewed as mere self-indulgent solitude; it is rather a mode of entry into the basic human condition.

The subject of much poetry is loneliness. The writing of poetry is a solitary operation. But that very loneliness is among the primary rewards of the poet. Writing to a young poet who complained of his loneliness, Rilke (1939) said:

> What is needed is just this. Loneliness, vast inner loneliness. To walk in one's self and to meet no one for hours on end. That is what one must be able to attain. To be lonely the way one was lonely as a child, when the grown-ups moved about, involved in things that appeared important and big because the big ones looked so busy and because one understood nothing of what they were doing. If one day one comes to perceive that their occupations are miserable, their professions moribund and no longer related to life, why not go on regarding them like a child as something alien, looking out from the depths of one's own world from the expanse of

one's own loneliness which is itself work and rank and profession. Why want to exchange a child's wise understanding for defensiveness and contempt when not understanding means being alone, while defensiveness and contempt mean participating in that from which one is trying by their means to separate one's self (pp. 99-100).

Rilke asks the young poet to return to the freedom of the child so that he might accept the conditions of life without defensiveness and contempt. The capacity for perceiving and accepting those conditions depends on the ability to recognize the basic reality of human loneliness.

In spite of the carrying power of tradition that allows any serious poet to live in a community that extends back to the earliest of human experience, the poet in action lives in essential loneliness. He shares this domain with all other discovering workers, whether artists or scientists. In work, in knowledge, even in love, we approach the loneliness of death in which the world ceases to function in any hitherto meaningful fashion. The world's modes and forms lose their inner authority, their power to support. The work of vision and knowledge destroys even those ties and affections that have made the work possible. Those powers are strangely depersonalized so the testimony to the force of revelation is possible only in the articulated, revealed artifacts. Looking back on the process of creation, the poet himself or his critic may perceive the weight of traditional lore, the habits of prosody that are the poet's personal style. But in honesty one has to admit that there is a leap, a point of breaking, where tradition and personality equally cease to have determining power. The loneliness of the poet and the loneliness of any discoverer is a form of death, both for the tradition of learning and the world it refers to, and for the personality itself.

What renders the poet's work specialized is the social character of language. Critics talk about the vocabulary of forms used by painters or architects or musicians, but poetry really has a vocabulary—a word hoard that all men can more or less employ for purposes of communication. The poet may aim beyond communication to communion. He may try to create linguistic silence, but he still does so with familiar materials. This reliance on a vocabulary of words cuts across the grain of normal human expectation to a greater extent than the vocabulary of forms developed by painters.

When language undergoes distortion, such as even the most conventional poetry must effect, men react to it very deeply or at least passionately. Nothing is more admired or resented than poetry. Like music, it is an incisive art that makes intimate impact. Poetry imposes a rhythm that entails the opening of new nervous channels. The range of human possibility is limited by kinesthetic habit, and part of the resistance to poetry comes from a deep and justified conviction that it will make an exorbitant claim, ask that we change our lives, or with overwhelmingly dangerous intimacy force us to move in designs that we had never previously imagined or entertained. The poet's lonely discovery menaces the social reliance on defensiveness and contempt because it is rendered in designs of language that have a design on the audience. The ideas are only as profound as their impact. Men are threatened only by incisive arts.

The loneliness described by Rilke as the poet's destiny and reward has its articulation in poetic forms that destroy solitude. The same loneliness was described by Yeats in many different essays as a descent into the true self that was deeper than anarchic individualism or social character. Yeats saw that deeper self as personal and typical, and as an embodiment of a universal role or function more meaningful than the social life. In his phrasing, "The rhetorician would deceive his neighbors,/The sentimentalist himself; while art/Is but a vision of reality" (Yeats, 1956, p. 159). Or in another passage derived from John Stuart Mill, "Rhetoric is heard, poetry overheard." T. S. Eliot, in distinguishing the voices of poetry, described first the poet speaking to himself. In Yeats's sense that activity would constitute poetry. Rilke, Yeats, and Eliot all insist on the solitude of the poet's activity, its asocial character, and Yeats exquisitely emphasizes the visionary nature of poetic art. Poets often stress that their art requires that one share the vision, undergo the experience of poetry. They are, in Susan Sontag's phrase, "against interpretation." They are convinced that the poem means exactly what it says. They share the kind of frustration that the scientist undergoes when he sees his work confused with technology and engineering, rather than related to the contemplative action of artist and saint. Anyone who has undergone the experience of science or of religion in a genuine manner understands immediately the irritation of a poet when asked to explain what he is communicating.

When we turn from the essential loneliness of the contemplative life in which the poet participates, we encounter another isolating factor —the relation of the poet to a paramount, transcendent structure, a vision of reality that at once underlies and is expressed or articulated in his artifacts. Embodying this vision in language is the aim of the prophetic poet. Many of the great poets, especially those since the eighteenth century, have been occupied in constructing a vision of the world that will have elegance, harmony, cogency, and inclusiveness. Living as we all do in a world where the standard options have become unacceptable to thinking people, each man has to construct a satisfactory accounting for phenomena. If that man has representative quality and great gifts of articulation, then he is paid attention. In the modern world, men live in multiple spheres to such an extent that each is a universe unto himself. This may be our greatest burden. The poet's singular vision serves to bring us an extension and subtilizing of our own limited and partial view, and once again the vision is communicated with unequalled incisiveness.

Modern men are bound by a special kind of loneliness that is related to the multiplicity of philosophical and religious options available to them. I have already mentioned the Age of Panic and the sense of isolated helplessness that is so prevalent as to be typical. Poets do have a socially representative role that to them is ancillary, but to readers often primary. The kind of loneliness that one finds in Robert Lowell's recent lyrics falls in the category that he calls "the existential dark night." And in the early poetry of Ginsberg, particularly in such well known poems as "Howl," there is a sense of moral and social outrage at his own solitude and the solitude of others he has known. He tries to utilize his sense of separation to identify himself with the insulted and injured of the world. Thus the refrain of "Howl" in the Rockland section is, "Carl Solomon, I am with you in Rockland," an insane asylum in New York (Ginsberg, 1956, p. 19). Ginsberg is saying that he identifies with the suffering, the mutilated, and the damaged. He projects his sense of outrage into a general social view.

Ginsberg's work is very complicated and there are other kinds of solitude and loneliness expressed in it. Some of it is the loneliness of the visionary and the loneliness of the man who is emotionally stifled and emotionally unsatisfied, both by the experience of his body and by the society in which he lives. You see that most clearly in his poem to the terribly sad loneliness of his mother, the Kaddish poem in which he describes a funeral service, her life and death. Then there is the kind of loneliness that comes from a vision that he cannot communicate. There is the loneliness that comes from the lack of love he feels in himself and in those with whom he associates. There is also a heroic loneliness of the sort that Walt Whitman exalted. In his extension of Whitman's vision, Ginsberg looks out a Pullman window and declares, "America, I will haunt you with my beard," a characteristic piece of wry wit. What he is really haunting America with is his eccentricity, his idiosyncracies, his isolating qualities that underline the national isolation and make possible the peculiarly American poem.

So far I have stressed the poet's attitude toward loneliness as a necessary condition of his work, as an arena for struggle where he can find his demons or angels, as the isolation of discovery, as a result of his effort to find and construct a controlling vision of experience, and as an inevitable consequence of his fierce perception of the immediate.

But loneliness is also a primary subject of poetry because it is a major human problem. Most human beings do not share the poet's protection against, or reward for, his loneliness. The poet moreover, as man rather than artist, suffers as all men do from loss, from the failure of communication, and from the sense of being locked within himself. The poet, too, is one of those that Matthew Arnold spoke of when he wrote, "We mortal millions live alone." Indeed many of Matthew Arnold's best poems have as their substance the fact of unrewarding solitude, the sense of strangeness in a strange land, or the conviction that his buried life may never emerge into a fruitful relation with his daily conscious self. In his poetry, nature becomes a backdrop for the tears of the solitary man. Love normally fails and leaves the individual isolated in the sea of life. Love merely embodies the construction of a sad duo, and the love of this duo is no more than an assertion against the violent dark world where ignorant armies clash by night. Arnold looks with envy on the community of silence of the Carthusian monks and sees it in contrast to the noisy, divided world of his own being as illustrated in a phrase often quoted from the "Stanzas from the Grand Chartreuse"; "Wandering between two worlds, one dead, /The other powerless to be born." Or Arnold takes the solitary gypsy scholar as a norm of happy loneliness that his lack of faith will not allow him to attain. He mourns the death of his friend, Arthur Hugh Clough, who did not bring to fullness his entire promise. Solitude is the normal human condition for Arnold. It fills him with misery and, alas, a certain amount of self-pity. This last, the tendency toward self-pity, was so disturbing to Arnold that he deleted one of his finest and most extensive poems, "Empedocles on Etna," from his first large collection, explaining the deletion in his preface on the following grounds:

> What are the situations, from the representations of which, though accurate, no poetical enjoyment can be derived? They are those in which the suffering finds no vent in action; in which a continuous state of mental distress is prolonged, unrelieved by incident, hope, or resistance; in which there is everything to be endured, nothing to be done. In such situations there is inevitably something morbid, in the description of them something monotonous. When they occur in actual life, they are painful, not tragic; the representation of them in poetry is painful also (Arnold, 1965, p. 592).

Most contemporaries might dismiss this as a priggish Victorian shying away from the difficulties of life. But William Butler Yeats justified excluding Wilfred Owen from *The Oxford Book of Modern Verse* on the grounds that passive suffering is not a proper subject for poetry. Something more than prudery lies behind Arnold's attitude; it was probably that very attitude that led Arnold to give up writing poetry entirely. From our point of view what is even more alarming is that the situation outlined in that selection from his 1853 preface is not very remote from the existential dark night that Robert Lowell described as underlying one of his most representative later poems. I have characterized Arnold's view at length because I should like to inspect the question of whether loneliness is not in fact a kind of passive suffering that poets as great as Arnold or Yeats found a subject so improper for poetry that when it became a dominant obsession of poetry, a man of such intellectual integrity as Arnold stopped writing poetry entirely and became an inspector of schools and a literary critic.

I shall now examine two extreme poetic perceptions of loneliness, Percy Shelley's "Stanzas Written in Dejection Near Naples," and William Carlos Williams' "Danse Russe." Shelley's poem used to be part of every survey course in English literature, but fashion has now decreed that it should be forgotten. The poem begins with the description of an exhilarating day, perfect in its Italian fullness of life, and then focuses on the poet, "I sit upon the sands alone." He reflects on the beauty of the scene and then he says with some ambiguity, "How sweet! did any heart now share in my emotion," which I take to mean that his loneliness makes it impossible for him really to experience the fullness of beauty. His loneliness casts a pall over the scene. He describes his inner condition, and when one tries to think about what the worst inner condition might be, one imagines it as a state without peace or calm, contentment, or inner glory, and certainly one lacking fame, power, love, or leisure. Other men may take pleasure in life, but as Shelley says, "To me that cup has been dealt in another measure." There follows the key stanza that has been widely discussed in literary criticism generally and by Shelleyans in particular. I shall reproduce the whole poem because I like it. I first read it when I was about sixteen and have come back to it over and over again. It is beautifully wrought and though not in the current style, still very lovely:

> The sun is warm, the sky is clear,
> The waves are dancing fast and bright,
> Blue isles and snowy mountains wear
> The purple noon's transparent might,
> The breath of the moist earth is light,
> Around its unexpanded buds;
> Like many a voice of one delight,
> The winds, the birds, the ocean floods,
> The City's voice itself, is soft like Solitude's.

> I see the Deep's untrampled floor
> With green and purple seaweeds strown;
> I see the waves upon the shore,
> Like light dissolved in star-showers, thrown:
> I sit upon the sands alone—
> The lightning of the noontide ocean
> Is flashing round me, and a tone
> Arises from its measured motion,
> How sweet! did any heart now share in my emotion.

> Alas! I have nor hope nor health,
> Nor peace within nor calm around,
> Nor that content surpassing wealth
> The sage in meditation found,
> And walked with inward glory crowned—
> Nor fame, nor power, nor love, nor leisure.
> Others I see whom these surround—

Smiling they live, and call life pleasure;
To me that cup has been dealt in another measure.

Yet now despair itself is mild,
Even as the winds and waters are;
I could lie down like a tired child,
And weep away the life of care
Which I have borne and yet must bear,
Till death like sleep might steal on me,
And I might feel in the warm air
My cheek grow cold, and hear the sea
Breathe o'er my dying brain its last monotony.

Some might lament that I were cold,
As I, when this sweet day is gone,
Which my lost heart, too soon grown old,
Insults with this untimely moan;
They might lament—for I am one
Whom men love not—and yet regret,
Unlike this day, which, when the sun
Shall on its stainless glory set,
Will linger, though enjoyed, like joy in memory yet.
                    (*Shelley, 1901, p. 363*)

The lovelessness of Shelley does bring him at that point to genuine self-pity, and his suffering is passive.

Now let us alter our humor entirely and turn from this poem to a celebration of loneliness written a century later by the jovial doctor of Rutherford, New Jersey, William Carlos Williams. The shift, let me warn you, is abrupt:

If I when my wife is sleeping
and the baby and Kathleen
are sleeping
and the sun is a flame-white disc
in silken mists
above shining trees,—
if I in my north room
dance naked, grotesquely
before my mirror
waving my shirt round my head

and singing softly to myself:
"I am lonely, lonely.
I was born to be lonely,
I am best so!"
If I admire my arms, my face
my shoulders, flanks, buttocks
against the yellow drawn shades,—

Who shall say I am not
the happy genius of my household?
                    (Williams, 1951, p. 148)

Williams' poem transcends its own subject by a happy denial of the very sufferings in the Shelley poem. It is amusing. It is fun and it has a cheerful objectivity about it that is charming. Yet I suspect that it is as objectionable to some as the Shelley poem is to others. At least I hope it is. It is autoerotic to the point of onanism. It is vulgar and smug and posturing as much as the Shelley lines are sentimental and self-pitying and posturing. Can we say, though, that these lines or the Shelley lines are excessive to their subjects? If we object to either poem, we might say that it is tasteless. We are reduced to making this matter a question of taste and judgment. It does not do much good to argue that the Shelley lines are immature. So are the Williams lines. Perhaps the concept of social maturity is simply not applicable to the poetic process.

Very few poems approach the question of loneliness as directly as these do. Often what we take to be loneliness resulting from the loss of love or the loss of an admired leader or friend becomes in the poet's hands something quite different. Catullus really is more concerned with his own passion and the character of Lesbia than with his loneliness. In his elegy for Lincoln, "When Lilacs Last in the Dooryard Bloom'd," Whitman is more concerned with the intimate panorama of the American nation unified in suffering than with the loss of Lincoln. There is only the most general reference to the character of Lincoln, while the sanctified earth of the nation and the nature of death itself are the real subjects of the poem. Loneliness, then, is the arena where the poet in his inner wandering finds his subject, where his angels and demons rise up for the creative clash that brings him to full awareness. Loss is antecedent to discovery. It is only the alienated who seek and create community either politically or imaginatively. Poems are based on the invisible, barely audible community of the great, lonely figures of tradition. When loneliness becomes the subject of poetry as it is in the works by Shelley and Williams, it does not embody the attitude of the poet or the controlling form of his poetic production. In these cases, the passive suffering of loneliness is thus not the poem, but what the poem treats or starts from. The Shelley poem, therefore, is not really about loneliness but about despair which is a much more important human condition. The Williams poem, conversely, is about joy.

What then do poets have to say about loneliness? Everything, I would say. For, once the poet has gone through the purifying process of his discipline, of which loneliness is no small part, he speaks to and for others. Man's fate is controlled and limited not only by the strictures of the social order or milieu, but by his nature—his limited capacity for knowing himself and the limited nature of his language.

I should like to consider in more detail two of the great poems of the twentieth century, Rilke's *Duino Elegies,* and D. H. Lawrence's "The Ship of Death." Thanks to the brilliant translation of Leishman and Spender, the *Duino Elegies* have become part of the English-speaking tradition. In the elegies, loneliness is a major subject which is now more and now less explicit, but always a resonant tone. One metaphor the elegies use (much as D. H. Lawrence uses death in "The Ship of Death") is love; the frustration of love and the reward that results from such frustration. For Rilke, requited love is insufficient. He reminds us that the human capacity for the unsatisfied may be our saving grace. It makes our loneliness meaningful. What is more important, "human beings do not love singly nor in pairs, /Their love wells up from immemorable instances" (Rilke, 1939, p. 39). It is invaded by memories they as men cannot evoke normally. In love, human beings look beyond the lover to a reality that the lover only suggests. For human beings, as Rilke sees it, love is a total action, a kind of thorough responsibility for the universe they inhabit. In love, the beloved is left behind. Rilke speaks of what lovers could see if only the other were not there always spoiling the view.

> Look, we don't love like flowers, with only a single
> season behind us; immemorial sap
> mounts in our arms when we love. Oh, maid,

this: that we've loved, *within* us, not one, still to come, but all
the innumerable fermentation; not just a single child,
but the fathers, resting like mountain-ruins
within our depths;—but the dry river-bed
of former mothers;—yes, and the whole of that
soundless landscape under its cloudy or
cloudless destiny:—*this* got the start of you, maid.

And you yourself, how can you tell,—you have conjured up
prehistoric time in your lover. What feelings
whelmed up from beings gone by! What women
hated you in him! What sinister men
you roused in his youthful veins! Dead children
were trying to reach you...Oh gently, gently
show him daily a loving, confident task done,—guide him
close to the garden, give him those counter-
balancing nights....
                    Withhold him...
                                    (Rilke, 1939, p. 39)

Love is therefore at its best when unsatisfied; it is most selfless and no-
ble when, like the arrow, it outlives the bowstring. It is described here
as total human action involving a temporal continuum that extends
back to the very origin of human beings.

Now this is a model of the way in which poetry effectively destroys
the loneliness of its reader. Poetry, like all literature, has the
therapeutic function of making the human condition more bearable,
even a source of fun and joy because it presents the full, incisive indication of human speech acting in the world. Poetry, and indeed all
literature, destroys our solitude by placing it intimately in contact with
another solitude. It embodies a spatial and temporal continuity. All
men may live in loneliness, but no one who can read need be alone. A
once useful word has unfortunately become a shibboleth recently: the
misuse of language has tainted a perfectly good word like "community." Yet the only way to describe what the *Duino Elegies* do is to say
that they provide an entry into a larger and more worthy community
of spirit.

The finished poem takes on a social function that contrasts with the
loneliness that fuels the poetic process. In talking about poetry on different occasions, I often find myself shifting back and forth from ex-

plaining poetry as the work of a poet involved in psychological and technological processes highly specialized and individualized, to explaining poetry as a social event. Poetry is a form of social action even when the poet writes only to be overheard. It may be, as Auden observed, that poetry makes nothing happen but it does make poetry happen. What happens in poetry concerns the courageous and joyful actions with which man faces the mystery of human destiny, of love or death, of external nature, of the otherness of things and beings. He may face his own death as Yeats does in the last stanza of one of his last poems:

> When a man grows old his joy
> Grows more deep day after day,
> His empty heart is full at length,
> But he has need of all that strength
> Because of the increasing Night
> That opens her mystery and fright.
> > *(Yeats, 1956, p. 332)*

Or the poet may face his own death with a quiet, insistent tone that makes it represent all deaths.

A paradigm of such poetry is Lawrence's "The Ship of Death." D. H. Lawrence is not adequately known as a poet, but some of his best energies went into the poetic enterprise. His stories and novels take much of their vigor from his deep, continuous immersion in the poetic process. Certainly Lawrence's greatest poems are media for seeing and apprehending the human condition and grant us entry to a more generous and delicate life than we could have imagined without them. The poems of death are poems in which the calmness of suffering and the acceptance of fate appear most tenderly. One of them is fairly short, "Bavarian Gentians." He wrote it during the last weeks of his life when he knew he was dying.

> Not every man has gentians in his house
> In soft September, at slow, sad Michaelmas.
>
> Bavarian gentians, tall and dark, but dark
> Darkening the day-time torch-like with the smoking blueness of
> > Pluto's gloom,

Ribbed hellish flowers erect, with their blaze of darkness
    spread blue,
Blown flat into points by the heavy white draught of the day.

Torch-flowers of the blue-smoking darkness, Pluto's dark-
    blue blaze
Black lamps from the halls of Dis, smoking dark blue
Giving off darkness, blue darkness, upon Demeter's yellow-
    pale day
Whom have you come for, here in the white-cast day?

Reach me a gentian, give me a torch!
Let me guide myself with the blue, forked torch of a flower
Down the darker and darker stairs, where blue is darkened on
    blueness
Down the way Persephone goes, just now, in first-frosted
    September
To the sightless realm where darkness is married to dark
And Persephone herself is but a voice, as a bride
A gloom invisible enfolded in the deeper dark
Of the arms of Pluto as he ravishes her once again
And pierces her once more with his passion of the utter dark.
Among the splendor of black-blue torches, shedding fathomless
    darkness on the nuptuals.

Give me a flower on a tall stem, and three dark flames,
For I will go to the wedding, and be wedding guest
At the marriage of the living dark.

                        (Lawrence, 1964, pp. 955-956, 24-29)

There is a curious pride in his uniqueness that is qualified and placed
in a wider perspective. His death becomes identified with the death of
the year and the reception into darkness that is inevitable and, as he
shows it, worthy of celebration. There is neither self-pity nor bravado
in treating a situation that tempts to both. The relation between man,
brief beautiful flower, and death becomes a sacramental rite.

"The Ship of Death" takes its origin in Etruscan burial practices,
but the association of the longest voyage and the voyage into death is
widely diffused throughout the various cultures of the world.
Lawrence places himself in the framework of these wide human
associations, and sees his individual death in the perspective of all

preceding voyagers. His use of the metaphor of the seasons makes for the identification of life and death; he sees the entire world in those terms. When we approach and face death we are reminded of our ultimate vulnerability and divested of armor. Death is the final democracy. The ship of the poem is the vehicle of the journey that is life, that is death, and that brings us to the verge of human possibility. What matters most in the poem is the expression of a love of life that makes death itself an object of love. There is a splendid mild resignation, an abdication of any property rights to experience. In such a poem, the poet consoles, reveals, and makes the exigencies of life endurable. He destroys our solitude.

I

Now it is autumn and the falling fruit
and the long journey towards oblivion.

The apples falling like great drops of dew
to bruise themselves an exit from themselves.

And it is time to go, to bid farewell
to one's own self, and find an exit
from the fallen self.

II

Have you built your ship of death, O have you?
O build your ship of death, for you will need it.

The grim frost is at hand, when the apples will fall
thick, almost thundrous, on the hardened earth.

And death is on the air like a smell of ashes!
Ah! can't you smell it?
And in the bruised body, the frightened soul
finds itself shrinking, wincing from the cold
that blows upon it through the orifices.

III

And can a man his own quietus, make
with a bare bodkin?

With daggers, bodkins, bullets, man can make
a bruise or break of exit for his life;
but is that a quietus, O tell me, is it quietus?

Surely not so! for how could murder, even self-murder
ever a quietus make?

IV

O let us talk of quiet that we know,
that we can know, the deep and lovely quiet
of a strong heart at peace!

How can we this, our own quietus make?

V

Build then the ship of death, for you must take
the longest journey, to oblivion.

And die the death, the long and painful death
that lies between the old self and the new.

Already our bodies are fallen, bruised, badly bruised,
already our souls are oozing through the exit
of the cruel bruise.

Already the dark and endless ocean of the end
is washing in through the breaches of our wounds,
already the flood is upon us.

Oh build your ship of death, your little ark
and furnish it with food, with little cakes, and wine
for the dark flight down oblivion.

VI

Piecemeal the body dies, and the timid soul
has her footing washed away, as the dark flood rises.

We are dying, we are dying, we are all of us dying
and nothing will stay the death-flood rising within us
and soon it will rise on the world, on the outside world.

We are dying, we are dying, piecemeal our bodies are dying
and our strength leaves us,
and our soul cowers naked in the dark rain over the flood,
cowering in the last branches of the tree of our life.

VII

We are dying, we are dying, so all we can do
is now to be willing to die, and to build the ship
of death to carry the soul on the longest journey.

A little ship, with oars and food
and little dishes, and all accoutrements
fitting and ready for the departing soul.

Now launch the small ship, now as the body dies
and life departs, launch out, the fragile soul
in the fragile ship of courage, the ark of faith
with its store of food and little cooking pans
and change of clothes,
upon the flood's black waste
upon the waters of the end
upon the sea of death, where still we sail
darkly, for we cannot steer, and have no port.

There is no port, there is nowhere to go
only the deepening blackness darkening still
blacker upon the soundless, ungurgling flood
darkness at one with darkness, up and down
and sideways utterly dark, so there is no direction an
and the little ship is there; yet she is gone.

She is not seen, for there is nothing to see her by.
She is gone! gone! and yet
somewhere she is there.
Nowhere!

VIII

And everything is gone, the body is gone
completely under, gone, entirely gone.
The upper darkness is heavy as the lower,
between them the little ship

is gone.
She is gone.

It is the end, it is oblivion.

IX

And yet out of eternity a thread
separates itself on the blackness,
a horizontal thread
that fumes a little with pallor upon the dark.

Is it illusion? or does the pallor fume
A little higher?
Ah wait, wait, for there's the dawn,
the cruel dawn of coming back to life
out of oblivion.

Wait, wait, the little ship
drifting, beneath the deathly ashy grey
of a flood-dawn.

Wait, wait! even so, a flush of yellow
and strangely, O chilled wan soul, a flush of rose.

A flush of rose, and the whole thing starts again.

X

The flood subsides, and the body, like a worn sea-shell
emerges strange and lovely.
And the little ship wings home, faltering and lapsing
on the pink flood,
and the frail soul steps out, into the house again
filling the heart with peace.

Swings the heart renewed with peace
even of oblivion.

O build your ship of death. Oh build it!
for you will need it.
For the voyage of oblivion awaits you.
                         (Lawrence, 1964, pp. 716-720)

One of the difficulties and challenges of writing about the poet's loneliness has been to make a narrow, arbitrary channel through the immense diversity of poetic literature. In a sense the only subject of poetry is human loneliness, seen under the aspect of an inclusive vision and rendered in language that incises its vision deeply and completely in the receptive mind. If we should like to be among those on whom nothing is lost, poetry can show us what we might be missing. Out of this enlightenment issues beauty and the only kind of power that matters, the power over ourselves that transforms mere external fate to inner destiny and gives us that sense of sudden growth, of love, and of courage that only the dignity of full human knowledge can grant. If after that moment of sharing in the sense of glory we find ourselves alone and perhaps lost and wondering, the example remains. The ability to know and appreciate and lovingly accept our loneliness may be the ability of the wisest and best men. At their best poets are precisely such men.

26

Loneliness and Creativity

JACOB LANDAU

WHEN I WAS INVITED to write this paper, my first reaction was "Who me?" I am, after all, only an artist without a solid, experimental base for my prejudices. Generally, artists couldn't care less about the subject of creativity. Barnett Newman's quip about esthetics being no more to the artist than ornithology to the birds could apply as easily to studies in creativity. Yet I was drawn to the chance to "tell it like it is," to report on my experience as a "creator," and to present my conviction, based on that experience and on much reading and meditating, that loneliness is, or can be, an important ally to the artist, to all creative people, and to the creative process in general.

I confess that I do not enjoy nit-picking, hyperspecialized studies that neglect the forest for the trees. I know that the trees are important and that highly focused studies are worthwhile in the long run if and when they contribute to the creation of new paradigms. But it is precisely the forest-tree relation in human perception that I want to examine as a metaphor both of the creative process and of all such bipolar processes. As I will try to argue, the compartmentalization of knowledge into highly specialized modes is dangerous at least in part because it serves to discredit the artist's input—it isn't considered "hard knowledge" or "cold fact." It is my belief, however, that metaphors, myths, and paradigms are just as important as hard knowledge or cold facts.

Putting the two terms loneliness and creativity together may seem at first glance an odd coupling. Loneliness is almost universally treated as a sickness, a negative experience to be avoided at all costs,

486

an evil condition for which we must find the remedy. Creativity, on the other hand, is a subject with infinite sex appeal, one that is everywhere regarded as healthy, positive, desirable, and one that must be studied carefully with the help of tests, rats, and computers not only to arrive at "predictive effectiveness" in Jerome Bruner's phrase (in Gruber, Terrill, and Wertheimer, 1962), but perhaps even to arrive at a form that can be produced, packaged, and sold along with underarm deodorant and the 3 R's. Yet, still more oddly, creativity in "exceptional" people is often ascribed to neurotic or pathological causes—to narcissism, egotism, paranoia, wish-fulfillment, or childishness; to obsessive-compulsive, depressive, or repressive states; to sublimation of sexuality or to hypersexuality; to the frustrations of childhood or the insensitivities of parents; to fear of death or the lack of fear of death; even to such things as astigmatism, syphilis, or alcohol.

As for loneliness, there are not many who would attribute it to healthy impulses in the human psyche, or claim that it may even be intimately, and not just casually or superficially, connected with creativity. Clark E. Moustakas (1972) is one, but because he writes from personal experience, with a poetic touch and without an experimental foundation, he tends to be discounted. For most of the other writers on the subject, loneliness is either a social or individual disease that can be cured if the right measures are taken. Riesman et al. (1950) believe people are lonely when cut off from the crowd of other-directed people, a condition which can be overcome through increased autonomy and inner-direction. Tanner (1973) feels we are lonely because of our fear of love, and because of the risks involved in letting ourselves go in building a love relationship. He claims that we overcome our loneliness by learning to take risks, by assuming "personal responsibility for the consequences of loving." Philip Slater (1970) believes we are too afraid of loneliness, and that our fear causes us to deny the "reality and importance of human interdependence." But he does not come to the defense of loneliness; instead he suggests we are lonely to the degree we allow ourselves to get disconnected. If rampant individualism produces our loneliness, then we must learn how to get reconnected. Leiderman (1969), in distinguishing loneliness from depression, concludes that it is associated with guilt, anxiety, hostility, or libidinal elements. It can be treated by increasing "self-object differentiation." Jules Henry (1973) thinks vulnerable people shrink from others, thus increasing their vulnerability. He states that this condition is aggravated by the inhumanity of our society, and implies that we must rehumanize society before we can remove the roots of loneliness. Robert S. Weiss (1973) calls "ordinary" loneliness one of our "most common distresses," but feels that the different forms of loneliness are "responsive to different remedies." Loneliness caused by the absence of an "engaging social network," for example, can be remedied by acquiring "access to such a network." John Bowlby (in Weiss, 1973) argues that our need for affectional bonds is, like our need for food, a biological survival mechanism, and that loneliness is our response to affectional deprivation. While he does not propose a remedy, he supports the value of "sheer familiarity in giving us a sense of security...confidence...identity" (p. 51), hence the value of stable families and stable communities. Helena Lopata (in Weiss, 1973) proposes a number of "solutions" to the different forms of loneliness she describes. Morton Hunt (in Weiss, 1973) feels that only the "severely wounded" (!) can treasure loneliness as a way of gaining strength; the rest of us have to make do with a variety of more or less useful remedies.

I do not wish to discount these excellent contributions to our understanding of loneliness. I think it is important to note, however, that none save Moustakas will grant full citizenship to loneliness among the cluster of essential qualities within what may be called the human condition.

In turning now to creativity, I will not attempt a survey of the voluminous literature, for it would not serve my purposes. Instead, I shall propose a trial definition. When I speak of creativity, I refer not only to its role in men and women of genius, but to its presence in all of us. Creativity is, in my opinion, the capacity to invent, to innovate, to come up with variations on preexisting themes, and, in the process, to break with established sets, habits, patterns, adaptations. The latter, in fact, seems to be a prerequisite for the former. I say we all have it because we are all part of a creative natural order; we wouldn't be here if this were not true. Yet, as self-evident as this idea seems, we know next to nothing about how creativity works in the universe, about how the emergence of novelty in fact takes place. We have some models, scattered over a dozen sciences from biology to astrophysics, but these constitute a fairly chaotic assemblage of suggestive but unintegrated material. For me, however, the working of creativity can best be approached "artistically," with infinite respect not only for the statements of artists, scientists, and "geniuses," but equally for the vast body of the world's literature, myth, legend, and folklore. The working of creativity can only be approached, moreover, through attempting to learn what ancient and modern ideas of development and process in the natural order have in common.

In my own view, we grow up with an experience of order—in our bodies, in the procession of days and nights and seasons, in the cycles of births and deaths, in our adaptations to the material conditions around us. We trust that our eyes do not lie to us, that our minds can make sensitive distinctions and intelligent choices. We believe in evolutionary change, in growth, progress, innovation, and the probability of self and social improvement. Our beliefs are reinforced by the society in which we live, for it is a society founded on the institutionalization of inventiveness itself.

But we also grow up with an experience of disorder, with an awareness that nature's evolutionary drive towards form is contradicted by an equal and opposite tendency towards disintegration, devolution, chaos. We experience it in hundreds of ways, and these ways include our awareness of the inevitable decay and death of all living creatures, including ourselves, the accumulation of unsolved and apparently insoluble problems in our daily lives, and the role of "accidents" and the unforeseen consequences of perfectly reasonable acts. Evolution and the idea of progress, it would seem, are contradicted by the second law of thermodynamics. In order to deal with increasing entropy, we must redouble our efforts (in thermodynamic terms, increase the input of energy to overcome the loss of available energy within the system). Occasionally, for a time, some of us do succeed in tricking our apparent fates, in creating enclaves of increased order in the midst of a general increase of disorder. Bucky Fuller calls this "doing more with less," or "more with lessing"—becoming more efficient, the only way, of course, to beat the second law, for a time. In the end, we know that we can win only temporary and conditional victories, though we do not know that we know this.

This tendency to ignore our fate is because of our "peculiar" bias in favor of winning over losing. We cannot conceive of a universe that is not designed to ensure our success as individuals. After all, no species would survive if its individual members did not have a built-in need to win. But we forget that we know about the natural order and the possibility of losing. We forget we know that nature contains both good and evil, tragedy and triumph, hope and despair, heaven and hell, god and devil, creativity and passivity, loneliness and togetherness, thesis and antithesis, stress and adaptation, evolution and the second law of thermodynamics.

The view that "man"[1] is born benign but is corrupted by society has always been a puzzle. How did society go bad? The converse is equally puzzling—that "man" is inherently evil, but can somehow conceive of the good, or create beneficent religions, arts, sciences. It is only as people come into conflict with each other over access to tools and wealth that technologies and their support-structures "autoamputate" (in Marshall McLuhan's term) human potentials for goodness, and strengthen tendencies toward evil. The evil is institutionalized as the environment to all who are born into society and who thereby come to experience society's wealth as illth, and its productivity as pollution. So both propositions about man's natural state turn out to be true—the benign are corrupted, and the corrupted dream dreams of beauty, grandeur, and eternal life. Autoamputation of one potential permits the autoamplification of others, producing a plethora of psychic specializations, part-people, people who think but do not feel, who feel but do not think, who hate without loving or love without hating, who act without reacting or respond with impotence.

The part-person is, by definition, a psychic monster. The technological society produces such people as a matter of course; it could not function without them. This fact is the basis of my fear that we are in danger of losing touch with the last vestiges of our humanity, of which the loss of the capacity to understand and endure the pain of loneliness and the loss of the ability to remain creative throughout our lives are prime symptoms. Let me try to illustrate what I mean.

Science in the industrial age, which is "scientistic" in its exclusion of

---

[1]Throughout this paper, I will put quotation marks around "his," "he," "man," except in direct quotes, as a way of circumventing the awkwardness of our language. In doing so, I am hoping that wherever these words appear, the reader will understand me to mean he/she, his/her, and man/woman. I did not wish to interrupt the flow with quantities of he/she's. Furthermore, it is sometimes inappropriate to use "one's" or "we's," and the expression "of her" is unsatisfactory, especially when referring to activities largely dominated by males in our society. Lastly, I don't like Slater's use of the masculine for negative and the feminine for positive values.

values, has created a world of facts and fact-worshippers. Technology has accepted one value as its foundation—the obsolescent but still reigning assumption of 19th century science that facts and only facts are valid, particularly if they aid productivity. This leads to two equal and opposite assumptions: one may either believe that only one value is valid (which is impossible) or that all values, as "facts," are equally valid and/or invalid. The so-called avant-garde artist has, in the main, embraced both assumptions, having already caught the bug of scientism. "His" ultimate value is "his" own validation through productivity and inventiveness, thus aping the technology as the producer of art or anti-art, both "arti-facts" of the marketplace. "He" has separated "his" producing system from "his" understanding system, as the scientist has separated "his" analytical functions from "his" interpreting functions. "He" is thus, like the scientist, transformed into a technician, a specialist. If philosophers reject the search for values as meaningless, and scientists reject art, philosophy, religion, and all other value-systems as arbitrary or inconsistent, and artists reject all but the forming process as worthless, they all become subject to technological forces. They are thereby transformed into "means" for the technological society, particles without true freedom to choose alternative pathways, enslaved to the inherent dynamics of the total field, and, in particular, to the dynamics of the marketplace.

Andy Warhol said, "I want to be a machine." Jacques Ellul, whose book *The Technological Society* (1964) seems increasingly prophetic, wrote: "When man himself becomes a machine, he attains to the marvelous freedom of unconsciousness, the freedom of the machine itself. . . Man feels himself to be responsible, but he is not. He does not feel himself to be an object, but he is" (p. 226). Power and power-play via manipulation of mass-media dominate the field, overriding even the values of objectivity and neutrality in science or productivity and estheticism in art. They appear to be abstract, uncontrollable forces as incomprehensible to modern "man" as natural forces were to archiac peoples. *Each particle-"man" seeks to validate "himself" by invalidating others*. Science-for-itself, art-for-itself, or anything-for-itself, even if serving only as fig leaves for co-optation, are separated from whole human meaning and value considerations; they produce individuals-for-themselves, people obsessed with self-preservation via their specialties, with success at all costs at the expense of the next person or of the "whole damn world" if necessary. It is tempting to point out that the greatest failure was Leonardo; the greatest success, the cockroach. Does "man" aspire toward the condition of the cockroach?

We seem, therefore, to have created the penultimate specialization, the mass-technological society of pure means, the evil society, the monstrous society, the society of *partial solutions* and inadequate fix-ups with no concern for side effects or long-range consequences, or of *"final solutions"* like the Nazi holocaust, or the bomb. It is in such a context that the problem of loneliness acquires a special poignancy. If "togetherness" implies "joining up," adjusting to and participating in the ritual dance of death, then loneliness is a holding action, a clinging to the still living roots of a dying plant. In a poisoned environment, only the poison-eaters survive. Creativity, at present, involves choosing the flip-side, thereby opting for life over death, pain over pleasure, and tragedy over triumph. One chooses this way not out of preference, but because in a world of entertainment-art, therapy-religion, "bought" science, public relations politics, and addictive consumption, these negative values seem more real than the pseudopositive values now being purveyed around the world, including the value of unlimited progress and its soft underbelly, the principle of triage.

The artist has, in the main, become a "salesman" of progress, and art has become the human face of technology. The dialectic of modern life obliges the artist to speak only for himself in a society emptied of genuine individual values and lacking authentic social values. But despite what "he" creates, even "his" most ardent protests are grabbed up and whirled around by the centrifugal forces of mass-communication, and dispersed in homogenized form. "He" and "his" esthetic have proclaimed that the individual is in fact the only social value, that "his" very isolation, suffering, and eccentricity carry a vital meaning for our time. This is true only as an image of desperation, as a last ditch attempt to resist homogenization. It is a negative value, and, in its own way, a heroic attempt to save humanity from being consumed by the machine. That is why the artist has seemed to be in love with perversity, madness, anger, isolation, despair, absurdity, suffering, violence, loneliness. Or "he" has been obliged to swing between the standpoints of critic-outsider and vanguard-insider.

There may indeed be survival value in such swings. The "esthetic" youth rebellion of the 1960s was the first sign of a swing towards rehumanization, an attempt to restore spontaneity, pain, love, hell, danger, loneliness, apocalypse to the alienated psyche. The second move, the Easternization of Western thought, is now in progress. I believe we are moving toward a reexamination of all our values in a swing away from the brink and toward survival. But it is the idea of wave motion itself as the dynamic of change and of creativity in the universe that I wish now to examine.

Early in my life, I became interested in what seemed to be the universal tendency towards paradox, ambivalence, duality. Artists are responsive to patterns of all kinds, but as one who was driven to find out why things worked as well as how they worked, I became involved with what I conceived of as the pattern of patterns, the meta-pattern of all motion and change.

The following image emerged for me: that all existence is comprised of processes and forms in more or less relatively transitory equilibrium states; that all forms are processes, and all processes are involved in the making of forms; and that forming tendencies (spatial organization) arise naturally from the interplay of contrary forces (temporal organization). I further envisioned this interplay taking form a rhythmic fluctuation between poles within a field, and I understood that all fields have boundaries and that form and fluctuation represent a universal duality of which the particle-wave duality is a special case. Finally, I saw that our inability to ever know the exact moment when red turns to orange in the spectrum, or when growth yields to decay in a living organism is a general principle of uncertainty of which Heisenberg's principle is a particular application, and that harmony and creativity in nature are the consequence of a universal war between contraries.

My experience as an artist has included: the gestalt character of perception, with its positive-negative, figure-field bipolarity; the flow between concrete and abstract ways of functioning; the struggle between my past conditioning and my future potentials, between being programmed and choosing among alternatives, between being a critic or outsider and being a creator or insider. It has also included both the gradual unfolding of my discontent with avant-gardist paths in the arts and the sudden leap to an independent vision against the ground of tradition; my need for security and my longing to be free; my swing from exploration of new territory to exploitation of of my discoveries. Every time I begin a work, I violate the purity of the surface in order to transcend it. When I invent a new image, I soon discover hidden links to earlier images, while all of my discoveries seem to be gathering their forces toward some as yet undisclosed transcendent illumination. Form in drawing seems often to contradict color in painting, and every painted work is a compromise between objects-in-themselves and objects bathed in the light of their surroundings. Painting is an act of withdrawing from others to realize oneself, which in turn is a means for drawing closer to others so that they may be helped to realize themselves. "Innering" myself is both a commitment to the abyss, to loneliness, and a passionate longing for understanding and acceptance, for "outering."

My experience has also included what I learned from the lives of other artists, from their encounters with ambiguity. I think of Beethoven's lifelong preoccupation with freedom and necessity, Blake's wedding of heaven and hell, El Greco's spiritualization of the material, and Lebrun's effort to counter the pain of awareness with the joy of forming. From such a ground, I came to believe that stress is the primal creative force in the universe.

Lancelot Law Whyte states that development occurs through the tension between opposing forces, between inner tendencies of an organism, which are conservative of past forms, and circumstance, which if it does not destroy the organism, succeeds in modifying it. In temporal terms, this involves a movement from asymmetry to symmetry; in spatial terms, only the simpler molecular systems, such as crystals, attain something like end-of-the-road "symmetries of relative stability, whereas, in hierarchical structures, where parts of a complex system interact, no such separation can occur." Instead, the emergent form is a "process-equilibrium" (L. L. Whyte, 1948, p. 18), a structure composed of interacting contraries operating on a number of levels simultaneously.

Remarkably, the parts of an organism in isolation would tend to disintegrate, but the processes of the wider system sustain and modify them by nourishing them, and by gradually increasing the "mutual conformity of organism and environment" (p. 22). In other words, the organism is *inseparable* from its environment, and its "life consists in that inseparability." The point, according to Whyte, is that "life is not autonomous" (p. 23). It is instead, *a rhythmic fluctuation between symmetry and asymmetry, structure and process, organism and environment—a wave motion in time.* And every concrete manifestation of the forming tendency, every emergent structure, every creature, gesture, idea, or work of art, every gestalt is *a particle in the wave front*, a spatial configuration. The cause of change is the *mutual stressing of each by the other*; environment stresses organism by obliging it to adapt, and organism stresses environment by feeding back to it the consequences of its adaptations.

I don't think we know how this works, but the stress-adaptation mechanism in human ecology proposed by Hans Selye is a possible link in the chain. He calls this mechanism the "General Adaptation Syndrome." According to Selye, creatures go through three distinct phases of adaptation to stress. The first is the "alarm" reaction; the second, a stage of "resistance" or getting used to the stress; and the third, exhaustion or the breakdown of adaptation. What interests me in this model is that during the second stage we experience *pick-ups* or *turn-ons* after each reexposure to the original stress. We also experience *hangovers*. Dr. Theron Randolph, in his book *Human Ecology and Susceptibility to the Chemical Environment* (1978), points out that a person may resort to stresses in "an addiction-like manner as often as necessary to remain 'picked-up.' Indeed, this may be the only way he knows to postpone or relieve his otherwise inevitable delayed 'hangover-like' reactions, for only thereby does he remain 'normal' and without complaints" (p. 8). Along with the *pick-up* and its addictive potential, adaptation also involves *mechanization*, the routinizing or automating of behavior—in other words, the formation of *habits* which can function unconsciously.

I find these ideas enormously suggestive. I believe there are positive and negative stresses. Love, for example, can be a positive stress. In describing their responses to love, poets have often resorted to language very much like clinical descriptions of the alarm reaction: rapid heart beat, sweating, loss of appetite, uncontrollable agitation or excitement, and so on. I believe there are positive and negative reactions to stress, such as creativity and passivity (the high or pick-up, the low or automatization). I believe that stress initially heightens awareness; we are aroused for fight or flight as adrenalin pours into the blood, and everything becomes vivid as we focus our total attention and sensitivity. I believe we are never more alive than when we experience stress. Animals are likewise "turned-on," but when the stress is removed they tend toward idleness, passivity, sleep. Humans, because they can remember the stress, paint pictures, write poems, invent theologies, solve problems. I believe that people can become addicted not only to allergens and other chemical irritants, but to other people, things, activities, environments. I believe that persons who take off on one-sided tangents are those who for different reasons become part-people unable to handle the normal stresses of ambiguity. These people say, in effect, "stop the wave, I want to get off."

I believe that flexibility, or the capacity to move *from positive to negative polarities*—from particle to wave orientations in rhythmic fashion—is the norm for survival purposes. I believe that the fanatics, suicides, geniuses, and other linear freaks, are needed as ecological correctives to society's self-consolidating, automating, habit-forming tendencies. I believe that "peak experiences," as well as chemically induced highs, come from stress and cause stress, and that they, too, can become addictive: people can want to perpetuate their highs as they seek to remain "picked-up" by tobacco, heroin, LSD, sugar, coffee, allergen, religion, art, politics, love, war. I believe that people get addicted because the body, in adjusting to stress, alters its structure in a way that incorporates the stress itself. It then needs the stress in order to continue to feel OK, or "picked-up," and it needs the stress in ever-increasing doses as the body's adaptive mechanism in time adjusts to each escalation, up to the point of final exhaustion or collapse. I am persuaded that, as the body suffers "withdrawal" symptoms when the stress is removed, so does the psyche—how we need our love or hate "fixes," and how we suffer when they are withdrawn!

I believe that boredom is a symptom of adaptation as vividness is a sign of stress. But I also believe that boredom may function as a stress and that it is part of the creative cycle. The stress of boredom stimulates the search for more exciting living, for an antidote to closure, for renewed openness and vulnerability. I believe that most people tend towards closure because they fear openness. They prefer to get trapped in their adaptations and behavioral rigidities while maintaining the relatively safe fiction of openness through entertainment: mediated titillations, petty hedonisms, consumerist novelties.

I believe that artists are people who prefer the open condition of perpetual maladaptation, of never quite settling down or becoming "established," which is perhaps why the humanist potential movement has adopted the "artistic" model of self-actualization in place of the more static notion of "adjustment." I believe there are social rhythms of adaptation which reflect and react upon the individual waves, that the history of our species is a history of cyclic swings from war to peace, life-loving to life-hating, "innering" to "outering," concreting to abstracting, ennobling to belittling, believing to doubting. I believe that the artist, like the scientist, in coming to terms with personal stresses, may help solve society's problems by inventing socially necessary paradigms which, of course, function in the realm of feeling and image.

And, finally, I believe that the exhaustion stage in personal or social adaptation patterns is at times a negation of life and growth, and at times a crisis of rebirth and transcendence. Or, perhaps both at the same time. Jantsch feels that all so-called nonequilibrium systems "mutate toward new dynamic regimes, which may be at a higher state of complexity" (1975, p. 38). This could be the pattern of all evolutionary development—either a rise in hierarchy (nature's strategy for overcoming the dissipative effect of rising entropy) driving the system to a new level of order and complexity, or a degradation towards the equilibrium state of rest or death, an evolutionary or developmental dead end. I believe that as development via fluctuation proceeds, as we move back and forth between our stresses and our adaptations, we are driven either to avoid stress, toward monotonously increasing entropy and the death-in-life of addictive dependency and eventual breakdown, or toward acceptance of, and interaction with, stress in nonaddictive, flexible ways, and therefore toward creation, transcendence, mutation, breakthrough.

Though we don't know how nature decides when to create a new mutation and when to crash, I believe that our human freedom to grow creatively involves the capacity to choose when to accept stress and when to evade it, when to take risks and when to play safe, when to end a habit and when to start one, when to open oneself to experience and when to buttress oneself against it, when to seek solitude and when to look for the company of others. Timing is all, in the cyclic dance of life, the universal coupling and uncoupling of opposites, the interpenetrating and interfecundating hierarchy of wave-motions which constitute both the history and present structure of the universe.

The foregoing excursus on the dynamics of creativity, sketchy as it is, provides the necessary underpinning for a fresh look at the significance of loneliness in our lives and, in particular, of its role in the act of creation. For me, loneliness can only mean how it feels to "inner" or to be "innered," to be inside of ourselves, to be located, lost, or trapped in our separate being, to feel cut off from adequate communication with others, to feel misunderstood or misjudged, to lose or fear the loss of our connectedness with the universe, other humans, or our own humanity. It pertains to the loss or fear of loss of our connectedness with the important and significant others who can understand or affirm us, or with that pure, natural, uncorrupted central core of our being which is the source of our life's dream and hope. In short, loneliness means to feel our apartness, our inability to bridge the gaps that exist or may arise between ourselves and others. And all of this is somehow related to the problem of meaning: do others understand what we mean, do we understand what we mean, do we grasp what our choices and their consequences mean, what life means, what separation and loss mean, what being misunderstood means, what death means, and what the whole endless succession of births and deaths of planets or people can possibly mean?

For me, there are only two kinds of loneliness—the social kind, and the individual kind which Moustakas calls "existential," and which I have sought to define above. Forms of loneliness such as the need for a friend, the desire to get married or to avoid being divorced or "put away" in an old-age home, though experienced psychologically, are all derivatives of social conditions and transactions, and they represent the socialized, or adapted, portions of the psyche. They may be viewed as inherently soluble: one can go to a therapist to overcome an inability to communicate with others, or one can fight in the social arena for the improvement of one's own situation or for the modification of social usages and structures. I am afraid that most of us tend to think that every kind of loneliness is in this way theoretically correctable. We do this because our technologically derived bias in favor of perpetual growth is based on our ability to solve problems.

I am not suggesting that we should not try to correct what is correctable. On the contrary, I do not think we have even begun to realize how much more we could accomplish in this direction if we could disengage ourselves from outdated paradigms, social structures, and procedures; if we could cut through the alienated web of interpersonal relationships and begin to move towards a rehumanized society based on caring and community. Castaneda's Don Juan says we cannot begin to face our lives until we have faced our deaths. Moustakas believes that "efforts to overcome or escape the existential experience of loneliness can result only in self-alienation" (1972, p. ix)—the worst kind of loneliness. Both are saying that we must get in touch with our human condition in order to avoid the dehumanizing effects of our social inventions. It is just barely possible that society itself must first face the likelihood of apocalyptic collapse before it can begin to live again on a new basis, or hope to find honest, effective, meaningful solutions for the worst manifestations of socially derived loneliness and alienation. It is quite likely that we cannot accomplish this reorientation without beginning to temper our hubris with humanity, without developing a concept of the irremediable in life.

I want briefly to illustrate with two anecdotes my conception of existential loneliness, and of the irremediable core of all forms of loneliness. The first is a recollection of childhood. I remember, when in first grade in a school in Baltimore, Maryland, that I had a dear friend named Leon. I was about to move to Philadelphia with my family and, on the last day, Leon and I walked arm-in-arm around the schoolyard. We were inconsolable. He said, "We'll never see each other again." I said, "Oh, but I'm sure we will." He said, crying, "But how will I know you?" And I had no answer, because I was not sure I knew how I would know him.

The second recollection dates from World War II. I was present at the burial of a buddy in Italy. At the precise moment when his body was lowered into the ground, I experienced a kind of clairvoyance, of seeing past the grass to the teeming life-forms hidden by it, even to the atoms and molecules of earth and sky.

In the first of these experiences, I encountered the loneliness of simple separation, one which I had encountered earlier on, and which I would reexperience countless times in the years to come. In the second, I faced the loneliness of death, of final separation. By not allowing myself to be diverted, I gained a great deal from both experiences. The moment of enhanced perception in the second, not unlike some hallucinogenic visions, was an expansion for me of the meaning and quality of life that followed my first full encounter with the reality and inevitability of death. And my memory of that schoolyard drama contains a bittersweet awareness of another kind of inevitability, one that equally enhanced my consciousness and sensitivity.

Such experiences of loneliness are rooted in our humanity, in the fact of our being born and dying alone, and in the absolute impossibility of achieving "perfect" communication with others in the absolute and irrevocable loneliness of our separate existence. As we grow, we learn, to our sorrow, that mothers, fathers, friends cannot always be there for us when we need them, that we cannot even be there all the time for ourselves, as we pay out our compromises in small coin, as we meet the basic paradox of choice—the possibility of increasing the "wrong" in the effort to do "right."

I am persuaded that most so-called primitive peoples knew how to face tragedy, by ritualizing the great separations and joinings of life, and by teaching people how to "live through" loneliness, pain, failure. Lord Krishna, in the *Bhagavad Gita*, put it this way: "Be not afflicted by the unavoidable." Our own teachings, our rituals of death, marriage, and separation contain none of this wisdom. They do not help us meet ourselves, one another, or our true existences.

The older civilizations of the East have institutionalized the irremediable as we have sanctified the idea of absolute progress. In one case, even what can be helped is not; in the other, even what cannot be helped, is. Both are examples of dichotomization carried to the point of absurdity. I am saying that we cannot suppress one pole of a bipolar field without paying a heavy price as reality avenges itself. I am saying that if we cannot face pain, then we are obliged to deal with it in unhealthy ways, by enjoying gratuitous violence on TV, by ignoring the pain we inflict on others, by becoming inhuman. I am saying that the only way to deal effectively with the pleasure-pain polarity is to transcend it. I am saying that transcendence is achieved in the natural order by mutation, by ascent to a higher level of organization, by reordering and reenergizing the field. I am saying that nature's creations come about only as a result of fully matured processes of conflict between contraries, not through the fudging, hedging, or evading of such conflicts. I am saying that partial resolutions of partially lived-through conflicts can only result in the abortion of change, or in pathological kinds of change.

I accept the idea of transcendence not as a way of suppressing or evading bipolarity, but as a way of going beyond opposites by encompassing them. I am convinced that as long as we are earthbound, all such acts of transcendence do not get rid of opposites, but rather substitute new opposites for old ones, new opposites that exist on higher levels of organization and therefore allow for greater freedom of excursion. I believe, with Jantsch, that we can transcend ourselves only by centering and grounding ourselves. People who are centered and grounded do not suppress or repress any of life's contraries. Such people can get in and out of pain, loneliness, or exaltation; they can ride the wave like surfers instead of drowning in it, or merely drifting in its currents and eddies; and they are free to drift instead of surfing when necessary, or even to become uncentered and ungrounded, if necessary. True freedom means, as Erich Fromm has written, acting on the basis of alternatives and their consequences. One cannot choose among alternatives if one is hooked or trapped. One must get unhooked first.

The artist is, perhaps, a person whose creativity is grounded in loneliness itself. "He" is frequently a person who begins life as someone endowed with greater than average sensitivity to stress. Possibly this means, among other things, a particular hormonal or nervous structural difference of significance—a hypothesis which, to me, is more sound than the various neurosis theories of creativity. As "he" develops, "he" experiences many agonies of adaptation if "he" chooses to indulge and encourage "his" difference, to step out of line, to be far-in or far-out, to zig when others are zagging. "He" learns to live within "himself," to listen to the chorus of inner voices, to shut "himself" away in solitary while others are playing or working, to throw "himself" into the void, in Picasso's phrase, with each poem or painting.

The fact that many creative people in our time have been amply rewarded, have become celebrities, even millionaires, does not necessarily protect them from loneliness. There is a story, perhaps apocryphal, that Franz Kline was afraid to get up, and that Rauschenberg is afraid to go to sleep. Apocryphal or not, it illustrates the point that even the famous are not immune to the loneliness of uncertainty and to doubts about their accomplishments or abilities.

Beyond all other factors, beyond the need to create forms, the need to win affection and approbation through one's striving, the need to keep reinvesting oneself, the artist is a person who, par excellence, is tuned into the need to find meaning in life, and to return meaning to life. I will not try to guess why art is important to us, but I am sure that it is, and to the extent that we have lost the art in ourselves, we have become an endangered species. Talent in the few, it would seem, has been purchased at the cost of its suppression in the many—a consequence of specialization which breeds, as its corollary, amateurism, the poor man's authenticity. The act of surrendering a part of oneself to the specialists is an act of autoamputation: because we gave religion to the church, we have no faith; because we gave art to the artist, we have no beauty; because we gave authority to politicians, we are not self-governing. The problem, of course, is that both professional and amateur are crippled in the process. In the conflict between an alienated art and an equally alienated, inartistic society, the artist is obliged to escalate "his" oddness, "his" difference, and, in consequence, "his" loneliness.

Avant-gardism is a modern myth of transcendence, of the artist-hero-prophet who offers "himself" as a lonely sacrifice so that society's fatal illness may be cured. Slater (1970) shows how society absorbs and incorporates the prophet's message even as it destroys the prophet. In the global media-environment, the NOW is a wave front in which the leading edge represents the locus of prophetic insight, the place where the action is. All problems and solutions appear to coexist in an eternal present, and anything which seems tied to the past lacks all meaning. To pursue the wave metaphor, the water behind the wave front is merely part of the ocean—only the wave front lives! In like fashion, the system has decreed: if you are not mediated, you are dead. And you are mediated only if you are news, NOW. In order to become and remain visible, all must strive for up-frontness, relevance. Obsolescence is built into such a system; the price you pay for relevance today is extinction tomorrow. When you are no longer news, you are dead. The prophet is expendable. The prophecy lives on, as myth, as pseudotranscendence. Because we gave our capacity for transcendence to our hero-prophets, we are doomed to pendulate forever between yes-no contraries. Their loneliness is only matched by our own. For the humanist artist, on the other hand, all questions become merged into the overriding question of "man's" survival, and all views about survival constellate around this central problem: is "man" exempt from the workings of natural law, the law that decrees the ceaseless rise and fall of life forms and the mortality of each, in which case history can be seen as progressive or teleological and "man" as superior to nature; or is "man" part of the natural order, which implies that "he" may, like all other species, come to an end by drowning in his own shit, or by transforming his own nature (a negative transcendence) in imitation of the machine, or by any of a number of other small or large apocalypses, in which case "his" history, after a progressive phase, may now be regressive and decadent. The humanist artist sees history as a "tragedy in which the uncompromising vision of the poet has demanded that 'his' art transcend 'his' mere opinions; each character is to be presented as simultaneously right and wrong, so that the truth will be expressed not in the characters but in the epic. And that is the timeless Homeric vision" (Thompson, 1971, p. 97).

The word tragic does not necessarily mean "unhappy ending." It refers to fatality and ambiguity, to the belief that no single position, philosophy, strategy, movement, or faith contains the final Truth. It means that none is either right or wrong, that all positions may be "simultaneously right and wrong" (Thompson, 1971, p. 97), or that some positions may be right at one time and wrong at another, including, of course, the artist's position. All art is above all particular ideologies, which is why art survives and ideologies do not. It transcends the artist's ideology by uniting the contraries, by revealing them in their true motion and conflict.

If in my work and in the writing of this article, I have stressed the negative or tragic values, it is in the above sense that I have done so. In addition, I share with many other artists a felt need to counter the fake cheerfulness of our culture, its smiles max-factored out of all resemblance to the human. Bertolt Brecht said: "The man who laughs has not yet been told the terrible news." Do I batten on misfortune? Do I relish tragedy? I am sure that I do to a degree. I contain both victim and executioner, life-wish and death-wish.

This is where my loneliness begins—at the point of intersection between my inhumanity and my dreams of a just social order. I can remember a crisis of loneliness in art school, when many of my friends were turning towards abstraction, while I clung to images of social comment and commitment. I felt bitter, abandoned, guilty, inadequate. I later came to feel that I had a right, even a responsibility, to be myself, to yield to my sense of justice and injustice and to be hierarchic about my moral and esthetic choices. Thus I acquired, out of loneliness, my first real sense of freedom. At a later date, when I found others winning awards, I experienced terrible feelings of rejection and self-rejection, of loneliness and estrangement from my earlier choices and from the world, which had begun to direct its injustice toward me. I learned how to accept the consequences of having chosen to be myself and of having rejected the path of innovation for its own sake, a game I could easily have played at the price of authenticity. When I began to win acclaim and awards and to sell widely, the critic who questioned the "sincerity" of my humanist motivation threw me into a panic of loneliness, of being cut off from the people I had chosen to represent and speak to in my work, and from my own humanity as well. Were my motives suspect? I came out of this crisis with the realization that they probably were, as are the motives of all reformers or revolutionaries. This insight helped me become less addictive in my self-righteousness, but it strengthened, as it deepened, my concern.

But beyond all of these cross-purposes, beyond the pleasure-pain polarity, beyond commitment and doubt, I felt a transcendent need to give expression to an even deeper kind of loneliness, one which is connected with the sheer magnificence and mystery of life beyond gadgetry and games. In earlier societies, where alienation had not yet become a problem, the self was actualized only in relation to social norms that were transcendent. It is the ability of the self to identify with the more-than-self, with the universal, the divine, the cosmic, and to find a role in this scheme which would shape and tax the self that seems to be missing today. The roles we play are indeed not our own, though we appear to choose them. The goals we are offered are more personal than ever before, yet we despise them inwardly, because we know they are insufficiently meaningful. It is precisely the lack of otherness that has created the widespread anxiety about self. In choosing not to parody my own essence in order to remain visible or viable in the information environment, I have encountered an order of loneliness which I believe to be prerequisite for change, but which is integral to the process of centering the self. The center of one's being contains the inner limits of what is or can be known in particular, and the outer limits of—the universal?—the divine?—the cosmic?—the natural?—that can only be glimpsed at rare moments of self-or-world denial, wherein lies the ultimate ambiguity of what it means to be human. This loneliness, at the boundary between time and eternity, is both awful and sublime. It is the loneliness of connection and disconnection, with humanity and the more-than-human, of knowing and not knowing whether we can see past the boundaries of existence. It is loneliness at the brink of the abyss which, as is true of all such nodal points, urges us either toward reversal of polarity, back the way we came toward (apparently) safer terrain, or onward toward—the hope of breakthrough and salvation?—the fear of breakdown and extinction?

For several generations, various assault-teams of artists have heralded the coming of our crisis of crises. From existentialism to the songs of Richard Farina ("For I am a wild and lonely child/ And the son of an angry land...") and Bob Dylan ("Heard the roar of a wave that could drown the whole world..."), among others, the loneliness of the revolutionary, the prophet, rings out. Though the flood of apocalyptic rock has receded, other tides are beginning to merge with the wave sweeping toward the opposite shore. These include the rather large and expanding field of future studies, the surviving and still developing alternate culture experiments, the humanist potential movement, and the grass roots political movement. In my view, no one of these probes is "the answer," the "right" path or pill, no more than any single mind or voice is the "right" leader or guru. Hegel saw the end of his dialectic in the Prussian State; Lenin saw the end of his in the dictatorship of the proletariat. I can no longer accept such panaceas; they are part of the problem.

I do not, therefore, wish to propose a "solution" for others to adopt. My life's work as a "humanist" artist is my trial solution. Yours will be different. I am a pluralist. I believe all individually conceived stresses heading us towards humanization are simultaneously valid and/or invalid. This is above all else a recognition of the possibility that we may lose, which is where I began. But this recognition does not argue for pessimism, any more than admitting the inevitability of evil, pain, or loneliness in the human condition argues for these negative values over and against the positive ones. As humans, we cannot help but choose to improve ourselves and our circumstances, provided we do so without continuing to violate the natural order, without destroying ourselves and our spaceship earth in the process.

I am sure there will continue to be stress-adaptation-breakout and/or breakdown cycles to the end of time. But there is, simultaneously, the hope of earthbound transcendence, the possibility of moving up a ladder of transcendence, of personal and social chakras or fields of fluctuating, contradictory energies, toward higher levels of more centered and grounded living. I am persuaded that getting in touch with the existential loneliness which underlies all other forms of loneliness can help shake us loose from our traps and "trips," our powerlessness and our pseudopower, and move us to unheard-of levels of creative, synergetic potency. The path out and up, if it exists, can only be followed if we achieve simultaneous rhythmic "outering" and "innering" of self and social transcendence, the recovery of our cosmic interconnectedness, not in vitro but in vivo, not by propaganda but by individual transformation, not by panacea but by probe.

27

Loneliness, Creativity,
and Vincent van Gogh

ALBERT J. LUBIN

IN THE PREFACE to *Stranger on the Earth: A Psychological Biography of Vincent van Gogh* (1972), I wrote, "As a psychiatrist involved in the study of van Gogh, the question I meet most frequently is, 'What was the matter with him?' Although it is a question that fascinates psychopathologists, professional and amateur alike, it is not very important. Countless human beings with similar frailties have long since been forgotten and such frailties can be better studied among the living. It is more pertinent to question what made it possible for him to accomplish such outstanding things. Therefore, while I have inevitably been concerned with van Gogh's problems, the stress has been put on his ability to transform them into incredible achievements" (p. xviii). In this vein I will discuss facets of van Gogh's creative processes that grew out of loneliness and related mental states.

This chapter is an edited selection from Dr. Lubin's book *Stranger on Earth: A Psychological Biography of Vincent van Gogh* (1972). This work has also appeared in a revised edition as *Stranger on the Earth: The Life of Vincent van Gogh* (1975). Translations of van Gogh's letters are from *The Complete Letters of Vincent van Gogh* (1958), as modified by Dr. Jacob Spanjaard. For location of individual quotations, see the references in *Stranger on the Earth.* Reproduction of "Madame Roulin with Her Baby" is by permission of The Philadelphia Museum of Art: Bequest of Lisa Norris Elkins (Mrs. William M. Elkins). Reproduction of "The Potato Eaters" and "The Pietà" is by permission of the National Museum Vincent van Gogh, Amsterdam.

LONELINESS, DEPRESSION, AND ARTISTIC CREATIVITY

"The only true wisdom lives far from mankind, out in the great loneliness, and it can be reached only by suffering. Privation and suffering alone can open the mind to all that is hidden in others." So spoke a primitive Eskimo shaman named Igjugarjuk, recorded by the Arctic explorer-scholar Knud Rasmussen and quoted by Joseph Campbell in *The Masks of God* (1959). "The 'grave and constant' in human suffering, then," Campbell writes, "leads—or *may* lead—to an experience that is regarded by those who have known it as the apogee of their lives and which is yet ineffable." He believes that this experience "is the ultimate aim of all religion, the ultimate reference of all myth and rite." "But all, certainly, will not be suffering," Campbell concludes, "...for the paramount theme of mythology is not the agony of the quest but the rapture of a revelation, not death but the resurrection: Hallelujah" (1959, pp. 54, 56).

Change the words "religion" and "mythology" to "artistic creativity" and these quotations might have been written by—or about—Vincent van Gogh. By reason of childhood experience, parental teaching, and religious conviction, he thoroughly believed in the value of suffering, sorrow, and loneliness.

In 1876, four years before he began his career as an artist, Vincent gave a sermon at a small Methodist church in Richmond, a humble London suburb. Preaching to the congregation, he was also preaching to himself—and of himself. The images he used were the same as those that were to be given powerful expression in his pictures. The text chosen for the sermon was Psalm 119:19, "I am a stranger on the earth, hide not Thy commandments from me." The young preacher then went on: "It is an old faith and it is a good faith, that our life is a pilgrim's progress—that we are strangers on the earth, but that though this be so yet we are not alone for our Father is with us." The psalm's text is an affirmation of isolation and loneliness, but they are summarily eliminated; for the community of the faithful, "I" becomes "we," and "we are not alone."

The theme of sorrow is woven through the sermon and seen as an inherent human trait: "Our nature is sorrowful." But painful as it may be, sorrow is a blessing in disguise, a quality to be cultivated: "Sorrow is better than joy," he asserts, and "by the sadness of the countenance the heart is made better''; hence one is ''sorrowful yet always rejoicing.''

The sermon shows Vincent freely accepting the existence of grief, loneliness, and death, but through the vehicle of religious faith he is able to glorify them as prerequisites for joy, acceptance, and immortality. Catalyzed by suffering, sorrow leads to joy, loneliness to togetherness, death to rebirth, darkness to light, and earth to heaven.

When his brother Theo remarked that being ill was no misfortune, Vincent replied, ''No, for 'Sorrow is better than laughter.' No, being ill when God's arm supports us is not bad, especially when we get new ideas and new intentions that would not have come to us if we had not been ill, and we achieve clearer faith and stronger trust.'' Even before he became an artist, when his father told him, ''Sadness does no harm, but makes us see things with a holier eye,'' Vincent remarked, ''*This* is the true 'still sadness,' the pure gold.'' Neither of them could have guessed at that time that this sadness would be transformed by Vincent's hand into the pure gold of art.

The desire to rid himself of depression—and the loneliness, despair, and fears that were part of it—was the most powerful force that motivated Vincent to become an artist and incited the intense energy that was so vital to this end. His pictures became his companions, his mistresses, and his children. ''The work is an absolute necessity for me,'' he wrote. He observed another time that hard work was the way to avoid ''that melancholic staring into the abyss.'' ''I feel inexpressibly melancholic without my work to distract me. . . . *I must forget myself in my work*, otherwise it will crush me.''

It was not simply that art made his suffering more tolerable, but Vincent regarded suffering itself as a virtue that contributed to his success as an artist. From The Hague he wrote, ''If momentarily I feel rising within me the desire for a life without care, for *prosperity*, each time I go fondly back to the trouble and the cares, to a *life full of hardship*, and think, it is better this way; I learn more from it.''

His fight against loneliness and his fear of intimacy set up opposing strivings that functioned alternately in activating his creative processes. On the one hand, he wanted to join hands with other painters ''because everyone who paints would almost sink down under it if alone.'' On the other, he gave credit for his accomplishments to the self-isolation that arose from his fear: ''I agree with what I recently read in Zola: 'If at present I am worth something, it is because I am alone, and I hate fools, the impotent, cynics, idiotic and stupid scoffers.'" Vincent could tolerate mutually opposing thoughts and manage to combine them to the benefit of his work, having at one time relations with other artists who provided him with new ideas and at another time the isolation in which his mind could function without outside interference.

Art was the one activity that enabled him to turn loneliness into solitude, the solitude that provided necessary time for fantasy, reflection, study, and reading. In his first letter to Theo after deciding to become an artist in 1880, he stressed the importance of his self-isolating proclivities, an explanation that was both a rationalization and an insight: his shocking appearance and his life of poverty and neglect, he said, "was a good way to assure the solitude necessary for concentrating on whatever study preoccupies one."

His position as an outsider also made it easier for him to create a new and unique style. Just as Freud praised his Jewishness as a valuable source of energy that helped to give him a "readiness to accept a situation of solitary opposition," Vincent praised his alienation as a necessary part of his creative life. Ignored in The Hague by his cousin-in-law and teacher Anton Mauve, he wrote that it was "not exactly a misfortune to struggle on alone. What one learns from personal experience is not learned so quickly, but it is imprinted more deeply on the mind." It is also more apt to have its origins in genuine, deeply rooted ideas and feelings.

During his ten years as an artist he lived in eleven different places, exposing him to a wide variety of people, ideas, and landscapes. His behavior, however, made it inevitable that relations with people would be short-lasting, and that he would never be so thoroughly attached to anyone or anyone's ideas as to become an imitator rather than an innovator.

Vincent, like many on the threshold of depression, tried to find solace in an inner world of fantasy. He recognized that this tendency grew out of his emotional problems, but it also enabled him to become an artist. Months of silence and contemplation, with his imagination given free rein, brought him a clear vision of his future, which he then proceeded to turn into action. "It is true that there may be moments when one becomes absent-minded, somewhat visionary; some become too absent-minded, too visionary," he wrote in 1880, when he announced his intention to become an artist. "This is perhaps the case with me, but it is my own fault; maybe there is some excuse after all—I was absorbed, preoccupied, troubled, for some reason—but one overcomes this. The dreamer sometimes falls into the well, but is said to get out of it afterward."

THEMES IN VINCENT'S ART

The two broad phases of Vincent's artistic life follow the antithetical themes of the sermon he preached in 1876. The works of the first phase, executed in Holland and Belgium between 1880 and 1885, tend to be somber and dark, with the emphasis on sorrow and isolation. Those of the second phase, executed in Paris, Provence, and Auvers between 1886 and his death in 1890, tend to be bright, colorful, and joyous. Some have tried to explain this transition from darkness to light in terms of his encounter with the French Impressionists and the southern sun, but it is more relevant that his own needs led him to seek them out.

From beginning to end, the depression that permeated Vincent's life cast an indelible stamp on his art. From The Hague in July, 1882, for instance, he wrote, "In either figure or landscape I should wish to express not sentimental melancholy but serious sorrow," and from Saint-Rémy-de-Provence in February, 1890, he described his pictures as "a cry of anguish." By becoming the recorder of sad people rather than one of them, he disclosed his sadness, but at the same time kept it at a distance.

The many solitary figures in van Gogh's work correspond to the lonely outcast—the stranger, the prisoner, and the vagabond—he saw himself to be. In some of his pictures each figure seems to have a private space around it that keeps others at a distance. *Landscape with Pollard Willows* shows a lonely figure standing in the center of a large expanse, neither in the immediate world of the viewer nor in the heavens beyond; in *Mending the Nets* each washerwoman is alone, alienated from the others; in *A Factory* a single man is seen in the midst of a barren, snow-covered field with a dreary factory in the distance; and in *Willows with Shepherd and Peasant Woman*, the lone peasant woman on the left is insulated from the lone shepherd on the right by three rows of trees.

Girl in the Woods, an 1882 oil depicting a girl dwarfed by giant oak trees, recalls young Vincent's solitary walks in the Zundert woods, where he escaped from his family. In *View from the Artist's Studio Window* two women are separated from each other by clotheslines, and they, in turn, are barricaded from the workmen beyond by tall fences. A man in the right upper corner pushing a wheelbarrow is enclosed in a tree-lined road, remote from all the others, heading toward the distant horizon. *View from the Studio Window in the Snow* shows a laborer digging in the snow; the figure is sandwiched between two fences, while someone in the distance disappears down the same tree-lined road. The rigidity and remoteness of Vincent's early figures might be attributed to defective technique if his work as a whole during the same period did not belie this. In fact, the same "fault" remains visible even at the peak of his technical development, as witness the mother and child in *Madame Roulin with Her Baby* (Figure 1) from Arles; the mother holds the stiff, awkward child at a distance, as if she was afraid to cuddle him. Perhaps Vincent's fear of closeness made it difficult for him to portray tender relationships, even though he wished to do so.

Vincent compared himself to "a prisoner who is condemned to loneliness." He gave this description artistic expression in *The Prison Courtyard*, after Doré. *The Weaver* was also a prisoner, one who spent "whole seasons alone." Like jail bars, the bars of the loom isolated the weaver from society; the weaver was "imprisoned in some cage," just as Vincent saw himself.

Sometimes he heightened the alienation of the solitary person by contrasting him with couples. In *Third-Class Waiting Room*, reminiscent of Daumier, a man and woman on the left sit at a discreet distance from each other, further separated by a vertical member of the window frame; in contrast, the two women on the right face each other, engaged in friendly conversation, and one of them holds a baby. The estranged man and woman gaze in unison toward them, attracted by the intimacy they themselves lack. Couples are seated tête-à-tête in *La Guingette*, an inn on the outskirts of Paris, while—like a standing corpse—a stiff waiter is entombed by the narrow wall behind and the lamppost beside him, forms that add to his separation from the couples. In the watercolor *Montmartre* a ghostly figure sits by herself on the right side, separated from the couple on the left by the porch posts and from the couple above by the porch floor; the estrangement is accentuated by placing the solitary woman at the extreme edge of the picture while the closeness of the couples is strengthened by superimposing one figure over another. In an oil from Auvers, *The Stairs*, two women and two girls stroll toward the stairs as a solitary man descends them, heading in the opposite direction. *The White House at Night*, also from Auvers, recalls the parsonage of Vincent's father in Nuenen. Two women enter the

FIGURE 1

Madame Roulin with Her Baby.

house together, while a solitary woman in the foreground walks away from it. She reminds one of the artist himself, who always yearned to return to his parents' house but whose discomfort in their presence compelled him to stay away.

Plagued by loneliness, Vincent never ceased to yearn for closeness with another human being. But closeness meant for him a merger that was both mental and physical, and his fierce, mystical determination to achieve this goal was so powerful that it threatened his intended partner. It frightened parents, relatives, women, artists, and even his brother Theo, contributing to the failure of every attempt at intimacy. Learning to expect these failures, he substituted nature, art, and books for friends, marriage, and children.

Fantasies of closeness and union were diverted into art. Vincent not only portrayed the sad, lonely person he felt himself to be, but also the companion he wished to be. The desire for intimacy in life was paralleled by an obsession with it in his art. He was forever sketching pairs of people—companions and lovers who stood together, walked together, sat together, worked together, grieved together, and lay together. Typically, one partner is close to the other; they are arm in arm, they embrace, or their bodies touch. In the most characteristic van Gogh pair, one figure overlaps the other, as if merged with it.

Since Vincent sometimes mentioned these couples in his letters, it is clear that they had special significance for him. Of one proposed drawing, similar to *The Old Couple*, he wrote from The Hague in 1883: "[T]he couple, arm in arm, against the hedge of beeches, are the type of man and woman who have grown old together and where love and faith remain." This drawing had its Provençal counterparts in *The Rhone River at Night*, *The Lovers*, and *The Poet's Garden*. The first of these three, Vincent wrote, shows "two colorful little figures of lovers in the foreground"; the second, "two lovers, the man in pale blue with a yellow hat, the woman with a pink bodice and a black skirt"; and the last, "two figures of lovers in the shade of the great tree." The old lovers from The Hague are in a simple somber setting, reinforcing the pathos of age, while the settings for the young lovers, from France, are vibrant and alive, with trees that are tall and lush.

Vincent's gift for seeing nature in terms of human form and feeling provided solace for living and a constant enrichment of his art. "The worse I get along with people," he wrote, "the more I learn to have faith in nature and concentrate on her." The expressive trunks and limbs of trees were easily translated in terms of youth and age, strength and weakness, beauty and ugliness, sorrow and joy, death and rebirth. He equated a lone tree with a lonely person, and he paired trees in the same way that he paired humans. He noted that *The Vicarage Garden*, in addition to its human pairs, has three other "couples": "to the right, two trees—orange and yellow; in the center, two bushes of grey-green; to the left, two trees of brownish yellow.'' Each of the paired trees of *Park along the Fence* and *Two Pines* gently touches its partner. *Souvenir de Mauve*, ''probably the best landscape I have done,'' shows ''two pink peach trees against a sky of glorious blue and white''; their limbs intertwine.

Cypresses are popular in Provence, where they are planted in hedgerows as windbreaks in the face of the powerful mistral. Paired cypresses are not common, but Vincent's personal vision led him to paint many of them, such as cypress couples standing side by side in *The Drawbridge* or overlapping in *Wheatfield with Cypresses*. In *Road with Cypress and Star*— the title its owner, the Kröller-Müller National Museum, gives it— the ''cypress'' turns out to be two cypresses when one discovers the two trunks at the base: the two trees have almost fused.

Other objects were also turned into symbolic human couples, with one partner touching or merging with the other. Vincent drew a pair of cottages, fully conscious of his intent: ''The subject struck me very much. Those two half-mouldered cottages under one and the same thatched roof reminded me of an old couple, worn with age, who have grown into one being, are seen leaning on each other. For you see there are two cottages and a double chimney.'' Similar twinned structures in *Barns and Houses at Scheveningen* complement the human couple to their left; like Siamese twins, the buildings are bound together by a connecting structure, the couple by the woman's arm. *The Yellow House*, from Arles, is also one of a pair; its partner on the left is structurally identical. They are tied together by a common segment, similar to the wall in *Barns and Houses at Scheveningen*. Vincent made several paintings of pairs of worn shoes; conceived in human terms, he called them ''a pair of decrepit ancients.'' ''Couples'' are also pictured in *Two Rats Eating*, *Two Sunflowers*, and *Sandbarges Unloading*, the latter showing a pair of river barges lying side by side along the quay at Arles.

The Bedroom is a painting of Vincent's bedroom in the Yellow House. He had purchased two ''country beds, big double ones'' for the house, and the bed in the painting—with its two pillows side by side—is undoubtedly one of them. By creating an illusion of depth in the picture which increases the bed's length, he makes the double bed look like a single bed. Similar to overlapping couples, merged trees, and cottages that ''have grown into one,'' the two would-be occupants of the bed are brought together, occupying the space of one. There are a pair of paintings on the wall above the bed (one a man, the other a woman), a pair of chairs, a pair of bottles on the table, and a pair of windows above the table. This pairing, repeated over and over again, expressed Vincent's wish that the Yellow House would end his isolation and become "a home of my own, which frees the mind from the melancholy of being out on the streets."

Vincent wrote that *Tree with Ivy and Stone Bench*, a painting of the garden of the sanitarium at Saint-Rémy, represented "eternal nests of greenery for lovers. Some thick tree trunks covered with ivy. . . ." Both the bench, where people sat together, and the ivy encircling the tree trunk represented closeness and love. But the ivy also stood for his fear of being engulfed and destroyed by love, as witness the words he had written six weeks before, while still in Arles: "The ivy loves the old branchless willow — every spring the ivy loves the trunk of the old oak tree — and in the same way cancer, that mysterious plant, so often fastens on people whose lives were nothing but ardent love and devotion."

The use of complementary colors, by itself, was still another means by which he symbolized the union of two human beings: "[T]here are colors which cause each other to shine brilliantly, which form a *couple*, which complete each other like man and woman." He reaffirmed this idea in declaring that he wished "to express the love of two lovers by a wedding of two complementary colors, their mingling and their opposition, the mysterious vibration of kindred tones." The orange background complementing the blue of the cap in *Self-Portrait with Bandaged Ear* is one example of such a "wedding." From the standpoint of technique and style, Rembrandt's chiaroscuro painting, *The Jewish Bride* (which had so fascinated Vincent in Amsterdam), and this strange Provençal work with its raw complementary colors side by side, were poles apart. In the former, the message—"the love of two lovers"—was carried by its expressive content; in the latter, by the "wedding" of colors. To Vincent van Gogh, they were psychological equivalents.

THE FIRST VINCENT AND THE SAD MOTHER

Vincent van Gogh was born, and died, on March 30, 1852. The baby was buried in the graveyard of the Dutch Reformed church in Zundert, the Brabant village where his father was minister. Exactly one year later, on March 30, 1853, another boy was born to the van Goghs.

He was also named Vincent, and he lived his early years just around the corner from his dead brother's grave.

Lr. Dr. V. W. van Gogh, Theo's son and Vincent's nephew, has remarked, "Until he left the parental home, Vincent saw this little grave at least once a week when he went to church, but he also saw it when he came home on weekends, holidays, etc. Besides it is certain that he heard the little boy mentioned continually." He wrote to the late Charles Mauron, an esteemed student of van Gogh, that the artist, "conceived and carried by a mother who was in deep mourning, was able to see the tomb of the one he was to replace every day from the time he was old enough to perceive." Dr. Mauron added, "The psychological importance of this detail is difficult to evaluate."

Vincent nowhere mentions his dead brother or his mother's reaction to the death. As an adult he probably had no conscious memories of her reaction and its consequences, yet the thoughts that preoccupied his mind—repetitiously expressed in his sermon, letters, and art—suggest that the first Vincent influenced the psychological development of the second, and that the latter's life was dominated by the idea that he was unloved and ignored by a mother who continued to grieve for her beloved dead son.

The grief that his mother suffered following the death may have persisted during the second Vincent's early years, for the transformation of mourning into a chronic state of melancholy is not rare among women whose children have died. This would make it difficult for her to satisfy the boy's needs for the warmth and intimacy that come from a happy mother's loving care. Sharing the brother's name, Vincent constantly reminded the mother of her loss. A dead child easily becomes an idealized child. The first Vincent did not live long enough to be bad, and a child who continued to live would inevitably fail in comparison. The mother's own guilt about the death would then be displaced to the next child: he became the guilty one. The depression the little boy suffered from this experience may have laid the foundation for the depressive, isolating tendencies he was to bear later in life.

His brother's example doubtless taught Vincent that being dead meant being loved and cherished, while being alive meant being rejected. Referring to another family with a similar tragedy, Erik Erikson has written, "For example, a mother whose firstborn son dies and who (because of complicated guilt feelings) has never been able to attach to her later surviving children the same amount of religious devotion that she bestows on the memory of her dead child, may well arouse in one of her sons the conviction that to be sick or to be dead is a better assurance of being 'recognized' than to be healthy and about'' (1956, p. 87). Such a pattern is in keeping with Vincent's preoccupation with the partial deaths of sickness and mutilation and with the anticipation and glorification of death. "It is better to go to the house of mourning," he preached at Richmond in 1876, "than to the house of feasts."

Vincent's deep misery seems to have been present from his earliest years. "My youth," he wrote, "was gloomy and cold and sterile...," and, as his sister Elizabeth noted, he was a stranger to his family. Although he sometimes fancied that his childhood was happy, second thoughts caused him to suspect that he only imagined it.

He had a theory about the origins of his chronic unhappiness, and he voiced it in a language that came easily to him—the pictorial language of nature: "The germinating seed must not be exposed to a frosty wind —that was the case with me in the beginning." He was saying, in effect, that during his earliest years he was deprived of those ingredients that comprise the mysterious entity called mother-love: the freely-given, cuddling, cooing, nourishing, protecting, reassuring behavior of a maternal figure. He was like a scraggy, stunted, deformed plant, constantly struggling for its life because it had been neglected by an unfriendly Mother Nature when it was beginning to root and grow.

Depression, to be sure, is a psychological reaction familiar to everyone. But the study of children and the psychoanalysis of adults indicate, as Vincent's explanation suggests, that extreme vulnerability to it may arise out of a defect in the nurture of the young child: the seed has been exposed to a frosty wind.

When the infant first opens his eyes, he cannot differentiate between himself and the people and things that surround him—a state that Freud called an "oceanic feeling." Gradually, the infant becomes aware that the most vital thing in his existence, his mother, is separate from himself. Then, one by one, he perceives the differences between himself and other people and objects around him. During the course of this learning experience, he builds a discrete mental image of himself. This image is composed in part of what he sees, feels, and hears about himself, in part of what others think about him, and in part by identifying himself with certain aspects of those close to him.

This process of self-differentiation is facilitated by a mutually close, trusting relationship between mother and child. The relationship may be deficient due to emotional distress in the mother, to her absence at crucial times, or to a stifling overprotectiveness. Anything that causes discomfort in the child, such as illness or feeding problems, may also impair the relationship. This impairment impedes the infant's development into a stable, integrated, self-respecting, self-sufficient human being. Instead he tends to feel inferior, unloved, lonely, hopeless, and hypersensitive to all kinds of stimuli. The mere possibility of unloving behavior from the outside world causes anxiety, and relatively mild displays of rejection cause depression, a predisposition that persists into adulthood.

In *Madame Roulin with Her Baby* (Figure 1), the tense, rigid baby is precariously positioned by a mother who holds him away from her body rather than cuddling him. This unhappy state of affairs is more a representation of his imagined relationship with his own mother than the actual situation between the affectionate Madame Roulin and her child. Being raised by a depressed mother who was unable to cuddle him securely may have given rise to a feeling of insecurity in space. Fears of heights associated with dizziness might impede the work of a landscape painter. But Vincent took adversity as a challenge, and—like depression—the symptom no doubt stimulated his creative functions. In what may have been an attempt to master this fear and attenuate the dizziness, he made pictures from high places, drew dizzying perspectives, and discovered for art the use of swirling line patterns. Instead of passively experiencing the symptom, he actively depicted it. Professor A. M. Hammacher expresses the belief that Vincent, who painted many pictures from windows, felt a strong need to use this safe enclosure because it made him dizzy to work in the open air (1962, p. 30). The window may have acted like a protective barrier on the edge of a dizzying cliff.

The oblique references recorded by Vincent and his sister Elizabeth are all that is known of his childhood relationship with his mother, but his relationship with her is better documented during the period of his published correspondence, from the age of nineteen until his death at thirty-seven. Of course, a grown man's relations with his mother do not openly reveal the childhood situation. Indeed, feelings and actions sometimes become reversed during the course of development. Still, they may supply valuable clues, especially when they form part of a larger pattern of behavior; for the compulsion to repeat earlier patterns, while it may be modified, is one of the deepest and most ineradicable processes in human nature—even if the pattern is detrimental to adult living.

One looks in vain through hundreds of Vincent's revealing letters to find a spontaneous, affectionate reference to his mother. The most flagrant breach in his wall of silence was a bitter outburst after his rejection by his widowed cousin Kee Vos-Stricker in 1881: he protested that his mother cut off every opportunity for him to discuss the unhappy situation with her; like his father, she did not understand him. Indeed, she took Kee's side rather than his own. He complained that "a man who wants to act cannot approve of the fact that his mother prays for his resignation." This was followed by a shotgun blast in her direction: "There really are no more unbelieving and hard-hearted and worldly people than clergymen and especially clergymen's wives."

Soon after he left the parsonage for The Hague in 1882, his resentment vanished. He rarely mentioned his mother; and when he did, a spirit of sadness and a willingness to share the blame permeated his thoughts. "[T]he disharmony between Father, Mother and me," he wrote, "has become a chronic evil because there has been misunderstanding and estrangement between us for too long"; as a result, he felt like a "half-strange, half-tiresome person."

When he left Holland and his mother in 1885, he protested that she had neglected him for a long time and complained that they had become "more estranged . . . than if they were strangers." Soon after, he interjected a poem that echoed these feelings, but added to them the opposing feelings of love:

> All evil has come from woman—Obscured by reason,
>   appetite for lucre, treachery...
> Golden cups in which the wine is mixed with lees,
> Every crime, every happy lie, every folly
> Comes from her. Yet adore her, as the gods
> Made her...and it is still the best thing they did.

When, a few months later, he described Xanthippe as "a woman of a soured love," he may have been describing the dangerous, untrustworthy nature of woman as he learned it from his mother.

Far away in France, he received a photograph of her; the confrontation stimulated him to paint two canvases. The words he chose to describe the first, based on a memory of the parsonage at Etten, indicate that Vincent saw his mother as depressed and angry: "[T]he deliberate choice of color, the *somber* violet *violently* blotched with the citron yellow of the dahlias, suggested Mother's personality to me" (italics added). The second, a portrait of his mother, was painted "ashen grey," as deadly a color as might be imagined. It brought to his mind a poem about a man's longing for a woman who, being cold and sad, cannot return his love. He included the poem in a letter to his sister Wil:

> Who is the maid my spirits seek
> Through cold reproof and slanders blight?
> . . . wan and sunken with midnight prayer
> Are the pale looks of her I love . . .

Mrs. van Gogh-Bonger, Theo's wife and Vincent's biographer, has pointed out that Theo's correspondence with the family was "preserved in full," but Vincent's was "unfortunately destroyed." Similarly, the way in which Vincent's mother dealt with his art reinforces the suspicion that his sense of rejection was not based simply on figments of his imagination. It appears that when Vincent quit Nuenen in November, 1885, he left almost all the drawings and paintings that remained to him in the Catholic sexton's house, where earlier he had rented a room in order to get away from his family. When his mother moved to Breda in May, 1886, they were brought there with the family furniture, packed in cases, and left with a carpenter. Upon hearing that "traces of woodworm" had been found in the packing cases, she developed a "fear of infection"; this "fear" gave her leave to abandon her son's work—estimated at "60 paintings on stretchers, 150 loose canvases, two portfolios with approximately 90 pen drawings, and some 100 or 200 crayon drawings." This large collection eventually fell into the hands of a junk dealer who destroyed some of them and sold others for pennies from a pushcart.

The Vicarage Garden in Winter is one of a group of drawings in which a solemn woman, garbed in black, stands in a garden facing a church steeple, a steeple that is set in the midst of a cemetery. Vincent annotated it *Mélancolie*. It shows a woman with a melancholic closeness to the earth who nevertheless is preoccupied with heaven, recalling the mother's grief for the dead son who is buried in the earth but is now in heaven.

Though Vincent does not mention it, *Peasant Burning Weeds*, a lithograph of 1883, was undoubtedly influenced by Millet's *The Angelus*, a painting that Vincent had copied three years earlier. Both *The Angelus* and the lithograph depict a man, a woman, and a wheelbarrow in a field. Considering that the lithograph is reversed from the original sketch from which it was printed, the three elements are in similar position in both works. But in *The Angelus*, the two people are standing; their heads are bowed in prayer; and the wheelbarrow is behind the woman. In Vincent's lithograph, the man is stooped over, tending the burning weeds; the woman is seated on the wheelbarrow, and her bowed head is supported by her hand. Another figure has been added to the lithograph—a youngster stands alone in the distance. The mood of thankful prayer in Millet's scene has been changed to one of quiet desperation. It is in keeping with Vincent's unconscious fixation: a woman is grieving for her dead son, ignoring the remote, isolated child. Like the first Vincent, the dead burnt weeds unite with the earth, but the fire and smoke arising from them carry their immortal spirits to heaven.

People who have been reared as replacements for a dead child tend, like Vincent, to be preoccupied with death, illness, and body-mutilating accidents. Like Vincent, they also have an inordinate interest in cemeteries (Cain and Cain, 1964). Cemeteries were the goal of many of his walks. He saw them not as receptacles for rotting bodies but as beautiful places where living things grow out of the ground. For example, his favorite walk in Amsterdam was to the Oosterbegraafplaats (East Cemetery), where he would pick snowdrops, "preferably from under the snow."

When Vincent returned home in 1877 because an old friend of the family was dying, he went directly to the cemetery: "It was very early [Sunday morning] when I arrived in the graveyard in Zundert: everything was so quiet. I went over all the dear old spots, and the little paths, and waited for the sunrise there. You know the story of the Resurrection—everything reminded me of it that morning in the quiet graveyard." Here, during the meditative hours of this early Sunday morning—under the sway of dawn, when the sun is reborn—he could become his brother, a reborn beloved Vincent.

Vincent depicted burial places even before he became an artist, and he continued to depict them in Nuenen, Paris, Arles, and Saintes-Maries-de-la-Mer. But these direct portrayals represent only a fragment of the fascination with burial places that he diverted into art. Using a variety of symbols, he elaborated the fantasies associated with his dead brother, both as a body buried in the earth and as a beloved child resurrected out of it. He drew, for example, many diggers, ditches, and objects (such as potatoes) that are buried and later retrieved from the earth. More significant to his work as a whole, this fascination evolved into a generalized artistic commitment to the earth.

His sketch of a Drenthe graveyard contrasts with the vibrant landscapes of the Provençal plains, such as *The Harvest*, yet the transition between them can be traced. The sketch is dark, small in scale, and melancholic. The landscapes are colorful, grand in scale, and often joyous. Both contain plots—burial plots in one and farm plots in the other. This similarity suggests that these van Gogh landscapes are derivatives of the graveyard. Vincent transformed a dark, unhappy scene based on dark, unhappy memories into bright, happy scenes.

VISUAL HUNGER

Visual activity was one of the devices that Vincent used to make his loneliness tolerable. Vision is a means by which an outsider can carry on a relationship with other people, even if at a distance and largely in fantasy.

People with strong depressive tendencies are especially prone to feel unloved and hated. They often have a highly developed perceptual sense, a built-in radar apparatus that detects dangers they fear will overcome them at any moment. Convinced that others wanted to hurt him, Vincent used his eyes to track movements in the ranks of the enemy. What was developed as a means of self-protection, however, ultimately became a means of understanding people that was useful in his work as an artist. As he wrote to his Dutch friend van Rappard, "You know that I am in the habit of observing very accurately the physical exteriors of people in order to get at their real mental makeup."

Many passages from Vincent's letters suggest that looking also represented a hungry devouring state. He had more pleasure nurturing himself through his eyes than through his mouth. His eating habits were ascetic, but he was ravenous in what he took in through his eyes. For example, he had "devoured" two chapters of a new book, adding, "Someone says instead of eating enough . . . I keep myself going on coffee and alcohol, and reading." He once remarked, "*How rich in beauty art is; if one can only remember what one has seen, one is never empty or truly lone-*

ly, never alone," and he heartily endorsed Delacroix's statement that "painting is a feast for the eyes."

I have suggested that the rejection that Vincent experienced with his mother was related to problems in feeding and cuddling: his mother did not actually abandon him; she was still there to be seen. As a result, a shift of interest from unsatisfied mouth-skin-body sensations to visual sensations may have occurred, as if the situation became frozen at the time before eating. He went on and on, gazing expectantly at his mother from a distance, anticipating being fed and held. But this gaze, because it was frustrated in its goal, became a hungry gaze. It is an old idea that such frustration leads to wish-fulfilling hallucinations. Such visual imagery, however, is ordinarily a precursor to the real goal and not the goal in itself. Out of frustration, Vincent made the imagery the goal, rather than the unobtainable final, intimate union with mother. In doing this he also denied the angry, devouring impulses he feared; it was his eye that was voracious, not his mouth.

Some clinical data suggest a connection between depression and ravenous use of the eye. The English pediatrician-psychoanalyst D. W. Winnicott observed visual states akin to Vincent's in depressed children (1944, pp. 85-90). The eyes of these unhappy children became fixed for long periods on near objects; later they became "slave drivers to their eyes" and developed a tremendous reading urge.

Vincent himself observed the child's pleasure in gazing—a baby, for instance, "looking for hours at the shuttle [of a loom] flying to and fro." He equated the warm rays of the morning sun with a mother's warmth: "[I] think I see something deeper, more infinite, and more eternal than an Ocean in the expression of the eyes of a little baby when he wakes in the morning and coos or laughs because he sees the sun shining in his cradle." This child, an extension of himself, is content and immortal because the mother-breast-face sun sends out its nourishing rays.

"[O]ld cab horses have large beautiful eyes," Vincent once wrote, "as heart-broken as Christians sometimes have." Round, large bulging eyes have long been empirically associated with a melancholic gaze, and Vincent drew many of them, such as those in *The Potato Eaters*. They beg, "Please don't hurt me. Please help me and love me." Like a hungry open mouth, they also ask to be fed.

In describing a portrait of his idol Millet, Vincent noted the "intense look of a painter—how beautiful it is—also that piercing gleam like in a cock's eye." Vincent, too, had "the intense look." During his bookselling days in Dordrecht in 1877, an acquaintance noted his "small, narrowed peering eyes," just as later on in Arles an observer said he was "continually stopping and peering at things." Gazing was the need Vincent could gratify most readily. When he was hospitalized in The Hague and forbidden to get out of bed, for instance, he could not stop breaking the rules in order to look at the "splendid" view from the window of the ward. He went to dances in Antwerp, not to dance but to look: "I still go often to those popular balls, to see the heads of the women and the heads of the sailors and soldiers. . . . [O]ne can amuse oneself a whole evening, at least I do, by watching these people enjoy themselves." And of the Provençal scenery he exclaimed, "I cannot tell you often enough, I am ravished, ravished by what I see."

During the periods in Provence when he was forced to stay indoors, he found he could draw upon his store of visual memories, much as one might look at home movies. This was especially helpful during winter when the weather would not let him work outside.

Fixing on paper or canvas what he gazed at was natural to Vincent: "It is splendid to look at something and admire it, to think about it and keep hold of it and then to say, I am going to draw it and work at it until I have it fixed on paper."

He also used the art of others as a substitute form of looking. When he was in England, long before he became an artist, he went every week to *The Graphic* and *The London News* to see the new issues. "The impressions I got on the spot," he recalled some 10 years later, "were so strong that notwithstanding all that has happened to me since, the drawings are clear in my mind." Painting was an extension of seeing: "I love to paint, to see people and things and everything that makes our life—artificial—if you like."

But even gazing gave rise to fear when there were insufficient barriers between him and people in whose presence he felt uncomfortable. His sister Elizabeth noted that as a child he kept his eyes half-closed when eating with his family. This childhood method of isolating himself seems to have been transformed into a technique that contributed to the development of his artistic style. He first mentioned it in 1883: "[N]ow that I let myself go a little, and look more through the eyelashes, . . . it leads me more directly to seeing things more like patches of color in mutual contrast."

Vincent readily saw actual surroundings as if they were paintings. A boat on the Rhone, for example, was "pure Hokusai" and figures on the beach were "like Cimabue." Being born in a country with a 400-year tradition that accepted art as an integral part of life and into a family that prized art seems likely to have encouraged such a disposition, and the dark, wet, flat Dutch countryside may have also contributed to it. Vincent equated this bleak environment with loneliness and depression, and it often provoked a melancholic state in him. Seeing it glorified through the eyes of a revered artist, however, transformed the scene into an aesthetic experience that alleviated boredom and depression. The fear that grew out of the very intensity of his gaze may have reinforced his perception of the world in this "as-if" way. Like keeping his eyes half-closed, seeing the object or person as a painting made it less real and less threatening.

UGLINESS AND BEAUTY

A strong sense of shame also played a key role in the development of Vincent's dependence on visual experience. While the feeling of shame is dependent on anatomical structures, its intensity depends upon the same factors that cause a child to develop a negative self-image, for they determine the ease with which these structures are used. Childhood situations that convince him of his own inferiority—whether physical or psychological, general or specific—lower his threshold for feeling shame. Shame is the emotion above all that relates to vision, for it is based on the feeling that one is seen as an inferior or despised person—ugly, dirty, repulsive, and helpless. To avoid being regarded in this way he wishes to disappear from sight.

The transformation of the visual core of shame, the pain of being looked at, into the awe of looking was especially important in Vincent's artistic development. Awe signifies a sense of being overwhelmed by the greatness and majesty of a person or object; feelings of reverence, wonder, or fear often accompany it. Shame and awe are related. Both are concerned with contrasts between superior and inferior and with vision, although in shame one is observed while in awe one is the observer. Vincent often described the intense awe that he felt in the presence of idealized figures and in the presence of nature, making explicit what one might surmise from his paintings. In the presence of an object of awe, he continued to feel small and inferior while the object of awe was felt as big and powerful, but he no longer experienced the shame of scorn and the terror of abandonment that would result from it.

In their place he felt a reverence, a oneness, and a ''consolation,'' as he put it, in the presence of a powerful image.

Awe, however, was not a completely satisfying substitute for shame. For he remained weak, inferior, and helpless in relation to the awesome object. Besides, the awe was sometimes accompanied by fear. The ability to see the object as a painting rather than the real thing was a further step in the transformation of shame. By visually containing the object within the bounds of a canvas and a frame, Vincent could then master the residue of shame and fear inherent in awe, transforming it into an aesthetic reaction. Now he could say, ''I have nothing to fear. It is not I but you who is small and helpless. But I do not take advantage of my power. Rather, I admire you and want to be your friend.''

One more step in this process remained for Vincent. The aesthetic reaction felt in looking made it easier to put the object on canvas and produce the same reaction in others. By becoming the painter rather than merely looking through the eyes of the painter, by the transformation from passivity to activity, further control was wrested from the object. He became the master, and the object was contained for eternity. By simplifying and modifying the picture, he became bigger in relationship to it, and the transformation was completed.

Compared with his father and Theo, whose features were refined, Vincent was not handsome. But without the melancholic conviction that he was unloved and therefore unlovable, he would not have been so certain he was ugly. Yet he instinctively knew the meaning of the aphorism in Robert Burton's *Anatomy of Melancholy*: ''Beauty alone is a sovereign remedy against fear, grief, and melancholic fits.'' It was in the struggle to relieve melancholy that he developed his concept of beauty.

The word *ugly* originally meant horrible, dreadful, or loathsome; a person who feels ugly feels repulsive, and, like Vincent, he will be cautious of making close ties. Part of Vincent's artistic task—as well as a remedy for ''melancholic fits''—was to transform the feeling of being ulgy and repulsive into a feeling of being beautiful and attractive. To accomplish this he used the masochistic device of glorifying this negative aspect of himself. Just as he was convinced that a show of suffering would bring him love, he was convinced that a show of ugliness would bring him admiration.

Michelangelo, small in stature and deformed of face, made monumental figures of classic beauty; Toulouse-Lautrec, partially immobilized by deformity, produced grace in motion. Vincent did it differently. While he was well aware of contemporary standards of beauty, he refused to be hog-tied by them. He admired the ugly, the poor, the aged, and the mutilated. And as soon as he began to draw, he drew them, doing it with a pathos that would stimulate compassion toward them and indirectly toward him. Michelangelo was encouraged in his direction by the classic aesthetic values of his Catholic Renaissance environment. Similarly, Vincent's masochistic glorification of ugliness was backed up by his Dutch artistic forebears; the self-portraits Rembrandt painted as he grew older, poorer, and uglier, for example, are commonly admired more than those painted when he was younger, wealthier, and handsomer.

Vincent once wrote, "I do not want the beauty to come from the material, but from within myself." Later in referring to the classic example of ugliness, Victor Hugo's Quasimodo, he thought of a saying: "In my soul I am beautiful." He saw Sien, "this ugly ???, faded woman," in the same light: "In my eyes she is beautiful." The Dutch word *schoon* means both clean and beautiful, illustrating the importance the Dutch place on cleanliness, but Vincent defied this idea, proving in his art that dirtiness can also be beautiful. He "saw drawings and pictures in the poorest huts, in the dirtiest corner. And my mind is drawn toward these things by an irresistible force." He liked to paint scenes "that people would pass by . . . even figure painters [would say] 'Oh, those dirty people.' "

Vincent's passionate desire to reconstruct himself and his relationships in his art made him seek new techniques and new figures with whom he could identify himself. It motivated him to assimilate and utilize the ideas of a broad spectrum of creative people in art and literature. But his inability to remain part of a closely-knit group, like his fear of intimacy in general, did not allow him to adhere to one school of art any more than to remain committed to one woman or one church; it also facilitated his fight against self-satisfied orthodoxies.

Vincent had no objection to being called an Impressionist, not so much because he felt he was one but because it gave him a free hand: "That is why I remain among the Impressionists, because it says nothing and pledges you to nothing, and as one of them I need not spell out my ideas." Here was a way of belonging to a group while not being bound to it.

The thick, deep brown paints that covered Vincent's earlier canvases were like the abundant Dutch mud that was not to be tracked inside the house or, to put it in the framework of an earlier period of his life, like feces that were not to be smeared willy-nilly on his surroundings. It would be a mistake, however, to imply that his molded forms and rough textures were motivated solely, or even mainly, by such defiant "anal" factors. More important, they were efforts to make contact with other people. Feeling repulsive, untouchable, rootless, and "dead," he tried to produce art that was touchable, solid, and alive. As he wished to be held, he wished the viewer to touch and hold this extension of himself, hoping in this roundabout way both to define himself and to make contact with others. He steered clear of visionary subjects that might precipitate latent feelings of unreality and depersonalization. His rejection of the customary practice of beginning the painting with the contour may have been based on similar fears. Perhaps the spaces within the contour lines reminded him of the emptiness that he felt inside himself, for he called such pictures "dead." Beginning the painting from the inside emphasized the life and substance of the portrayed object and, indirectly, of himself.

THE POTATO EATERS AND THE PIETÀ

Vincent's work in the North culminated in *The Potato Eaters* (Figure 2), a "composition of those peasants around a dish of potatoes." More study went into this painting than any other in his career. After a long series of preliminary studies of heads and hands, he made a rough sketch in March, 1885, a preliminary oil in April, and the definitive version in May. He had mastered the model and the scene so well that he painted this last version from memory; "[T]he thing is so fixed in my mind," he wrote, "that I can literally dream it." In contrast to Vincent's usual humility about his work, he had no qualms about praising *The Potato Eaters*. Looking back on his achievements more than two years later, he called it "the best one after all." When van Rappard criticized it, Vincent's resentment led to a rupture of their friendship. *The Potato Eaters* was the focus of all his energy, talent, and hope—a situation suggesting that it depicted a central issue in his life.

The painting was a sermon on the unjust treatment of the peasant by the Dutch ruling class and an ode to the peasant's endurance. But it was more. While the painting depicts a family group seated around a small table united by the rays of a single lamp above them, their closeness is

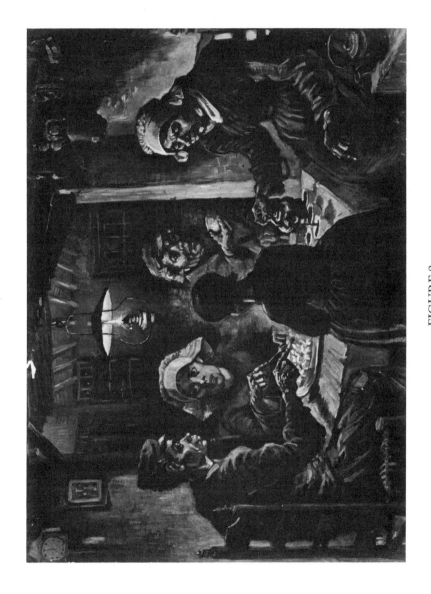

FIGURE 2
The Potato Eaters.

only physical. Emotionally, they are remote from each other, unable to communicate, lonely. Vincent identified himself with these coarse peasants, with their suffering and their isolation. Meyer Schapiro observes that "each figure retains a thought of its own and two of them seem to be on the brink of an unspoken loneliness" (1950, p. 40). This same sense of isolation is common to many of Vincent's Dutch works. A wall separates the woman on the right from the rest of the family—Professor Schapiro says that it "creates a strange partition of the inner space." I have suggested that Vincent often used such partitions to portray a feeling of isolation.

Such are a few of the messages conveyed by *The Potato Eaters*. But these same messages are contained in other van Gogh pictures; they do not account for the elaborate detail. Preliminary studies were sketched at the hut of the de Groot family, and the family posed for them. The painting itself, however, was done in his studio, using his memory and imagination. The sketches drawn directly from the models were "*food for one's imagination,*" he wrote, "but in the painting I give free scope to my own head." Such freely elaborated thinking, like the content of dreams, has roots both in the present and in the distant past, and is derived from conscious as well as unconscious thoughts. Vincent began his work on the painting immediately after his father's death. Perhaps the renewed confrontation with his mother's grief reactivated memories of the childhood situation.

If we look at *The Potato Eaters* from this point of view, the younger man on the left represents Vincent: the name "Vincent" is inscribed on the top slat of the back of his chair. The older woman on the right represents his mother. Her head is bowed, seemingly because she is intent on pouring coffee. But it is modeled from the melancholic heads that Vincent had been drawing in preparation for the painting. The act of pouring coffee diverts attention from her downcast expression; at a deeper level, melancholy accounts for her inability to show interest in those around her. The goggle-eyed "Vincent" gazes at her, vainly trying to make contact.

The enigmatic figure of a child in the foreground—faceless and ethereal—stands between Vincent and his mother. No chair is visible, and the child is a ghostly presence, not a flesh-and-blood human being. Curiously, steam arises from only one side of the plate, forming an aureole that envelops the child's head and shoulders. It would seem that Vincent was portraying the grieving mother who could not mother him; her spirit remained with the dead but perfect child who stood between them, separating them in the painting as in life.

It is interesting to compare *The Pietà* of 1889 (Figure 3) with *The Potato Eaters* of 1885. *The Pietà*, based on a painting of Delacroix, depicts the dead Christ lying in the entrance of a cave. His grieving mother stretches out her arms toward him in a "large gesture of despair"; because he has suffered and died, she shows him her love. The contrast between the two heads causes them "to seem like one somber-hued flower and one pale flower, arranged in such a way as to intensify the effect." Death and grief were on Vincent's mind at the time he painted *The Pietà*. He had just painted *The Reaper*, the one in yellow that he called "the image of death," and a self-portrait in which he pictured himself "thin and pale as a ghost." He was also concerned about his mother's grief, then occasioned by the loss of her last son, Cor, who had gone off to South Africa.

The red-headed, red-bearded dead Christ of *The Pietà* shares the same brilliant colors, the same pathos, the same shadow effects as the ghostly self-portrait. While the crucifix above Vincent's head only hints at his identification with Christ in *The Potato Eaters*, he has become Christ in *The Pietà*. Even as the somber hues of *The Potato Eaters* have been replaced by the brilliant blues and yellows, the downcast rejecting mother has been replaced by the adoring mother and the live rejected son has been replaced by the dead adored son. The haloed self-portrait painted shortly before *The Pietà* reveals that the red-headed Christ is also Vincent. Anticipating the death he is soon to bring upon himself, Vincent proclaims once again that it is better to be dead than alive, for death is the prerequisite for a state of perpetual bliss in which a good mother loves her adored child.

FROM DARKNESS TO LIGHT

With *The Potato Eaters* in May, 1885, the first half of Vincent's career came to a natural conclusion, and he was then free to seek new solutions to his life problems and new approaches to art. His chief psychological task between May and his departure from Nuenen six months later was to weaken his attachment to Holland and to find other attachments that would facilitate his move to a brighter, more friendly land.

Holland had become for him a dark, antagonistic place that was an extension of his antagonistic family. He still felt like an outsider in his

FIGURE 3

The Pietà.

own country and in its world of art—"banished because of my wooden shoes." He warded off feelings of neglect and loneliness, however, by convincing himself that he had no real need for these ostentatious hypocrites. "The real thing that makes one happy," he wrote, ". . . does not exist here."

His artistic task paralleled this psychological task. It was to find the technical means to express not only sorrow but other intense emotions, including the joy he was unable to experience in life. The dark tones of Dutch chiaroscuro could not do this. In July he announced that he had seen too much gray in his life: "Painting gray as a *system* is becoming intolerable and we shall certainly get to see the *other side of the coin.*"

He decided to go south, an idea that symbolized his search for light and joy and his intent to change from an art of dark tones to one of bright contrasts. One of his last Dutch paintings was a still life with a large dark Bible and a small, bright, yellow copy of Zola's *The Joy of Life*. The Bible is open to Isaiah LIII, in which the description of the Messiah resembles Vincent's own self-image: "One who grew up like a root out of dry ground . . . [who] had no beauty. . . . He was despised and rejected by men; a man of sorrows, acquainted with grief." This was the Vincent of the dark North. The Bible, his father's, suggests the suffering he associated with his rigid Calvinistic parents, their church, and their country. *The Joy of Life* suggests the acceptance he hoped to find in France. There in the bright light his sorrow would disappear and be transformed into joy. But the message is ambiguous, for the Bible also expresses his hope for a joyous future, and the title on the cover of Zola's book is an ironical one, as there is no joy at all inside it.

After leaving Holland, Vincent's moods continued to fluctuate. On May 29, 1888, he wrote from Arles that he suffered "from unaccountable but involuntary emotions or from dullness on some days." Two months later he said that he "hadn't advanced one inch in the heart of the people," that "many days pass without speaking a word to anyone, only to ask for dinner or coffee. . . . But up to now," he added, "the loneliness has not worried me much because I have found the brighter sun and its effect on nature so absorbing." In August and September his life was "disturbed and restless" and the isolation was "pretty serious." But, he explained to Emile Bernard, this was to be expected, for exile is the lot of the artist.

Although he complained bitterly of his isolation, Vincent did not lack companions in Arles, suggesting that his misery was provoked more by inner feelings of desolation and abandonment than by the actual circumstances of his life. Besides, Vincent added to his unhappiness and isolation by continuing to dress and behave in a way that excited the ridicule of the townspeople. The children, being franker than most, openly poked fun at him.

Joseph Roulin, a postal agent whom Vincent compared to Socrates, was probably his closest friend in Arles. Vincent was drawn to Roulin's big family, similar to his own in size. But whereas his own family, he felt, was unhappy and rejecting, the Roulins seemed the opposite. In becoming one of them, Vincent gained substitute parents, a substitute family, and a substitute childhood. He had a loving mother who did not neglect, criticize, and humiliate her child. He acquired new parents whom he did not fear, who did not intensify his guilt or shame him for his rough ways, and who paid attention to him in spite of their own tribulations.

Although he made very few paintings of his family, he made many of the Roulins. At the time of the ear incident, he was painting *The Cradle*, using Madame Roulin for his model. This was the first of five similar paintings of a mother rocking a cradle, the cradle being outside the painting. His envious identification with happy babies even affected the way he saw his subject: "I have just said to Gauguin about this picture that when he and I were talking about the fishermen of Iceland and of their mournful isolation . . . the idea came to me to paint a picture in such a way that sailors, who are at once children and martyrs . . . would feel the old sense of being rocked come over them and remember their own lullabies." He thought of himself as he thought of the fishermen. He too was the child and the martyr who lived in mournful isolation, wanted to be rocked and loved. In painting *The Cradle*, he identified himself with the beloved child who is rocked by the full-breasted mother.

HOMESICKNESS AND SUICIDE

Vincent went to the sanitarium in Saint-Rémy-de-Provence on May 8, 1889. Soon after, he expressed the wish to return to the colors he had used in the North. By September, however, the idea became more explicit: "I have a terrible desire coming over me to see my friends and to see the northern countryside again." In April, 1890, his homesickness was reflected in the group of paintings and drawings depicting thatch-roofed huts and peasants with wooden shoes that he called "memories of the North" and in a revised version of *The Potato Eaters* drawn in his new linear style. He wrote to his mother that he had some pictures that "remain just as if they were painted say in Zundert, or Calmpthout [another Brabant village]. . . . It would have been simpler if I had stayed quietly in North Brabant''; and he told Theo that his present studies were links ''with our distant memories of our youth in Holland.''

He continued these ''memories of the North'' after he moved to Auvers-sur-Oise in 1890. The first painting that Vincent described from there was a study of one of the few remaining thatch-roofed houses, and he persisted in painting these houses to the end. By recreating scenes that resembled his childhood environment, he was probably acting out frustrated wishes to return home. Two other buildings that he depicted in Auvers—the town hall and the church—may have been part of the same reconstruction, for their counterparts in Zundert played an important visual role during his childhood. *The Town Hall of Auvers* is remarkably similar to the view from the house in Zundert he had left about twenty-five years before, and *The Church at Auvers* no doubt reawakened memories of the church in Zundert where his father preached and the first Vincent was buried.

While Vincent did not link these two churches in his letters, he did note that the painting of the church in Auvers was intended to be ''nearly the same thing as the studies I did in Nuenen of the old [church] tower and the cemetery''—studies I have traced to the influence of the Zundert church and cemetery (see Lubin, 1972, chapter 5; 1975, chapter 5). The cemetery of the Nuenen studies, however, is not present in the Auvers rendition. Perhaps this is explained by the fact that the cemetery looks down on the rear of the church, the side depicted in the painting. This suggests that he was symbolically looking at the Zundert church from his envied brother's burial place. Soon, he was to commit suicide and have himself buried in the same cemetery.

The unconscious, according to psychoanalysts, conceives of death as the ''good sleep'' of a baby following a satisfying feeding or as a state of happiness in which the dead one is united with a good mother (Lewin, 1970, pp. 150-155). Martin Grotjahn writes, ''The unconscious may not know death but it knows peace and sleep and longs for reunion with mother'' (1960, pp. 147-155). This is the latent meaning behind much of Vincent's art, perhaps most obvious during the last year of his life when his brush strokes move ecstatically into the heavens. For it is in heaven where this happy union will occur. *Landscape with Olive Trees*, for instance, painted at about the same time as *The Reaper* and *The Pietà*, continues the theme of death and a mother's love: The cloud in the sky, toward which anguished trees are reaching, resembles ''a wraith-like mother and child'' (1950, p. 108), as Professor Schapiro put it. In a picture sketched just before Vincent killed himself, *Thatched Roof with Man on Top*, a man stands on a rooftop, and a breast-shaped cloud formation awaits him in the sky above.

In dying, Vincent hoped to rid himself of loneliness and depression by uniting in heaven with the loving mother he had never been able to find on earth. His suicide continued the search for togetherness he had carried on in his art.

28

Hermits and Recluses:
Healing Aspects of
Voluntary Withdrawal from Society

ILZA VEITH

In solis sis tibi turba locis.[1]
Montaigne, "On Solitude"

WHEN GRETA GARBO arrived in the United States in the early thirties, much of her immediate success was due not only to her unusual beauty or acting ability, but also to the mysterious reserve with which she surrounded herself. When pursued, and indeed besieged, by the press, she was quoted as having said, "I want to be alone." What she really said was, "I want to be *left* alone." But the belief in her expressed desire to be alone was in large part responsible for the creation of the Garbo mystique: a boundless admiration for a beautiful woman who had the inner resources to find contentment in her own company instead of the constant, fawning presence of reporters, journalists, and all the other camp followers of the famous and great.

It is odd and leads to speculation that Americans, usually so sociable and gregarious, exulting in cocktail parties and vast entertainments, were so intrigued by a Swedish woman who ran counter to many of the

---

An expanded version of this paper appeared in H. Riese, ed. (1978), *Historical Explorations in Medicine and Psychiatry.* New York: Springer.
[1]In solitude be your own crowd.

537

local customs, a woman who preferred long solitary walks in unfashionable flat-heeled shoes when others only took their walks on golf courses, in foursomes, pursuing golf balls. Garbo was not censured for her refusal to join the crowd, but was in fact admired for her social and emotional independence. Naturally, the admiration was enhanced by her uncommon beauty.

The phenomenon was, of course, more than the veneration of an extraordinarily beautiful and successful film star. It sprang from a faint and nostalgic memory of periods and personalities who made solitude a desirable state of contemplation and self-knowledge. Such personalities have existed since time immemorial—those who feel that they are closer to their gods when they withdraw temporarily or permanently from society, and either establish themselves as hermits in nature or join institutions devoted to the religious withdrawal from the affairs of the world.

But the American reaction to Greta Garbo's desire for absolute privacy and independent solitude also calls to mind an observation that few visitors to the United States fail to make: one of the most striking features of the American landscape for the newcomer crossing the continent, by train, plane, or even automobile, is the enormous isolation, the distance of human settlements from each other. This geographical isolation makes for a solitude that nowadays is the main distinguishing feature of American life in the country. Most Americans tend to feel uncomfortable in solitude and equate it with solitariness and rejection that deprive them of creativity. In a city or town, anyone who desires solitude has to pay for it by being called odd, a recluse, or perhaps only an eccentric. (And yet there is talk of "the need for privacy," and Americans revere the memory of Henry David Thoreau, whose contemplative moods took him to the solitude and beauty of Walden Pond; see Thoreau, this volume.)

Many Europeans, on the other hand, still consider it desirable to remove themselves from the densely populated cities, towns, even villages and territories of their relatively small countries, and consider solitude a luxury and a stimulus to creativity that could be attained only by the great landowners of the past.

The veneration of solitude so frequent in the Europe of the past centuries was, of course, a romanticization of religious beliefs and practices, and the philosophers of the Enlightenment who, like Rousseau in his *Rêveries d'un promeneur solitaire*, stressed—even if they did not feel it—

that a return to nature and removal from the defiling influence of fellowman would insure the intellectually and morally cleansing effect of the original simplicity of human society. Even Goethe, who was in fact quite dependent upon human interaction, indulged in reveries of the joys of solitude.

An important seeker of solitude in the past was the French essayist and philosopher Michel de Montaigne (1533-1592), whose incomparable *Essais* include "On Solitude" (1580) which reveals Montaigne's intricate knowledge of that state of being. He says that in solitude "our soul may return to itself; it may keep its own company; it is able to lead an attack, to defend itself; it is able to receive and to give; let us not be afraid to wither in this solitude of monotonous idleness." And then he exhorts his readers, "*In solis sis tibi turba locis*" (1580, p. 235).

Going back further, it is clear that the belief in the desirability of solitude has generally been derived from the religious hermits or holy men who, like Christ in the desert, felt closer to their god if their devotion was not deflected by the business of the world. Even the word *monastery* is derived from the Greek word *monastērion*, a community group of *monastēs*, or persons who live in solitude, from *monos*, alone. And even today a monastery is a "house of religious retirement," or of seclusion from the world for persons under religious vows, especially monks. In further pursuance of this philological interpretation, it is of interest to note that monasticism equals organized asceticism, which implies a state of self-imposed self-denial carried out toward the achievement of a higher ideal.

It is clear that in all the examples mentioned so far, mundane and sublime, solitude was chosen, and spiritual loneliness or isolation surely was not. Greta Garbo wanted to be left alone by the interfering exponents of what is now called "the media." Jean Jacques Rousseau enhanced his "image" by advocating a "return to nature." Religious hermits, monks, and ascetics chose solitude because they believed that it would bring them closer to their deity. A revival of most of the solitudinous strivings of the past may be found among the many modern youths, who seek their fulfillment in solitary campsites along mountain ranges, rivers, and lakes. Whether they are simply flirting with a mysticism of nature—going through the rituals of nature worship with a desire to impress the public—or have truly made nature their shrine, no one can really know.

A Dutch contemporary of Montaigne's, a prominent merchant,

vastly disturbed the burghers of Amsterdam when it appeared in print that he had given up his work "in order better to serve his God." This man, deeply affected by the death of his closest friend, moved to the country and lived there in absolute solitude. There he was criticized by his former colleagues, who tried all means to restore him to his role as a wealthy merchant in Amsterdam. This attack by his former colleagues expresses the hostility of the majority toward those who are different, especially the solitary ones, *die Einzelgänger*. The story of this hermit, like that of many others who deliberately chose the life of a religious recluse, is difficult to find in the monastic literature because the histories of such individuals, or even of groups of individuals who live in monasterylike communities or communes, are usually unrecorded and would scarcely be included in official church histories.

The distinguished German religious historian Professor Ernst Benz (1966) theorizes that the evolution of the hermitage as an institution was part of the history of occidental colonization, mainly because hermits prefer solitude to the organized church and state. Thus, large parts of Italy and Germany were colonized by hermits. Similarly, the history of the colonization of Siberia is a history of the hermits, who, as nonconformists, withdrew from the worldly established church and gradually pushed eastward and set up their domicil. Other similarly inclined religious men and even families followed the initial hermits, and thus by accretion villages came into being. When eventually the tax collectors and soldiers arrived, the hermits packed up and moved farther east.

The history of the principle of the hermitage has been neglected because the individual hermits were intent on withdrawing not only from their fellowman but also from the records of the church. Hermits, as a rule, do not leave any traces; they are not inclined to write autobiographies, nor do they leave any records as a bishop would. As far as source material is concerned, hermits can scarcely ever be traced. The true hermits are the ones about whom nothing whatsoever is known, who were unknown even while they lived, and who are now totally unremembered. Nevertheless, Güttenberger and Nigg compiled histories of the Christian hermit movement up to the late nineteenth century, and in fact the movement continues today.

Although it would seem logical to dissociate Protestantism from the hermit movement, Professor E. Benz's studies on the radical pietism of the eighteenth century uncovered traditions of a hermit-like movement in the Egyptian desert. In his work on the Protestant movement towards eremitism, Professor Benz was particularly struck by the realization that the movement includes the very man whom one would be least inclined to connect with the hermitic movement, Martin Luther. As Professor Benz shows, Martin Luther joined the sixteenth century continuation of the old-Christian hermit movement when he entered the hermitic branch of the Order of St. Augustine after his shattering encounter with the stroke of lightning in which the presence of God was revealed to him. Oddly enough, most students of Luther have so far assumed that he was a member of the regular Order of St. Augustine. In fact, he belonged to a separate branch, the Order of Augustinian Hermits, founded in the Middle Ages by communities of Italian hermits. Like Luther himself, the medieval founders of these hermitic sects reacted to the feudal aspects of the traditional Roman Catholic Church. Solitariness and the striving towards hermitical life was a distinguishing feature not only of most branches of Christianity but also of other religious movements that originated in the Near and the Far East.

The Coptic Church of Ethiopia put its monasteries on nearly inaccessible mountain tops which could be reached only by extraordinary feats of climbing cliffs. This mode of access reinforced one of the most important tenets of the Coptic Church, namely, the total restriction of the monastery to males. So abhorrent was the idea of female intrusion onto the monasterial mountain top that even animals hauled up by a rope for slaughtering had to be males. Similarly extreme in its quest for purity is the tradition of the Greek Orthodox monastery on top of Mount Athos, which is also inaccessible to females of any species.

Such purity may also be found in some Japanese Zen monasteries, although as a whole Buddhist monasteries do not insist on celibacy, and many permit monks to have wives and engage in a modicum of family life. This is in interesting contrast to Gautama Buddha, the founder of the Buddhist religion, who left his wife and worldly connections to seek solitude and safety from distractions. In Zen Buddhism, which teaches its adherents to cope with solitariness, there is no doubt that the state of being alone does not mean loneliness, which implies a somewhat negative quality, but means being able to cope with being solitary, which can be a highly distinctive and positive ability. It might mean being *primus inter pares,* first among equals, and might therefore account for the frequently reiterated statement of several of the presidents of the United States that the presidency is a "lonely office."

A similarly lonely office is that of a Zen monk. It is in the Zen monastery that men have been exposed to a healing isolation, a solitariness that was meant to, and often did, heal patients of incapacitating neuroses.

The form of Buddhism best known to the West under the Japanese name of *Zen* originated, like Buddhism itself, in India, where it was known in Sanskrit as *dhyāna.* When, somewhat later, it migrated eastward to China, it became known as *ch'an,* a character which is pronounced *Zen* in Japanese. The central element of Zen is the act of meditation, an act of deliberate solitariness that must stem from the devotee's feeling of self-sufficiency. Meditation in Zen is not only a means of achieving ultimate truth, it is an end in itself—it is truth in action.

While other Buddhist schools have relied mainly on certain texts of the scriptures, Zen forgoes literary bridges and transmits teaching "from mind to mind"—that is, from the master directly to his disciple without the intervention of rational argumentation or formulation in conceptual terms. Above all, *ch'an,* or *Zen,* is a religious discipline that requires complete submission to the will of the master, who alone can guide authoritatively and insure the correct transmission of the Truth. Zen teaches "becoming a Buddha just as you are," believing that "Buddha-nature" is inherent in all human beings and can be reached through meditative introspection. To attain Buddhahood, the great Zen masters advocated "absence of thought" in order to free the mind from the bonds of the external world. They also taught the need to ignore one's emotions. This is the significant element in Morita psychotherapy (described below by Kiefer, in chapter 23) that has evolved from the doctrine.

The two basic beliefs of Zen Buddhism pertain to the importance of nature and life in and with nature, and to the immersion of the individual in the family, the group, and the community. Deviance from these tenets is deemed an alienation from the religious and social ideals and also from mental health in general. This attitude especially prevails among the Zen adherents in Japan.

According to these beliefs, Zen monasteries constituted a focal point for the practice of such proper conduct. Life in the monastery counteracted alienation from nature and society. Probably it was for this reason that the Zen monks found on their hands not only the devout but also numerous mentally disturbed individuals who sought refuge. Psychotherapy is not a part of Zen doctrine nor were the monks conversant with, or eager to undertake, any form of therapy. To all comers, healthy or disturbed, they applied the same treatment: insistence upon strict conformity with the rules of Zen conduct.

As the results often were surprisingly favorable, Shōma Morita, a Japanese physician at Jikei University, conceived the idea of extracting the essential elements from Zen conduct and constructing from them a form of psychotherapy. Thus Morita therapy was born: an absolutely typical Japanese mode of dealing with neurotic patients that has few parallels in the Western world, inasmuch as it is openly derived from a specific religion. Its first major element is the combatting of the egocentricity that is the most striking symptom of the patient's neurosis. The second element of Morita therapy is the correction of the patient's alienation from nature, inasmuch as dependence on and love of nature characterize the Japanese in physical and emotional health.

It is remarkable, of course, that there can be a form of therapy that restores love of nature and abolishes egocentricity, and it stands to reason that both these major emotional adjustments can be achieved only with the iron discipline that is practiced in the Zen communities. To illustrate what I mean by "iron discipline," I wish to explain the basic tenets of Morita therapy. From my description it will be realized that this form of therapy is entirely impossible on an outpatient basis.

Regardless of the age or sex of the patient, Morita therapy follows a specific schedule, or ritual, on which recovery is said to depend. Upon his arrival at the hospital, the neurotic patient—overt psychotics are not accepted—must have complete bed rest for up to a week. During this time he is not permitted to associate with anyone else. He must not read or write, smoke, telephone, listen to the radio, or watch television. The patient is left alone with his illness until he and his illness become one—he has to accept his illness in complete solitude. This initial period of absolute isolation and immobility in bed is the most difficult phase of Morita therapy. Subsequently, the patient is gradually restored to the world. He is encouraged to work in the garden surrounding the hospital. This, however, is not the occupational therapy known in hospitals of the Western world; rather, it is intended to encourage the patient's emotional return to nature. Gradually, also, the patient is permitted renewed contact with other persons. Rather late, he also meets with the therapist, not in the intimate setting of the doctor's office, but on a walk through the garden, during a game of table tennis or a similar diversion. In short, there is no occasion, or encouragement, for the patient to bare his soul, because that would only serve to reinforce the egocentricity that is the essence of his neurosis. Furthermore, in a subsequent stage of therapy when the patient is given the task of keeping a diary, he is enjoined to refrain from recording anything that relates to his emotions or to his illness. The physician who checks the daily diary entries, somewhat in the manner of a severe teacher, applauds the patient if he is able gradually to free himself from the hypochondriacal self-importance that had held him in bonds. In fact, it is the physician's explicit task to induce the patient to become once more a part of the society from which he has been alienated. The patient must learn to associate with his fellow men without friction, and to perform his work as best he can, even up to the standards of healthy society. To be sure, the patient is never permitted in the course of his treatment to think of himself as an emotional invalid, or as different from the rest of the community.

There was, oddly enough, an American antecedent to the Morita method of healing by isolation, but it appears to have been wholly unrelated to any religious notions. It was conceived by the brilliant and versatile Philadelphia neurologist Dr. S. Weir Mitchell (1881, 1888).

Born in 1829, a descendant of a well-born Philadelphia family, S. Weir Mitchell began his medical education in his native city and completed it with a year of postgraduate studies in Paris. On his return to Philadelphia he gradually moved into neurology, which was then called neuropsychiatry. As a neurologist, Mitchell saw veterans of the Civil War, many of whom had sustained incapacitating nerve injuries. Mitchell's psychiatric practice was made up largely of men and women of his own social class who were unable to function in their appointed roles in life. As was to be expected in his day and age, the majority of Mitchell's psychiatric patients were women who suffered from an indefinite malaise that included constant fatigue, headaches, and backaches. Since, as a rule, this pattern of delicacy began in childhood or youth, the women patients usually had a close female relative, a mother or sister, who tended to the patient's every need and catered to her weaknesses and complaints.

Mitchell designed his own very different regimen for these patients. He saw "the self-sacrificing love and over-careful sympathy of a mother, a sister or some other devoted relative" as aggravating the condition. Like the Japanese Morita practitioners who considered malign egocentricity the prominent feature of the neurosis, Mitchell spoke of the neurotic woman patient as a sort of "vampire" who sucks the strength of the healthy people around her.

In order to break the vicious cycle Mitchell decided that it was essential to separate the patient from her overly solicitous relatives and to isolate her completely. Termed a "Rest-Cure"—not the pleasurable escape that neurotic patients sought so frequently—Mitchell's treatment brought about the isolation that forced the patients to draw upon their own emotional and physical resources. During this month of enforced rest when the patient was not permitted to read, write, or engage in any of the other usual time-consuming occupations, there was also the absence of any of the patient's accustomed attendants, but simply an unfamiliar though capable and professional nurse. Although there occasionally were patients who took a "morbid delight" in this enforced inactivity and isolation, most came to look forward to its gradual termination with pleasure. Towards the end of the period of complete inactivity and isolation, the patient went through a regimen of reconditioning by means of passive and active exercise. All this was accompanied by a light and nutritious diet. At the end of a month the patient began to receive actual psychotherapy, which was then called "moral treatment." It consisted of lengthy conversations with the physician and even of the patient's writing her life history and the circumstances that had preceded—and frequently caused—the neurosis.[2]

So far as the modern world is concerned, "voluntary withdrawal from society" has become somewhat less frequent in the West than in the days of eremitism and religious withdrawal into monastic institutions. It does, however, occur in response to the involuntary isolation—largely experienced by women—that is imposed by society on the victims of our social system, namely, widows, divorcées, invalids, and the aged. The fact that the last mentioned are generally referred to as the "elderly," or, euphemistically, the "golden age group," reveals the feeling of guilt of those who permit the imposition of isolation on such a large part of society. It is doubtless the result not only of far-reaching urbanization but also of the retrenchment of active religious expression, for in earlier centuries the tenets of Christianity demanded

---

[2]The use of artificially induced solitude in modern psychotherapy is well described by the Dutch psychiatrist, W. J. J. de Sauvage Nolting, and forms one of the many important chapters *("Arzt und Seelsorger")* in the Symposium on Loneliness held in 1966 by the *Stuttgarter Gemeinschaft*.

the succoring of the aged, the lonely, and, above all, the ill. Here it is important to contemplate that both Christ and Buddha washed the feet of lepers, the most isolated of all human beings, and thus by their mere contact restored those to society who had been removed from, and shunned by, their communities and even their families.

29

Loneliness and Solitude

PAUL TILLICH

I

"HE WAS THERE, ALONE" — so are we. Man is alone, because he is man!
In some way every creature is alone. In majestic isolation each star
travels through the darkness of endless space. Every tree grows according to its own law, fulfilling its unique possibilities. Animals live, fight,
and die for themselves, caught in the limits of their bodies. Certainly,
they appear as male and female, in families, in flocks. Some of them are
gregarious. But all of them are alone! Being alive means being in a
body—a body separated from all other bodies. And being separated
means being alone.

This is true of every creature, and it is true of man more than of any
other creature. He is not only alone; he also *knows* that he is alone.
Aware of what he is, he therefore asks the question of his aloneness. He
asks why he is alone and how he can overcome his being alone. He cannot stand it; but cannot escape it either. It is his destiny to be alone and
to be aware of it. Not even God can take away this destiny from him.

In the paradise story we read: "Then the Lord God said, It is not
good that man should be alone." And he creates the woman from the
body of Adam. An old myth is used, showing that originally there was
no bodily separation between man and woman. In the beginning they

were one; now they are longing to be one again. But, although they recognize each other as flesh from their own flesh, each remains alone. They look at each other, and, although longing for each other, they see their strangeness. In the story God himself makes them aware of this when he speaks to each of them separately, when he makes them responsible each for his own guilt, when he listens to their excuses and mutual accusations, when he pronounces a different curse over each of them and leaves them to the experience of shame in face of their nakedness. They are alone. The creation of the woman has not conquered the situation which God describes as not good for man. He remains alone, and the creation of the woman, although providing a helper for Adam, has only added to the one human being who is alone another human being who is equally alone, and out of them all the others, each of whom is also alone.

But is that really so? we ask. Did not God do better than that? Is our aloneness not largely removed in the encounter of the sexes? Certainly it is for hours of communion and moments of love. The ecstasy of love can absorb one's own self in its union with the other self. Separation seems to be overcome. But after such moments the isolation of self from self is more deeply felt than before, even to the point of repulsion. We have given too much of ourselves, and now we want to take it back. An expression of our desire to protect our aloneness is the feeling of shame. We are ashamed if our intimate self is opened, mentally as well as bodily. We try to cover our nakedness as Adam and Eve did after they had become conscious of themselves. Man and woman remain alone even in the most intimate union. They cannot penetrate each other's innermost center. If this were not so, they could not be helpers to each other; they could not have human community.

And this is the answer to the question of why God himself could not liberate man from his aloneness: It is man's greatness that he is centered within himself. He is separated from his world and able to look at it. Only because this is so can he know the world and love it and transform it. God, making him the ruler of the earth, has to separate him and put him into aloneness. Therefore, man can be spoken to by God and by man; therefore, man can ask questions, give answers, and make decisions. Therefore, he has the freedom for good and evil. Only he who has an impenetrable center in himself is free. Only he who is alone can claim to be a man. This is the greatness and this is the burden of man.

II

The wisdom of our language has sensed these two sides of man's being alone. It has created the word "loneliness" in order to emphasize the pain of being alone. And it has created the word "solitude" in order to emphasize the glory of being alone. In daily life these words are not always distinguished; but we should do so consistently, thus deepening the understanding of our human predicament.

In the Twenty-fifth Psalm we read: "Turn thou to me and be gracious; for I am lonely and afflicted." The psalmist feels the pain of loneliness. We do not know the character of *his* loneliness, but we know about the many facets our loneliness can have. We all have experienced some of them.

Most widespread is the feeling of loneliness when those who helped us to forget that we are alone leave us, be it by separation, be it by death. This refers not only to those who are nearest to us but also to the groups which gave us the feeling of communion—groups with which we worked, groups with which we had social contact, groups with which we had spiritual communication. For many people such loneliness has become a permanent state and a continuous source of melancholy feeling and profound unhappiness. The sighing of numberless lonely people all over the world and in our nearest neighborhood fills those ears which are opened by love.

And now let us turn to those among us who are surrounded by friends and neighbors, by co-workers and co-citizens, who live in a family group and have the communion of the sexes—all that the others do *not* have! And here we ask: Are they without the pain of loneliness? Is their aloneness covered up by the crowd within which they move? Perhaps this is our own situation, and we may be able to give an answer to this question. And this might be our answer: I never felt so lonely as in a particular hour when I was surrounded by people and suddenly realized my ultimate isolation. And I became silent; I retired into a corner and left the group in order to be alone with my loneliness. I wanted my external predicament to match my internal one. Do not minimize such an experience by saying that people often do not feel strong enough to obtain a significant place with a group and that their withdrawal is nothing but an expression of their weakness calling for counseling or psychiatric help. Such people certainly do exist in large numbers, and they need help. But I am speaking of the strong ones who have their place within the crowd and who nevertheless have this terrifying experience of ultimate loneliness. They are aware in a sudden breakthrough of man's real predicament. Do not minimize such an experience by saying that people often feel misunderstood in spite of their urgent desire to make themselves understandable and that this gives them the feeling of loneliness in the crowd. No one can deny that there are such people and, even more, that they are not altogether wrong; for who is really understood, even by himself? The mystery of a person cannot be dissolved into a neat description of his character. But those who feel always misunderstood confuse the mystery of every person with imaginary treasures they believe they possess within themselves, demanding of others that they recognize them. But the others do not, and so they feel lonely and withdraw. They also need help; but let us instead consider those people whose real treasures are great enough to find expression and who are understood and received but who nevertheless have the terrifying experience of ultimate loneliness. In such moments they break through the surface of their average life into the depth of man's predicament.

Many feel lonely because their love is rejected, although they try hard to love and to be loved. Often this loneliness is self-created. There are people who claim as their right what only can come to them as a gift. They withdraw into a self-chosen loneliness, taking revenge through bitterness and hostility upon those by whom they feel rejected, enjoying at the same time the pain of their loneliness. There are many such persons, and they greatly contribute to the growth of neurotic loneliness in our days. They, above all, need help; for they easily become the prey of a demonic force which keeps them completely secluded within themselves. There is also the genuine experience of rejected love. No claim was made, but hope was at work. And the hope was disappointed. A community of love came to an end or never came into existence. Such loneliness cuts the ties with our world; it becomes manifest that we are ultimately alone and that even love cannot take this burden from us. He who can stand the loneliness of disappointed love without bitterness has experienced the depths of man's predicament in a most radical and creative way.

There are two forms of loneliness which do not permit any cover or any escape: the loneliness of guilt and the loneliness of death. Nobody can take from us what we have done against our true being. We feel our hidden and open guilt as *ours,* and ours *alone.* We cannot make anybody else responsible for what has happened through us. We cannot run away from our guilt; we cannot honestly cover it up. We are alone with it; and it is this loneliness which permeates all other forms of loneliness, transforming them into experiences of judgment.

Above all, this is true of the loneliness in which we have to die. We remain alone in the anticipation of our death. No communication with others can remove this loneliness, as no presence of others in the actual hour of our dying can hide the fact that it is *our* death, and *our* death *alone,* that we die. In the hour of death we are cut off from the whole universe and everything in it. We are deprived of all things in the encounter in which we forgot our being alone. Who can stand this loneliness?

III

Loneliness can be conquered only by those who can bear solitude. We have a natural desire for solitude because we are men; we want to feel what we are, namely, alone, not as a matter of pain and horror but as a matter of joy and courage. There are many ways in which solitude can be sought and experienced. And every way is that of "religion"—if it is true what a philosopher has said, "Religion is what a man does with his solitariness."

One of these ways is the desire for the silence of nature. Here we can speak without voice to the trees and the clouds and the waves of the ocean. They answer without words in the rustling of the leaves and the moving of the clouds and the murmuring of the waves. This can be solitude. But only for a brief time. Then we realize that the voices of nature have no answer to the questions of our mind. Our solitude in nature easily becomes loneliness, and we return to the world of man.

Solitude can be found in the reading of a poem, the hearing of music, the seeing of a picture, the thinking of significant thoughts. We are alone, perhaps in the midst of multitudes, but we are not lonely. Solitude protects us like an armor, without isolating us. But life calls us back to its empty talk, its unavoidable demands, its daily routine, its loneliness and the cover it spreads over our loneliness.

There can be no doubt that this is not only a description of man's general predicament. It is also, and emphatically so, a description of our time. Today more than in preceding periods man is so lonely that he cannot bear solitude. So he tries to become a part of the crowd. And everything in our day supports him. It is a symptom of our disease that everything is done by teachers and parents and the managers of public communication to deprive us more and more of the external conditions for solitude, the simplest aids to privacy. Even our houses, instead of protecting the solitude of every member of the family or the group, are built in such a way that privacy is almost excluded. And the same holds true of the forms of communal life in school, college, office, and factory. A never ceasing pressure tries to kill even our desire for solitude.

But sometimes God pushes us out of the crowd into a solitude which we did not desire but which takes hold of us. As the prophet Jeremiah says: "I sit alone, because thy hand was upon me." God sometimes lays hands upon us. He wants us to ask the question of truth which may isolate us from most men and which can be asked only in solitude. He wants us to ask the question of justice which may bring us suffering and death and which can grow in us only in solitude. He wants us to break through the ordinary ways of man which may bring disrepute and hate upon us, a breakthrough which can happen only in solitude. He wants us to penetrate to the limits of our being, where the mystery of life appears, and it can appear only in the moments of solitude.

There are some among you who want to become creative in some realm of life. You cannot become and cannot remain creative without solitude. One hour in conscious solitude does more for your creativity than many hours of learning how to become creative.

What is it that happens when we are in solitude? Let us hear the few words of Mark about Jesus' solitude in the desert: "And he was in the wilderness forty days, tempted by Satan; and he was with the wild beasts, and the angels ministered to him." He is alone, facing earth and sky, the wild beasts around him and in him, he himself the battlefield of divine and demonic forces. This is what first of all happens in our solitude. We meet ourselves, not as ourselves, but as the battlefield of creation and destruction, of God and the demons. Solitude is not easy. Who can bear it? It is not easy even for Jesus. We read: "He went up into the hills to pray. When evening came, he was there alone." When evening comes, loneliness becomes more lonely. We feel this when a single day, or a period, or all the days of our life come to an end. Jesus went up to pray. Is this the way to transform loneliness into solitude and to stand solitude? We should not answer this question too easily. Most prayers have not such power. They make God into the partner of a conversation, useful in *preventing* the only true way to solitude. They go easily from the mouth of ministers or laymen. But they are not born out of a solitary encounter of God with man. This certainly is not the prayer for which Jesus went up to the hills. We had better remain silent and let our soul, which is always longing for solitude, sigh without words to God. And this all of us can do even in a crowded day and in a crowded room, even under most difficult external conditions; this can give us moments of solitude which nobody can take from us.

In the moments of solitude something is done to us. The center of our being, the inner self which is the ground of our aloneness, is elevated to the divine center and taken into it. Therein we can rest without losing ourselves.

And now we have reached the point where we can answer a question which you may have already asked: How can communion grow out of solitude? We have seen that we can never reach the innermost center of another being. We always are alone, each for himself. But we can reach it in a movement which rises first to God and then returns from him to the other self. In this way man's aloneness is not removed but taken into the community with that in which the centers of all beings are resting and so into a community with all of them. Even love is reborn in solitude, for only in solitude are those who are alone able to reach those from whom they are separated. Only the presence of the eternal can break through the walls which isolate the temporal from the temporal. In one hour of solitude we may be nearer to those we love than in many hours of communication. We take them with us to the hills of eternity.

And perhaps if we ask what the innermost nature of solitude is, we should answer: It is the presence of the eternal upon the crowded roads of the temporal. It is the experience of being alone but not lonely, in view of the eternal presence which shines through the face of the Christ and which includes everybody and everything from which we are separated. In the poverty of solitude all riches are present. Let us dare to have solitude: to face the eternal, to find others, to see ourselves. *Amen.*

30

Prospect: What Is Man?

MARTIN BUBER

IN TWO SIGNIFICANT MODERN ATTEMPTS we have seen that an individualistic anthropology, an anthropology which is substantially concerned only with the relation of the human person to himself, with the relation within this person between the spirit and its instincts, and so on, cannot lead to a knowledge of man's being. Kant's question *What is man?* whose history and effects I have discussed in the first part of this work, can never be answered on the basis of a consideration of the human person as such, but (so far as an answer is possible at all) only on the basis of a consideration of it in the wholeness of its essential relations to what is. Only the man who realizes in his whole life with his whole being the relations possible to him helps us to know man truly. And since, as we have seen, the depths of the question about man's being are revealed only to the man who has become solitary, the way to the answer lies through the man who overcomes his solitude without forfeiting its questioning power. This means that a *new* task in life is set to human thought here, a task that is new in its context of *life*. For it means that the man who wants to grasp what he himself is, salvages the tension of solitude and its burning problematic for a life with his world, a life that is renewed in spite of all, and out of this new situation proceeds with his thinking. Of course this presupposes the beginning of a new process of overcoming the solitude—despite all the vast difficulties—by reference to which that special task of thought can be perceived and expressed. It is obvious that at the present stage reached by mankind such a process cannot be effected by the spirit alone; but to a certain extent knowledge will also be able to further it. It is incumbent on us to clarify this in outline.

Criticism of the individualistic method starts usually from the standpoint of the collectivist tendency. But if individualism understands only a part of man, collectivism understands man only as a part: neither advances to the wholeness of man, to man as a whole. Individualism sees man only in relation to himself, but collectivism does not see *man* at all, it sees only "society." With the former man's face is distorted, with the latter it is masked.

Both views of life—modern individualism and modern collectivism—however different their causes may be, are essentially the conclusion or expression of the same human condition, only at different stages. This condition is characterized by the union of cosmic and social homelessness, dread of the universe and dread of life, resulting in an existential constitution of solitude such as has probably never existed before to the same extent. The human person feels himself to be a man exposed by nature—as an unwanted child is exposed—and at the same time a person isolated in the midst of the tumultuous human world. The first reaction of the spirit to the awareness of this new and uncanny position is modern individualism, the second is modern collectivism.

In individualism the human being ventures to affirm this position, to plunge it into an affirmative reflexion, a universal *amor fati;* he wants to build the citadel of a life-system in which the idea asserts that it wills reality as it is. Just because man is exposed by nature, he is an individual in this specially radical way in which no other being in the world is an individual; and he accepts his exposure because it means that he is an individual. In the same way he accepts his isolation as a person, for only a monad which is not bound to others can know and glorify itself as an individual to the utmost. To save himself from the despair with which his solitary state threatens him, man resorts to the expedient of glorifying it. Modern individualism has essentially an imaginary basis. It founders on this character, for imagination is not capable of actually conquering the given situation.

The second reaction, collectivism, essentially follows upon the foundering of the first. Here the human being tries to escape his destiny of solitude by becoming completely embedded in one of the massive modern group formations. The more massive, unbroken, and powerful in its achievements this is, the more the man is able to feel that he is saved from both forms of homelessness, the social and the cosmic. There is obviously no further reason for dread of life, since one needs only to fit oneself into the ''general will'' and let one's own responsibility for an existence which has become all too complicated be absorbed in collective responsibility, which proves itself able to meet all complications. Likewise, there is obviously no further reason for dread of the universe, since technicized nature—with which society as such manages well, or seems to—takes the place of the universe which has become uncanny and with which, so to speak, no further agreement can be reached. The collective pledges itself to provide total security. There is nothing imaginary here, a dense reality rules, and the ''general'' itself appears to have become real; but modern collectivism is essentially illusory. The person is joined to the reliably functioning ''whole,'' which embraces the masses of men; but it is not a joining of man to man. Man in a collective is not man with man. Here the person is not freed from his isolation, by communing with living beings, which thenceforth lives with him; the ''whole,'' with its claim on the wholeness of every man, aims logically and successfully at reducing, neutralizing, devaluating, and desecrating every bond with living beings. That tender surface of personal life which longs for contact with other life is progressively deadened or desensitized. Man's isolation is not overcome here, but overpowered and numbed. Knowledge of it is suppressed, but the actual condition of solitude has its insuperable effect in the depths, and rises secretly to a cruelty which will become manifest with the scattering of the illusion. Modern collectivism is the last barrier raised by man against a meeting with himself.

When imaginings and illusions are over, the possible and inevitable meeting of man with himself is able to take place only as the meeting of the individual with his fellow man—and this is how it must take place. Only when the individual knows the other in all his otherness as himself, as man, and from there breaks through to the other, has he broken through his solitude in a strict and transforming meeting.

It is obvious that such an event can only take place if the person is stirred up as a person. In individualism the person, in consequence of his merely imaginary mastery of his basic situation, is attacked by the ravages of the fictitious, however much he thinks, or strives to think, that he is asserting himself as a person in being. In collectivism the person surrenders himself when he renounces the directness of personal decision and responsibility. In both cases the person is incapable of breaking through to the other: there is genuine relation only between genuine persons.

In spite of all attempts at revival the time of individualism is over. Collectivism, on the other hand, is at the height of its development, although here and there appear single signs of slackening. Here the only way that is left is the rebellion of the person for the sake of setting free the relations with others. On the horizon I see moving up, with the slowness of all events of true human history, a great dissatisfaction which is unlike all previous dissatisfactions. Men will no longer rise in rebellion — as they have done till now — merely against the false realization of a great effort, the effort towards community, in the name of the genuine realization. Men will fight against the distortion for the pure form, the vision of the believing and hoping generations of mankind.

I am speaking of living actions; but it is vital knowledge alone which incites them. Its first step must beto smash the false alternative with which the thought of our epoch is shot through—that of "individualism or collectivism." Its first question must be about a genuine third alternative—by "genuine" being understood a point of view which cannot be reduced to one of the first two, and does not represent a mere compromise between them.

Life and thought are here placed in the same problematic situation. As life erroneously supposes that it has to choose between individualism and collectivism, so thought erroneously supposes that it has to choose between an individualistic anthropology and a collectivist sociology. The genuine third alternative, when it is found, will point the way here too.

The fundamental fact of human existence is neither the individual as such nor the aggregate as such. Each, considered by itself, is a mighty abstraction. The individual is a fact of existence in so far as he steps into a living relation with other individuals. The aggregate is a fact of existence in so far as it is built up of living units of relation. The fundamental fact of human existence is man with man. What is pecularily characteristic of the human world is above all that something takes place between one being and another the like of which can be found nowhere in nature. Language is only a sign and a means for it, all achievement of the spirit has been incited by it. Man is made man by it; but on its way it does not merely unfold, it also decays and withers away. It is rooted in one being turning to another as another, as this particular other being, in order to communicate with it in a sphere which is common to them but which reaches out beyond the special sphere of each. I call this sphere, which is established with the existence of man as man but which is conceptually still uncomprehended, the sphere of "between." Though being realized in very different degrees, it is a primal category of human reality. This is where the genuine third alternative must begin.

The view which establishes the concept of "between" is to be acquired by no longer localizing the relation between human beings, as is customary, either within individual souls or in a general world which embraces and determines them, but in actual fact *between* them.

"Between" is not an auxiliary construction, but the real place and bearer of what happens between men; it has received no specific attention because, in distinction from the individual soul and its context, it does not exhibit a smooth continuity, but is ever and again reconstituted in accordance with men's meetings with one another; hence what is experience has been annexed naturally to the continuous elements, the soul and its world.

In a real conversation (that is, not one whose individual parts have been preconcerted, but one which is completely spontaneous, in which each speaks directly to his partner and calls forth his unpredictable reply), a real lesson (that is, neither a routine repetition nor a lesson whose findings the teacher knows before he starts, but one which develops in mutual surprises), a real embrace and not one of mere habit, a real duel and not a mere game—in all these what is essential does not take place in each of the participants or in a neutral world which includes the two and all other things; but it takes place between them in the most precise sense, as it were in a dimension which is accessible only to them both. Something happens to me—that is a fact which can be exactly distributed between the world and the soul, between an "outer" event and an "inner" impression. But if I and another come up against one another, "happen" to one another (to use a forcible expression which can, however, scarcely be paraphrased), the sum does not exactly divide, there is a remainder, somewhere, where the souls end and the world has not yet begun, and this remainder is what is essential. This fact can be found even in the tiniest and most transient events which scarcely enter the consciousness. In the deadly crush of an air-raid shelter the glances of two strangers suddenly meet for a second in astonishing and unrelated mutuality; when the All Clear sounds it is forgotten; and yet it did happen, in a realm which existed only for that moment. In the darkened opera house there can be established between two of the audience, who do not know one another, and who are listening in the same purity and with the same intensity to the music of Mozart, a relation which is scarcely perceptible and yet is one of elemental dialogue, and which has long vanished when the lights blaze up again. In the understanding of such fleeting and yet consistent happenings one must guard against introducing motives of feeling: what happens here cannot be reached by psychological concepts, it is something ontic. From the least of events, such as these, which disappear in the moment of their appearance, to the pathos of pure indissoluble tragedy, where two men, opposed to one another in their very nature, entangled in the same living situation, reveal to one another in mute clarity an irreconcilable opposition of being, the dialogical situation can be adequately grasped only in an ontological way. But it is not to be grasped on the basis of the ontic of personal existence, or of that of two personal existences, but of that which has its being between them, and transcends both. In the most powerful moments of dialogic, where in truth "deep calls unto deep," it becomes unmistakably clear that it is not the wand of the individual or of the social, but of a third which draws the circle round the happening. On the far side of the subjective, on this side of the objective, on the narrow ridge, where *I* and *Thou* meet, there is the realm of "between."

This reality, whose disclosure has begun in our time, shows the way, leading beyond individualism and collectivism, for the life decision of future generations. Here the genuine third alternative is indicated, the knowledge of which will help to bring about the genuine person again and to establish genuine community.

This reality provides the starting point for the philosophical science of man; and from this point an advance may be made on the one hand to a transformed understanding of the person and on the other to a transformed understanding of community. The central subject of this science is neither the individual nor the collective but man with man. That essence of man which is special to him can be directly known only in a living relation. The gorilla, too, is an individual, a termitary, too, is a collective, but *I* and *Thou* exist only in our world, because man exists, and the *I*, moreover, exists only through the relation to the *Thou*. The philosophical science of man, which includes anthropology and sociology, must take as its starting point the consideration of this subject, "man with man." If you consider the individual by himself, then you see of man just as much as you see of the moon; only man with man provides a full image. If you consider the aggregate by itself, then you see of man just as much as we see of the Milky Way; only man with man is a completely outlined form. Consider man with man, and you see human life, dynamic, twofold, the giver and the receiver, he who does and he who endures, the attacking force and the defending force, the nature which investigates and the nature which supplies information, the request begged and granted—and always both together, completing one another in mutual contribution, together showing forth man. Now you can turn to the individual and you recognize him as man according to the possibility of relation which he shows; you can turn to the aggregate and you recognize it as man according to the fullness of relation which he shows. We may come nearer the answer to the question what man is when we come to see him as the eternal meeting of the One with the Other.

31

Solitude

HENRY DAVID THOREAU

THIS IS A DELICIOUS EVENING, when the whole body is one sense, and imbibes delight through every pore. I go and come with a strange liberty in Nature, a part of herself. As I walk along the stony shore of the pond in my shirt-sleeves, though it is cool as well as cloudy and windy, and I see nothing special to attract me, all the elements are unusually congenial to me. The bullfrogs trump to usher in the night, and the note of the whip-poor-will is borne on the rippling wind from over the water. Sympathy with the fluttering alder and poplar leaves almost takes away my breath; yet, like the lake, my serenity is rippled but not ruffled. These small waves raised by the evening wind are as remote from storm as the smooth reflecting surface. Though it is now dark, the wind still blows and roars in the wood, the waves still dash, and some creatures lull the rest with their notes. The repose is never complete. The wildest animals do not repose, but seek their prey now; the fox, and skunk, and rabbit, now roam the fields and woods without fear. They are Nature's watchmen—links which connect the days of animated life.

When I return to my house I find that visitors have been there and left their cards, either a bunch of flowers, or a wreath of evergreen, or a name in pencil on a yellow walnut leaf or a chip. They who come rarely to the woods take some little piece of the forest into their hands to play with by the way, which they leave, either intentionally or accidentally. One has peeled a willow wand, woven it into a ring, and dropped it on

Reprinted from *Walden and Other Writings of Henry David Thoreau*, ed. B. Atkinson, New York, Modern Library, 1937, 1950, pp. 117-126.

my table. I could always tell if visitors had called in my absence, either by the bended twigs or grass, or the print of their shoes, and generally of what sex or age or quality they were by some slight trace left, as a flower dropped, or a bunch of grass plucked and thrown away, even as far off as the railroad, half a mile distant, or by the lingering odor of a cigar or pipe. Nay, I was frequently notified of the passage of a traveler along the highway sixty rods off by the scent of his pipe.

There is commonly sufficient space about us. Our horizon is never quite at our elbows. The thick wood is not just at our door, nor the pond, but somewhat is always clearing, familiar and worn by us, appropriated and fenced in some way, and reclaimed from Nature. For what reason have I this vast range and circuit, some square miles of un-frequented forest, for my privacy, abandoned to me by men? My nearest neighbor is a mile distant, and no house is visible from any place but the hilltops within half a mile of my own. I have my horizon bounded by woods all to myself; a distant view of the railroad where it touches the pond on the one hand, and of the fence which skirts the woodland road on the other. But for the most part it is as solitary where I live as on the prairies. It is as much Asia or Africa as New England. I have, as it were, my own sun and moon and stars, and a little world all to myself. At night there was never a traveler passed my house, or knocked at my door, more than if I were the first or last man; unless it were in the spring, when at long intervals some came from the village to fish for pouts—they plainly fished much more in the Walden Pond of their own natures, and baited their hooks with darkness—but they soon retreated, usually with light baskets, and left "the world to darkness and to me," and the black kernel of the night was never profaned by any human neighborhood. I believe that men are generally still a little afraid of the dark, though the witches are all hung, and Christianity and candles have been introduced.

Yet I experienced sometimes that the most sweet and tender, the most innocent and encouraging society may be found in any natural object, even for the poor misanthrope and most melancholy man. There can be no very black melancholy to him who lives in the midst of nature and has his senses still. There was never yet such a storm but it was Aeolian music to a healthy and innocent ear. Nothing can rightly compel a simple and brave man to a vulgar sadness. While I enjoy the friendship of the seasons I trust that nothing can make life a burden to me. The gentle rain which waters my beans and keeps me in the house today is not drear and melancholy, but good for me too. Though it prevents my hoeing them, it is of far more worth than my hoeing. If it should continue so long as to cause the seeds to rot in the ground and destroy the potatoes in the low lands, it would still be good for the grass on the uplands, and, being good for the grass, it would be good for me. Sometimes, when I compare myself with other men, it seems as if I were more favored by the gods than they, beyond any deserts that I am conscious of; as if I had a warrant and surety at their hands which my fellows have not, and were especially guided and guarded. I do not flatter myself, but if it be possible they flatter me. I have never felt lonesome, or in the least oppressed by a sense of solitude, but once, and that was a few weeks after I came to the woods, when, for an hour, I doubted if the near neighborhood of man was not essential to a serene and healthy life. To be alone was something unpleasant. But I was at the same time conscious of a slight insanity in my mood, and seemed to foresee my recovery. In the midst of a gentle rain while these thoughts prevailed, I was suddenly sensible of such sweet and beneficent society in Nature, in the very pattering of the drops, and in every sound and sight around my house, an infinite and unaccountable friendliness all at once like an atmosphere sustaining me, as made the fancied advantages of human neighborhood insignificant, and I have never thought of them since. Every little pine needle expanded and swelled with sympathy and befriended me. I was so distinctly made aware of the presence of something kindred to me, even in scenes which we are accustomed to call wild and dreary, and also that the nearest of blood to me and humanest was not a person nor a villager, that I thought no place could ever be strange to me again.—

"Mourning untimely consumes the sad;
Few are their days in the land of the living,
Beautiful daughter of Toscar."

Some of my pleasantest hours were during the long rainstorms in the spring or fall, which confined me to the house for the afternoon as well as the forenoon, soothed by their ceaseless roar and pelting; when an early twilight ushered in a long evening in which many thoughts had time to take root and unfold themselves. In those driving northeast rains which tried the village houses so, when the maids stood ready with mop and pail in front entries to keep the deluge out, I sat behind my door in my little house, which was all entry, and thoroughly enjoyed its protection. In one heavy thunder-shower the lightning struck a large pitch pine across the pond, making a very conspicuous and perfectly regular spiral groove from top to bottom, an inch or more deep, and four or five inches wide, as you would groove a walking-stick. I passed it again the other day, and was struck with awe on looking up and beholding that mark, now more distinct than ever, where a terrific and resistless bolt came down out of the harmless sky eight years ago. Men frequently say to me, "I should think you would feel lonesome down there, and want to be nearer to folks, rainy and snowy days and nights especially." I am tempted to reply to such—This whole earth which we inhabit is but a point in space. How far apart, think you, dwell the two most distant inhabitants of yonder star, the breadth of whose disk cannot be appreciated by our instruments? Why should I feel lonely? Is not our planet in the Milky Way? This which you put seems to me not to be the most important question. What sort of space is that which separates a man from his fellows and makes him solitary? I have found that no exertion of the legs can bring two minds much nearer to one another. What do we want most to dwell near to? Not to many men surely, the depot, the post-office, the bar-room, the meeting-house, the school-house, the grocery, Beacon Hill, or the Five Points, where men most congregate, but to the perennial source of our life, whence in all our experience we have found that to issue, as the willow stands near the water and sends out its roots in that direction. This will vary with different natures, but this is the place where a wise man will dig his cellar. . . . I one evening overtook one of my townsmen, who has accumulated what is called "a handsome property"—though I never got a *fair* view of it—on the Walden road, driving a pair of cattle to market, who inquired of me how I could bring my mind to give up so many of the comforts of life. I answered that I was very sure I liked it passably well; I was not joking. And so I went home to my bed, and left him to pick his way through the darkness and the mud to Brighton—or Bright-town—which place he would reach some time in the morning.

Any prospect of awakening or coming to life to a dead man makes indifferent all times and places. The place where that may occur is always the same, and indescribably pleasant to all our senses. For the most part we allow only outlying and transient circumstances to make our occasions. They are, in fact, the cause of our distraction. Nearest to all things is that power which fashions their being. *Next* to us the grandest laws are continually being executed. *Next* to us is not the workman whom we have hired, with whom we love so well to talk, but the workman whose work we are.

"How vast and profound is the influence of the subtile powers of Heaven and of Earth!"

"We seek to perceive them, and we do not see them; we seek to hear them, and we do not hear them; identified with the substance of things, they cannot be separated from them."

"They cause that in all the universe men purify and sanctify their hearts, and clothe themselves in their holiday garments to offer sacrifices and oblations to their ancestors. It is an ocean of subtile intelligences. They are everywhere, above us, on our left, on our right; they environ us on all sides."

We are the subjects of an experiment which is not a little interesting to me. Can we not do without the society of our gossips a little while under these circumstances—have our own thoughts to cheer us? Confucius says truly, "Virtue does not remain as an abandoned orphan; it must of necessity have neighbors."

With thinking we may be beside ourselves in a sane sense. By a conscious effort of the mind we can stand aloof from actions and their consequences; and all things, good and bad, go by us like a torrent. We are not wholly involved in Nature. I may be either the driftwood in the stream, or Indra in the sky looking down on it. I *may* be affected by a theatrical exhibition; on the other hand, I *may not* be affected by an actual event which appears to concern me much more. I only know myself as a human entity; the scene, so to speak, of thoughts and affections; and am sensible of a certain doubleness by which I can stand as remote from myself as from another. However intense my experience, I am conscious of the presence and criticism of a part of me, which, as it were, is not a part of me, but a spectator, sharing no experience, but taking note of it, and that is no more I than it is you. When the play, it may be the tragedy, of life is over, the spectator goes his way. It was a kind of fiction, a work of the imagination only, so far as he was concerned. This doubleness may easily make us poor neighbors and friends sometimes.

I find it wholesome to be alone the greater part of the time. To be in company, even with the best, is soon wearisome and dissipating. I love to be alone. I never found the companion that was so companionable as solitude. We are for the most part more lonely when we go abroad among men than when we stay in our chambers. A man thinking or working is always alone, let him be where he will. Solitude is not measured by the miles of space that intervene between a man and his fellows. The really diligent student in one of the crowded hives of Cambridge College is as solitary as a dervis in the desert. The farmer can work alone in the field or the woods all day, hoeing or chopping, and not feel lonesome, because he is employed; but when he comes home at night he cannot sit down in a room alone, at the mercy of his thoughts, but must be where he can "see the folks," and recreate, and, as he thinks, remunerate himself for his day's solitude; and hence he wonders how the student can sit alone in the house all night and most of the day without ennui and "the blues"; but he does not realize that the student, though in the house, is still at work in *his* field, and chopping in *his* woods, as the farmer in his, and in turn seeks the same recreation and society that the latter does, though it may be a more condensed form of it.

Society is commonly too cheap. We meet at very short intervals, not having had time to acquire any new value for each other. We meet at meals three times a day, and give each other a new taste of that old musty cheese that we are. We have had to agree on a certain set of rules, called etiquette and politeness, to make this frequent meeting tolerable and that we need not come to open war. We meet at the post office, and at the sociable, and about the fireside every night; we live thick and are in each other's way, and stumble over one another, and I think that we thus lose some respect for one another. Certainly less frequency would suffice for all important and hearty communications. Consider the girls in a factory—never alone, hardly in their dreams. It would be better if there were but one inhabitant to a square mile, as where I live. The value of a man is not in his skin, that we should touch him.

I have heard of a man lost in the woods and dying of famine and exhaustion at the foot of a tree, whose loneliness was relieved by the grotesque visions with which, owing to bodily weakness, his diseased imagination surrounded him, and which he believed to be real. So also, owing to bodily and mental health and strength, we may be continually cheered by a like but more normal and natural society, and come to know that we are never alone.

I have a great deal of company in my house; especially in the morning, when nobody calls. Let me suggest a few comparisons, that some one may convey an idea of my situation. I am no more lonely than the loon in the pond that laughs so loud, or than Walden Pond itself. What company has that lonely lake, I pray? And yet it has not the blue devils, but the blue angels in it, in the azure tint of its waters. The sun is alone, except in thick weather, when there sometimes appear to be two, but one is a mock sun. God is alone—but the devil, he is far from being alone; he sees a great deal of company; he is legion. I am no more lonely than a single mullein or dandelion in a pasture, or a bean leaf, or sorrel, or a horse-fly, or a bumblebee. I am no more lonely than the Mill Brook, or a weathercock, or the north star, or the south wind, or an April shower, or a January thaw, or the first spider in a new house.

I have occasional visits in the long winter evenings, when the snow falls fast and the wind howls in the wood, from an old settler and original proprietor, who is reported to have dug Walden Pond, and stoned it, and fringed it with pine woods; who tells me stories of old time and of new eternity; and between us we manage to pass a cheerful evening with social mirth and pleasant views of things, even without apples or cider—a most wise and humorous friend, whom I love much, who keeps himself more secret than ever did Goffe or Whalley; and though he is thought to be dead, none can show where he is buried. An elderly dame, too, dwells in my neighborhood, invisible to most persons, in whose odorous herb garden I love to stroll sometimes, gathering simples and listening to her fables; for she has a genius of unequalled fertility, and her memory runs back farther than mythology, and she can tell me the original of every fable, and on what fact every one is founded, for the incidents occurred when she was young. A ruddy and lusty old dame, who delights in all weathers and seasons, and is likely to outlive all her children yet.

The indescribable innocence and beneficence of Nature—of sun and wind and rain, of summer and winter—such health, such cheer, they afford forever! and such sympathy have they ever with our race, that all Nature would be affected and the sun's brightness fade, and the winds would sigh humanely, and the clouds rain tears, and the woods shed their leaves and put on mourning in midsummer, if any man should ever for a just cause grieve. Shall I not have intelligence with the earth? Am I not partly leaves and vegetable mould myself?

What is the pill which will keep us well, serene, contented? Not my or thy great-grandfather's, but our great-grandmother Nature's universal, vegetable, botanic medicines, by which she has kept herself young always, outlived so many old Parrs in her day, and fed her health with their decaying fatness. For my panacea, instead of one of those quack vials of a mixture dipped from Acheron and the Dead Sea, which come out of those long shallow black-schooner looking wagons which we sometimes see made to carry bottles, let me have a draught of undiluted morning air. Morning air! If men will not drink of this at the fountain-head of the day, why, then, we must even bottle up some and sell it in the shops, for the benefit of those who have lost their subscription ticket to morning time in this world. But remember, it will keep quite till noonday even in the coolest cellar, but drive out the stopples long ere that and follow westward the steps of Aurora. I am no worshipper of Hygeia, who was the daughter of that old herb-doctor Aesculapius, and who is represented on monuments holding a serpent in one hand, and in the other a cup out of which the serpent sometimes drinks; but rather of Hebe, cup-bearer to Jupiter, who was the daughter of Juno and wild lettuce, and who had the power of restoring gods and men to the vigor of youth. She was probably the only thoroughly sound-conditioned, healthy, and robust young lady that ever walked the globe, and wherever she came it was spring.

References

Abraham, K. (1911), Notes on the psycho-analytical investigation and treatment of manic-depressive insanity and allied conditions. In: *Selected Papers on Psycho-Analysis*. New York: Basic Books, 1953.

———— (1924), Short study of development of the libido, viewed in light of mental disorders. In: *Selected Papers on Psycho-Analysis*. New York: Basic Books, 1953, pp. 418–501.

Albrecht, R. E. (1962), *Aging in a Changing Society*. Gainesville: University of Florida Press.

Ames, R. (1953), Protest and irony in Negro folk song. In: *Mother Wit from the Laughing Barrel*, ed. A. Dundes. Englewood Cliffs, N.J.: Prentice-Hall.

Ariès, P. (1962), *Centuries of Childhood*, trans. R. Baldick. New York: Knopf.

Arnold, M. (1965), *The Poems of Matthew Arnold*, ed. K. Allott. London: Longmans.

Asch, S. E. (1952), Effects of group pressure upon the modification and distortion of judgments. In: *Readings in Social Psychology*, ed. G. E. Swanson, T. M. Newcomb, & E. L. Hartley. New York: Holt.

Atchley, R. C. (1972), *The Social Forces in Later Life*. Belmont, Cal.: Wadsworth.

Audy, J. R. (1969), *Red Mites and Typhus*. London: Athlone.

Bally, G. (1964), Psychoanalysis and social change. *Amer. J. Psychoanal.*, 24:145–152.

Bart, P. B. (1969), Why women's status changes in middle age: The turns of the social ferris wheel. *Soc. Sympos.*, 1:1–18.

Becker, E. (1964), *The Revolution in Psychiatry: The New Understanding of Man*. Glencoe, Ill.: Free Press.

Becker, T. (1974), On latency. *The Psychoanalytic Study of the Child*, 29:3–11. New York: International Universities Press.

Bell, A. (1973), A drag queen's fantasy of a man's conception of women? *The Village Voice*, April 12, 1973, pp. 81–82.

Benedek, T. (1950), Climacterium: A development base. *Psychoanal. Quart.* 12:1–27.

Benedict, R. (1946), *The Chrysanthemum and the Sword: Patterns of Japanese Culture*. Boston: Houghton Mifflin.

Benz, E. (1966), *Evolution and Christian Hope: Man's Concept of the Future from*

569

the Early Fathers to Teilhard de Chardin, trans. H. Frank. Garden City, N.Y.: Doubleday.

Berger, E. M. (1952), The relation between expressed acceptance of self and expressed acceptance of others. *J. Abnorm. Soc. Psychol.,* 47:778–782.

―――― (1955), Relationships among acceptance of self, acceptance of others, and MMPI scores. *J. Counsel. Psychol.,* 2:279–284.

Berger, P. L. & Berger, B. (1975), *Sociology: A Biographical Approach.* New York: Basic Books.

Berne, E. (1964), *Games People Play: The Psychology of Human Relationships.* New York: Grove.

Bernicot, L. (1953), *The Voyage of the Anahita.* London: Rupert-Hart-Davis.

Bettelheim, B. (1969), *The Children of the Dream.* New York: Macmillan.

Bexton, W. H., Heron, W., & Scott, T. H. (1954), Effects of decreased variation in the sensory environment. *Canad. J. Psychol.,* 8:70–76.

Bibring, E. (1953), The mechanism of depression. In: *Affective Disorders: Psychoanalytic Contribution to Their Studies,* ed. P. Greenacre. New York: International Universities Press, pp. 13–48.

Billingsley, A. (1968), *Black Families in White America.* Englewood Cliffs, N.J.: Prentice-Hall.

Binswanger, L. (1942), *Grundformen und Erkenntnis Menschlichen Daseins.* Zurich: Niehans.

―――― (1957), *Schizophrenie.* Pfüllingen: Neske.

―――― (1963), *Being-in-the-World,* trans. & ed. J. Needleman. New York: Basic Books.

Blain, D. (1965), Novalescence. *Amer. J. Psychiatry,* 122:1–12.

Blau, Z. S. (1973), *Old Age in a Changing Society.* New York: New Viewpoints.

Blenkner, M. (1963), Social work and family relationships in later life with some thoughts on filial maturity. In: *Social Structure and the Family: Generational Relations,* ed. E. Shanas & G. F. Streib. Englewood Cliffs, N.J.: Prentice-Hall, pp.46–59.

Blum, R. H. et al. (1972), *Horatio Alger's Children: The Role of the Family in the Origin and Prevention of Drug Risk.* San Francisco: Jossey-Bass.

Blyth, R. H. (1949), *Haiku. Vol. 1: Eastern Culture.* Tokyo: Hokuseido.

Bohannan, P. (1970), The six stations of divorce. In: *Divorce and After,* ed. P. Bohannan. Garden City, N.Y.: Doubleday.

Bornstein, B. (1951), On latency. *The Psychoanalytic Study of the Child,* 6:279–285. New York: International Universities Press.

Botwinick, J. & Thompson, L. W. (1968), A research note on individual differences in reaction time in relation to age. *J. Genet. Psychol.,* 112:73–75.

Bowlby, J. (1960), Separation anxiety. *Internat. J. Psycho-Anal.,* 41:89–113.

_____ (1963), Pathological mourning and childhood mourning. *J. Amer. Psychoanal. Assn.,* 11:500–541.

_____ (1969), *Attachment and Loss. Vol. I: Attachment.* New York: Basic Books.

_____ (1973), *Attachment and Loss. Vol. II: Separation: Anxiety and Anger.* New York: Basic Books.

Bowman, C. C. (1955), Loneliness and social change. *Amer. J. Psychiatry,* 112:194–198.

Bradley, R. (1970), Measuring loneliness. *Dissert. Abst. Int.,* 30:3382.

Brown, M. (1974), Keeping marriage alive through middle age. In: *Growing Older,* ed. M. H. Huyck. Englewood Cliffs, N.J.: Prentice-Hall, pp. 95–101.

Brown, S. A. (1937), *Negro Poetry and Drama.* Washington, D.C.: Associates in Negro Folk Education Bronze Booklet No. 7, p. 18.

Bruch, H. (1957), *The Importance of Overweight.* New York: Norton.

Buber, M. (1947), *Dialogisches Leben: Gesammelte Philosophische und Pädagogische Schriften.* Zurich: Muller.

_____ (1952), *Eclipse of God.* New York: Harper & Row.

Burney, C. (1952), *Solitary Confinement.* New York: Coward-McCann.

Cain, A. C. & Cain, B. S. (1964), On replacing a child. *J. Amer. Acad. Child Psychiat.,* 3:443–456.

Calhoun, J. B. (1963a), *The Ecology and Sociology of the Norway Rat.* Bethesda, Md.: U.S. Department of Health, Education and Welfare.

_____ (1963b), The social use of space. In: *Physiological Mammalogy,* ed. W. V. Mayer & R. G. Van Gelder. New York: Academic Press, pp. 1–187.

_____ (1976), A scientific quest for a path to the future. *Populi.,* 3:19–28.

_____ (1977), Looking backward from the beautiful ones. In: *Discovery Processes in Biology — A Collection of Autobiographies,* ed. W. R. Klemm. New York: Krieger, pp. 26–65.

_____ (1978), Biological basis of the family. In: *Georgetown Family Symposium,* vol. 3. Washington, D.C.: Georgetown University Family Center, pp. 52–67.

_____ & Ahuga, D. R. (1979), Population and environment: An evolutionary perspective to development. In: *World Population and Development: Challenges and Prospects,* ed. P. M. Hauser. New York: Syracuse University Press.

_____ & Casby, J. U. (1958), *Calculation of Home Range and Density of Small Mammals.* Bethesda, Md.: U.S. Department of Health, Education and Welfare/Public Health Service Monograph No. 55.

Campbell, J. (1959), *The Masks of God: Primitive Mythology.* New York: Viking.

Carnegie, D. (1936), *How to Win Friends and Influence People.* New York: Simon & Schuster.

Carroll, J. B., ed. (1956), *Language, Thought and Reality: Selected Writings of*

B. L. Whorf. Cambridge: M.I.T. Press.

Carter, H. & Glick, P. C. (1970), *Marriage and Divorce: A Social and Economic Study.* Cambridge: Harvard University Press.

Caudill, W. (1962), Patterns of emotion in modern Japan. In: *Japanese Culture: Its Development and Characteristics,* ed. R. J. Smith & R. K. Beardsley. Chicago: Aldine, pp. 115–131.

Cervantes, M. (1613), Man of glass. In: *The Portable Cervantes,* trans. & ed. S. Putnam. New York: Viking, 1951, pp. 760–796.

Clark, R. W. (1976), *The Life of Bertrand Russell.* New York: Knopf.

Coleman, J. C. (1964), *Abnormal Psychology and Modern Life,* 3rd. ed. Glenview, Ill.: Scott, Foresman.

Coles, R. (1971), *The Middle Americans.* Boston: Little, Brown.

Comer, J. P. (1971), *Beyond Black and White.* New York: Time.

Courtauld, A. (1932), Living alone under polar conditions. *The Polar Record,* no. 4. Cambridge: Harvard University Press.

Cumming, E. & Henry, W. E. (1961), *Growing Old: The Process of Disengagement.* New York: Basic Books.

Czernik, A. & Steinmeyer, E. (1974), Experience of loneliness in normal and in neurotic subjects. *Archiv. Psychiat. Nervenkrank.,* 218:141–159.

Dante, A. (1308–1312), *The Inferno,* trans. J. Ciardi. New Brunswick, N.J.: Rutgers University Press, 1954.

—— (1308–1321), *The Divine Comedy of Dante Alighieri: The Carlyle Wiksteed Translation.* New York: A. S. Barnes, 1944.

Defoe, D. (1719), *Robinson Crusoe.* London: Oxford University Press, 1972.

Deutsch, H. (1945), *The Psychology of Women: A Psychoanalytic Interpretation,* vol. 2. New York: Grune & Stratton.

DeVos, G. (1964), *Role Narcissism and the Etiology of Japanese Suicide.* Mimeo, University of California, Berkeley.

Doi, T. (1962), Amae: A key concept for understanding Japanese personality structure. In: *Japanese Culture: Its Development and Characteristics,* ed. R. J. Smith & R. K. Beardsley. Chicago: Aldine, pp. 132-140.

—— (1973), *The Anatomy of Dependence,* trans. J. Bester. Tokyo, New York, San Francisco: Kodansha International.

Dole, S. H. (1970), *Habitable Planets for Man,* 2nd ed. New York: American Elsevier.

Douglass, F. (1855), *My Bondage and My Freedom.* New York: Miller, Orton & Mulligan.

Durkheim, E. (1893), *The Division of Labor in Society,* trans. G. Simpson. New York: Free Press.

—— (1897), *Suicide: A Study in Sociology,* trans. J. A. Spaulding & G. Simpson. Glencoe, Ill.: Free Press.

Ehrenwald, J. (1971), Mother-child symbiosis: Cradle of ESP. *Psychoanal. Rev.,* 58:455-466.

Eiseley, L. (1969), *The Unexpected Universe.* New York: Harcourt, Brace & World.

Eliot, T. S. (1952), *The Complete Poems and Plays, 1909-1950.* New York: Harcourt, Brace.

Ellam, P. & Mudie, C. (1953), *Sopranino.* New York: Norton.

Ellison, R. (1967), A very stern discipline. *Harper's Magazine,* 234:76-95.

—— (1952), *Invisible Man.* New York: New American Library.

Ellul, J. (1964), *The Technological Society,* trans. J. Wilkinson. New York: Knopf.

Erikson, E. H. (1950), *Childhood and Society,* rev. ed. New York: Norton 1963.

—— (1956), The problem of ego identity. *J. Amer. Psychoanal. Assn.,* 4:56-121.

—— (1959), Identity and the life cycle. *Psychol. Issues,* Monogr. 1. New York: International Universities Press.

—— (1963), Youth: Fidelity and diversity. In: *The Challenge of Youth,* ed. E. H. Erikson. New York: Anchor, pp. 1-29.

Farber, M. L. (1968), *Theory of Suicide.* New York: Funk & Wagnalls.

Ferreira, A. J. (1962), Loneliness and psychopathology. *Amer. J. Psychoanal.,* 22:201-207.

Forer, L. K. (1969), *Birth Order and Life Roles.* Springfield, Ill.: Thomas.

Frazier, E. F. (1966), *The Negro Church in America.* New York: Schocken.

French, T. (1952), *The Integration of Behavior. Vol. I: Basic Postulates.* Chicago: University of Chicago Press.

Freud, A. (1954), About losing and being lost. In: *Writings,* vol. 4. New York: International Universities Press, 1968, pp. 302-316.

Freud, S. (1916-1917), Introductory lectures on psycho-analysis (Part III). *Standard Edition,* 16. London: Hogarth Press, 1963.

—— (1917), Mourning and melancholia. *Standard Edition,* 14:239-260. London: Hogarth Press, 1961.

—— (1923), The ego and the id. *Standard Edition,* 19:3-66. London: Hogarth Press, 1961.

—— (1926), Inhibitions, symptoms and anxiety. *Standard Edition,* 20:77-175. London: Hogarth Press, 1959.

—— (1930), Civilization and its discontents. *Standard Edition,* 21:59-145. London: Hogarth Press, 1961.

Fromm, E. (1941), *Escape from Freedom.* New York: Farrar & Rinehart.

Fromm-Reichmann, F. (1959), Loneliness. *Psychiat.,* 22:1-15.

Ginsberg, A. (1956), *Howl and Other Poems.* San Francisco: City Lights.

Glick, I. O., Weiss, R. S., & Parkes, C. M. (1975), *The First Year of Bereavement.* New York: Wiley.

Glick, P. & Norton, A. (1977), Marrying, divorcing and living together in the U.S. today. *Popul. Ref. Bur.,* 32(5).

van Gogh, V. (1958), *The Complete Letters of Vincent van Gogh,* trans. J. van Gogh-Bonger & C. de Dood. Greenwich, Conn.: New York Graphic Society.

Gorer, G. (1948), *The American People: A Study in National Character,* rev. ed.

New York: Norton, 1964.

Gould, R. L. (1972), The phases of adult life: A study in developmental psychology. *Amer. J. Psychiat.*, 129:521-531.

Greenblatt, M. L. (1972), Two hearts in three-quarter time. *Psychiat. Ann.*, 2:6-11.

Grier, W. H. & Cobbs, P. M. (1968), *Black Rage*. New York: Basic Books.

Grotjahn, M. (1960), Ego identity and the fear of death and dying. *J. Hillside Hosp.*, 9:147-155.

Gruber, H. E., Terrell, G., & Wertheimer, M. (1962), *Contemporary Approaches to Creative Thinking*. New York: Atherton.

Hall, E. T. (1966), *The Hidden Dimension*. Garden City, N. Y.: Doubleday.

––––––– (1968), Proxemics. *Curr. Anthropol.*, 9:83-108.

Halmos, P. (1969), *Solitude and Privacy: A Study of Social Isolation, Its Causes and Therapy*. New York: Greenwood.

Hammacher, A. M. (1962), *Van Gogh's Life in his Drawings: Van Gogh's Relationship with Signac*. London: Marlborough Fine Art Ltd.

Hammer, M. (1972), A therapy for loneliness. *Voices*, 8:24-29.

Handlin, O. (1951), *The Uprooted*. New York: Grosset & Dunlap.

Harlow, H. F. & Harlow, M. (1966), Learning to love. *Amer. Sci.*, 54:244-272.

Harris, I. (1959), *Normal Children and Mothers*. Glencoe, Ill.: Free Press.

Havinghurst, R. J. et al. (1949), *Personal Adjustment in Old Age*. Chicago: Science Research Associates.

––––––– & Albrecht, R. (1953), *Older People*. New York: Longmans, Green.

Hayflick, L. (1975), Why grow old? *Stanford Mag.*, 3:36-43.

Hegel, G. W. (1793-1800), *Theologische Jugendschriften*. Tübingen: Mohr, 1907.

––––––– (1795), The positivity of the Christian religion. In: *On Christianity: Early Theological Writings*, trans. T. M. Knox. Gloucester, Mass: Smith, 1970.

––––––– (1807), *The Phenomenology of Mind*, 2nd ed., trans. J. B. Baillie. New York: Humanities Press, 1964.

––––––– (1837), *The Philosophy of History*, trans. J. Sibree. New York: Dover, 1956.

Heidegger, M. (1967), *Being and Time*, trans. J. Macquarrie & E. Robinson. Oxford: Blackwell.

Hendin, H. (1969), Black suicide. *Arch. Gen. Psychiat.*, 21:407-422.

Henry, J. (1973), *On Sham, Vulnerability and Other Forms of Self-Destruction*. New York: Random House.

Heron, W. (1957), The pathology of boredom. *Sci. Amer.*, 196:52-56.

––––––– Bexton, W. H., & Hebb, D. O. (1953), Cognitive effects of a decreased variation in the sensory environment. *Amer. Psychol.*, 8:366 (abstract).

Hesse, H. (1929), *Steppenwolf*, trans. B. Creighton. New York: Holt.

Hilgard, J. (1969), Depressive and psychotic states at anniversaries to sibling death in childhood. *Internat. Psychiat. Clin.*, 6:197-211.

Hirsch, G. (1941), Die Erziehungsprage der ekstatischen Jugend. *Z. Pädog. Psychol.*, 42:1-13.

Hobson, R. F. (1974), Loneliness. *J. Anal. Psychol.*, 19:71-89.

Hodgins, E. (1964), *Episode: Report on the Accident Inside My Skull.* New York: Atheneum.

Hoggart, R. (1957), *The Uses of Literacy.* Fairlawn, N.J.: Essential Books.

Homans, G. C. (1950), *The Human Group.* New York: Harcourt, Brace.

Hoshino, A. & Atsumi, R. (1960), The relationships between self-attitudes of children and the adjustment levels as rated by peer group members. *Jpn. Psychol. Res.*, 4:135-138.

Howard, J. (1975), *The Flesh-Colored Cage: The Impact of Man's Essential Aloneness on His Attitudes and Behavior.* New York: Hawthorn.

Howes, C. B. (1970), Job travel isn't glamorous for him — or her. *Today's Health*, 48:27-29, 83.

Hsu, F. L. K. (1961), American core value and national character. In: *Psychological Anthropology*, ed. F. L. K. Hsu. Homewood, Ill.: Dorsey, pp. 209-230.

Hughes, L. (1958), *The Langston Hughes Reader.* New York: Braziller.

——— (1967), *The Panther and the Lash: Poems of Our Times.* New York: Knopf.

Hunt, M. M. (1966), *The World of the Formerly Married.* New York: McGraw-Hill.

Hutchinson, J. (1975), What Alice said about John at tea. "This Week in Review." *The New York Times*, August 17, 1975, p. 15.

Huyck, M. H. (1974), *Growing Older.* Englewood Cliffs, N.J.: Prentice-Hall.

Hyppolite, J. (1946), *Genesis and Structure of Hegel's Phenomenology of Spirit*, trans. S. Cherniak & J. Heckman. Evanston, Ill.: Northwestern University Press, 1974.

Jacobson, E. (1957), Normal and pathological moods: Their nature and function. *The Psychoanalytic Study of the Child*, 12:73-113. New York: International Universities Press.

James, W. (1902), *The Varieties of Religious Experience.* New York: Modern Library, 1929.

——— (1925), *The Philosophy of William James.* New York: Modern Library.

Jantsch, E. (1975), *Design for Evolution.* New York: Braziller.

Jarvik, L. F. (1975), Thoughts on the psychobiology of aging. *Amer. Psychol.*, 30:576-583.

Jaspers, K. (1965), *Nietzsche: An Introduction to the Understanding of His Philosophical Activity*, trans. C. F. Wallraff & F. J. Schmitz. Tucson, Ariz.: University of Arizona Press.

Johnson, J. W. (1927), *God's Trombones.* New York: Viking, 1969.

Johnson, T. B., Jr. (1969), *An Examination of Some Relationships Between Anomia and Selected Personality and Sociological Correlates in a Sample of High School Dropouts.* Unpublished Doctoral Dissertation, University of California, Berkeley.

Josephson, E. & Josephson, M. (1962), *Man Alone: Alienation in Modern Society*. New York: Dell.

Jung, C. G. (1933), *Modern Man in Search of a Soul*, trans. W. S. Dell & C. F. Baynes. London: Paul, Trench, Trubner.

———— (1951), Aion: Researches into the Phenomenology of the Self. *Collected Works*, vol. 9. Princeton: Princeton University Press, 1968.

Kahler, E. (1957), *The Tower and the Abyss*. New York: Braziller.

Kalish, R. A. (1975), *Late Adulthood: Perspectives on Human Development*. Monterey, Cal.: Brooks/Cole.

Kaplan, S., rep. (1957), Panel on the latency period. *J. Amer. Psychoanal. Assn.*, 5:525-538.

Kastenbaum, R. J. (1973), Loving, dying, and other gerontologic addenda. In: *The Psychology of Adult Development and Aging*, ed. C. Eisdorfer & M. P. Lawton. Washington, D.C.: American Psychological Association.

Kaufmann, W., ed. (1958), *Existentialism from Dostoevsky to Sartre*. New York: Meridian.

Kelly, J. B. & Wallerstein, J. S. (1976), The effects of parental divorce: Experiences of the child in early latency. *Amer. J. Orthopsychiat.*, 46:20-32.

Kiefer, C. W. (1968), *Personality and Social Change in a Japanese "Danchi."* Unpublished Doctoral Dissertation, University of California, Berkeley.

———— (1976), The *danchi-zoku* and the evolution of metropolitan mind. In: *Japan, The Paradox of Progress*, ed. L. Austin. New Haven: Yale University Press, pp. 279-300.

Kierkegaard, S. (1843), *Fear and Trembling*. Garden City, N.Y.: Doubleday, 1954.

———— (1844), *The Concept of Dread*, trans. W. Lowrie. Princeton: Princeton University Press, 1944.

———— (1849), *The Sickness Unto Death*, trans. W. Lowrie. Princeton: Princeton University Press, 1945.

King, M. L. (1963), Letter from a Birmingham jail. *The Christian Century*, 80:767-773.

Knowles, L. & Prewitt, K., eds. (1969), *Institutional Racism in America*. Englewood Cliffs, N.J.: Prentice-Hall.

Kohlberg, L. (1964), Development of moral character and moral ideology. In: *Review of Child Development Research*, vol. 1, ed. M. L. Hoffman & L. W. Hoffman. New York: Russell Sage Foundation, pp. 383-433.

Kohut, H. (1971), *The Analysis of the Self: A Systematic Approach to the Psychoanalytic Treatment of Narcissistic Personality Disorders*. New York: International Universities Press.

Krantzler, M. (1973), *Creative Divorce*. New York: M. Evans.

Kuhn, M. H. & McPartland, T. S. (1954), An empirical investigation of self-attitudes. *Amer. Soc. Rev.*, 19:68-76.

Lanham, B. B. (1956), Aspects of child care in Japan: Preliminary report. In: *Personal Character and Cultural Milieu*, ed. D. G. Haring. Syracuse:

Syracuse University Press, pp. 565-583.

Lawrence, D. H. (1964), *The Complete Poetical Works*. New York: Viking.

Leary, T. (1957), *Interpersonal Diagnosis of Personality: A Functional Theory and Methodology for Personality Evaluation*. New York: Ronald.

Leiderman, P. H. (1969), Loneliness: A psychodynamic interpretation. *Internat. Psychiat. Clin.*, 6:155-174.

Levinson, B. M. (1966), Subcultural studies of homeless men. *Transac. N.Y. Acad. Sci. II*, 29:165-182.

Levinson, D. J. et al. (1974), The psychosocial development of men in early adulthood and the mid-life transition. In: *Life History Research in Psychopathology*, vol. 3, ed. D. F. Ricks, A. Thomas, & M. Roff. Minneapolis: University of Minnesota Press, pp. 243-258.

Lewin, B. D. (1970), *The Psychoanalysis of Elation*. New York: Norton.

Lifton, R. J. (1965), Youth and history: Individual change in postwar Japan. In: *The Challenge of Youth*, ed. E. Erikson. Garden City, N.Y.: Doubleday, pp. 260–290.

———— (1967), *Death in Life: Survivors of Hiroshima*. New York: Random House.

Lilly, J. C. (1956), Mental effects of reduction of ordinary levels of physical stimuli on intact, healthy persons. *Psychiat. Res. Rep.*, 5:1-9.

Lindemann, E. (1944), Symptomatology and management of acute grief. *Amer. J. Psychiat.*, 101:141-148.

Lindner, R. (1955), *The Fifty-Minute Hour: A Collection of True Psychoanalytic Tales*. New York: Rinehart.

Locke, A. (1936), *The Negro and His Music*. Washington, D.C.: Bronze Booklet No. 2, Associates in Negro Education.

Loewenberg, J., ed. (1957), *Hegel Selections*. New York: Scribner's.

———— (1965), *Hegel's Phenomenology: Dialogues on the Life of the Mind*. LaSalle, Ill.: Open Court.

Lopata, H. Z. (1969), Loneliness: Forms and components. *Soc. Prob.*, 17:248-262.

———— (1971), *Occupation: Housewife*. New York: Oxford University Press.

———— (1973a), *Widowhood in an American City*. Cambridge, Mass.: Schenkman.

———— (1973b), The effect of schooling on social contacts of urban women. *Amer. J. Soc.*, 79:604-619.

———— (1975a), Couple companionate relationships in marriage and widowhood. In: *Old Family/New Family*, ed. N. Glazer-Malbin. New York: D. Van Nostrand, pp. 119-149.

———— (1975b), Grief, the sanctification process and support systems involving widows. Unpublished paper presented at Duke University, January 1974.

Lovell, J., Jr. (1953), The social implications of the Negro spirituals. In: *Mother Wit from the Laughing Barrel*, ed. A. Dundes. Englewood Cliffs, N.J.: Prentice-Hall, pp. 452-464.

Lowe, C. M. & Damankos, F. J. (1965), The measurement of anomie in a psychiatric population. *Newsl. Res. Psychol.*, 7:19-21.

_____ & _____ (1968), Psychological and sociological dimensions of anomie in a psychiatric population. *J. Soc. Psychol.*, 74:65-74.

Lowenthal, M. F. (1964), Social isolation and mental illness in old age. *Amer. Soc. Rev.*, 29:54-70.

_____, Thurnher, M., & Chiriboga, D. (1975), *Four Stages of Life*. San Francisco: Jossey-Bass.

Lubin, A. J. (1972), *Stranger on the Earth: A Psychological Biography of Vincent van Gogh*. New York: Holt, Rinehart and Winston.

_____ (1975), *Stranger on the Earth: The Life of Vincent van Gogh*. St. Albans, Herts, England: Paladin.

Ludwig, A. M. (1972), Psychedelic effects produced by sensory overload. *Amer. J. Psychiat.*, 128:1294-1297.

Lynch, J. J. (1977), *The Broken Heart: The Medical Consequences of Loneliness*. New York: Basic Books.

MacIver, R. M. (1960), *Life: Its Dimensions and Its Bounds*. New York: Harper.

Mahler, M. S. & LaPerriere, K. (1965), Mother-child interaction during separation-individuation. *Psychoanal. Quart.*, 34:483-499.

Marmor, J. (1958), The psychodynamics of realistic worry. In: *Psychoanalysis and the Social Sciences*, vol. 5. New York: International Universities Press, pp. 155-263.

Marris, P. (1958), *Widows and Their Families*. London: Routledge & Kegan Paul.

Maslow, A. H. (1962), *Toward a Psychology of Being*. New York: Nostrand.

May, R. (1953), *Man's Search for Himself*. New York: Norton.

McClosky, H. & Schaar, J. (1965), Psychological dimensions of anomy. *Amer. Soc. Rev.*, 30:14-40.

Mead, M. (1959), *Four Families*. National Film Board of Canada. Film distributed by McGraw-Hill, New York.

Menninger, K. (1930), *The Human Mind*. New York: Knopf.

_____ (1959), *A Psychiatrist's World*. New York: Viking.

Merleau-Ponty, M. (1962), *Phenomenology of Perception*, trans. C. Smith. London: Routledge & Kegan Paul.

_____ (1964), *Signs*, trans. R. C. McCleary. Evanston, Ill.: Northwestern University Press.

Merton, R. K. (1938), Social structure and anomie. *Amer. Soc. Rev.*, 3:672-682.

_____ (1957), *Social Theory and Social Structure*. Glencoe, Ill.: Free Press.

_____ (1964), Anomie, anomia, and social interaction: Contexts of deviant behavior. In: *Anomie and Deviant Behavior: A Discussion and Critique*, ed. M. B. Clinard. Glencoe, Ill.: Free Press.

Mijuskovic, B. (1971a), Descartes' bridge to the external world. *Studi Internazionali de Filosofia*, Autumn: 65-81.

_____ (1971b), Hume and Shaftesbury on the self. *Philosoph. Quart.* (St. Andrews), 21:324-336.

_____ (1973), Spinoza's ontological proof. *Sophia*, 12:17-24.

_____ (1974), Personal identity in the 17th and 18th centuries. In: *The Achilles of Rationalist Arguments*. The Hague: Nijhoff, pp. 93-118.

_____ (1975a), Locke and Leibniz on personal identity. *Southern J. Philos.*, 23:205-214.

_____ (1975b), The simplicity argument and absolute morality. *J. Thought*, 20:292-305.

_____ (1976a), Camus and the problem of evil. *Sophia*, 15:11-19.

_____ (1976b), The simplicity argument *versus* a materialist theory of mind. *Philos. Today*, 20:292-305.

_____ (1978), The simplicity argument and the freedom of consciousness. *Ideal. Stud.*, 8:62-74.

Millay, E. St. V. (1956), *Collected Poems*, ed. N. Millay. New York: Harper & Row.

Mitchell, L. S. (1953), *Two Lives: The Story of Wesley Clair Mitchell and Myself*. New York: Simon & Schuster.

Mitchell, S. W. (1881), *Lectures on the Diseases of the Nervous System, Especially in Women*. Philadelphia: Lea.

_____ (1888), *Doctor and Patient*. Philadelphia: Lippincott.

Montaigne, M. E. (1580), On solitude. In: *Les Essais*. Paris: Edition de la Pléiade, 1962.

Moore, J. A. (1972), *Loneliness: Personality, Self Discrepancy and Demographic Variables*. Unpublished Doctoral Dissertation, York University.

_____ & Sermat, V. (1974), Relationship between self-actualization and self-reported loneliness. *Can. Counsel.*, 8(3):194-196.

Morioka, K. (1968), Life history and social participation of families in danchi, public housing project in a suburb of Tokyo. *ICU J. Soc. Sci.*, 7:92-158.

Morsbach, H. (1972), *Aspects of Non-Verbal Communication in Japan*. Mimeo, Department of Psychology, University of Glasgow.

Mosse, E. P. (1957), *The Conquest of Loneliness*. New York: Random House.

Moustakas, C. E. (1961), *Loneliness*. Englewood Cliffs, N.J.: Prentice-Hall.

_____ (1972), *Loneliness and Love*. Englewood Cliffs, N.J.: Prentice-Hall.

Nemiah, J. C. & Sifneos, P. E. (1970), Affect and fantasy in patients with psychosomatic disorders. In: *Modern Trends in Psychosomatic Medicine*, vol. 2, ed. O. W. Hill. London: Butterworths, pp. 26-34.

Neugarten, B., ed. (1968), *Middle-Aged and Aging: A Reader in Social Psychology*. Chicago: University of Chicago Press.

New York Times (1973), Article on alcoholism, April 29, 1973.

Nie, N., et al. (1975), *Statistical Package for the Social Sciences*. New York: McGraw-Hill.

Nihon Jūtaku Kōdan (1972), *Survey of Wives' Perceptions of "Home": Danchi and Apartment. (Sumai nī kan suru shūfu no ishiki chōsa—danchi, apāto.)* Tokyo: Nihon Jūtaku Kōdan.

Offer, D. (1971), *The Offer Self-Image Questionnaire for Adolescents: Revised Manual.* Chicago: Special Publication.

———— & Offer, J. B. (1975), *From Teenage to Young Manhood: A Psychological Study.* New York: Basic Books.

———— & Sabshin, M. (1974), *Normality: Theoretical and Clinical Concepts of Mental Health,* 2nd ed. New York: Basic Books.

Osgood, C. E. (1971), Methodological issues in cross cultural research (Discussant). Annual Convention of the American Psychological Association, Washington, D.C.

Packard, V. O. (1972), *A Nation of Strangers.* New York: McKay.

Pelzel, J. (1954), The small industrialist in Japan. *Explor. Entrepren. Hist.,* 7:79-93.

Peplau, L., Russell, D., & Heim, M. (1979), An attributional analysis of loneliness. To appear in: *Attribution Theory: Applications to Social Problems,* ed. I. Frieze, D. Bar-Tal, & J. Carroll. San Francisco: Jossey-Bass.

Perlman, D., Gerson, A., & Spinner, B. (1978), *Loneliness Among Senior Citizens: An Empirical Report.* Paper presented at the 86th Annual Convention of the American Psychological Association, Toronto, Canada, August 1978.

Pettigrew, T. F. (1964), *A Profile of the Negro American.* Princeton, N.J.: Nostrand.

Phillips, D. P. (1977), Deathday and birthday: An unexpected connection. In: *Statistics: A Guide to the Biological and Health Sciences,* ed. J. M. Tanur et al. San Francisco: Holden-Day, pp. 111-125.

Piaget, J. (1967), *Six Psychological Studies,* trans. A. Tenzer & D. Elkind. New York: Random House.

Plath, D. W. & Sugihara, Y. (1968), A case of ostracism — and its unusual aftermath. *Trans-Action,* 5:31-36.

Potok, C. (1969), *The Promise.* New York: Knopf.

Prescott, J. W. & McKay, C. (1972), Paper presented at 27th Annual Convention of the Society of Biological Psychiatry, Dallas, April 28-30, 1972.

Press, I. (1969), Ambiguity and innovation: Implications for the genesis of the culture broker. *Amer. Anthropol.,* 71:205-217.

Randolph, T. (1978), *Human Ecology and Susceptibility to the Chemical Environment.* Springfield, Ill.: Thomas.

Rank, O. (1929), *The Trauma of Birth.* New York: Harcourt Brace.

Rees, W. D. & Lutkins, S. G. (1967), Mortality of bereavement. *Brit. Med. J.,* 4:13-16.

Riesman, D., Denny, R., & Glazer, N. (1950), *The Lonely Crowd.* New Haven: Yale University Press.

Rilke, R. M. (1939), *Duino Elegies,* trans. J. B. Leishman & S. Spender. New York: Norton.

Rogers, C. R. (1961), *On Becoming a Person.* Boston: Houghton Mifflin.

———— (1970), *On Encounter Groups.* New York: Harper & Row.

Rosenberg, M. (1965), *Society and the Adolescent Self Image.* Princeton:

Princeton University Press.

Rosow, I. (1962), Retirement housing and social integration. In: *Social and Psychological Aspects of Aging,* ed. C. Tibbitts & W. Donahue. New York: Columbia University Press.

———— (1974), *Socialization to Old Age.* Berkeley: University of California Press.

Rossi, A. S. (1972), Family development in a changing world. *Amer. J. Psychiat.,* 128:1057-1066.

Rubins, J. L. (1964), On the psychopathology of loneliness. *Amer. J. Psychoanal.,* 24:153-166.

Russell, B. (1967), *The Autobiography of Bertrand Russell,* vol. 1. Boston: Little, Brown.

———— (1968), *The Autobiography of Bertrand Russell,* vol. 2. Boston: Little, Brown.

Sabine, G. (1961), *A History of Political Theory.* New York: Holt, Rinehart & Winston.

Sadler, W. A., Jr. (1969a), Creative existence: Play as a pathway to personal freedom and community. *Humanitas,* 5:57-80.

———— (1969b), *Existence and Love: A New Approach in Existential Phenomenology.* New York: Charles Scribner's Sons.

Sarano, J. (1970), *La Solitude Humaine.* Paris: Centurion.

Sarnoff, C. (1971), Ego structure in latency. *Psychoanal. Quart.,* 40:387-414.

Schachter, S. (1959), *The Psychology of Affiliation.* Stanford: Stanford University Press.

Schapiro, M. (1950), *Vincent van Gogh.* New York: Abrams.

Scheerer, E. (1949), An analysis of the relationship between acceptance of and respect for self and acceptance of and respect for others in ten counseling cases. *J. Consult. Psychol.,* 13:169-175.

Schrut, A. (1968), Some typical patterns in the behavior and background of adolescent girls who attempt suicide. *Amer. J. Psychiat.,* 125:69-74.

Schutz, A. (1962), *The Problem of Social Reality.* The Hague: Nijhoff.

———— (1964), *Collected Papers. Vol. II: Studies in Social Theory,* ed. M. Natanson. The Hague: Nijhoff.

Sears, P. (1975), In: *Campus Report, Stanford University,* 3:1, 6.

Seiden, R. H. (1972), Why are suicides of young blacks increasing? *HSMHA Reports,* 87:3-8.

Seidenberg, R. (1960), Interpersonal determinants of reality-testing capacity. *Arch. Gen. Psychiat.,* 3:368-372.

———— (1967), Fidelity and jealousy: Sociocultural considerations. *Psychoanal. Rev.,* 54:583-608.

———— (1973), *Corporate Wives—Corporate Casualties?* New York: Amacon.

Seidensticker, E. (1961), *Japan.* New York: Time.

Seifer, N. (1973), *Absent from the Majority: Working Class Women in America.* New York: American Jewish Committee.

Seligman, M. E. (1975), *Helplessness: On Depression, Development and Death.*

San Francisco: Freeman.

Sennett, R. (1972), Women: What is to be done? *N.Y. Rev. Books,* 13:22–26.

———— & Cobb, J. (1972), *The Hidden Injuries of Class.* New York: Knopf.

Sermat, V., Cohen, M. & Pollack, H. (1970), Helping freshmen adjust to the university. *Internal Report No. 25, Psychological Services Department.* York University.

Shaftesbury, A. A. C. (1964), *Characteristics of Men, Manners, Opinions, Times,* ed. J. M. Robertson. Indianapolis: Bobbs-Merrill.

Shanas, E. & Streib, G. F., eds. (1965), *Social Structure and the Family: Generational Relations.* Englewood Cliffs, N.J.: Prentice-Hall.

———— et al. (1968), *Old People in Three Industrial Societies.* New York: Atherton.

Shannon, W. V. (1972), Article on the suburban housewife. *New York Times,* August 3, 1972.

Shaver, P. & Freedman, J. (1976), Your pursuit of happiness. *Psychol. Today,* August: 10:26–32, 75.

Shelley, P. B. (1901), *The Complete Poetical Works.* Cambridge, Mass.: Houghton Mifflin.

Shostrom, E. L. (1966), *Manual: Personal Orientation Inventory.* San Diego: Educational and Industrial Testing Service.

Siassi, I., Crocetti, G., & Spiro, H. R. (1974), Loneliness and dissatisfaction in a blue collar population. *Arch. Gen. Psychiat.,* 30:261–265.

Simmel, G. (1962), The metropolis and mental life. In: *Man Alone: Alienation in Modern Society,* ed. E. Josephson & M. Josephson. New York: Dell, pp. 151–165.

Singer, E. (1968), Hypocrisy and learning disability. Unpublished paper presented at the William Alanson White Institute of Psychiatry, Psychoanalysis, and Psychology, New York City, N. Y., October 19–20, 1968.

Sisenwein, R. J. (1964), *Loneliness and the Individual as Viewed by Himself and Others.* Unpublished Doctoral Dissertation, Columbia University.

Slater, J. (1973), Suicide: A growing menace to black women. *Ebony,* 11:152–159.

Slater, P. E. (1970), *The Pursuit of Loneliness: American Culture at the Breaking Point.* Boston: Beacon.

Slocum, J. (1905), *Sailing Alone Around the World.* New York: Century.

Smith, R. J. (1956), Kurusu: A Japanese agricultural community. University of Michigan Center for Japanese Studies. *Occas. Papers,* 5:1–112.

Solomon, P., Leiderman, P. H., Mendelsohn, J. H., & Wexler, D. (1957), Sensory deprivation: A review. *Amer. J. Psychiat.,* 114:357–363.

Southern, E. (1971), *The Music of Black Americans: A History.* New York: Norton.

Spencer-Booth, Y. & Hinde, R. A. (1971), Effects of brief separations from mothers during infancy on behaviour of rhesus monkeys 6–24 months later. *J. Child Psychol. Psychiat.,* 12:157–172.

Spitz, R. A. (1945), Hospitalism. *The Psychoanalytic Study of the Child,* 1:53–74. New York: International Universities Press.

―――― (1946), Anaclitic depression. In: *The Psychoanalytic Study of the Child,* 2:313–342. New York: International Universities Press.

Srole, L. (1956), Social integration and certain corollaries. *Amer. Soc. Rev.,* 21:709–716.

Staples, R. (1976), *Introduction to Black Sociology.* New York: McGraw-Hill.

Steinbeck, J. (1951), *The Grapes of Wrath.* Harmondsworth: Penguin.

Sullivan, H. S. (1953), *The Interpersonal Theory of Psychiatry.* New York: Norton.

―――― (1956), *Clinical Studies in Psychiatry.* New York: Norton.

Suttie, I. D. (1952), *The Origins of Love and Hate.* New York: Julian.

Szalita-Pemow, A. (1955), The "intuitive process" and its relation to work with schizophrenics. *J. Amer. Psychoanal. Assn.,* 3:7–18.

Szasz, T. (1973), *The Second Sin.* Garden City, N.Y.: Doubleday.

Tabor, E. (1950), *The Cliff's Edge: Songs of a Psychotic.* New York: Sheed & Ward.

Takenaka, T. (1964), *The Seven Deadly Sins of the Apartments (Danchi Nantsu no Daizai).* Tokyo: Kobundo, Frontier Books.

Tanner, I. J. (1973), *Loneliness: The Fear of Love.* New York: Harper & Row.

Teicher, J. D. & Jacobs, J. (1966), Adolescents who attempt suicide: Preliminary findings. *Amer. J. Psychiat.,* 122:1248–1257.

Thigpen, C. H. & Cleckley, H. M. (1957), *The Three Faces of Eve.* New York: McGraw-Hill.

Thomas, A. & Sillen, S. (1972), *Racism and Psychiatry.* New York: Brunner/Mazel.

Thompson, W. I. (1971), *At the Edge of History.* New York: Harper & Row.

Tillich, P. (1952), *The Courage to Be.* New Haven: Yale University Press.

Toffler, A. (1970), *Future Shock.* New York: Random House.

Townsend, P. (1957), *The Family Life of Old People.* London: Routledge & Kegan Paul.

―――― (1962), Isolation, loneliness, and the hold on life. In: *Man Alone: Alienation in Modern Society,* ed. E. Josephson & M. Josephson. New York: Dell.

Turner, D. (1960), *Lonely God, Lonely Man.* New York: Philosophical Library.

Turner, V. W. (1969), *The Ritual Process: Structure and Anti-Structure.* Chicago: Aldine.

United States Senate (1963), *Developments in Aging: 1959 to 1963.* A Report of the Special Committee on Aging. Washington, D.C.: U.S. Government Printing Office.

Vahanian, G. (1966), *The Death of God.* New York: Braziller.

Voth, H. M., Voth, A. C., & Canero, R. (1969), Suicidal solution as a function of ego-closeness — ego-distance. *Arch. Gen. Psychiat.,* 21:536–545.

Wallerstein, J. & Kelly, J. (1974), The effects of parental divorce: The adolescent experience. In: *The Child in His Family,* ed. E. J. Anthony & C. Koupernik. New York: Wiley, pp. 479–505.

_____ & _____ (1975), The effects of parental divorce: Experiences of the preschool child. *J. Amer. Acad. Child Psychiat.,* 14(4).

Ward, M. J. (1946), *The Snake Pit.* New York: Random House.

Weiss, R. S., ed. (1973), *Loneliness: The Experience of Emotional and Social Isolation.* Cambridge: M.I.T. Press.

West, L. J. (1969), Unpublished paper read at Northern California Psychiatric Society, November 19, 1969, San Francisco, Cal.

Whitehorn, J. C. (1961), On loneliness and the incongruous self-image. *Ann. Psychother.,* Monogr. 3, pp. 15–17.

Whitman, W. (1855), *Leaves of Grass.* New York, Harper, 1950.

Whyte, L. L. (1948), *The Next Development in Man.* New York: Holt.

Whyte, W. H. (1956), *The Organization Man.* New York: Simon & Schuster.

Will, O. A. & Cohen, R. A. (1953), A report of a recorded interview in the course of psychotherapy. *Psychiat.,* 16:263–282.

Williams, F. S. (1970), Alienation of youth as reflected in the hippie movement. *J. Amer. Acad. Child Psychiat.,* 9:251–263.

Williams, W. C. (1951), *The Collected Earlier Poems.* Norfolk, Conn.: New Directions.

Winnicott, D. W. (1944), Ocular psychoneuroses of childhood. In: *Collected Papers.* New York: Basic Books, 1958, pp. 85–90.

_____ (1953), Transitional objects and transitional phenomena. *Internat. J. Psycho-Anal.,* 34:89–97.

_____ (1958), The capacity to be alone. *Internat. J. Psycho-Anal.,* 39:416–420.

Witzleben, H. D. von (1958), On loneliness. *Psychiat.,* 21:37–43.

Wolfe, T. (1957), *The Face of a Nation.* New York: Scribner's, pp. 179–180.

_____ (1976), The me decade and the third great awakening. In: *Mauve Gloves and Madmen, Clutter and Vine, and Other Stories, Sketches, and Essays.* New York: Farrar, Straus & Giroux.

Woodward, J. & Woodward, H. (1972), *Loneliness Among the Elderly.* Paper presented at the 9th International Congress of Gerontology, Kiev, U.S.S.R.

Work, J. W. (1969), *Folk Song of the American Negro.* New York: Negro Universities Press.

Wright, R. H. (1971), The stranger mentality and the culture of poverty. In: *The Culture of Poverty: A Critique,* ed. E. Leacock. New York: Simon & Schuster, pp. 315–337.

Yeats, W. B. (1956), *Collected Poems.* New York: Macmillan.

Zilboorg, G. (1938), Loneliness. *Atlan. Month.,* 161:45–54.

Znaniecki, F. (1965), *Social Relations and Social Roles: The Unfinished Systematic Sociology.* San Francisco: Chandler.

Supplementary Reading List

Aaron, N. S. (1967), Some personality differences between asthmatic, allergic, and normal children. *J. Clin. Psychol.,* 23:336–340.

Abel, T. (1930), The significance of the concept of the consciousness of kind. *Soc. Forces,* 9:1–10.

Abrahams, R. B. (1972), Mutual help for the widowed. *Soc. Work,* 17:55–61.

Adams, F. R. (1967), Stereotype, social responsiveness, and arousal in a case of catatonia. *Brit. J. Psychiatry,* 113:1123–1128.

Adler, A. (1927), *Understanding Human Nature,* trans. W. B. Wolfe. Greenwich, Conn.: Fawcett.

Alexander, L. (1967), Clinical experiences with hypnosis in psychiatric treatment. *Internat. J. Neuropsychiat.,* 3:118–124.

Altman, I. (1975), *The Environment and Social Behavior: Privacy, Personal Space, Territoriality, Crowding.* Monterey, Cal.: Brooks/Cole.

———, Taylor, D. A., & Wheeler, L. (1971), Ecological aspects of group behavior in social isolation. *J. Appl. Soc. Psychol.,* 1:76–100.

Amat Aguirre, E. (1967), Anxiety in depressive syndromes. *Rev. Esp. Otoneurooftalmol. Neurocir.,* 26:347–356.

Anthony, E. J. & Koupernik, C. eds. (1974), *Children at Psychiatric Risk.* New York: Wiley.

Ardrey, R. (1966), *The Territorial Imperative.* New York: Atheneum.

Arlen, M. J. (1970), *The Exiles.* New York: Farrar, Straus & Giroux.

Arling, G. (1976), The elderly widow and her family, neighbors and friends. *J. Marr. Fam.,* 38:757–768.

——— (1976), Resistance to isolation among elderly widows. *Internat. J. Aging Hum. Develop.,* 7:67–86.

Armstrong, R. (1972), *Themselves Alone.* Boston: Houghton Mifflin.

Bakan, D. (1968), *Disease, Pain, and Sacrifice: Toward a Psychology of Suffering.* Chicago: University of Chicago Press.

Bakwin, H. (1942), Loneliness in infants. *Amer. J. Dis. Child.,* 63:30–40.

Barry, M. J. (1962), Depression, shame, loneliness and the psychiatrist's position. *Amer. J. Psychother.,* 16:580–590.

Barthell, C. N. & Holmes, D. S. (1968), High school yearbooks: A nonreactive measure of social isolation in graduates who later became schizophrenic. *J. Abnorm. Psychol.,* 73:313–316.

Basquin, M. & Trystram, D. (1966), Exhibitionism in the adolescent. *Ann. Med. Psychol.,* 2:534.

Beard, B. H. (1969), Fear of death and fear of life: The dilemma in chronic renal failure, hemodialysis, and kidney transplantation. *Arch. Gen. Psychiat.,* 21:373–380.

Becker, E. (1967), *Beyond Alienation: A Philosophy of Education for the Crisis of Democracy.* New York: George Braziller.

——— (1969), *Angel in Armor: A Post-Freudian Perspective on the Nature of Man.* New York: George Braziller.

——— (1973), *The Denial of Death.* New York: Free Press.

——— (1974), The spectrum of loneliness. *Humanitas,* 10:237–246.

Belcher, M. J. (1973), *The Measurement of Loneliness: A Validation of the Belcher Extended Loneliness Scale (BELS).* Unpublished Doctoral Dissertation, Illinois Institute of Technology.

Bell, R. G. (1956), Alcohol and loneliness. *J. Soc. Ther.,* 2:171–181.

Bem, S. L., Martyna, W., & Watson, C. (1976), Sex typing and androgyny: Further explorations of the expressive domain. *J. Pers. Soc. Psychol.,* 34:1016–1023.

Bennett, A. M. H. (1961), Sensory deprivation in aviation. In: *Sensory Deprivation. A Symposium Held at Harvard Medical School,* ed. P. Solomon, P. E. Kubzansky, P. H. Leiderman, J. H. Mendelson, R. Trumbull, & D. Wexler. Cambridge: Harvard University Press, pp. 161–173.

Bennett, R. (1973), Social isolation and isolation-reducing programs. *Bull. N.Y. Acad. Med.,* 49:1143–1163.

Berblinger, K. W. (1968), A psychiatrist looks at loneliness. *Psychosomatics,* 9:96–102.

——— (1970), Loneliness and the depressive perspective: The chronically depressed patient. In: *Depression in Medical Practice,* ed. A. J. Enelow. West Point, Pa.: Merck, Sharp & Dohme.

Berdiaev, N. (1976), *Solitude and Society,* trans. G. Reavey from Russian reproduction of 1938 ed. Westport, Conn.: Greenwood Press.

Berezin, M. A. & Cath, S. H., eds. (1965), *Geriatric Psychiatry: Grief, Loss, and Emotional Disorders in the Aging Process.* New York: International Universities Press.

Berg., I., Nichols, K., & Pritchard, C. (1969), School phobia: Its classification and relationship to dependency. *J. Child Psychol. Psychiat.,* 10:123–141.

Bettelheim, B. (1960), *The Informed Heart. Autonomy in a Mass Age.* Glencoe, Ill.: Free Press.

Bitter, W. (1967), *Loneliness From a Medical-Psychological, Theological, and Social Point of View.* Stuttgart, Germany: Ernst Klett.

Black, K. (1973), Social isolation and the nursing process. *Nurs. Clin. North Amer.,* 8:575–586.

Blackwell, A. & Rollins, N. (1968), Treatment problems in adolescents with anorexia nervosa: Preliminary observations on the second phase. *Acta Paedopsychiat.,* 35:294–301.

Blanc, M., Bourgeois, M., & Henry, P. (1966), The suicide attempt: Current aspects (apropos of 500 cases). *Ann. Med. Psychol.,* 1:554–559.

Blau, Z. S. (1961), Structural constraints on friendships in old age. *Amer. Soc. Rev.,* 26:429–439.

Bliss, E. L., ed. (1962), *Roots of Behavior. Genetics, Instinct, and Socialization in Animal Behavior.* New York: Harper, pp. 235–245, 277–320.

Blum, H. P. (1969), A psychoanalytic view of "Who's Afraid of Virginia Woolf?" *J. Amer. Psychoanal. Assn.,* 17:888–903.

Board, F., Wadeson, R., & Persky, H. (1957), Depressive affect and endocrine functions. *Arch. Neurol. Psychiat.,* 78:612–620.

Bombard, A. (1954), *The Voyage of the Hérétique.* New York: Simon & Schuster.

Bonney, M. E. (1971), Assessment of efforts to aid socially isolated elementary school pupils. *J. Educ. Res.,* 64:359–364.

Bot, B. W. (1968), The nursing-home patient and his environment. *Gawein,* 16:163–186.

Bowlby, J. (1961), Separation anxiety: A critical review of the literature. *J. Child Psychol. Psychiat.,* 1:251–269.

Bowskill, D. (1974), *All the Lonely People.* New York: Bobbs-Merrill.

Boyd, H. (1968), Love versus omnipotence: The narcissistic dilemma. *Psychother. Theory Res. Pract.,* 5:272–277.

Boyer, S. L. (1967), George Orwell: The pursuit of decency. *Soc. Work,* 12:96–100.

Braceland, F. (1967), Psychological analysis of solitude. *Actas Luso Esp. Neurol. Psiquiatr.,* 26:12–23.

Bradburn, N. (1969), *The Structure of Psychological Well-Being.* Chicago: Aldine.

Bradley, R. (1970), Measuring loneliness. *Dissert. Abst. Int.,* 30:3382.

Brain, R. (1976), *Friends and Lovers.* New York: Basic Books.

Brand, H. (1976), Kafka's creative crisis. *J. Amer. Acad. Psychoanal.,* 4:249–260.

Brenton, M. (1974), *Friendship.* New York: Stein & Day.

Brod, M. (1963), *Franz Kafka: A Biography,* 2nd ed., trans. G. H. Roberts & R. Winston. New York: Schocken.

Brown, N. O. (1959), *Life Against Death: The Psychoanalytical Meaning of History.* Middleton, Conn.: Wesleyan University Press.

Brown, R. W. (1929), *Lonely Americans.* New York: Coward-McCann.

Brownfield, C. (1965), *Isolation: Clinical and Experimental Approaches.* New York: Random House.

Buber, M. (1958), *I and Thou,* 2nd ed., trans. R. G. Smith. New York: Scribner's.

Bugbee, H. G. (1974), Loneliness, solitude and the twofold way in which concern seems to be claimed. *Humanitas,* 10:313–328.

Buhl, H. (1956), *Lonely Challenge,* trans. H. Merrick. New York: Dutton.

Buhler, C. (1969), Loneliness in maturity. *J. Hum. Psychol.,* 9:167–181.

Burgess, P. (1940), *Who Walk Alone.* New York: Holt.

Burke, C., ed. (1970), *Loneliness,* photos by N. Provost. Winona, Minn.: St. Mary's College Press.

Burnside, I. M. (1971), Loneliness in old age. *Mental Hyg.*, 55:391–397.

Burton, A. (1961), On the nature of loneliness. *Amer. J. Psychoanal.*, 21:34–39.

―――― & Heller, L. G. (1964), The touching of the body. *Psychoanal. Rev.*, 51:122–134.

Butler, R. N. & Lewis, M. I. (1973), *Aging and Mental Health: Positive Psychosocial Approaches.* St. Louis: Mosby.

Bychowski, G. (1970), Psychoanalytic reflections on the psychiatry of the poor. *Internat. J. Psycho-Anal.*, 51:503–509.

Byrd, R. E. (1938), *Alone.* New York: Putnam.

Calhoun, J. B. (1963), Population density and social pathology. In: *The Urban Condition. People and Policy in the Metropolis,* ed. L. J. Duhl & J. Powell. New York: Basic Books, pp. 33–43.

―――― (1965), Ecological factors in the development of behavioral abnormalities. *Amer. Psychopathol. Assn. Proc.*, 55:1–53.

―――― (1966), A glance into the garden. In: *Three Papers on Human Ecology.* Mills College Assembly Series 1965–1966. Oakland, Cal.: Mills College, pp. 19–36.

―――― (1971), Space and the strategy of life. In: *Behavior and Environment: The Use of Space by Animals and Men,* ed. A. H. Esser. New York: Plenum, pp. 329–387.

Camus, A. (1946), *The Stranger,* trans. S. Gilbert. New York: Knopf.

―――― (1964), *The Fall,* trans. J. O'Brien. New York: Modern Library.

Caplan, G. & Killilea, M., eds. (1976), *Support Systems and Mutual Help: Multidisciplinary Explorations.* New York: Grune & Stratton.

Carr, V. S. (1975), *The Lonely Hunter: A Biography of Carson McCullers.* Garden City, N.Y.: Doubleday.

Carthy, J. D. & Ebling, F. J., eds. (1964), *Natural History of Aggression.* Institute of Biology Symposia, No. 13. New York: Academic Press.

Cashar, L. & Dixson, B. K. (1967), The therapeutic use of touch. *J. Psychiat. Nurs. Ment. Hlth. Serv.*, 5:442–451.

Chandler, M. J. (1975), Relativism and the problem of epistemological loneliness. *Hum. Develop.*, 18:171–180.

Chapman, R. (1963), *The Loneliness of Man.* Philadelphia: Fortress.

Christensen, J. A. (1972), Fiction of loneliness. *Media Methods,* 8:24–28.

Clark, M. & Anderson, B. C. (1967), *Culture and Aging.* Springfield, Ill.: Thomas.

Coleman, J. C. (1969), The perception of interpersonal relationships during adolescence. *Brit. J. Educ. Psychol.*, 39:253–260.

Collier, R. M. & Lawrence, H. P. (1951), The adolescent feeling of psychological isolation. *Educ. Theory,* 1:106–115.

Conti, M. L. (1970), The loneliness of old age. *Nurs. Outlook,* 18:28–30.

Corson, S. A. & Corson, E. O. (1969), Neuroendocrine and behavioral correlates of constitutional differences. *Cond. Reflex,* 4:265–286.

Coser, L. A. & Rosenberg, B. (1964), Alienation and anomie. In: *Socio-*

logical Theory: A Book of Readings, 2nd. ed. New York: Macmillan, pp. 519-582.

Cotton, J. M. (1973), Problems of older people: Forced idleness, impoverishment, ill health, isolation. *Bull. N. Y. Acad. Med.,* 49:1023-1027.

Cox, H. G. (1965), *The Secular City.* New York: Macmillan.

Cunningham, B. (1972), Growing old in New York. Article V: Loneliness and love. *New York Post,* Oct. 13, 1972, p. 39.

Curran, J. P. (1977), Skills training as an approach to the treatment of heterosexual-social anxiety: A review. *Psychol. Bull.,* 84:140-157.

D'Aboy, J. E. (1972), *Loneliness: An Investigation of Terminology.* Unpublished Doctoral Dissertation, Arizona State University.

Davis, K. (1940), Extreme social isolation of a child. *Amer. J. Sociol.,* 45:554-565.

———— (1947), Final note on a case of extreme isolation. *Amer. J. Sociol.,* 52:432-437.

Davis, T. N. (1968), *The Loneliness of Man.* Chicago: Claretian.

Dean, L. R. (1962), Aging and the decline of affect. *J. Gerontol.,* 17:440-446.

Dean, W. F. (1954), *General Dean's Story.* New York: Viking.

De Araujo, H. A. (1968), Neurotic anxiety and its treatment. *Ann. Med. Psychol.,* 2:25-40.

Decaux, F., Rodriguz Tome, H., & Zlotowicz, M. (1970), "Difficult situations" for adolescents: Analysis of content, vocabulary and affectivity themes. *Enfance,* 3:365-396.

DeJanos, S. (1971), *Loneliness and Communication.* Toronto: New Press.

DeJong-Gierveld, J. (1971), Social isolation and the image of the unmarried. *Sociol. Neerland.,* 7:1-14.

DeLaczay, E. (1972), *Loneliness.* New York: Hawthorn.

DeNelsky, G. Y. & Denenberg, V. H. (1967), Infantile stimulation and adult exploratory behavior. *J. Comp. Physiol. Psychol.,* 63:309-312.

Denenberg, V. H., Hudgens, G. A., & Zarrow, M. X. (1964), Mice reared with rats: Modification of behavior by early experience with another species. *Science,* 143:380-381.

Dénes, Z. (1975), Loneliness and old age. *Z.F.A.,* 29:305-310.

Dennis, W. (1941), *Infant Development Under Conditions of Restricted Practice and of Minimum Social Stimulation.* Provincetown, Mass.: Journal Press.

Dlabocova, E. (1967), Free drawings in anxious children. *Psychol. Patopsychol. Dietata.,* 3:33-40.

Dominick, J. R. & Stotsky, B.A. (1969), Mental patients in nursing homes: IV. Ethnic influences. *J. Amer. Geriatr. Soc.,* 17:63-85.

Donson, C. & Georgés, A. (1967), *Lonely-land and Bedsitter-land.* Bala, New Wales: Chapples.

Dostoevsky, F. (1864), Notes from the underground. In: *Existentialism from Dostoevsky to Sartre,* ed., W. A. Kaufmann. New York: Meridian,

1958, pp. 52–82.

Dreyfus, E. A. (1967), The search for intimacy. *Adoles.,* 2:25–40.

Dubrey, R. J. & Terrill, L. A. (1975), The loneliness of the dying person: An exploratory study. *Omega: J. Death Dying,* 6:357–371.

Duhl, L. J. & Powell, J., eds. (1963), *The Urban Condition. People and Policy in the Metropolis.* New York: Basic Books.

Dusenbury, W. L. (1960), *The Theme of Loneliness in Modern American Drama.* Gainesville, Fla.: University of Florida Press.

Duvall, E. M. (1945), Loneliness and the serviceman's wife. *Marr. Fam. Liv.,* 7:77–81.

Dyer, B. M. (1974), Loneliness — there's no way to escape it. *Alpha Gamma Delta Quart.,* Spring, pp. 2–5.

Eberhard, K. (1969), Characteristic syndromes of neglect. *Prax. Kinderpsychol. Kinderpsychiatr.,* 18:60–66.

Eckardt, M. H. (1960), The detached person: A discussion with a phenomenological bias. *Amer. J. Psychoanal.,* 20:139–163.

Eddy, P. D. (1961), *Loneliness: A Discrepancy with the Phenomenological Self.* Unpublished Doctoral Dissertation, Adelphi College.

Edwards, M. & Hoover, E. (1974), *The Challenge of Being Single.* Los Angeles: Tarcher.

Eisenstadt, J. M. (1978), Parental loss and genius. *Amer. Psychol.,* 33:211–223.

Ekman, P. & Friesen, W. V. (1967), Head and body cues in the judgment of emotion: A reformulation. *Percept. Motor Skills,* 24:711–724.

Ellis, R. A. & Lane, W. C. (1967), Social mobility and social isolation: A test of Sorokin's dissociative hypothesis. *Amer. Soc. Rev.,* 32:237–253.

Enachescu, C. (1968), Ideo-affective complexes and their representation in the drawings of mental patients. *Encéphale,* 57:195–226.

Engelhardt, H. T. (1974), Solitude and sociality. *Humanitas,* 10:277–288.

Ephron, D., ed. (1978), Loneliness: The New York condition. *New York,* 11:40–48 (March 20).

Farberow, N., ed. (1963), *Taboo Topics.* New York: Atherton.

Farrell, J. T. (1966), *Lonely for the Future.* Garden City, N. Y.: Doubleday.

Ferrell, D. R. (1971), Anxiety and the death of God. *Natl. Catholic Guidance Conf. J.,* 15:200–205.

Fidler, J. (1976), Loneliness — The problems of the elderly and retired. *R. Soc. Hlth. J.,* 96:39–41, 44.

Fingarette, H. (1963), *The Self in Transformation.* New York: Basic Books.

Fischer, C. S. (1977), *Networks and Places: Social Relations in the Urban Setting.* New York: Free Press.

Flanders, J. P. (1976), From loneliness to intimacy. In: *Practical Psychology.* New York: Harper & Row, pp. 21–43.

Ford, E. & Zorn, R. L. (1975), *Why Be Lonely?* Niles, Ill.: Argus Communications.

Forer, B. R. (1969), The taboo against touching in psychotherapy. *Psychother. Theory Res. Pract.,* 6:229–231.

Forer, L. K. (1969), *Birth Order and Life Roles.* Springfield, Ill.: Thomas.

Francel, C. G. (1961), Loneliness. In: *Some Clinical Approaches to Psychiatric Nursing,* ed. S. F. Burd & M. A. Marshall. New York: Macmillan.

Francis, G. M. (1976), Loneliness: Measuring the abstract. *Internat. J. Nurs. Stud.,* 13:153–160.

Frank, L. K. (1954), *Feelings and Emotions.* Garden City, N.Y.: Doubleday.

_____ (1958), Tactile communication. *ETC Rev. Gen. Semant.,* 16:31–79.

Freedman, D. A. et al. (1976), Further observations on the effect of reverse isolation from birth on cognitive and affective development. *J. Amer. Acad. Child Psychiat.,* 15:593–603.

Freedman, S. J. (1961), Sensory deprivation: Facts in search of a theory: Perceptual changes in sensory deprivation: Suggestions for a conative theory. *J. Nerv. Ment. Dis.,* 132:17–21.

Friedenberg, E. (1963), The isolation of the adolescent. In: *The Adolescent: His Search for Understanding,* ed. W. C. Bier. New York: Fordham University Press, pp. 11–20.

Fromm, E. (1956), *The Sane Society.* London: Routledge & Kegan Paul.

Furchner, C. S. & Harlow, H. F. (1969), Preference for various surrogate surfaces among infant rhesus monkeys. *Psychonom. Sci.,* 17:279–280.

Gaev, D. M. (1976), *The Psychology of Loneliness.* Chicago: Adams.

Gajdusek, D. C. (1953), The Sierra Tarahumara. *Geogr. Rev.,* 43:15–38.

Gallico, P. (1949), *The Lonely.* New York: Knopf.

Garcia, J. S. (1966), Some considerations on agoraphobia. *Rev. Psicoanal. Psiquiatr. Psicolog.,* 4:34–39.

Gerard, R. W. (1955), The academic lecture. The biological roots of psychiatry. *Amer. J. Psychiatry,* 112:81–90.

Gibson, J. E. (1967), You don't have to be lonely. *Sci. Digest,* 62:33–36.

Gibson, W. (1953), *The Boat.* Boston: Houghton Mifflin.

Gilger, K. (1976), Loneliness and the holidays. *Holiday News Story* (No. 19). University of Nebraska-Lincoln, Department of Agricultural Communications.

Gladwin, T. (1958), Canoe travel in the Truk area. Technology and its psychological correlates. *Amer. Anthropol.,* 60:893–899.

Glaser, B. G. & Strauss, A. (1965), *Awareness of Dying.* Chicago: Aldine.

_____ & _____ (1968), *Time for Dying.* Chicago: Aldine.

Glasser, W. (1972), Loneliness and failure. In: *The Identity Society.* New York: Harper & Row, pp. 72–101.

Glatzel, J. (1967), Über eine Beobachtung von Trichloänthylen-Sucht. (An observation regarding addiction to trichloroethylene.) *Psychiatr. Neurol. Med. Psychol.,* 19:366–371.

Godown, J. (1978), Loneliness. *Fort Meyers (Southwest Florida) News Press,* Sunday, Aug. 6, 1978, pp. 1D–7D.

Goffman, E. (1963), *Stigma: Notes on the Management of Spoiled Identity.* Englewood Cliffs, N.J.: Prentice-Hall.

Goldman, G. D. (1955), Group psychotherapy and the lonely person in our changing times. *Group Psychother.,* 8:247–253.

Gonzalez Duro, E. (1968), The genetic structure of paranoid delirium. *Actas Luso Esp. Neurol. Psiquiatr.,* 27:416–432.

Gordon, S. (1976), *Lonely in America.* New York: Simon & Schuster.

Gotesky, R. (1965), Aloneness, loneliness, isolation, solitude. In: *An Invitation to Phenomenology,* ed. J. M. Edie. Chicago: Quadrangle.

Gottman, J., Gonso, J., & Schuler, P. (1976), Teaching social skills to isolated children. *J. Abnorm. Child Psychol.,* 4:179–197.

Götz, I. L. (1974), Loneliness. *Humanitas,* 10:289–300.

Gratton, C. (1974), Summaries of selected works on loneliness and solitude. *Humanitas,* 10:329–334.

_____ (1974), Selected subject bibliography on loneliness (covering the past ten years). *Humanitas,* 10:335–340.

Green, M. & Kaplan, B. L. (1978), Aspects of loneliness in the therapeutic situation. *Internat. Rev. Psychoanal.,* 5:321–330.

Greenbaum, M. (1962), The displaced child syndrome. *J. Child. Psychol. Psychiat.,* 3:93–100.

Greer, I. M. (1955), Roots of loneliness. *J. Pastoral Psychol.,* 9:27–31.

Greer, S. (1966), Parental loss and attempted suicide: A further report. *Brit. J. Psychiat.,* 112:465–470.

Griffiths, W. J., Jr., Lawrence, D., & Benson, E. (1967), Tactile preferences in the rat. *Percept. Mot. Skills,* 24:33–34.

Grinspoon, L. (1969), Psychosocial constraints on the important decision-maker. *Amer. J. Psychiat.,* 125:1074–1082.

Groat, H. T. & Neal, A. G. (1967), Social psychological correlates of urban fertility. *Amer. Sociol. Rev.,* 32:945–959.

Gubrium, J. F. (1974), Marital desolation and the evaluation of everyday life in old age. *J. Marr. Fam.,* 36:107–113.

Gunn, A. D. G. (1968), Vulnerable groups: Lives of loneliness. The medical-social problems of divorce and widowhood. *Nurs. Times,* 64:391–392.

Hall, M. P. (1978), *Ways of the Lonely Ones.* Los Angeles: Philosophical Research Society.

Hamer, J. H. (1965), Acculturation stress and the functions of alcohol among the Forest Potawatomi. *Quart. J. Stud. Alcohol,* 26:285–302.

Harlow, H. F. & Harlow, M. (1966), Learning to love. *Amer. Sci.,* 54:244–272.

_____ & _____ (1966), Affection in primates. *Discovery,* 27:11–18.

_____ & Zimmermann, R. R. (1959), Affectional responses in the infant monkey. *Science,* 130:421–432.

Harper, R. (1974), The concentric circles of loneliness. *Humanitas,* 10:247–254.

Hartog, J. (1974), A transcultural view of sibling rank and mental disorder. *Acta Psychiatr. Scand.,* 50:33–49.

Hau, T. F. von (1973), Psychology and psychopathology of loneliness. *Z. Psychosom. Med. Psychoanal.,* 19:265–271.

Hediger, H. (1950), *Wild Animals in Captivity*, trans. G. Sircom. London: Butterworths.

Hendrix, M. J. (1971), *Toward an Operational Definition of Loneliness*. Unpublished Doctoral Dissertation, Boston University School of Nursing.

Hilgard, J. R. & Newman, M. F. (1961), Evidence for functional genesis in mental illness: Schizophrenia, depressive psychoses and psychoneuroses. *J. Nerv. Ment. Dis.*, 132:3–16.

Hill, C. T., Rubin, Z., & Peplau, L. A. (1976), Breakups before marriage. The end of 103 affairs. *J. Soc. Issues*, 32:147–168.

Hinde, R. A., Leighton-Shapiro, M. E. & McGinnis, L. (1978), Effects of various types of separation experience on rhesus monkeys five months later. *J. Child Psychol. Psychiat.*, 19:199–211.

Hoover, E. (1976), Few are shaken by prediction of L. A. earthquake, most psychologists believe. *Los Angeles Times*, April 22, 1976, pp. 1, 3.

Horney, K. (1937), *The Neurotic Personality of Our Time*. New York: Norton.

————— (1950), *Neurosis and Human Growth: The Struggle Toward Self-Realization*. New York: Norton.

Horowitz, M. J. (1968), Spatial behavior and psychopathology. *J. Nerv. Ment. Dis.*, 146:24–35.

Horrocks, J. E. & Benimoff, M. (1967), Isolation from the peer group during adolescence. *Adoles.*, 2:41–52.

Howells, J. G. & Layng, J. (1955), Separation experiences and mental health. *Lancet*, ii:285–288.

Hulme, W. E. (1977), *Creative Loneliness*. Minneapolis, Minn.: Augsburg.

Hunt, M. M. (1973), Alone, alone, all, all, alone. In: *Loneliness: The Experience of Emotional and Social Isolation*, ed. R. S. Weiss. Cambridge: M.I.T. Press, pp. 125–133.

Hunter, E. (1953), *Brain-Washing in Red China*. New York: Vanguard.

Jacobs, J. (1971), *Adolescent Suicide*. New York: Wiley.

————— & Teicher, J. D. (1967), Broken homes and social isolation in attempted suicides of adolescents. *Internat. J. Soc. Psychiat.*, 13:139–149.

Jourard, S. M. & Rubin, J. E. (1968), Self-disclosure and touching: A study of two modes of interpersonal encounter and their interaction. *J. Hum. Psychol.*, 8:39–48.

Kafka, F. (1949), *The Diaries of Franz Kafka 1914–1923*, ed. M. Brod, trans. M. Greenberg with the cooperation of H. Arendt. New York: Schocken.

Kanner, L. (1968), Autistic disturbances of affective contact. *Acta Paedopsychiatr.*, 35:98–136.

Kaufman, B. (1965), *Solitudes Crowded with Loneliness*. New York: New Directions.

Kaufman, P. D. (1978), *Paddling the Gate: A Kayak Trip on San Francisco Bay*. Santa Monica, Cal.: Mara.

Keniston, K. (1965), *The Uncommitted: Alienated Youth in American Society*. New York: Harcourt, Brace & World.

Kennedy, E. (1973), *Living with Loneliness*. Chicago: Thomas More.

———— (1977), *Loneliness*. Chicago: Thomas More.

Kerken, L. V. (1967), *Loneliness and Love*. New York: Sheed & Ward.

Kernberg, O. (1975), *Borderline Conditions and Pathological Narcissism*. New York: Aronson.

Kersten, F. (1974), Loneliness and solitude. *Humanitas,* 10:301–312.

Keyes, R. (1973), *We, the Lonely People*. New York: Harper & Row.

Klein, M. (1963), On the sense of loneliness. In: *Our Adult World and Other Essays*. New York: Basic Books.

Knapp, P. H., ed. (1960), *Expression of the Emotions in Man* (Symposium). New York: International Universities Press.

Knoblock, P. & Goldstein, A. P. (1971), *The Lonely Teacher*. Boston: Allyn & Bacon.

Koluchova, J. (1970), Severe mental deprivation of long duration in two children in a family. *Psychol. Patopsychol. Diet.,* 5:161–170.

Korner, A. F. (1971), Individual differences at birth: Implications for early experience and later development. *Amer. J. Orthopsychiat.,* 41:608–619.

Kosten, A. (1961), *How You Can Conquer Loneliness: A Modern Guide to Affirmative Living*. New York: Twayne.

Krebs, J. S. (1974), *The Infinite Spaceship: A Phenomenological Analysis of the Experience of Loneliness*. Unpublished Doctoral Dissertation, The George Washington University. *Dissert. Abst. Int.,* 35:1052B.

Krulik, T. (1978), *Loneliness in School-Age Children with Chronic Life-Threatening Illness*. Unpublished Doctoral Dissertation, School of Nursing, University of California, San Francisco.

Laing, R. D. (1960), *The Divided Self*. Chicago: Quadrangle.

Lederer, W. J. & Jackson, D. D. (1968), False assumption 6: That loneliness will be cured by marriage. In: *Mirages of Marriage*. New York: Norton.

Lee, S. C. & Brattrud, A. (1967), Marriage under a monastic mode of life: A preliminary report on the Hutterite family in South Dakota. *J. Marr. Fam.,* 29:512–520.

Leger, J. M., et al. (1969), It is easy to relate an erotomatic syndrome to its etiology on the clinical level apropos of four cases, two of which developed toward a schizophrenic process. *Ann. Med. Psychol.,* 2:442.

Lester, D. (1967), Psychology and death. *Continuum,* 5:550–559.

Levy, E. Z. (1962), The subject's approach: Important factor in experimental isolation? *Menn. Clin. Bull.,* 26:30–42.

Leyhausen, P. (1965), The sane community—A density problem? *Discovery,* 26:27–33.

Liebner, K. (1969), Beitrag zum Problem der Selbstmordverhütung. (A contribution to the problem of suicide prevention.) *Psychiatr. Neurol. Med. Psychol.,* 21:472–474.

Liebow, E. (1967), *Tally's Corner: A Study of Negro Streetcorner Men*. Boston: Little, Brown.

Lifton, R. J. (1967), *Death in Life: Survivors of Hiroshima.* New York: Random House.

Lilly, J. C. (1956), Mental effects of reduction of ordinary levels of physical stimuli on intact, healthy persons. *Psychiat. Res. Rep.,* 5:1–9.

Linden, J. I. (1968), On expressing physical affection to a patient. *Voices,* 4:34–38.

Lindenauer, G. G. (1970), Loneliness. *J. Emot. Educ.,* 10:87–100.

Lindsley, D. B. (1950), Emotion and the electroencephalogram. In: *Feelings and Emotions,* The Mooseheart Symposium in Cooperation with the University of Chicago, ed. M. L. Reymert. New York: McGraw-Hill, pp. 238–246.

Lopata, H. Z. (1969), Loneliness: Forms and components. *Soc. Prob.,* 17:248–262.

_____ (1977), The meaning of friendship in widowhood. In: *Looking Ahead: A Woman's Guide to the Problems and Joys of Growing Older,* ed. L. E. Troll, J. Israel, & K. Israel. Englewood Cliffs, N.J.: Prentice-Hall, pp. 93–105.

Lorenz, K. (1966), *On Aggression,* trans. M. Latzke. London: Methuen.

Lotz, J. B. (1967), *The Problem of Loneliness.* New York: Alba.

Loucks, S. (1974), *The Dimensions of Loneliness: A Psychological Study of Affect, Self-concept, and Object-relations.* Unpublished Doctoral Dissertation, The University of Tennessee. *Dissert. Abst. Int.,* 35:3024B.

Loveland, M. & Hillman, H. (1971), Survey of people over 65 years of age living alone in contact with welfare authorities. *Med. Officer,* 126:93–97.

Lystad, M. H. (1969), *Social Aspects of Alienation: An Annotated Bibliography.* Washington, D.C.: National Institute of Mental Health.

Madden, J. P., ed. (1977), *Loneliness: Issues of Emotional Living in an Age of Stress for Clergy and Religious.* Whitinsville, Mass.: Affirmation.

Mahler, M. S. (1968), *On Human Symbiosis and the Vicissitudes of Individuation.* New York: International Universities Press.

Maisel, R. (1969), *Report of the Continuing Audit of Public Attitudes and Concerns.* Cambridge, Mass.: Harvard Medical School, Laboratory of Community Psychiatry.

Mannin, E. E. (1966), *Loneliness: A Study of the Human Condition.* London: Hutchinson.

Margolis, G. J. (1967), Postoperative psychosis on the intensive care unit. *Compr. Psychiat.,* 8:227–232.

Mark, F. R. (1972), America's major diseases: Loneliness, anxiety and boredom. *Rehabil. Rec.,* 13:5–8.

Mason, W. A. (1970), Motivational factors in psychosocial development. *Nebr. Symp. Motiv.,* 18:35–67.

Masserman, J. H. (1969), A planarian behaviorist's view of science and human behavior. *J. Biol. Psychol.,* 11:10–14.

Masterson, J. F. (1976), *Psychotherapy of the Borderline Adult: A Developmental Approach.* New York: Brunner/Mazel.

May, R. (1953), The loneliness and anxiety of modern man. In: *Man's Search for Himself.* New York: Norton.

―――― (1958), The origins and significance of the existential movement in psychology. In: *Existence: A New Dimension in Psychiatry and Psychology,* ed. R. May, E. Angel, & H. F. Ellenberger. New York: Basic Books, pp. 3–36.

Mehrabain, A. (1967), Orientation behaviors and nonverbal attitude communication. *J. Commun.,* 17:324–332.

―――― (1968), Inference of attitudes from the posture, orientation, and distance of a communicator. *J. Consult. Clin. Psychol.,* 32:296–308.

Meredith, C. P. (1970), *A Comparative Examination of Anxiety, Guilt, Prejudice and Loneliness in Selected Scriptural and Psychological Writings.* Unpublished Doctoral Dissertation, Florida State University.

Michaux, L. (1970), Child and death. *Acta Paedopsychiatr.,* 37:137–147.

Mijuskovic, B. (1979), *Loneliness in Philosophy, Psychology and Literature.* The Netherlands: Van Gorcum.

Miller, P. R. (1969), Outcasts and conformers in a girls' prison. *Arch. Gen. Psychiat.,* 20:700–708.

Mishara, T. T. (1975), *A Social Self Approach to Loneliness among College Students.* Unpublished Doctoral Dissertation, University of Maine. *Dissert. Abst. Int.,* 36:1446B.

Mitchell, G. D. & Clark, D. L. (1968), Long-term effects of social isolation in nonsocially adapted rhesus monkeys. *J. Genet. Psychol.,* 113:117–128.

Money, J., Wolff, G., & Annecillo, C. (1972), Deficiency (psychosocial dwarfism). *J. Autism Child Schiz.,* 2:127–139.

Moore, J. A. (1974), Relationship between loneliness and interpersonal relationship. *Can. Counsel.,* 8:84–89.

―――― (1976), Loneliness: Self discrepancy and sociological variables. *Can. Counsel.,* 10:133–135.

Moreno, J. L. (1934), *Who Shall Survive?* Washington, D.C.: Nervous & Mental Disease Publ.

Mosher, L. R. (1969), Father absence and antisocial behavior in Negro and white males. *Acta Paedopsychiatr.,* 36:186–202.

Moustakas, C. E. (1974), *Portraits of Loneliness and Love.* Englewood Cliffs, N.J.: Prentice-Hall.

―――― (1975), *The Touch of Loneliness.* Englewood Cliffs, N.J.: Prentice-Hall.

―――― (1977), The creative path of loneliness. In: *Turning Points.* Englewood Cliffs, N.J.: Prentice-Hall.

Munnichs, J. M. A. (1964), Loneliness, isolation and social relations in old age. *Vita Hum.,* 7:228–238.

Munz, P. (1965), *Relationship and Solitude.* Middletown, Conn.: Wesleyan University Press.

Myers, L. (1978), Too good is unhealthy. *The New Yorker,* Oct. 16, 1978, pp. 41–45.

McCullers, C. (1940), *The Heart is a Lonely Hunter*. Boston: Houghton Mifflin.

_____ (1949), Loneliness, an American malady. "This Week Magazine." *New York Herald Tribune*, Dec. 19, 1949, pp. 18–19.

McDevitt, J. & Settlage, C., eds. (1971), *Separation — Individuation: Essays in Honor of Margaret S. Mahler*. New York: International Universities Press.

Nagy, M. H. (1959), The child's view of death. In: *The Meaning of Death*, ed. H. Feifel. New York: McGraw-Hill, pp. 79–98.

National Council of Social Service, London (1973), *Loneliness: A New Study*. London: International Publications Service.

Neal, A. G., Ivoska, W. J., & Groat, H. T. (1976), Dimensions of family alienation in the marital dyad. *Sociometry*, 39:396–405.

Nerviano, V. J. & Gross, W. F. (1976), Loneliness and locus of control for alcoholic males: Validity against Murray Need and Cattell trait dimension. *J. Clin. Psychol.*, 32:479–484.

Ochiai, Y. (1974), The structure of loneliness in current adolescents. *Jpn. J. Educ. Psychol.*, 22:162–170.

Olford, S. F. (1977), *Encounter with Loneliness*. Kalamazoo, Mich.: Masters.

Olson, S. F. (1961), *The Lonely Land*. New York: Knopf.

Orbach, C. E. (1959), The multiple meanings of the loss of a child. *Amer. J. Psychother.*, 13:906–915.

Ortega, M. J. (1969), Depression, loneliness, and unhappiness. *Internat. Psychiat. Clin.*, 6:143–153.

Ostow, M. (1970), *The Psychology of Melancholy*. New York: Harper & Row.

Packard, V. (1972), *A Nation of Strangers*. New York: McKay.

Park, J. (1975), *Loneliness and Existential Freedom* (Existential Freedom Series No. 4). Minneapolis, Minn.: Existential Books.

Parker, D. & d'Usseau, A. (1954), *The Ladies of the Corridor, A Play*. New York: Viking.

Parkes, C. M. (1972), *Bereavement: Studies of Grief in Adult Life*. New York: International Universities Press.

Pattison, E. M. (1967), The experience of dying. *Amer. J. Psychother.*, 21:32–43.

Paull, H. (1972), Rx for loneliness: A plan for establishing a social network of individual caring. *Crisis Interv.*, 4:63–73.

Penn, W. (1976), *Some Fruits of Solitude in Reflections and Maxims*. (Reproduction of 1903 ed.) Folcroft, Pa.: Folcroft.

Peplau, H. E. (1955), Loneliness. *Amer. J. Nurs.*, 55:1476–1481.

_____ (1966), Loneliness and the lower socioeconomic psychiatric patient. Presented at the Meeting of the Interdivisional Council of Psychiatric and Mental Health Nursing, New York, May, 1966.

Peplau, L. A. & Caldwell, M. (1979), Loneliness: A cognitive analysis. *Essence*, 10 (In press).

_____ & Perlman, D. (1979), Blueprint for a social psychological theory of loneliness. In: *Proc. of the Swansea Conference on Love and Attraction,* ed. G. Wilson. Oxford: Pergamon, pp. 99–108.

———, Russell, D., & Heim, M. (1978), Loneliness: A biography of research and theory. *JSAS Catalog of Selected Documents in Psychology* (Ms. No. 1682), vol. 8, p. 38.

Peterson, G. H. & Mehl, L. E. (1978), Some determinants of maternal attachment. *Amer. J. Psychiat.,* 135:1168–1173.

Petrarca, F. (1977), *The Life of Solitude,* trans. J. Zertlisi. Westport, Conn.: Hyperion.

Plugge, H. (1967), Concerning the types of human embarrassment. *J. Psychol. Psychother. Med. Anthropol.,* 15:1–12.

Poe, E. A. (1956), The man of the crowd. In: *Selected Writings of Edgar Allen Poe,* ed. E. H. Davidson. Boston: Houghton Mifflin, pp. 131–139.

Polansky, N. A. (1967), On duplicity in the interview. *Am. J. Orthopsychiat.,* 37:568–579.

Pollack, G. H. (1962), Childhood parent and sibling loss in adult patients. *Arch. Gen. Psychiat.,* 7:295–305.

Pomeroy, W. B. (1967), A report on the sexual histories of twenty-five transsexuals. *Trans. N.Y. Acad. Sci.,* 29:444–447.

Potthoff, H. H. (1976), *Loneliness: Understanding and Dealing With It.* Nashville, Tenn.: Abingdon.

Powell, C. H. (1961), *The Lonely Heart: The Answer to the Problem of Loneliness through Life.* New York: Abingdon.

Rapoport, J. L. (1969), A case of congenital neuropathy diagnosed in infancy. *J. Child Psychiat. Psychol.,* 10:63–68.

Rasmussen, J. E., ed. (1973), *Man in Isolation and Confinement.* Chicago: Aldine.

Retterstol, N. (1968), Paranoid psychoses associated with unpatriotic conduct during World War II. *Acta Psychiatr. Scand.,* 44:261–279.

Rheingold, H. L., ed. (1963), *Maternal Behavior in Mammals.* New York: Wiley.

——— & Eckerman, C. O. (1970), The infant separates himself from his mother. *Science,* 168:78–83.

Riesman, D. (1969), "The lonely crowd" twenty years after. *Encounter,* 33:36–41.

Riley, L. (1975), Loneliness—A consideration in community health. *Imprint,* 22:38–39.

Ritter, C. (1954), *A Woman in the Polar Night,* trans. J. Degras. New York: Dutton.

Robert, M. (1973), *Loneliness in the Schools (What To Do About It).* Niles, Ill.: Argus.

Roberts, J. M. (1972), Loneliness is. *Perspect. Psychiat. Care,* 10:226–231.

Robertson, J. (1958), *Young Children in Hospitals.* New York: Basic Books.

Robinson, A. M. (1971), Loneliness. *J. Prac. Nurs.,* 21:18–20, 40–42.

Rogers, C. G. (1970), The use of alienation in crisis work. *J. Psychiat. Nurs. Ment. Hlth. Serv.,* 8:7–11.

Rohner, R. P. (1975), *They Love Me, They Love Me Not: A Worldwide Study of the Effects of Parental Acceptance and Rejection.* New Haven, Conn.: Human Relations Area Files Press.

Rosenbaum, J. & Rosenbaum, V. (1973), *Conquering Loneliness.* New York: Hawthorn.

Rosenberg, C. M. (1969), Young alcoholics. *Brit. J. Psychiat.,* 115:181-188.

———— (1969), Young drug addicts: Background and personality. *J. Nerv. Ment. Dis.,* 148:65-73.

Rosenblatt, C. (1972), Isolation and resistance in the elderly: A community mental health problem. *J. Psychiat. Nurs. Ment. Hlth. Serv.,* 10:22-25.

Rosenhan, D. (1967), Aloneness and togetherness as drive conditions in children. *J. Exp. Res. Pers.,* 2:32-40.

Roskolenko, H., ed. (1977), *Solo: The Great Adventures Alone.* New York: Playboy.

Ross, M. (1970), Death at an early age. *Can. Ment. Hlth.,* 18:7-10.

Rubins, J. L. (1964), On the psychopathology of loneliness. *Amer. J. Psychoanal.,* 24:153-166..

Rubinstein, C. M. (1978), Portraits of the lonely in southwest Florida. *Fort Myers (Southwest Florida) News Press,* Sunday, Aug. 6, 1978, pp. 1D, 6D.

———— (1978), Who are the lonely people? *Sunday News Magazine,* New York, June 25, 1978, pp. 7-9, 12.

———— & Shaver, P. (1978), Who are the lonely? Telegram readers share their views. *Worcester Sunday Telegram,* July 2, 1978, pp. 12-15.

Russell, D., Peplau, L. A., & Ferguson, M. L. (1978), Developing a measure of loneliness. *J. Pers. Assess.,* 42:290-294.

Sadler, W. A., Jr. (1974), On the verge of a lonely life. *Humanitas,* 10:255-276.

———— (1975), The causes of loneliness. *Sci. Dig.,* 78:58-66.

Saito, S.-I., Kitamura, S., & Tada, H. (1970), A study of social isolation. *Tohoku Psychol. Fol.,* 28:104-111.

Santana Carlos, V. (1967), Rehabilitative medicine and geriatrics. *Inform. Social,* 2:56-65.

Satran, G. (1978), Notes on loneliness. *J. Amer. Acad. Psychoanal.,* 6:281-300.

Saunders, J. T. (1969), In defense of a limited privacy. *Philos. Rev.,* 78:237-248.

Schmalohr, E. (1966), Effects of early social isolation on humans and animals. *Prax. Kinderpsychol. Kinderpsychiatr.,* 15:246-252.

Schneemann, N. (1970), Reflections concerning the formative story of a hippie based on an analysis of struwwelpeter. *Z. Psychother. Med. Psychol.,* 20:213-223.

Schorr, A. L. (1966), On selfish children and lonely parents. *Publ. Interest,* 4:8-12.

Schossberger, J. A. (1976), Depersonalization and estrangement: Individual or social processes? *Brit. J. Psychiat.,* 118:138-140.

Schuetz, A. (1944), The stranger: An essay in social psychology. *Amer. J. Sociol.,* 49:499–507.

Schultz, T. (1976), *Bittersweet: Surviving and Growing from Loneliness.* New York: Crowell.

Schulz, R. (1976), Effects of control and predictability on the physical and psychological well-being of the institutionalized aged. *J. Pers. Soc. Psychol.,* 33:563–573.

Schwartz, B. (1968), The social psychology of privacy. *Amer. J. Sociol.,* 73:741–752.

Schwarz, H. (1968), Contribution to symposium on acting out. *Internat. J. Psycho-Anal.,* 49:179–181.

Schwarzrock, S. & Wrenn, C. G. (1970), *Living with Loneliness.* Circle Pines, Minn.: American Guidance Service.

Seabrook, J. (1973), *Loneliness.* London: Trinity.

Searles, H. F. (1960), *The Nonhuman Environment in Normal Development and in Schizophrenia.* New York: International Universities Press.

Seeman, M. (1971), The urban alienation: Some dubious theses from Marx to Marcuse. *J. Pers. Soc. Psychol.,* 19:135–143.

Segal, J. & Yahraes, H. (1978), *A Child's Journey.* New York: McGraw-Hill.

Shapiro, J. (1966), Single-room occupancy: Community of the alone. *Soc. Work,* 11:24–33.

Shaver, P., Rubenstein, C., & Pullis, C. (1978), Are you lonely? A special questionnaire for News readers. *Sunday News Magazine,* New York, March 19, 1978, pp. 21–26.

Sheehy, G. (1976), *Passages: Predictable Crises of Adult Life.* New York: Dutton.

Shein, H. M. (1974), Loneliness and interpersonal isolation: Focus for therapy with schizophrenic patients. *Amer. J. Psychother.,* 28:95–107.

Sheldon, J. H. (1948), *The Social Medicine of Old Age.* London: Oxford University Press.

Shevrin, H. & Toussieng, P. W. (1965), Vicissitudes of the need for tactile stimulation in instinctual development. *The Psychoanalytic Study of the Child,* 20:310–339. New York: International Universities Press.

Shoben, E. J. (1960), Love, loneliness and logic. *J. Individ. Psychol.,* 16:11–24.

Sigg, E. B., Day, C., & Colombo, C. (1966), Endocrine factors in isolation-induced aggressiveness in rodents. *Endocrinology,* 78:679–684.

Singer, I. B. (1973), Neighbors. In: *A Crown of Feathers and Other Stories.* New York: Farrar, Straus & Giroux, pp. 288–298.

Singh, J. A. L. & Zingg, R. M. (1942), *Wolf-children and Feral Man.* New York: Harper.

Sinha, T. C. (1969), On aloneness. *Samiksa,* 23:1–8.

Skoglund, E. (1975), Loneliness. Downers Grove, Ill.: Inter-Varsity.

Small, M. H. (1900), *On Some Psychical Relations of Society and Solitude.* Thesis, Clark University.

Solomon, P. et al., eds. (1961), *Sensory Deprivation. A Symposium Held at*

Harvard Medical School. Cambridge: Harvard University Press.

Sorokin, P. A. (1959), *Social and Cultural Mobility.* Glencoe, Ill.: Free Press.

Spence, I. (1975), *Coping with Loneliness.* Grand Rapids, Mich.: Baker.

Sperber, M. (1974), Interlude. In: *Masks of Loneliness: Alfred Adler in Perspective.* New York: Macmillan, pp. 113–121.

Spitz, R. A. (1946), Hospitalism: A follow-up report. *The Psychoanalytic Study of the Child,* 2:113–117. New York: International Universities Press.

Stanley, E. J. & Barker, J. T. (1970), Adolescent suicidal behavior. *Amer. J. Orthopsychiat.,* 40:87–96.

Stark, S. (1968), Suggestion regarding *Gemeinschaft,* inner creation, and role-taking (empathy): I. David Bakan on "Epistemological Loneliness." *Psychol. Rep.,* 22:275–282.

Steig, W. (1970), *The Lonely Ones.* New York: Windmill.

Stierlin, H. (1965), The dialectic of related loneliness. *Psychoanal. Rev.,* 52:367–380.

Stoddard, T. L. (1932), *Lonely America.* Garden City, N.Y.: Doubleday, Doran.

Taves, I. (1968), *Women Alone.* New York: Funk & Wagnalls.

Taylor, D. A. et al. (1969), Personality factors related to response to social isolation and confinement. *J. Consult. Clin. Psychol.,* 33:411–419.

———— Wheeler, L., & Altman, I. (1968), Stress relations in socially isolated groups. *J. Pers. Soc. Psychol.,* 9:369–376.

Teicher, J. D. (1972), The alienated, older, isolated male adolescent. *Amer. J. Psychother.,* 26:401–407.

Thorpe, J. G. (1961), Sensory deprivation. *J. Ment. Sci.,* 107:1047–1059.

Tournier, P. (1962), *Escape from Loneliness,* trans. J. S. Gilmour. Philadelphia: Westminster.

Townsend, P. (1968), Isolation, desolation and loneliness. In: *Old People in Three Industrial Societies,* ed. E. Shanas et al. New York: Atherton.

———— (1973), Isolation and loneliness in the aged. In: *Loneliness: The Experience of Emotional and Social Isolation,* ed. R. S. Weiss. Cambridge: M.I.T. Press, pp. 175–188.

Traven, B. (1962), *The Death Ship.* New York: Collier.

Tribou de Thomaso, M. (1971), "Touch power" and the screen of loneliness. *Perspect. Psychiat. Care,* 9:112–118.

Tunstall, J. (1966), *Old and Alone: A Sociological Study of Old People.* London: Routledge & Kegan Paul.

Turnbull, C. M. (1963), *The Lonely African.* Garden City, N.Y.: Doubleday.

Urick, R. V. (1970), *Alienation: Individual or Social Problem?* Englewood Cliffs, N.J.: Prentice-Hall.

Vella, G. (1967), On the religiosity of psychotics. *Riv. Psichiatr.,* 2:333–343.

Vivante, A. (1978), A gallery of women. *The New Yorker,* Nov. 13, 1978, pp. 50–53.

Vollmerhausen, J. W. (1961), Alienation in the light of Karen Horney's theory of neurosis. *Amer. J. Psychoanal.,* 21:144–155.

Walker, H. B. (1966), *To Conquer Loneliness.* New York: Harper & Row.

Walsh, R. P. (1968), Parental rejecting attitudes and control in children. *J. Clin. Psychol.,* 24:185–186.

Wayne, D. (1968), The lonely school child. *Amer. J. Nurs.,* 68:774–777.

Weigert, E. (1960), Loneliness and trust—Basic factors of human existence. *Psychiat.,* 23:121–131.

Weil, S. (1960), *The Need for Roots: Prelude to a Declaration of Duties Toward Mankind,* trans. A. Wills. Boston: Beacon.

Weinberg, A. A. (1964), Mental ill-health, consequent to migration and loneliness, and its prevention. *Psychother. Psychosom.,* 15:69.

———— (1969), Beeinträchtigung der geistigen Gesundheit infolge von Wohnortwechsel und Einsamkeit und Möglichkeiten der Prävention. (Injury to mental health as the result of environmental change and loneliness and possibilities of prevention.) *Z. Psychother. Med. Psychol.,* 19:45–51.

Weinstein, E. A. & Lyerly, O. G. (1969), Symbolic aspects of presidential assassination. *Psychiat.,* 32:1–11.

Weiss, F. A., ed. (1961), A symposium on alienation and the search for identity. *Amer. J. Psychoanal.,* 21:117–279.

———— (1961), Self-alienation: Dynamics and therapy. *Amer. J. Psychoanal.,* 21:207–218.

Weiss, R. S. (1975), The provisions of social relationships. In: *Doing Unto Others: Joining, Molding, Conforming, Helping, Loving,* ed. Z. Rubin. Englewood Cliffs, N.J.: Prentice-Hall.

———— (1975), *Marital Separation.* New York: Basic Books.

———— (1976), The emotional impact of marital separation. *J. Soc. Issues,* 32:135–146.

Weissman, M. M. & Paykel, E. S. (1974), *The Depressed Woman: A Study of Social Relationships.* Chicago: University of Chicago Press.

Weltman, A. S. et al. (1962), Endocrine aspects of isolation stress on female mice. *Fed. Proc.,* 21:184.

Wenz, F. V. (1977), Seasonal suicide attempts and forms of loneliness. *Psychol. Rep.,* 40:807–810.

West, N. (1969), *Miss Lonelyhearts* and *The Day of the Locust.* New York: New Directions.

Westin, A. F. (1967), *Privacy and Freedom.* New York: Atheneum.

Wheelis, A. (1958), *The Quest for Identity.* New York: Norton.

Whitehorn, J. C. (1961), On loneliness and the incongruous self-image. *Ann. Psychother.,* 3:15–17.

Whitney, E. D. (1965), *The Lonely Sickness.* Boston: Beacon.

Wilson, C. (1956), *The Outsider.* Boston: Houghton Mifflin.

Winnicott, D. W. (1965), The capacity to be alone. In: *The Maturational Processes and the Facilitating Environment.* New York: International Universities Press, pp. 29–36.

———— (1966), Psycho-somatic illness in its positive and negative aspects. *Internat. J. Psycho-Anal.,* 47:510–516.

Witzleben, H. D. von (1958), On loneliness. *Psychiat.*, 21:37–43.

Women's Group on Public Welfare (1972), *Loneliness: A New Study.* London: Bedford Square.

Wood, L. A. (1976), *Loneliness and Social Structure.* Unpublished Doctoral Dissertation, York University, Ontario, Canada.

Wood, M. M. (1953), *Paths of Loneliness: The Individual Isolated in Modern Society.* New York: Columbia University Press.

Wood, R. S. (1976), *Goodbye Loneliness.* New York: Dell.

Woodward, H., Gingles, R., & Woodward, J. C. (1974), Loneliness and the elderly as related to housing. *Gerontologist,* 14:349–351.

Wright, L. M. (1975), A symbolic tree: Loneliness is the root; delusions are the leaves. *J. Psychiat. Nurs. Ment. Hlth. Serv.,* 13:30–35.

Young, L. D. et al. (1973), Early stress and later response to separation in rhesus monkeys. *Amer. J. Psychiat.,* 130:400–405.

Young, M., Benjamin, B., & Wallis, C. (1963), The mortality of widowers. *Lancet,* ii:454.

Zavitzianos, G. (1967), Problems of technique in the analysis of a juvenile delinquent. Therapeutic alliance and transference neurosis. *Internat. J. Psycho-Anal.,* 48:439–447.

Zawadski, B. & Lazarsfeld, P. (1935), The psychological consequences of unemployment. *J. Soc. Psychol.,* 6:224–251.

Zimbardo, P. G. (1977), *Shyness: What Is It, What to Do about It.* Reading, Mass.: Addison-Wesley.

Ziskind, E. (1958), Isolation stress in medical and mental illness. *JAMA,* 168:1427–1431.

Zubek, J. P., ed. (1969), *Sensory Deprivation: Fifteen Years of Research.* New York: Appleton-Century-Crofts.

Zuckerman, M. (1964), Perceptual isolation as a stress situation. *Arch. Gen. Psychiat.,* 11:255–276.

Index

Index

passivity as constituent of, 465
pre-eighteenth century sense of,
463–464
retirement and, 461
roles and, 461
sacrifice as constituent of, 463
sexuality as criterion of, 460
social categories and, 461
urban locales and, 464–465
work as source of, 461–462

Identity confusion, 53
Immortality, desire for, 88–89
Individuality
community and, 422
effect of Renaissance on, 409
gregariousness versus, 13–14
Individuation, 81
Infancy, 112
aloneness in, 397–400
demands of, 398
depression in, 343
lack of skin contact during, 398
paranoid-schizoid position in, 363
persecutory anxiety during, 363
relationship with mother during, 363
security in, 363
self-differentiation in, 517–518
separation and, 16
sleeping alone during, 397–398
tolerance of loneliness in, 398–399
see also Children
Innovation
anomie and, 120
loneliness as requirement for, 455–456
Integration, 363–372
guilt and, 369
idealization and, 367–368
male and female elements in, 368–370
manic-depressive illness and, 368
omnipotence and, 373
pain of, 367
role of internalized breast in
achieving, 376
schizophrenic illness and, 365
superego and, 376
Intimacy
commitment and, 416
community and, 415–416
fantasy as substitute for, 343–344
fear of, 344

mystery of, 450
need for, 342
"swinging" as, 416
Introversion, 184
Isolation
animals and reaction to, 117–118
anxiety and, 24–25
collectivism and, 556
communication following, 355
decapsulation and, 79–80
derangement caused by, 117–118
of elderly, 545–546
emotional, 237, 289–290
enforced, 353–356
extreme, 68
hallucinations caused by, 116–117,
354, 357
healing by, 544
incorporation and, 79–80
individualism and, 555
loneliness and, 36–37, 329, 332
nationalism and, 80–81
physical, 307–308
in polar expeditions, 354
in prisons and concentration camps,
354–355
religion and, 80–81
"Rest Cure" as form of, 545
routine as defense against, 355
self-imposed, 118–119, 354
sensory limitation experiments and,
356–357
social, 237, 289, 290
in solitary seafarers, 354
tolerance of, 353–357

Japan, 425–450
aesthetics in, 430, 433
amae concept in, 9, 443
America contrasted with, 429–430
anonymity in, 436–437
apartment (*danchi*) living in, 439
atomic bomb survivors in, 445
bodily pleasures in, 430
commitment to relationships in,
435–437
consciousness of lonely feelings in,
429–435
drunkenness in, 443
education of wives in, 447
elderly in, 445, 446